The Employment Practitioner's Guide to Taxation

The Employment Practitioner's Guide to Taxation

Third edition

Ryan Hawthorne
Devereux Chambers

Jolyon Maugham
Devereux Chambers

Jonathan Peacock QC
11 New Square

Bloomsbury Professional

Bloomsbury Professional, Maxwelton House, 41–43 Boltro Road, Haywards Heath, West Sussex, RH16 1BJ

Bloomsbury Professional is an imprint of Bloomsbury Publishing plc

British Library Cataloguing-in-Publication Data

A CIP Catalogue record for this book is available from the British Library.

ISBN 978 1 78043 454 4

Printed in Great Britain by Hobbs the Printers, Totton, Hampshire

Preface

It is now almost five years since the second edition of this book was published (as *Taxation for Employment Specialists*, 2nd edition). There have been a number of developments in the field that made the case for a third edition of this book overwhelming.

Fully updated to the Finance Act 2013, this third edition features the following recent case law: *R (oao Gaines-Cooper) v HMRC*; *ITV Services v HMRC*; *Autoclenz v Belcher*; *HMRC v PA Holdings* and *Kuehne & Nagel Drinks Logistics v HMRC*. It also covers the Statutory Residence Test as it relates to expatriates and the disguised remuneration provisions in Part 7A of ITEPA 2003.

Another important development has been the growth of resources on the taxation of employment earnings available on the internet, particularly the website of Her Majesty's Revenue & Customs. These have made the task of the employment specialist who seeks some familiarity with the provisions of tax law operating in his or her field a great deal simpler. This book signposts to a number of those resources.

We have endeavoured to state the law as at 14 February 2014.

Ryan Hawthorne
Devereux Chambers

Contents

Table of Cases

Table of Statutes

[All references are to paragraph numbers]

Table of Statutory Instruments

[All references are to paragraph numbers]

Chapter 1

Introduction

1.1 PURPOSE

The sheer complexity of the modern employment relationship – driven in the direction of greater flexibility and less security by international competitive pressures and in the direction of greater employee rights by (largely European Union) regulation – means that the numbers of people who at some stage of their working lives will consider their strict contractual entitlement is greater than ever before. Whether in the context of signing a new contract, varying an existing one or seeking compensation for a contract brought to an end, employees are more readily seeking professional advice as to their legal position. Inevitably this has led to a more litigious approach, both by employers and employees, and thus to a greater frequency of non-standard payments made or demanded by one party or another.

A number of further factors have, alongside this increasing assertiveness of employees, contributed to the need for employment advisers to have some understanding of the principles governing the taxation of employment earnings. Employment advisers cannot but encounter sophisticated remuneration packages, mobile – often internationally mobile – workforces, and individuals and 'employers' choosing a relationship which is neither clearly employment nor self-employment. The employment adviser who works in these areas without some grasp of the tax factors which drive these sorts of structures cannot hope properly to serve his or her clients.

For a long time, the United Kingdom tax code tended to lag behind the development of the law around the employment relationship. Successive Finance Acts focused on closing off avenues whereby recipients of large bonuses could escape a liability to pay higher rate tax rather than updating the employment tax code at large. This led to a creakingly backward fiscal framework, barnacled about by complex and lengthy statutory provisions designed to counteract specific tax avoidance schemes which had often, by the time the next Finance Act came along, already fallen into disuse.

However, three recent developments have reversed this trend.

First, a report presented to Parliament by the then Inland Revenue – now HM Revenue and Customs (referred to here as 'HMRC') – in 1995 entitled 'The Path to Tax Simplification' was the spur to a modernisation of that code. The main recommendation – that UK direct tax legislation should be written in clearer and simpler language – has led to a succession of Acts codifying various aspects of the UK tax system, amongst which being the Income Tax (Earnings and Pensions) Act 2003 (ITEPA 2003).

The fact of publication of a new edition of this book renders redundant any further comment from the authors as to whether the avowed aim of what is popularly known as the Tax Law Rewrite project – namely, a *simplification* of the tax code – has been achieved. What ITEPA 2003 certainly did do was (at least for a moment in time) to gather together in one place the various enactments which impose the charge to employment income tax and, to a greater or lesser degree, modernise their terms. Farewell, then, the reference to 'keeping and maintaining a horse' (for the purposes of business travel) which survived until 1997.

Second, rather than continuing with detailed technical solutions, the draftsman is increasingly using motive tests to counteract tax avoidance. Those statutory tests generally ask the question whether a particular contract, or feature of a contract, has tax avoidance as its sole or main purpose. Where it does, any tax advantage arising by reason of that contract or feature is reversed.

Third, the statutory draftsman has imposed a statutory requirement for 'promoters' of tax avoidance schemes in the field of employment income tax to report those schemes to HMRC to enable an early assessment of the efficacy of those schemes and speedy legislation to counteract their effect. Moreover, the Chancellor has indicated that, where tax avoidance is encountered in the instant field, legislation will be introduced which both closes the 'loophole' for the future and operates retrospectively to claw back any tax efficiencies which have been achieved in the past.

In writing this book we have deliberately set ourselves a limited goal. Our aim has been to produce an easily accessible guide to the types of tax issue which frequently arise in the context of the modern employment relationship. The guide is designed primarily for the non-tax specialist who needs some understanding of the UK tax treatment of payments made in anticipation, under, in variation, as compensation for breach and after completion, of a contract of employment.

Some of the material – particularly that appearing in Part A – will be familiar to many advisers with a basic grasp of the UK tax code; what we have attempted to do is to tailor the material – particularly in Part B– to specific situations so that this work can be used as a quick reference prior to further research in more specialist tax textbooks. Inevitably, this work cannot be a substitute for a more detailed specialist work or (in appropriate cases) for specialist tax advice. Instead it aims to be a comprehensive starting point.

1.2 STRUCTURE

In line with the basic purpose and object of the work, this book is divided into two parts.

1.3 Part A

Part A sets out some of the fundamental principles of tax law, and specifically income tax law, without an understanding of which it will be difficult to appreciate some of the more technical points made in later chapters. Thus there are chapters dealing with general principles (Chapter 2), sources of tax law (Chapter 3), an introduction to income tax itself (Chapter 4), the PAYE system, by which much of the tax due on employment income is collected in the UK (Chapter 5), an introduction to national insurance contributions which are, in all but name, an additional tax on employment income (Chapter 6) and the basic provisions dealing with challenges to assessments to tax (Chapter 7).

1.4 Part B

Part B then considers the relevant tax treatment of various scenarios which arise in common employment disputes and the tax issues which they give rise to. Thus there are chapters dealing with remuneration from employment in the form of benefits in kind (Chapter 8), taxation of shares and share options (Chapter 9), the taxation of sums paid in the context of the termination and variation of the employment contract (Chapter 10), taxation of damages for breach of the employment contract (Chapter 11), expatriate taxation (looking both at the UK position of those who leave the UK to work abroad and those who come to the UK to work here) (Chapter 12) and the taxation of pension payments (Chapter 13).

We have endeavoured to state the law as at 19 December 2013.

Chapter 2

General Principles

2.1 INTRODUCTION

As is set out in Chapter 1, this book aims to provide a basic guide to the relevant provisions of the UK tax code which will most commonly arise in practice. However, before looking at the provisions in detail, it is necessary to have a basic understanding of a number of principles of tax law which form the backdrop to the legislative code. This chapter considers those relevant principles in outline; if *specific* issues arise, reference should be made to the standard work dealing with the particular issue.

In the words of the famous dictum 'income tax … is a tax on income'.[1] The tax legislation does not define 'income' (as opposed to 'capital'); instead it identifies a number of types of receipt – monies received from property (eg rent), from investment (eg interest), from employment (eg salary) – and levies tax according to rules based upon the nature of the sum received. What is charged to tax under each category is the gross receipt of income – that which 'comes in' – subject to certain specific permitted deductions (eg for expenses). Once a particular sum has been identified as flowing to a person, then a number of other factors are taken into account in determining whether (and how) that person is to be liable to tax on the sum concerned. In broad terms, the UK tax system taxes such income as follows:

(1) All 'UK source' income is taxed in the UK irrespective of the residence of the person to whom the income arises.

(2) UK residents who are also domiciled in some part of the UK are taxed on their worldwide income as it arises whether or not the source of the income is in the UK.

(3) UK residents who are not domiciled in some part of the UK are taxed on their worldwide income as it arises whether or not the source of the income is in the UK (ie as in (2)), *subject to* special rules which provide that no tax falls due in certain cases until the sums concerned are remitted to the UK.

1 See Lord Macnaghten in *LCC v Attorney General* [1901] AC 26 at 35, 36.

Thus, as will be seen, it is important in any given situation to identify whether the sum is *income* or *capital* in nature, the status of the taxpayer (*resident* or non-resident, UK *domiciled* or not), the *source* of the income and whether the tax charge operates on an *arising* or *remittance* or *receipts* basis. These terms are considered below.

2.2 INCOME AND CAPITAL

The UK tax code differentiates, both in terms of receipts and expenses between income and capital. Thus, in very broad terms, income – after the deduction of income, or 'revenue', expenditure – is charged to income tax; a gain, of a capital nature – after deduction of capital expenditure – is charged to capital gains tax. In determining the liability of a taxpayer to tax on a particular receipt, it is important for this reason to establish – as the first step in the inquiry – whether the sum concerned is income or capital in nature.

For a detailed discussion of the numerous cases on this capital: income distinction (the subject of over 100 years of keenly fought jurisprudence), it is necessary to refer to the standard tax textbooks.[2] For present purposes, it is important to note that the courts have – over time – considered a number of relevant factors or tests in determining between capital and income. This question is one of law so that the opinions of, for example, an expert accountancy witness, cannot be determinative of the issue: see *Heather v P-E Consulting Group*.[3]

2.3 The starting point

The traditional starting point is the judgment of Viscount Cave in *British Insulated and Helsby Cables Ltd v Atherton*[4] where his Lordship stated:

> 'when an expenditure is made, not only once and for all, but with a view to bringing into existence an asset or an advantage for the enduring benefit of a trade, I think there is very good reason … for treating such an expenditure as properly attributable not to revenue but to capital.'

Although that case was concerned with identifying the nature of expenditure, the tests set out apply equally when determining the nature of a sum received. Thus if the sum is received as a one off payment in consideration of the giving up of a right which was of a capital nature, then the payment is likely to be capital in nature itself.

2 Particularly useful in this regard is *Whiteman & Sherry on Income Tax* with updates.
3 [1973] 1 Ch 189.
4 [1926] AC 213.

2.4 One off payments

A one off payment, made 'once and for all' is, *prima facie*, taken to be a capital payment. This however is not universal since there are cases in which a one off payment has been held to be a revenue sum and, likewise, a recurrent receipt has been held to be of a capital nature. The relevant question in examining the nature of a payment under this heading is whether the sum can be regarded as either a single one off payment (capital), one of a number of instalments of a one off payment (almost certainly capital), or the regular receipt of ongoing payments (revenue) – see *IRC v Land Securities Investment Trust Ltd*[5] and *Heather v P-E Consulting Group*.[6]

The 'once and for all' factor is not itself determinative of the issue – see *Lawson v Johnson Matthey plc*.[7] The second limb of the test set out in *Atherton* – namely whether the payment secures any enduring benefit for the payer – is frequently of greater importance. Although there are a number of difficult questions as to the circumstances in which a benefit can be said to 'endure' for these purposes, the courts generally recognise that payments leading to long term advantages are capital in nature at least as regards the payer – see *IRC v Carron*[8] and *ECC Quarries Ltd v Watkis*.[9] Where the advantage endures for approximately five years it is unlikely that this will automatically be regarded as capital in nature – see *BP Australia Ltd v Australian Commissioner of Taxation*.[10]

2.5 Capital asset

Equally, the courts will often have regard to whether the expenditure in the hands of the payer acquires, modifies or procures the sale of an identifiable capital asset. This can be seen in the judgment of Millett LJ (as he then was) in *Vodafone Cellular Ltd v Shaw*.[11]

2.6 What does the payment produce?

Alternatively, the courts have also taken a slightly different approach of looking at particular payments to see what they were calculated to effect 'from a practical and business point of view', irrespective of a strict legal analysis. This can be seen in the recent decision of the Privy Council in *Inland Revenue*

5 [1969] 1 WLR 604.
6 [1973] Ch 189. See also *JT Dove Ltd v Revenue & Customs Commissioners* [2011] UKFTT 16 (TC).
7 [1992] STC 466.
8 (1968) 45 TC 18.
9 [1975] STC 578.
10 [1966] AC 224.
11 [1997] STC 734.

Commissioner v Wattie.[12] This accords with some of the older authorities where the courts had regard to the 'flavour' or 'character' of the particular payment and determined the issue largely as a matter of impression.

2.7 Capital and income

It should, however, be born in mind that a particular payment can be capital in the hands of the payer and income in the hands of the recipient and vice versa. Thus, that an employer regards a particular sum as income is not itself conclusive of the treatment of the sum in the hands of the employee. Conversely, if the employer regards a sum as capital, this does not of itself mean that the sum cannot be income in the hands of the recipient employee. When advising the employee/recipient of the sum, it is thus necessary to determine – on the basis of first principles – whether the item concerned is capital or income in his hands taking account of – but not determined by – the treatment of the sum in the hands of the employer/payer.

2.8 Capital and income in an employment context

Although it will be relatively rare in the employment field for a taxpayer successfully to contend that a particular receipt from his employer (directly or indirectly) is capital in nature and thus not taxable, the following are examples of circumstances which have been considered by the courts – a payment by a company to an actor to refrain from appearing in films for an 18 month period was not regarded as taxable income since the actor had given up a part of his vocation (*Higgs v Olivier*);[13] a signing-on fee payable when an amateur sportsman turned professional was regarded as a capital sum for relinquishing his amateur status (*Jarrold v Boustead*);[14] a sum payable to an accountant to give up his profession and enter employment was regarded as a taxable (income) receipt (*Glantre Engineering v Goodhand*);[15] a payment to procure the retirement of a director was regarded as revenue in nature in the hands of the payer since it was paid to benefit the trade of the company (*Mitchell v BW Noble Ltd*).[16]

2.9 RESIDENCE

The relevance of an individual's tax residence was discussed earlier in this chapter. In summary the relevance is as follows: first, an individual is liable

12 [1998] STC 1160.
13 [1952] Ch 311.
14 [1964] 1 WLR 1357. Compare this with *Riley v Coglan* [1967] 1 WLR 1300.
15 [1983] STC 1.
16 [1927] 1 KB 719.

to UK income tax with respect to his worldwide income if he is resident in the country for the tax year. On the other hand, if he is not resident in the UK for the tax year then he is only liable to UK income tax with respect to so much income as arises from sources within the country. Second, the question of residence also dictates whether or not an individual is eligible for personal allowances and other relief.

From 6 April 2013, the key source of rules which governs an individual's residence status is the statutory residence test (SRT) contained in Schedule 45 to the Finance Act 2013 (FA 2013). The sources of the rules which governed an individual's residence status for the purposes of UK income tax prior to 6 April 2013 were statute,[17] common law principles, and HMRC publication, IR20 (subsequently HMRC6). What follows is a discussion on the SRT. Then the common law principles and HMRC6 will be considered as these will be relevant to disputes prior to 6 April 2013.

However, three points should be borne in mind: first, the SRT is said to legislate the effects of the previous legislation, tax cases and practice, and so it is intended that the status of the majority of individuals would be unaffected by the statutory residence test.[18] Second, the SRT can be applied by election to certain earlier tax years in order to determine an individual's pre-April 2013 residence status for the purposes of the new rules, in particular for the three preceding tax years under the sufficient ties test.[19] Third, guidance on the statutory residence test is provided in HMRC booklet RDR3 'Guidance Note: Statutory Residence Test (SRT)'. An HMRC online residence indicator tool provides a definitive residence status, provided accurate information is used and subject to the interpretation of any subjective issues.

2.10 THE STATUTORY RESIDENCE TEST FROM 6 APRIL 2013

Schedule 45 to the FA 2013 is split into four parts. Part 1 contains the rules applicable for determining UK residence for a particular tax year and operates by identifying a basic residence rule: an individual is resident in the UK if he meets the *automatic residence test* or the *sufficient ties test*. If he meets neither he is not resident for UK tax purposes for that tax year. He will meet the automatic residence test if he meets any of the *automatic UK tests* and does not meet any of the *automatic overseas tests*. A hierarchy of conclusive tests is thereby established and these should be approached as follows:

17 ITA 2007, Ch 2, ss 829, 831 and 832.
18 HMRC Statement: 'Statutory definition of residence and reform of ordinary residence' June 2012.
19 FA 2013, Sch 45, para 154.

(a) Meeting any one of the Automatic Overseas Tests will mean the individual is conclusively non-resident in the UK for the tax year in question.

(b) If he meets none of those, he will be conclusively resident in the UK if he meets any one of the Automatic UK tests.

(c) If he meets none of those, consideration will need to be given to the Sufficient Ties test in order to determine his residence status.

Part 2 of Schedule 45 deals with key concepts in the legislation, such as 'home' and 'full-time work'. Part 3 of Schedule 45 deals with split-year treatment; and Part 4 of Schedule 45 deals with anti-avoidance, putting the rules relating to temporary non-residence on a statutory footing.

2.10A Automatic overseas tests

There are three key automatic overseas tests in FA 2013, Sch 45, paras 11–16 and an individual who meets any one of them is non-resident. The tests are that:

(1) The individual was UK-resident in one or more of the three previous tax years, and is present in the UK for a maximum of 15 days (and does not die) in the current tax year.[20]

(2) The individual was UK-resident in none of the three previous tax years and is present in the UK for a maximum of 45 days in the current tax year.[21]

(3) The individual works sufficient hours overseas from which work there are no significant breaks, in the current tax year and he or she is present in the UK in the current tax year for no more than 90 days (of which no more than 30 are days on which more than three hours' UK work is done).[22]

It is not necessary to apply either the automatic UK test or the sufficient UK ties test to an individual who falls within one of the automatic overseas tests at (1)–(5) because he or she is definitively non-resident for the tax year.

2.10B Automatic UK tests

An individual is UK-resident for the tax year where none of the automatic overseas tests above are met and the individual meets one of the following four tests in Sch 45, paras 6–10:

20 FA 2013, Sch 45, para 12.
21 FA 2013, Sch 45, para 13.
22 FA 2013, Sch 45, para 14. See Chapter 12 (Expatriate Taxation).

(1) They spend at least 183 days in the UK in the tax year.[23]

(2) They have a home in the UK and are present there on at least 30 separate days [The days can be consecutive or intermittent and there is no time minimum for presence] in the tax year, and in a period of at least 91 consecutive days (part of which falls in the tax year) they either have no home abroad or they have one or more non-UK home(s) in which they are present for less than 31 separate days in the tax year. [FA 2013, Sch 45 para 8.] If the individual has more than one UK home, each is considered separately for the 30-day and 91-day counts.

(3) They work in the UK over a period of at least 365 days (part of which falls in the tax year) in which there are no significant breaks [A significant break from UK work is a continuous period of at least 31 days during which there is no day on which there is more than three hours of UK work, or on which the individual would have done more than three hours' UK work, but for being on annual, sick or parenting leave:[24] from UK work, and more than 75% of the days on which they do more than three hours' work are days on which more than three hours are worked in the UK, and there is at least one day that falls in the period and in the tax year on which they do three hours' work in the UK.[25]]

If the individual has a relevant job on board a vehicle, aircraft or ship at any time in the tax year, this test does not apply.[26] A relevant job is an employment with duties personally performed (and required to be personally performed) on board a vehicle, aircraft or ship while it is travelling, on trips substantially all of which trips involve crossing an international border.[27]

(4) They die in the tax year and were UK-resident under the automatic residence test in each of the three previous tax years, and their home was in the UK when they died, or they had more than one home and at least one of them was in the UK, and if they had a home overseas during all or part of the tax year they did not spend a sufficient amount of time there in the tax year.[28]

It is not necessary to apply the sufficient UK ties test below to an individual who falls within one of the automatic UK tests at (1)–(4) but meets none of the automatic overseas tests, because they are definitively resident for the tax year.

23 FA 2013, Sch 45, para 7.
24 FA 2013, Sch 45, para 29.
25 FA 2013, Sch 45, para 9. This is described as 'full-time UK work' in RDR3 paragraph 1.33.
26 FA 2013, Sch 45, para 30.
27 FA 2013, Sch 45, para 27(3).
28 FA 2013, Sch 45, para 10.

2.10C Sufficient ties test

The sufficient ties test in Sch 45, paras 17–20 only applies where an individual meets none of the automatic overseas tests and none of the automatic UK tests above, but they visit the UK and have one or more UK ties.

The test comprises two separate sliding scales that use the UK days and the individual's UK ties in the tax year. The scale that applies depends on the individual's residence status in the previous three tax years.

A previously-resident individual (or 'leaver') can spend up to 15 days in the UK in the tax year without becoming resident, regardless of the number of UK ties that they have. A previously non-resident individual (or 'arriver') can spend up to 45 days in the UK in the tax year without becoming resident, regardless of the number of UK ties that they have.

The sliding scale that applies to the tax year depends on the individual's residence status in the previous three tax years, as follows:[29]

Individual not resident in UK in the three preceding tax years

UK days	Residence status/UK ties
45 or less	Non-resident
45-90	4 or more ties = resident
91-120	3 or more ties = resident
More than 120	2 or more ties = resident

Individual UK-resident in any of the three preceding tax years

UK days	Residence status/UK ties
15 or less	Non-resident
16–45	4 or more ties = resident
45–90	3 or more ties = resident
91–120	2 or more ties = resident
More than 120	1 or more ties = resident

The UK ties taken into account in the sufficient ties test above are as follows.

(a) A family tie with a UK-resident spouse, civil partner (or the common-law equivalent), or a child aged under 18;[30]

29 Table taken from *Simon's Taxes*, 'E6.102A Statutory residence test (SRT) 2013–14 onwards'.
30 FA 2013, Sch 45, para 32. See also RDR3 Annex C para C6.

(b) A UK work tie, ie the individual works in the UK for at least 40 days in the tax year;[31]

(c) A UK accommodation tie, ie the individual has a place to live in the UK that is available to them for a continuous period of 91 days, and they actually spend one day there;[32]

(d) A 90 UK days tie, ie spending more than 90 days in the UK in either or both the two preceding tax years;[33] and

(e) A UK country tie, ie the UK is the country in which the individual spends the greatest number of midnights in the tax year (only applicable to individuals previously UK-resident).[34]

2.10D Definitions

A UK day means UK presence at midnight, with the exception of UK in-transit days where the individual leaves the UK on the following day and does not engage in activities unrelated to their passage through the UK.[35] A maximum of 60 days of UK presence can be ignored if due to exceptional circumstances.[36]

A home can be any building or part of a building, such as a vehicle, vessel or structure of any kind, but not a holiday home or temporary retreat.[37] The facts of each case will determine whether there is sufficient permanence or stability about the individual's arrangements to make a place their home.

'Work' and 'full-time work' are considered in Chapter 12 (Expatriate Taxation).

2.11 Common law principles prior to 6 April 2013

Prior to 6 April 2013 the term 'residence' was not defined anywhere in the tax legislation, however, a considerable body of case law developed over the years as to what the word meant. This body of law was helpfully summarised by the Court of Appeal in *Grace v Revenue and Customs Commissioners*[38] in a number of propositions thus:

(1) The word 'reside' is a familiar English word which means 'to dwell permanently or for a considerable time, to have one's settled or usual

31 FA 2013, Sch 45, paras 35 and 36.
32 FA 2013, Sch 45, para 34. See also RDR3 Annex A paras A27 to A42.
33 FA 2013, Sch 45, para 37.
34 FA 2013, Sch 45, paras 31(2) and 38.
35 FA 2013, Sch 45, para 22. Also note the deeming rules in FA 2013, Sch 45, para 23.
36 FA 2013, Sch 45, para 22(4). See also RDR3 Annex B paras B8 to B20 for what is meant by 'exceptional circumstances'.
37 FA 2013, Sch 45, para 25. See also RDR3 paras A11 to A22.
38 [2009] EWCA 1082 per Lloyd LJ at paragraphs 6 and 7.

abode, to live in or at a particular place': *Levene v IR Commrs* (1928) 13 TC 486, 505. This is the definition taken from the *Oxford English Dictionary* in 1928, and is still the definition in the current on-line edition.

(2) Physical presence in a particular place does not necessarily amount to residence in that place where, for example, a person's physical presence there is no more than a stop gap measure: *Goodwin v Curtis* [1998] BTC 176, 180; 70 TC 478, 510.

(3) In considering whether a person's presence in a particular place amounts to residence there, one must consider the amount of time that he spends in that place, the nature of his presence there and his connection with that place: *IR Commrs v Zorab* (1926) 11 TC 289, 291.

(4) Residence in a place connotes some degree of permanence, some degree of continuity or some expectation of continuity: *Fox v Stirk* [1970] 2 QB 463, 477; *Goodwin v Curtis* [1998] BTC 176, 180; 70 TC 478, 510.

(5) However, short but regular periods of physical presence may amount to residence, especially if they stem from performance of a continuous obligation (such as business obligations) and the sequence of visits excludes the elements of chance and of occasion: *Lysaght v IR Commrs* (1928) 13 TC 511, 529.

(6) Although a person can have only one domicile at a time, he may simultaneously reside in more than one place, or in more than one country: *Levene v IR Commrs* (1928) 13 TC 486, 505.

(7) 'Ordinarily resident' refers to a person's abode in a particular place or country which he has adopted voluntarily and for settled purposes as part of the regular order of his life, whether of short or long duration: *R v Barnet LBC, ex parte Shah* [1983] 2 AC 309, 343.

(8) Just as a person may be resident in two countries at the same time, he may be ordinarily resident in two countries at the same time: *Re Norris* (1888) 4 TLR 452; *R v Barnet LBC, ex parte Shah* [1983] 2 AC 309, 342.

(9) It is wrong to conduct a search for the place where a person has his permanent base or centre adopted for general purposes; or, in other words to look for his 'real home': *R v Barnet LBC, ex parte Shah* [1983] 2 AC 309, 345 and 348.

(10) There are only two respects in which a person's state of mind is relevant in determining ordinary residence. First, the residence must be voluntarily adopted; and second, there must be a degree of settled purpose: *R v Barnet LBC, ex parte Shah* [1983] 2 AC 309, 344.

(11) Although residence must be voluntarily adopted, a residence dictated by the exigencies of business will count as voluntary residence: *Lysaght v IR Commrs* (1928) 13 TC 511, 535.

(12) The purpose, while settled, may be for a limited period; and the relevant purposes may include education, business or profession as well as a love of a place: *R v Barnet LBC, ex parte Shah* [1983] 2 AC 309, 344.

(13) Where a person has had his sole residence in the United Kingdom he is unlikely to be held to have ceased to reside in the United Kingdom (or to have 'left' the United Kingdom) unless there has been a definite break in his pattern of life: *IR Commrs v Combe* (1932) 17 TC 405, 411.

The meaning of 'definite break in his pattern of life' was recently considered by the Supreme Court in *Gaines-Cooper v HMRC* [[2011] UKSC 47]. Lord Wilson held that where an individual claims to have shed his UK residences, the requirement of a distinct break mandates a 'multifactorial inquiry'. This is because:

> 'The distinct break relates to the pattern of the Appellant's life in the UK and no doubt it encompasses *a substantial loosening of social and family ties*; but the allowance, to which I will refer, of limited visits to the UK on the part of the Appellant who has become non-resident, clearly foreshadows their continued existence in a loosened form. "Severance" of such ties is too strong a word in this context.'

2.12 HMRC's view up to 5 April 2013

HMRC6 (previously IR20) provided that a person would be regarded as being resident here if he is physically present in the UK for 183 days or more.[39] But it is also possible to be resident here if you are present for less than 183 days depending on such other factors as the location of your residential property, family and other social or business connections. In calculating whether or not someone has been physically present for 183 days or more, it is presence in the UK at midnight which counts,[40] unless that person is just in transit in which case his presence in the UK at midnight can be ignored.[41]

2.13 Resident for less than a year

By Extra Statutory Concession A11, HMRC are (for certain purposes) prepared to split years so that a person can be regarded as resident for part of a year only (eg on arrival in or departure from the UK) where a person *arrives* in the UK to live permanently or for at least two years (not having been ordinarily resident in the UK before that) or to take up employment for at least a two year period or *leaves* the UK to live abroad permanently (not being ordinarily resident at the time of departure) or to take up full time employment abroad and meet certain conditions).

39 See paragraph 2.2 thereof.
40 See paragraph 2.2.
41 See paragraph 2.3.

2.14 'Ordinary residence'

The concept of ordinary residence was abolished from 6 April 2013. Prior to 6 April 2013, the term 'ordinary residence' was not defined in the legislation but was, instead, a standard term which has been the subject of considerable case law. Before looking at those cases it is important to stress that a person's residence is quite different from his or her ordinary residence, since the latter is a broader, more elastic, term. Thus a person could be resident in the UK but not ordinarily resident (eg because he has moved from Paris to work in London on a 15-month contract); conversely, a person could be ordinarily resident in the UK but not resident (eg because he has moved from London to Paris to work on a 15-month contract). Equally, a person who left the UK in March 2004 to work abroad and did not return until June 2007 would not have been regarded as resident in the UK in 2004–2005 or 2005–2006; he would, in all likelihood, have been regarded as ordinarily resident in the UK during this period unless he could demonstrate that he has gone abroad to take up 'permanent residence' outside the UK (see below).

A person would be regarded as 'ordinarily resident' in the UK if it was his normal or habitual place of residence for a series of tax years.[42] This has been applied in practice by looking primarily at the time period spent in the UK – see *Levene v IRC*[43] (habitual visitor for 20 weeks per year held to be ordinarily resident) and *Elmhirst v IRC*.[44] A person would thus have been treated as ordinarily resident in the UK if he was regularly in the UK and had accommodation available for his use. There was no split year concession for ordinary residence (see Extra Statutory Concession A11) so that ordinary residence operated from the commencement of the tax year of arrival until the end of the tax year of departure.

2.15 'DOMICILE'[45]

English law – like virtually all other major legal systems – has a concept of 'domicile' which is separate from a person's residence in a particular country or citizenship of that country. Thus, every individual has a domicile (see *Udny v Udny*)[46] throughout their life either in a particular country or, where a country is made up of separate states, in a particular state. A person can have domicile in England and Wales, or in France, or (in an Australian context) in, say, Western Australia. A person can only have one domicile at any given time (*Udny v Udny*).

42 *R v London Borough of Barnet ex parte Shah* [1983] 1 All ER 226.
43 [1927] 2 KB 38.
44 [1937] 2 KB 551.
45 For a discussion of domicile in a tax context see: *Gaines-Cooper v Revenue and Customs Commissioners* [2008] STC 1665.
46 (1869) LR 1 Sc & Div 441.

2.16 Permanent home

A person's domicile is, put simply, the place in which he has his 'permanent home', that is, the place in which he resides without any intention of moving from it permanently or for an indefinite period – see *Winans v Attorney General*.[47] Thus there are two elements to the legal notion of domicile – first the element of a permanent base and second the element of the requisite intention. As will be seen, domicile is not altered merely by changing one without the other. If a person moves from Spain to the UK without intending to stay in the UK at least indefinitely he has not thereby lost his Spanish domicile; conversely, if he stays in Spain but determines to move to the UK indefinitely he does not thereby lose his Spanish domicile unless and until he actually moves to the UK. This notion of a permanent home should not be taken too far however since, as will be seen, a person can – by virtue of a number of 'deeming' rules – have a domicile in a country which he has never visited never mind lived in.

In broad terms, a person's domicile will be one of three types (see HMRC6 paragraph 4.3): a domicile of origin; a domicile of choice; or a domicile of dependence.

2.17 Domicile of origin

A person's domicile of origin is acquired at birth and is normally taken from the father. For example a person born to a father with a French domicile acquires a domicile of origin in France by virtue of birth – see *Udny v Udny*. A person born to parents who are not legally married (or born to married parents but after the death of the father) does not acquire a domicile of origin from the father but, instead, acquires the mother's domicile – see *Udny v Udny*. This concept of a domicile of origin means that a person may be born in London to a father who has English citizenship but may still acquire a domicile of origin in, say, France if that is the father's domicile at the time of birth. Equally, although it may disappear at various times (see below), a person's domicile of origin is never lost. It can, at various times and in various circumstances, merely be superseded by a domicile of choice or (now rarely) a domicile of dependence.

2.18 Domicile of choice

A person can acquire a domicile of choice (usually at the age of 16) when he or she becomes physically present in another country with a settled intention to reside permanently in that country – see *Bell v Kennedy*[48] and *IRC v Bullock*.[49]

47 [1904] AC 287.
48 (1868) LR 1 Sc & Div 307.
49 [1976] 1 WLR 1178.

This intention must be clearly established on the evidence and must have a high degree of permanence about it since it is difficult for one domicile to be displaced by another except on the clearest of evidence – see *Winans v Attorney General*.[50] Thus if a person merely lives in the UK for a considerable period of time, he will not necessarily acquire a domicile of choice in, say, England and Wales if he has a realistic intention of returning to, say, France on the happening of some specific event. If and when he no longer has such an intention he becomes UK domiciled – see *Gulbenkian v Gulbenkian*.[51] Common examples include a non UK domiciliary who resides in this country for many years always intending to return to a different country on the termination of employment, on the death of a spouse (see *IRC v Bullock*), or on the breakdown of marriage.

Although the position arises more frequently in the context of HMRC contending that a person has acquired a domicile of choice in the UK, the relevant factors in considering whether this has occurred, or (conversely) whether a person with a UK domicile of origin has acquired a domicile of choice abroad, are the same. In practice, HMRC will look for actual *residence* in a particular country (something which is usually easily demonstrated) and then examine a person's business and family relationships to determine the range and strength of a person's ties with a particular country and thus his *intention*. Thus, for a person to contend that he has maintained a domicile of origin in, say, France, he will have to demonstrate that he continues to have family links with people in France, some measure of business or financial affairs in France and some specific evidence of a clear intention (contingent on particular events or not) to return to France at some stage. Where all such ties have been cut, HMRC will frequently contend that a domicile of choice in the UK has been acquired. It is however open to a person to contend that residence in a particular country should be discounted since it was not freely chosen or was in some way precarious (see *Udny v Udny*) – eg because he is a refugee or a prisoner or he is a diplomat or a member of the armed forces.

Should a person acquire a domicile of choice in a particular country (say Germany) thereby losing his domicile of origin in the UK (say Scotland) that domicile of choice will continue unless and until it is lost. Where that is the case, the person's domicile of origin revives (on this example, in Scotland) and remains in place unless and until a different domicile of choice is acquired. For tax purposes, this can be important in that a person who has ceased to have domicile in the UK can find that the domicile of origin has revived in the 'gap' period between one domicile of choice and another.

50 [1904] AC 287.
51 [1937] 4 All ER 618.

2.19 Domicile of dependence

A domicile of dependence applies now primarily to children. A child has a domicile of dependence until he attains the age of (generally) 16; that is until he is capable of acquiring a domicile of choice of his own. Thus a child born to German domiciled parents would acquire a German domicile from his father (assuming the parents are married); should the father acquire a new domicile in, say, Spain while the child is under the age of 16, the child would acquire a domicile of dependence in Spain. Although strong evidence is normally required to displace an existing domicile this presumption in favour of continuity is weaker in the case of a domicile of dependence – *Re Scullard*.[52]

Prior to 1 January 1974, a married woman could not acquire a domicile of choice of her own but, instead, she gained a domicile of dependence – the domicile of her spouse – on getting married to her husband. Although this rule was repealed by the Domicile and Matrimonial Proceedings Act 1973, there is one crucial transitional provision which ensures that a woman who married prior to 1 January 1994 – and thus acquired her husband's domicile on marriage – retained that domicile as a domicile of choice unless and until she acquires a new domicile of choice of her own or abandons her domicile of dependence (eg on divorce) thereby reviving her domicile of origin. This continues to be the case for all women married prior to 1 January 1974. A widow will retain her husband's domicile unless she acquires a domicile of choice of her own – see *Duchess of Portland v IRC*.[53]

2.20 THE BASES OF TAXATION

A number of factors which effect the determination of a person's liability to tax have already been considered – eg the rules of residence and domicile. Once a particular person has been categorised by reference to such concepts (eg as UK resident but non-UK domiciled), the basis upon which the tax liability will be calculated can be determined by reference to these three terms – arising, remittance and receipt. For example, a person who is domiciled and resident in the UK is (absent specific statutory provision) liable to income tax in the UK on all income which 'arises' in the UK and upon all income which 'arises' abroad. Conversely, a person who is resident but not domiciled in the UK will only be liable to tax on income which 'arises' abroad, to the extent that this income is 'remitted to' the UK.

52 [1957] Ch 107.
53 [1982] 2 WLR 367.

2.21 The 'arising basis'

Where the 'arising basis' applies there is a tax liability as soon as the income is due to the recipient. For example, once a particular payment is due in discharge of a legal obligation – eg a payment of rent falls due to the landlord under a lease –that income has 'arisen' such that a UK resident and domiciled person is (in general terms) chargeable to tax in respect of it.

2.22 The 'remittance basis'

As will be familiar to all but the most casual reader, there have been profound changes in the remittance basis of taxation in the UK. The rules are now to be found in Part 14, Chapter A1 of the Income Tax Act 2007 (ITA 2007). They apply to an individual who is UK resident in a tax year but not UK domiciled or not ordinarily UK resident and who makes a claim to be taxed under the remittance basis (which very broadly taxes income and gains brought into the UK rather than those arising worldwide).[54]

Anything other than the most cursory examination of the remittance basis – since the Finance Act 2008 changes, one of the most complex parts of the statutory code – is beyond the scope of this book. However, if an individual's unremitted foreign gains and income – essentially those which he leaves outside the country – are less than £2,000 he can use the remittance basis without having to make a claim and he will not lose his entitlement to UK personal tax allowances or to the annual exempt amount for capital gains tax. Moreover, he will not have to pay the Remittance Basis Charge.

Where an individual's unremitted foreign income or gains arising in a tax year are more than £2,000 he will have to make a claim if he wants the remittance basis to apply. If he does not make such a claim he will be taxed on the arising basis. If he does claim the remittance basis then, in most cases, he will lose his entitlement to UK personal allowances and reliefs for income and capital gains tax. Moreover, depending on how long he has been resident in the UK, he may also be liable to pay a 'remittance basis charge' (which is currently £30,000).

A longer and more detailed discussion of the remittance basis post the changes made by the Finance Act 2008 can be found in Chapter 12 (Expatriate Taxation).

2.23 THE SOURCE DOCTRINE

The third main factor in determining the tax liability attaching to any particular stream of income (over and above residence of the recipient and whether the

54 ITA 2007, s 809B.

remittance or arising basis applies) is the 'source' or location of the particular income. The UK tax system operates by identifying the particular source and then charging that source to tax.

There is one major consequence of this 'source' doctrine. As a matter of principle, a taxpayer cannot be taxed on the receipt of monies from a particular source of income where that source has ceased or the taxpayer has ceased to possess it unless the particular receipts are referable to a period in which the source existed and was possessed by the taxpayer.[55] Although this principle has been abrogated by specific statutory provision to tax post cessation receipts of trades and professions and sums paid to former directors or employees, it remains good in the absence of such specific provisions.

55 See *Brown v National Provident Institution* [1921] 2 AC 222; *Carson v Cheyney's Executors* [1959] AC 412; *Bray v Best* [1988] STC 103.

Chapter 3

Sources of Tax Law

3.1 INTRODUCTION

To the casual venturer, tax law often seems an impenetrable thicket – indeed a jungle – of provisions densely drafted and haphazardly organised. The problem is made worse by the compound of interlocking definitions and the apparent primacy of the strict rule of interpretation which leaves the reader without a compass, as it were.

This state of affairs has arisen largely in consequence of the technical nature of the subject matter and the yearly round of amendments to the primary legislation following the Budget. In order to relieve the difficulties somewhat, HMRC have issued an array of extra-statutory materials which serve a multitude of functions including clarifying HMRC's view on points of difficulty, relieving perceived unfairness around the margins of the legislation and indicating how HMRC will exercise their powers of control and management.

There are a number of discrete series of extra statutory materials: Statutory Interpretations, Extra Statutory Concessions, Statements of Revenue Practice, Leaflets, Press Releases, Commentaries on Finance Bills and Tax Bulletins. However, the most significant measure of recent years has been the publication of the internal manuals used by Inspectors in performing their functions.

3.2 TAX STATUTES

The main statute in the instant context is the Income Tax (Earnings and Pensions) Act 2003 ('ITEPA 2003'). ITEPA contains the substantive charging provisions of relevance to the taxation of employment income. The machinery for the assessment and collection of tax on that income is primarily to be found in the Taxes Management Act 1970 (although see also the Income Tax (Pay as You Earn) Regulations 2003 which are discussed in Chapter 5).

3.3 Interpretation of statutes

There has been a lot written about the interpretation of taxing statutes. Much of it is misleading: it rarely proves beyond the wit of a tax adviser arguing a point of construction before the Tax Chamber of the First-tier Tribunal to find high judicial authority apparently supportive of the interpretative approach advocated.[1] However, it is useful to recite a few broad principles which inform the judicial approach to taxing statutes.[2]

In the past, there had always been an averred preference for the literal rule of interpretation, although it tended to give way in appropriate instances.[3] However, it is doubtful whether this is any longer the case.

As levels of public opprobrium attached to 'artificial' tax avoidance schemes, relying on a literal interpretation of taxing statutes, have increased, judges have become more and more bold in assuming that a particular result cannot have been the intention of the statutory draftsman and proceeding to search (generally successfully) for a construction which avoids that result. The case of *HMRC v Scottish Provident Institution*[4] provides a good recent example. In an elegant passage in *IRC v McGuckian*,[5] Lord Steyn recounts more generally how this change was brought about.

The meaning of a word or expression must be ascertained from the intention and schema of the Act as a whole.[6] To take but one example, the word 'gains' used in the Income and Corporation Taxes Act 1988 (ICTA) refers to revenue profits rather than, as would otherwise be arguable, capital gains.[7]

It is also worth recalling the rule in *Pepper v Hart*:[8]

> '… subject to any question of Parliamentary privilege, the exclusionary rule should be relaxed so as to permit reference to Parliamentary materials where:
>
> (a) legislation is ambiguous or obscure, or leads to an absurdity;
>
> (b) the material relied on consists of one or more statements by a minister or other promoter of the Bill together if necessary with such other Parliamentary material as is necessary to understand such statements and their effects; and
>
> (c) the statements relied on are clear.'

1 See, to this effect, Viscount Simonds in *A-G v Prince Augustus of Hanover* [1957] AC 436, 464.
2 The reader anxious to follow the debate in greater detail is referred to *Simon's Direct Tax Service* at paragraph A2.115.
3 See, for example, Lord Reid in *IRC v Luke* [1963] AC 557 apparently contradicting his fierce adherence to the literal rule in *IRC v Hinchy* [1960] AC 748, 767.
4 [2005] 1 WLR 3172.
5 [1997] STC 908, 915–916.
6 *IRC v Priestley* [1901] AC 208, 213.
7 This is, of course, because the taxation of capital gains is, almost exclusively, the province of the Taxation of Chargeable Gains Act 1992 (TCGA 1992).
8 [1992] STC 898, per Lord Browne-Wilkinson 922–923.

Searching through Hansard – and in particular the Standing Committee debates in relation to the Finance Bill which introduced the measure in question – occupies a significant proportion of most tax specialists' time. However, although Hansard has been cited to the court in a tax context on a large number of occasions, it very rarely proves decisive.

Influencing the manner in which taxing statutes are read is an underlying presumption against double taxation. Lord Denning went so far on one occasion as to say that the courts would 'not allow' it.[9] A further tide running under the surface of statutory interpretation is that of standard commercial accountancy practice. Rules such as the matching principle and accruals principle have an influence which extends beyond such notions as 'profit' and 'loss' to include the entirety of principle driven revenue law. Indeed, this tide now finds statutory expression in the Finance Act 1998 which provides that the profits of a trade, profession or vocation must be computed on an accounting basis which gives a true and fair view.[10]

3.4 CASE LAW

Decisions on points of revenue law create precedents in the normal way. It is worth noting that taxing statutes apply across the United Kingdom and so Scottish decisions stand as authorities in English courts.

It is only recently – 1995 – that decisions of the Special Commissioners (and its replacement, the Tax Chamber of the First-tier Tribunal) have started to be published. As is noted elsewhere,[11] the First-tier Tribunal is one from which generally there exists no appeal on the grounds of fact,[12] and so care has to be taken in ascertaining the facts which underpinned the decision before it may be relied upon as a general principle.

3.5 EXTRA-STATUTORY SOURCES

As has already been indicated, there are a variety of extra-statutory sources of tax law which perform a variety of functions, ranging from clarification to disapplication of statutory provisions. These sources are reproduced in a number of tax handbooks.[13] Before turning to consider these individual series in more detail, it will be helpful to examine their legal status.

9 *IRC v Cleary* (1966) TC 399, 412. See also TCGA 1992, s 37(1) which states there shall be excluded from the consideration taken into account for capital gains tax purposes any sum chargeable as income.
10 TCGA 1992, s 42, subject to any adjustment required or authorised by law.
11 See Chapter 7 (Challenging Revenue Decisions).
12 Save for the normal quasi-factual appeals such as bias and perversity.
13 For example, the *Tolley's Yellow Tax Handbook* Part II and *Simon's Direct Tax Service* Binder 9.

3.6 Legal status of extra-statutory sources

It has been clear since *IRC v National Federation of Self Employed*[14] that HMRC has a public law duty to act fairly as between the body of taxpayers. One specific application of this duty is a public law obligation to make good on extra statutory concessions – whether published or not[15] – indeed, HMRC does not generally argue otherwise.[16] The obligation has been formulated variously as a duty to make good on general representations made to all taxpayers[17] and as a prohibition against discriminating against particular taxpayers.[18] What is clear is that the taxpayer must show HMRC have acted in a way which is *Wednesbury* unreasonable before he can succeed.[19]

Needless to say, this is not an easy test to satisfy. The comment of Lord Templeman in *IRC v Preston* is apposite:[20]

> 'The court can only intervene by judicial review to direct the commissioners to abstain from performing their statutory duties or from exercising their statutory powers if the court is satisfied that "the unfairness" of which the taxpayer complains renders the insistence by the commissioners on performing their duties or exercising their powers an abuse of power by the commissioners.'

It is unclear, however, whether this rule applies to the whole spectrum of extra statutory material.[21] There are some powerful arguments to be made that revenue interpretations, for example, do not have the same legal effect.[22]

Proceedings to secure the enforcement of extra-statutory materials must be brought by way of judicial review. As the first instance tax tribunals have

14 [1982] AC 617, see in particular Lord Scarman at 651. See also *Preston v IRC* [1985] AC 835, 866–67; *R v IRC, ex parte MFK Underwriting Agencies Limited* [1990] 1 WLR 1545, 1569; *R v IRC, ex parte Kaye* [1992] STC 581.

15 A variety which has greatly diminished in importance post-publication of HMRC Manuals. However, see for confirmation, *R v Inspector of Taxes, ex parte Brumfield* [1989] STC 151, per Peter Gibson J 155f. Tending to go the other way is the judgment of Kennedy J in *R v IRC, ex parte Allen* [1997] STC 1141, 1152e.

16 See *R v Inspector of Taxes, ex parte Brumfield* [1989] STC 151, per Peter Gibson J 155.

17 See *R v IRC, ex parte SG Warburg* [1994] STC 518, 527.

18 *Ex parte S G Warburg* [1994] STC 518 ; see also the *National Federation of Self-Employed* case [1982] AC 617.

19 *R v IRC ex parte S G Warburg* [1994] STC 518, 540f.

20 [1985] STC 282, 293.

21 It has, however, been held to apply or been accepted by HMRC as applying to Statements of Practice (*R v IRC, ex parte Kaye*, *ex parte Brumfield* and *ex parte S G Warburg*) and Revenue Manuals (*ex parte Allen*).

22 The arguments are essentially two-fold. First, public bodies may not bind themselves to act ultra vires. Secondly, it is doubtful whether HMRC's view of what the law is ought to give rise to the same expectation as an extra statutory concession. To the best of the authors' knowledge, the question has not been raised to date.

remarked on any number of occasions, they are creatures of statute and do not have jurisdiction to consider abuse of power type arguments.

It should be said, however, that the recent Supreme Court cases of *R (on the application of Davies and another) v R&C Commissioners; and R (on the application of Gaines-Cooper) v R&C Commissioners*,[23] where taxpayers argued unsuccessfully that they had relied on HMRC clear wording, do not set a very auspicious precedent. Accordingly, it is not wise to rely, in the authors' view, on the manual or the frequently answered questions when seeking to find an answer, particularly where otherwise significant amounts of tax would be payable, and probably the most prudent course is to obtain a specific clearance in relation to any particular points of concern.

3.7 Extra-statutory concessions

Extra-statutory concessions are, in essence, derogations from particular statutes. In a note to a concession published in 1989,[24] the Revenue (now HMRC) explained the purpose – and limits on the use – of extra-statutory concessions:

> 'An extra-statutory concession is a relaxation which gives the taxpayer a reduction in tax-liability to which he is not entitled under the strict letter of the law. Most concessions are made to deal with what are, on the whole, minor or transitory anomalies under the legislation and to meet cases of hardship at the margin of the code where a statutory remedy would be difficult to devise or would run to a length out of proportion to the intrinsic importance of the matter.
>
> Inland Revenue extra-statutory concessions are of general application, but in a particular case there may be special circumstances which must be taken into account in considering the application of the concession. A concession will not be given in any case where an attempt is made to use it for tax avoidance.'

There are four series of extra-statutory concessions (A to D) numbering some 230 in total. The most important for present purposes is 'A' which contains concessions applicable to individuals.

Extra-statutory concessions are tightly drafted and, naturally, it will be necessary for the taxpayer to show that he comes within its terms. That having been said, HMRC is generally receptive to an argument that the taxpayer clearly came within the intendment of the concession, if not its literal wording. Naturally this purposive approach to construction cuts both ways. The Revenue will deny

23 [2011] UKSC 47.
24 On the Tax Treatment of Adoption Allowances, Press Release of 16 February 1989.

the benefit of a concession to a taxpayer who may come within its wording but falls outside the intendment.

3.8 Statements of Practice and Press Releases

Prior to 18 July 1978 the Revenue had no formal procedure for issuing Statements of Practice. Generally, these would be published by way of written answers and oral statements in Parliament and letters to professional bodies and trade journals. The procedure has become somewhat more formal since then; new Statements of Practice are generally given a reference number in the following form 'number/year'. Meanwhile, however, HMRC continues to issue press releases and send letters to professional bodies and trade journals.

It is difficult to discern any real distinction in terms of approach or subject matter as between Statements of Practice and Press Releases. Perhaps it is true to say that Statements of Practice are of more general interest. Both tend to be drafted in broad terms and will generally contain an exposition of HMRC's underlying reasoning.

The most important set of Press Releases is the huge bundle released every year on budget day. These generally contain the devilish detail to the points mentioned by the Chancellor in his budget speed.

3.9 HMRC Interpretations

New HMRC Interpretations are published in the HMRC Tax Bulletin. Their purpose is to clarify HMRC's understanding of particular statutory provisions. HMRC have stated that Interpretations will normally be applied in relevant cases, however, they reserve their right not to follow the published Interpretation where the particular facts of the case demand it or in the context of an appeal on the law.[25]

3.10 Manuals

The Revenue Manuals, as they then were, were first published in 1995 for the perusal of taxpayers and their advisers as part of the Code of Practice on Access to Government Information. They contain (almost all of) the guidance prepared for the staff of HMRC. The guidance is reasonably comprehensive but in difficult or complex cases staff can obtain further, specific, guidance from specialists at Head Office or HMRC Solicitor's Office.

25 Indeed, they are legally obliged so to do by the obligation on public bodies not to bind themselves to act outside their power.

They are published in paper form and on the internet[26] and contain a helpful exposition of how HMRC approach particular questions, frequently supported with worked examples. Frequent reference has been made in the 'hard law' Chapters of this book to the Employment Income Manual.

The status of Manuals was first addressed in *R v IRC ex parte Allen*[27] where Kennedy LJ pointed out that it might in some circumstances be possible successfully to challenge by means of judicial review a decision taken either in accordance with the Manual (presumably on the usual *British Oxygen* grounds of failing to have regard to the particular circumstances of an individual case) or where a decision was not taken in accordance with the Manual (presumably on the grounds that, as is outlined above, HMRC were not behaving in an even handed way as between the body of taxpayers).

26 At http://www.hmrc.gov.uk/thelibrary/manuals.htm.
27 [1997] 1141, 1152.

Chapter 4

Introduction to Income Tax

4.1 INTRODUCTION

In broad terms, the income tax liability of an employee or office holder is calculated upon the earnings he receives in a year of assessment from the employment or office less his deductible expenses. This Chapter will examine each of these elements save for the question, what is income, which is dealt with in Chapter 2 (General Principles).[1] It should be recalled that if a sum received is not of an income nature, then no question of income tax arises, irrespective of whether the sum in question might otherwise be said to fall within one of the heads of charge in the relevant part of the income tax code.

4.2 IDENTIFYING EMPLOYMENT INCOME

4.3 'The old world'

The rules for determining many of the above matters differ according to the nature of the source of the income. This is because income tax was originally levied on the basis of a schedular system.

Prior to the changes made as part of the re-write of the tax code under the Tax Law Rewrite Project, there were a number of separate Schedules (primarily, in recent times, Schedule A dealing with income from land, Schedule D dealing with trading and other business profits and Schedule E dealing with employment income), those schedules being mutually exclusive.[1a] Where, unusually, income fell within more than one head of charge, the Revenue had to elect a Schedule under which to charge that sum.[2] Different rules for assessing income applied to each of the individual Schedules. Although that scheduler system has been replaced, for income tax purposes it is helpful to refer to it briefly at least, since it explains much of the case law in this area which is still relevant to the current legislation.

1 At **2.2–2.8** thereof.
1a See discussion in *HMRC v PA Holdings* [2011] EWCA Civ 1414 per Moses LJ at [26]–[31].
2 See, for example, *Bye v Coren* [1985] STC 113; *IRC v Wilkinson* [1992] STC 454.

As regards Schedule D, this schedule had sub-categories known as 'Cases'. The tax liability attaching to a particular source of income potentially differed according to which Case the income is taxed under. In order to assess whether the income is taxable it is, therefore, necessary to have some familiarity with the individual Cases. Schedule D was to be found in section 18 of the Income and Corporation Taxes Act 1988 ('ICTA 1988'). It comprised six Cases. Case I taxed the profits of any trade carried on in the United Kingdom. Case II taxed the profits of any profession or vocation and Case III taxed interest, annuities and other annual payments. Cases IV and V dealt with income from property outside the United Kingdom and Case VI was a residual category taxing 'any other' annual profits or gains.

As regards Schedule A, this schedule taxed profits arising from a business carried on for the exploitation of land: see section 15 of ICTA.

As regards Schedule E, this schedule taxed emoluments from any office or employment.

4.4 'The new world'

As a result of the Tax Law Re-write Project, the structure of the income tax code is now different.

Taking matters in chronological order, with effect from 2003, the Income Tax (Earnings and Pensions) Act 2003 ('ITEPA 2003') restructured the employment income regime by abolishing emoluments, Cases and Schedule E and replacing this system with a general charge on employment income. HMRC provides guidance on the interpretation and application of ITEPA in its Employment Income Manual.[3] The charging section in ITEPA 2003 is section 9. This imposes a charge on 'general earnings' (covering income that was previously charged under ICTA 1988, s 19(1)) and 'specific employment income' (covering income that was previously charged under ICTA 1988, 19(5)). Together these are called 'employment income'.

In 2005 new provision was made for trading, professional and property income (the former Schedules D and A) in the Income Tax (Trading and Other Income) Act 2005 ('ITTOIA 2005').

In 2007 the remaining, more general, rules dealing with the collection and levying of income tax were re-written into the Income Tax Act 2007 ('ITA 2007').

3 www.hmrc.gov.uk.

This book is predominantly concerned with employment income. However, it will also be useful to outline, briefly, the scope of self-employment income in order better to delineate the ambit of Chapter 2 of ITEPA 2003.

4.5 Trading profits

The basis of taxation under trading profits is set out in ITTOIA 2005, ss 5–8 as follows:

(1) provision is made for the taxation of profits of a trade, profession or vocation (section 5);

(2) which arise to a UK resident wherever the trade etc is carried on or to a non-UK resident if the trade etc is carried on in whole or in part in the UK (section 6);

(3) on the full profits of the year computed by reference to a basis (typically, an accounting) period (section 7);

(4) whereby the person liable to the tax is the person in receipt of the profits (section 8).

So far as sections 5–8 are concerned, the question for present purposes is whether the income in question is one which derives from the exercise by the individual in question of a trade etc or, on the other hand, an employment. This question is addressed in **4.20** below.

4.6 Chapter 2 of ITEPA 2003

The basis of taxation under Chapter 2 of ITEPA 2003 is set out in section 6(1), which provides that the charge to tax on employment income is a charge on general earnings and specific employment income.

4.7 General earnings

General earnings are defined in ITEPA 2003, s 62 as follows:

> '(2) "earnings" means (a) any salary, wages or fee, (b) any gratuity or other profit or incidental benefit of any kind obtained by the employee if it is money or money's worth, or (c) anything else that constitutes an emolument of the employment.
>
> (3) "money's worth" means something that is (a) of direct monetary value to the employee, or (b) capable of being converted into money or something of direct monetary value to the employee.'

Since ITEPA 2003 rewrites, but does not generally reform, the law, all the old case law concerning the word 'emolument' still applies.

In the case of general earnings the actual amount charged under ITEPA 2003 is 'the net taxable earnings from an employment' for the year.[4] Only general earnings which are 'for a tax year' in which the employee is resident and/or domiciled in the UK fall within Part 2 of ITEPA 2003. Such earnings are subject to a charge when they are received (rather than when they are earned).

4.8 Specific employment income

'Specific employment income' means any amount which, by virtue of Part 6 or 7 of ITEPA 2003 or any other enactment, counts as employment income. This covers that previously charged by section 19, which taxed income which another provision of the Tax Acts directed should be charged under Schedule E.

In the case of specific employment income the actual amount charged under ITEPA 2003 is 'the net taxable specific income from an employment for the year'.[5] To ascertain 'taxable specific income' one has to look at the terms of the relevant provision.

Where the employee pays foreign tax on his employment earnings, relief against United Kingdom tax will be available under the conditions outlined in Chapter 12 (Expatriate Taxation), at **12.2**.

4.9 YEAR OF ASSESSMENT

A year of assessment – or tax year – runs from 6 April to 5 April. Tax is charged under Chapter 2 of ITEPA 2003 on income *received* in the tax year.[6] Section 18 provides that general earnings consisting of money shall be treated as received at the earliest of the following times:

Rule 1: the time when payment is made of or on account of the earnings.

Rule 2: the time when a person becomes entitled to payment of or on account of earnings.

Rule 3: If the employee is a director of a company and the earnings are from employment with the company (whether or not as director), whichever is the earliest of:

4 ITEPA 2003, ss 9(2), 11(1), 14 and 15(1).

5 ITEPA 2003, ss 9(4) and 12.

6 See ITEPA 2003, ss 15(2) and 18 for money earnings and 19 for others. For a practical application of these rules in unusual circumstances, see *White v IRC* [2003] STC (SCD) 161 (housing allowance paid on a 'back-dated' basis to officers of the RUC).

(a) the time when sums on account of the earnings are credited in the company's accounts or records (whether or not there is any restriction on the right to draw the sums);

(b) if the amount of earnings for a period is determined by the end of the period, the time when the period ends;

(c) if the amount of earnings for a period is not determined until after the period has ended, the time when the amount is determined.

Section 19 provides that general earnings not consisting of money are to be treated as received at the following times:

> '(2) If an amount is treated as earnings for a particular tax year under any of the following provisions, the earnings are to be treated as received in that year:
>
> | | |
> |---|---|
> | section 81 | (taxable benefits: cash vouchers), |
> | section 94 | (taxable benefits: credit-tokens), |
> | Chapter 5 of Part 3 | (taxable benefits: living accommodation), |
> | Chapter 6 of Part 3 | (taxable benefits: cars, vans and related benefits), |
> | Chapter 7 of Part 3 | (taxable benefits: loans), |
> | Chapter 10 of Part 3 | (taxable benefits: residual liability to charge), |
> | section 222 | (payments treated as earnings: payments on account of tax where deductions not possible), |
> | section 223 | (payments treated as earnings: payments on account of director's tax). |
>
> (3) If the amount is treated as earnings under section 87 (taxable benefits: non-cash vouchers), the earnings are to be treated as received in the tax year mentioned in section 88.'

If section 19(2) or (3) does not apply to general earnings not consisting of money, the earnings are treated as received at the time when the benefit is provided.[7]

4.10 CALCULATIONS

Once the income received in the tax year has been determined, the calculation of the tax liability for the year is relatively simple. The first step is to deduct

7 ITEPA 2003, s 19(4).

such allowances as are available to the individual employee. Allowances are uprated every year in accordance with rises in the retail price index unless Parliament determines otherwise.[8] The second is to apply the rates of tax applying to each of the taxable bands of income to the remaining income.

In effecting these calculations in a situation where an employee has more than one source of income – either from another employment or any other source – it must be born in mind that allowances can be claimed only once. Moreover, generally,[9] any income additional to employment income must be taxed at the employee's marginal rate. In other words, that income will represent an accretion to his employment income and must be taxed at the appropriate rate ('top sliced').

4.11 Personal allowance

For the tax year 2013–14, every individual – whether single or married – is entitled to a deduction from his total income of £9,440 Where the individual is, at any time within the tax year, aged 65 or above, he shall be entitled to a deduction from his total income of £10,500 Where the individual is, at any time within the tax year, aged 75 or above, he shall be entitled to a deduction from his total income of £10,660.

4.12 Other allowances

4.13 Married Couple's Allowance

Persons married before 5 December 2005

Where a couple is married and living together and at least one spouse was born before 6 April 1935, the husband can claim Married Couple's Allowance. This gives rise to a reduction in the husband's tax bill by 10% of the Married Couple's Allowance to which he is entitled. The actual amount depends on the husband's income.

Persons married on or after 5 December 2005 or are in a civil partnership

Where a couple is married or in a civil partnership and living together and at least one spouse or partner was born before 6 April 1935, the person with

8 ICTA 1988, s 257C(1) and subject to the phased removal of personal allowances for certain taxpayers announced in the Budget 2009.

9 Certain types of non-employment income are taxed at the basic rate of tax irrespective of the recipient's other earnings.

the higher income can claim Married Couple's Allowance. Again this gives rise to a reduction in the claimant's tax bill by 10% of the Married Couple's Allowance to which he or she is entitled. The actual amount depends on the income of the spouse or civil partner with the higher income.

Period from which Married Couple's Allowance is effective

In the year of marriage or civil partnership a proportion of the allowance is available depending upon the number of complete months of marriage or partnership in the tax year.

Amount of Married Couple's Allowance

The maximum amount of Married Couple's Allowance is £7,915 and the minimum amount is £3,040 for the tax year 2013–14. Claimants receive 10% of the allowance amount – ie at least £304 and up to £791.50 – depending upon their income and, specifically, the extent to which it exceeds £26,100 (2013–14). Each £2 of income over this figure reduces the Married Couple's Allowance by £1.

Blind person's allowance

If the individual is registered blind he is entitled to a 'blind person's allowance' which, for the tax year 2013–14 is £2,160.

4.14 Employee's national insurance contributions

Employee's national insurance contributions are addressed at Chapter 6. However, broadly speaking, they are charged at 12% on all income between £5,668 and £41,444 per annum where the employee has not 'contracted out' of the State Earnings Related Pension Scheme, and 10.4% where he has.

4.15 The taxable bands

For the tax year 2013–14 the taxable bands are as follows:

Rate	Taxable income (£)
20% (basic)	0 – 34,370
40% (higher)	34,371 – £150,000
45% (additional)	Over £150,000

4.16 Examples

Example 1

In the year 2013–14 Tom, a 29 year old single male with no children, receives gross pay of £50,000 from employment. His tax liability will be calculated as follows.

Gross pay	50,000
less personal allowance	9,440
Taxable income	40,560
20% basic rate on £34,370	6,874
untaxed income	6,190
40% higher rate on £6,190	2,476
Income tax liability	£9,350

Example 2

Julia, a blind single mother, receives income from employment of £25,000. Her tax liability, ignoring tax credits, will be calculated as follows.

Gross pay	25,000
less personal allowance	9,440
less blind person's allowance	2,160
Taxable income	13,400
20% basic rate on £13,400	2,680
Income tax liability	£2,680

4.17 OFFICE OR EMPLOYMENT

Neither 'office' nor 'employment' was defined in ICTA and it makes no difference for the purposes of Chapter 2 of ITEPA 2003 whether an individual is in employment or is an office holder. There is, however, a considerable body of case law on the subject which remains of some relevance for the purposes of ITEPA 2003.

4.18 Office

An 'office' is a post which can be recognised as existing and continuing to exist whether or not it is occupied at any given time; if occupied, the office should not owe its existence in any way to the identity of the person who holds it at that given time. Thus it is a post which goes on and is filled by successive holders.[10] Thus, merely by a way of example, the following are holders of an 'office' – Members of Parliament, local councillors, employees of the Crown, police officers, magistrates, judges, bishops and clergymen, a consultant in the National Health Service whether full time or part time,[11] a director of a company – even if he has a contract of employment and holds all the shares therein[12] – an auditor,[13] trustees and executors;[14] a solicitor holding an appointment as registrar of a company;[15] and a clerk holding an appointment as local land charges registrar.[16]

The following have been held not to be offices: an inspector appointed by the Department of the Environment to hold a public local enquiry,[17] a barrister's clerk[18] and the foreign agent of a company.[19]

4.19 Employment

The notion of 'employment' will, presumably, be second nature to readers. What follows, therefore, is: (1) a brief discussion of several lines of cases; (2) a breakdown of the factors HMRC regard as determinative; (3) an analysis of several questions which will arise in a specific tax context; and (4) a short analysis of several occupations which raise particular problems. There are, however, a number of preliminary points which can usefully be made.

First, the parties cannot alter the true nature of the contract between them merely through the words used in the contract. The courts have repeatedly insisted that the mere label cannot be determinative of the tax treatment of the contract.[20] This point was recently emphasised by the Supreme Court in *Autoclenz v Belcher*[21] where Lord Clarke[22] stated as follows:

> 'So the relative bargaining power of the parties must be taken into account in deciding whether the terms of any written agreement in truth represent

10 ITEPA 2003, s 5(3). See also *Great Western Railway v Bater* [1920] 3 KB 266, *McMillan v Guest* [1942] AC 561 and *Edwards v Clinch* [1981] 3 WLR 707.
11 *Mitchell and Edon v Ross* [1960] Ch 145.
12 *McMillan v Guest* [1942] AC 561. See also *Berry v Farrow* [1914] 1 KB 632; *Watson v Rowles* (1926) 11 TC 171; *Proctor v Ryall* (1928) 14 TC 204; *Goodwin v Brewster* (1950) 32 TC 80.
13 *Ellis v Lucas* [1967] Ch 858.
14 *Attorney General v Eyres* [1909] 1 KB 723; Dale v IRC [1951] Ch 893.
15 *IRC v Brander and Cruickshank* [1970] SLT 159.
16 *Ministry of Housing and Local Government v Sharp* [1970] 2 QB 223.
17 *Edwards v Clinch* [1981] Ch. 1.
18 *McMenamin v Diggles* [1991] STC 419.
19 *Pickles v Foster* [1913] 1 KB 174.
20 *Massey v Crown Life Insurance Co* [1978] 1 WLR 676.
21 [2011] UKSC 41.
22 [2011] UKSC 41 at para 35.

what was agreed and the true agreement will often have to be gleaned from all the circumstances of the case, of which the written agreement is only a part. This may be described as a purposive approach to the problem. If so, I am content with that description.'

Second, it is, strictly speaking, irrelevant that another government department – typically HMRC – have treated a particular contract as being, say, an employment contract rather than a contract for services. In practice however, a ruling for the purposes of income tax that a person is self-employed is unlikely to be challenged for the purposes of national insurance contributions and vice versa. The same symmetry of treatment is not however always apparent when one compares the income tax treatment with the value added tax treatment.[23]

Third, a written contract can be disregarded where it does not reflect the true relationship between the parties[24] or because the parties did not intend it to be a complete record of their understanding.[25] The written contract is however the starting point – and the best evidence in cases of ambiguity – in determining the true nature of the legal rights and obligations between the parties.[26]

Fourth, as a matter of construction, the contract must be examined in light of the words used by the parties with a view to determining the true, objective, intention of the parties at the time the contract was signed. As with the interpretation of any contract, extraneous evidence (eg of subjective intention or of prior negotiations) cannot be considered.[27]

4.20 The case law

In determining whether a person is employed or self-employed, the courts have traditionally applied a number of tests. These will be familiar to readers such that it is merely necessary to outline the relevant factors. It should, however, be noted that certain tests may be more appropriate in some circumstances than others – there is no single correct approach.[28]

4.21 Mutual obligations test

Under the mutual obligations test a person will be properly regarded as an employee where the contract imposes certain minimum, irreducible, obligations

23 *Reed Personal Services v Commissioners of Customs and Excise* [1995] STC 588.
24 *Autoclenz v Belcher* [2011] UKSC 41; *Global Plant Ltd v Secretary of State for Health and Social Security* [1972] 1 QB 139 and *Protectacoat v Szilagyi* [2009] EWCA Civ 98.
25 *Carmichael v National Power plc* [1999] ICR 1226.
26 *Massey v Crown Life Insurance Company* [1978] 1 WLR 676.
27 *Chartbrook Ltd v Persimmon Homes Ltd* [2009] 1 AC 1101; *Prenn v Simmonds* [1971] 1 WLR 1381.
28 *Hall v Lorimer* [1994] STC 23 and see *Montgomery v Johnson Underwood Ltd* [2001] ICR 819.

upon him and the person with whom he has entered into the contract. Thus, if the person concerned is obliged to accept and carry out certain duties for the counterparty (ie the employer) and he makes himself available to work for that counterparty, thereby cutting himself off from seeking or accepting work from another employer it is likely that he will be regarded as an employee.[29] Equally, if the counterparty is obliged to offer continuing employment to the person concerned which the person is obliged to accept it is likely that the counterparty will be regarded as an employer properly so called. Thus in *O'Kelly v Trust House Forte plc*,[30] it was clear on the evidence that regular temporary waiters who would be asked to provide work for particular shifts but were free to refuse the work offered, were not employees properly so called even though the offers of work were regular (and highly regulated) and frequently accepted (and see also in this regard *Express & Echo Publications Ltd v Tanton*[31]).

It is possible that, over a period of time, the absence of the necessary mutual obligations which would found an employment relationship will gradually be replaced by expectations that work will be offered and accepted and/or economic dependence by the worker concerned upon the provider of that work. In such circumstances, what was originally a contract for services may become a contract of service.[32] The other possibility to be born in mind is that what may appear to be single, separate but repeated contracts for services are – in all the circumstances – in fact merely a part of a greater, 'umbrella', contract of service by which the employee is required to accept work offered to him from time to time.[33]

4.22 The economic reality/integration test

Under these tests (whether separately considered or, more commonly now, applied as one), the courts ask themselves whether a particular person has become so integrated into the business of the company concerned that he or she has become a part *of* that business rather than someone who provides services *to* it. The court will look at such factors as whether a person has become part of sick pay schemes, maternity pay schemes, holiday regulations, staff social clubs and other general work place activities.

Approaching the same matter from a purer economic point of view, the courts have similarly asked whether the person concerned can be said to be 'in business on his own account'[34] or whether he or she has surrendered their

29 *Nethermere (St Neots) Ltd v Gardiner* [1984] ICR 615 and *Hellyer Brothers Ltd v McLeod* [1966] ICR 122.
30 [1983] 3 All ER 456.
31 [1999] ICR 693.
32 *Airfix Footwear Limited v Cope* [1978] ICR 1210.
33 *Stringfellow Restaurants Limited v Quashie* [2012] EWCA Civ 1735 per Elias LJ at paras 10 to 14. See also *Hellyer Brothers Ltd v McLeod* [1966] ICR 122.
34 *Market Investigations Ltd v Minister of Social Security* [1969] 2 QB 173.

identity so as to become economically a part of an employing company. Here the courts have looked at whether a person takes financial risk, whether he or she takes responsibility for the management of the activities, whether he or she has an opportunity of profiting from the efficient performance of the obligations imposed upon them, whether he or she hires additional helpers (and can substitute someone else to perform the tasks) and whether he or she provides their own equipment. For a decision of the Court of Appeal – in a tax context – which can be regarded as encapsulating the correct approach, see *Hall v Lorimer*[35] where the court considered a number of factors with a view to building up an overall picture including provision of equipment, engagement of helpers, financial risk, responsibility for management and the opportunity to profit.

4.23 The control test

In determining whether a person who has contractual obligations to another is providing a service or services (ie is employed or self-employed) it remains relevant, to some degree, to ask whether the person concerned is subject to another's control to such an extent as to render the relationship that of employer and employee.[36]

This test looks at two separate issues. First, whether a person is obliged to do the work himself (or whether he is able, as a self-employed person would usually be, to substitute another to perform the services on his behalf). And, second, whether in carrying out the obligations under the contract the person has no practical freedom as to how the work is to be done. As an example the courts have looked at the way in which a person has been paid (whether weekly, monthly or by reference to the job as a whole) and the number of hours worked, namely whether there is a set number to be worked in a given period (beyond which, for example overtime pay may be due) or whether the contract merely requires the performance of a job by a fixed deadline.

As will be appreciated, the significance of the control test has declined over recent years for a number of reasons, the primary one being that greater specialisation in the workplace has meant that the degree of control which can be exercised over specialist employees is necessarily limited. In addition, there are more flexible working patterns throughout industry generally which make it difficult to determine, merely from an examination of contract, that a person is subject to sufficient 'direct' control to be properly regarded as an employee. For these reasons the control test should not be applied alone in determining a person's status, except in the clearest of cases.

35 [1994] STC 23.
36 *Ready Mixed Concrete (South East) Ltd v Minister of Pensions and National Insurance* [1968] 2 QB 497.

4.24 HMRC's approach

HMRC's Employment Status Indicator (ESI) tool enables an individual or group of workers to check their employment status, that is, whether they are employed or self-employed for income tax, National Insurance Contributions or VAT purposes.[36a]

The matters to which HMRC will have regard in determining whether an individual is in employment are set out in the Employment Status Manual,[37] and include the following:

- The worker's job description;
- Whether there is a written contract or whether handbooks were issued to the worker;
- How are the parties described in the contract;
- The manner in which control is exercised over the work done, eg who decides what work is done; where is the work done; who decides when the work is to be done etc;
- How is the work supervised;
- Must the worker do the job himself or can he use a stand;
- Is there exclusivity about the working arrangement, eg does the worker provider similar services on a short term basis to many 'employers';
- Has the worker taken on any financial risk such as investing capital or meeting expenses, eg who provides the equipment;
- On what basis is pay calculated;
- Is provision made for holiday pay, sick pay or pensions;
- How does the worker fit in to the organisational structure of the business;
- Does the 'employer' have the right to dismiss the employee;
- Is there a mutuality of obligation to provide and accept further work;
- If the engagement is part time, is it related to any existing business of the worker; and
- What National Insurance Contributions are paid by the worker?

4.25 Tax aspects of the notion of employment

It will be recalled from the discussion of the architecture of the tax code (see **4.3** above) that the legislation draws two distinctions: first, that between a

36a http://www.hmrc.gov.uk/calcs/esi.htm.
37 See Employment Status Manual, paragraph 00500 at www.hmrc.gov.uk.

'trade' and employment. Earnings from a trade are taxable under ITTOIA 2005 and not ITEPA 2003. Second, that between a 'profession or vocation' and employment. Again, in respect of the former, the earnings are taxable under ITTOIA 2005 and not ITEPA 2003.

The foundation for the two distinctions is identical: it lies not in the nature of the occupation – to use a neutral expression – but rather *how* that occupation is carried on. Although, for example, the exercise of an activity which could be described as a profession or vocation is a pre-requisite to a tax liability under ITTOIA 2005 it is not, as ITTOIA 2005, s 4(2) (priority provisions) makes clear, sufficient to take the earnings therefrom outside Chapter 2 of ITEPA 2003. Persons exercising a profession are frequently taxed under Chapter 2.[38] It is necessary to ask, first, whether the individual undertakes an 'employment' or occupies an 'office'.[39] It is only if the answer lies in the negative that ITTOIA 2005 is called into operation.

The position is identical when it comes to distinguishing between a trade and employment: it is the manner in which the occupation is carried on rather than the occupation itself which is of importance.

4.26 Solicitor and accountants

One area which gives rise to particular difficulty is that of solicitors and accountants. As recounted above, the income made by professionals in private practice is taxable under ITTOIA 2005. However, if they hold an office or employment, the receipts therefrom are taxable under Chapter 2 of ITEPA 2003. So where an accountant was an auditor of a limited company he held an office[40] as did a solicitor who acted as court clerk.[41] Assistant solicitors and accountants (other, of course, than partners) both being employees, are taxable under Chapter 2 of ITEPA 2003.

However, where a professional in private practice takes an office or employment the duties of which would normally fall within the scope of his private practice as an incident of his practice, the Revenue will usually agree, as a matter of concession, that receipts therefrom may be taxed under ITTOIA 2005. However, this treatment is usually available only where:

(a) the duties of the office or employment (in terms of time taken) are small in relation to other practice work (of the individual or partner) which is clearly of a professional nature;

38 See, for example, *Fall v Hitchen* (1972) 49 TC 433 where it was held that the income derived by a ballet dancer from a contract with Sadler's Wells was taxable under Schedule E notwithstanding that she was carrying on a profession.

39 *Mitchell and Edon v Ross* (1959) 40 TC 11 per Upjohn J at 34.

40 *Walker v Carnaby* [1970] 1 All ER 502; *Ellis v Lucas* [1967] Ch 858.

41 *IRC v Brander & Cruickshank* [1970] SLT 159.

(b) the office or employment is in a field related to the profession and particular practice concerned;

(c) in a case involving a partner, there is an agreement between the partners that the fees are included as income of the partnership and pooled for division amongst the partners – and that agreement is acted upon;

(d) the individual and any partners agree that the income be treated for tax purposes in this manner and agree to pay tax on the fees on that basis (where appropriate as part of the partnership profits);

(e) the fees are not derived from the directorship of a company and are small in relation to the receipts of the practice generated by the individual or partner.

The limits of this treatment can be seen in the famous case of *Ricketts v Colquhoun*[42] where a barrister who accepted an appointment as Recorder was taxable in respect of earnings therefrom under Schedule E (now Chapter 2).

Directors' fees received by members of professional partnerships are subject to a formal Revenue concession.[43] Upon the making of a request, the Revenue will agree that those fees may be taxed under ITTOIA 2005 provided that: (a) the directorship is a normal incident of the profession and the particular practice concerned; (b) the fees are only a small part of the profits; and (c) under the partnership agreement the fees are pooled for division amongst the partners.

The same concession applies to companies which appoint a director to the board of another company and the fees for which are remitted to the appointing company. Such fees are taxable as trading income of the company concerned.

4.27 NHS doctors and dentists

It is clear that doctors and dentists holding full time employment in the NHS are taxed under Chapter 2 as are those holding part time employment: see *Mitchell and Edon v Ross*.[44] Following that decision a statement was agreed between the Revenue and British Medical Association of which the following is an extract:

'(1) Last July [1961], the House of Lords gave its decision in the test cases about the income-tax treatment of part-time consultants. The effect of the decision is that part-time hospital doctors are taxable under Schedule E and not under Schedule D on the emoluments of their hospital appointments (and of any other office or employment within

42 *Ricketts v Colquhoun* (1925) 10 TC 118
43 Extra Statutory Concession A37.
44 [1962] AC 813.

the scope of Schedule E) and that the expenses attributable to their duties for the hospital can be deducted only if they qualify under the Schedule E expenses rule.

(2) This decision applies to all the emoluments of a part-time hospital doctor from his hospital appointment, with the qualification that fees for lecturing (other than lecturing in teaching hospitals under the ordinary terms of the appointment) and fees for outside domiciliary consultants undertaken for a hospital board by which the doctor is not employed would continue to be assessable under Schedule D …'

Appointments held outside the NHS are also strictly assessable under Chapter 2, however, where the criteria specified in the Statement are satisfied, HMRC will agree that they may be taxed as professional income under ITTOIA 2005.

4.28 Casual and freelance workers in film, television and radio

HMRC have tended to argue that the majority of casual and freelance staff engaged on making films, television and radio are taxable under Chapter 2. However, a list of those whom HMRC is prepared to accept may be taxed on professional or trade income under ITTOIA 2005 can be found in the Film, Television and Production Industry Guidance Notes.[45] These notes (updated in August 2013) have been expanded to confirm that workers in certain grades (a comprehensive list is included in the guidance, from animal handlers to warm up acts) may be regarded as self-employed provided that they are engaged:

(a) For a one-off production such as a feature film or a single drama or documentary (if the worker is to be engaged on a separate production following the completion of the one-off production then, where this is known at the outset of the second production, PAYE should be considered from the commencement of the second production. If this happens after a break, where it can be shown that the worker was seeking or worked elsewhere, then the worker can be treated as self-employed. A break is a natural break rather than a contrived one such as Christmas holiday or an annual vacation); or

(b) For less than nine months on a series or a specific strand of a programme (if the worker is engaged for nine months on a series and a second series is commissioned then as the series are linked, the worker can continue to be treated as self-employed on the second series.)

The position of a freelance vision mixer was considered by the Court of Appeal in *Hall v Lorimer*.[46] He worked on a series of short-term contracts lasting one or two days. He worked in studios and did not provide any of his

45 Film and TV Guidance Notes: www.hmrc.gov.uk.
46 [1994] STC 23.

own equipment. His work involved selecting the most appropriate camera shot from a range of shots subject to the overall wishes of the director. He did not generally hire staff but could provide a substitute with the consent of the production company concerned. He did not contribute to the production costs. Having regard, in particular, to the fact that the taxpayer customarily worked for 20 or more production companies and that the vast majority of his assignments, as appears from the documentary evidence, lasted only for a single day,[47] the Court of Appeal was not prepared to overturn the decision of the Special Commissioners that the individual in question was not 'employed' and was taxable under Schedule D. (See *also ITV Services Ltd v HMRC* [2013] EWCA Civ 687.)

4.29 Workers supplied by or through intermediaries

The position of workers supplied by or through agencies is addressed in Part 2, Chapters 7, 8 and 9 of ITEPA 2003. Broadly, the intention of these Chapters is that workers who would be employees if engaged directly by those who use their labour should be taxed as if they are actually employees.

4.30 Agencies

Chapter 7 deals with agency workers. It applies where an individual personally provides, or is under an obligation personally to provide his services to another (the Client); the services are supplied by or through a third person (the Agency) under the terms of an 'agency contract'; the worker is subject to (or to the right of) supervision, direction or control as to the manner in which the services are provided; and remuneration receivable under or in consequence of the agency contract is not otherwise employment income.[48]

Where the chapter applies, the services provided by the worker are to be treated for income tax purposes as duties of an employment held by the worker with the agency (ie the agency is to be as the employer) and all remuneration payable under or in consequence of the agency contract shall be treated as earnings from that employment.[49]

These provisions are apt to catch most employment agency type arrangements. However, should one wish to avoid them, doing so is relatively straightforward. An agency contract is defined as one made between the worker and the agency under the terms of which the worker is obliged to personally provide services to the client.[50] If the contract between himself and the agency gives him a right

47 Per Nolan LJ at 30g.
48 Section 44.
49 Section 44(2).
50 Section 47(1).

to substitute the labour of another for his own then, irrespective of whether he exercises that right, the relationship between him and the agency will not be under an agency contract and so the agency provisions will not apply.

If the services in question are services as an actor, singer, musician or other entertainer, or as a fashion, photographic or artist's model then the section does not apply[51] Nor will it apply if the services are rendered wholly in the worker's own home or at other premises which are neither controlled or managed by the client nor prescribed by the nature of the services.[52]

If a company is interposed between the worker and the agency, HMRC accepts that it is not necessary for the agency to deduct PAYE income tax at source because the interposed company is itself an agency.[53]

4.31 IR35

This obvious route to escaping from the operation of the agency provisions was increasingly utilised by individual 'contractors', typically although not exclusively in the IT sector, who set up wholly owned companies through which they would supply their services to the end user. Their contract with the intermediary company would not oblige them to supply their services personally.

The Revenue's response was Chapter 8 of ITEPA 2003 (colloquially known as IR35, after the Revenue publication that announced its adoption). Chapter 8 stands to apply where a worker does personally perform or is under an obligation personally to perform services for another person (the 'Client') and the services are not provided under a contract between the client and the worker but under arrangements involving a third party (the 'intermediary'). Where those conditions are satisfied and 'the circumstances' are such that, if the services were provided under a contract directly between the client and the worker, the worker would be regarded for income tax purposes as an employee of the client.[54] The circumstances include (but, implicitly, are not confined to) the terms on which the services are provided:[55] under these provisions one is 'not considering an actual contract between the service company and the client, but imagining or constructing a notional contract which does not in fact exist.'[56]

HMRC has published (May 2012) guidance in the form of a 12-point assessment for answering the difficult hypothetical questions raised.[57]

51 Section 47(2)(a).
52 Section 47(2)(b).
53 See Revenue Decision 4.
54 Section 49(1).
55 Section 49(4).
56 *R (oao Professional Contractors Group) v IRC* [2001] STC 629.
57 http://www.hmrc.gov.uk/ir35/guidance.pdf.

Where Chapter 8 applies, the intermediary is treated as paying to the worker, and the worker is treated as receiving from the intermediary, an amount which is to be treated as earnings from employment (referred to in the legislation as the 'deemed employment payment')[58] and that payment is liable to employment income tax and national insurance contributions. The quantum of the deemed employment payment is calculated by reference to a statutory formula in section 54 of ITEPA 2003 and (very broadly) is 95% of the payments and benefits received by the intermediary, less expenses that would be deductible if the worker were an employee.

However, although far more robust in theory than Chapter 7, Chapter 8 proved equally difficult in practice. Workers, often advised by providers of intermediaries who had a vested interest in the continuation of the *status quo*, continued to proceed on the basis that the facts were such that the arrangements fell outside the scope of Chapter 8. Investigating whether such a stance was justified was, from the Revenue's perspective, extremely resource intensive. Moreover, even where such an investigation did reveal a failure on the part of the intermediary properly to account for tax and NICs on a deemed employment payment, because primary liability for the tax and NICs rested on the intermediary, the worker would often simply let that company fail and start up a new one. All, from the Revenue's perspective, highly unsatisfactory.

4.32 Managed Service Companies

The Revenue's response was Chapter 9: the Managed Service Company regime. This applies where there is a 'managed service company' and a 'managed service company provider'. A managed service company is a company in the business of providing the services of an individual to others; payments are made to that individual of an amount equal to the greater part or all of the consideration for the provision of the services; the payments are made in such a way as to result in the individual receiving a higher net of tax and NICs sum than he would if the payments were employment income; and a 'managed service provider' is involved with the company.[59] There is then a list of the circumstances in which a third person will or will not be involved with the company.[60]

Where the services of a worker are provided directly or indirectly by a managed service company, the worker receives a payment or benefit which can reasonably be taken to be in respect of the services and the payment is not otherwise employment income, the managed service company is treated

58 Section 50(1).
59 Section 61B.
60 Section 61B(2)–(5).

as making and the worker is treated as receiving a payment which is treated as earnings from an employment.[61] The amount of that payment is calculated by reference to the formula in section 61E.

There are two material differences between the MSC provisions and IR35. First, the MSC provisions are not triggered by the presence or absence of some quasi-employment relationship. Thus, certain relationships will fall within IR35 which would not fall within the MSC provisions and vice versa. Second, unlike with IR35, the MSC code contains provision which enables the debts of MSC companies to be traced through to a range of other persons, including: (a) directors, office holders or associates of the MSC; (b) the MSC provider; (c) a person who encouraged or was actively involved in the provision by the MSC of the services of the individual; and (d) a director or other office holder or associate of (b) or (c).[62]

These extensive tracing provisions certainly succeeded in catching the attention of the promoters of intermediary companies in a way that the IR35 provisions never did. Whilst it is open to question whether compliance with the MSC code is better than compliance with IR35, anecdotal evidence suggests that the tracing provisions have caused many intermediaries to leave the market.

4.33 EARNINGS

The definition of earnings in section 62 is a broad one. Commission is a form of earnings. So are all benefits-in-kind which, although not taking the form of a money payment, are capable of being turned into money.[63] Discretionary and contractual bonuses are earnings.[64]

The source of the payment is irrelevant[65] and payments received from third parties attributable to the employment such as, for example, tips received from customers constitute earnings.[66] Monies improperly diverted by an employee to his own use may constitute assessable earnings.[67] Where, however, monies are received by a person owing a fiduciary obligation to the party from whom the monies are diverted (for example, a director to a company), that person will hold those monies as trustee and, hence, they will not constitute earnings.[68]

61 Section 61D.
62 Section 688A.
63 *Tennant v Smith* [1892] AC 150. See discussion below.
64 *Denny v Reed* (1933) 18 TC 254.
65 Although if the source is otherwise than the employer, it will raise the question whether the payment can be said to be 'from' the employment: see the discussion below.
66 See *Calvert v Wainwright* [1947] KB 526. See *also Wright v Boyce* (1958) 38 TC 160 (CA).
67 See, for example, *Billows v Robinson* [1990] STC 162.
68 See *Rose v Humbles* 48 TC 103, 117H.

Payments applied for the benefit of the employee are just as much his income as money paid directly to him.[69] So where an employer makes good a financial obligation of his employee, the sum paid is treated as income. Where the financial obligation is the employee's income tax liability – as in the case of an obligation to pay monies free of all income tax – the sum paid over must be 'grossed up' so as to discharge the employee's tax liability on the additional income comprised of the settlement of his tax bill.[70]

Example 3

An employer is to pay his employee £75,000 per annum free of income tax. Assuming that the employee is liable to income tax at 40% on the entirety of that sum, the question which arises is: what is the gross sum (x) which, before deduction of tax at 40%, leaves £75,000 net?

60% of x = £75,000

x = £125,000

(40% of £125,000 = £50,000)

4.34 Gifts, bonuses and other voluntary payments

Prima facie, a gift is not chargeable to income tax as it is not 'income'.[71] As a matter of law, a gift made by employer to employee in consequence of a personal relationship – to take an obvious example, a gift from a father to his employee son – will tend not to be earnings because it does not derive from the employment relationship.[72] The point is well illustrated by Atkinson J's example that a tip to a taxi driver was taxable but that a tip of £10 would not be taxable if paid at Christmas or when the driver was going on holiday and was intended to acknowledge the driver's qualities and faithfulness.[73] Ultimately the question is one of fact and degree. A payment to relieve poverty[74] or to mark the passing of an examination in principle falls outside the charge to tax.[75]

Where, however, the gift is attributable to services rendered, it will be an earnings. For example, a Christmas bonus paid to all members of staff at the

69 See, for example, *Drummond v Collins* [1915] AC 1011.

70 See *North British Railway Co v Scott* [1923] AC 37; *Jaworski v Institute of Polish Engineers* [1951] 1 KB 768. It is not unusual in certain sectors (eg professional football) for contracts to provide for payment 'netto' (ie free of UK tax).

71 *R v Supplementary Benefits Commission ex parte Singer* [1973] 1 WLR 713.

72 See, for example, *Bridges v Hewitt* (1957) 37 TC 289.

73 *Calvert v Wainwright* [1947] 1 All ER 282.

74 *Turton v Cooper* (1905) 5 TC 138.

75 *Ball v Johnson* (1971) 47 TC 155.

end of a successful year – whether contractual or *ex gratia*[76] – will be taxable,[77] as will a 'long service award'.[78] Quite where this leaves gifts to departing employees purchased following a collection from colleagues is unclear. Strictly speaking, the position would appear to be that one must consider the relationship between donee and donor, however, it is considered unlikely that the Revenue would take the point.[79]

In *Moorhouse v Doland*,[80] monies collected for a professional cricketer for meritorious performances at matches were held to be assessable, where the cricketer had a contractual right to a collection 'for any meritorious performance by the professional with bat and ball in certain matches'. In *Seymour v Reed*,[81] on the other hand, where a benefit match was held for a professional cricketer on his retirement following a lifetime's service to cricket, the gate money was held not to be taxable. Lord Cave said:

> 'Its purpose is not to encourage the cricketer to further exertions, but to express the gratitude of his employers and of the cricket-loving public for what he has already done, and their appreciation of his personal qualities.'

A useful summary is provided by Jenkins LJ in *Moorhouse v Dooland*:[82]

(1) The test of liability to tax on a voluntary payment made to the holder of an office or employment is whether, from the standpoint of the person who receives it, it accrued to him by virtue of his office or employment or, in other words, by way of remuneration for his services.

(2) If the recipient's contract of employment entitled him to receive the voluntary payment that is a strong ground for holding that it accrued by virtue of his office or, in other words, is a remuneration for his services.

(3) The fact that the voluntary payment is of a periodic or recurrent character affords a further, although less cogent, ground for the same conclusion.

(4) On the other hand a voluntary payment may be made in circumstances which show that it is given by way of present or testimonial on grounds personal to the recipient, as for example a collection for the particular individual who is at the time vicar of a given parish because he is in

76 *Denny v Reed* (1933) 18 TC 254.

77 *Laidler v Perry* [1965] 2 All ER 121.

78 *Weston v Hearn* [1943] 2 All ER 421. Note, however, this is subject to relief provided in ITEPA 2003, s 322 which excludes from income tax long service awards of £50 per year of service. This applies where the employee has served not less than 20 years and no similar award has been made to the recipient within the previous ten years.

79 One should, of course, never say never. A considerable body of case law has grown up in relation to the tax treatment of additions to the Church collection plate: see *Blakiston v Cooper* [1909] AC 104; *Moorhouse v Dooland* [1955] Ch 284, 299; *Slaney v Starkey* [1931] 2 KB 148; *Seymour v Reed* [1927] AC 554, 569; *Corbett v Duff* [1941] 1 KB 730, 740.

80 [1955] Ch 284 (CA).

81 [1927] AC 554.

82 [1955] Ch 284.

> straightened circumstances, or a benefit held for a professional cricketer in recognition of his long and successful career in first class cricket. In such a case, the proper conclusion is likely to be that the voluntary payment is not a profit accruing to the recipient by virtue of his office or employment but a gift to him as an individual paid and received by reason of his personal needs or by reason of his personal qualities or attainments.

Where the donor is the employer, one must also consider his intention.[83] The value of the gift will cast some light upon this fact.[84]

There is an exemption operating on gifts made to employees or office holders by third parties to the value of £250.[85] In order for the treatment to apply, the following conditions must be satisfied: (a) the gift consists of goods or a voucher or token only capable of being used to obtain goods; (b) the person making the gift is not the employer or a person connected with the employer; (c) the gift is not made either in recognition of the performance of particular services in the course of the employment or in anticipation of particular services which are to be performed; (d) the gift has not been directly or indirectly procured by the employer or a person connected with the employer; and (e) the total cost of all gifts made by the same donor to the employee during the income tax year is £250 or less.

The same treatment excludes from tax an annual Christmas party or alternative annual function of a similar nature open to all staff where the expenditure is less than £150 per person per annum.[86] However, where the expenditure is above that threshold the entire amount falls into tax.

4.35 Payments on commencement of employment

Payments made on or before the commencement of employment will be chargeable as earnings if they are made in respect of services to be rendered to the employer. Payments which are, properly analysed, given in exchange for the employee giving up some personal advantage will not be taxable. In *Jarrold v Bousted*[87] it was held that lump sum payments made to former rugby union players for switching to league were given in respect of their resigning their amateur status and were not taxable. A 'Golden Handcuffs' payment, repayable in the event that the employee leaves the employment, would, however, be taxable.[88]

83 Per Lord Hodson in *Laidler v Perry* [1966] AC 16, 35.
84 See *Seymour v Reed* [1927] AC 554, 569, *Calvert v Wainwright* [1947] 1 All ER 282 and *Laidler v Perry* [1965] Ch 192, 199.
85 ITEPA 2003, ss 264, 270 and 324.
86 ITEPA 2003, s 264.
87 41 TC 701 (CA).
88 The limits of this principle are exposed in *Riley v Coglan* 44 TC 481, 489.

4.35A Employment income provided by third parties

The Finance Act 2011 introduced a new Part 7A into ITEPA 2003 containing wide-reaching anti-avoidance provisions, commonly referred to as the 'disguised remuneration provisions'. Under Part 7A, a charge to income tax (and liability to NICs) arises on the value of a 'relevant step' taken by a third party as part of an arrangement which is (wholly or partly) a means of providing recognition or rewards or loans to an employee or a person linked with him or her. The value of the relevant step counts as employment income of the employee.

The 'relevant step' can take various forms. It can be the earmarking of a sum or money or an asset, a payment of a sum of money or the transfer of an asset, or the act of making an asset available.[88a] As a relevant step can include the earmarking of a sum or an asset it is possible for a charge to tax on employment income to arise before the employee has received anything or become entitled to use any asset.

Part 7A takes precedence over the other provisions of ITEPA 2003,[88b] so should always be considered first when a third party is involved in delivering any form of valuable consideration to an employee.

4.36 PAYMENTS FOR ENTERING INTO A RESTRICTIVE COVENANT

Payments made to an employee or officer for entering into a restrictive covenant are dealt with specifically at section 225 of ITEPA 2003. Where an individual who holds, has held, or is about to hold an office or employment gives an undertaking which restricts him as to his conduct or activities,[89] and receives a sum in respect of the giving of the undertaking or its total or partial fulfilment,[90] that sum shall be treated as earnings of his office or employment. The section applies whether the undertaking is enforceable or not.[91]

HMRC has confirmed that a financial settlement relating to litigation commenced or to be commenced by the employee in respect of the termination of his employment which binds the employee not to pursue the litigation is taxable under the termination payments provisions[92] rather than section 225.[93]

88a ITEPA 2003, ss 554B–554D.
88b ITEPA 2003, s 554Z6.
89 Section 225(1)(a).
90 Section 225(1)(b).
91 Section 225(8).
92 See Chapter 10.
93 Statement of Practice 3/96.

Where the subject of that litigation is the enforceability of a restrictive covenant contained in the contract, the authors' view is that any payment by the employer in return for which the employee agreed to abide by that covenant will fall into tax under section 225.

4.37 CLAWBACK ARRANGEMENTS

An employee may receive earnings, taxable as earnings in the year in which they are paid, which he is nonetheless required to repay to his employer in a subsequent tax year. Such a situation might arise where a bonus is subject to a clawback provision, or where an employee acts in breach of a term of compromise agreement, triggering some condition which defeats his entitlement to the payment. There is no general entitlement to a refund of tax which was properly charged and paid when it was due. But this may amount to 'negative earnings'.[94] In *Martin v HMRC*,[95] the employee had received a signing bonus of £250,000 in return for committing to work for a five-year period. On giving early notice of termination, he was required, under the terms of his contract of employment, to repay £162,500, on which he had already paid tax. The First-tier Tribunal, without the assistance of authority, decided that the reference to negative taxable earnings in section 11 of ITEPA 2003 referred to a contractual reversal, under the terms of employment, of what had constituted taxable earnings.

4.37A Benefits in kind

The taxation of benefits in kind – ie non-monetary perks received by employees from their employment – is discussed at Chapter 8.

4.38 Salary sacrifice

Arrangements whereby employer and employee agree that the latter should forego part of his monetary remuneration in exchange for the receipt of a benefit in kind (usually of a type attracting a lower charge to tax on receipt than the monetary remuneration foregone) are increasingly commonplace.

The general rule is that if a person holds an office or employment, no application of the income therefrom which he may make as between himself and any other person can affect his tax liability[96] In *Dolan v 'K' National School Teacher*[97] a nun employed as a teacher but bound by the constitution of her Order to hand over all earnings was properly assessed under Schedule E. However, where it is

94 ITEPA 2003, s 11.
95 [2013] UKFTT 40 (TC).
96 See, for example, *Reade v Brearley* 17 TC 687, 693.
97 [1944] IR 470.

clear from the facts that there was never any intention to pay or receive a salary, no liability will arise.[98]

As a general rule, salary sacrifice arrangements are effective when: (i) the contractual right to monetary remuneration is removed before it is treated as received for tax purposes; and (ii) on a proper reading of the revised contract, the employee is entitled only to that lower cash remuneration and the benefit. The question of when earnings are treated as received for tax purposes is addressed at **4.9** above.

Obviously, the reduction in cash remuneration will have a number of employment law consequences. Will the revised wage still be higher than the statutory minimum? Will the revised wage still be above the lower earnings limit for national insurance purposes so as to give rise to a right to statutory sick pay, and so on? HMRC's website at http://www.hmrc.gov.uk/specialist/salary_sacrifice.htm contains a number of discussions of the sometimes complex issues that can arise around salary sacrifice schemes.

4.39 Sick pay

Generally, no difficulty arises in respect of sick pay, including statutory sick pay.[99] It is taxable in the same way as any other earnings from employment

However, in certain industries – the building industry, for example – where it is common for employees to work for short periods of time in successive employments, employers contribute to a central fund during the period they employ an individual so that if he is off sick the cost of sick pay is spread amongst all the employers, not merely the one who happened to be employing him at the time. Where such arrangements are in place, it is the central fund rather than the employer which pays the sick pay.

Section 221 provides, for the avoidance of doubt, that such a payment shall be chargeable to income tax as earnings of the employment.[100] Where, however, the employee has contributed to the fund only such payments as are attributable to the employer's contributions shall be so taxable.[101]

4.40 Payments on death or disablement in service

The tax treatment of a payment made on the employee's death or disablement is as follows. Such a payment will not be taxable under Chapter 2 of ITEPA

98 See *Reade v Brearley* 17 TC 687, 693 and *Oliver v Chuter* 18 TC 570.
99 Section 660.
100 Section 221(3).
101 Section 221(4).

2003 as it follows not from the employment but from the fact, as it were, that the employee can no longer be employed.[102] Moreover, it will not be taxable under Chapter 3 of ITEPA 2003 as a termination payment.[103] If however, the sums are paid by or pursuant to an arrangement made for a pension or other retirement benefit, regard should be had to the pensions code, addressed in Chapter 13.

4.41 Not earnings

The following have, by way of example, been held not to be earnings: payment as consideration for entering into a restrictive covenant,[104] payments to rugby league players for relinquishing their amateur status,[105] monies diverted by a director from a company in breach of his fiduciary duty,[106] an award to a bank clerk for passing his professional examinations[107] and the sum of £1,000 paid to Bobby Moore (and the other members of the team) as an accolade for winning the World Cup.[108]

4.42 ARISING FROM THE EMPLOYMENT

Not every payment made to an employee constitutes taxable earnings. It is also necessary that 'the payment must be made in reference to the services the employee renders by virtue of his office, and it must be something in the nature of a reward for services, present or future'.[109] It is not enough to show that the employee would not have received the sum had he not been an employee. To be earnings arising from the employment, the payment must be a reward for services rendered or to be rendered.[110] Historically, the approach adopted by the courts was to require the employment be a *causa causans* of the payment and not merely a *causa sine qua non*. However, recently the Court of Appeal in *Kuehne + Nagel Drinks Logistics Ltd v Commissioners for HMRC*[111] held that such archaic language – described as judicial glosses on the statutory words – was unhelpful. Mummery LJ took a simpler, more expansive, view on the meaning of causation in this context and held as follows:[112]

> 'When considering the cause of, or the reason for, an event or an act in a particular case, the courts steer clear of involvement in general theories of

102 See *Duncan's Trustee v Farmer* 5 TC 417, 422
103 Section 401(4).
104 *Beak v Robson* [1943] AC 352 but see ITEPA 2003, s 225 discussed at **4.36** above.
105 *Jarrold v Boustead* (1964) 41 TC 701, 729 discussed at **4.35** above.
106 *Rose v Humbles* (1971) 48 TC 103, 117H discussed at **4.33** above.
107 *Ball v Johnson* (1971) 47 TC 155.
108 *Moore v Griffiths* (1972) 48 TC 338.
109 *Hochstrasse v Mayes* [1960] AC 376, 388.
110 *Hochstrasse v Mayes* per Lord Cohen.
111 [2012] EWCA Civ 34.
112 Ibid at paragraph 32.

causation. Instead they apply a mix of general principle, legal policy and good-sense pragmatism to determine whether legal liability in accordance with the conditions set by the relevant rules has been established on the particular facts of the case.'[113]

This question is most frequently litigated in the context of termination payments and the reader is referred to the discussion in Chapter 10.

4.43 INCOME OUTSIDE THE CHARGE TO TAX

A number of specific provisions exempt certain sums which would otherwise fall into charge as earnings from tax. These are now gathered together in Part 4 of ITEPA 2003; the main areas addressed are transport and travel, recreational benefits, non-cash vouchers and removal benefits, such benefits being addressed in Chapter 8 below (Benefits in Kind). Provision is also made in Part 4 of ITEPA 2003 for special categories of employees (eg MPs, members of the armed forces etc, see Part 4, Chapter 8) to which reference should be made in appropriate cases.

Particular aspects of the exemption provisions which may be most relevant in practice, are as follows:

4.44 Education

Section 776(1) of ITTOIA 2005 provides as follows:

> 'No liability to income tax arises in respect of income from a scholarship held by an individual in full-time education at a university, college, school or other educational establishment.'

'Scholarship' includes an exhibition, bursary or any other similar educational endowment.[114] This is generally assumed to include local authority grants However, the section is limited in its application to the person receiving the scholarship.[115] So, for example, a scholarship provided to a family member of a higher paid employee[116] will generally constitute earnings of that employee.

Loans made to student employees will not, upon being released or forgiven, benefit from this exemption.[117]

113 See also *Commissioners for HMRC v PA Holdings Limited* [2011] EWCA Civ 1414.
114 Section 776(3).
115 Section 215 of ITEPA 2003.
116 Ie an employee earning over £8,500 per annum or a director. See Chapter 8 (Benefits in Kind).
117 *Clayton v Gothorp* (1971) 47 TC 168.

HMRC's practice[118] is to treat as exempt from income tax certain payments made by employers to employees undertaking full-time educational courses, including 'sandwich' courses. The practice operates only in respect of payments for periods of attendance at the educational establishment; payments made to the employee for periods spent at work during vacations or otherwise are taxable in the normal way and the following conditions must be satisfied:

(a) the period for which the employee is enrolled at the educational establishment is at least one academic year and the actual full-time attendance at that establishment during that period amounts on average to at least 20 weeks a year;

(b) the rate of payment including lodging, subsistence and travelling expenses but excluding any university, etc, fees payable by the employee, does not exceed for the academic year.

Payments are taxable in full where the rate exceeds that specified in (b) above. An employer's own internal training school or centre, or one run by an employer's association, is not regarded by the Revenue as an educational establishment for present purposes.

4.45 Strike pay

Payments made by a trade union to members who are on strike are not earnings from the employment and are not taxable.[119]

4.46 Training

There is no charge to tax on payments made to young people taking part in government or other work experience schemes if they hold the status of trainee and not employee.[120]

In *Revenue & Customs Commissioners v Banerjee*[121] the costs of training undertaken by a NHS registrar were held to be allowable, on the basis that Dr Banerjee's contract was essentially a training contract, the duties of which included attendance at training events. (See also HMRC's Guidance at EIM32535 on deductibility of training costs where undertaking education is part of the contractual duties of the employment.)

118 Statement of Practice 4/86.
119 See Employment Income Manual, paragraph 06500.
120 See Employment Income Manual, paragraph 10500. See, in this regard, the rules dealing with work-related training at ITEPA 2003, s 250.
121 [2010] STC 2318.

4.47 DEDUCTIONS

Deductions from Chapter 2 earnings are dealt with by Part 5 of ITEPA 2003. Section 336 provides that:

The general rule is that a deduction from earnings is allowed for any amount if:

(a) the employee is obliged to incur and pay it as a holder of the employment; and

(b) the amount is incurred wholly, exclusively and necessarily in the performance of the duties of the employment.

There are two separate regimes in place: the first covers travelling expenses and the second, all other expenses.

4.48 Travelling expenses

The key provision is section 337 of ITEPA 2003, which provides that:

A deduction from earnings is allowed for travel expenses if:

(a) the employee is obliged to incur and pay them as holder of the employment; and

(b) the expenses are necessarily incurred on travelling in the performance of the duties of the employment.

Section 338 provides a similar provision for expenses attributable to an employee's necessary attendance at any place in performance of the duties of the employment. However, this does not apply to expenses of ordinary commuting or travel between any two places that is for practical purposes substantially 'ordinary commuting'.

> '338(3) …"Ordinary commuting" means travel between –
>
> (a) the employee's home and a permanent workplace, or
>
> (b) a place that is not a workplace and a permanent workplace.'

Furthermore, section 338 does not apply to expenses of private travel or travel between any two places that is for practical purposes substantially private travel.

> '338(5) … "private travel" means travel between –
>
> (a) the employee's home and a place that is not a workplace, or
>
> (b) two places neither of which is a workplace.'

And 'workplace' means 'a place at which the employee's attendance is necessary in the performance of the duties of employment.'[122] The section goes on to provide a definition of 'permanent' workplace.[123]

The intention is to allow deductions where the employee incurs expenditure in travelling either to a 'temporary' workplace[124] or from one workplace to another. Where, however, the employee incurs expenditure in normal commuting, that expenditure will not be deductible.

4.49 Other expenses

The general rules governing the deduction of expenses incurred by an employee are notoriously rigid and narrow and frequently lead to unfairness in individual cases. As Vaisey J has remarked:

> 'An expenditure may be "necessary" for the holder of an office without being necessary to him in the performance of the duties of that office; it may be necessary in the performance of those duties without being exclusively referable to those duties; it may perhaps be both necessarily and exclusively, but still not wholly so referable The words are indeed stringent and exacting; compliance with each and every one of them is obligatory if the benefit of the Rule is to be claimed successfully. They are to my mind, deceptive words in the sense that when examined they are found to come to nearly nothing at all.'[125]

The provision for deduction of expenses for trades, professions and vocations under ITTOIA 2005[126] is, relatively speaking, relaxed. The word 'necessarily' is omitted and the expression 'for the purposes of the trade' is substituted for 'in the performance of the duties'. Fiscally, therefore, it is usually advantageous for the putative employer to incur himself such expenditure as he can without giving a benefit in kind to his employees.

4.50 'In the performance of duties'

The distinction drawn by this phrase is between expenditure incurred in the performance of the duties and expenditure which merely enables the duties better

122 Section 339(1).

123 Section 339(2), '"permanent workplace" means a place which the employee regularly attends in the performance of the duties of the employment and which is not a temporary workplace.'

124 Section 339(3). For a practical application of these rules see *Kirkwood v Evans* [2002] EWHC 30 (Ch) (Civil Servant at the DSS) and *Warner v Prior* [2003] STC (SCD) 109 (supply teacher).

125 *Lomax v Newton* (1953) 34 TC 558, 562.

126 ITTOIA 2005, s 34..

to be performed.[127] It precludes, for example, deduction of the cost of a child-minder or housekeeper.[128] Under the common law, subscriptions to professional bodies were disallowed even though the journals published by those bodies enabled the taxpayer to keep up to date with developments in his field.[129] The effect of this decision has been counteracted, in part, by section 344 of ITEPA 2003.[130] A history teacher who attended a series of weekend lectures at a college of adult education for the purposes of improving his background knowledge was not allowed to deduct the cost thereof.[131] An employee was not allowed to deduct the costs of a record player and records which he had purchased in order to provide musical stimulus whilst working late at night[132] notwithstanding that, as Cross J observed, 'it may well be that [he] was stimulated to work better by hearing good music, just as other people may be stimulated to work better by drink'.[133] Fees paid to an employment agency to obtain a job are not incurred in the employment of the duties of that job.[134]

The distinction is explored with some detail in two House of Lords decisions, both concerning the deductibility of expenditure incurred on newspapers and magazines by journalists in *Smith v Abbott*[135] and *Fitzpatrick v IRC (No 2)*.[136]

4.51 'Necessarily'

The case law has tended not to focus on this requirement: claims for deduction tending to fall at the other hurdles. However, several general observations may nevertheless be made.

It is clear that the test is an objective one.[137] It follows from this that an employee with defective eyesight cannot recover the cost of his glasses.[138] The tax tribunal must find that any and every holder of the employment would have had to incur the expenditure in question.[139]

The fact that the employment requires the expenditure does not suffice. As Donovan LJ puts the matter: 'The test is not whether the employer imposes the expense but whether the duties do, in the sense that irrespective of what

127 *Lupton v Potts* [1969] 3 All ER 1083; *Elderkin v Hindmarsh* [1988] STC 267.
128 *Bowers v Harding* [1891] 1 QB 560.
129 *Simpson v Tate* [1925] 2 KB 214.
130 See 'Professional membership fees' at Chapter 8 (Benefits in Kind).
131 *Humbles v Brook* (1962) 40 TC 500.
132 *Newlin v Woods* (1966) 42 TC 649.
133 (1966) 42 TC 649 at 658.
134 See *Shortt v McIlgorm* 26 TC 262.
135 [1991] STC 661.
136 [1994] STC 237.
137 *Ricketts v Colquhoun* [1926] AC 1, 10.
138 *Roskams v Bennett* (1950) 32 TC 129.
139 *Smith v Abbott* [1991] STC 661 per Warner J 683–4.

the employer may prescribe, the duties cannot be performed with incurring the particular outlay'.[140] So a student assistant who worked in the laboratories of a particular company who was performing his duties whilst attending classes in preparation for an external degree from the University of London was not allowed to deduct his expenses.[141] In *Griffiths v Mockler*[142] the fact that a Major in the Royal Army Pay Corps would have been subject to disciplinary action had he not paid his mess membership did not mean the mess bill was necessarily incurred in the performance of his duties as an officer.

4.52 'Wholly and exclusively'

A further barrier is thrown up by the words 'wholly and exclusively' which preclude deduction of any sum from emoluments where there is some element of personal benefit.[143] In the famous[144] case of *Mallalieu v Drummond*[145] a barrister was unable to recover the cost of black dresses, suits, tights and shoes and white shirts or blouses notwithstanding her evidence that she would never wear black or white in anything other than a work context. The House of Lords heard that there was a dual motive for incurring the expenditure, namely, the normal human requirements of warmth and decency.

However, so long as the sole object of incurring the expenditure is the performance of the duties, the fact that it may, incidentally, bring about some other result or effect is irrelevant. A particular item of expenditure may be apportioned only where it is possible to point to a particular benefit therefrom which is wholly and exclusively 'work-related'. Telephone expenses aptly illustrate the point: the price of business calls made from a home telephone are deductible, however, no part of the cost of the line rental will be.[146]

4.53 Business entertainment

It should be noted that section 356 of ITEPA 2003 specifically precludes any deduction being taken for any expenses incurred in providing business entertainment.[147] 'Business entertainment' is defined as hospitality of any kind and entertainment or a gift, or expenses incurred in providing anything incidental to the provision of entertainment or a gift.[148]

140 *Brown v Bullock* 40 TC 1, 10.
141 *Blackwell v Mills* (1945) 26 TC 468.
142 (1953) 35 TC 135.
143 *Griffiths v Mockler* (1953) 35 TC 135, 137.
144 Or, at least, famous to barristers.
145 57 TC 330.
146 *Lucas v Cattell* (1972) 48 TC 353.
147 ITEPA 2003, s 356(1).
148 ITEPA 2003, s 356(3).

4.54 Specifically permitted deductions

In order to ameliorate the severity of the rule, ITEPA 2003 specifically authorises several types of deduction from Chapter 2 earnings. A number of specifically authorised statutory deductions are addressed in Chapter 8 (Benefits in Kind). However, the remainder are addressed here.

4.55 Capital allowances

Where an employee has to make a purchase of an item of plant and machinery which is 'necessary'[149] for use in the performance of his duties, he may claim a capital allowance in respect thereof.[150] A full discussion of the complex subject of capital allowances is beyond the scope of this work, however, in essence, the employee will be entitled to claim a deduction against his earnings of a percentage of the cost of the capital item in the year in which he purchases the item and in each of the three subsequent years. Broadly speaking, an item will be capital if it has a working life of at least two years.

4.56 Liability and indemnity insurance

Sections 346–348 of ITEPA 2003 permit the deduction of liabilities incurred by employees in respect of any act or omission of a person in his capacity as the holder of that employment. Moreover, premiums paid by an employee in order to indemnify himself against the consequences of incurring, *inter alia*, such a liability are deductible.

4.57 Clergymen and ministers of any religious denomination

Any person from time to time holding any full-time office as clergyman or minister of any religious denomination may make certain deductions in addition to those satisfying the wholly, exclusively and necessarily test.[151] Section 351(2) of ITEPA 2003 permits the deduction of one quarter of the rent paid by him in respect of a dwelling-house, any part of which is used wholly or mainly and substantially for the purposes of his duty as such clergyman or minister. Section 351(3) extends this to permit the deduction of a proportion of the expenses of maintaining, repairing, insuring or managing such residences.

Moreover, where such a person (assuming he is 'lower-paid') is provided with a residence in premises from which to perform his duties, no tax liability arises in respect of sums paid on his behalf or reimbursed in respect of heating, lighting,

149 Capital Allowances Act 2001, ss 36 and 262.
150 Capital Allowances Act 2001, s 15(1).
151 ITEPA 2003, s 351.

cleaning and gardening expenses which are the contractual liability of the minister. If an allowance is paid to him to meet such costs, that allowance will not be taxed except to the extent that it exceeds the costs actually incurred.[152]

4.58 Security assets and services

By section 377 of ITEPA 2003 an employee who faces a 'special threat to his personal physical security' which threat arises 'wholly or mainly by virtue of the particular employment concerned' may obtain a deduction in respect of the cost of a security asset or security service. The deduction is, however, available only in respect of expenditure incurred by the employer either directly on the employee's behalf or indirectly through reimbursing the employee.

4.59 Charitable contributions

The effect of the 'Getting Britain Giving' package of measures has been to extend the scope of a number of legislative provisions which enabled employees to make donations and claim a deduction from their gross income in the amount of that donation.

There are now two main schemes. Under the first ('Gift Aid') employees can make one-off gifts (of income net of income tax, which income is subsequently grossed up in the hands of the charity) with no upper limit on the amount of the gift.[153] Under the second ('Payroll Giving') employers will, with the permission of individual employees, make regular payments to charities from employees' 'before tax' pay under the conditions prescribed by the payroll deduction scheme.[154]

152 See Extra Statutory Concession A61.
153 ITA 2007, Ch 2, Pt 8.
154 ITEPA 2003, ss 713–715.

Chapter 5

The PAYE System

5.1 INTRODUCTION

Pay as you earn – or 'PAYE' – does not impact upon an employee's underlying tax burden; rather it is a mechanism by which the Revenue collect tax on income from employment and Class 1 and 1A employees' and employers' national insurance contributions ('NICs').[1]

PAYE is the most widely used of a number of regimes under which tax due is deducted from income at, and usually by, the source of that income. Other examples of deduction at tax at source include deductions from payments made to construction industry sub-contractors and deductions from interest paid on cash balances at banks and building societies. The deduction of tax at source is founded upon two distinct aims. First, it protects the Revenue's position so far as the payment of that tax is concerned. Secondly, it places the initial burden of calculation and collection on a party better placed to bear this burden than the actual taxpayer, namely, in the case of PAYE, the employer. It can, however, leave the employer with the burden of paying tax properly chargeable to the employee when the employer under-deducts.

The core statutory provisions are in Part 11 of the Income Tax (Earnings and Pensions) Act 2003 (ITEPA 2003), (ss 682–715) which are, in turn, supplemented by the Income Tax (Pay As You Earn) Regulations 2003, SI 2003/2682 (the 'Regulations'). The provisions apply to employment income, pension income and social security income for the year.[2] However, the focus of this Chapter will, obviously, be on the former.

The objective of the legislation is to match the tax deducted over the course of the tax year – the period from 6 April one year to 5 April next – to the employee's liability to pay tax on the income received during the year.[3] Tax is deducted on an on-going basis – week by week or month by month as the

1 To avoid repetition, save for where the context requires the contrary, references to tax in this Chapter should be taken as referring to both income tax and Class 1 and 1A NICs.
2 ITEPA 2003, s 683(1).
3 ITEPA 2003, s 685(1)(a).

employee is paid – so it will necessarily be deducted *before* his liability to pay tax for that year is finally assessed.

Calculations as to the amount of tax to be deducted are carried out by reference to a code allocated HMRC to each employee. This code is applied to a set of tables issued by HMRC to calculate the amount of tax to be deducted from each payment made to the employee. The tables operate on a cumulative basis. They show, for each week or month and by reference to each code, the cumulative amount of tax due from the beginning of the tax year from the cumulative earnings. Although tax cannot be deducted from non-cash earnings, such as benefits in kind, these are taken into account in setting the code so as to enable the tax liability in respect of such benefits to be collected through PAYE.

The codes represent the amount of the total allowances and reliefs less deductions, omitting the last digit; thus code 475 will cover allowances between £4,750 and £4,759 inclusive. The code also includes an alphabetical suffix which enables the employer to make an automatic adjustment in the event of a change in the allowances.

The tax deducted is then accounted for by the employer making payments to HMRC at regular intervals – monthly in the case of all but the smallest of employers[4] – of the income tax that he has or ought to have deducted from payments made to his employees. Moreover, at the end of the year the employer is required to make a return to HMRC showing details of the earnings and tax deductions of each employee employed during the year.[5] The employer is also required to give a certificate (known as a Form P60) to every employee specifying the payments made and tax deducted[6] along with a record of all benefits in kind provided to the employee.[7]

The machinery of PAYE is also used to collect employees' national insurance contributions under the Social Security Contributions and Benefits Act 1992, Schedule 1.[8]

The PAYE legislation is lengthy, detailed and prescriptive. It is also the subject of a section of HMRC's website: www.hmrc.gov.uk/paye/index.htm and a large number of carefully drafted guides prepared for employers by HMRC.[9] The authors have therefore confined themselves to presenting an overview of how the PAYE system operates with references to statutes and statutory instruments to facilitate the reader's further researches.

4 Broadly, those employers the quantum of whose obligation to remit income tax and national insurance contributions to HMRC is less than £1,500 per month.
5 SI 2003/2682, regs 73 and 85.
6 SI 2003/2682, reg 67.
7 SI 2003/2682, reg 94.
8 See Chapter 6 (National Insurance Contributions).
9 A full list of which can be found here: www.hmrc.gov.uk/paye/forms-publications.htm.

5.2 THE SCOPE OF PAYE

The scope of PAYE is the scope of income taxed as employment income.[10] A full account of the scope of employment income will be found elsewhere in this book – see Chapter 4 (Introduction to Income Tax).

Regulation 21(1) of the Regulations requires every employer on making any 'relevant payments' to an employee during a tax year to deduct (or repay) tax in accordance with the Regulations. A number of questions thus arise: payments to what employees; who are 'employers'; and what constitute 'relevant payments'?

5.3 What employees?

The PAYE machinery is designed to effect deductions in respect of all income liable to employment income tax. It should, therefore, affect any person in receipt of employment income. This result is brought about by regulation 2(1) of the Regulations as supplemented by regulation 12(1). Regulation 2(1) achieves the result that an employee is someone who is in employment including apprentices, those employed in the service of the Crown and office holders.[11] And regulation 12(1) treats 'other payees' – persons receiving 'relevant payments'[12] in a category other than employee or agency worker[13] – as employees for the purposes of the Regulations.

Where an individual holds more than one office or employment assessable to income tax – perhaps a number of directorships – the PAYE regime will be applied separately to each. The employee will typically be given different codes for each with the allowances available to him reflected in the code for his principal employment with tax being deducted at the appropriate rate without taking allowances into account from each of the subsidiary employments.

PAYE is also applied in the ordinary way to an employee who is not resident in the UK in respect of payments for duties performed in the UK and an employee resident in the UK who is working abroad.

5.4 Agency workers

Section 44 of ITEPA 2003 treats, for the purposes of income tax, the relationship between certain[14] employment agencies and workers as a relationship of

10 ITEPA 2003, Part 11, Chapter 1.
11 ITEPA 2003, ss 4 and 5
12 In respect of which, see below.
13 SI 2003/2682, reg 2(1).
14 A fuller discussion of employment agencies can be found in Chapter 4 at **4.29**.

employment. By regulation 10 of the Regulations, the PAYE machinery is also extended to such agency workers.[15] In other words, the agency is required to operate PAYE in respect of the remuneration which it pays to that person.

5.5 Payments made after termination

That obligation to deduct PAYE continues after the termination of employment ie the employer must still deduct in respect of payments made to his former employee. No difficulty arises where the employee is paid before Form P45 is issued because PAYE operates in the normal way. However, where they are paid subsequent to Form P45 being issued, employers are required to operate PAYE using the 0T code (rather than the basic rate code used prior to 6 April 2011).

The 0T code requires the employer to tax the payment, on the basis that no personal allowance is available, at 20%, 40% and 45%. The employer is required to operate the 0T code on a non-cumulative basis.[16] So an individual receiving a termination payment will have 1/12th of the basic rate band available and, if applicable, 1/12th of the higher rate (40%) and additional rate (45%) bands available, irrespective of his or her current level of salary.

Example

If a taxable payment of £25,000 is made after Form P45 is issued in tax year 2013–14, the employer is required to deduct approximately £10,052 in tax calculated as follows:

£0 – 2,864.17 (1/12 of the 20% rate threshold from 6 April 2012 £34,370) at 20% = £572.83

£2,864.18 – £12,500.00 (1/12 of the 40% rate threshold £150,000) at 40% = £3,854.33

£12,500.01 – £25,000 at 45% = £5,625

For many employees this means that they pay too much tax initially and have to claim a refund of tax from HMRC. This effectively gives a cash flow advantage to HMRC (rather than the employee prior to 6 April 2011).

If immediately prior to the termination of their employment, the employee had a No Tax (NT) code, the employer should continue to operate the NT code on all payments made after leaving.

15 As defined by SI 2003/2682, reg 2(1).
16 SI 2003/2682, reg 37(2).

There are some potential advantages for higher and additional rate taxpayers. If more than one termination payment is made in a year, provided they are in different tax months, each is treated independently for PAYE purposes. Staggering the payments may therefore result in a cash-flow advantage in that more of the basic rate band will be available. However, it is crucial to remember that it is the date when the individual becomes entitled to the payment that is relevant for PAYE purposes[17], not when the payments are actually received. Also, even if only one termination payment is made, there is likely to still be a cash-flow advantage for additional rate taxpayers who are not entitled to personal allowances anyway.

5.6 New employees

The treatment of new employees depends upon whether they are in possession of a Form P45. If a new employee has in his possession the form P45 supplied by a previous employer, he should give it to his new employer.[18] The employer has then to comply with a series of notification obligations.[19] The new employer then proceeds to operate PAYE in the normal way, taking into account the code number and cumulative pay and tax as recorded on the form P45.

There are, however, several circumstances in which a new employee may not produce a form P45; this may be his first employment, he may have lost the form or he may not wish his new employer to know his previous pay. Where the new employee does not produce Form P45 at the time he takes up the new employment, the new employer must prepare Form P46 (on the basis of statements made by the employee) to show the employee's name, address, national insurance number and the date the employment commenced. Deductions or repayments of tax from subsequent payments of emoluments are then calculated according to the statement made by the employee.

5.7 Students

By concession, where an employer engages a student on a course in the UK to work for him during the holidays, he should ask the student to complete form P38(S). On satisfactory completion of the form, no tax need be deducted from his earnings. However, as soon as his earnings go above his personal allowance, you will need to start deducting PAYE tax from your payments to the employer.

17 SI 2003/2682, reg 37(1).
18 SI 2003/2682, reg 40(1).
19 Set out in SI 2003/2682, regs 42 et seq.

5.8 What employers?

Again, the intention of the PAYE legislation is to deduct tax at source from all payments of income assessable to employment income tax.[20] In order to achieve this objective, the Regulations define as employers a number of persons who could, in no normal sense of the word, be described as such. As with the definition of employees, this result is achieved by extending the concept of 'employer'[21] to include those who make relevant payments.[22]

5.9 Non-resident employers

Part 11 of ITEPA 2003 is, on its face, of general effect and not confined to employers resident in any geographical area. However it has been clear since *Clark v Oceanic Contractors*[23] that, before the obligation to operate PAYE can bite, the employer must have a sufficient geographical nexus with the United Kingdom. As Lord Scarman put the matter, in an unusual inversion of the maxim *ubi jus ibi remedium*,[24] '[t]he only critical factor, so far as collection is concerned, is whether in the circumstances it can be made effective. A trading presence in the United Kingdom will suffice.'[25] Lord Wilberforce regarded the presence in the United Kingdom of a branch or agency against whom the PAYE obligation might be enforced as a pre-requisite. Where the employer has neither a branch or agency or any address for service in the United Kingdom, it will not be obliged to operate PAYE.[26] Naturally, HMRC will view with scepticism any attempt to argue that an employer with employees or an address in the UK falls outside the PAYE net.

5.10 What payments?

PAYE applies to 'relevant payments' made by an employer to an employee during a tax year.[27] The concept of 'relevant payments' is a complex one but, at least so far as income from employment is concerned,[28] it encompasses payments of almost all employment income except for payments of certain relocation expenses, business expenses, certain notional payments of non-

20 See *Booth v Mirror Group Newspapers* [1992] STC 615.
21 See the definition of 'employment' in SI 2003/2682, reg 2(1).
22 See SI 2003/2682, reg 12 and the definition of 'other payer' in reg 2(1).
23 [1983] STC 37. See more recently *Telfer v Sakellarios* [2013] EWHC 1556 (Comm) and *Goldman Sachs International v Revenue & Customs Commissioners* [2010] UKFTT 205 (TC).
24 Where there is a right there must be a remedy.
25 [1983] STC 37 at 43.
26 See *Bootle v Bye* [1996] STC (SCD) 58.
27 See SI 2003/2682, reg 21(1).
28 Because the concept also extends to certain pension and social security income: ITEPA 2003, s 683(1)(b)–(c).

cash vouchers or credit tokens, and meeting certain pecuniary liabilities of an employee.[29] However, it does not include allowable pension contributions and allowable donations to charity.[30]

The other point to bear in mind is that to be a relevant payment, there has to be a 'payment'. Employment income that is not a payment (for example, most benefits in kind) cannot be subject to deduction of tax.[31]

In *Garforth v Newsmith Stainless*[32] it was held that the placing of sums at the disposal of a director was a 'payment'. In *Paul Dunstall Organisation Ltd v Hedges*[33] the Special Commissioners held that the word 'payments' is a word which takes its meaning from its context and that transferring emoluments other than cash might, if those emoluments were readily convertible into cash, amount to 'payments' thus requiring PAYE to be operated in respect thereof. The facts of that case were rather unusual and probably the better view is that it does not upset the general rule that – save where there is a specific deeming provision – employers are only obliged to make deductions from cash payments.

Employers are required to operate PAYE for income tax for all employees whose pay *exceeds* a prescribed weekly or monthly amount. That amount is known as the 'PAYE threshold' (there is another threshold for NICs). The PAYE threshold for income tax is based on a pro-rata proportion (either 1/52 or 1/12 depending on whether the employee is paid weekly or monthly) of the single person's allowance.[34] Where, in other words, the income to be received by an employee in a year of assessment is less than his personal allowance, he will have no income tax liability and there is, therefore, no tax to be deducted at source. The NIC thresholds are outlined in paragraph 4 of Chapter 6.

5.11 When is a payment made?

The time when the payment is treated as being made – and hence when the obligation to deduct and remit the appropriate sum arises – is specified by section 686 of ITEPA 2003. The general rule is that the payment is treated as made when it is in fact made or, if earlier, the time when the person becomes entitled to the payment. However, there are rules which deem the payment to be made earlier where the PAYE income is income of a person who is a director.

29 See SI 2003/2682, reg 4, ITEPA, ss 683(1) and 10.
30 SI 2003/2682, reg 3(1).
31 It can only be taken into account in calculating the employee's PAYE code.
32 [1979] STC 179.
33 [1999] STC (SCD) 26.
34 See SI 2003/2682, reg 9. The personal allowance for 2012–2013 is £9,440.

The statutory predecessor to this provision was introduced in 1989 to prevent early corporation tax deductions being taken by employers for staff costs without there arising a corresponding PAYE liability at the same time.

5.12 Benefits in kind

PAYE applies to 'payments' of emoluments. At first glance, therefore, it would not seem to apply to a benefit in kind – a company car or gym membership, for example – which is not 'paid' to the employee. However, the inspector will take any benefits in kind into account by setting the employee's code so that the receipt of non-cash benefits in kind is taken into account. In other words, if the employee is expected to receive £3,000 of taxable benefits in kind during the course of the tax year, his code will reflect that by instructing the employer to make deductions as if his personal allowances were £3,000 lower than, in fact, they are.

Where the taxable value of the benefits in kind received by a particular employee exceeds that employee's personal allowance, he will be given a negative (K) code.[35] Where an employee receives a K code, an amount will be notionally added to his pay in order to calculate the PAYE which should be deducted.[36]

For a number of years, employers operated the practice of remunerating employees in assets – such as gold bars, fine wines, etc – in order to avoid the PAYE regime[37] and, by so doing, achieve a delay in the time at which income tax was paid by the employee. This practice was, effectively, brought to an end by the statutory predecessor to section 696 of ITEPA 2003 which provides that certain 'readily convertible assets' are to be treated as payments of income in the amount likely to be PAYE income in respect of the provision of the asset.[38]

5.13 Tips, service charges and troncs

If the employer operates a scheme under which he pays employees tips from customers or service charges, he must include these in the amount of remuneration entered on the deductions working sheet.

In some businesses, gratuities are commonly shared amongst employees through an arrangement known as a tronc. The person administering the tronc

35 See 'Coding' at **5.16** below.
36 For clarification, it should be noted that this notional extra pay does not affect the employer or employee's liability to NIC.
37 The transfer of such an asset did not give rise to a 'payment' and hence the PAYE regime was not, previously at least, triggered.
38 ITEPA 2003, s 696(2).

– the tronc master – will be treated as an employer[39] and required to operate PAYE in respect of the distributions of tips, including his own share.

If a tronc system is started, the principal employer[40] must advise the inspector of its existence and give him the name of the tronc master. If the tronc master fails to operate PAYE in respect of tips which he distributes, and where the tips are given to the tronc master by the principal employer, the Revenue may direct the main employer to operate PAYE in respect of the tips;[41] the tronc master is then required to advise the main employer of the amounts paid to each employee, and the main employer will deduct the appropriate amount of tax from the tips given to the tronc master.[42] The nature of the liability upon the employer is explored by the Court of Appeal in *Figael v Fox*.[43] In that case, the taxpayer company, which operated a restaurant, unsuccessfully appealed against an assessment raised on it for unpaid PAYE.

5.14 Expenses

Formally speaking, when an employer reimburses business expenses that an employee has incurred, an employee receives taxable income from which he can then claim a deduction. And that taxable income is income which is subject to PAYE.

However, this system creates an unfair cashflow disadvantage to the employee: a payment to reimburse an employee for expenses he has incurred is not truly income of the employee and the employee ought not to suffer the deduction of tax at source from that payment.

Accordingly, there is provision for HMRC to authorise the employer by 'dispensation' to exclude from 'relevant payments' certain 'excluded business expenses'.[44] The effect of such exclusion is to remove the obligation on the part of the employer to deduct tax on reimbursing such expenses.

To apply for a dispensation employers can either complete a form (P11DX) and send it to their tax office or simply write setting out the employees or groups of employees for whom they would like a dispensation, the types and amounts of expenses payments or reimbursements which the employer wishes to be covered and the employer's system for controlling and authorising payments of expenses and reimbursements.

39 SI 2003/2682, reg 100(3).
40 Defined by SI 2003/2682, reg 100(7) as the person under whose general control and management the employees in question work.
41 See SI 2003/2682, reg 100(4).
42 SI 2003/2682, reg 100(5).
43 [1992] STC 83.
44 SI 2003/2682, reg 5.

HMRC will issue the dispensation if they are satisfied that the employees would be able to obtain a deduction for the expenses in arriving at their tax liability and the employer properly controls the system for authorising expenses. A dispensation can cover any type of expense payment such as qualifying travel expenses, reasonable scale rate payments for subsistence, entertaining, subscriptions to professional bodies, etc.

5.15 COMMON FORMS

There are a number of forms issued by HMRC to facilitate uniformity and efficiency in the management of PAYE. Whilst a comprehensive recitation of those documents is beyond the scope of this work, the principal forms are as follows.

Where an employee ceases to work for an employer, that employer must provide him with a certificate on Form P45 which shows the code and the cumulative pay and tax up to the date of leaving.[45] The employee can then produce the form P45 to his next employer to enable him to continue the cumulative system of tax deduction.

Form P46 is used by the employer to tell the Inspector about a new employee who fails to produce Parts 2 and 3 of Form P45.[46]

By 19 May following the end of the tax year, the employer has to make a return to HMRC on Form P35 giving, in respect of every employee in respect of whom he is required to operate PAYE, the name of the employee together with the amount of tax deducted or refunded during the year.

By 31 May following the end of the tax year, the employer is required to give to each employee who was employed by him at the end of the tax year a certificate on Form P60.[47] That certificate must specify, *inter alia*, the total amount of the emoluments paid by the employer to the employee during the year and the total net tax deducted from those emoluments.[48]

By 6 July following the end of each tax year, the employer is required to make a return to HMRC (on Form P11D in respect of higher paid employees and on Form P9D in respect of all others) showing particulars of benefits in kind received by the employee, together with deductible expenses.[49]

45 SI 2003/2682, reg 36.
46 SI 2003/2682, reg 46.
47 SI 2003/2682, reg 67.
48 A full list of the matters required to be specified may be found in SI 2003/2682, reg 67(2) and (3).
49 SI 2003/2682, regs 86 and 87.

Forms P9 and P2 are used by HMRC to notify, respectively, employers and employees of their tax code.

5.16 CODINGS

Codes allocated to particular employees derive from tax tables constructed by HMRC.[50] The tables are compiled to ensure that, so far as possible, the total income tax payable in respect of broad employment income for any tax year is deducted from that income paid during that year.[51] The codes, not surprisingly, take into account all reliefs as well as adjustments for income tax overpaid or remaining unpaid on previous years, other income of the employee, and 'such other adjustments as may be necessary' to secure that the correct tax is deducted.[52]

Ordinarily a code is comprised of two elements: a number and a suffix. The number represents the total allowances available to the employee without the last figure – so, for example, a code of 420 would represent allowances in the range £4,200 to £4,209 – and the letter suffix refers to the nature of the personal allowance. Finally there are three-letter only codes: BR indicates the employer should deduct tax at the basic rate from all pay, NT means that the employer should not deduct tax at all and OT gives credit for no personal allowance and effectively divides the different tax bands into twelfths.

Generally codes are used in a cumulative way, using the pay and tax deducted since the start of the tax year. This ensures that the correct proportion of lower, basic and higher rate tax is deducted on each payday. Where, exceptionally, a code is used in a non-cumulative fashion, previous earnings in the tax year may be ignored. Non-cumulative codes will be denoted as such by the letters (Wk 1) or (Month 1) after the code.

Where the 'L' code is used *after* a number, this indicates that an emergency code is being applied, usually because the employer does not have a code for the employee. The code is applied on a non-cumulative basis and takes into account the employee's personal allowance only. The application of an 'L' code will typically lead to over-deduction or acceleration of deduction of income tax, which over-deduction or acceleration is then remedied when HMRC notify the employer of the employee's proper code.

In calculating the numerical portion of the code, the inspector will take into account any personal allowances, expenses which he is satisfied are deductible

50 ITEPA 2003, s 685.
51 ITEPA 2003, s 685(1).
52 SI 2003/2682, reg 14.

from income, together with any other deductions such as, for example, tax overpaid in a previous year.

Where an employee does not agree with the coding he has been given, he may send a notice of objection to the Inspector stating the grounds thereof.[53] If the Inspector continues to maintain the coding the employee may appeal.[54]

5.17 REFUNDS

The objective of the PAYE system is to ensure that there has, at the end of the tax year, been deducted from the employee's earnings an amount equivalent to his tax liability for that year. As has been stated, this is achieved through the use of tables which spread the employee's personal allowances – and the starting and basic rate tax bands – across the whole of the earnings in a tax year. However, it will occasionally be apparent that the PAYE deductions exceed the employee's tax liability.

The most frequent cause of over-deductions is where an employee ceases employment prior to the conclusion of the tax year. PAYE is operated on the assumption that the employee is to remain in employment all year and spreads his personal allowance throughout the year. Accordingly, some part will remain unutilised.

By regulation 65, where any person who has ceased to be employed produces to HMRC: (1) parts 2 and 3 of Form P45; (2) a certificate that he is or will not claim certain social security benefits;[55] and (3) such evidence of his unemployment as HMRC may require, HMRC shall make any repayment which is appropriate.

5.18 RESPONSIBILITY FOR UNDER-DEDUCTIONS

Regulation 69 of the Regulations imposes an obligation on the employer to pay monthly or quarterly to HMRC all money which the employer was *liable* to deduct under the Regulations. The obligation is not to remit to HMRC such sums as actually have been deducted from payments to employees. In other words, if the employer actually deducts £10 where he ought to have deducted £100, the employer remains liable to remit £100 to HMRC. The question therefore arises whether the shortfall may be recovered from the employee. There are two possible routes. The first is to procure HMRC to make a

53 SI 2003/2682, reg 18.
54 SI 2003/2682, reg 18(3).
55 As defined in SI 2003/2682, reg 81.

direction that the employee, rather than the employer, remit the shortfall to HMRC. The second, obviously applying only where HMRC refuses to make such a direction, is to seek to recover the money direct from the employee by way of an action in restitution.

5.19 HMRC direction

The question when a direction will be made is addressed by regulation 72 of the Regulations. There are three situations in which the employer may escape liability for a shortfall. The first is where the employer took reasonable care to comply with the Regulations and the failure to deduct the appropriate amount of tax was due to an error made in good faith.[56] The second is where the employee has received his emoluments knowing that the employer has wilfully failed to deduct the amount of tax which he was liable to deduct.[57] In either situation, HMRC may estimate the shortfall and direct that the appropriate amount be recovered from the employee rather than the employer. The third is where the employee has paid the tax anyway.

The question whether these requirements are satisfied has led to a welter of case law. The important general point to emerge is that the issue is not whether HMRC is correct or incorrect in the view it forms. Rather it is whether there is sufficient material to enable HMRC reasonably to form the view that it formed.[58]

The error made in good faith provision is the less frequently used. It applies where, first, the employer took reasonable care to operate PAYE correctly and, second, the under-deduction was due to an error made in good faith. Application of the provision depends, therefore, upon an error being made by the employer and will not apply where, for example, the employer was misinformed as to the employee's status. HMRC practice is also to refuse to make a direction where the employer continues to maintain that the PAYE regime does not apply. This provision is typically used where the employer makes an arithmetical error in good faith.

The leading case on a 'wilful failure to deduct' is *ex parte Chisholm*[59] where McNeill J said:

> 'The material words in the passage I read, if I may stress them again, are "The employee has received his emoluments knowing that the employer has wilfully failed to deduct", those last four words also I stress, "therefrom the amount of tax which he was liable to deduct."

56 SI 2003/2682, reg 72(3).
57 SI 2003/2682, reg 72(4).
58 A point which emerges powerfully from the decision of Nolan J in *R v IRC ex parte Cook* [1987] STC 434, 444.
59 *R v IRC, ex parte Chisholm* [1981] STC 253, per McNeill J 256.

> I accept that, for the purpose of construing that regulation, the word "knowing" means what it says and does not mean "ought to have known" or "should have been suspicious" or any other weakening of knowledge. Although I shall have to refer to authority on the interpretation of that word in the criminal law, I do not think it is necessary to refer to authority for the proposition that the word "knowing" means "knowing" and nothing else. I also accept – and it is not really in dispute between the parties – that the word "wilfully" means "intentional" or "deliberate", and may, in the context of the PAYE scheme and the collection of tax, import a measure of blameworthiness, at least in the sense that it is blameworthy not to pay the tax that is due.'

In other words, 'actual' knowledge is required and 'Nelsonian' blindness is not enough.

5.20 Restitution

The leading case on actions brought by employer against employee to recover a shortfall of tax was *Bernard & Shaw Ltd v Shaw*.[60] In that case, Lynskey J held that the money was paid under a mistake of law and hence was not recoverable. However, there must be real doubt about whether this remains good law in the light of the decision of the House of Lords in *Kleinwort Benson v Lincoln City Council*[61] to abolish the rule that payments made under a mistake of law are irrecoverable. In the authors' view, under-deductions of PAYE may now, where the normal conditions for an action in restitution are satisfied, be recovered by the employer from the employee. In *McCarthy v McCarthy & Stone plc*[62] the Court of Appeal held that in the absence of an express contractual provision for recoupment from the employee, there is no reason in logic or justice for withholding a restitutionary remedy from the employer.[63]

60 [1951] 2 All ER 267. See, also, the unusual case of *Philson & Partners Ltd v Moore* (1956) 167 Estates Gazette 92.
61 [1998] 3 WLR 1095.
62 [2007] EWCA Civ 664.
63 Ibid at [39].

Chapter 6

National Insurance Contributions

6.1 INTRODUCTION

Until relatively recently, national insurance contributions (NICs) had largely escaped the attention of tax advisers. NICs were relatively unimportant when compared with income tax and were, in any event, unavoidable. However, the position has altered in recent years as a result of three main developments.

First, the UK Government has radically changed its approach to NICs, treating them more as the 'tax' they always were rather than as contributions to a common social security fund. Second, and following on from the first development, employers and employees have shown a greater willingness to avoid a liability to pay NICs and greater ingenuity in devising avoidance strategies. This has inevitably led, third, to the Government taking a more aggressive and pro-active approach to the collection of NICs and, particularly, in the targeting of anti-avoidance schemes, whether aimed at large industrial concerns or City-driven annual bonuses.

The result has been a welter of new law and a growing willingness on the part of advisers – whether acting for employer or employee – to take account of the NICs consequences of all payments made under, or arising out of, the employment relationship.

This Chapter cannot be a substitute for a specialist work on NICs. Instead, it aims to provide a basic introduction to the subject. All advisers should be aware, in any event, that the law relating to NICs changes frequently – sometimes even from week to week – and that much of the relevant legislation is difficult to find and (on occasions) even harder to interpret. This is a result of the trend, followed by all recent Governments, of amending the various parts of the legislative code piecemeal to deal with specific situations without the fundamental reform which this area of the law so desperately requires.

6.2 THE CONTRIBUTION SYSTEM

NICs are – like all taxes – charged entirely under statute; there is no 'common law' applicable to contributions. The primary legislation to which reference will be made in this Chapter can be found in the Social Security Administration Act 1992 (SSAA 1992) and the Social Security Contributions and Benefits Act 1992 (SSCBA 1992) supplemented by the Social Security (Categorisation of Earners) Regulations 1978, SI 1978/1689 ('the Categorisation Regulations') and the Social Security (Contributions) Regulations 2001, SI 2001/1004 ('the Contributions Regulations'). In addition, HMRC regularly publishes press releases, booklets and leaflets setting out the 'official' view of particular parts of the legislation. As is rehearsed elsewhere in this book,[1] these expressions of opinion are just that and have no binding legal force. They do, however, represent a useful starting point in checking liability.

Although there can, on occasions, be minor differences between the treatment in the different home nations, it should for present purposes be assumed that this Chapter addresses the liability to NICs in all parts of the United Kingdom (Northern Ireland having its own system which mirrors in all material respects that in Great Britain).

Before turning to the structure of the system itself it is important to bear in mind the territorial scope of that system. Contributions have to be paid by or in respect of those in employment or self-employment in Great Britain and, for these purposes, special provision is made for territorial waters and the continental shelf activities in the North Sea (see, eg, section 172 of SSCBA 1992) and for those who are, or have been, outside Great Britain for a period (Contributions Regulations, regulations 145–148). The remainder of the world can then be divided into three separate categories: European Economic Area countries (plus Switzerland) where the social security position is governed by EC Regulations (principally Regulation 1408/71); those countries with whom the UK has a bilateral agreement (eg the USA); and finally, the rest of the world. The liability to make contributions in, or in respect of, other jurisdictions is extremely complex and outside the scope of this work. For present purposes it is merely sufficient to note that 'individual' liability (eg primary class 1 or classes 2–4) requires employment or self-employment in Great Britain and 'corporate' liability requires either a presence or place of business in Great Britain.

6.3 A common fund

The original idea behind the contribution system was that NICs would be payable by those in employment (and self-employment) for the purpose of providing funds to the Government from which the Government could pay certain contributory benefits as part of the social security system. This remains the underlying principle behind the modern legislation (see section 1 of SSCBA 1992). Thus, for example, unemployment benefit (Jobseeker's

1 See Chapter 3 (Sources of Tax Law).

Allowance), statutory sick pay, statutory maternity pay and certain retirement pensions are paid out of the fund derived from NICs. There are, in contrast, other non- contributory benefits paid under the social security system – such as child benefit, housing benefit and income support – which are not funded by NICs. Each of the contributory benefits is available only when the person concerned has paid a minimum amount of contributions into the fund before drawing out benefits from it. These minimums are usually set at relatively low levels to ensure, for example, the availability of Jobseeker's Allowance to most of the unemployed[2].

6.4 A unified system

With effect from 1 April 1999, various changes were made to the system of appeals (see paragraph 7 below) in an effort to bring the contribution system, so far as possible, into line with the PAYE and income tax collection mechanisms. Further changes were made in 2009 with the adoption of the uniform system of tribunals covering, in this context, both tax and national insurance contributions.

Although there have in the past been – and there continues to be – variances between the liabilities to income tax in a given situation and the liabilities to NICs, the clear intent of the Government is to remove these wherever possible. As a general principle, which will gain greater force over time, if a person is liable to income tax in a given situation, the likelihood is that he or she will also be liable to national insurance contributions. In a clear move in this direction, the scope of Class 1A contributions now extends to include all emoluments which do *not* give rise to a contributions liability under Class 1 (see **6.7** below).

6.5 The classes of contributions

The basic feature of the contribution system is that all persons in employment or self-employment are required to pay a certain amount – usually calculated by reference to each week of employment/self-employment – into the national insurance fund in accordance with the specific rules attaching to the different types of contribution. In order to deal with the broad categories of economic activity and with those who may wish (unusually in the tax field) to pay voluntary sums so as to ensure future entitlement to social security benefits, provision is made for a number of separate classes of contribution.[3]

What follows is a brief description of the classes of contribution, together with their ambit. The remainder of this Chapter will concentrate on contributions

2 See *Stec v UK*, ECHR 65731/01, April 2006 for a discussion of the nature of the UK social security system and the application to it of human rights legislation.

3 See SSCBA 1992, s 1.

payable by, or in respect of, persons in employment. These are known as Class 1 contributions and account for approximately 95% of the National Insurance Fund's contribution income.

6.6 Class 1 contributions

Class 1 contributions are due[4] where 'earnings' are paid to or for the benefit of an 'earner' who is over the age of 16 but below pensionable age in respect of any one 'employment' of his which is 'employed earner's' employment and the amount paid is equal to or exceeds the current earnings thresholds (limits set, primarily, so as to preclude a liability for those on very low incomes).[5]

'Earnings' includes (ie the definition is not an exhaustive one) any remuneration or profit derived from an employment and 'earner' is to be construed accordingly.[6]

'Employment' includes (again, this is not an exhaustive definition) any trade, business, profession, office or vocation and 'employed' has a corresponding meaning.[7]

An 'employed earner' is a person gainfully employed in Great Britain either under a contract of service or in an office (including elective office) with employment income chargeable to income tax under Part 2 of ITEPA 2003.[8]

Class 1 contributions are further divided into two categories, *primary* contributions payable by employees and *secondary* contributions payable by employers;[9] these are considered, together with the rates applicable thereto, at **6.24** below.

6.7 Class 1A contributions

Prior to the Child Support, Pensions and Social Security Act 2000, Class 1A contributions extended only to cars made available by employers for private use and car fuel provided by employers. However, section 73 of that Act

4 See SSCBA 1992, ss 1 and 6
5 See SSCBA 1992, s 5 discussed at **6.24** below.
6 SSBCA 1992, s 3(1)(a).
7 SSCBA 1992, s 122(1). It should be noted that where a person occupies an 'office' he or she is only liable to national insurance contributions to the extent that he or she receives employment income chargeable to income tax (see Chapter 4) in respect of that office. Consideration should therefore be given to **4.33** in Chapter 4 which deals with the concept of office and employment income 'therefrom' in the context of income tax.
8 SSCBA 1992, s 2(1)(a). The question 'what is employment income subject to tax under Part 2 of ITEPA' is addressed at Chapter 4.
9 SSCBA 1992, s 1(2)(a).

dramatically increased the scope of the Class 1A contributions so that they extend to a far broader range of benefits in kind.

They are now payable[10] where a 'higher paid' employee[11] receives a benefit taxable as an 'emolument' under ITEPA 2003,[12] the receipt of which does not give rise to a liability to pay Class 1 contributions.[13] In other words, *prima facie*, any emolument paid to a higher paid employee will either give rise to a liability to pay Class 1 (primary and secondary contributions) or a liability to pay Class 1A contributions. It will, of course, continue to be advantageous for employees to receive benefits falling outside the definition of 'earnings' (see **6.14** below) because, under Class 1A, there is no liability upon the employee to make contributions.

The rates applicable to Class 1A contributions are considered at **6.25** below.

6.8 Class 1B contributions

Class 1B contributions are payable (from 6 April 1999) by any person who is accountable to HMRC for income tax on earnings under a PAYE settlement agreement.[14] This provision is designed to ensure that, where an employer reaches agreement with the Revenue about previous underpayments of income tax on emoluments – and discharges all liabilities by making payment of tax, plus interest and penalties – the amount of NICs which would have been due from the employer as the secondary contributor can also be collected. This replaced an administrative practice of somewhat unsound legislative basis. Contributions will thus be due on the amount of the emoluments included in the settlement agreement and the amount of the income tax payable by the employee.[15]

The rate applicable to Class 1B contributions is considered at **6.26** below.

6.9 Class 2 contributions

Class 2 contributions are paid at a flat weekly rate by all 'self-employed earners' who are over the age of 16 and under pensionable age.[16] As with Class 1 contributions, there is a lower earnings limit below which no contributions are payable.

10 See new SSCBA 1992, s 10(1).
11 SSCBA 1992, s 10(1)(b). See **8.4** for a definition of this term.
12 SSCBA 1992, s 10(1)(a).
13 SSCBA 1992, s 10(1)(c).
14 SSCBA 1992, ss 1(2)(bb) and 10A. PAYE settlement agreements are not dealt with elsewhere in this text, but see ITEPA 2003, Part 11, Chapter 5.
15 SSCBA 1992, s 10A(2) and (3).
16 SSCBA 1992, ss 1(2)(c) and 11.

A 'self-employed earner' is a person gainfully employed in Great Britain otherwise than in employed earner's employment (whether or not he is also employed in such employment).[17]

6.10 Class 3 contributions

Class 3 contributions are contributions voluntarily paid by those who wish to ensure that they have full entitlement to those contributory benefits which require payment of a certain amount of contributions.[18] Class 3 contributions, not surprisingly, form a tiny fraction of the overall payments in any given year.

6.11 Class 4 contributions

Class 4 contributions are payable by self-employed earners in respect of 'profits or gains' immediately derived from the carrying on of a trade, profession or vocation, the profits from which are chargeable to income tax under Chapter 2, Part 2 of ITTOIA 2005 and at least part of which is carried on in the UK.[19] No contributions are payable by those who are under the age of 16 or over pensionable age.

Main Class 4 contributions are payable at a fixed percentage rate on so much of class 4 earnings (ie the profits) as exceed a lower annual limit[20] but do not exceed an upper annual limit.[21] In effect, the fixed percentage of a certain band of profits is payable, the current rate being 9%. Additional Class 4 contributions are due at a rate of 2% for earnings in excess of a threshold, currently £41,450[22]. Class 4 contributions are, in general, collected by HMRC along with the income tax due under ITTOIA 2005.[23]

Class 4 contributions are also payable by a person who, although in employment rather than self-employment as a matter of general law, is deemed to be self-employed for national insurance purposes. Contributions are due in such circumstances where the earnings from the employment exceed a certain figure, being the class 4 lower annual limit.[24]

The phrase 'profits or gains' – is not defined in the legislation. However, the courts have – in the income tax field – long taken a broad approach to

17 SSCBA 1992, s 2(1)(b).
18 SSCBA 1992, ss 1(2)(d) and 13.
19 SSCBA 1992, ss (1)(2)(e) and 15.
20 For the year 2013–14: £7,755.
21 For the year 2013–14: £41,450.
22 SSCBA 1992, s 18(1A)(b).
23 SSCBA 1992, ss 15 and 16.
24 For the tax year 2013–14: £7,755.

the meaning of the term, whether by reference to what accountants would recognise as a profit or (here) by reference to the ordinary meaning of the term.

6.12 Employed or self-employed

The key distinction for present purposes is whether a person is an 'employed earner' or someone who is a 'self-employed earner'. The distinction between an employee and a self-employed person is a familiar one both to tax lawyers and non-tax lawyers and has been the subject of much case law. When considering the position for national insurance purposes the courts have traditionally adopted the tests used in a wider employment context so that (subject to some specific statutory exceptions) there are no special considerations to take into account in this context. The distinction is considered at some length at **4.19** *et seq* of Chapter 4, Introduction to Income Tax.

The exceptions come in the form of specific NICs provisions deeming as employed earners certain earners who would otherwise be self-employed earners. Those exceptions, broadly, take the form of NICs equivalents to Chapters 7, 8 and 9 of ITEPA 2003 (discussed in **4.29** in Chapter 4, Introduction to Income Tax).

The specific provisions can be found in three sets of statutory provisions. First, the Social Security (Categorisation of Earners) Regulations 1978, SI 1978/1689 which deem a certain class of person who would otherwise be regarded as self-employed under general law to be 'employed earners' for the purposes of Class 1 contributions.[25] The regulations also make limited provision for the converse situation where certain categories of person are deemed to be self-employed when otherwise, under general law, they would be regarded as employed.[26] The regulations deal with (*inter alia*) examiners, ministers of religion, office cleaners, part time or visiting lecturers and teachers and employment of a person by his or her spouse.[27] These regulations should thus be considered once the status of a particular person has been determined as a matter of general law.

Second, the Social Security Contributions (Intermediaries) Regulations 2000, SI 2000/727 which are the NICs equivalents to Chapter 8 of Part 2 of ITEPA 2003 (or IR35). And, third, the Social Security Contributions (Managed Service Company) Regulations 2007, SI 2007/2070 which are the NICs equivalent to Chapter 9 of Part 2 of ITEPA 2003.

25 See SI 1978/1689, reg 2(2).

26 SI 1978/1689, reg 2(3).

27 See SI 1978/1689, Sch 1 thereto and, for a practical application of the rules, *St John's College School Cambridge v Sec State Social Security* [2001] ELR 103. The application of the 1978 Regulations to entertainers was recently considered by the Court of Appeal in *ITV Services Limited v HMRC* [2013] EWCA Civ 867. Revenue & Customs Brief 35/13 sets out HMRC's proposal to remove entertainers from the ambit of the 1978 Regulations from 6 April 2014.

6.13 CLASS 1 CONTRIBUTIONS: 'EARNINGS'

It will be recalled that Class 1 NICs are charged on 'earnings' 'paid' to or for the benefit of an earner.[28] The two key concepts are, therefore, the definition of 'earnings' and 'paid'.

6.14 What are 'earnings'?

Section 3 of SSCBA 1992 provides:

> '"earnings" includes any remuneration or profit derived from an employment …'

It should be noted as a preliminary point that it follows from this definition that Class 1 NICs are charged on gross earnings, rather than those net of income tax.[29]

There are then four matters to be considered in determining whether a particular sum should be treated as 'earnings':

(1) Is the sum a 'remuneration' or 'profit'?

(2) Is the sum derived from the employment?

(3) If not, is the sum specifically deemed to be earnings from the employment by express provision?

(4) If so, is the sum specifically excluded from the definition by express provision?

These will be addressed in turn.

6.15 Remuneration or profit

The word 'remuneration' is not defined in the legislation. However it is a broad term (note the reference in the definition of 'earnings' to '*any* remuneration') and was clearly intended by the draftsman in this instance to cover all forms of economic benefit derived from the employment activity. It is, however, thought not to include non-money payments such as benefits in kind.[30]

Neither is 'profit' defined in the legislation. However, the courts have – in the income tax field – long taken a broad approach to the meaning of the term whether by reference to what accountants would recognise as a profit or (here) by reference to the ordinary meaning of the term. In any event, it is arguable

28 See SSCBA 1992, s 6(1).
29 See also SI 2001/1004, reg 24.
30 See *S & U Stores Ltd v Wilkes* [1974] 3 All ER 401.

that a benefit in kind which is capable of being turned into money is a 'profit' for these purposes.[31] Certainly this is the view of HMRC.

It should be pointed out that any debate about whether benefits in kind fall within the definition of earnings would be – at least for present purposes – academic given the effect of regulation 25 of and Schedule 3 to the Contributions Regulations, considered at **6.20** below, which excludes benefits in kind from the definition of earnings.

6.16 Derived from the employment

The question whether the earnings are derived from the employment is addressed in an income tax context in Chapter 10 (Termination and Variation Payments). The reader is directed to that discussion.

6.17 Deemed earnings

The Contributions Regulations contain a number of provisions deeming certain payments, which would otherwise not fall within the definition above, to be earnings. A full discussion of those provisions is outside the scope of this work. However, they include, most materially, payments in kind falling within Schedule 3, Parts II-IV to the Contributions Regulations.[32]

6.18 Excluded earnings

The Contributions Regulations – and in particular regulation 25, Schedule 3 discussed at **6.20** below – exclude from charge certain benefits in kind subject to a list of exclusions from that general exception.

6.19 When are they 'paid'?

Unlike income tax, Class 1 NICs liability arises in relation to earnings 'paid' not emoluments 'earned'. It is, therefore, important to determine when, in law, a 'payment' of earnings takes place.

The word 'paid' is not defined in the legislation. However, it is clear that each term must be interpreted broadly, taking its colour from the definition of 'earnings'.[33] The general rule is that earnings are 'paid' when they are placed at

31 See *Tennant v Smith* [1892] AC 150.

32 See below at **6.20**.

33 See *Elmdene Estates Ltd v White* [1960] AC 528, *Garforth v Newsmith Stainless Ltd* [1979] 1 WLR 409 and *Paul Dunstall Organisation Ltd v Hedges* [1999] STC (SCD) 26 (payment in the form of a plot of land).

the disposal of the earner.[34] It should also be noted that, by section 6 of SSCBA 1992, it suffices if earnings are paid to 'or for the benefit' of an earner over the age of 16.

6.20 Payments in kind

The question whether benefits in kind give rise to a liability to make Class 1 contributions is answered by section 25 of and Schedule 3 to the Contributions Regulations[35] which provide:

> 'A payment in kind, or by way of the provision of services, board and lodgings or other facilities is to be disregarded in the calculation of earnings.
>
> This is subject to paragraph 2 and also to any provision about a payment in kind of a particular description or in particular circumstances in any other Part of this Schedule.'

This general exemption for payments in kind is then made subject to a bewildering number of specific exceptions – see Schedule 3 – which bring the provision of certain (indeed most) types of benefits in kind back into charge for Class 1 contribution purposes.

6.21 The general rule

Looking first at what is included within the general rule in Schedule 3, paragraph 1 to the Contributions Regulations it is important to note that:

(1) The phrase 'services or other facilities' is deliberately broadly drafted and is, on its face, capable of applying to a vast range of non-cash benefits provided to employees.

(2) The width of the general exclusion is cut down by the fact that the service or other facility provided to the employee must be 'in kind'. Thus if the employer acquires an asset – eg a yacht – and gives that to the employee, that is the provision of a benefit in kind. Conversely, if the employee contracts with the boatbuilder to buy the yacht and the employer discharges the debt by paying cash to the builder for the yacht, there is no provision of a benefit in kind; instead, the employer has paid cash to discharge a pre-existing obligation of the employee. For a consideration of the use of employer-provided credit cards in the purchase of petrol for 'company cars' see *R v Department of Social Security ex p Overdrive Credit Card Ltd*.[36]

34 *Garforth v Newsmith Stainless Ltd* [1979] 2 All ER 73.
35 See the Social Security (Contributions) Regulations 2001, SI 2001/1004.
36 [1991] STC 129.

(3) Following from (2) above, a payment will only be 'in kind' where it cannot be exchanged for cash by mere surrender or otherwise negotiated for a known cash value. HMRC have long held the view (on balance, correctly) that anything that can be turned into cash through mere surrender – eg a voucher exchangeable for cash – is not a payment in kind. A similar stance has always been taken in relation to premium bonds, national savings certificates, store vouchers and frequent flyer programmes which are all virtually cash.

(4) With effect from 6 April 1999, the national insurance contributions position for non-cash vouchers follows that applicable for income tax purposes (see Chapter 8 (Benefits in Kind) 'Vouchers') so that most non-cash vouchers attract a liability to contributions. The types of voucher excluded from the charge are those entitling the employee to childcare (up to the age of 16), transport (provided to employees earning less than £8,000 per annum), sport or recreational facilities, subsidised meals on site and the first 15p per day of (eg) Luncheon Vouchers. The changes to the Contributions Regulations which make these amendments appear in the Schedule 1C to those Regulations.

(5) If, properly analysed, what is provided to the employee is cash, the fact that such a payment has been 'disguised' through a number of other steps or transactions which purport to provide for payment in kind will not be relevant: see *DTE Financial Services Ltd v Wilson*[37] (purported award of interest in non-resident trust in satisfaction of cash bonus) and *Paul Dunstall Organisation Ltd v Hedges*[38] (payment in the form of a plot of land). The Revenue (and the courts) are showing a greater willingness to apply such an approach – and specifically the principles of purposive statutory construction in cases such as *Ramsay v IRC*[39] and *Furniss v Dawson*.[40]

6.22 The exceptions

However, there are a large number of specific exceptions to the general exemption for benefits in kind set out in the preceding paragraph. In short, a payment of these exceptions will constitute earnings and thus give rise to a liability to pay Class 1 NICs. These specific exceptions are set out in Schedule 3, Parts II–IV to the Contribution Regulations.

37 [1999] STC (SCD) 121.
38 [1999] STC (SCD) 26.
39 [1982] AC 300.
40 [1984] AC 474.

6.23 RATES OF CONTRIBUTION

6.24 Class 1 contributions

In the case of Class 1 contributions, there is a dual liability imposed under the NICs system. First, the employed earner concerned has an obligation to make primary contributions to the national insurance fund and it is these contributions which are, traditionally, deducted from an employee's salary prior to payment. At the same time, the employer of a person who is an employed earner under a contract service or the person who is, in fact, the employer of an office holder, is required to make secondary contributions to the fund. Secondary contributions are those paid by the employer in respect of sums paid to particular employees.

Although the amounts payable by employee (primary contributions)[41] and employer (secondary contributions)[42] vary from year to year according to the rates and particular earnings brackets, the general picture can be seen from the class 1 contributions for the tax year 2013–14:

Primary contributions	
Total weekly earnings	*Contributions*
Less than £109	Nil
£109 – £797	12%
More than £770	2%

Different rates apply to those employees who have contracted out of the State Earnings Related Pension Scheme ('SERPs'). There is, in effect, a discount of 1.4% given on primary contributions.

Secondary contributions	
Total weekly earnings	*Contributions*
Less than £136	Nil
£136 or more	13.8%

There is a lower rate for employers operating Contracted-out Salary Related (COSR) Schemes of 10.4%. A COSR Scheme is one whereby the employer undertakes to provide the employee in question with a guaranteed minimum pension related to earnings.

41 SSCBA 1992, s 8(1).
42 SSCBA 1992, s 9(1).

6.25 Class 1A contributions

Class 1A contributions are paid by the employer only. By subsections 10(4) and 10(5) of SSCBA 1992, Class 1A contributions shall be calculated on such emoluments as are left out of account for Class 1 contributions. The rate applicable to those emoluments under Class 1A is the 'secondary percentage', or in other words, the percentage rate payable on secondary Class 1 contributions, namely 13.8%. It should also be noted that no Class 1A contributions are payable in respect of so much of any emolument as attracts a liability to pay Class 1B contributions.[43]

6.26 Class 1B contributions

Class 1B contributions are payable by the employer on any emoluments included in the PAYE settlement agreement and any amount of income tax payable by the employee thereunder. They are payable at the percentage rate payable on secondary Class 1 contributions, namely 13.8%.[44]

6.27 TERMINATION AND VARIATION PAYMENTS

Before looking at the details relating to payments made on a termination or variation of contract, it is important to stress that there is only a liability to pay Class 1 contributions where the payment is made to someone who "is" in employed earner's employment at the time.[45] Thus, on the face of it, payments made to someone before employment begins or after employment has ceased fall outside the charge to contributions. However, it should be noted that HMRC take the view that the word 'is' must be read as 'is, was, or will be'.

6.28 Payments on arrival

It should be noted that the national insurance contributions treatment of 'golden hellos' and signing on fees is virtually identical to that which applies for income tax purposes. In effect, payments made prior to the commencement of employment[46] will be liable to contributions where they can be said to be a reward for, or referable to, services to be performed in the future. If, however, the sum paid is an inducement for the surrendering of some other right eg (amateur status) the sum should not be treated as 'earnings' for contribution purposes.[47]

43 SSCBA 1992, s 10(6).
44 SSCBA 1992, s 10A.
45 SSCBA 1992, s 6(1).
46 Assuming that the argument considered in **6.27** above on the meaning of the word 'is' in SSCBA 1992, s 6(1) is rejected.
47 See *Jarrold v Boustead* [1964] 1 WLR 1357 (amateur rugby league player turning professional).

6.29 Other termination and variation payments

There is no direct NIC equivalent to section 401 of ITEPA 2003[48] or sections 393–394 of ITEPA 2003.[49] The position, therefore, is that the question whether Class 1 contributions are payable on a termination payment will be substantially identical to the question whether such payments are taxable generally as earnings.

6.30 COLLECTION

The method of collection of contributions depends upon the Class concerned. The position is as follows.

6.31 Class 1 contributions

Class 1 contributions are collected through the PAYE system from the secondary contributor.[50] Thus, where an employer pays an employee, the employer has an obligation to deduct primary contributions from the payment and to account for the sums deducted and his secondary contributions to HMRC in accordance with the usual PAYE time limits. There are a number of obligations on the secondary contributor to keep detailed records of the amounts of primary and secondary contributions.[51]

An employer cannot recover sums due from an employee as primary contributions in any manner other than by deduction and from deducting secondary contributions from sums due to an employee.[52]

Should the secondary contributor fail to make the relevant payments of Class 1 contributions, HMRC can require him to render a return within 14 days setting out the amounts of contributions due.[53] If no return is made, HMRC can require a production of a detailed record or estimate the amounts due and serve notice upon the secondary contributor.[54] The same remedies are available where an amount of class 1 contributions have been paid but HMRC is not satisfied that the correct amount has been accounted for. Should the amount still remain unpaid, HMRC may certify the amount due and, relying on that certificate, commence proceedings against the employer. Considerable penalties can

48 Which subjects termination and variation payments to income tax: see Chapter 10.
49 Which subject 'relevant benefits' given under non-approved retirement benefits schemes to income tax: see Chapter 13.
50 SSCBA 1992, s 6(1), and Sch 1, para 3 and SI 2001/1004, reg 66.
51 SSCBA 1992, Sch 1, para 6.
52 SSCBA 1992, Sch 1, para 3(3) and the SI 2001/1004, Sch 4, para 6(2).
53 SI 2001/1004, Sch 4, para 14.
54 SI 2001/1004, Sch 4, paras 15 and 16.

be imposed for failure to comply with the payment and collection system.[55] Finally, provision is also made for direct collection of primary contributions from the employed earner in certain, limited, circumstances.[56]

6.32 Class 1A contributions

The position here is for all practical purposes identical to that in relation to Class 1 considered above, save that provision is made for the direct payment of class 1A contributions by employers.[57]

6.33 Class 1B contributions

Class 1B contributions are collected at the same time as sums payable under the relevant PAYE settlement agreement.

6.34 Other classes

Class 2 contributions are collected on a weekly basis, albeit now, typically by way of monthly direct debit. Class 3 contributions are paid voluntarily. Class 4 contributions are collected through the self-assessment income tax system.

6.35 APPEALS

Prior to 1 April 1999 there was a confused and unwieldy appeals and review structure for those persons wishing to challenge any contention by the contributions agency that contributions, or further contributions, were due. With the transfer of responsibility for the levying and collection of NICs from the Department of Social Security to the Revenue, a new appeals procedure was introduced with the aim of aligning the treatment of disputes relating to income tax with those relating to contributions. The system has been amended again with effect from 1 April 2009 on the introduction of the new unified tribunal system. This is addressed in more detail at Chapter 7.

The most frequent category of appeals in relation to NICs includes appeals connected with employment status (employed or self-employed), liability to pay contributions, entitlement to pay voluntary contributions and disputes relating to contributions already paid.

55 SSCBA 1992, Sch 1, para 6(7), 7 and SI 2001/1004, Sch 1, paras 30(7), 51(10).
56 SI 2001/1004, regs 60, 84, 86, Sch 4, paras 30–31.
57 See SI 2001/1004, regs 70–80.

As the appeals procedure post 1 April 2009 accords with that applicable for income tax appeals, reference should be made to Chapter 7. The following points should however be noted in relation to NICs appeals:

(1) Class 4 contributions are payable notwithstanding that an appeal has been lodged, unless an application has been made to postpone payment. The postponement provisions do not apply to appeals against decisions relating to classes 1, 1A and 2 contributions so that an appellant can therefore choose to pay such contributions prior to the appeal or put off payment until after the appeal has been determined. Should the former course be adopted, any contributions overpaid will be repaid; should the latter course be adopted any contributions which become due as a result of the determination of the appeal will normally carry interest so that interest will be payable in addition from the date upon which the contribution should have been paid until the date when they are actually paid.

(2) An employer who has appealed against a decision relating to the national insurance contributions of his employee is not required to pay the contributions pending the appeal. Any contributions which are found to be due must be paid immediately the appeal has been determined together with interest from the original date upon which the amounts were payable.

Chapter 7

Challenging HMRC Decisions

7.1 INTRODUCTION

Although a detailed consideration of the tax appeal system is outside the scope of this work, this Chapter considers, in outline, the key matters involved in bringing an appeal against an assessment to tax. HMRC publishes a guidance note on how to challenge their decisions which can be found at www.hmrc.gov.uk/factsheets/hmrc1.pdf.

The old machinery whereby an employee had, broadly, a choice whether to appeal to the Special Commissioners or the General Commissioners has been swept away by the Tribunals, Courts and Enforcement Act 2007 (TCEA 2007). Under TCEA 2007, those two venerable tribunals were replaced by the Tax Chamber of the First-tier Tribunal (and, exceptionally, the Upper Tribunal).

The Rules governing the practice of the Tax Chamber can be found in the Tribunal Procedure (First-tier Tribunal) (Tax Chamber) Rules 2009, SI 2009/273 (the 'Rules').

From the Tax Chamber, an appeal lies, on a point of law and with permission, to the Upper Tribunal. Then there is an even more limited right of appeal to the Court of Appeal.

7.2 Appeals and PAYE

Appeals are generally brought against an assessment by HMRC of a taxpayer's tax liability or against a closure notice following an enquiry into a taxpayer's self-assessment return. This is somewhat problematic when it comes to appeals against taxation of employment earnings as the whole point of the PAYE system[1] is to deduct tax at source from the taxpayer's income and thus obviate the need for him to make a self-assessment return.

1 Considered in Chapter 5.

In order to side-step this difficulty, there is a long-winded procedure – which commences with the taxpayer requiring[2] HMRC to serve upon him a notice – to enable any person who has suffered deductions of tax at source to procure a closure notice against which he can appeal.

7.3 A REVIEW BY HMRC

The changes consequential on the TCEA 2007 include statutory provision for a review by HMRC of the decision prior to the appeal. The statutory code containing that procedure can be found in sections 49A–49I of the Taxes Management Act 1970 (TMA 1970). As shall be seen, the review is at the taxpayer's option.

Broadly the procedure prescribed has two stages: first, HMRC indicate their view of the matter and then that view is reviewed. These terms 'view' and 'review' are used in the statutory code in contradistinction to one another. The result of that review is then one against which the taxpayer can, should he choose, appeal to the Tax Chamber.

Where the review is triggered by one of the routes described following, HMRC review their view but the nature and extent of that review are 'such as appear appropriate' to HMRC.[3] HMRC are supposed to take account of any representations made by the taxpayer and may conclude that HMRC's view of the matter is to be upheld, varied, or cancelled.[4] HMRC are required to notify the taxpayer of the outcome of the review, and their reasoning, within the period of 45 days or such other period as may be agreed.[5] If they do not so notify the taxpayer, the review is to be treated as having concluded that HMRC's view of the matter is upheld and HMRC must notify the taxpayer of their deemed conclusion.[6]

The outcome of the review will produce a result which the taxpayer can either accept or appeal against.[7] If he wishes to appeal, he must do so within 30 days of the document in which HMRC give notice of the conclusions of the review.[8]

The review regime is very similar to that which obtains under the Finance Act 1994 for customs duties and excise matters. The authors' experience of that regime suggests that occasions on which the nominally independent review will actually lead to any different an outcome from the original view are very

2 Under ITEPA 2003, s 711.
3 TMA 1970, s 49E(2).
4 TMA 1970, s 49E(5).
5 TMA 1970, s 49E(6).
6 TMA 1970, s 49E(8) and (9).
7 TMA 1970, s 49F(2) and (4).
8 TMA 1970, ss 49G(2) and (5) and 49H.

rare indeed. Moreover, it will almost invariably be the case that HMRC fail to complete the review within the prescribed 45 day period leading, as has been stated, to a deemed upholding of HMRC's original view.

There are, however, a number of specific points to be noted depending on whether the taxpayer notifies HMRC that he requires them to review the decision;[9] HMRC offers to review the decision;[10] or the taxpayer notifies the appeal to the Tax Chamber.[11]

7.4 The taxpayer requires a review

As will be seen below, an appeal is made by giving notice to the relevant officer of HMRC.[12] The taxpayer can, at the same time, notify HMRC that he requires HMRC to review the matter in question.[13] In such circumstances, HMRC must, within 30 days or such longer period as is reasonable, notify the taxpayer of HMRC's view.[14] And then HMRC must review the matter in accordance with the procedure described above.[15]

7.5 HMRC offer a review

If, at the same time as giving notice to the relevant officer of HMRC, the taxpayer does not notify the appeal to the Tax Chamber,[16] HMRC can notify the taxpayer of an offer to review the matter in question, which offer must be accompanied by HMRC's view of the matter.[17] There is then an 'acceptance period' within which the taxpayer must accept the offer.[18] If the offer is accepted, HMRC review their original view in the manner described above; if there is no acceptance within that period (encompassing, implicitly, a rejection), then HMRC's view is formalised[19] but the taxpayer retains the ability to appeal against that formalised view.[20]

7.6 The taxpayer notifies the appeal to the Tax Chamber

Finally, if the taxpayer notifies the Tax Chamber of his appeal, without requiring a review, or before HMRC offer one, then the Tax Chamber becomes

9 TMA 1970, s 49A(2)(a).
10 TMA 1970, s 49A(2)(b).
11 TMA 1970, s 49A(2)(c).
12 TMA 1970, ss 31 and 31A.
13 TMA 1970, s 49A(2)(a).
14 TMA 1970, s 49B(2).
15 TMA 1970, s 49B(3).
16 In respect of which, see the following paragraph.
17 TMA 1970, s 49C(2).
18 TMA 1970, s 49C(3).
19 By being treated as an agreement under TMA 1970, s 54(1): see s 49C(4).
20 TMA 1970, s 49C(6).

seized of the appeal and a review is avoided.[21] If the authors' experience of the Finance Act 1994 procedure is replicated in employment income tax matters, then unless the taxpayer has some strategic reason for wishing to slow down the hearing of the appeal, this will invariably be the sensible course to opt for.

7.7 APPEALS TO THE TAX CHAMBER

As has been stated, the twin regimes of the General and Special Commissioners were replaced by the Tax Chamber with effect from 1 April 2009.

The Tax Chamber is composed of one or more of either or both of 'judges' and 'members' depending on which level of complexity the case falls into. The precise configuration of members in each of those levels is prescribed by a Practice Statement issued by Lord Justice Carnwath, the first Senior President of Tribunals, on 10 March 2009 entitled, snappily, 'Composition of Tribunals in Relation to Matters that fall to be decided by the Tax Chamber of the First-tier Tribunal and the Finance and Tax Chamber of the Upper Tribunal on or after 1 April 2009'. Broadly speaking, judges are legally qualified, whereas members need not be.

When a taxpayer receives an assessment or determination which falls into one of the categories of decision over which the Tax Chamber has an appellate jurisdiction, and he decides that he wishes to appeal against it, the procedural steps fall broadly into the following categories: (1) starting proceedings and allocation to a category; (2) preparation for the hearing before the Tax Chamber; (3) the hearing; (4) the decision; and possibly (5) review and appeal.

7.8 What does one appeal against?

The first, and surprisingly complex, step is to identify an appealable decision. Not every HMRC decision on a tax matter carries with it a right of appeal. When HMRC does make a decision against which a taxpayer has a right of appeal, the letter containing that decision ought to state that it is a decision against which the taxpayer has a right of appeal. However, it may be helpful briefly to outline the principal ways, relevant for present purposes, in which an appealable decision may arise.

Where the grounds of complaint is that too much income tax has been deducted at source by the employer, and the individual has not been asked to make a self-assessment return, the individual in question may at any stage[22] require HMRC to ask him to make a self-assessment return. In completing the return,

21 TMA 1970, s 49D.
22 TMA 1970, s 7l1.

the individual will self-assess what he regards as being the correct amount of tax and will claim a refund. If HMRC disagrees with this self-assessment, they will issue a notice of enquiry and then, having completed their enquiry, a closure notice showing what they regard as being the correct amount of tax payable and effectively disallowing the refund. That closure notice is then an appealable decision.

Where the individual already makes a self-assessment return, the procedure is as outlined above save only that, obviously, there is no need for the individual to require HMRC to ask him to make a self-assessment return.

Where the dispute is not in relation to an amount of tax that has been deducted but is in relation to an amount that HMRC assert is due but which has not been paid, the same holds true. The individual should self-assess on the basis that he considers correct, and HMRC will in the manner described amend the self-assessment and the taxpayer can then appeal against that amendment.

The other appealable decision that an advisor is likely to encounter is where HMRC 'discover'[23] that an amount of tax which they consider to be due has not been paid. In those circumstances, they issue what is generally known as a 'discovery' assessment against which the taxpayer can appeal.

7.9 Commencing an appeal

An appeal is commenced by the taxpayer sending or delivering a notice of appeal to the relevant officer of HMRC within the time limit prescribed by the particular enactment.[24] The 'relevant officer' will be the officer who issued the closure notice or assessment. If the taxpayer knows he does not wish to utilise the statutory review procedure, he should send notice of the appeal to the Tax Chamber at the same time.[25]

Typically the time limit is 30 days,[26] however, both HMRC and the Tax Chamber have power to extend time.[27] The contents of the notice of appeal are prescribed by rule 20 of the Rules. The notice of appeal must include the name and address of the taxpayer and his representative (if any), an address where documents may be sent, details of the decision being appealed against, the result the taxpayer is seeking and his grounds for making the appeal. The taxpayer must also provide a copy of any written record of the decision appealed against and any statement of the reasons for that decision that the taxpayer has or can reasonably obtain.

23 To use the parlance of TMA 1970, s 29.
24 TMA 1970, s 31A(1).
25 See **7.22** below.
26 TMA 1970, s 31A.
27 Under, respectively, TMA 1970, s 49 and SI 2009/273, rr 5(3)(a) and 20(4).

When the Tribunal receives the notice of appeal, it gives notice of the proceedings to HMRC.[28]

Despite the fact that an appeal has been lodged, the tax due remains payable unless the taxpayer applies to HMRC (and if that application is unsuccessful the Tax Chamber) for some or all of the tax to be postponed under section 55 of TMA 1970. That application will succeed where there are 'reasonable grounds for believing that the appellant is overcharged to tax'. In practice, postponement is usually agreed by HMRC.

7.10 Listing and notice of hearing

Following the lead of the Civil Procedure Rules 1998, SI 1998/3132 (the CPR), when the Tax Chamber receives the notice of appeal, it must give a direction allocating the appeal to one of four categories: default paper, basic, standard and complex. Different rules apply to each category, as set out below. However, broadly, default paper cases will usually be disposed of without a hearing, basic cases will generally be disposed of after a hearing with minimal exchange of documents before the hearing, standard cases will benefit from detailed case management and be disposed of after a hearing and complex cases likewise but these may be transferred to the Upper Tribunal.

Lord Justice Carnwath has issued a Practice Statement, the 'First-tier Tribunal Categorisation of Cases in the Tax Chamber,' which sets out what is essentially a presumption[29] that certain prescribed types of case will be dealt with under the default paper or basic rules. Formally, however, each appeal will be allocated to one of these different categories at the point in time when the Tribunal receives the notice of appeal.

It is the authors' opinion that most cases relating to the taxation of employment income tax are likely to be 'standard' cases.

7.11 Standard cases

The procedure for standard cases is set out in the following paragraphs. Following allocation of the appeal to the standard case category, and within 60 days of the notice of appeal being sent to HMRC, HMRC must file with the Tax Chamber a Statement of Case setting out the legislative position under which the decision under appeal was made and their position in relation to the case.

28 Rule 20(5).

29 'Unless the Tribunal considers that there is a reason why it is appropriate to allocate the case to a different category': see paragraphs 2 and 3 of the Practice Statement.

Under the old rules there was no obligation to send in a Statement of Case in direct tax cases. However, there was in indirect tax cases, and the obligation was to serve a Statement of Case within 30 days. That obligation was invariably ignored by HMRC and that was almost invariably tolerated by the VAT Tribunal. Whilst the extension to 60 days can be seen as a reflection of HMRC's inability to comply with the shorter time limit, it is probably fair to anticipate the Tax Chamber continuing to be tolerant of failures on the part of HMRC to comply even with this longer time limit.

Within 42 days of service of the Statement of Case, both HMRC and the taxpayer must serve on each other and the Tribunal a list of documents upon which each proposes to rely. Each side then has a right to inspect or take copies of the documents on that list.[30]

It should be noted that, in contrast to the CPR, there is no obligation to serve on the other side a list of documents which one does not place reliance on, even if they are relevant to the appeal.[31] Specifically, there is no obligation to include in the list documents having an adverse effect on one's case. The reasons for this omission are not clear to the authors. However, several points should be noted.

First, HMRC have extensive powers in the TMA to compel the taxpayer and others to produce documents in advance of any appeal and before they make their appealable decision. It may, therefore, have been anticipated by the author of the Rules that, if HMRC wanted specific documents, they would already have obtained them.

Second, the practice in the predecessor tribunals has been for HMRC informally to ask during the course of the hearing, or immediately prior to it, for any documents they then consider they wish to see and, if those documents are not produced promptly, to invite the Tribunal to draw inferences from the non-production of those documents. It is probably reasonable to anticipate a continuation of this practice.

It is also likely that the Tax Chambers will direct that the parties together produce a Statement of Agreed Facts. This particular feature of tax litigation is probably a function of the absence of any formal pleadings of facts relied upon coupled with the fact that tax disputes are usually (although not invariably) primarily disputes on the law rather than on the facts.

30 SI 2009/273, r 27. Somewhat nonsensically, the right to inspect or take copies of documents is expressly not extended to any documents which are privileged: r 27(3). However, if documents are privileged and the party serving the list is not waiving privilege, those documents cannot be ones upon which the party providing the list intends to rely on or produce at the hearing (r 27(2)(b)) and so ought not to have been on the list in the first place.

31 And the procedure before the predecessor tribunals was the same.

7.12 Case management powers

The Rules give the Tax Chamber power to regulate its own procedure, including by giving a direction in relation to the conduct or disposal of proceedings, and at any time,[32] and by giving directions as to the issues on which it requires evidence or submissions. The structure of the Rules is to outline, at rule 5(3), some of the specific directions that the Tax Chamber may give. It is also specifically given power to amend, suspend or set aside an earlier direction that it has made.

It is worth noting, specifically, that the Rules mimic High Court practice by giving to the Tax Chamber an active role in case management. As rule 6(1) makes clear, the Tax Chamber may give a direction either on the application or one or more of the parties or on its own initiative. If a party seeks a direction, it can either make a written application to the Tax Chamber or apply orally during the course of a hearing including, it would seem, a directions hearing. Whilst the Rules state that any application must 'include the reasons for making that application',[33] that requirement has not always been strictly adhered to under the predecessor rules.[34]

Although the CPR do not apply to the Tax Chamber, the principles articulated by those Rules and the decisions of the High Court (and above) on their application tend to guide the Tax Chamber in exercising its discretion. In interpreting the Rules, and considering how the Tax Chamber will exercise its discretion thereunder, it will always, therefore, be worth exploring the current High Court practice.

A failure to comply with any requirement in the Rules, a practice direction or a specific direction made in the proceedings by the Tax Chamber is met by the Tribunal taking 'such action as it considers just' which can extend from waiving the requirement[35] to striking out a party's case.[36] The Tax Chamber also has power to refer the matter to the Upper Tribunal in relation to contempt-like failures to comply with a requirement imposed by the Tax Chamber to attend, give evidence, or produce documents.[37] The Upper Tribunal, in turn, has all the powers that the High Court has to punish such failures.

32 SI 2009/273, r 5(1) and (2).
33 SI 2009/273, r 6(3).
34 The typical instance is of HMRC applying for an extension of time for complying with a direction because they 'need more time' to do so.
35 SI 2009/273, r 7(2)(a).
36 SI 2009/273, r 7(2)(c), in respect of which see below.
37 SI 2009/273, r 7(3).

7.13 Consolidation of proceedings and lead cases

Provision is made, similar to the procedure in the High Court, for the Tax Chamber, either on the application of any party or on its own initiative, to consolidate or hear together two or more sets of proceedings or parts of proceedings raising common issues.

There are also, now, express powers for the Tax Chamber to treat a case as a lead case. Rule 18 provides that where two or more cases have been started before the Tax Chamber and those cases give rise to common or related issues of fact or law, the Tax Chamber may specify one or more of those cases as a lead case or as lead cases and staying the remainder. Where the Tax Chamber makes a decision in respect of that or those common or related issue or issues it must then send a copy of the decision to each party and, with one proviso, it is treated as binding on those parties. The proviso is that a litigant in a 'following' case can within 28 days apply for a direction that the decision does not apply to, and is not binding upon, the parties to that case.

It should also be noted that rule 5(3)(b) seems to envisage that rule 18 is merely indicative of how arrangements involving lead cases may operate and that, where appropriate, other arrangements can operate instead.

The flexibility inherent in the operation of these rules in practice is likely, very quickly, to become encrusted by precedent. Disputes between taxpayers and HMRC frequently raise issues which are of importance to large numbers – in employment tax cases often thousands – of taxpayers, each of which has a formal right to pursue its own appeal and each of which may be pressing for payment or repayment of sums held by the Revenue. In practice, procedural disputes around lead and following cases tend to be a rich vein of work for junior members of the tax bar.

7.14 Preliminary matters

The Tax Chamber has power to deal with an issue in the proceedings as a preliminary matter.[38] Generally a preliminary hearing – essentially a mini hearing of a substantive issue in the main proceedings and taking place prior to the main proceedings – will be directed in circumstances where it may result in a saving of time or costs in determining the main proceedings.

7.15 Postponements and adjournments

The Tax Chamber has a general power to postpone or adjourn proceedings.[39] Moreover, there is, implicit in rule 33, a power to postpone a hearing as a result

38 SI 2009/273, r 5(3)(e).
39 SI 2009/273, r 5(3)(h).

of the failure of either side to attend at a hearing. In that latter instance, the Tribunal will proceed with the hearing if, broadly, it is satisfied that reasonable steps have been taken to notify the non-attending party of the hearing and it considers it is in the interest of justice to proceed. Typically, this involves a brief investigation of such factors as the amount of tax at stake, the merits of the case, and the question whether the non-attending litigant is a repeat offender.

7.16 Power to obtain further information

Supplementing the automatic, but relatively relaxed, permissive disclosure regime outlined above is a power for the Tax Chamber, either on its own application or that of either party, to compel any person to attend as a witness or answer any questions or produce any document in that person's possession or control which relate to any issue in the proceedings.[40]

7.17 Other case management powers

The Tax Chamber has a number of further case management powers, including the ability to extend or shorten time for complying with any rule, practice direction or direction,[41] substitute or add parties to the appeal,[42] permit or require any party to amend a document,[43] permit or require a party to provide documents, information or submissions to the Tax Chamber or another party,[44] decide the form of any hearing[45] (by which, presumably, is meant by telephone, in person or otherwise), and so on.

7.18 Striking out applications

The Rules give the Tax Chamber power to strike out[46] proceedings. The powers can be grouped into a number of sub-categories.

First, there is an automatic strike out if there is a failure to comply with what is vernaculously referred to as an 'unless' order.[47] Second, the proceedings

40 SI 2009/273, r 16.
41 SI 2009/273, r 5(3)(a) (unless to do so would conflict with a provision of another enactment setting down a time limit).
42 SI 2009/273, r 9, a power which will usually be exercised where the wrong person has been named as a party but can also be exercised where the substitution 'has become necessary because of a change in circumstances'.
43 SI 2009/273, r 5(3)(c).
44 SI 2009/273, r 5(3)(d).
45 SI 2009/273, r 5(3)(g).
46 Or, in the case of such a sanction imposed on HMRC, a direction barring HMRC from taking any further part in the proceedings: see SI 2009/273, r 8(7)(a).
47 SI 2009/273, r 8(1).

must be struck out if the Tax Chamber does not have jurisdiction in relation to proceedings and does not exercise its jurisdiction to transfer them.[48] These two provisions are unexceptional.

Third, and most importantly, there are three grounds pursuant to which the Tax Chamber *may* strike out the whole or part of proceedings. Those grounds are set out in rule 8(3) and are, basically: (1) failure to comply with a direction that states that a failure to comply could lead to the striking out of proceedings, (2) failure to co-operate with the Tribunal to such an extent that the Tribunal cannot deal with the proceedings fairly and justly, and (3) a lack of any reasonable prospect of the case, or part of it, succeeding.

Whilst ground (3) will be familiar to most practitioners, and is a welcome development, questions do arise in relation to grounds (1) and (2). As to (1), the Rules seem to envisage that not all failures to comply with directions will be capable of leading to an appeal being struck out – it will only be those where the direction itself says that a failure to comply may lead to the appeal being struck out. Parenthetically, it follows that the Rules envisage a three stage hierarchy of directions: those a failure to abide by which cannot be the subject of meaningful sanction (and which one is tempted to say can safely be ignored); those which say that a failure to abide by them *may* lead to the appeal being struck out; and those which say that a failure to abide by them *will* lead to the appeal being struck out.

It should also be noted that there is a power for a litigant whose appeal has been struck out (or, in the case of the Revenue, barred from taking any further part in the proceedings) to apply for the appeal to be reinstated.[49] No doubt all of this will constitute fertile ground for dispute.

As to (2), this appears to extend only to failures to co-operate *with the Tax Chamber* (rather than non-compliance with the Rules themselves) and, thus, does not appear to constitute a power to strike out for non-compliance with the Rules. Moreover, the threshold for strike out is set at an impractically high level: that the failure is such that the Tribunal cannot deal with the proceedings fairly and justly. Frankly, whilst it is easy to envisage circumstances where non-cooperation makes dealing with cases fairly and justly more difficult, it is far from easy to envisage circumstances where non-cooperation makes such impossible.

The final point that should be noted is that where it is HMRC's failure which is at issue, the appeal is, of course, not struck out, but rather HMRC is barred from taking further part in the proceedings.[50] However, this barring means only

48 SI 2009/273, rr 8(2) and 5(3)(k).
49 SI 2009/273, r 8(5)
50 SI 2009/273, r 8(7)(a).

that the Tribunal need not consider any response or other submissions made by HMRC. In practice, of course, HMRC will make submissions and there will, at the lowest, be a very real possibility that the Tribunal will consider those submissions.

7.19 The substantive hearing

Hearings before the Tax Chamber are relatively informal; however, they are adversarial in nature: the Tax Chamber is required to determine the issue between the parties by reference to the evidence put before it and on the basis of the legal submissions made to it. It has no independent investigative function.

There is a presumption that hearings will be in public.[51] Hearings (or parts of hearings) can be heard in private where such is justified on certain grounds including[52] the protection of a right to respect for private or family life and to maintain the confidentiality of sensitive information. Applications to hold hearings in private are more likely to be sympathetically received by the Tax Chamber in circumstances where the issue in the hearing is one other than whether a tax avoidance scheme entered into by the appellant succeeds or fails. The Tax Chamber is, in other words, and understandably, increasingly sympathetic to the submission advanced by HMRC that there is a particular public interest in exposing to scrutiny details about those who engage in tax avoidance.

Parties may be represented at that hearing by barristers, solicitors or any other representative, whether professionally qualified or not, that they choose.[53] The Rules appear to make provision either for someone to be appointed a representative in advance of the hearing or for a taxpayer to be accompanied by someone who, with the Tribunal's permission, may act as a representative.[54]

The Tax Chamber has the power to regulate its own procedure[55] and parties can be asked to present their cases in whatever order the Tax Chamber considers appropriate. However, typically the order will follow that which would obtain in the High Court. Generally, because it is the taxpayer who bears the burden of proof, it is also, generally, the taxpayer who presents his arguments first. The taxpayer must show why the disputed assessment or closure notice is wrong. This may involve putting evidence before the Tax Chamber to establish the facts, figures and dates, etc and making any arguments of law as to why HMRC's decision is wrong. If the taxpayer needs to call witnesses or produce

51 SI 2009/273, r 32(1).
52 There are five grounds in total: see SI 2009/273, r 32(2).
53 SI 2009/273, r 11.
54 SI 2009/273, r 11(4).
55 SI 2009/273, r 5(1).

documents, he will need to ensure that they are all available at the hearing. Self-evidently, any witnesses giving evidence may be cross-examined.

HMRC's representative will then be asked to present its case, explaining it in detail and offering any evidence it relies on to support its decision. Finally the taxpayer will be given the opportunity to deal with those submissions of law or fact.

7.20 Costs

The Tax Chambers has a limited costs jurisdiction. It may make an order for costs where a party (or its representative) has acted 'unreasonably' in bringing, defending or conducting proceedings, or where the case falls into the category of complex cases and the taxpayer has not made a written request to the Tribunal to oust the costs jurisdiction.[56]

This last, unusual, jurisdiction obviously advantages the taxpayer (who appears to have a right to choose[57] whether the costs jurisdiction applies in complex cases) over HMRC. The taxpayer who is able to conduct litigation cheaply (so that his downside is bigger than his upside) or who wishes carefully to manage risk (so that, at least in the Tax Chamber, he is only liable to his own costs) or who believes that his prospects are poor (so that the likelihood is that he would otherwise pay his opponent's costs rather than vice versa) may be well advised to make a request under rule 10(1)(c)(ii).

It may also make a wasted cost order against any person exercising a right of audience.[58]

7.21 THE DECISION

The Tax Chamber has power to give a decision orally at a hearing.[59] This power will tend to be exercised after case management hearings and at the conclusion of simple substantive hearings. It also has power to give a decision notice which must state the Tribunal's decision and notifies the parties of any right of appeal against the decision and the time within which, and the manner in which, the right of appeal may be exercised.[60]

56 SI 2009/273, r 10(1).
57 The Tax Chamber appears not to have any discretion whether to accede to a request that the costs jurisdiction in complex cases be ousted. If request is made, the request must be adhered to.
58 SI 2009/273, r 10(1)(a) and the Tribunal, Courts and Enforcement Act 2007, s 29(4).
59 SI 2009/273, r 35(1).
60 SI 2009/273, r 35(2).

The decision notice must (unless both sides agree it is unnecessary) include a summary of the findings of fact and reasons for the decision or be accompanied by full written findings of fact and reasons for the decision.[61] If only a summary is given, a party may apply for full written findings and reasons (and, indeed, must do so before making any application for permission to appeal).[62]

The Tax Chamber can also, at the request of the parties, and if it considers it appropriate, dispose of the proceedings by consent order.[63] The requirement for the Tribunal to 'consider it appropriate'[64] presumably enables the Tax Chamber to refuse where the appeal raises issues of importance extending beyond the parties to the appeal.

7.22 REVIEWS AND APPEALS

The system of review and appeal in the TCEA 2007 is as follows: first, there is an obligation on the Tax Chamber itself to consider whether to 'review' its decision and, secondly, there is a need to obtain permission to appeal.

7.23 Reviewing the original decision

Following the making of its decision, the Tax Chamber now has no fewer than three wholly separate jurisdictions to correct its original decision.

7.24 The slips rule

Rule 37 gives voice to the so-called 'slips' rule whereby, if the Tax Chamber has made a clerical mistake, or other accidental slip or omission in a decision, direction or document produced by it, it may send notification of the amended decision to all the parties. This power, which is essentially administrative in nature, is unremarkable and will be familiar to most legal advisers.

It would appear[65] that such a correction may be made by the Tax Chamber either on the application of any party or of its own volition.

7.25 Power to set aside a decision and remake it

Rule 38 of the Rules gives to the Tax Chamber power to set aside a decision which disposes of proceedings, or part of proceedings, and to remake that

61 SI 2009/273, r 35(3).
62 SI 2009/273, r 35(4)
63 SI 2009/273, r 34(2).
64 SI 2009/273, r 34(1).
65 From the words 'at any time' in SI 2009/273, r 37.

decision where it considers that the interests of justice so require and one of the conditions in sub-rule (2) was not satisfied. Those conditions in sub-rule (2) go, broadly, to the presence of some procedural irregularity – such as a document not being sent to a party or the Tribunal at an appropriate time or some other such procedural irregularity, or a party not being present at the hearing.

It would appear that this jurisdiction is triggered by an application being made by a party[66] within 28 days after the date on which the Tribunal sends notice of the decision to the applicant.

Whilst it is not entirely clear whether the Tribunal has power to set aside its decision without immediately remaking it, in the opinion of the authors, the better view is probably that it does, even though such power is implicit.[67]

7.26 Power to review a decision

Third, and finally, there is a novel, and somewhat curiously drafted, review jurisdiction.

On receiving an application for permission to appeal, the Tribunal must consider whether to review the decision.[68] However, it may only actually review the decision where: (a) there is an appeal against the decision of the Tribunal, and (b) the Tribunal is satisfied that there is an error of law in the decision.[69]

It is clear from the TCEA 2007,[70] that, even though the Tribunal is obliged to consider whether to review the decision, even if it is satisfied that there is an error of law in the decision, it retains a discretion not to review the decision. How that discretion will be exercised in practice is not easy to predict. It may be that, where the conditions for a review are satisfied, there is a presumption that there will be a review but that, perhaps in circumstances where a review is unlikely to conclude the litigation, the Tribunal may form the view that the overriding objective is unlikely to be served by a review.

A further question which must await determination is whether a decision to review is itself an appealable decision. Certainly the Tax Chamber may not

66 SI 2009/273, r 38(3) and it should be noted that the power in r 6(1) for the Tribunal to make a direction on its own initiative applies only to 'directions'.
67 Such seems to be the only logical consequence of a power to set aside a decision because a party or his representative was not present. The counter view follows from the presence of the words 'and re-make the decision' in SI 2009/273, r 38(1) and the apparent absence of any mechanism in SI 2009/273 dealing with what is to happen should the Tribunal want to set aside the Decision without immediately remaking it.
68 SI 2009/273, r 40(1).
69 SI 2009/273, r 41(1).
70 TCEA 2007, s 9(1) and the word 'may'.

take any action in relation to a decision following a review without first giving every party an opportunity to make representations in relation to the proposed action.[71]

The difficult questions raised by the Tax Chamber's review jurisdiction are not confined to procedural ones. Of course, at the point in time at which it is considering whether to review a decision, all it will have is the putative appellants' list of alleged errors in the decision, which list comprises that putative appellants' application for permission. It will not have a full skeleton from the appellant and it will have nothing from the putative respondent. In other words, the materials it will have in considering whether to review the decision might be said to be inadequate for that purpose.

On a review, the Tax Chamber may correct accidental errors in the decision or in a record of the decision, amend the reasons given for the decision, or set the decision aside.[72] Given that the Tax Chamber is plainly entitled to tidy up a decision in consequence of an application for permission, and given a likely disinclination on the part of Tax Chambers to admit they got it wrong, there must at the very least be a possibility that Tax Chambers will use the review jurisdiction to seek to appeal-proof their decisions. This possibility is likely to present the advisor of a putative appellant with a difficult balance to strike in drafting any application for permission.

7.27 Appealing against the original decision

The right to appeal is triggered by the putative appellant receiving full written findings and reasons. It is only once these have been received that he can apply for permission to appeal.[73] It follows that the first step for a putative appellant wishing to appeal is to check that he has received the 'full written findings of fact and reasons for the decision'.[74] If he has not, he must request these within 28 days after the date the Tribunal provided the decision notice[75] and they must be provided by the Tribunal within 28 days of receiving the request.

7.28 Permission to appeal

The Rules impose a requirement for a putative appellant to seek permission before appealing against a decision of the Tax Chamber.[76] An application for permission must be received by the Tax Chamber not later than 56 days after

71 SI 2009/273, r 41(3)
72 TCEA 2007, s 9(4).
73 SI 2009/273, rr 35(4) and 39(1).
74 SI 2009/273, r 35(3)(b).
75 SI 2009/273, r 35(5).
76 SI 2009/273, r 39(1).

the date on which the putative appellant receives the later of: (a) full written reasons for the decision; (b) notification of amended reasons for, or correction of, the decision following a review;[77] or (c) notification that an application to set aside has been unsuccessful.[78]

If the Tax Chamber refuses permission, the application may be renewed before the Upper Tribunal.[79] An application can only be made to the Upper Tribunal if the Tax Chamber has refused or not admitted the application for permission made to itself.[80] The application must be made in writing within one month of the date upon which the Tax Chamber sent notice of its refusal of permission or it refused to admit the application for permission to the putative appellant.

The formal requirements for the renewed application are set out in Rule 21(4) and (5) of the Upper Tribunal Rules but, materially, the application must state the grounds on which the appellant relies.

If the Upper Tribunal also refuses permission without a hearing, the putative appellant can ask for that refusal to be reconsidered at a hearing.[81] Any application for reconsideration at a hearing must be in writing and made within 14 days of the refusal of permission by the Upper Tribunal.[82] However, if permission is again refused, that is the end of the road.

7.29 Appealing to the Upper Tribunal

The would-be appellant who has obtained permission must provide a notice of appeal to the Upper Tribunal within one month of the giving of permission.[83] The matters stated in the notice of appeal must include the matters included in the application for permission to appeal. The respondent may provide a response to the notice of appeal and there is also procedure for the appellant to reply thereto.[84] However, given that the Upper Tribunal Rules do not appear to impose any sanction for not responding (or replying) it is not immediately clear why the respondent (or appellant) would wish to give the other side advance notice of his arguments.

On an appeal, by section 12 of TCEA 2007, if the Upper Tribunal finds that the decision involved an error of law, it may set aside the decision of the Tax

77 It would seem that, if the Tribunal reviews a decision, this starts the 56-day clock running and it may be sensible to renew the application for permission that triggered the review.
78 SI 2009/273, r 39(2).
79 TCEA 2007, s 11(4)(b) and the Tribunal Procedure (Upper Tribunal) Rules 2008, SI 2008/2698 (the 'Upper Tribunal Rules'), r 21(1).
80 SI 2008/2698, r 21(2)(b).
81 SI 2008/2698, r 21(4).
82 SI 2008/2698, r 21(5).
83 SI 2008/2698, r 23(1).
84 SI 2008/2698, rr 24 and 25 respectively.

Chamber. If it does, it must either remit the case to the Tax Chamber with directions for its reconsideration or re-make the decision. If the case is remitted back to the Tax Chamber, the Upper Tribunal may also direct that the members of the First-tier Tribunal who are chosen to reconsider the case are not to be the same as those who made the decision that has been set aside or give procedural directions in connection with the reconsideration of the case by the First-tier Tribunal.

If it re-makes the decision, the Upper Tribunal may make any decision which the Tax Chamber could make if the Tax Chamber were re-making the decision, and may make such findings of fact as it considers appropriate.

7.30 Appeals on a question of law

As has been stated, an appeal to the Upper Tribunal lies on a point of law[85] rather than on the facts. This will be a distinction familiar to most readers and which serves to prevent the endless rehearing of cases on appeal: see the judgement of Lord Gifford in one of the earliest reported tax cases, *Caledonian Railway Company v Banks*,[86] where his Lordship stated:

> 'It appears that it is only on proper questions of law that there is any appeal to this Court as the Court of Exchequer in Scotland. All reviews upon questions of fact which are to be ascertained by evidence of any kind are excluded, review being allowed only upon pure and proper questions of law; and in order that the law and the fact may be kept entirely separate, it is provided that the case to be stated by the Commissioners shall "set forth the facts, – that is it shall specify all the matters of fact upon which the legal determination proceeds and shall also set forth 'the determination" – that is, the decision in law – which the Commissioners have pronounced upon the facts proved or admitted before them; and it is this determination, so far as proceeding upon grounds of law, which alone is the subject of appeal to this Court …'

In practice, deciding between errors of law and errors of fact is, of course, not always straightforward, particularly when parties are faced with a decision of the Commissioners in a particular case which has to be dissected and analysed to see what, if any, errors of law have been made.

Any decision of the Tax Chamber can, as a matter of analysis, be separated into five different elements: (1) the evidence presented to the Tax Chamber; (2) the primary facts found by the Tax Chamber as a result of hearing the evidence; (3) inferences and conclusions drawn from such findings of fact; (4) the relevant legal principles; and (5) the application of such principles to the facts found

85 TCEA 2007, s 11(1).
86 (1880) 1 TC 487 at 498.

and inferences drawn. Whether a particular item of evidence was actually presented to the Tax Chamber is clearly a question of fact, just as the relevant legal principles and their application to the facts found and inferences drawn are clearly questions of law. The elements which are difficult to categorise are the remaining two – findings of primary fact, and inferences from such facts – as it is these elements in any decision which straddle the dividing line between fact and law. The proper categorisation of each can, however, be done by drawing upon some of the older authorities in tax and other areas of the law where these issues have been considered.

It is a question of fact as to whether, on balance, the Tax Chamber was entitled to make a finding of primary fact on the basis of contradictory evidence presented to them. As such, a finding of primary fact is effectively unappealable. This is clear from the judgement of Rowlatt J in *Cape Brandy Syndicate v CIR*[87] where his Lordship stated:

> 'I do not think, by telling me all the evidence, that the Commissioners can make me, or indeed give me authority – because they cannot give me authority if I do not possess it by law – to determine the question of fact.'

Similarly, see also the judgement of Lord Reid in *JP Harrison (Watford) Limited v Griffiths*:[88]

> 'Where the question is a question of fact, that means that the decision of the Commissioners cannot be reviewed by this Court.'

However, a finding of primary fact can be challenged as a question of law if there was *no* evidence at all before the Tax Chamber upon which they could have relied. On this point see Fletcher Moulton LJ in *The New Zealand Shipping Company v Stephens*[89] where he stated 'it is, as a rule, a point of law whether or not there is any evidence on which a certain finding of fact can be made'. This accords with the classic statement on this point in a case concerned with the case stated procedure for appeals from the magistrates court – see Lord Goddard CJ in *Bracegirdle v Oxley*:[90]

> 'In this Court we only sit to review the magistrates, decision on points of law, being bound by the facts which they have found, provided always that there is evidence on which they could come to the conclusion of fact at which they arrive.'

Similar statements can be found in cases concerning appeals from the decisions of arbitrators – see Mocatta J in *Re 'Effy'*.[91] Although the distinction between

87 [1921] 1 KB 64.
88 (196) 40 TC 281 at 296.
89 (1907) 5 TC 553 at 566.
90 [1947] KB 349.
91 [1972] 1 Lloyd's Reports 18 at 33, 34.

'no evidence' and 'some evidence' will often not be a clear one, there is no doubt that findings of fact in a case in which both parties put in *relevant* contradictory evidence are beyond the scope of challenge by way of case stated.

Inferences or conclusions drawn from findings of primary facts can be challenged as questions of law if no reasonable tribunal, properly directed, could have reached such inferences or conclusions in the light of the primary facts found. There are many authorities for such a proposition; for example, see Scott LJ in *British Samson Aero Ltd v CIR*[92] where his Lordship stated:

> 'Where the Commissioners put before the Court in the Special Case the whole of the materials from which they drew their final inference, then it is a question of law as to whether, from that material, their inference was correct or not.'[93]

7.31 Redefining the boundary between questions of law and fact

The recent Supreme Court decision in *R (Jones) v First-tier Tribunal (Social Entitlement Chamber)*[94] appears to redraw the line between the jurisdiction of the First-tier and Upper Tribunals; it gives to the latter an enhanced supervisory role over the decisions of the former. Lord Carnwath envisages[95] a genuinely flexible approach to the question 'fact or law' in which the Upper Tribunal is empowered to ask how the interests of justice generally – and not just between the parties in an individual case – would be served by a decision to entertain (or not) a particular appeal.

This decision has already been wielded by Judge Berner in the Upper Tribunal in his recent (impressively reasoned) decision in *Ramsay v HMRC*[96] to thwart a submission from Counsel for the respondent that the Upper Tribunal had no place intervening because the question was one of fact. It has also been referred to in a number of other judgments addressing first or second appeals against decisions of the Tax Chamber[97].

7.32 Further appeals

There is then an appeal, with permission, from a decision of the Upper Tribunal to the Court of Appeal. The rules governing such an appeal are contained in the CPR and section 13 of TCEA 2007 and are not repeated here.

92 (1938) 22 TC 29 at 49.
93 (1938) 22 TC 29 at 296. See also *JP Harrison (Watford) Ltd v Griffiths*, per Lord Reid at 296, Lord Denning at 298, 299 and Lord Morris at 301.
94 [2012] 2 AC 48.
95 [2012] 2 AC 48 at paras 41, 43 and 46.
96 [2013] STC 1764.
97 See *HMRC v Arkeley Ltd* [2013] UKUT 0393 (TCC) at para 29 and *HMRC v Lloyds TSB Equipment Leasing (No 1) Ltd* [2013] UKUT 0368 (TCC) at para 36.

7.33 OTHER FORMS OF RELIEF

7.34 Other forms of legal challenge

Although outside the scope of this work, it should be noted that – as in other areas involving citizens and government departments – a disgruntled taxpayer has a right to seek judicial review of HMRC's action or (in an appeal context) of the actions of the Tax Chamber. The courts are now very familiar with such challenges in a tax context – see for example *R v IRC ex p National Federation of Self Employed and Small Businesses*[98] and *R v IRC ex p Matrix Securities Ltd*[99] – but it remains the case that successful applications for judicial review in this field are relatively rare. As with other areas of law, relevant factors will include availability of alternative remedies, standards of behaviour or performance to be expected from HMRC, the degree to which HMRC can be required to abide by a public statement of practice or policy and whether the application has been brought 'promptly' and within the three month time limit.

7.35 Administrative remedies

Equally, taxpayers are also entitled to pursue complaints – particularly those framed in terms of the Taxpayers' Charter – to the Parliamentary Commissioner for Administration (the 'Ombudsman') and to HMRC's own Adjudicator who is charged with the investigation and reporting of alleged abuses of power or failure to provide proper and adequate service to taxpayers. Although HMRC will commonly adopt the recommendations of both the Ombudsman and the Adjudicator – paying compensation where appropriate – they are not bound in law to do so.

7.36 Error or mistake claims

Much more relevant in practice are the provisions contained in section 33 of TMA 1970 which allow a taxpayer to make a claim for overpaid tax within a specific time of the overpayment. By section 33(1), a person who has overpaid income tax under an assessment (whether a self-assessment or otherwise) by reason of an error or a mistake in a tax return can give notice seeking repayment. He must do so within five years of the 31 January which follows the year of assessment in which the return was made. HMRC are required to inquire into the matter and to give such relief by way of repayment of tax as is reasonable and just. No relief is however available if the return was made in accordance with the generally prevailing practice at the time (subsection (2A)) and in considering repayment HMRC can have regard to the taxpayer's overall tax position in the relevant year and other years (subsection (3)).

98 [1981] 2 WLR 722.
99 [1994] STC 272. For other examples, see **3.6** in Chapter 3.

Chapter 8

Benefits in Kind

8.1 INTRODUCTION

The taxation of benefits in kind is comprised of essentially three regimes. The first – the general regime[1] – applies to all employees. The second – the residual regime[2] – applies only to employees earning £8,500 or more and directors and application of it will usually, although not invariably, lead to a higher charge to tax than an application of the general regime.[3] The third regime is basically a collection of specific statutory provisions, some of which apply only to employees earning £8,500 or more and company directors and some of which apply to all employees. Not surprisingly, where specific statutory provision is made, the common law and residual regimes tend to give way.

The structure of this Chapter is, first, to identify the basis upon which income tax is calculated where the general regime applies and, second, to identify the basis of charge which will apply where the residual regime obtains. There will then be a discussion of the more frequently encountered benefits in kind which will take in a discussion of the more important specific statutory provisions referred to in the previous paragraph.

The primary relevance of the distinction between the first and second regimes described above is for 'lower paid employees' who are not directors and who have no material interest in their employer.[4] For such individuals, save for where special provision is made (under the third regime), if they are not taxable under the first regime, they are not taxable at all. This might mean that they escape tax altogether or they are taxed on a much smaller sum.

This category of employees is delineated by sections 216, 217 and 220 of ITEPA 2003. The conjoint effect of those rules is broadly that you are a lower paid employee in respect of an employment if: (a) you earn less than £8,500 from that and related[5] employments; and (b) are not a full time director of

1 Which can be found in ITEPA 2003, s 62.
2 Which can be found in ITEPA 2003, s 203.
3 ITEPA 2003, ss 63(2), 216 and 217.
4 See **8.4** below for a description of the employees to whom this Chapter applies.
5 ITEPA 2003, s 220(3).

your employer; or (c) you are a director but have no material interest in your employer and are either a full time director or the company is charitable or non-profit making. A fuller discussion of this category can be found below at **8.4** below.

Finally, it should be noted that HMRC's Employment Income Manual contains further details of the taxation of specific benefits in kind. That Manual provides, by way of example, a description extending to something in excess of eighty pages on how living accommodation is taxed (from paragraphs 11301 to 11522 of that Manual) and goes into more detail than can usefully be provided in this book.

8.2 THE GENERAL REGIME

The general regime taxes an employee recipient as if he had received the money's worth of that benefit, by which is meant the price at which that benefit could be sold on the date of receipt. Thus if a benefit cannot be turned to account in some way, the employee will escape income tax thereon. The reason why this regime tends to lead to a lower charge to tax is that the open market value may either be nothing or considerably lower than the value of the benefit to the employee.

This principle stems from the case of *Tennant v Smith*[6] which concerned an agent for a bank whose duties included residing at a particular house provided rent-free but which he had no power to sub-let. Held, the value of the house was not an emolument in the agent's hands as the benefit was not convertible into money. Lord Macnaghten said:

> 'On examining that Schedule it became obvious that it extends only to money payments or payments convertible into money.'

In *Wilkins v Rogerson*[7] a company decided to give certain employees a suit, overcoat or raincoat as a Christmas present. The tailor was instructed to give each employee a fitting and send the account to the company. Held, this was a perquisite or profit of the employment and that the measure of the emolument was the value of the suit to the employee, ie its second-hand value. If, by contrast, the employer had paid for a suit previously ordered by the employee, the measure of the emolument would have been the cost of the suit.

In *Ede v Wilson*[8] a number of employees were allotted shares on the condition that, for so long as they continued to work for the company, they could not sell

6 [1892] AC 150.
7 [1961] Ch 133.
8 26 TC 381.

them without permission. The court held that the shares were earnings even though there was a restriction on sale. The restriction was, however, a factor to be taken into account in determining the amount of the earnings.

This principle has now acquired statutory voice in section 62 of ITEPA 2003. 'Earnings' is defined to include things of 'money's worth'[9] and 'money's worth' is defined as 'something that is: (a) of direct monetary value to the employee; or (b) capable of being converted into money or something of direct monetary value to the employee'.[10]

Where the employee has the right to give up the benefit altogether in return for a higher financial remuneration, the amount taxable as earnings under section 62 is the amount of the wage or salary that would be paid in lieu of the benefit.

In *Heaton v Bell*[11] an employee was provided with the use of a car by his employer, but an agreed sum was deducted from his wages for that use. He could give up the right to use the car at any time with the result that the wage he received would be increased. It was held that the use of the car was earnings in the sum deducted from his wages.

8.3 THE BENEFITS CODE REGIME

The residual regime (or the 'higher paid regime' as it might also be described), imposed by sections 201–203 of ITEPA 2003, is considerably more stringent. It taxes 'higher paid employees,'[12] as they might for the sake of convenience be described, on the 'cash equivalent' of the particular benefit. The cash equivalent is, in essence, the expense incurred in or in connection with the provision of the benefit by the employer.[13] These provisions – contained within Chapter 10 of Part 3 of ITEPA 2003 – were enacted to counter what were felt to be abuses of the general regime.

Whenever there is: (1) supplied to a person to whom this Chapter applies or other members of his family or household; (2) any benefit to which section 201 applies; (3) by reason of the employment; and (4) the cost of providing that benefit is not otherwise chargeable to tax as income; there is (5) to be treated as employment income an amount equal to the cash equivalent of the benefit.

9 ITEPA 2003, s 62(2)(b).
10 ITEPA 2003, s 62(3).
11 (1967) 46 TC 211.
12 Ie those who are not lower paid employees (see **8.4** below). The term, although not found in the legislation, is frequently used.
13 ITEPA 2003, s 204.

8.4 Which persons are affected?

The rules apply to employees earning £8,500 or more and to company directors.[14] The £8,500 figure refers to earnings from the specific employment rather than the earnings of the person holding it. Therefore, where an individual holds a number of part-time positions with separate employers, he may fall outside this provision notwithstanding that his aggregate earnings comfortably exceed it. Equally, his benefits in kind received from some positions may be taxed under the general regime and others under the higher paid regime.

The figure of £8,500 has not been increased for many years and is now such, evidently, as to include all full-time employees. Broadly speaking, the application of the £8,500 figure is calculated by ignoring any deductions which may be made from emoluments[15] and including all sums which would be included if the employee fell above the threshold.[16]

Although the threshold is determined by reference to the income derived from the particular employment rather than the aggregate earnings derived from all employments by the employee, it is not open to an employee to avoid application of these rules by entering into a number of separate contracts between the employee and a single employer or a number of employers in the same group.[17] Separate employments with the same employer are treated as one employment, as are separate employments with employers under common control.

For present purposes, 'director' has a definition *sui generis* which is to be found in section 67 of ITEPA 2003:

> '(1) In the benefits code "director" means –
>
> (a) in relation to a company whose affairs are managed by a board of directors or similar body, a member of that board;
>
> (b) in relation to a company whose affairs are managed by a single director or similar person, that director or person; and
>
> (c) in relation to a company whose affairs are managed by the members themselves, a member of the company,
>
> and includes any person in accordance with whose directions or instructions the directors of the company (as defined above) are accustomed to act.

14 ITEPA 2003, s 216(4).
15 ITEPA 2003, s 218(1) and EIM 20102.
16 ITEPA 2003, s 218(1).
17 ITEPA 2003, s 220.

(2) For the purposes of subsection (1) a person is not to be regarded as a person in accordance with whose directions or instructions the directors of the company are accustomed to act merely because the directors act on advice given by that person in a professional capacity.'

The person in accordance with whose instructions the others are instructed to act may be a director or a shadow director.[18] It is also worth noting that the definition is comprehensive, so that if a company has a board of directors, but in practice its affairs are managed by only one of those directors, the remainder will not be directors as that word is used in the benefits code.

Finally, an individual who: (a) either works full-time as a director[19] or is a director of a company which is non-profit making or is established for charitable purposes only; (b) earns under £8,500 pa; and (c) has no material interest[20] in the company for which he works, will fall outside the regime.[21]

This regime applies both to benefits provided for higher paid employees and for members of his family or household.[22] Section 721 of ITEPA 2003 defines who is a member of a person's family:

'(a) the person's spouse or civil partner;

(b) the person's children and their spouse or civil partner;

(c) the person's parents; and

(d) the person's descendants.'[23]

And who is a member of a person's household, being a member of a person's family and his domestic staff and guests.[24]

8.5 To what benefits does section 201 of ITEPA 2003 apply?

Section 201 of ITEPA 2003 applies to all benefits except 'excluded benefits' and 'excluded benefits' are those for which specific statutory provision is made in Chapters 3 to 9 of the benefits code save for where an exception means that one of those Chapters does not apply.[25] In other words, it is a residual category

18 The definition of which has been considered in a tax context by the House of Lords in *R v Allen* [2001] STC 1537, per Lord Hutton at paras 19–20.
19 A full time working director is a director who is required to devote substantially the whole of his time to the service of the company in a managerial or technical capacity: ITEPA 2003, s 67(3).
20 'Material interest' is defined by ITEPA 2003, s 68.
21 ITEPA 2003, s 216(3).
22 ITEPA 2003, s 201(2)(b).
23 ITEPA 2003, s 721(4).
24 ITEPA 2003, s 721(5).
25 ITEPA 2003, ss 201–202.

that applies only to those benefits for which specific provision is not otherwise made.

8.6 By reason of his employment

All provision which is made for an employee or members of his family or household[26] by his employer is deemed to be made to them 'by reason of the employment' except any such provision which is made by the employer, being an individual, in the normal course of his domestic, family or personal relationships.[27] This exception addresses the situation where an individual employs a friend or family member and he then makes provision for them in his capacity as a friend or family member rather than as an employer.

The phrase 'by reason of the employment' has a wider meaning than 'from the employment' (being the equivalent applying to the general regime rather than the higher paid regime).[28] In *Wicks v Firth*[29] Lord Denning said that 'by reason of the employment' covered cases where an employee would not have received a benefit unless he had been an employee. The employment must be one of the causes of the benefit being provided. It need not be the sole cause or even the main one. But it must be an operative cause in the sense that it was a condition of the benefit being granted.[30] In the same case Lord Oliver said that the question to ask is 'what is it that enables the person concerned to enjoy the benefit?' If the answer to that question properly includes 'the employment' as one of the factors then that is 'by reason of' the employment. This question was before the Special Commissioners in *Sports Club plc v Inspector of Taxes*.[31] The Special Commissioners expressed the view that payments in respect of image rights to a football player were not made 'by reason of the employment' and stated: '[i] n our view the expression 'benefit'… must exclude anything provided in return for good consideration under a separate commercial contract.'

HMRC states that, in practice, it is reasonable to assume where a benefit is provided by someone other than the employer and it is plainly connected with the employment, it has been provided 'by reason' of the employment.[32] However, the aforementioned decision of the Special Commissioners in *Sports Club plc v Inspector of Taxes* gives very real reason to doubt whether the courts would agree with the breadth of such an assertion.

26 And see **8.4** above for a definition of members of an employee's family or household.
27 ITEPA 2003, s 201(3).
28 ITEPA 2003, s 9.
29 [1983] STC 25.
30 The House of Lords in that case declined to express a view on the question.
31 [2000] STC (SCD) 443.
32 See EIM 20503.

8.7 Is the cost otherwise chargeable to income tax?

The inter-relationship between the section 62 regime and the higher paid regime is governed by section 64 of ITEPA 2003. If the same benefit constitutes both money's worth under section 62 and an amount to be treated as earnings under the higher paid regime, then the money's worth is taxable under section 62 and the amount by which the amount to be treated as earnings under the benefits code exceeds the money's worth is taxed under the higher paid regime. As will be seen, this has the net effect of ensuring that the higher of the cost of providing the benefit or its market value is chargeable to tax.

8.8 What is the cash equivalent of the benefit?

The cash equivalent of the benefit is defined as the cost of the benefit less so much of it (if any) as is made good by the employee to those providing the benefit.[33]

The 'cost of a benefit' is the amount of any expense incurred in or in connection with its provision, and includes a proper proportion of any expense relating partly to the benefit and partly to other matters. There are specific provisions which further define the 'cost of the benefit' where the benefit in question is the benefit of use of an asset without transferring property in it[34] or the transfer of an asset which has been used or depreciated since its acquisition by the transferor.[35]

How the cost of an in-house benefit is calculated was the subject of the decision, famous for other reasons, in *Pepper v Hart*.[36] In that case, a number of teachers had their children educated at Malvern College and paid concessionary fees of no more than 20% of those paid by other parents. However, the children occupied surplus places only and their right to do so was at the discretion of the College.

The House of Lords held that the expense of providing the benefit of the children's education was the marginal additional cost of its provision and not, as the Revenue had contended, a proportion of the full costs of providing an education to all pupils at the College.

In reaching this decision, Lord Browne-Wilkinson distinguished two types of benefit, first, a benefit bought in from outside the employer's business and, second, services or facilities which it is part of the employer's business to sell to the public. The cost of an external benefit is easy to calculate: it is the

33 ITEPA 2003, s 203(2).
34 ITEPA 2003, s 203(3)(a).
35 ITEPA 2003, s 203(3)(b) and 206.
36 65 TC 421.

amount the employer has to pay to the third party supplier to, for example, buy medical insurance.

The cost of an in-house benefit is more difficult to quantify because the employer already incurs costs on providing the goods or service to the public and the cost of providing the same service to an employee is only a marginal additional expense. In the case of a school, the fixed costs to the employer of the classroom and teacher are the same whether the class comprises 19 pupils paying full fees, or those 19 plus one child of an employee paying reduced fees. The only additional costs are those relating specifically to the extra child, for instance, his books and writing materials.

8.9 SPECIFIC BENEFITS IN KIND

The remainder of this Chapter addresses the taxation of specific benefits in kind including, but not confined to, those the subject of specific statutory provisions.

8.10 Accommodation[37]

Where an employee is provided with accommodation by reason of his employment, he cannot normally convert into money the benefit of that accommodation. It follows that the general regime in section 62 of ITEPA 2003 cannot apply to that benefit and special rules are needed to bring it into charge.

So far, so good. However, the special rules adopted by the draftsman (in Chapter 5 of Part III of ITEPA 2003) to address this difficulty are amongst the most arcane remaining in the entire fiscal code. What follows is an attempt at a useful summary.

Where living accommodation is provided for an employee or a member of his family or household at low or no rent, that employee will be assessed to tax on the 'cash equivalent of the benefit of the accommodation'.[38] The charge applies irrespective of whether the employee is low paid.[39] Calculation of the cash equivalent depends on whether the cost of providing the accommodation exceeds £75,000.[40]

The formula for calculating the cost of providing accommodation is given by section 104 as A+I–P where A is the expenditure involved in acquiring the

37 It should be noted that this section deals only with the taxation of living accommodation. Other accommodation, such as board and lodging, is taxed under the benefits code.
38 ITEPA 2003, s 102(1).
39 ITEPA 2003, ss 63(2) and 216(1) and (4).
40 ITEPA 2003, s 103.

estate or interest; I is any expenditure on improvements to the property before the tax year in question; and P is any reimbursements by the employee of A or I.

Where the cost of providing the accommodation is less than £75,000, the 'cash equivalent' – at least if one simply follows the language of ITEPA 2003 – is a function of the rental value of the accommodation for the tax year less any sum made good by the employee to the person at whose cost the accommodation is provided.[41] There are rules for calculating the rental value of the accommodation[42] which is basically a market value rent assuming the tenant pays all taxes, rates and charges usually paid by a tenant and the landlord bears the costs of repairs and insurance and such other expenses as are necessary for maintaining the property in a state to command that rent.

However, by long-standing practice, the amount of the annual value is treated as being the 1973 gross-rating value.[43] This leads to a very low cash equivalent in respect of properties the cost of provision of which is less than £75,000.

However, where the cost of providing the accommodation is greater than £75,000, the 'cash equivalent' is calculated by reference to the complex formula set out in section 106. Basically, that formula produces a cash equivalent of the aggregate of: (a) the 1973 gross rating figure; and (b) a sum representing a yield[44] on the surplus of the cost of providing the accommodation over £75,000 less the amount of any rent paid by the employee.

Where the cost of providing the property exceeds £75,000 and the property has been held by the person providing the accommodation for a period of more than six years, section 107 operates to revalue the cost of providing the property to the open market value.

There is also a provision to apportion the cash equivalent between more than one employee if it is provided for more than one.[45]

8.11 Exceptions

The living accommodation charge is displaced where:

(a) it is necessary for the proper performance of the employee's duties that he should reside in the accommodation;[46]

41 ITEPA 2003, s 105(2).
42 ITEPA 2003, s 105(3), 110.
43 Employment Income Manual, paragraphs 11432–11434.
44 Of the official rate of interest in force for the purpose of calculating the beneficial loans charge.
45 ITEPA 2003, s 108.
46 ITEPA 2003, s 99(1).

(b) the accommodation is provided for the better performance of the duties of employment and the employee holds a kind of employment for which it is customary for accommodation to be provided;[47]

(c) there is a special threat to the employee's security, special security arrangements are in force, and he resides in the accommodation as part of those arrangements;[48] or

(d) there is an exception for social housing provided by a local authority to someone who is employed by it.[49]

These exemptions are applied narrowly.

If (a) is to apply the employee must show that the necessity to reside in the accommodation arises from the need properly to perform his duties rather than his personal need, such as an inability to afford accommodation near the area where he is required to work.[50]

There are two limbs which must be satisfied before (b) can apply. First, the accommodation must be provided for the better performance of the duties. This is, effectively, a rather less strict version of the test in (a). Second, the employment must be of a kind for which the employer customarily provides accommodation. There are three factors to this: how common is the practice statistically, how long has the practice gone on, and has it achieved acceptance generally. In *Vertigan v Brady*[51] two out of every three workers were provided with accommodation, however, in all the circumstances of the case Knox J felt unable to disrupt the Special Commissioners' finding of fact that the 'customary' limb was not satisfied. This might include accommodation provided for a nanny, housekeeper, hotel staff, etc.

Exemption (c) is self-explanatory and will apply only in exceptional circumstances. Exemption (d) is plainly intended to cover the coincidental supply of council housing to one of its employees.

If the employee in question is a director[52] of the company providing the accommodation[53] then, in respect of exemptions (a) and (b) above, the following additional conditions must be satisfied. First, the director must have

47 ITEPA 2003, s 99(2)(a).
48 ITEPA 2003, s 100.
49 ITEPA 2003, s 98.
50 *Vertigan v Brady* [1988] STC 91, 99.
51 [1988] STC 91, 99.
52 The definitions of director and full-time working director operative for present purposes are given by ITEPA 2003, ss 67(1), (2) and (3) and 223(8). See ITEPA 2003, s 721(5).
53 Or an associated company. A company is associated with another for the purposes of this provision if one has control of the other or both are under the control of the same person: see ITEPA 2003, s 99(5).

no material interest[54] in the company.[55] Second, he must either be employed as a full-time working director of the company or the company must be non-profit making or charitable.[56]

8.12 The 'higher paid employee' charge

A higher paid employee will also be assessable under the second 'higher paid employee' regime in section 201 on the value of the following services if they are provided for him by reason of his employment:

(a) heating, lighting or cleaning;

(b) repairs, maintenance or decoration; and

(c) furniture or other effects normal for domestic occupation.

Where the employee satisfies one of conditions (a), (b) or (c) for exemption[57] from the charge, the amount assessable in respect of these additional services is limited to 10% of net emoluments,[58] less any contribution by the employee.[59] If the accommodation is provided for part of a year of assessment, the amount assessed is proportionately reduced.

A similar exemption from the charge applies where the employer pays council tax, rates or water or sewerage charges in respect of accommodation satisfying one of conditions (a), (b) or (c) for exemption.[60]

8.13 Structural repairs

Finally, it should be noted that there is no deemed emolument where the employer makes structural alterations or additions to living accommodation occupied by reason of employment[61] or makes repairs to the premises of a kind which would be the obligation of the landlord under the covenants implied by section 11(1) of the Landlord and Tenant Act 1985.[62]

8.14 Car benefits

The provisions taxing company car usage are drafted in detail so arduous that they could – and indeed they do – form the subject of an entire book. After the

54 A material interest is defined by ITEPA 2003, ss 68 and 223(8).
55 ITEPA 2003, s 99(3).
56 ITEPA 2003, s 99(3).
57 Set out in ITEPA 2003, s 99(1), (2) and 100.
58 Net emoluments for present purposes are defined in ITEPA 2003, s 315(3).
59 ITEPA 2003, s 315(1) and (2).
60 See ITEPA 2003, s 314.
61 Section 313(2).
62 Section 313(3).

rationalisation of the old rules effected by ITEPA 2003, they remain lengthy, detailed and prescriptive but are no longer particularly complex.[63] What follows is a brief outline. However, it should be noted that significant changes to the taxable sum can arise from relatively insignificant alterations to the type of car that is made available and the arrangements pursuant to which it is made available. This is, therefore, likely to be an area where the cost of specialist advice may be money well spent.

There are essentially two questions to consider. First, are the conditions necessary for the application of the charge present and if so, second, what is the cash equivalent of the benefit.

It should be noted that there are separate regimes for cars and vans (being terms which are defined by section 115) and also separate regimes for the provision of fuel for cars and vans. There are, in other words, four regimes in all. However the conditions necessary for the application of the charge are common to all four. The regime in Chapter 6 of Part 3 applies where a car or van: (1) is made available (without any transfer of property in it) to an employee or a member of the employee's family or household;[64] (2) is so made available by reason of the employment; and (3) is available for the employee or member's private use.[65]

Where these conditions are satisfied, the Chapter treats as earnings the cash equivalent of the benefit of the car or van and any fuel provided for the car or van as earnings.[66]

As to these conditions:

(1) The question whether a car or van is *made available* to an employee is addressed in section 116 of ITEPA 2003. That section does little more than restate the language of section 114. However, a car is likely to be 'made available' if the employee (or a member of his family or household)[67] is able to use it (irrespective of whether he actually does).

(2) The question whether it is made available *by reason of employment* is addressed in section 117. Where the car is made available by an employer to an employee or a member of his family or household it is to be regarded as available by reason of the employment unless, in the familiar formulation, the employer is an individual and the vehicle is made available in the normal course of the employer's domestic, family or personal relationships.

63 In *Apollo Fuels Ltd v HMRC* [2013] UKFTT 350 (TC), the Tribunal found that the employees had proprietary rights over the vehicles, which meant that the car benefit charge did not apply. In addition, since market value rentals were charged there could be no 'benefit'.

64 The definition of those who are in an employee's family or household can be found in ITEPA 2003, s 721.

65 ITEPA 2003, s 114(1).

66 ITEPA 2003, s 114.

67 And for the definition of these terms see **8.4** above.

(3) The question whether the car is available for private use is the subject of section 118. Private use is defined as any use other than for the 'employee's business travel', a term which is the subject of extensive statutory provisions[68] limiting the use to that which is (very broadly) necessary for work and which does not form part of the pattern of ordinary commuting or travel. A car or van is available for private use unless the terms on which it is made available prohibit such use and it is not so used.[69]

The quantification of the cash equivalent of the benefit can be found at sections 120 to 148 (in respect of the benefit of the car), sections 149 to 153 (in respect of the benefit of any fuel provided for the car), sections 154 to 159 (in respect of the benefit of the van) and sections 160 to 164 (in respect of the benefit of any fuel provided for the van).

8.15 The benefit of the car

The cash equivalent of the benefit of the car is calculated as a percentage (the 'appropriate percentage') of the price of the car. The appropriate percentage is based on the carbon dioxide emissions of the car and is calculated according to a method statement at section 121(1) of ITEPA 2003 but will typically be between 10% and 35%. An adjustment is made where either the employee contributes a capital sum to expenditure on the provision of the car[70] or he makes a payment for private use.[71] A reduction is also made where a car is shared.[72]

8.16 Car fuel

The cash equivalent of the benefit of fuel is the appropriate percentage of £21,100. The appropriate percentage is calculated in the same way as that for the benefit of the car.[73]

There are reductions to this figure if the employee makes good the cost of providing the fuel for his private use,[74] where the car for which the fuel is provided is unavailable for a period of time,[75] or where the car is shared.[76]

68 ITEPA 2003, ss 118, 171(1), 337 to 342, 353 and Chapter 5 of Part 5 (other than section 377).
69 ITEPA 2003, s 118(1).
70 ITEPA 2003, s 132.
71 ITEPA 2003, s 144.
72 ITEPA 2003, s 148.
73 ITEPA 2003, s 150(2).
74 ITEPA 2003, s 151.
75 ITEPA 2003, s 152.
76 ITEPA 2003, ss 148 and 153.

8.17 The benefit of the van

The cash equivalent of the benefit of the van is £3,000 unless either the 'commuter use requirement' or the 'business travel requirement' is satisfied.[77] The commuter use requirement requires that the terms on which the van is made available prohibit its private use otherwise than for ordinary commuting and there is no use other than that use. The business travel requirement is satisfied if the van is available to the employee mainly for use for the purposes of the employee's business travel.[78]

This sum is reduced in respect of periods where the van is unavailable,[79] where the van is shared,[80] or where payments are made for private use.[81]

8.18 Van fuel

The cash equivalent of the benefit of van fuel is, at least in respect of a year after 2006–07, £564.[82] This figure is reduced to nil if either the employee is required to and does make good the cost of providing the fuel for his private use or the fuel is only made available for business travel.[83] There is also a proportionate reduction to this charge where the van is unavailable for a period of time.[84]

8.19 Car and van pools

Where a car is included in a car pool for the use of employees of one or more employers, no tax charge arises in respect of use of the car.[85]

A car is treated as being included in a car pool if:

(a) the car was made available to, and actually used by, more than one employee;

(b) the car was made available by reason of the employee's employment;

(c) the car was not ordinarily used by one of those employees to the exclusion of the others;

77 ITEPA 2003, s 155.
78 A term which is defined identically to that obtaining in respect of cars (see above).
79 ITEPA 2003, s 156.
80 ITEPA 2003, s 157.
81 ITEPA 2003, s 158.
82 ITEPA 2003, s 161.
83 ITEPA 2003, s 162.
84 ITEPA 2003, s 163.
85 ITEPA 2003, s 167(2).

(d) any private use of the car was merely incidental to the employee's other use; and

(e) the car was not normally kept overnight on or in the vicinity of any residential premises where any of the employees were residing.[86]

A discussion of the important 'merely incidental' condition forms the subject of a Statement of Practice SP 2/96 which contains a number of examples of use which HMRC consider will and will not be considered 'merely incidental'.

Section 168 of ITEPA 2003 contains equivalent provision for van pools.

8.20 Parking spaces for employees

The cost of providing parking spaces for employees – or the reimbursement of parking expenses incurred by employees – at or near the place of work is deemed not to constitute earnings from the office or employment.[87]

8.21 Childcare

Save to the extent that one of the statutory exceptions outlined below applies, the cost to an employer of providing childcare to higher paid employees will give rise to earnings from employment under the residual regime in section 203 of ITEPA 2003. The amount of the earnings will be a proportion of the aggregate cost incurred by the employer in providing all of that care. By contrast, where childcare facilities are provided to a lower paid employee, there will be no charge to tax as the benefit is not transferable.

There are also several schemes exempting higher paid employees from the charge.

No liability to income tax arises in respect of the provision for an employee of childcare by an employer where certain conditions are satisfied.[88] Those conditions are:

(1) as to the nature of the relationship between the child and employee;[89]

(2) that the premises on which the childcare is provided are not used wholly or mainly as a residential dwelling and the applicable registration requirements (which in England and Wales are in Part 10A of the Children Act 1989) are met;[90]

86 ITEPA 2003, s 167(3).
87 ITEPA 2003, s 237(2).
88 ITEPA 2003, s 318.
89 ITEPA 2003, s 318(3).
90 ITEPA 2003, s 318(4), (5).

(3) that the premises on which the care is provided are made available by the employer alone or the partnership requirements are met.[91] The partnership requirements are intended to enable the employer to provide the care in partnership with others. Established nursery providers not infrequently operate schemes which seek to bring employers within the partnership requirements so as to enable those employers to offer tax free childcare to their employees;[92] and

(4) that the scheme is open to the scheme employer's employees generally or to those generally at a particular location.

There is also a separate statutory scheme in section 318A enabling employers to pay up to £55 per week, free of tax, to an employee in respect of qualifying childcare (essentially registered childcare).

HMRC's website has an entire section dedicated to childcare: http://www.hmrc.gov.uk/childcare/.

8.22 Computer equipment

Where computer equipment is transferred to a lower paid employee, the amount of earnings will be the resale value of the computer equipment at the date of transfer. If, on the other hand, it is lent to a lower paid employee on condition that he is to maintain control of it, there will be no charge to tax.

Where computer equipment is 'placed at the disposal' of an employee or a member of his family or household for the employee or member's use, or is used wholly or partly for the purposes of the employee, a charge to tax can arise under section 205 of ITEPA 2003. This charge to tax arises only where, effectively, there is non-work related use by the employee or member of his family or household, however, it is thought that immaterial personal use would be ignored.

Where computer equipment is transferred to a higher paid employee, the charge to tax will be calculated on the basis set out in section 203 (either the cost to the employer or, if second hand, the market value at the time of transfer).

8.23 Cycles and cycle safety equipment

No liability to income tax arises in respect of the provision to employees of cycles or cycle safety equipment where there is no transfer of property in the cycle or equipment in question, the employee uses the cycle or equipment

91 ITEPA 2003, s 318(6).
92 ITEPA 2003, s 318(7).

mainly for the purpose of qualifying journeys and cycles are available generally to employees of the employer concerned.[93]

8.24 Discounts for staff

The position in respect of employees given a discount on goods or services purchased or received from their employer depends upon the employee's status.

In respect of lower paid employees, the discount cannot be converted into money *per se*, however, there will nevertheless be a chargeable emolument if what the employee pays is less than the second-hand value of the goods. The value of the emolument is the excess, if any, of the second hand value over the price paid by the employee.

As to higher paid employees, the emolument is the excess, if any, of the cost to the employer of the product over the price paid by the employee. If the amount the employee pays exceeds the expense incurred by the employer in providing the goods or services, the cash equivalent of the benefit will be nil. This is because the employee has made good more than the expense of provision of the benefit.

8.25 Education and training[94]

There is no charge to tax where an employer incurs expenditure in providing work-related training for an employee.[95] The exemption extends to 'related costs' of that training.[96] It applies irrespective of whether the training is paid for by the employee and defrayed by the employer or paid for directly by the employer.

The central concept is the definition of work-related training. In relation to an employee, it means:

> 'a training course or other activity designed to impart, instil, improve or reinforce any knowledge, skills or personal qualities which –
>
> (a) are likely to prove useful to the employee when performing the duties of the employment or a related employment, or
>
> (b) will qualify or better qualify the employee –
>
> (i) to perform those duties, or

93 ITEPA 2003, s 244.
94 See also, 'Retraining' below for education and training provided by the employer in the aftermath of an employee ceasing to be employed.
95 ITEPA 2003, s 250(1).
96 ITEPA 2003, s 250(1).

(ii) to participate in any charitable or voluntary activities that are available to be performed in association with the employment or a related employment.'[97]

And a related employment means:

> 'another employment with the same employer, or with a person connected with the employer, which the employee –
>
> (a) is to hold;
>
> (b) has a serious opportunity of holding; or
>
> (c) can realistically expect to have a serious opportunity of holding in due course.'[98]

This language is extremely broad and would extend to various activities – such as, for example, psychotherapy – which might not obviously fall within the description. This combination of broad language and value to the employee of receiving the monies free of tax makes it an extremely attractive benefit for employers to promote. However, it should be noted that section 253 of ITEPA 2003 contains provision for the exemption from income tax to be disapplied where the reason for the provision of the training satisfies one of the unallowable purposes described therein.

According to HMRC,[99] there is no restriction on the way the training can be delivered. Self-tuition packages, computer based training, distance learning, work experience or work placement and informal teach-ins are all acceptable as are more formal classroom based methods. It does not matter whether training is delivered internally or externally, or on a part-time or full-time basis.

A wide range of practical and/or theoretical skills will qualify for exemption so long as the skills are relevant to the employee. Where leadership and team skills are appropriate to the employee, participation in activities such as Outward Bound, Raleigh International, or Prince's Trust will qualify. Work-related first aid and health and safety courses will also qualify. Some employers operate Employee Development Schemes, often aimed at those employees with low skills levels. These seek to improve an employee's attitude towards training by commencing with enjoyable courses as an introduction to more concentrated job-related training. All elements of genuine schemes will qualify.

8.26 What expenditure falls within the exemption?

The costs which are covered are costs of the training or any benefit incidental to it, the costs which are incidental to the employee undertaking the training,

97 ITEPA 2003, s 251(1).
98 ITEPA 2003, s 251(2).
99 Employment Income Manual, 01220.

expenses incurred in connection with an examination or other assessment of what the employee has gained from the training, and the cost of obtaining any qualification, registration or award to which the employee becomes entitled as a result of the training.[100] Moreover, travel or subsistence expenses satisfying the conditions in section 252 of ITEPA 2003 qualify for the exemption from liability to income tax.

8.27 Expenses, payments and allowances

Sums paid to higher paid employees in respect of expenses are dealt with in sections 70–72 of ITEPA 2003. The structure adopted by the legislation is to treat as earnings from employment all sums paid to the employee in respect of expenses. However, if the expenses are ones in respect of which a deduction is available, the employee can claim that deduction and return to a position where he has no tax liability on those sums.

The effect is to throw the burden of establishing the conditions for deductibility onto the employee.[101] So if an employee gives the office junior (earning over £8,500 per annum) a pound to go and buy some milk, that pound will be treated as an emolument of his employment. The slightly cumbersome nature of the structure means that generally it will be preferable for the employer directly to meet the expenses.

It should be noted that section 65 contains a procedure whereby an officer of the Revenue may give to an employer a dispensation in respect of particular classes of payments. The effect is that neither the employee nor the employer need include them in their respective end of year returns.

Where an employee is provided with a company credit card for making such purchases it will also be necessary to consider the provisions applying to 'Vouchers' below.[102]

8.28 Health care and health insurance

The provision of private health care benefits – directly or indirectly – is not covered by the terms of any relief.[103] Accordingly, where the same forms part of an employee's benefits package, it is taxed in the same fashion as any other benefit in kind.

So, if an employee has medical treatment, the hospital bills the employee and the employer pays the bill, the employer has discharged the employee's debt so

100 ITEPA 2003, s 250(1)(b).
101 See *McLeish v IRC* (1958) 38 TC 1.
102 ITEPA 2003, section 92 discussed under 'Vouchers' below.
103 The relief in sections 54–57 of the Finance Act 1989 was abolished by the Finance (No 2) Act 1997.

the amount is taxable as earnings under section 62 of ITEPA 2003 irrespective of whether the employee is higher paid. The same treatment applies, and to all employees, if the employer gives the employee money to pay the hospital bill.

Where the employer arranges with the hospital to meet the bill directly so that the bill is in the name of the employer, no tax charge arises on lower paid employees who have no received cash or money's worth. However, all other employees and directors are chargeable under section 203 on the amount paid by the employer. This is the tax treatment whether the employer pays the bill from its own funds or out of the proceeds of an insurance policy under which it is the insured person.

If the employer pays the premiums on a group insurance policy under which the employees and/or their families are the insured persons such that their medical bills are met directly by the insurer, there is no tax charge on lower paid employees. However, again, all other 'higher paid' employees are chargeable under section 203 on the premiums paid by the employer under the policy.

There are, however, various modest exemptions which might be dealt with under this heading. By section 320B, where an employer offers all employees one health screening/medical check-up a year and meets the cost itself, the cost of provision is exempt from charge as earnings.

Moreover, where regulations made under the Health and Safety at Work Act 1974 require an eye and eyesight test and what the legislation describes as 'special corrective appliances' are shown to be necessary, the cost of providing that test and those appliances does not give rise to earnings.[104] HMRC interpret this provision as extending to those who are required to use VDUs in the course of their normal work and extending to the cost only of the test and a special prescription for VDU use.[105]

Finally, where an employee is outside the United Kingdom for the purposes of performing the duties of his employment and he requires medical treatment the cost of which, or the cost of insuring against which, is met by the employer, no charge to income tax will arise.[106]

8.29 Incidental overnight expenses

Incidental overnight expenses[107] incurred by an employee during a qualifying absence away from home will not constitute emoluments of his employment.[108]

104 ITEPA 2003, s 320A.
105 Employment Income Manual, 21765.
106 ITEPA 2003, s 325.
107 Overnight expenses are incidental if they are paid wholly or exclusively for the purpose of defraying or being used to defray any expenses which are incidental to that person's being away from his usual place of abode: ITEPA 2003, s 240 (1).
108 ITEPA 2003, s 240(1).

A qualifying absence is, broadly, any continuous period during which the employee is obliged to stay away from his usual place of abode and during which he has at least one overnight stay away.[109] However, the relief is limited in the case of overnight expenses incurred within the United Kingdom to £5 per night and, in the case of travel outside the United Kingdom, to £10 per night.[110] If the payment is above this sum, the entirety of it ceases to benefit from the exemption.[111]

8.30 Late night journeys home

Generally, the payment of taxi expenses by an employer to take an employee home will give rise to a taxable benefit in kind. However, by section 248 of ITEPA 2003,[112] where: (1) an employee is occasionally required to work later than usual and until at least 9 pm; and (2) by the time the employee can go home either no public transport would be available or it would not be reasonable of the employer to expect the employee to use it; or (3) there has been a breakdown of a car sharing arrangement, the employee will not be charged income tax on the cost of a taxi or 'similar private road transport'.

The requirement that the use be 'occasional' means that it must be neither frequent (defined as occurring on more than 60 occasions in a tax year) nor regular.

8.31 Loans

The beneficial loan provisions only apply to higher paid employees.[113] They tax the provision by an employee of any loan made at an interest rate below that obtaining on the market and 'making' a loan extends to situations where the employer guarantees, arranges or facilitates a loan.[114]

8.32 Low interest loans

The starting point is that there has to be an 'employment related loan'. This is a loan made to an employee or relative of an employee and the loan is of a described class.[115] The class includes loans made by the employer; loans

109 ITEPA 2003, s 240(4)–(7).
110 ITEPA 2003, s 241(3).
111 ITEPA 2003, ss 240(3) and 241(1).
112 ITEPA 2003, s 248(2).
113 ITEPA 2003, s 216(1), (4).
114 ITEPA 2003, s 173.
115 ITEPA 2003, s 174(1).

made by companies or partnerships controlled by the employer; loans made by companies or partnerships which control the employer; and loans made by a person having a material interest in certain companies controlling or being controlled by the employer.[116] As has been stated, references to making a loan include references to arranging, guaranteeing or in any way facilitating a loan.[117]

Where the employment-related loan is a taxable cheap loan, the cash equivalent of the loan is treated as earnings.[118] A taxable cheap loan is broadly a loan upon which the interest paid is less than the 'official rate'.[119] The 'cash equivalent' is the difference between the amount of interest that would have been payable on the loan for that year at the official rate and the amount of interest (if any) actually paid on the loan for the year.[120] 'Loan' includes any form of credit.[121]

There is a *de minimis* exception for advances for the purpose of paying for necessary expenses or incidental overnight expenses where certain conditions are met[122] where the amount of the advance does not exceed £1,000.

Moreover, the cash equivalent of the benefit of an employment-related loan is not to be treated as earnings if the amount outstanding on the loan does not exceed £5,000.[123] However, where the employee enjoys a number of low interest loans connected with his employment, those loans must be aggregated before looking to see whether the *de minimis* exception has any application. There is also an exception for loans made in the ordinary course of business if comparable loans were available to members of the public.[124]

The rules for calculating the amount of the emolument are set out in section 175 of ITEPA 2003. Broadly, the calculation is the amount of interest which would have been payable on the loan if interest at the official rate been payable, less the amount of interest actually paid on the loan.[125]

116 ITEPA 2003, s 174(2).
117 ITEPA 2003, s 173(2)(b).
118 ITEPA 2003, s 175(1).
119 The official rate is that prescribed by ITEPA 2003, s 181. The most recent rate can be found on www.hmrc.gov.uk/rates/interest.htm .
120 ITEPA 2003, s 175(3) and (4).
121 ITEPA 2003, s 173(2)(a). As a matter of strict construction, the definition extends beyond 'any form of credit', however, it is difficult to see what else might be included within the description 'loan' which is not 'any form of credit'. An advance on a salary has been held to fall within this provision: *Williams v Todd* [1988] STC 676, 60 TC 727.
122 ITEPA 2003, s 179.
123 ITEPA 2003, s 180.
124 ITEPA 2003, s 176.
125 ITEPA 2003, s 175(3).

8.33 Forgiveable loans

If a higher paid employee has an employment-related loan and in any year an amount of that loan is released or written off, the employee will be treated as having received earnings in the amount released or written off.[126]

The usual derogation applies for loans made by individuals in the normal course of their domestic, family or personal relationships.[127] Moreover, a loan is not an employment-related loan if it is made to a relative of the employee and the employee derives no benefit from it.[128]

8.34 Meal allowances and staff canteens

The provision of meals or of board and lodging by the employer is common in certain occupations, eg, those working in hospitals, schools and domestic servants. Where the employee is lower paid, no charge to tax will arise as the benefit is not transferable.

So far as higher paid employees are concerned, no charge to tax arises where meals are provided by the employer in a canteen in which meals are provided for staff generally.[129] In all other cases, however, the provision of meals will give rise to a charge in the amount of the cost to the employer in providing that meal.

Vouchers will be taxed as non-cash vouchers.[130]

8.35 Mileage allowance payments

Approved mileage allowance payments ('MAPs') are exempt from income tax. MAPs are amounts paid to an employee for expenses relating to the use of cars, vans, motor cycles and cycles for business travel.[131] MAPs are approved if they do not exceed the approved amounts for such payments.[132]

The approved amount for a car or van is 45p for the first 10,000 miles and 25p after that. For motorcycles it is 24p and for cycles 20p.[133]

126 ITEPA 2003, s 188.
127 ITEPA 2003, s 174(5).
128 ITEPA 2003, s 174(5)(b).
129 ITEPA 2003, section 317(1).
130 See 'Vouchers' below.
131 Sections 229(1) and 235.
132 Section 229(3).
133 ITEPA 2003, s 230.

Where the MAPs are less than these approved amounts, an employee can claim mileage allowance relief in respect of the difference. That relief is allowable as a deduction.[134]

The code also makes provision for 'approved passenger payments' ('APPs') to be exempt from tax.[135] Approved passenger payments are payments made to an employee receiving MAPs who is also paid for carrying a passenger. The approved rate is 5p per mile.[136] Sadly, one cannot receive APPS for 'dubbing' someone on one's bicycle as, unlike MAPs, APPs can only be made for use of a car or van.[137]

8.36 Mobile telephones

Where a mobile telephone is made available – without any transfer of property in it – to an employee, there will be no liability to income tax on that provision.[138] This exemption from charge covers the mobile telephone itself, any line rental and the cost of private calls paid for by the employer in respect of one mobile telephone number.[139]

8.37 Outplacement counselling

When an employee is made redundant, his employer may pay for him to receive professional advice and assistance designed to help him cope with his new situation and find a new job. Such professional advice is known as outplacement counselling and may consist of anything from a single advisory interview to ongoing assistance for a period of several months. It has, in recent years, become an increasingly common feature of redundancy packages offered by employers.

Prima facie, a payment for outplacement counselling will comprise a termination payment and will be taxable to the extent that it, taken in combination with other payments made on the termination of employment, exceeds £30,000.[140] However, payments for outplacement counselling which meet certain conditions have been exempted from tax under sections 62 and 203 of ITEPA 2003. The exemption is found in section 310 and applies to the provision of services to a person in connection with the cessation of his employment or the payment or reimbursement of fees for such provision or travelling expenses incurred in connection with such provision.

134 Sections 231 and 232.
135 Sections 233 and 234.
136 ITEPA 2003, s 234.
137 ITEPA 2003, s 233(1)
138 ITEPA 2003, s 319.
139 ITEPA 2003, s 319(3).
140 See Chapter 10 (Termination and Variation Payments).

The conditions that must be met before the exemption applies are set out in section 310(2)–(5) and are as to the purpose of the services, their nature, the duration of employment prior to the termination and the extension of the opportunity to either all other employees or other employees of a particular class.

8.38 Parties

Where an employer funds the cost of an annual party or similar annual function which is available to employees generally, no liability to income tax arises in respect of its provision if the cost per head of the party or function does not exceed £150.[141]

8.39 Professional membership fees

Section 343 of ITEPA 2003 permits the deduction from employment income of certain types of fees paid by professionals to their authorising body. Subsection (2) lists a number of types of fee; however, the section also enables HMRC to approve the deduction of other fees upon the applicant body satisfying conditions set out in subsection (3).

8.40 Removal and relocation packages

Sections 271 to 289 in Chapter 7 of Part 4 of ITEPA 2003 outline an exemption from income tax in respect of earnings for certain expenses connected with moving to take up a new job. The provisions are relatively detailed and no attempt is made here to do more than summarise their effect.

Section 271 exempts from income tax the provision of certain 'removal benefits' and the payment or reimbursement of certain 'removal expenses'. There is an upper cap on deducibility of £8,000.[142]

Removal benefits must satisfy two main conditions.

First, they must be reasonably provided in connection with a change of the employee's residence which satisfies the condition that either: (i) the change of residence results from the employee becoming employed, his duties altering, or the place where he is to perform those duties altering; or (ii) the change of residence is made wholly or mainly to allow him to reside within a reasonable daily travelling distance of the place where he normally performs or is normally to perform the duties of his employment; or (iii) the employee's

141 ITEPA 2003, s 264.
142 ITEPA 2003, ss 271 and 287.

former residence is not within a reasonable daily travelling distance of that place.[143]

Second, they must be provided on or before the last day of the tax year after that in which the employee begins to perform the duties of the employment after the change in the first condition.[144]

The types of benefit which qualify are ancillary expenses in connection with acquiring a new residence;[145] expenditure incurred in an abortive attempt to acquire a new residence;[146] ancillary expenses in connection with disposing of the old residence;[147] expenditure of transporting belongings from the old to the new residence;[148] travel and subsistence benefits in connection with the move;[149] and the replacement of domestic goods used at the old residence but unsuitable for use in the new.[150]

Part 4, Chapter 7 of ITEPA 2003 specifies a detailed regime for taxing payments of removal and transfer expenses.[151] The schema is to provide that 'qualifying removal expenses' – whether payable to or on behalf of the employee – are not emoluments of his employment.[152] Similarly, 'qualifying removal benefits' provided for the employee or members of his family or household do not comprise emoluments.

Removal expenses, the payment or reimbursement of which is exempt from income tax, are those reasonably incurred by the employee in connection with a change of residence satisfying the first condition for removal expenses above.[153] And they must be incurred within the time limit, the subject of the second condition above.[154]

In addition to covering expenditure on the provision by the employee of the sorts of benefits which would be removal benefits if provided by the employer,[155] they also cover expenses in connection with bridging loans.[156]

143 ITEPA 2003, ss 272(1)(a) and 273.
144 ITEPA 2003, ss 272(1)(b), 274 and 275.
145 ITEPA 2003, s 277.
146 ITEPA 2003, s 278.
147 ITEPA 2003, s 279.
148 ITEPA 2003, s 280.
149 ITEPA 2003, s 281.
150 ITEPA 2003, s 285.
151 ITEPA 2003, s 271.
152 ITEPA 2003, s 271.
153 ITEPA 2003, ss 272(3)(a) and 273.
154 ITEPA 2003, ss 272(3)(b) and 274.
155 ITEPA 2003, ss 373(3)(c).
156 ITEPA 2003, ss 284.

Where the provision of a benefit falls outside the terms of the statutory exemption, the lower paid employee is likely to escape the charge to tax on it (because it is likely to be personal to the employee and inalienable and thus not of money or money's worth). The higher paid employee will be charged to tax on the cost to the employer of providing the benefit. Where the employer either reimburses the cost to the employee of him providing the benefit himself, or meets a bill in the employee's name, both higher and lower paid employees will have earnings in the amount of the cost or bill.

8.41 Retraining packages

The payment or reimbursement by an employer of retraining course expenses is exempt from income tax if the course condition and the employment condition are met. Where the expenses are travel expenses, there is also a further condition to be met.[157]

Retraining course expenses are fees for the attendance of the employee at a training course, travelling expenses in connection with it, examination fees at the end of it, and the cost of any books that are essential for a person attending it.[158]

The course condition is that the course provides training designed to impart or improve skills relevant to and intended to be used in the course of gainful employment of any description;[159] the course must be entirely devoted to the teaching or practical application or both of the skills or knowledge;[160] and it must last not more than two years.[161]

The employment condition is that the employee begins the course whilst employed or within one year of ceasing to be employed; the employee ceases to be employed by the employer within two years of finishing the course and is not re-employed within two years of that cessation; the employee is employed in the employment which is ceasing throughout the period of two years ending when he begins the course or (if earlier) when the employment ceases; and the opportunity to undertake the course is available to the employer's employees generally or to a particular class or classes of them.[162] The further limitation in respect of travel expenses is outlined in section 311(5) of ITEPA 2003.

157 ITEPA 2003, s 311(1).
158 ITEPA 2003, s 311(2).
159 ITEPA 2003, s 311(3)(a).
160 ITEPA 2003, s 311(3)(b).
161 ITEPA 2003, s 311(3)(c).
162 ITEPA 2003, s 311(4).

8.42 Scholarships

Section 776 of the Income Tax (Trading and Other Income) Act 2005 (ITTOIA 2005) exempts from income tax income from a scholarship[163] held by an individual in full-time education at a university. However, where the scholarship is provided by reason of employment, the exemption extends to the scholarship holder alone.[164] If the scholarship is provided by reason of another person's employment, that other person can be liable under the benefits code. In other words, if an employer provides a scholarship to a daughter of one of its employees, the employee can still be chargeable to tax in respect of it.

HMRC have promulgated a helpful Statement of Practice 4/86 setting out the conditions that must be satisfied in order for payments by an employer to an employee for periods of attendance on a full-time course to be exempted from income tax.

Those conditions are broadly as follows.

First, the employee must be enrolled for at least one academic year and must attend the course for at least twenty weeks of that academic year. If the course is longer, the employee must attend for an average of at least twenty weeks per year.

Second, the educational establishment must be a recognised university, technical college or similar educational establishment which is open to members of the public generally and which offers more than one course of instruction. In other words an employer's in-house training school will not qualify and nor will attendance at a trade organisation.

Third, the payments, including lodging, subsistence and travelling allowances must normally be below a variable figure which was £15,480 for the academic year. However, if they exceed this, HMRC may look at the arrangements in detail.

The exemption does not apply to payments of earnings derived from working for the employer during vacations or otherwise.

8.43 Season tickets

The provision of a season ticket for ordinary commuting constitutes a 'non-cash voucher' taxable under section 87(4) of ITEPA 2003. See 'Vouchers'

163 And scholarship includes a 'bursary, exhibition or other similar educational endowment': ITTOIA 2005, s 776(3) and ITEPA 2003, s 211(3).
164 ITEPA 2003, s 215.

below. However, the provision of an interest free loan to buy a season ticket may well come within the *de minimis* threshold and so escape charge to tax (see 'Loans' above).

8.44 Security arrangements

There is a special exemption for living accommodation provided to an employee who faces a special threat to his security.[165]

Moreover, there is an exemption for assets or services which improve personal security in circumstances where there is a 'special threat to an employee's personal physical security which arises wholly or mainly because of the employee's employment'.[166]

The high water mark of qualification for the exemption is the case of *Hanson v Mansworth*[167] where the Special Commissioners held that his prominence as a businessman was such as to entitle him to the benefit of the exemption. HMRC's view, not entirely without justification, is that this a case which should be regarded as being, as lawyers politely say when they mean probably wrongly decided, on its own facts.

8.45 Shares and share options

These are dealt with in Chapter 9 (Taxation of Shares and Share Options).

8.46 Sporting and leisure facilities

The provision by an employer of certain recreational and sporting facilities (or right to make use of such facilities) for an employee – or a member of his family or household – will escape charge to tax subject to certain conditions being satisfied.[168]

The conditions are that the facilities are made available generally to employees; that they are not available to members of the public generally; and that they are used wholly or mainly by persons whose right or opportunity to use is employment-related.[169]

The following benefits are expressly excluded from the scope of the exemption:

165 Section 100.
166 Section 377(1)(a).
167 [2004] STC (SCD) 288.
168 ITEPA 2003, s 261.
169 ITEPA 2003, s 261(3)–(6).

(a) an interest in, or the use of, a mechanically propelled vehicle (including a mechanically propelled boat, ship or other vessel, aircraft or hovercraft);

(b) an interest in, or the use of, holiday or overnight accommodation or other facilities which include or are provided together with the right or opportunity to use the accommodation;

(c) a facility provided on domestic premises (that is, premises used wholly or mainly as a private dwelling or land belonging to or enjoyed with such premises);

(d) a facility which is available to the general public; or

(e) a facility which is not used mainly by persons whose right to use it derives from their employment (ie by virtue of being an employee of a particular employer or a member of the family or household of such an employee).[170]

Where the sports or leisure facilities provided fall outside this exemption – perhaps because the employer makes provision for its employees to have the right to use a public gymnasium – a charge to tax will arise.

Where the employee joins a gym or other leisure club and is reimbursed for the cost thereof by the employer, this will amount to a defrayal of a liability of the employee by the employer and will be chargeable in full under the terms of section 62 of ITEPA 2003.

Where the subscription is taken out directly by the employer, a higher paid employee will be taxed on the cost thereof under the higher paid regime. Other employees will, assuming the subscription is not transferrable, escape any charge to tax on the benefit. Where the employer takes out a group subscription for his employees, the cost thereof will need to be apportioned between all the employees – both higher paid and others – concerned. Higher paid employees will then be treated as if they had received an emolument in the amount of the cost as apportioned.

8.47 Suggestion scheme rewards

By section 321 and 322 of ITEPA 2003, HMRC will not tax certain awards made to employees under the terms of a company-wide suggestion scheme. Where the award is an encouragement award, ie one made for a suggestion with intrinsic merit or showing special effort, the maximum exemption is £25. However, where the award is for a suggestion leading to an improvement in efficiency and effectiveness which the employer has decided to adopt and

170 ITEPA 2003, s 262.

reasonably expects to result in a financial benefit the maximum is £5,000 or a share of the financial benefit over a prescribed period of time if that is less.

8.48 Vouchers

Sections 81, 87 and 94 of ITEPA 2003 taxes, respectively, 'cash vouchers', 'non-cash vouchers', and 'credit tokens'. These provisions were enacted to counter the avoidance of tax by paying lower paid employees otherwise than in cash. Whenever an employee receives goods or services by reason of his employment which he does not pay for in full, the first step should always be to consider whether a voucher or credit-token was used to obtain them.

8.49 Cash vouchers

Section 81 of ITEPA 2003 was enacted in order to counter specific holiday pay stamp schemes and is unlikely to have wide application elsewhere.

A cash voucher is any voucher, stamp or similar document capable of being exchanged for a sum of money greater than, equal to or not substantially less than the expense incurred by the person at whose cost the voucher is provided.[171] An employee who receives a cash voucher is treated, unsurprisingly, as being in receipt of an emolument at the time of receipt of that voucher.[172] This displaces the charge to section 62 which would otherwise attach when the cash was obtained in consequence of exchange of the voucher.

There are several restrictions to the ambit of this provision. First, there is no charge to income tax where the sum, the receipt of which the voucher makes provision for, would not, if received directly have been chargeable to income tax.[173] This provision ensures that the receipt by an employee of a petty cash slip or expenses claim form does not give rise to a section 62 emolument. Second, the section is disapplied where the cash voucher is a savings certificate, the accumulated interest in which would be free from income tax.[174] So where an employee is given a national savings certificate, he will not face an immediate charge to income tax on the face value of that certificate which incorporates a large element of tax-free growth.

8.50 Non-cash vouchers

A non-cash voucher is any voucher, stamp or similar document or token which can be exchanged for money, goods or services but is not a cash voucher.[175] It is

171 ITEPA 2003, s 75(1).
172 ITEPA 2003, s 81.
173 ITEPA 2003, s 80.
174 ITEPA 2003, s 80.
175 ITEPA 2003, s 84(1).

expressly stated to include a childcare voucher, transport voucher and a cheque voucher. A childcare voucher is means 'a voucher, stamp or similar document or token intended to enable a person to obtain the provision of care for a child (whether or not in exchange for it)'.[176] A transport voucher is 'any ticket, pass or other document or token intended to enable a person to obtain passenger transport services (whether or not in exchange for it)…'.[177] A cheque voucher is defined as 'a cheque provided for an employee and intended for use by him wholly or mainly for payment for particular goods or services or for goods or services of one or more particular classes …'.[178] The most common type of non-cash voucher will, of course, be season tickets for public transport such as the Underground. However, such items as tickets at Twickenham or for the theatre will also clearly constitute non-cash vouchers.

Where an employee – whether highly paid or not – is provided with a non-cash voucher he shall be treated as having received an emolument equivalent to the expense incurred in providing that voucher and the money, goods or services for which it is capable of being exchanged.[179] The earnings shall be treated as received, in the case of a cheque voucher, in the tax year in which the voucher is 'cashed in',[180] and in the case of any other non-cash voucher, in the tax year in which the cost of provision is incurred or, if later, in which the voucher is received by the employee.[181] If, however, there is an appropriation of the voucher to the employee's use – whether by attaching it to a card held for him or in any other way – the emolument shall be treated as received at the time it was so appropriated.[182]

There are a number of exemptions from the deemed earnings. Any payment made for the voucher will go to reduce the amount of the deemed earnings.[183] If the non-cash voucher is used to pay for expenses which would otherwise be deductible, the employee can claim relief in the normal way. There is an exemption where a non-cash voucher is used to obtain entertainment of any kind, it is provided at the cost of someone other than the employer[184] and is not given in recognition of particular services performed or to be performed by him.[185] This is intended to cover the provision by clients of tickets to sports matches, etc. There are also exemptions in respect of non-cash vouchers for parking provisions, transport between home and work for disabled employees, transport home for late night working or on the failure of car-sharing

176 ITEPA 2003, s 84(2A).
177 ITEPA 2003, s 84(3).
178 ITEPA 2003, s 84(4).
179 ITEPA 2003, s 87(1).
180 ITEPA 2003, s 88.
181 ITEPA 2003, s 88.
182 ITEPA 2003, s 82(3).
183 ITEPA 2003, s 87(2).
184 Or a person connected with the employer.
185 ITEPA 2003, s 266(1).

arrangements, cycles and cycle safety equipment, mobile phones, and various other items.[186]

8.51 Credit tokens

A credit token is a card, token, document or other thing given to a person by another person who undertakes: (1) that on the production of it he will supply money, goods or services on credit; or (2) that where, on the production of it to a third party, that third party will supply money, goods or services, he will pay the third party for them.[187] It does not, however, include cash vouchers or non-cash vouchers.[188] The most obvious example of a credit token is a company credit card.

If a credit token is provided to an employee by reason of his employment then, on each occasion he uses the credit token, he shall be treated as having received an earnings from his employment.[189] The amount of those earnings shall be an amount equal to the expense incurred by the person at whose costs the money, goods or services were provided[190] in or in connection with that provision.[191]

There are a number of exemptions similar to those obtaining in respect of non-cash vouchers[192] where the credit token is used to obtain goods and services the cost of which would have been deductible,[193] the expense incurred by the person at whose cost the goods or services are provided is made good by the employee,[194] or the credit token is used to obtain hospitality from some third person.[195]

8.52 Dispensations

An employer can apply for a dispensation from the non-cash voucher and credit token provisions.[196] In order to do this, he must satisfy the Inspector that no tax would be payable in respect of those circumstances where non-cash vouchers or credit tokens are provided because, for example, they are only used for deductible business expenses or the employee will fully reimburse any non- deductible goods or services obtained.

186 ITEPA 2003, s 266.
187 ITEPA 2003, s 92(1).
188 ITEPA 2003, s 92(4).
189 ITEPA 2003, s 94(1).
190 ITEPA 2003, s 94(2).
191 ITEPA 2003, s 94(3).
192 See above.
193 ITEPA 2003, s 363.
194 ITEPA 2003, s 94(1)–(3).
195 ITEPA 2003, s 267.
196 ITEPA 2003, s 96.

Chapter 9

Taxation of Shares and Share Options

9.1 INTRODUCTION

Employee share plans are arrangements that enable employees to acquire shares, typically in their employing company or its parent. These arrangements are very common in both the UK and US and are becoming very widespread elsewhere. Participation in employee share plans has been an established part of the remuneration package offered to employees of UK-listed companies for quite some time and certainly since 1978, when the then Labour Government introduced the first tax beneficial plan.

Employee share incentive plans are not only used to recruit, retain and motivate employees but also to help align the interests of employees, particularly senior executives, with those of shareholders and other stakeholders in the company. Employee share incentive plans can also reduce employment costs. Since the first tax beneficial plan was introduced, successive governments have endorsed the view that encouraging equity incentives can help increase profitability and thus improve the general economy. Tax legislation has therefore been used to introduce particular employee share plan structures which enjoy valuable tax reliefs.

However, there has been an ever increasing tension between, on the one hand, introduction and Government support of tax beneficial share plans and, on the other hand, stricter measures designed to combat arrangements intended to exploit opportunities for tax and NIC avoidance. At the sharp end, this has increasingly focused on ensuring gains are taxed as capital (at, presently, 18% or 28% depending on the total taxable income of the individual) rather than income (at, presently, up to 45% plus Employers and Employees NICs). Although HMRC does recognise the concept of capital growth in the context of share plans, it has nevertheless become increasingly stringent in tackling arrangements which it considers ought to be taxed pursuant to general remuneration principles.

The principles behind the taxation of employee share plans can be traced back to the case of *Weight v Salmon*.[1] That case established that shares are taxed

1 (1935) 19 TC 174.

as a benefit in kind so that, when employees are given an opportunity to buy shares in their employer at less than their prevailing market value, the issue of those shares at a discount is an immediate profit, received as remuneration chargeable to income tax.

The general principles attaching to the taxation of equity based plans for employees were further endorsed in the early 1960s by the then Inland Revenue (now HMRC) as a direct consequence of the House of Lord's decision in the case of *Abbott v Philbin (Inspector of Taxes)*.[2] In that case, the House of Lords held that an employee was subject to income tax on the value of an option as assessed at the time of grant – any gain subsequently realised when the option was exercised was not to be regarded as earnings from the employment and was therefore free of income tax. Although the position was subsequently reversed through the introduction of legislation[3] the general *Abbott v Philbin* position still remains the default position under common law.

All shares and other securities acquired in connection with an employment now come within the scope of a specific regime to tax employment-related securities, including shares acquired by directors or employees on the formation of a company. The rules also extend to rights or opportunities to acquire securities (eg share options), and to benefits in connection with shares and securities that are not otherwise chargeable to tax. They cover cases where the securities, or opportunities, or rights to acquire the securities, are provided by a person other than the employer, and where the securities are not directly received by the employee.

In 2003, the legislation governing the tax treatment of share plans made available to employees was radically altered by the introduction of the Income Tax (Earnings & Pensions) Act 2003 (ITEPA 2003) which consolidated the majority of the relevant provisions in the Income and Corporation Taxes Act 1988 (ICTA 1988) and various supporting enactments, insofar as they applied to the implementation and operation of employee share plans. Almost immediately following its introduction, ITEPA 2003 was amended very significantly by Schedule 22 to the Finance Act 2003 (Schedule 22) so as to, amongst other things, broaden the scope of taxation and anti-avoidance legislation.

The scope of the UK's tax favourable employee share plans legislation currently extends to four discrete types of plan:

(i) the company share option plan (CSOP);

(ii) the savings-related share option or 'save as you earn' plan (SAYE);

2 [1961] AC 352.
3 Re-enacted as ITEPA 2003, ss 477–478 (originally ICTA 1988, s 135).

(iii) the Share Incentive Plan (SIP); and

(iv) Enterprise Management Incentives (EMI).

Apart from EMI, each type of tax-favoured plan must be approved in advance by HMRC. Hence, these arrangements are generally referred to as 'approved' plans. Any other share or option plan which does not offer tax- favoured treatment is typically referred to as 'unapproved'.

This Chapter will begin by examining how the relevant sections of ITEPA 2003 now operate to tax shares and options. Consideration is then given to the specific taxing provisions set out in Chapters 2 to 4 of Part 7 of ITEPA 2003, followed by an analysis of the tax consequences of granting unapproved share options or similar rights concerning a future acquisition of shares. It will then turn to identifying the principal conditions attaching to the tax-favoured plans, together with the tax advantages which follow.

For the sake of completeness, mention is also made of the use of Employee Benefit Trusts (EBT's), which are principally used as a vehicle for holding shares to be used to satisfy share-based incentive awards. However, it is important to emphasise that the following descriptions are set out mainly to illustrate UK taxation of employee share plans and not to provide a full analysis of the taxation of equity based arrangements. The complexity of this technical (and constantly changing) area of tax law must not be underestimated. Finally, it should also be noted that this analysis has been prepared on the basis that employees are, at all relevant times, resident for UK tax purposes.

It is always recommended that specialist advice is sought whenever employee share plans are being considered, implemented, or amended.

9.2 BY REASON OF EMPLOYMENT?

Prior to the Finance Act 2003, the test as to whether the legislation could charge gains to income tax as opposed to capital gains tax (CGT), was usually whether the shares or other securities were acquired 'by reason of employment'. This made it very easy for directors to claim that their shares were not acquired by reason of their employment but, rather, were 'founder shares' acquired in consequence of their investment in the relevant company. Accordingly, any future gain would fall outside any charge to income tax. In order to address this potential loophole, a deeming provision was introduced by Schedule 22. This provision states that, if an individual's employer (or someone connected with the individual employer) makes available a right or opportunity to acquire any securities, interests in securities or options, then the individual is deemed to have acquired the securities or interest or option by reason of his or her employment. So if a spouse, distant relative or friend acquires securities under a right or an opportunity because of another individual's employment, then it is the employee who is subject to taxation. The 'employment', in relation to employment-related securities or employment-related securities options, means the employment by reason of which the right or opportunity to acquire the employment-related securities or options is available (the 'employee' and the 'employer' being construed accordingly). References in the legislation to employees include directors and other office-holders, so that they are taxed in the same way.

The rules also apply to prospective employees or former employees.[4] So an option granted to a director before taking office will be potentially liable to tax on exercise. A share package awarded to an employee after retirement will also be within the legislation, although it is notable that securities will generally cease to be 'employment-related' seven years after the employee leaves employment, subject to certain limits.

9.3 SECURITIES AND INTERESTS

Before carrying out a more detailed review of the UK tax treatment of employee share plans, it is important to clarify a number of fundamental concepts.

As a direct consequence of the introduction of ITEPA 2003 and subsequent legislation including, but not limited to, Schedule 22, there are a number of provisions which are embodied within ITEPA 2003 and which have developed old, and introduced new, concepts concerning the acquisition, retention and disposal of securities and rights to acquire such, ie options. These provisions are now contained within discrete chapters of Part 7 of ITEPA 2003 (Part 7) which categorise different types of securities as follows:

(a) Chapter 2 restricted securities.

(b) Chapter 3 convertible securities.

(c) Chapter 3A securities with artificially depressed market value.

(d) Chapter 3B securities with artificially enhanced market value.

(e) Chapter 3C securities acquired for less than market value.

(f) Chapter 3D securities disposed of for more than market value.

(g) Chapter 4 post-acquisition benefits from securities.

All these categories fall under the general umbrella term 'employment-related securities'.

4 ITEPA 2003, s 421B(2)(b).

We will now briefly consider the principles behind the taxation under each chapter of Part 7 and look at the principal charging provisions.

9.4 RESTRICTED SECURITIES

9.5 Introduction

Companies often provide their senior executives with the opportunity to acquire shares as a means of aligning executives' interests with those of the existing shareholders and to encourage capital growth. In order to protect the Company, and its shareholders, in the event that the relationship does not develop as originally intended, it is not unusual for such shares or awards to be subject to various restrictions or conditions which may, for example, prohibit transfer of the shares, limit voting or dividend rights or result in the shares or awards being forfeited if the executive ceases to be an employee.

Chapter 2 of Part 7 of ITEPA 2003 contains the rules governing taxation of 'restricted securities' acquired by a person by reason of his employment or that of any other person.

For employment-related securities to be classified as 'restricted' under ITEPA 2003, there must be the possibility of a transfer, reversion or forfeiture of the securities, or the interest in them, whereby:

(a) the holder will cease to have any beneficial interest in them;[5] and

(b) that person will receive less than the market value that the securities would have had without the forfeiture provision.[6]

ITEPA provides a wide definition of the term 'restricted'. However, in practice, the first consideration is whether or not the restriction has any effect on the market value of securities. If the value is not reduced, then even if there is a restriction, the securities are not within Chapter 2.

A typical example of such a restriction is where an employee holder is required to sell his shares at the lesser of cost or the prevailing market value if he ceases employment in certain circumstances.

In essence, if there is a chance that less than market value will be received and the employee is not entitled to retain the shares, they will be treated as both restricted and forfeitable. It is important to identify whether or not any risk of forfeiture will fall away within five years or not. To the extent that any such risk may apply for five years or more, then, for tax purposes, no distinction is

5 ITEPA 2003, s 423(2)(b).
6 ITEPA 2003, s 423(2)(c).

made between restricted or forfeitable shares. Accordingly, the tax treatment of restricted shares that carry a risk of forfeiture will follow that described immediately below. However, if restricted securities are subject to a risk of forfeiture which will definitely apply within five years from acquisition, then the tax treatment is significantly different. This is considered further in **9.7** below.

9.6 General taxation principles for restricted securities

Where restricted securities are acquired for less than their actual market value (ie the market value taking account of the restrictions), an initial money's worth charge arises under the general earnings charge of ITEPA 2003.[7]

A further charge to income tax and, if applicable, NICs will occur on the occasion of a subsequent chargeable event. Such chargeable events are set out in Chapter 2 of Part 7[8] and, in summary, comprise:

(a) the lifting of all restrictions from the shares;

(b) the variation of any of the restrictions; and

(c) the disposal of the securities to an unconnected person.

It is important to note that the amount on which an individual is taxed as a consequence of acquiring restricted shares at an undervalue is not determined by reference to the full increase in value on the occasion of a subsequent chargeable event. Rather, the taxable amount is the increase in value on the proportion of the security that is not fully taxed on acquisition.

In order to explain this further, a worked example based on the calculation formula which is set out in ITEPA 2003[9] is set out below.

Example 1

Assume that a share has an unrestricted market value (ie a market value ignoring the effect of any restrictions) at the time of acquisition of £20. The restrictions reduce the market value of the share to £15, and the employee pays

£15 for the share. Consequently, the initial uncharged proportion will amount to:

$$\frac{£20 - £15}{£20} = 0.25, \text{ i e } 25\%$$

7 ITEPA 2003, s 62.
8 ITEPA 2003, s 427.
9 ITEPA 2003, s 428.

If the unrestricted market value of the shares is £40 when the shares are sold, the employee will then pay income tax on: £40 × 0.25 = £10, ie on 25% of the unrestricted market value.

9.7 Forfeitable securities

Contrary to the general taxation of restricted securities, a charge to income tax does not arise on the acquisition of a restricted security if it carries a risk of forfeiture which will definitely cease within five years of the date of acquisition.[10] This is the case whether or not other restrictions continue to apply after this five-year period.

Instead, the employee will be subject to income tax on the full unrestricted market value of the securities (less any amount already paid for them) at the time the shares are sold or the restrictions are lifted.

However, an employee may choose to pay income tax on either the actual market value on acquisition of the forfeitable security or on the full unrestricted market value on acquisition.

Although there is a specific election regime that applies to forfeitable securities,[11] it is typically the case that employees adopt the election procedure set out in section 431(1) of ITEPA 2003, which applies to all types of restricted security, rather than just those shares which carry a risk of forfeiture lasting less than five years. These elections are considered further in the following section.

9.8 Restricted securities – elections

Just as an employee and employer can jointly elect out of the deferral of a charge on the acquisition of a forfeitable security, elections can be made to accelerate the taxation of any restricted share. An election may be either on acquisition or on a later chargeable event.

There are a number of provisions under ITEPA 2003 which permit different elections to be made. However, the most common approach is to elect under section 431(1) of ITEPA 2003 so that income tax (and NICs if applicable) will be charged to the full market value of the security, ignoring the effect of all restrictions that apply at the time the securities are acquired. No further charge to income tax (or NICs) will arise when the restrictions are lifted, regardless of

10 ITEPA 2003, s 425(2).
11 ITEPA 2003, s 425(3).

any capital growth in the value of the security. Rather, any such future capital growth will fall under the capital gains tax regime.

Although the potential advantages for employees are clear given the current disparity in rates under the income tax and capital gains tax regimes, employees should note that there is no refund of income tax (or NICs) paid if the market value of the securities is lower at the time when a subsequent income tax charge would ordinarily arise, ie on lifting of restrictions or disposal shares. Similarly, there is no tax refund if the shares are subsequently forfeited.

The elections must be in a form approved by HMRC and must not be made more than 14 days after the date of acquisition or, in certain circumstances, the relevant chargeable event. Standard form elections are available on the HMRC website.

Once signed, the original and copies of the election(s) are ordinarily kept by the employer and employee respectively. These forms do not have to be submitted to HMRC unless so requested.

Optionholders who acquire restricted securities on the exercise of options under CSOP, SAYE and EMI, are deemed to have made a section 431 election on exercise.[12]

9.9 Convertible securities

Chapter 3 of ITEPA 2003 imposes a charge to income tax on any increase in value arising from the conversion of securities of one description to securities of a different description. Chargeable events also arise from the receipt of consideration in connection with the conversion rights. The charges set out in Chapter 3 of ITEPA 2003 apply irrespective of when the securities were acquired.

In practice, there might often be circumstances which potentially give rise to a charge under Chapter 3 as well as Chapter 2 of Part 7. In these cases, HMRC would typically not seek to charge under both but, rather, would expect the Chapter 2 charge on restricted securities to be preferred by the employee.

9.10 Share rights and enhancements

Chapters 3A to D and Chapter 4 of Part 7 contain various tax avoidance based provisions in recognition of the fact that share values (including shares in subsidiary companies) can be manipulated. These provisions seek to impose

12 ITEPA 2003, s 431A.

charges to income tax (rather than capital) where things may have been done other than for genuine commercial reasons.

For example, Chapter 3A of Part 7 is designed to counter tax avoidance through companies artificially reducing the value of their shares. Chapter 3A treats the artificial reductions as employment income and generally works by replacing the reduced market value in the calculation for each chargeable event with a figure of market value, ignoring the artificial reduction.

Similarly, Chapter 3B of Part 7 treats value realised by artificial increases to the value of securities as employment income. There was a forerunner to the Chapter 3B provisions in the dependent subsidiary legislation which was introduced in 1988.

Chapter 3C of Part 7 is, on the face of it, a very straightforward provision in that it seeks to impose a charge to income tax in circumstances where securities are acquired by reason of employment for less than their market value. Historically, this provision was first introduced in 1976 and sought to tackle avoidance using partly-paid shares. The Chapter 3C provisions however interact very closely with other similar taxing provisions and often apply in cases where certain circumstances are not fully caught by those other provisions. That being said, there are many circumstances where, even if securities have been acquired for less than their market value, no charge will arise under Chapter 3C, because Chapter 3C is a sweeping up provision over which other provisions take priority.

The charging mechanism under Chapter 3C mirrors that for beneficial loans. The undervalue or unpaid element is treated as a notional loan on which there is an annual charge under the beneficial loans legislation[13] and a final charge on the sale of the shares or release of liability.

Chapter 3D of Part 7 applies where employment related securities are disposed of by an associated person for more than their market value. In this case, the difference between the disposal proceeds and market value is charged to income tax. The additional sale proceeds may come from:

(a) the employer buying back the securities at an agreed value;

(b) the employer making up the difference where securities are sold to a third party;

(c) arrangements that enable employees to sell their shares at an inflated price over that achieved by other shareholders; or

(d) exchanges of existing securities for more valuable securities.

13 ITEPA 2003, Chapter 7, Part 3.

This provision has proved to be particularly relevant in recent years and has given rise to various arguments concerning determination of market value and whether or not rights that are not inherently included in a class of shares (through, say, the articles of association) can be taken into account for HMRC's fiscal valuation purposes. The short answer appears to be that HMRC will seek to impose an income tax charge under Chapter 3D in cases where an employee receives a return on a disposal of his shares which has been determined, at least in part, by reference to a separate side agreement which is not binding on all other holders of the same class of shares.

The final element of the tax-avoidance provisions principally affecting restricted securities is Chapter 4 of Part 7 (Chapter 4), which seeks to tax 'post-acquisition' benefits.

Unfortunately, the term 'benefits' is not expressly defined and the scope is potentially wide, although it should be noted that a benefit can only come within the Chapter 4 charge if not otherwise chargeable to income tax.[14] According to the Revenue guidance on this, a common benefit would be the provision of bonus shares in certain circumstances. In which case, the amount of the benefit would be the market value of the bonus shares, less any reduction in value of the original holding caused by the issue of bonus shares. Another example given is where an employer improves the rights of shares owned by employees by altering the articles of association. However, it is generally now accepted that, as the Chapter 4 charge is essentially a sweeping-up charge, its application in practice is like to be increasingly limited.

9.11 UNAPPROVED OPTION PLANS

A share option is a right to acquire shares (by subscription or purchase) at some time in the future at a predetermined price, normally fixed at the time of grant. Unless and until the option is exercised, the optionholder bears no economic risk (other than any premium, paid for the grant of the option – a premium is very rare in an employment context).

The provisions governing the income tax treatment of unapproved share options are set out in Chapter 5 of Part 7 of ITEPA 2003. Chapter 5 also covers other rights which entitle employees to receive shares or other securities at some time in the future and which will become exercisable (ie 'vest') automatically without any action to be taken by the employee. For the remainder of this chapter, any references to unapproved options will equally apply to other such rights concerning possible future acquisition of shares.

14 ITEPA 2003, s 447.

Typically, there will be no charge to income tax on the grant of the option;[15] but income tax will be payable on any gain realised by the exercise, assignment, or release of the option.[16]

Where the right has been exercised, the 'gain' is the difference between the market value of the shares at the date of exercise and the amount paid for the shares. Where the right has been assigned or released, the 'gain' is the difference between the amount paid for the assignment or release and the amount paid for the grant of the right.[17]

Example 2

In 2009, an employee is granted an option to purchase 1,000 shares at £1.50 each. He pays £300 for the option. In January 2013, he exercises the option. At the time of exercise, the market value of the shares is £4.50 each. His liability to income tax is calculated as follows:

£	£
Market value on exercise (1000 × £4.50)	4,500
Less: price paid on grant	(300)
Option exercise price	(1,500)
Amount subject to income tax and, possibly, NICs	2,700

9.12 PHANTOM OPTIONS

Many of the same benefits to be gained from granting share options to employees can be achieved through granting phantom – essentially notional – rights. These are contractual arrangements which do not give participants any right to acquire shares but which provide benefits to an employee which mimic, to the extent provided in those arrangements, those the employee would enjoy if he were in possession of such a right to acquire actual shares. In addition to granting phantom options, a company may also make an award of notional shares. Therefore, in the case of notional shares, where the company declares a dividend the employer makes a payment of an equivalent amount to the employee. Where the employee wishes to 'sell' his phantom shares, the employer will make a payment to the employee of an amount equal to the difference between the value of those shares at the time of sale and the notional price at which they were notionally granted.

15 ITEPA 2003, s 475.
16 ITEPA 2003, s 478(1).
17 ITEPA 2003, s 479(5).

Clearly there may be considerable administrative and cost benefits to using phantom arrangements. Moreover, from an employee's perspective, there may be advantages in an employer being able to operate the PAYE system,[18] deducting income tax at the time payments are made (although there will also be commensurate NIC liabilities).

No particular difficulty arises in respect of such plans. A contractual right to receive income on the satisfaction of certain contingencies is not, itself, taxable. The employee will, therefore, be taxed under the general taxable remuneration provisions as and when he receives a cash payment in accordance with the terms of the phantom option plan.

9.13 TAX FAVOURED SHARE OPTION PLANS

There are currently three types of tax favoured share option plan – SAYE, CSOP and EMI. To date, all three have been well received in the UK and each, in their own way, has often formed a solid foundation to any company's employee incentive policies and practice.

9.14 Savings related share option plan

Under an SAYE plan the employee enters into a certified contractual savings scheme with a bank, building society or other approved financial institution.[19] This contract commits him to save a regular monthly amount of up to £250 per month for a fixed three- or five-year term. At the end of the contract, he is credited with a tax free bonus.[20] If the contract is a five year contract and the employee leaves the sum to accumulate for a further two years (if so permitted by the employer), he will be entitled to an enhanced bonus.

At the same time as he starts his savings contract, the employee is granted an option to subscribe for or acquire shares in the employer company which he can exercise at the expiry of the contract.

The main governing provisions concerning the implementation and operation of an SAYE plan are set out in Schedule 3 to ITEPA 2003 (Schedule 3). In summary, the cost of the shares must be satisfied out of the proceeds of the savings contract, which may include the bonus. The exercise price of the option must be fixed at the date of grant and cannot be for less than 80% of the

18 See ITEPA 2003, Chapter 5 of Part 7.
19 ITEPA 2003, Part 5, Schedule 3.
20 In a three year contract, the bonus is three monthly payments and in a five year contract, nine payments. The bonus is free of income tax by virtue of ITTOIA 2005, s 702 and is disregarded for capital gains tax purposes by virtue of TCGA 1992, s 271(4).

market value of the shares at the time the option is granted. A SAYE plan must be open to all employees and full time directors.

The rules governing taxation of SAYE plans are set out in Chapter 7 of Part 7. In outline:

(a) no income tax will arise on the grant of an SAYE option;

(b) no tax is charged on the bonus of any interest received under the related savings contract. This touches on a significant advantage of SAYE plans – even if the option is not ultimately exercised, the employee is still entitled to receive a tax free return on the savings which he has accumulated;

(c) if the option is exercised in accordance with the plan rules (which, in turn, must follow the requirements set out in Schedule 3) then no income tax will generally arise on the exercise;[21] but

(d) the favourable tax treatment will not apply if the option is exercised within three years from the date of grant in the event of a takeover, corporate restructuring or winding up of the company, or the optionholder leaving the group because his employing company is sold outside that group. In these cases, a charge to income tax will arise[22] on broadly the amount of the option gain (ie the difference between the market value on the date of exercise and the option exercise price); and

(e) if the option is exercised within three years in circumstances where the optionholder has left the employment by reason of injury, disability, retirement or redundancy, then no income tax liability will arise provided such exercise is effected within six months from cessation.

Shares acquired upon the exercise of an SAYE option in circumstances that qualify for income tax relief will have a base cost for capital gains tax purposes that is equal to the exercise price paid.[23]

9.15 Company share option plan

A CSOP, otherwise known as an executive share option plan, enables participation to be offered to selected groups of employees or indeed individual employees.

The governing provisions concerning the implementation and operation of an approved CSOP are set out in Schedule 4 to ITEPA 2003 (Schedule 4). An

21 ITEPA 2003, s 519.
22 ITEPA 2003, s 476.
23 TCGA 1992, ss 38(1)(a), 144 and 144ZA.

option granted under a plan that has been approved by HMRC under Schedule 4 is known as an approved option.

In order for a selected plan to benefit from the favourable tax treatment, a number of conditions must be satisfied which concern not only the terms of the options to be granted, but also the type of shares, corporate structure and criteria for participation. One of the most important of these conditions is that the value of the shares underlying an option at the date of grant must not exceed £30,000.[24] Other preconditions include a requirement that the exercise price of the option must be stated at the time the option is granted and not be manifestly less than the market value of shares of the same class at that time.[25] The CSOP cannot provide for options to be granted otherwise than to employees or full time directors. The company whose shares are to be put under option must be either an independent company (ie not under the control of another company) or under the control of a listed company which is not a close company for tax purposes.

Where the preconditions for approval are satisfied, tax will not be charged on grant of the option. Moreover, if the option is held for more than three but less than ten years before being exercised, income tax shall not be charged under any provision of ITEPA 2003 in respect of the exercise. Instead capital gains tax may arise on a disposal of the resulting shares, and is charged (subject to the availability of allowances) on the difference between the full cost of the option shares and the disposal proceeds.

The exercise of an approved share option will qualify for relief from the charge to income tax which generally arises upon the exercise of unapproved options (as set out in Chapter 5 of Part 7) if the exercise is:

(a) in accordance with the rules of the plan at a time when it remains approved;

(b) no later than the tenth anniversary of the date of grant;

(c) except when exercised after the optionholder has died or where the rules of the plan otherwise provide, not before the third anniversary of the date of grant; and

(d) if the CSOP rules so provide, before the third anniversary of the date of grant and provided that such exercise takes place within six months after the optionholder ceasing to be an employee or full time director by reason only of injury, disability, redundancy or retirement.

If an approved share option is exercised outside the statutory time limits, a charge to income tax arises under section 476(2) of ITEPA 2003. Alternatively,

24 ITEPA 2003, Sch 4, Part 2.
25 ITEPA 2003, Sch 4, Part 5.

albeit in limited circumstances, the optionholder could also be taxed under Chapter 3C of Part 7 as having had a notional interest-free loan.

The shares acquired upon the exercise of an approved share option will have a base cost for capital gains tax purposes equal to the exercise price paid.

9.16 Enterprise Management Incentives

Employees of independent trading companies with gross assets not exceeding £30 million are eligible to receive tax relief for EMI share options. To qualify, the company must not be carrying on certain disqualifying activities and must not have more than 250 employees. There is a limit of (currently) £250,000 on the maximum initial market value of the shares over which EMI options may be granted. These restrictions are also subject to an overall limit of £3 million on the aggregate of the initial market value of shares in a company under all outstanding EMI options.

The main governing provisions concerning the implementation and operation of EMI options are set out in Schedule 5 to ITEPA 2003. The relevant taxation provisions concerning income tax relief are set out in Chapter 9 of Part 7 of ITEPA 2003.

In summary, if the exercise price at least equals actual market value of the shares (taking restrictions into account) at the date of grant, the subsequent exercise of an EMI option will not give rise to any liability for income tax, provided certain qualifying conditions relating to the options have not been breached and the option is not exercised more than ten years after grant.

The exercise of an EMI option with an exercise price set at below the market value at the date of grant will give rise to an income tax liability on the lesser of:

(a) the market value at the date of grant; and

(b) the market value at the date of exercise unless the sum of the exercise price and any amount otherwise paid for the option.

Following the standard rules, if the shares under option are readily convertible assets (see section 15 below), any income tax arising on exercise will be collected under PAYE and a commensurate liability to NICs will also arise at the same time.

It is notable that, contrary to the standard position referred to above there is no deemed section 431 election in the case of the exercise of an EMI option which has been granted at less than market value. Consequently, if an employee acquires any restricted securities on the exercise of an EMI option and is subject to income tax as a result of the grant, he may also be subject to restricted securities income tax charges later (ie when such restrictions are lifted or the securities are disposed). Consequently, it is generally accepted that optionholders should be required to enter into a section 431 election as a condition of exercise.

For the purposes of CGT, shares acquired upon the exercise of an EMI option will have a base cost equal to the exercise price paid for them plus, if any income tax was payable upon the exercise of the option, the amount on which income tax was so charged.[26]

9.17 SIP

In his 2000 Budget, the Chancellor announced details of a new all-employee share scheme. The SIP replaced the prevailing profit sharing scheme.

A SIP requires the establishment of a trust with one or more trustees, all of whom must be resident in the UK. The rules of the SIP and the relevant trust deed are invariably set out in a single document and must meet the specific requirements set out in Schedule 2 to ITEPA 2003.

SIPs provide employees with the opportunity to acquire shares in their employing company. SIPs are established and operated HMRC tax favoured plans.

Four distinct types of award can be made under a SIP:

(a) free shares;

(b) partnership shares;

(c) matching shares; and

(d) dividend shares.

Companies can choose to offer both free shares and partnership shares or either of the two. Awards of free shares are limited to a value of £3,000 per employee in a tax year.[27] Allocations can be varied by references to performance so long as the measures are objective. Partnership shares are shares that are offered to employees for purchase out of their pre-tax salary up to a limit of the lesser of £1,500 per year and 10% of salary.[28]

If a company chooses to offer partnership shares, it may also offer matching shares, which are free shares awarded on a basis that is proportionate to the

26 TCGA 1992, ss 38(1)(a), 144 and 144ZA.
27 ITEPA 2003, Sch 2, Part 5.
28 ITEPA 2003, Sch 2, Part 6.

number of partnership shares that an employee purchases. The maximum match is two matching shares for every one partnership share bought.

Companies can also determine that any dividends payable on the shares in the SIP will be reinvested in dividend shares. Reinvestment may be compulsory or the company may permit participants to choose whether or not they wish to reinvest the dividends.

For the employee, there are no income tax/NICs liabilities when partnership, free or matching shares are awarded or purchased. However, a participant who ceases to be in 'relevant employment' must withdraw all of his plan shares from the SIP. If the shares are withdrawn from the SIP within five years of the date of award (except in certain circumstances set out below) a charge to income tax, and potentially NICs, will arise. The charge depends on when the shares are withdrawn in this five year period. If the shares are withdrawn within three years of award (or acquisition in the case of partnership shares), the employee will be liable to income tax on the value of the shares at that time. However, if the shares are withdrawn on or after the third anniversary, but before the fifth anniversary, of the date of award (or acquisition in the case of partnership shares), income tax is payable on the lesser of their value at the date of award and their value when they are withdrawn from the SIP.

There is no charge to tax on shares withdrawn from a SIP if such withdrawal is in consequence of cessation of employment by reason of:

(a) injury or disability;

(b) redundancy;

(c) a transfer to which the Transfer of Undertakings (Protection of Employment) Regulations 2006, SI 2006/246 apply;

(d) a change of control of the employing company;

(e) retirement ; and

(f) death in service.[29]

In the case of dividend shares, these are subject to a fixed holding period of three years.[30] At the end of the holding period, no income tax (or, if appropriate NICs) are chargeable on the removal of the dividend shares from the SIP. However, if dividend shares are withdrawn from the SIP within three years, income tax will be charged on the amount of the original dividend unless the participant has left for one of the reasons specified above.[31]

29 ITEPA 2003, s 498.
30 ITEPA 2003, Sch 2, Part 8.
31 ITTOIA 2005, Part 4, Chapters 3 (UK resident companies) and 4 (non-UK resident companies).

Whilst the shares are held in the SIP, any growth in value is not liable to CGT. On a sale of shares, any gain over their value when they came out of the SIP is a chargeable gain for CGT purposes.

An employer company will, under general first principles, be entitled to relief from corporation tax for that part of salary payments that are deducted to pay for partnership shares. A deduction is also allowed for the cost of acquiring additional partnership shares that may be necessary to satisfy an employee's entitlement should the need arise because, say, the market value of the shares when acquired on behalf of the employee exceeds the partnership share money available.

Corporation tax relief is given for an amount equal to the market value of any free and matching shares at the time they are acquired by the trustee.

However, HMRC has power under the legislation to clawback corporation tax relief that is given for the cost of providing free and matching shares if approval of the plan is withdrawn at any time. If any free or matching shares are forfeited, then no further corporation tax relief is offered even if those shares are subsequently allocated to other participants of the SIP.

9.18 Application of Part 7A of Chapter 2 ('the disguised remuneration provisions')

There are a number of exclusions from Part 7A. Any steps taken by a third party in relation to one of the share schemes recognised in Part 7 (SAYE schemes, Company Share Ownership Plans, Approved Share Incentive Plans or Enterprise Management Incentives) do not give rise to a charge to tax under Part 7A.[32]

9.19 CORPORATION TAX DEDUCTIONS

For most UK companies a statutory corporation tax (CT) deduction is available for awards of shares and share options made in accounting periods starting in 2003.

The statutory relief from corporation tax for employee share acquisitions was introduced by Schedule 23 to the Finance Act 2003 for accounting periods beginning on or after 1 January 2003. As a general rule, companies are entitled to receive corporation tax relief equal to the gain that employees achieve when they exercise options or receive shares under employee share plans.

32 ITEPA 2003, ss 554E and 554I–554M.

The statutory rules for corporation tax deductions in connection with employee share plans are set out in Part 12 of the Corporation Act 2009, for accounting periods ending on or after 1 April 2009. In the case of accounting periods ending before 1 April 2009, the original enactment under Schedule 23 still prevails.

If all relevant conditions set out in the respective legislation are satisfied, relief is given as a deduction in computing the profits of the business for the purposes of which the option was granted in an amount equal to the difference between:

(a) the market value of the shares at the time they are acquired pursuant to the option; and

(b) the total amount or value of the consideration being given for the shares or the grant of the option.

It is notable that companies receive this corporation tax relief even if they have not incurred any costs or the optionholder does not suffer a charge to income tax upon exercise of the option because it is a CSOP, SAYE or EMI share option.

The relief is given for the accounting period of which the recipient acquires a beneficial interest in the shares (and not, if different, when they are conveyed or transferred).

It should be noted that different rules apply for corporation tax relief in relation to the operation of SIPs. In the case of a SIP, the company will obtain corporation tax relief under the general corporation tax rules for the amount of employees' salaries used to pay for partnership shares under a SIP. The company will (or may) also obtain corporation tax relief related to the value of shares awarded under the SIP for awards of free and matching shares, in which case the relief will equal the market value of the shares at the time they were acquired by the SIP trustee.

To satisfy share awards under employee share plans of various types, companies may fund an employee benefit trust (EBT) to enable it to purchase shares. EBTs are widely used by quoted companies to purchase shares in the market which will be used to satisfy long-term incentive plan awards (or, less often, share options). Private companies may also use them to support the operation of their employee share plans.

The tax and accounting implications of funding an EBT to acquire shares for use in share plans have changed considerably in recent years.

In relation to contributions made on or after 27 November 2002, no claim for corporation tax relief for a contribution to an EBT is allowed under general principles unless, and to the extent that, in that period (or within nine months after the end of it) 'qualifying benefits' or 'qualifying expenses' are paid out of the contributions that have been made to the EBT. If no such benefits or expenses have been made, relief is deferred until the accounting period in which such qualifying benefits or expenses are paid out.[33] However these new provisions do not apply so as to restrict the deductibility of the deductions allowed for contributions to a share incentive plan or any deduction allowed under the rules governing relief for employee share acquisitions.

9.20 CAPITAL GAINS TAX

When employment-related securities are sold, the base cost for CGT purposes is generally taken to be the aggregate of the actual amount or value given for the securities and any amount already charged to income tax under the general charging provisions of ITEPA 2003 and any amount which counts, or has so counted, as employment income under the specific charging provisions of Part 7.

Where shares are acquired under a SIP, the base cost of those shares for capital gains tax purposes will be their value at the date they are appropriated to an individual employee.[34] Where shares are acquired under an approved share option scheme, the base cost of those shares for capital gains tax purposes will be the cost of the option plus the cost of exercising it.[35]

With effect from 6 April 2008, and the abolition of taper relief, calculation of CGT liabilities is now generally very straight forward, ie the application of a flat rate of tax at 18% or 28% (depending on the individual's income tax liability) on the chargeable gain after deduction for permitted allowances.

9.21 COLLECTION OF INCOME TAX AND REPORTING

Income tax arising under the operation of ITEPA 2003 will be collected by HMRC either through the pay-as-you-earn system (PAYE) or by self- assessment.

Typically, the employer is strictly liable to account to HMRC for PAYE income tax on share benefits and there are well established rules governing timings, liability, penalties for non- or late payment, etc. On the other hand, liability for payment of income tax under self-assessment rests entirely with the employee. Whether or not income tax is collected through PAYE or under self-assessment is generally dependent on whether the shares (or other securities) acquired

33 Finance Act 2003, Sch 24.
34 That is the date when the employee acquires beneficial ownership of the shares.
35 TCGA 1992, s 144.

are readily convertible securities (RCAs). Furthermore, it typically follows that primary (i e employee's) and secondary (ie employer's) Class 1 NICs are payable on an employee's earnings and other benefits giving rise to a PAYE income tax charge.

In outline, an RCA is defined in ITEPA 2003[36] as meaning:

(a) shares (and any other assets) capable of being sold on a number of specified markets (including the London Stock Exchange and the New York Stock Exchange); and

(b) in respect of which trading arrangements are in existence or are likely to come into existence.

However, even if there are no trading arrangements in place or likely to come into existence, shares will still be treated as RCAs unless the company by which the employee is employed is entitled to relief from corporation tax in respect of the shares, as set out under Schedule 23 to the Finance Act 2003.

This additional limb, which was introduced by the Finance Act 2003, has significantly extended the application of PAYE and NICs to employee share acquisitions. For example, it now means that shares in private equity backed companies are likely to be RCAs.

Employers in the UK have a statutory obligation to file annual returns to HMRC in respect of the operation of share incentive arrangements.

The information to be provided is set out in standard forms provided by HMRC in respect of approved and unapproved plans. Under various provisions set out in ITEPA 2003, HMRC can withdraw approval of the plans as a direct result of the employer's failure to provide the information required. Furthermore, under the Taxes Management Act 1970, penalties may also be imposed if there is a failure to provide the information requested or if that information is inaccurate or not provided within the required time limit.

In the case of the approved plans, HMRC will invariably provide the company with the requisite form at the end of each tax year and the employer will have three months from the date of issue in which to complete.

36 ITEPA 2003, s 702.

Chapter 10

Termination and Variation Payments

10.1 INTRODUCTION

Payments made to an employee on termination of his employment tend to be comprised of a variety of distinct elements. Payment in lieu of notice, compensation or damages for a failure to serve due notice, statutory or contractual redundancy pay, compensation for statutory employment claims such as unfair dismissal or unlawful discrimination, ex gratia payments and retirement benefits may all fall within the broad category of termination payments. A termination payment may take either a non-cash form – for example transfer of ownership of a company car – or a variety of cash forms such as lump sums, enhanced pension rights or forgivable loans. The analysis of such payments raises a number of discrete questions of tax law, both in terms of income tax and national insurance contributions.

As a matter of tax law, the payment of sums by an employer in consideration of an employee agreeing to a change to his rights or duties under his contract of employment raises very similar issues, although this is much less frequently encountered in practice for reasons explained within this Chapter.

The risk for the employer in failing properly to account to HMRC for any tax due on a termination or variation payment is that HMRC will use its powers to recover unpaid tax and national insurance contributions from the employer rather than the former employee, and may also impose penalties on the employer of up to 100% of the unpaid tax (plus interest).[1] Whilst this risk can be mitigated to a certain extent by limited rights of recovery against the former employee and by the inclusion of a tax indemnity from the former employee to the employer in a compromise agreement, there may be practical difficulties for the employer in enforcing the indemnity and, in any event, the employer will be prohibited from recovering any secondary (ie employer's) national insurance contributions from the former employee.[2]

1 See the Income Tax (Pay As You Earn) Regulations 2003, SI 2003/2682 and the Social Security (Contributions) Regulations 2001,SI 2001/1004.
2 Social Security Contributions and Benefits Act 1992, Sch 1, paras 3(2), 3A.

The principles involved in determining the tax treatment of any termination or variation payment can be stated simply. However, difficult questions are, to follow the familiar formulation, raised in their application.

10.2 THE ANALYSIS UNDER ITEPA 2003

There are four stages of analysis under ITEPA 2003 in respect of the tax treatment of any termination payment, and the order of priority is as follows:

(i) Does the sum fall within the category of general earnings under Part 2 of ITEPA 2003?[3]

(ii) If not, is the payment for a restrictive covenant?[4]

(iii) Is the payment a relevant benefit under a retirement benefits scheme?[5]

(iv) If not, is the payment in connection with the termination of a person's employment, a change in the duties of a person's employment or a change in the earnings from a person's employment under section 401(1)?

Sections 401 to 416 of ITEPA 2003 are effectively charging provisions, as they impose a charge to tax on payments that would not otherwise be chargeable under ITEPA 2003. In general terms, if a termination payment falls within section 401(1), then to the extent that it exceeds £30,000 it will be charged to tax. As any sum falling within sections 401 to 416 is not generally liable to national insurance contributions, there will invariably be a significant benefit both to the employer and the employee if a termination payment falls within these sections. If the sum falls outside of both Part 2 and section 401(1) then it will not generally be subject to any tax deductions – however, it is extremely rare for this to be the case in respect of a payment made on or following termination of employment, particularly given the breadth of the provisions under section 401(1).

10.3 Is the payment taxable under Part 2?

Section 6 of ITEPA 2003 specifies the nature of charge to tax on employment income as follows:

> '(1) The charge to tax on employment income under this Part is a charge to tax on:
>
> (a) general earnings, and
>
> (b) specific employment income.'

3 In respect of which, generally, see Chapter 4 (Introduction to Income Tax).
4 In respect of which, generally, see Chapter 4 (Introduction to Income Tax).
5 In respect of which, generally, see Chapter 13 (Taxation of Pension Provision).

The definitions of 'employment income', 'general earnings' and 'specific employment income' are set out in section 7, and the key to these definitions is whether a payment constitutes 'earnings', which is defined by section 62 of ITEPA 2003 as:

> '(a) any salary, wages or fee,
>
> (b) any gratuity or other profit or incidental benefit of any kind obtained by the employee if it is money or money's worth, or
>
> (c) anything else that constitutes an emolument of employment.'

It is necessary to turn to the case law relating to Schedule E to ICTA 1988 (the predecessor to sections 6 and 62 of ITEPA 2003) for the purposes of determining what constitutes an 'emolument of employment' and whether the emolument arises from employment. It is clear that the requirement for an emolument to arise from employment is not satisfied merely because the employee would not have received the sum had he not been an employee: *Hochstrasser v Mayes*.[6] To be an emolument arising from the employment, the payment must be made for services the employee renders by virtue of his employment.

Hochstrasser v Mayes concerned a payment made by ICI pursuant to an indemnity given to an employee against any loss he might sustain on the sale of his house. The indemnity was granted pursuant to a scheme introduced by ICI to give financial peace of mind to any employees asked to move. It in no way affected his salary. The payment was not taxable as an emolument arising from employment because, as Lord Radcliffe explained:[7]

> 'The essential point is that what was paid to [the employee] was paid to him in respect of his personal situation as a house owner, who had taken advantage of the housing scheme and had obtained a claim to indemnity accordingly. In my opinion, such a payment is no more taxable as a profit from his employment than would be a payment out of a provident or distress fund set up by an employer for the benefit of employees whose personal circumstances might justify assistance.'

From this point in, however, the line starts to get 'a little wobbly': per Evershed MR in *Dale v de Soissons*.[8] Rather than trying to trace the wobbles, this Chapter examines the tax treatment of common categories of termination and variation payments. In this task, Viscount Simonds' warning must be kept in mind: 'the question is one of substance, not form'.[9] It is, moreover, necessary

6 (1959) 38 TC 673. Per Lord Cohen at 709.

7 (1959) 38 TC 673 at 392.

8 (1950) 32 TC 118, 126. Or, as the matter is shyly put by Carnwath J in *Wilcock v Eve* [1995] STC 18, 25: 'It may not be possible to devise a completely logical basis for distinguishing between these different factual situations.'

9 See *Hochstrasser v Mayes* (1959) 38 TC 673 at 706.

to recognise that, as has been observed above, termination payments are frequently composed of a number of different elements. The question must be asked in relation to each one of these elements: is it taxable as 'earnings' under section 62 of ITEPA 2003?

One final preliminary point needs to be borne in mind: Hochstrasser v Mayes is one of a number of older cases that required that the employment be the causa causans of the payment rather than merely a causa sine qua non. However, in *Kuehne & Nagel Drinks Logistics Ltd v Commissioners for HMRC*[10] the Court of Appeal found this language unhelpful and developed the concept of causation as follows:[11]

> 'When considering the cause of, or the reason for, an event or an act in a particular case, the courts steer clear of involvement in general theories of causation. Instead they apply a mix of general principle, legal policy and good-sense pragmatism to determine whether legal liability in accordance with the conditions set by the relevant rules has been established on the particular facts of the case.'

10.4 Payments in lieu of notice

The phrase 'payments in lieu of notice' or PILONS is not a term of art and has commonly been used to describe at least four different 'categories' of payment:

(1) An employer gives proper notice of termination to his employee, tells the employee that he need not work until the termination date and gives him his wages attributable to the notice period in a lump sum. In this case (commonly called 'garden leave') there is no breach of contract by the employer. The employment continues until the expiry of the notice: the lump sum payment is simply advance payment of wages.

(2) The contract of employment provides expressly that the employment may be terminated either by notice or, on payment of a sum in lieu, summarily. In such a case if the employer summarily dismisses the employee he is not in breach of contract provided that he makes the payment in lieu. But the payment in lieu is not a payment of wages in the ordinary sense, since it is not a payment for work to be done under the contract of employment.

(3) At the end of the employment, the employer and the employee agree that the employment is to terminate forthwith on payment of a sum in lieu of notice. Again, the employer is not in breach of contract by dismissing summarily and the payment in lieu is not strictly wages since it is not remuneration for work done during the continuance of the employment.

10 [2012] EWCA Civ 34.

11 Per Mummery LJ at para 32; See also *Commissioners for HMRC v PA Holdings Limited* [2011] EWCA Civ 1414.

(4) Without the agreement of the employee, the employer summarily dismisses the employee and tenders a payment in lieu of proper notice. This is by far the most common type of payment in lieu. The employer is in breach of contract by dismissing the employee without proper notice. However, the summary dismissal is effective to put an end to the employment relationship, whether or not it unilaterally discharges the contract of employment. Since the employment relationship has ended, no further services are to be rendered by the employee under the contract. It follows that the payment in lieu is not a payment of wages in the ordinary sense since it is not a payment for work done under the contract of employment.[12]

The question of the taxability of PILONs categories (1)–(3), ie those upon the payment of which there is no breach of contract, was addressed by Chadwick LJ in *EMI Group Electronics Ltd v Coldicott*.[13] Following a helpful review of the authorities, his Lordship, in a judgment with which the other Lords Justices agreed, concluded that such payments were fully taxable as emoluments arising from employment.

More recently, in *Cerberus Software Ltd v Rowley*[14] the Court of Appeal held that an employer, dismissing summarily without cause in circumstances in which the contract provided for the employer to exercise its discretion to make a PILON (ie a category (2) PILON), is not obliged to make a payment in lieu of notice in full and without regard to whether the employee has successfully mitigated his loss. Although this case was not specifically about the tax treatment of any sums to be paid to Mr Rowley, it confirms that there may be circumstances in which the employer neither serves notice nor exercises its discretion to make a PILON, and any sums paid to the employee as a result of such termination will not be fully taxable as earnings but will be more properly characterised as damages for wrongful dismissal and therefore taxable under section 401(1) (see below). Such cases must be examined critically to ensure there is evidence that the employer did in fact choose to breach the contract. The case of *Richardson v Delaney*[15] is an example of a case where the High Court rejected the employer's claim that such a breach had occurred. From a practical perspective, it is unlikely that HMRC will agree that the link between the damages payment actually made and the PILON which could have been made has been broken unless there is: (1) some clear evidence of the employer choosing to terminate the contract in breach; (2) the damages payment is made after employment has terminated; and (3) this payment is for a considerably smaller sum than the employer would have been obliged to pay under the PILON.

12 See *Delaney v Staples* [1992] 1 AC 687, per Lord Browne-Wilkinson at 692.
13 [1999] STC 803, 811.
14 [2001] IRLR 160.
15 [2001] 74 TC 167.

Lord Browne-Wilkinson's categories of PILON were also considered in *Redundant Employee v McNally.*[16] In this case there had been some uncertainty as to whether the employee in question had been served notice and placed on garden leave – ie where the employee remained employed but was not required to work during her notice period – or summarily dismissed and paid in lieu of notice in instalments. On the facts, Park J found that the employee had been placed on garden leave, and commented that although a category 1 PILON describes a case where wages for the notice period are given to the employee in a lump sum, it will be exactly the same if the wages are paid monthly or weekly (whatever the intervals were under the particular employment). This case illustrates the importance of making it clear in any termination letter whether employment is being terminated summarily with damages for any loss of notice period being paid in instalments (therefore falling within a category 4 PILON) or whether an employee is being served notice and placed on garden leave until the expiry of the notice period.

In determining whether or not there is a contractual PILON, it is necessary to consider all documentation which may have been expressly or impliedly incorporated into the contract of employment. In *SCA Packaging Ltd v Her Majesty's Customs & Excise*[17] the High Court held that a memorandum of agreement between SCA and recognised trade unions representing the employees which had been incorporated into the contracts of employment created rights for employees to receive a PILON if SCA chose to give them short notice or no notice upon the termination of employment by reason of redundancy. As a result any such PILONs were deemed to be emoluments arising from employment and therefore fully taxable as earnings.

Where an employer has a custom of making PILON payments as an automatic response to termination, such payments may be deemed by HMRC to be earnings and so fully taxable. However, more recently HMRC appears to accept more readily that an implied right to make a PILON conflicts with an express obligation to serve notice, and therefore it will be rare for such an implied term to become incorporated into the contract of employment by reason of custom and practice.[18]

So far as the question of category (4) PILONS – those made in breach of contract – HMRC's view is that they are not fully taxable as earnings.

10.5 Statutory redundancy payments

Statutory redundancy payments are exempted from Part 2 by section 309 of ITEPA 2003, as are 'approved contractual payments'. Approved contractual

16 [2005] ALL ER (D) 389 (Mar).
17 [2007] EWHC 270 (Ch).
18 The Revenue's Tax Bulletin 63 (February 2003).

payments are those made pursuant to certain agreements approved by order of the Secretary of State between an employer or employers and a trade union or trade unions giving employees a right to a payment on the termination of their contract of employment: see the Employment Rights Act 1996, Part XI, Chapter IV.

The leading case in respect of non-statutory redundancy payments is *Mairs v Haughey*.[19] In that case, the House of Lords held that non-statutory redundancy payments are not emoluments arising from employment. Two reasons were given for this conclusion. First, such payments could not fairly be described as compensation for services rendered. Rather they were compensation or relief from the consequences of an employee not being able to continue to earn a living in his former employment. Secondly, the entitlement to a redundancy payment is never more than a contingent entitlement. It is HMRC's view that the decision covers both contractual and *ad hoc* redundancy payments.[20]

Generally, other types of contractual termination payments fall to be fully taxed as earnings, a state of affairs which raises the possibility of abuse. HMRC have accordingly stressed the importance of ensuring that the redundancy payment in question is, in reality, a payment made to compensate for loss of employment through redundancy.[21] Payments which are remuneration for services rendered – such as retention bonuses or bonuses for meeting production targets or doing extra work in the run-up to redundancy – dressed up as redundancy payments remain fully taxable as earnings. In practice, this can cause difficulties if the employer and the employee enter into a compromise agreement many months before the actual date of termination of employment which contains provisions relating to an enhanced redundancy payment which the employee will receive following termination. In certain circumstances it may be necessary to satisfy HMRC that there was a true redundancy situation and to make any necessary distinction from any incentive paid to the employee to complete the job in a satisfactory manner.

To assist employers, HMRC operates an *ad hoc* advance clearance procedure whereby employers can confirm the tax position on redundancy. The employer should apply to the local HMRC office in writing enclosing the scheme document(s) and any letter to be issued to employees.[22]

10.6 Contractual termination payments

Generally, contractual termination payments will fall within the ambit of section 62 of ITEPA 2003 In *Dale v de Soissons* (see above), Colonel de Soissons had

19 (1993) TC 273.
20 See SP 1/94, paragraph 2
21 See SP 1/94 and IR Tax Bulletin Issue 24. See also the Employment Income Manual EIM13775–13790.
22 See paragraph 5 of SP 1/94.

a fixed three-year contract of service. However, the employer was given the right to terminate at the end of the first year on a payment of £10,000. The employer exercised the option to terminate and Sir Raymond Evershed MR held that, properly analysed, this sum was part of the remuneration that Colonel de Soissons was entitled to get under his contract of service. Accordingly, it was fully taxable as an emolument arising from employment.[23] This serves as a reminder to distinguish clearly in any enhanced redundancy policy which elements may be in respect of redundancy and which elements may be in respect of a contractual termination payment or payment in lieu of notice.

The issue of a contractual liquidated damages provision raises a further question. By its nature, such a clause should reflect the parties' genuine pre-estimate of any loss which would flow from a breach of contract, and any damages in such circumstances would not normally be treated as 'earnings' under section 62. However, if the provision is deemed to be a payment contingent on the occurrence of a specific event as opposed to a genuine liquidated damages payment, then the sum will be treated as 'earnings' and will be chargeable to tax under Part 2 in the normal way.

10.7 Other cash payments on termination

Where the employer makes a non-contractual termination payment, this is generally not taxable as an emolument from the employment. As Lord Dunedin puts the matter in *Duncan's Trustees v Farmer*[24] it is difficult to see how a payment can be said to be in respect of an office when the whole reason it is given is that the payee is no longer in the office.

For examples of cases where *ex gratia* payments on termination have been held not to be fully taxable as earnings or emoluments see *Cowan v Seymour*;[25] *Beynon v Thorpe*;[26] *Heywood v Comptroller General*;[27] *Resolute Management Services Ltd v Commissioner for Her Majesty's Revenue and Customs*.[28] However, where it is the employer's practice to make termination payments calculable by reference to a certain formula, one must examine carefully the question whether or not this practice has matured into a contractual right: see *Thorn EMI Electronics v Coldicott*.[29] If it has then, of course, the payment will be taxed as a contractual one and thus subject to tax as an emolument arising from employment.

23 See by way of contrast the decision of the House of Lords in *Hunter v Dewhurst* (1932) 16 TC 605.
24 5 TC 417, 422.
25 (1920) 7 TC 372.
26 (1927) 14 TC 1.
27 [1975] AC 229.
28 [2008] SPC 710.
29 [1996] STC (SCD) 455.

The cases of *Du Cross v Ryall*[30] and *Henley v Murray*[31] suggest that where an employee is awarded damages or compromises a claim against his employer on termination of employment, any sum received in consequence of that agreement will not be earnings. However, despite the generality of the assertions in those cases, it is most unlikely that any element of the payment relating to unpaid wages would escape tax under section 62. Any legal costs incurred by an employee in bringing proceedings against a former employer are, strictly speaking, not deductible against monies recovered therefrom. In *Warnett v Jones*[32] the taxpayer recovered £500 in respect of his wrongful dismissal claim, however, he had incurred £1,300 in irrecoverable legal expenses. On appeal, the High Court found that the sum of £500 was properly brought into charge under section 401. Extra Statutory Concession A81 entitled 'Termination payments and legal costs' provided an extra-statutory exemption from income tax levied by virtue of ITEPA 2003, Chapter 3 Part 6 until 5 April 2010. The concession has been enacted as ITEPA 2003, s 413A which applies to payments made on or after 6 April 2011 (see **10.21**).[33]

10.8 Variation payments

The analysis is more complex where a payment is made by employers in the context of an on-going employment relationship in order to induce agreement to some change in the terms and conditions of employment. An initial distinction must be drawn between changes in the manner in which the employee's remuneration is calculated and changes in other terms and conditions.

Where a change is made to the employee's remuneration, any payment made in consideration thereof will be fully taxable: see *McGregor v Randall*.[34] The taxpayers in that case were directors of the Miln Masters Group. That company was purchased by a third party which made an offer of lump sums ranging from £3,000 to £6,000 to the taxpayers in order to induce their agreement to an end to profit share arrangements. Those sums were accepted by the directors and Scott J, as he then was, had little difficulty finding that the sums were properly brought into charge as emoluments from their employment.

See also *Prendergast v Cameron*[35] where the taxpayer was a long-serving director. He intended to resign but an offer of a £45,000 lump sum induced

30 (1935) 19 TC 444.
31 (1950) 31 TC 351.
32 (1980) 53 TC 283.
33 Note that the employer will not be able to recover any VAT payable in respect of such contribution to legal fees, as the lawyer's services are provided to the employee as his client, not the employer. This should therefore be factored into any amount of the overall contribution.
34 [1984] 1 All ER 1092.
35 [1940] AC 549.

him to change his mind. The money was paid and he continued to serve as a director at a reduced remuneration. The House of Lords was in no doubt that this lump sum was taxable as an emolument arising from employment.

However, where the change concerns any other right, it would seem that a further (and more nebulous) distinction has to be drawn between payments in commutation of rights 'directly connected' with the employment and payments in commutation of other rights. Only the former are taxable.

The authority for this proposition is the case of *Hamblett v Godfrey*.[36] Following the decision of the then government to deny union representation to civil servants working at GCHQ, employees were offered £1,000 in recognition of the loss of this statutory right. The question arose whether this sum was taxable as an emolument arising from employment. Delivering the leading judgment in the Court of Appeal, Purchas LJ stated:

> 'The rights, the loss of which was being recognised, were rights under the employment protection legislation, and the right to join a union or other trade protection association. Both those rights, in my judgment, are directly connected with the fact of the taxpayer's employment. If the employment did not exist, there would be no need for the rights in the particular context in which the taxpayer found herself. So, I start from the position that those are rights directly connected with employment.'

He then went on to contrast the situation where payments were made to employees for agreeing to abandon membership of a golf club. The fact that the rights were directly connected with the employment meant, as a matter of construction, that they were derived therefrom and as such were taxable.

The decision is not beyond criticism. Although, as Purchas LJ points out, the payments were for release of a right directly connected with the employment, it is difficult to see how they might be said to be for services rendered.[37]

From HMRC guidance it seems highly unlikely that a variation payment will not be fully taxable as earnings unless the change is sufficiently fundamental to the employment relationship, in which case the payment may fall within section 401(1).[38]

36 [1987] 1 WLR 357.

37 A factor stressed by the House of Lords in *Hochstrasser v Mayes* [1960] AC 376, 389–390, 391, 391–392; *Tyrer v Smart* [1979] STC 34, per Lord Diplock at 38; *Laidler v Perry* [1966] AC 16, per Lord Donovan at 35–36, etc. Against this, the case is commented upon in passing in two House of Lords decisions without adverse comment: *Bray v Best* [1989] 1 WLR 167 per Lord Oliver at 176; *Shilton v Wilmshurst* [1991] 1 AC 684, 694.

38 EIM 00680.

10.9 Damages in the context of an ongoing relationship

There is also a question whether damages recovered by the employee in the context of an ongoing relationship are fully taxable as earnings. This category would include, for example, statutory claims which are not connected with the termination of employment such as an unlawful deduction of wages claim or a claim of being subject to a detriment by reason of unlawful discrimination, victimisation or harassment.

It is therefore important to establish the nature of the employee's claim, and the type of award that the Tribunal orders. These facts are best found by obtaining a copy of the employee's complaint to the Tribunal and a copy of the Tribunal's decision setting out the grounds under which the compensation is ordered.

Approached as a matter of principle, of the heads of damage listed above, only an unlawful deduction of wages claim would fall within section 62. The remainder do not arise from the employee 'being or becoming an employee'[39] but rather from a breach of the fundamental rights he has as an employee.[40]

10.10 Sums paid by a third party

Taxable earnings are confined to earnings provided by the employer or a person who has an interest in the performance by the employee of the services he contracts to provide. It follows from this that the same questions must be asked in respect of termination payments made by third parties as those made by the employer.

This proposition emerges from *Shilton v Wilmshurst*,[41] a case which concerned the tax consequences of footballer Peter Shilton's transfer from Nottingham Forest to Southampton for a fee of £325,000. In addition to the transfer fee, Southampton agreed to pay Peter Shilton £80,000 for agreeing to play at the Dell. Moreover, Nottingham Forest contracted to pay Mr Shilton a further sum of £75,000 if he agreed to leave the City Ground.

It was conceded that the sum of £80,000 paid by Southampton was fully taxable. However, the question whether the sum paid by Nottingham Forest was an emolument arising from employment went all the way to the judicial Premier League. Lord Templeman put one past the former England goalkeeper by holding that the section was not confined to emoluments from the employer but embraced all emoluments arising from employment. In this light, the Special Commissioner's finding that the payment was an inducement to play for Southampton and nothing else was conclusive of the point.

39 Per Lord Templeman in *Shilton v Wilmshurst* [1991] 1 AC 684 at 689.
40 See also **10.8** below.
41 (1991) 64 TC 78.

It should be noted that, even if Peter Shilton had succeeded in the House of Lords, the payment made by Nottingham Forest would have been taxable under the precursor to section 401 of ITEPA 2003.

10.11 Benefits

Severance packages frequently include tangible and/or intangible benefits, for example a company car or continuation of medical insurance cover. Other than certain specific categories such as outplacement counselling (considered below) these are taxed in exactly the same way as cash payments. Generally, unless an employee has a contractual entitlement to receive a benefit, it will be taxable under section 401 of ITEPA 2003.

The only distinct question which arises is that of valuation. The question of the value of assets transferred is considered in Chapter 8, Taxation of Benefits in Kind.

10.12 Payments on retirement

The tax treatment of termination payments made from retirement benefit schemes is considered at Chapter 13, Taxation of Pension Provision.[42]

10.13 Writing off loans

If a loan is written off by an employer, whether during the employment or on termination as part of a settlement package, it shall still be fully taxable as earnings under section 188 of ITEPA 2003. There is no obligation on the employer to deduct income tax under PAYE, but the write off should be reported by the employer to HMRC on form P11D. As national insurance contributions are also due on any written off loan, it would often be more tax efficient for the employee to pay off the loan and be given additional compensation which may fall under section 401(1).

10.14 Apportionment of payments

Where, as will frequently be the case, a termination payment relates to a number of items, some of which fall within section 62 and others not, the payment will need to be apportioned and clearly distinguished in any compromise agreement: see *Wales v Tilley*.[43]

42 See also **10.21** below.
43 (1942) 25 TC 136.

10.15 Restrictive covenants

Payments in consideration of new restrictive covenants will be charged under section 225 of ITEPA 2003 even if paid on or following termination of employment[44] in consideration of the employee entering into new covenants under a compromise agreement. It is important to identify clearly what consideration is being given in return for any new covenants and to keep this separate from any termination payment, as a failure to do so could result in HMRC seeking to tax the termination payment under section 225.

10.16 The charging provisions applicable to section 401 payments

Section 401 of ITEPA 2003 brings within the charge to income tax any amount by which a termination payment not otherwise chargeable to tax exceeds £30,000. Subsection (1) provides as follows:

> 'This Chapter applies to payments and other benefits which are received directly or indirectly in consideration or in consequence of, or otherwise in connection with –
>
> (a) the termination of a person's employment,
>
> (b) a change in the duties of a person's employment, or
>
> (c) a change in the earnings from a person's employment,
>
> are chargeable to tax under this section if and to the extent that their amount exceeds £30,000.'

A benefit is defined in section 402(1) as follows:

> 'In this Chapter "benefit" includes anything in respect of which, were it received for performances of the duties of the employment, an amount which –
>
> (a) would be taxable earnings from the employment, or
>
> (b) would be earnings apart from an earnings only exemption.'[45]

Section 403(1) of ITEPA then confirms:

> 'The amount of any payment or benefit to which this Chapter applies counts as employment income of the employee or former employee for the relevant tax year if and to the extent that it exceeds the £30,000 threshold.'

44 See *RCI Europe v Woods (HM Inspector of Taxes)* [2003] EWCA 3129 (Ch).
45 The benefits which fall outside of this definition are described in ITEPA 2003, s 402(2)–(4).

As already indicated, section 401 applies only to payments not otherwise chargeable to tax. Where a payment or benefit granted on termination would be taxed under any of the other charging provisions under ITEPA, those other charging provisions will take precedence over section 401.

It should be noted that the application of section 401 is also reduced or even exempted in several specific instances by sections 405 to 414 of ITEPA 2003 (see **10.21** below).

10.17 Application of the £30,000 limit

The section applies if and only to the extent that the amount of the termination payment exceeds £30,000 in value. Where there has been an apportionment of a termination payment, and part of the payment is chargeable under section 62, the £30,000 threshold applies only to the part not chargeable under section 62.

Example 1

Ben is selected for redundancy. His contract gives his employer the option of making a payment in lieu of notice. The payment made to him on redundancy is composed of the following elements:

(1) payment in lieu of notice – £6,000

(2) enhanced redundancy payment – £32,000

Element (1) is taxable under section 62. Element (2) is, however, taxable only under section 401. Only £2,000 of this sum will exceed the £30,000 threshold and therefore be taxable.

It would appear from section 401 that the £30,000 limit applies to each contract of employment which is altered or terminated. In other words, if an individual received termination payments from more than one employer in a year – and those employers were not 'associated' within the meaning of section 404 – there would be no need to aggregate the payments before applying the £30,000 limit.

However, in principle, if an employee receives a payment following a change in his duties or emoluments, that payment must be aggregated with any subsequent termination payment, whenever received, before applying the £30,000 limit. Where the facts are such as to raise this question, consideration ought to be given to the difficult issue whether the contractual variation which gave rise to the earlier payment was such as to bring that contract to an end: see, for example, *Marriott v Oxford and District Co-operative Society (No 2)*.[46]

46 [1969] 1 WLR 254, 259.

10.18 'Otherwise in connection with' the termination or change

The words 'otherwise in connection with' give section 401 of ITEPA 2003 a very broad application encompassing awards for discrimination, denial of trade union rights, compensation for failure to re-engage, etc.

In *Mimtec Ltd v CIR Sp C* it was held that a protective award for a failure to inform and consult on collective redundancies[47] was not earnings but was a payment received in connection with the termination of a person's employment, and was therefore charged to tax under the equivalent of section 401(1). The Employer's Further Guide to PAYE and NICs[48] makes it clear that income tax is only charged on any amount of a protective award over £30,000, although unusually for a payment falling under section 401(1) national insurance contributions are payable on the full amount of the award.[49]

Although it is unusual, it is not impossible for a payment made following termination of employment to be deemed not to be 'in connection with' that termination. In *Cromptom v Revenue & Customs*[50] the Tribunal Judge of the First-tier Tribunal determined that compensation paid in respect of the Army Selection Board's failure to follow proper procedures in connection with Mr Cromptom's application for five different posts was not 'connected with' the termination of Mr Crompton's employment, notwithstanding that Mr Crompton took voluntary redundancy shortly after his applications had been unsuccessful. The compensation was therefore not taxable as earnings or under section 401(1), and was therefore free of tax.

In *A v Her Majesty's Revenue and Customs*[51] the taxpayer sought to argue that of a total gross sum of £250,000 received from his employer under the terms of a settlement agreement, £200,000 was payment of compensation for loss of reputation and injury to feelings resulting from disciplinary proceedings and therefore fell outside of the scope of sections 62 and 401(1) of ITEPA 2003 and was not taxable. The Special Commissioner disagreed with the characterisation of the payment and, applying the *Vento*[52] guidelines applicable to the assessment of injury to feelings awards in employment claims, accepted that £10,000 was fairly attributable to injury to feelings by reason of being subject to a detriment (and therefore not employment income or a payment

47 Section 189 of the Trade Union and Labour Relations (Consolidation) Act 1992 provides for a protective award of up to 90 days' full pay.

48 CWG2 (2009).

49 Social Security Contributions and Benefits Act 1992, s 112(3)(c).

50 [2009] UKFTT 00012 (TC) (7 April 2009).

51 [2009] SPC 00734 (4 February 2009).

52 *Vento v Chief Constable of West Yorkshire Police* [2003] IRLR 102.

in connection with the termination of his employment),[53] but held that the remaining £240,000 was chargeable to income tax under section 401(1) as a termination payment.

It is therefore extremely important when settling a number of claims under a compromise agreement, some of which may be argued are not 'in connection with' the termination of employment, to set out clearly the compensation attributable to each and the tax treatment of such compensation, and to remember that where several elements of compensation fall within section 401(1) these must be aggregated for the purpose of the £30,000 limit.

10.19 Non-monetary benefits

It is clear from the words 'and other benefits' in section 401(1) of ITEPA 2003 that the transfer of non-monetary benefits on termination or an alteration in conditions of employment may also give rise to a charge to tax under section 401. For example, where, following the termination of employment, the employee is permitted to keep the company car, there is a potential charge to tax under section 401.

10.20 Other recipients of a termination payment

Section 401(1) applies whether the payment is received by the employee or former employee, by his or her spouse or civil partner, or any blood relative or dependent of the employee or former employee or by the personal representatives of the former employee.

10.21 EXCEPTIONS AND REDUCTIONS TO PAYMENTS UNDER SECTION 401

There is an important group of exceptions and reductions to the charge under section 401, and these are set out in sections 405–414 of ITEPA 2003. For the purposes of this Chapter, the main provisions are as follows:

10.22 Death and disability

Under section 406, tax is not charged under section 401 where a payment is received: (i) in connection with the termination of the employment by death; or (ii) on account of injury or disability.[54] The meaning of the phrase 'on account of injury or disability' has been clarified by Lightman J in *Horner v Hasted*:[55]

53 A similar finding was made in *Walker v Adams* [2003] STC 269 and see HMRC Employment Income Manual EIM12965.

54 ITEPA, s 406(a) and (b).

55 (1995) 67 TC 439, 485.

'[I]t must be established: (1) that the disability alleged by an employee is a relevant disability, that is to say, a total or partial impairment (which may arise from physical, mental or psychological causes) of his ability to perform the functions or duties of his employment; and (2) that the person making the payment does so not merely in connection with the termination of employment … but on account of the disability of the employee. In short, there must be established as an objective fact a relevant disability and as a subjective fact that the disability is the motive for payment by the person making it.'

HMRC accepts that the exception applies both to sudden disability and the inability to perform the duties of an office or employment arising out of a gradual decline.

In *Orthet Ltd v Vince-Cain*[56] the EAT held that this exemption extends to compensation for injury to feelings (equating injury to feelings, short of psychiatric damage, with injury to the person). The startling reasoning is highly suspect, and might well not survive a challenge by HMRC. The point that a payment in respect of injury to feelings is not taxable was conceded by HMRC in Northern Ireland in *Walker v Adams*[57] but that was in a case where all the discrimination took place pre-termination.

10.23 Pension scheme payments (in)

Where, as part of an arrangement relating to the termination of employment, an employer makes a special contribution to the employee in question's pension scheme, such a payment will escape tax subject to the satisfaction of certain conditions.[58] Those conditions are that the payment is made into an 'approved retirement benefits scheme' or an 'approved personal pension scheme' and is in a form permitted by the scheme.[59] The payment does not use any of the £30,000 exemption for section 401. So the employer could pay £30,000 into pension, and another £30,000 directly, and there would be no charge under section 401.

10.24 Pension scheme payments (out)

Where an employee receives a payment from a 'tax-exempt pension scheme' in consequence of the termination of his employment, that payment will be taxable under the provisions in section 403 unless either:

56 [2005] ICR 374.
57 [2003] STC (SCD) 269.
58 ITEPA 2003, s 407.
59 In respect of which, see Chapter 13 (Taxation of Pension Provision).

(a) the payment or other benefit is by way of compensation –

  (i) for loss of employment, or

  (ii) for loss or diminution of earnings, and the loss or diminution is due to ill-health; or

(b) the payment or other benefits are properly regarded as earned by past service (in other words, where the payment really is part of his pension).

10.25 Legal costs

The element of a termination payment which represents legal costs is within section 401 as if is made in connection with the termination. However, it is not charged by virtue of section 413A, provided three conditions are met:

(a) The payment meets the whole or part of legal costs incurred by the employee exclusively in connection with the termination of the employee's employment.

(b) The termination of the employee's employment results in a settlement agreement between the employer and the employee.

(c) The settlement agreement provides for the payment to be made by the employer and the payment is made directly to the employee's lawyer.

The old definition of 'compromise agreement' in section 413A, which imported the formalities of the Employment Rights Act 1996 (ERA 1996), section 203(3) even in a case to which ERA 1996 did not apply, has been removed. The relevant agreement is now a 'settlement agreement', which is not defined in terms of the ERA 1996 definition, or any other. The amending instrument is the Enactment of the Extra Statutory Concessions Order 2013, SI 2013/234, article 3. This applies to payments made on or after 1 March 2013.

'Legal costs' means fees payable for services and disbursements of a lawyer.

10.26 Other exceptions

Other exceptions include the provision of outplacement counselling to employees,[60] certain payments provided in connection with approved retirement benefit schemes (section 407), to members of Her Majesty's forces (section 411) or by governments of overseas territories within the Commonwealth (section 412). Finally, payments made to employees with foreign service may be wholly or partially exempt: see section 414.[61]

60 ITEPA 2003, s 310 and Chapter 8 (Taxation of Benefits in Kind).
61 Discussed in Chapter 12 at **12.17**.

10.27 QUANTIFYING THE CHARGE UNDER SECTION 401

Quantifying the charge to income tax under section 401 is relatively straightforward: all amounts caught by section 401 above £30,000[62] are added to the employment income of the employee in the year in which he receives the payment. They are taxed as if they were the 'top slice' of the employee's income in the year of assessment in which they are received.

In the main, non-monetary benefits are treated in an identical fashion to cash payments. However, a question does arise as to what value should be attributed to these benefits.

Section 415 of ITEPA 2003 provides that, where a non-cash benefit is given, the amount of a payment or other benefit is taken to be the greater of:

(a) the amount of earnings (as defined in Chapter 1 of Part 3) that the benefit would give rise to if it were received by an employee within section 15 for performance of the duties of employment (money's worth), and

(b) the cash equivalent of the benefit under the benefits code if it were so received and the code applied to it.

10.28 Time of receipt

Section 403(3) provides that a cash benefit is treated as received when it is paid or a payment is made on account of it, or when the recipient becomes entitled to require payment of or on account of the benefit. A non-cash benefit is treated as received when it is used or enjoyed.

Determining the moment of receipt of a cash benefit is, therefore, straightforward. However, two points arise when it comes to non-cash benefits. First, where the employee continues to use a non-cash benefit which he enjoyed before the termination of his employment, it appears that the time of receipt must be the time of termination of employment. Secondly, where the employee receives a cash and non-cash benefit, it is quite possible that those two benefits will fall to be taxed in different years of assessment.

Section 404(4) makes it clear that, where the payments and benefits are received in different tax years, the £30,000 is set off against the amount of payments and other benefits received in earlier years before those received in later years. Nevertheless, there still may be a benefit to the employee receiving payments and benefits in different tax years, as he or she will be obliged to account to

62 See section 403(1).

HMRC for any marginal rate of tax due over and above basic rate of income tax deducted at source for any sums in excess of £30,000, and therefore there may be the ability to set off any such marginal rate against his or her personal allowances over two (or more) tax years.

10.29 THE GOURLEY PRINCIPLE AND TERMINATION PAYMENTS

The application of the *Gourley* principle is considered in more detail in Chapter 11, Taxation of Damages Awards. However, it is vital to note that the fact that a *Gourley* deduction is made from a termination payment does not mean that the damages awarded escape further taxation. HMRC's view – and it is clearly the correct one – is that the sum awarded falls into charge under section 401. Therefore advisers must be careful to ensure that the sum awarded reflects the fact that the employee will be liable to tax thereon to the extent that the sum takes him beyond the £30,000 limit for that employment. The difficulties raised thereby are addressed further in Chapter 11.

10.30 DRAFTING COMPROMISE AGREEMENTS

In practice, the majority of users of this book will be applying the forgoing principles when negotiating and drafting compromise agreements. Therefore the following general points should be borne in mind when drafting such agreements:

(a) Any compromise agreement should make provision for the incidence of PAYE on the settlement sum where relevant, for example where the settlement includes taxable earnings or to the extent that the sum exceeds £30,000 and is taxable under s 401. Consider an appropriate form of wording such as:

> 'The employer is entitled and bound to satisfy the sum payable hereunder by deducting tax and accounting to HM Revenue & Customs in accordance with the Income Tax (Pay as You Earn) Regulations 2003.'

Failure to make any provision at all may lead the disappointed employee to sue for the gross sum on the (totally incorrect) assumption that he was entitled to receive the full amount without deduction. This happened in *Barden v Commodities Research Unit International*.[63] After mediation, the employer settled a High Court claim made by a former employee by way of an agreement scheduled to a Tomlin order. The terms of the

63 [2013] EWHC 1633.

settlement were that the employer would pay a sum of £1,350,000 to an identified bank account by a specified date. The settlement agreement made no reference to PAYE and the employer belatedly appreciated the extent of its obligations to deduct, since the payment exceeded £30,000 and there was an income tax charge under s 401 of ITEPA 2003 to which PAYE applied. Rather than pay the contractual amount into the identified bank account, the employer paid that amount, less PAYE. The employee sought to enforce the Tomlin order, claiming to be entitled to receive the sum of £1,350,000 with the employer bearing the burden of the tax. Vos J drew a parallel with a contractual salary – no-one expects the salary to be paid without deduction of PAYE – and PAYE was deductible here despite the agreed mechanics of payment.

(b) Do not agree a global compromise sum under the misapprehension that the sum can, after the event, be re-allocated in a more tax-efficient way between different heads of claim. The tax character of a sum cannot lawfully be altered by calling it something different afterwards; however, a fair apportionment between taxable and non-taxable heads of loss may be achieved by seeking the agreement of you client's tax inspector, usually under CAP 1.

10.31 CLEARANCE FROM HMRC

One way to manage risk is to use HMRC's 'Clearance and Approvals' process (CAP 1) to seek a ruling by HMRC (generally given by a specialist) on the correct treatment of the termination payments. [Clearances and Approvals 1: http://www.hmrc.gov.uk/cap/cap1.htm. For the CAP 1 checklist, see http://www.hmrc.gov.uk/cap/annex-a-cap1-checklist.pdf.] HMRC will regard itself as bound by its ruling but the taxpayer is free to disagree with it. It is essential to make full disclosure of the circumstances and available arguments, or the ruling cannot be relied on.

Example 1

Alice was employed as an investment banker for Golding Bros Bank ('the employer') for ten years. Her base salary was £200,000; she was entitled to consideration for a discretionary annual bonus, and generally received a bonus of the order of £300,000, payable on 1 February. She has always been a member of the employer's registered pension scheme. From November 2012 Alice was sexually harassed by her manager. She was off work on sick leave continuously from 10 January 2013 and sustained serious psychiatric damage of indefinite duration, which led to her resignation on 1 December 2013. She was not paid a February 2011 bonus. She commences High Court and tribunal proceedings, claiming arrears of bonus both as debt and wrongful deduction, damages, sex discrimination, unfair dismissal. Her legal costs reach £30,000.

After disclosure and witness statements, including medical evidence, Golding Bros Bank is willing to settle for £500,000. It makes an offer comprised in a settlement agreement expressly on the basis that Alice will receive a lump sum of compensation of £200,000 plus arrears of bonus for last year at £300,000.

For Golding Bros Bank the cost will be £200,000 plus £300,000 plus Class 1 secondary NIC on the arrears of bonus at 13.8%, being £41,440. Total cost £541,440.

Alice, an additional rate taxpayer in 2013–14, would pay tax at 45% on £470,000, and Class 1 primary NIC of 2% on the bonus amounting to £6,000.[64] She is also taxable in full on the compensation payment to the extent it exceeds £30,000. The settlement will therefore cost her £211,500 of tax and another £6,000 of NIC,[65] in addition to her own costs of £30,000.

Now, considering the principles set out above, a settlement for the same sum of £500,000 might be better structured for everyone as follows:

(a) £80,000 for the psychiatric injury: tax free.[66]

(b) £30,000 for injury to feelings in respect of the harassment by Alice's manager during her employment: tax free as has no connection with termination.

(c) £30,000 for Alice's legal costs, paid directly to her solicitors under a settlement agreement: tax free.[67]

(d) The balance of £330,000[68] is paid as a lump sum of compensation.

So Alice's tax position is £170,000 tax free. Then, of the balance, she pays tax on £330,000 at 45%, namely £148,500. This has saved Alice £99,000 (as opposed to the £211,500 she would have paid had the payment not been restructured).

The parties could go further. Alice might want to divert some tax free cash into her pension arrangements.[69] She might need outplacement support[70]. It is clearly the case that if the payment is tax free and not considered earnings, the employer will pay less NICs on the payment.

---

64 This is because the bonus is arrears of earnings.

65 Deducted under PAYE using the OT Code – see Chapter 4 (The PAYE System).

66 ITEPA 2003, s 406(b).

67 ITEPA 2003, s 413A.

68 £500,000 minus £140,000 and minus the £30,000 tax free slice under ITEPA 2003, s 401, being £350,000.

69 ITEPA 2003, s 408.

70 ITEPA 2003, s 310.

10.32 SUMMARY

The taxation treatment of termination and variation payments contains a number of traps for the unwary. Advisers must be particularly careful to structure settlements or advance claims for damages in such a manner that allows elements of the overall termination package or sums claimed to be separately identified, particularly where those elements are being afforded different tax treatment. For example, it would not be impossible for a settlement agreement to include sums which are taxable under section 62 (eg unpaid wages prior to the termination date), sums which are taxable under section 225 (e g consideration for a new restrictive covenant), sums which are taxable under section 401 (eg compensation for an unfair dismissal) and sums which are not taxable at all (e g an amount for injury to feelings relating to harassment during employment). Add to this a contribution to legal fees and outplacement services and an exemption or reduction to any payment under section 401 and it becomes clear that tax planning becomes a central issue to any claims or settlements upon the termination of employment.

Chapter 11

Taxation of Damages Awards

11.1 INTRODUCTION: THE RULE IN GOURLEY'S CASE

The principle in *Gourley's* case[1] will be familiar to readers. The object of awarding damages for a breach of contract is to place the claimant in the position – so far as money can do it – that he would have been in had the contract been performed. Where the effect of the breach is to deny the claimant income, the damages, broadly, will comprise a sum equivalent to the income lost. *Gourley* establishes that, if tax would have been paid on the income, the court must, in assessing the damages, take that fact into account. The court will reduce the damages by a sum representing the tax which would have been paid on the income.[2] This sum is generally referred to as the 'notional tax'.

The question how to assess notional tax is probably the most complex addressed in this book. This complexity follows from difficult questions over which rate of tax to apply and how to deal with future and concurrent income streams. It arises against a background where it is not clear when it is appropriate to take *Gourley* deductions.

In certain situations, after damages have been reduced by notional tax, the claimant will have a further liability to pay tax to HMRC on receipt of the damages themselves. Without adjustment to take account of this fact, his damages will have been reduced twice over on account of tax and he will be under compensated. A question therefore arises whether to apply the *Gourley* rule and then gross the resultant sum up to take account of tax that will be paid on the damages, or simply not to apply *Gourley* at all. It is, of course, far simpler not to apply *Gourley*. However, as will be seen, this will lead to only a rough estimate of the claimant's true loss.

1 *British Transport Commission v Gourley* [1956] AC 185.
2 On the facts of *Gourley*, the damages for lost income were £37,720 gross and £6,695 net of notional tax.

11.2 WHEN DOES GOURLEY APPLY?

There are, therefore, two questions:

(1) Are the damages compensation for loss of income which, if in fact it had been received, would have been taxed?

(2) Will the damages themselves be taxed in the recipient's hands?

Where only the first question is answered in the affirmative, the position is clear, the rule in *Gourley* must be applied.

Example 1

Angela, a higher rate (40%) taxpayer is dismissed in breach of contract. She sues and her damages are assessed at £15,000 before *Gourley* deduction. Because her 'termination payment' is less than £30,000, no tax liability arises upon receipt:

Gross loss	£15,000
Less Gourley deduction at 40%	6,000
Net receipt	9,000

However, as has been mentioned, where both are answered in the affirmative, there is a question mark over the application of *Gourley*.

There are two schools of thought in relation to the matter. The first, propounded by Phillimore J in *Bold*,[3] is that *Gourley* should not apply where the damages will be taxed upon receipt by the claimant. Why bother, the argument goes, taking account of tax which would have been paid when the resultant award of damages will be taxed anyway. Just ignore the whole thing.[4] This was the result eventually arrived at in the non-employment income case of *Pennine Raceway Ltd v Kirklees Metropolitan Borough Council (No 2)*[5] where, at first instance, damages were awarded on the basis that they should be reduced by the notional tax in the belief that the award itself would not be subject to tax. Later the taxpayer was advised by the Revenue that the damages would be taxable on receipt, and the Court of Appeal determined accordingly that the damages should be recalculated without any deduction for notional tax.

3 *Bold v Brough, Nicholson & Hall Limited* [1964] 1 WLR 201

4 See in this regard, *Deeny v Gooda Walker Ltd* [1996] STC 299, HL and, as regards the tax treatment of damages taken into account in computing interest on those damages, *Deeny v Gooda Walker Ltd (No 4)* [1995] STC 696, QB.

5 [1989] STC 122.

The alternative view, propounded *inter alia* by Sheen J in *Shove v Down Surgical plc*,[6] is that *Gourley* should be applied and the resultant sum grossed up to reflect the tax which will in due course be paid on the damages because this will most closely place the claimant in the position he would have been in had the wrong not been done.

At first glance, it would appear to make little difference which approach is adopted (ignoring personal allowances and other reliefs):

Example 2 – the Bold approach

Dominic, a higher rate (40%) taxpayer, is dismissed in breach of contract. He sues and his loss is assessed at £55,000 before *Gourley* deduction.

Gross loss	£55,000
No *Gourley* deduction	
Sum awarded	£55,000
Less tax liability on receipt	
40% =	£22,000
Net receipt	£33,000

Example 3 – the Shove approach

Dominic, a higher rate (40%) taxpayer, is dismissed in breach of contract. He sues and his loss is assessed at £55,000 before *Gourley* deduction.

Gross loss	£55,000
Less Gourley deduction	£22,000
	£33,000
Plus grossing up	£22,000
Sum awarded	£55,000
Less tax liability on receipt 40% =	£22,000
Net receipt	£33,000

However, although the above calculations illustrate why the debate is generally redundant, they are misleading when the tax which would have been paid is income tax. *Bold* assumes that the tax liability on receipt of the damages in,

6 [1984] ICR 532. See also the powerfully argued judgment of Lord Hunter in *Stewart v Glentaggart Limited* (1963) SC 300.

say, the tax year 2009–10 will be the same as the tax liability would have been had the income have been received over the course of, say, 2006–07, 2007–08 and 2008–09. However, where the tax to be deducted is income tax, it is only infrequently that this assumption will be correct. This is principally because different slices of income are taxed at different rates but also because personal allowances for each of the three years in which the income would have been received need to be taken into account.

Under Chapter 3 of Part 6 of ITEPA 2003, and in particular, section 403(1) and (2),[7] the provision under which damages received will generally be taxed, makes clear that termination payments in excess of the statutory figure of £30,000 are treated as employment income for the year in which 'the payment or other benefit is *received*' (emphasis added). Tax on damages is, therefore, calculated on the basis that the damages constitute income for the year in which they are received. The *Bold* approach takes no account of the fact that the award may be made in respect of income lost from a wholly different period – or indeed more than one period – than that in which the damages are received. Effectively, therefore, it compresses income which may have accrued over a number of years into a single year of assessment. Accordingly, there is a chance that more of the income will be taxed at a higher rate of tax and the claimant will be under compensated. Moreover, the *Bold* approach will generally lead to damages being taxed in a different year to that in which the lost income would have been earned. It will depend on all the circumstances – ie the rate of tax obtaining in the year of lost income (eg 40%) as opposed to the rate obtaining in the year of receipt of damages (eg 45%) – whether this works to the claimant's advantage or disadvantage or indeed is tax neutral. However, there is clearly a risk that the damages award will not properly compensate the claimant for his loss of income.

The *Shove* approach, by contrast, calculates the tax which would have been paid had the income been earned. Moreover, it is calculated having regard to the year or years in which the income would have been earned.

The *Shove* approach will give rise to a more accurate assessment of the employee's loss, however, in contrast *Bold* is less complex. A number of decisions have evinced a strong preference for simplicity in the calculation (and thus the *Bold* approach): see, for example, *Gourley*[8] itself; *Parsons v BNM Laboratories*;[9] *John v James*.[10] However, it is clear that, where damages will not be taxed in the recipient's hands (typically because they are less than £30,000), *Gourley* must be applied and a deduction made on payment of the damages themselves. If this is not done the income will be received entirely

7 Discussed at Chapter 10 (Termination and Variation Payments).
8 [1956] AC 185, per Lord Jowitt 203.
9 [1964] 1 QB 95, 139.
10 [1986] STC 352.

free of tax. The attraction of the *Bold* approach – ie simplicity – appears to the authors to lose much of its force when this fact is borne in mind. To follow *Bold* leads to a somewhat anomalous situation where the calculation in lower value cases is both more detailed and more accurate than in higher value cases.

In summary, because the matter cannot be regarded as closed, both approaches will be considered.

11.3 WOULD THE LOST INCOME HAVE BEEN TAXABLE?

The question whether the lost income would have been taxable if received is addressed at length in Chapter 4, Introduction to Income Tax, to which reference should be made.

The only complication arises where the lost income would have been taxable if received in connection with a termination of employment or a change in the duties of or emoluments from employment.[11] An example might be where damages are sought in connection with a failure to make a contractual redundancy payment. The contractual redundancy payment would, if received, have been taxable as employment income only to the extent that its value exceeds £30,000. The notional tax must be calculated in respect of damages above this £30,000 sum.

11.4 WILL THE DAMAGES BE TAXABLE?

Damages count as employment income only to the extent that they exceed £30,000 (and hence are brought into tax as termination payments by section 403 of ITEPA 2003).[12]

Section 403(1) provides that any payment received in connection with the termination of a person's employment[13] or any change in the duties of or emoluments from a person's employment[14] and not otherwise chargeable to tax, shall be taxable as employment income to the extent that it exceeds £30,000.[15] It follows that, where the damages award exceeds £30,000, there will be a charge to tax on receipt.

Two questions then arise. The first – should *Gourley* be applied to payments over £30,000 – has been addressed at **11.2** above. The second is how to manage *Gourley* deductions when damages awards exceed this £30,000 limit.

11 See Chapter 10 for a detailed discussion of termination and variation payments.
12 See the leading case of *Henley v Murray* (1950) 31 TC 351 per Sir Raymond Evershed MR.
13 Section 401(1)(a).
14 Section 401(1)(b).
15 See Chapter 10 for a full discussion of Part 6, Chapter 3 of ITEPA 2003.

11.5 Damages over £30,000: the *Shove* approach

If the *Shove* approach is followed, the position can be stated simply.[16] First, the rule in *Gourley* is applied to the entirety of the damages award. Second, the damages award, as reduced by notional tax, must be grossed up to the extent that it exceeds £30,000 to take account of the tax to be paid under section 403.

Example 4 – the Shove approach

Dominic, a higher rate (40%) taxpayer, is dismissed in breach of contract. He sues and his loss is assessed at £55,000 before *Gourley* deduction.

Gross loss	£55,000
Less Gourley deduction	£22,000
	£33,000
Plus grossing up on £3,000 (ie amount exceeding £30,000)	£ 2,000
Sum awarded	£35,000
Less tax liability on monies over £30,000	£ 2,000
Net receipt	£33,000

11.6 Damages over £30,000: the *Bold* approach

However, there is a potential trap in the *Bold* approach. If *Gourley* is applied only to the first £30,000 of the damages award, the employee will be overcompensated.

Example 5 – the Bold approach

Dominic, a higher rate (40%) taxpayer, is dismissed in breach of contract. He sues and his loss is assessed at £55,000 before *Gourley* deduction.

Gross loss	£55,000
Less Gourley deduction on first £30,000	£12,000
Sum awarded	£43,000
Less tax liability on monies over £30,000	£ 5,200
Net receipt	£37,800

---

16 Albeit applied only with difficulty.

The reason for the difference is that, in Example 5, there is a £12,000 slice of untaxed income. The rule in *Gourley* reduces the first £30,000 of damages to £18,000. Section 403 then charges to tax the damages *as reduced by notional tax* only to the extent they exceed £30,000.

In order to avoid this consequence, it is necessary to apply the rule in *Gourley* to such sum which, after deducting notional tax, will leave £30,000 as the tax free element of the damages. For a 40% taxpayer this is £50,000.

Example 6 – the correct Bold approach

Dominic, a higher rate (40%) taxpayer, is dismissed in breach of contract. He sues and his loss is assessed at £55,000 before *Gourley* deduction.

Gross loss	£55,000
Less Gourley deduction on £50,000	£20,000
Sum awarded	£35,000
Less tax liability on monies over £30,000	£ 2,000
Net receipt	£33,000

11.7 CALCULATING THE NOTIONAL TAX

The task facing the court when assessing the notional tax liability is summed up by the following passage from the judgment of Orr LJ in *Lyndale Fashion Manufacturers v Rich*:[17]

> 'In my judgment, two calculations fall to be made, the first as to the tax which the defendant was liable to pay in respect of his actual income of the year in question, and the second as to the tax which he would have been liable to pay if he had earned by way of additional commission the sum of £495 in the same year; and the difference between these two liabilities will be the amount to be deducted in making the award.'

However, easy though the task may be to describe, it is far from simple to perform. The calculation 'depends on the combination of a number of factors that may vary with each case – allowances, reduced rates, surtax rates, other income of the claimant or his wife, charges or reliefs'.[18]

17 [1973] STC 32, 34.
18 See *Gourley* [1956] AC 185 per Lord Goddard 208.

11.8 What rate to apply?

The first task – and the most important in practical terms – will be to decide what rate to apply in calculating the notional tax. In a situation where the employee has little or no other income, the question is simple to answer. Following *Lyndale*, above, an assessment is made of the income tax which would have been paid by the employee on the lost income and the income is reduced by that sum.

However, where the employee has other income streams, it is necessary to reach a determination of whether the lost income should be taxed as if it were additional to all other income ('top slicing') or as if it were the only income earned by the employee in that year ('bottom slicing'). The difference between the two approaches can give rise to a difference in notional tax of many thousands of pounds, depending on rates of tax and, for example, the availability of personal allowances.

The leading case on the point is *Re Houghton Main Colliery Co Ltd*,[19] where

Wynn-Parry J observed:

> 'I can find no good reason for the suggestion that the notional amounts which as a result of the calculations are to be added to the actual incomes of Mr Brass and Mr Francis should be regarded in either case as representing the top slice of those incomes. To my mind, the proper way of looking at the matter is to say that, if, taking the case of Mr Brass, the company had continued to function, his income would have been greater by the amount which will emerge from the calculations to be performed, but it cannot be said that it represents the top slice, or for that matter the bottom slice, of his income; the only effect of making the calculation for the purposes of applying *British Transport Commission v Gourley* will be that his income for the relevant period must be treated as *larger than in fact it was* (emphasis added).'

This paragraph – and in particular the first sentence – is generally cited as authority for the proposition that, in calculating notional tax, the lost income should not be treated as the top-slice of the employee's income. However, it is submitted that this reading is incorrect.

Although the case is somewhat inadequately reported, it is clear that Messrs Brass and Francis were in receipt of other income during the period for which the lost income should have been paid. Moreover, it was to be paid irrespective of other earnings. In such circumstances, the appropriate calculation is to treat the lost income as comprising the top slice of income which *would have been earned had the contract been performed*. In other words, the lost income *is*

19 [1956] 1 WLR 1219 at 1224–5.

treated as the top slice of income. Indeed, this is what Wynn-Parry J goes on to observe after the first sentence above cited.

The only exception to top slicing comes where the employee has replaced some of the lost income with some other source; perhaps he has taken a new job. In such a situation, this replacement income should be ignored in calculating the notional tax on the damages awarded.

Where the other income derives from disposable investments which might be sold, little regard should be had to it.[20]

Possible changes of rates of tax in the future must be ignored in so far as they are matters of pure speculation, and the tax for the future should normally be calculated on the rates of tax in existence at the present.[21] However, if there is a reasonable expectation that the rates of tax are likely to change, for example, as a result of budget proposals, this can be taken into account in assessing notional tax.[22]

11.9 Period of lost income

The second task is to calculate the period of lost income in respect of which damages are paid. As Wynn-Parry J observed in *Re Houghton Main Colliery*,[23] it would be wrong to assess notional tax on income which would have been earned over a period of years without taking that fact into account. If notional tax is assessed on the basis that the entirety of the income be brought into account in a single year, this will likely lead to it being over-assessed. Notional tax must be calculated whilst having regard to the rates of tax and allowances which would have been available to the claimant in each of the tax years from which income was lost.

11.10 Tax mitigation by employees

Regard can also properly be had to methods by which the employee could legitimately have reduced his tax liability.[24] However, the employee must

20 [1956] AC 185, per Lord Goddard 209: 'In cases where surtax is payable and the rate has been affected by private income the nature of that private income will be relevant. If it is a life annuity under a will or settlement it may well be expected to continue. If it is disposable investments which might be sold at any time or transferred to a child, less, perhaps little, regard should be had to it'. See, to the same effect, Pilcher J in *Beach v Reed Corrugated Cases Ltd* [1956] 2 All ER 652.
21 [1956] AC 185 per Lord Goddard at 209.
22 *Daniels v Jones* [1961] 1 WLR 1103, per Willmer LJ at 1114.
23 [1956] 1 WLR 1219 at 1225.
24 *Beach v Reed Corrugated Cases Ltd* [1956] 1 WLR 807.

satisfy the court that he would have availed himself of such methods had he remained in employment.[25] Given the increasing sophistication of the tax system, this factor is unlikely to be of much practical significance.

11.11 Deductible expenses

Finally, any deductible expenses[26] which would have been incurred in earning the lost income may be set against that income in calculating the notional tax figure.[27] However, generally those expenses will reduce the damages figure rather than the notional tax figure.[28]

11.12 National insurance contributions

The question of notional national insurance contributions was considered in *Cooper v Firth Brown Ltd*[29] where Lawton J held that the rule in *Gourley* required that there be a reduction in the damages award to account for the national insurance contributions which would have been deducted from the employee's pay packet – ie that there be a reduction for notional national insurance contributions.[30]

However, in the authors' opinion, national insurance contributions are, pertinently for present purposes, distinguishable from income tax.[31] As is explained elsewhere in this book,[32] the payment of employee's national insurance contributions entitle the relevant employee to draw certain 'contributory benefits' such as the Jobseeker's allowance, State Earnings Related Pension, etc. Without paying those contributions, he cannot draw those benefits. Therefore, unlike income tax, the employee derives a benefit from the continuing payment of employee's national insurance contributions. It appears to the authors that the employee will be under compensated if he suffers both:

(1) a reduction on account of notional national insurance contributions, and (2) a disentitlement to draw contributory benefits.

25 See [1956] 1 WLR 807 at 814.
26 See **4.47** et seq, Chapter 4.
27 Because these would have reduced his tax liability in the event that he had received the income the subject of the claim: see *Lyndale Fashion Manufacturers v Rich* [1973] STC 32, per Orr LJ 35a.
28 A point made by Orr LJ in *Lyndale*.
29 [1963] 1 WLR 418.
30 Ie Class 1 primary contributions. See **6.24**, Chapter 6 for calculation details.
31 Indeed, there is a suggestion to this effect in the decision of Sir John Donaldson MR in *Dews v National Coal Board* [1986] 3 WLR 227, 231H: 'The decision that national insurance contributions are to be treated similarly (to income tax)… is open to review in this court, although it was not challenged by either party.'
32 See Chapter 6.

In this light, the appropriate way to proceed may be either: (1) not to make any deduction on account of notional national insurance contributions; or (2) where appropriate, to make such a deduction but also compensate the employee for loss of contributory benefits. On balance, the authors prefer the second solution.

11.13 Other deductions and adjustments

Finally, it is often difficult for courts to determine the particular extent to which the tax treatment of damages should be influenced by the detailed position that the claimant did enjoy in the actual world or would have enjoyed in the hypothetical world had he received that which he seeks damages for not receiving.

In a non-employment income case (see *Deeny v Good Walker Ltd (No 4))*[33] the Judge was prepared to take account, at least in assessing the quantum of interest to be awarded on damages, of the 'fact' that although the claimants had suffered losses in their business (as Lloyd's names), they would be able to enjoy tax benefits as a result of those losses. Accordingly, and on a broad-brush approach, the interest due was reduced by 25%.

A similar problem arises if a claimant suffers a loss of earnings in a particular year of assessment such that the amount of PAYE tax suffered in that year on earnings before the event giving rise to the claim is seen to be excessive. Where a repayment of PAYE is then due to the claimant, should this be factored in when calculating damages for loss of income? In *Hartley v Sandholme Iron Co Ltd*[34] the Court said that such an adjustment should be made since the repayment of PAYE income tax was a direct consequence of the event giving rise to the claim, it could be accurately quantified and was not completely collateral. While this seems correct as a matter of principle (a receipt of damages replacing lost income should not be permitted without taking account of the benefit enjoyed by the claimant because of the lost income), it should, however, be noted that this course has not been universally adopted.[35]

33 [1995] STC 696, QB.
34 [1975] QB 600.
35 *Adda International Ltd v Curcio* [1976] ICR 407, *MBS Ltd v Calo* [1983] ICR 459: per the EAT: sums of tax rebates are likely to be small and should thus be ignored in ordinary cases before the tribunals.

Chapter 12

Expatriate Taxation

12.1 INTRODUCTION

This Chapter considers the position of two groups of employees. First, those foreign nationals who come to the UK to work for a period of time and, second, those UK nationals who go abroad to work for a period of time. The position in each case can, depending on the exact circumstances, be complex so that it is only possible – within the scope of this work – to set out the basic analysis. Reference will be made to the 'residence', 'ordinary residence' and 'domicile' of the employees in question; further explanation of the scope of these terms appears respectively in Chapter 2 at **2.10**, **2.13** and **2.15** above.

There is one further preliminary matter which needs to be addressed before looking at the detailed position of expatriate employees, namely the concept of 'double taxation relief'.

12.2 DOUBLE TAXATION RELIEF

12.3 Introduction

As will be appreciated from a basic understanding of the rules on residence it is possible, and not uncommon, for a person to be resident for tax purposes in two different countries. Thus a French national who comes to work in the UK for a period will be regarded by the French Revenue authorities as being resident in France for French tax purposes and by UK HMRC as being resident in the UK for UK tax purposes. Equally it is possible for a person who is resident in one country to have a source of income in another country – such as a German national who carries out certain employment activities in the UK (without becoming resident in the UK for tax purposes). In the absence of special relief both the French national and the German national would be liable to tax in two different countries (by reference to the source of the income and by reference to their residence) on the same amount of income – classic 'double taxation'. The same principles apply for UK nationals who either become resident for tax purposes in another country or who work in that country – thereby becoming entitled to income liable to tax in that country – without becoming resident there.

Whatever the position in the foreign country (and the tax treatment of foreign nationals in their 'home' country is, of course, a matter for local advice) the UK tax system deals with this potential double taxation in one of two ways. First, provision can be made by agreement (a 'Double Tax Agreement') between the UK and (say) France under which the employee can only be taxed in one country and not in the other or (occasionally) for there to be a cap on the amount of tax which can be suffered in one of the countries or for both countries to levy tax but for one to give relief for tax suffered in the other. Alternatively – and sometimes in addition – provision is made in the UK tax code for relief from UK tax to be given for foreign tax suffered (here) in France. These different methods of giving relief from double taxation are known colloquially as 'bilateral' (or 'Treaty') relief and 'unilateral' relief.

12.4 Bilateral relief

Double tax agreements are incorporated into UK law by section 2 of the Taxation (International and Other Provisions) Act 2010. Nearly all of the UK's agreements follow the basic form of the OECD Model Tax Agreement, with amendments to that model to suit individual cases. The UK has agreements in one form or another with over 100 other jurisdictions; the agreement in any particular case should be carefully considered since it cannot be assumed that a provision in one agreement is necessarily present in another.

It is, however, safe to generalise to some degree. Most agreements define the scope of the taxes covered, provide for specific definitions, set out the criteria under which a person is to be regarded as resident in one country or another for the purposes of the agreement, set out the criteria under which a person will be regarded as having sufficient connection to a country to attract taxation in that country (a 'permanent establishment' or 'fixed base') and then provide specifically for the tax treatment of particular types of income. As a general rule certain types of income – eg that from land – are so closely tied to the country in which the income has its source that the 'natural' place for it to be taxed is in that country. Conversely, some types of income are more 'naturally' taxed in the country of residence of the recipient of the income – eg royalties. Many agreements determine the appropriate treatment by categorising the income concerned subject to the over-riding principle (close to the hearts of all Revenue authorities) that income should be taxed in the country of residence of the recipient with due credit being given for tax suffered elsewhere on that income. Finally provision is usually made – in the fuller agreements – for elimination of residual double taxation, non-discrimination against foreign nationals, dispute resolution and exchange of information.

12.5 An example

To take the UK: France Double Tax Agreement as an example for the purposes of this Chapter, the Agreement provides that:

- the agreement covers UK income, corporation and capital gains tax and French income and corporation tax (Article 1);
- the 'UK' extends, for these purposes, to the UK sector of the North Sea, and 'France' extends to its overseas Departments (e g Martinique) (Article 2);
- a 'resident' of either contracting state is a person who is (broadly) treated as tax resident under the laws of that state; where a person would be regarded as resident in both states there is a 'tie-breaker' clause to confer sole tax residence on that person for the purposes of the agreement (Article 3);
- capital gains arising to a resident of one contracting state from the sale of land are taxable in the contracting state in which the land is situated; capital gains arising to a resident of one contracting state from the sale of any asset forming part of a permanent establishment/fixed base (broadly a business venture) are taxable in the contracting state in which the permanent establishment/fixed base is situated; all other capital gains are only taxable in the contracting state in which the vendor is resident (Article 13);
- income from professional activities is only taxable in the contracting state of the person's residence unless he or she has a 'fixed base' in the other contracting state (when the income referable to that fixed base can be taxed in that state) (Article 14);
- income from employment (save for special provision set out below) is only taxable in the contracting state of the person's residence unless that person derives income from employment in the other contracting state and spends more than 183 days there in any period of 12 months, is paid by an employer who is not resident in that contracting state and the remuneration is not borne by a permanent establishment/fixed base in that state (Article 15). In applying these provisions, HMRC take a fairly aggressive line in relation to identifying the person who is the true 'economic' employer of the person concerned. Thus, if an employee is nominally employed by a German company based in Berlin, he will not get the benefit of exemption from UK tax under the UK: Germany Double Tax Agreement if, in reality, his true employer – the person to whom he owes direct responsibilities – is a London based subsidiary of the German company;[1] and

1 See the Revenue's 'Tax Bulletin' of June 1995.

- special provision is made for directors (Article 16), artistes and athletes (Article 17), pensions (Article 18), government employees (Article 19), teachers (Article 20) and students (Article 21).

12.6 Unilateral relief

In the first instance it will usually be advantageous for the employee to claim bilateral relief from double taxation. If such relief is not available, the employee has two remaining courses open to him – first, to rely on the provisions for unilateral relief set out in the UK tax code at sections 8 to 18 of the Taxation (International and Other Provisions) Act 2010 or (as a last resort) to deduct the foreign tax suffered from the income liable to UK tax under section 18 of the Taxation (International and Other Provisions) Act 2010. The first course – unilateral relief – involves the UK resident recipient of income getting credit against his UK tax liability for the foreign tax suffered up to a maximum of the UK tax. Thus a person who suffers foreign tax at 60% can set that against his liability to UK tax at 40% up to a maximum of the 40% – the remaining 20% of tax credit is lost. In effect, under unilateral relief a person's overall tax bill will always equate to the highest tax liability (whether in the UK or abroad).

The second course – of taking credit under section 18 – is however not particularly attractive since the taxpayer is not getting credit for foreign tax suffered against UK *tax* but, instead, against UK *income* liable to tax.

Example 1

Tim has employment income from an Italian employment of £10,000 upon which he is liable to Italian tax at 35%; he is also liable to tax in the UK at 40%. Ignoring bilateral relief, unilateral relief allows Tim to compute his UK liability to tax – £4,000 (ignoring reliefs and allowances etc) – and then to deduct the Italian tax suffered (£3,500). The additional sum due in the UK is thus limited to £500; Tim's overall tax bill is £4,000. If no unilateral relief is available for some reason, Tim must deduct the Italian tax suffered (£3,500) from the income liable to UK tax (£10,000) leaving a net sum of £6,500 upon which UK tax at 40% (ie £2,600) is due. Tim's overall tax bill is thus £6,100 (ie £3,500 plus £2,600).

Although the issue of double tax relief is considered here before a detailed consideration of the UK tax position, in practice the better course – when analysing the 'overseas' element in any employment taxation situation – is to determine the position under the normal UK rules and then to consider whether any applicable double tax agreement or the provisions for unilateral relief alter the position.

12.7 COMING TO WORK IN THE UK – INCOME TAX

HMRC's policy in relation both to those who come to the UK and those who leave is set out in an invaluable booklet, HMRC6 (formerly IR20).

12.8 Triggering UK residence

HMRC6, although it does not itself have the force of law, is widely recognised to be an accurate description of the law in this area, leavened in appropriate cases by HMRC concession and policy. In most cases it is therefore of mere academic interest as to what the strict legal position is; what is more important is the approach HMRC will adopt – derived from HMRC6 – in any given situation. The first port of call in any discussion as to residence and non-residence for tax purposes should be this booklet. Note, however, the statutory residence test and associated revisions to the earnings legislation contained in the Finance Act 2013, effective from 6 April 2013, which superseded (but generally continues) the principles in much of the previous HMRC practice.

12.8A Statutory residence rules from 6 April 2013

The statutory rules that determine an employee's residence position from 6 April 2013[2] include conditions for individuals coming to work in the UK. The third of the five automatic UK residence tests in FA 2013, Sch 45 applies to an individual who works in the UK over a period of at least 365 days (part of which falls in the tax year) in which there are no significant breaks from UK work, and more than 75% of the days on which they do more than three hours' work are days on which more than three hours are worked in the UK, and there is at least one day that falls in the period and in the tax year on which they do three hours' work in the UK. This is described as full-time UK work in the HMRC Guidance Note (RDR3, paragraph 1.33).

A significant break from UK work is a continuous period of at least 31 days during which there is no day on which there is more than three hours of UK work, or on which the individual would have done more than three hours' UK work, but for being on annual, sick or parenting leave.[3] This means that residence by reason of full-time UK work can be avoided by a period of work abroad, but not by simply taking leave periods outside the UK.

If the individual has a relevant job on board a vehicle, aircraft or ship at any time in the tax year and at least six of their trips in the tax year as part of their job are cross-border trips that either begin in the UK, end in the UK or both, this test does not apply.[4] A relevant job is an employment with duties

2 FA 2013, s 218 and Sch 45.
3 FA 2013, Sch 45, para 29.
4 FA 2013, Sch 45, para 9(3).

personally performed (and required to be personally performed) on board a vehicle, aircraft or ship while it is travelling, on trips substantially all of which trips involve crossing an international border.[5]

The legislation splits the tax year on the individual's arrival in the UK to begin work.[6] Split year Case 5 (starting full-time work in the UK)[6] applies where an individual was non-resident in the UK in the previous tax year and a period of at least 365 days begins in the tax year on a day on which they do more than three hours' UK work. In the 365-day period they must work sufficient hours in the UK (a 35-hour average week), there must be no significant breaks from UK work, and more than 75% of the days on which they do more than three hours' work must be days on which more than three hours are worked in the UK. The individual must not have sufficient UK ties to be UK-resident before the day in the tax year on which the period begins. The maximum UK days and other connections in all parts of the sufficient UK ties test are applied to the period from the start of the tax year up to the date that the only home test is met (with the exception of the family tie, which can be met on a single day in the tax year). The maximum UK days are pro-rated to the number of whole months in the overseas period.

On leaving the UK for full-time employment overseas, split year Case 1[7] should apply to make the individual non-resident from the day after the date of their departure and their accompanying spouse or partner should be covered by split year Case 2.[8]

12.8B HMRC practice up to 5 April 2013

Up to 6 April 2013, there were four ways in which an employee who came to work in the UK could become UK-resident for tax purposes. These were: (1) the '183-day rule'; (2) the '91-day rule'; (3) the 'two-year rule'; and (4) the 'three-year rule'.

The '183-day rule'[9]

Where such a person spent at least 183 days in the UK in the tax year, they were UK-resident, otherwise they were non-resident. Thus, their residence position was determined on a year by year basis and any living accommodation in the UK for their use is ignored.[10] Days of UK arrival and departure and exceptional UK days could normally be ignored up to 5 April 2008 (under IR20) in

5 FA 2013, Sch 45, para 30.
6 FA 2013, Sch 45, para 48.
7 FA 2013, Sch 45 para 44.
8 FA 2013 Sch 45, para 45.
9 HMRC6, paragraph 7.5.
10 *Nicholas Ogden v Revenue and Customs Comrs* [2011] UKFTT 212 (TC) TC01077.

calculating the 183 days. However, from 6 April 2008 (under HMRC6) all days on which the individual is in the UK at midnight in the tax year must normally be counted, subject to an exception for certain in-transit days.

The '91-day rule'[11]

Where an individual made regular UK visits up to 5 April 2013 which totalled an average of 91 days or more in the UK in each UK tax year (calculated over a maximum total period of four tax years), up to 2012–13 the individual was UK-resident from the start of the fifth tax year, unless it was their intention to make these visits, in which case they were resident from an earlier tax year.

Example

Adam, an non-resident individual visits the UK for 90 days in the year ended 5 April 2008, 90 days in the year ended 5 April 2009, 75 days in the year ended 5 April 2010 and 115 days in the year ended 5 April 2011 (excluding days of UK arrival and departure before 6 April 2008 and three days in 2008–09 because of flu caught when in the UK).

The annual average UK days are:

$$\frac{90 + 90 + 75 + 115}{365 + 365 + 365 + 366} \times 365 = 92.44 \text{ days}$$

Adam is UK resident from 6 April 2011 onwards.

However, two points should be noted. First, an individual who intended to make regular UK visits totalling an average of 91 days or more a year and fulfilled that intention was UK-resident from the start of the tax year in which the individual formed that intention, where that decision was made before the start of the fifth tax year, provided those visits took place.

Second, an individual was likely to be treated as ordinarily resident from the beginning of the year in which the third anniversary of their UK arrival fell, if they remained in the UK beyond that anniversary,[12] because it was presumed that a settled pattern of life had been established in the UK.[13]

The 'two-year rule'[14]

An individual who comes to the UK for the purposes of employment for a period which exceeds two years will be resident from the date of his arrival

11 HMRC6, paragraph 7.5.
12 HMRC6, paragraph 7.7.4.
13 *Genovese v Revenue & Customs Comrs* [2009] STC (SCD) 373.
14 HMRC6, paragraph 7.2.]

in the UK. Such an individual would not be regarded as ordinarily resident in the UK unless he intended – on arrival – to stay for more than three years. In applying this three year test, HMRC's practice[15] is to contend that a person became 'ordinarily resident' on the earliest of the following dates: (a) the date of arrival in the UK if the employee has purchased accommodation in the UK or leased a property for a period of three years or more; (b) the beginning of the tax year in which such accommodation first becomes available; (c) the beginning of the tax year after the tax year straddling the third anniversary of arrival in the UK; or (d) the beginning of the tax year in which the taxpayer first has an intention to stay in the UK for more than three years from the original arrival date.

If an individual comes to the UK part way through a tax year, the year may by concession be split.[16] This means that income tax is calculated on the basis of the period the individual is living here rather than the whole of that tax year. This has the effect of splitting the tax year into resident and not resident periods for the purposes of calculating the tax due.

The 'three-year rule'[17]

An individual working in the UK up to 2012–13 could have become UK-resident throughout their UK stay by establishing a pattern of living that indicated more than temporary residence in the UK. An example was an individual who arrived in the UK for a period of three or more years, who was normally both resident and ordinarily resident from date of UK arrival to date of UK departure.

12.9 Employees resident in the UK

Employees who are resident in the United Kingdom (and up to 5 April 2013 ordinarily resident and domiciled in the United Kingdom) are chargeable to United Kingdom tax under section 15 of ITEPA 2003 on general earnings wherever received for duties performed in the United Kingdom. However, if the employee was resident but not ordinarily resident up to 5 April 2013, and was assessable on the remittance basis, and performed both UK and non-UK duties under a single contract of employment, the total earnings from the employment were apportioned and the earnings for the non-UK duties could be assessed under section 26 of ITEPA 2003 on the remittance basis.

Employees who are resident in the United Kingdom are also charged under section 26 of ITEPA 2003 on general earnings for duties performed outside

15 See Statement of Practice SP17/91.
16 Extra-Statutory Concession A11.
17 HMRC6, paragraph 7.2.

the United Kingdom but only to the extent that the earnings are remitted to the United Kingdom. The employee could be UK-domiciled or non-UK domiciled up to 5 April 2013, but the section is generally restricted to non-domiciles from 6 April 2013. If a remittance basis employee performs both UK and non-UK duties under a single contract of employment, the total earnings from the employment are apportioned and the earnings for the UK duties will be assessed under section 15. If the employee is not assessed under the remittance basis, all of the earnings from the contract are assessed under section 15.

12.10 Employees who were resident but not ordinarily resident up to 5 April 2013

Employees who were resident but not ordinarily resident in the United Kingdom were chargeable to United Kingdom tax under section15 of ITEPA 2003 on general earnings wherever received for duties performed in the United Kingdom. They are also chargeable under section 26 ITEPA 2003 on general earnings for duties performed outside the United Kingdom but only to the extent that the earnings are remitted to the United Kingdom.

Statement of Practice SP1/09 provided that – for employees who: were resident but not ordinarily resident in the United Kingdom; performed duties of a single employment both in and outside the United Kingdom, so that they were potentially chargeable under both sections 15 and 26 of ITEPA 2003 in respect of general earnings from that employment; and received part of their general earnings in the United Kingdom and part abroad – HMRC was prepared to accept that a charge under section 26 will arise only where the aggregate of general earnings remitted to the United Kingdom exceeds the amount chargeable under section 15 for that year; and to restrict the charge under section 26 to the excess of the aggregate over the charge under section 15.

12.11 Employees who are not UK-resident

The *general rule* is that foreign nationals who come to the UK to work without becoming either resident or ordinarily resident here are chargeable to tax in the UK upon employment income for the duties performed by them in the UK – section 27 of ITEPA 2003. Thus any employee who comes to the UK for even a few days in each tax year will be liable to tax in the UK on any employment income referable to the duties performed in the UK. However, this is subject to the main *exception* in section 39(1) and (2) of ITEPA 2003, namely that no charge arises where the duties performed in this country are 'merely incidental' to duties performed abroad.[18]

18 And for a discussion of the words 'merely incidental' see *Robson v Dixon* [1972] 1 WLR 1493.

Although not itself a determinative factor, it is the practice of HMRC to regard any duties performed in the UK for periods exceeding 90 days in a particular tax year as duties which cannot be regarded as 'merely incidental'.[19]

It is also relevant to ascertain whether the employee can take advantage of any double tax agreement so as to avoid a liability to tax in the UK. As is set out above, a person who is present in the UK for less than 183 days in the tax year and who is paid by a foreign employer in such circumstances that his remuneration is not connected with a permanent establishment/fixed base in the UK, will – in the case of many treaties – be exempt from UK income tax. In applying these provisions, HMRC take a fairly hard line specifically in relation to identifying the person who is the true 'economic' employer of the person concerned.

In applying the PAYE system, HMRC's policy – for administrative convenience consistent with its obligations to protect the revenue – is that those who are employed in the UK for short periods should be treated as follows:

(1) Any person who is in the UK for less than 30 days in a particular tax year has no reporting obligations and no obligation under the PAYE system.

(2) For a person who is in the UK for 31–60 days in a tax year, PAYE is not applied provided that the person submits a tax return covering worldwide income to a country with which the UK has a double tax agreement and the remuneration is paid by a non-UK resident employer and is not borne by a permanent establishment/fixed base of the employer in the UK.

(3) For a person who is in the UK for 61–90 days in a tax year, PAYE is not applied provided that the requirements in (2) above are met and the employee was not present in the UK in the proceeding tax year for more than 90 days and does not expect to be here in the following year for 90 days or more, the 90 day average rule is not broken looking at the four most recent years and the employee has no accommodation in the UK available on an ongoing basis.

(4) For persons in the UK for 91–183 days in a tax year, PAYE is not applied provided that the requirements in (2) and (3) are met and: (a) the employee can provide a statement from a foreign Revenue authority confirming his residence (or a copy of a tax return) or (in the case of US citizens) that the person is a US resident under the US: UK Double Tax Agreement, the employment income concerned relates to a period of 11 months or less spent in the UK and the period in the UK represents an interval between two periods of US residence; (b) the employee was not resident in the UK in the preceding tax year; nor (c) expects to be resident here in the following tax year.

19 See HMRC 6, paragraph 10.6.

12.12 Employment income of foreign nationals

In applying the various different tax treatments by reference to the residence and ordinary residence of foreign national employees, HMRC will bring into charge (on one basis or another) the full 'emoluments' of the employment. Although the scope of the term 'emoluments' has been considered in Chapter 4 above it is necessary to consider a number of specific items provided to employees, in the context of expatriate taxation:

(1) HMRC approval could be given up to 5 April 2006 for a pension scheme which corresponded to a scheme that would be approved by HMRC, provided the earnings of the employees were overseas earnings. Expatriate employees in receipt of UK tax relief for corresponding scheme contributions up to 5 April 2006 can continue to receive UK tax relief after that date. In addition, if the scheme meets such a test, the employee will be able to obtain a deduction for any additional contributions he makes to the scheme.

(2) Employment income is chargeable to tax in the UK under Chapter 2 of ITEPA 2003 by reference to the residence (and ordinary residence prior to 6 April 2013) of the employee concerned in the year in which the remuneration is earned. The employee's residence status in the year in which the emolument is received is not relevant for these purposes. Thus if a foreign national comes to work in the UK in a particular tax year and receives, during that year, a bonus or other form of deferred consideration for his services in a preceding tax year when he was not resident or ordinarily resident in the UK, no UK tax arises.

(3) If a person liable to tax on foreign emoluments within section 23(2) of ITEPA 2003 makes payments which 'correspond' to those which would have been tax deductible in a purely UK context, HMRC may allow the corresponding payments as a deduction in computing the amounts of the foreign emoluments.[20] A 'corresponding' payment would be, for example, a contribution to a foreign pension scheme, maintenance payments made under a foreign court order and some types of foreign interest payments.

(4) Special provision still remains for seafarers.[21] Any seafarers, whose duties of employment are performed wholly or partly outside the UK on terms whereby the duties are performed in the course of a qualifying period of at least 365 days,[22] will be liable to tax under Chapter 2 on the employment income from that employment attributable to that qualifying period and is subject to a deduction equal to the whole of that amount. In effect, the 100% deduction available to those persons whose foreign

20 ITEPA 2003, s 355(1) and (5).
21 ITEPA 2003, s 40(3)–(6).
22 ITEPA 2003, s 378(2).

employment activities lasted for a period of 365 days spent outside the UK is now limited to 'seafarers', defined as those in employment consisting of performance of duties on a ship or of such duties and others incidental to them. The term 'ship' does not include oil rigs.[23]

12.13 GOING TO WORK ABROAD

The position of an individual who is resident in the UK but who leaves the UK to work abroad for a period of time will now be considered. Again, the statutory residence test and associated revisions to the earnings legislation contained in the Finance Act 2013, effective from 6 April 2013, supersedes (but generally continues) the principles in much of the previous HMRC practice.

12.13A Statutory Residence rules from 6 April 2013

Schedule 45 to the Finance Act 2013 provides rules to determine an employee's residence position from 6 April 2013. At least three of the automatic overseas tests in Sch 45, paras 11–16 potentially apply to an employee and their accompanying spouse or partner who leave the UK for employment reasons (and make them non-resident), as follows:

(1) The individual was UK-resident in one or more of the three previous tax years, and is present in the UK for a maximum of 15 days (and does not die) in the current tax year.[24]

(2) The individual was UK-resident in none of the three previous tax years and is present in the UK for a maximum of 45 days in the current tax year.[25]

(3) The individual works sufficient hours overseas in the current tax year from which there are no significant breaks, and they are present in the UK in the current tax year for no more than 90 days (of which no more than 30 are days on which more than three hours' UK work is done).[26] This is described as full-time work overseas in HMRC guidance booklet RDR3 paragraph 1.5.

The work tests are applied to the tax year. If the individual has a relevant job on board a vehicle, aircraft or ship at any time in the tax year and at least six trips that they make in the tax year as part of that job are cross-border trips that either begin in the UK, end in the UK or both, this automatic UK test does

23 Exactly what is a ship and what is an oil rig is the subject of much debate: see most recently, in the context of NICs, *Oleochem (Scotland) Ltd v HMRC* [2009] UKSPC 731.

24 FA 2013, Sch 45, para 12.

25 FA 2013, Sch 45, para 13.

26 FA 2013, Sch 45, para 14.

not apply.[27] A relevant job is an employment with duties personally performed (and required to be personally performed) on board a vehicle, aircraft or ship while it is travelling, on trips all of which involve crossing an international border.[28]

Where one of the overseas employment non-residence tests applies, the tax years of UK departure and UK return can be split into periods of residence and non-residence under the following split year Cases in the legislation.[29]

12.13B Split year Case 1 (starting full-time work overseas)

Split year Case 1 applies to an individual who was resident in the previous tax year (whether or not it was a split year). In the tax year there must be a period that begins with a day on which they work for more than three hours overseas and continues to the end of the tax year, and which satisfies the overseas work criteria. The individual must be non-resident for the following tax year because they meet the automatic overseas test for full-time employment abroad.

The period satisfies the overseas work criteria if the individual works an average 35-hour week, there are no significant breaks from overseas work, there are no more than 90 annualised UK days after UK departure, of which no more than 30 annualised days are UK workdays (of three hours or more). Deemed UK midnight days are ignored for this purpose.

The normal annual maximum UK workdays are pro-rated to the number of whole months in the tax year after UK departure (or before UK arrival).

12.13C Split Year Case 2 (accompanying partner of individual starting full-time work overseas)

Split year Case 2 applies to an individual who was resident in the previous tax year and has a spouse, civil partner or the common law equivalent who meets the conditions of split-year Case 1 for either the current or the previous tax year.

The individual must move overseas to live together with their partner while they are working overseas and be non-resident for the following tax year, and have no UK home at any time, or have homes both in the UK and abroad but spend the greater part of their time living in the overseas home.[30]

27 FA 2013, Sch 45, para 14(4).
28 FA 2013, Sch 45, para 30.
29 FA 2013, Sch 45, paras 39–53.
30 The accompanying partner must not exceed the limit of UK days that applies to split year Case 1.

12.13D Split year Case 6 (ceasing full-time work overseas)

Split year Case 6 applies to an individual who was non-resident in the previous tax year because they met the third automatic residence test (full-time work abroad for the tax year), but was resident in the UK for one or more of the four tax years immediately preceding that year.

In the tax year there must be a period of one or more days that begins on the first day of the tax year and ends with a day on which the individual does more than three hours' work overseas and which satisfies the overseas work criteria. The individual must be resident for the following tax year.

The period satisfies the overseas work criteria if the individual works an average 35-hour week, there are no significant breaks from overseas work, and there are no more than 90 annualised UK days after UK departure, of which no more than 30 annualised days are UK workdays (of three hours or more). Deemed UK midnight days are ignored for this purpose.

The normal annual maximum and UK workdays are pro-rated to the number of whole months in the tax year after UK departure or before UK return.

12.13E Split Year Case 7 (accompanying partner of individual ceasing full-time work overseas)

Split year Case 7 applies to an individual who was non-resident in the previous tax year and has a spouse, civil partner or the common law equivalent who meets the conditions of split-year Case 6 for either the current or the previous tax year.

The individual must move to the UK to live together with their partner and be UK-resident for the following tax year. The accompanying partner's UK arrival day is the later of the day on which they move to join their partner in the UK and the first day of the UK part of their partner's Case 6 split tax year of UK arrival. In the part of the tax year before their deemed UK arrival day, the accompanying partner must either have no UK home at any time, or have homes both in the UK and abroad but spend the greater part of their time living in the overseas home.[31]

12.14 Breaking the tie with the UK up to 5 April 2013

Up until 5 April 2013, HMRC6 provided that an employee who: (a) worked full-time abroad under a contract of employment; (b) where all the duties of the

31 The accompanying partner must not exceed the limit for UK days that applies to split-year Case 6, in the part of the tax year before their UK arrival.

employment are in fact performed abroad (save for any duties he performs here which are 'incidental' to his duties abroad); and (c) that employment lasted for at least one complete tax year; and (4) visits to the UK do not break the 183 days rule or the 91 days rule in each tax year; then (e) he or she was usually regarded by HMRC as neither resident nor ordinarily resident in the UK from the day following departure until the day preceding return at the termination of the employment.[32] Such rules applied equally to those going abroad to carry on a trade, profession or vocation and to accompanying spouses.[33]

There is no definition of what constitutes 'full time' employment for these purposes. HMRC has however given some guidance.[34] 'Full-time' must be construed in accordance with its ordinary meaning, depending always on the particular facts of each case. If the person's employment or business activity involves a regular pattern of hours, it will be regarded as full-time if the hours he or she works each week equate to a typical UK working week (now, presumably, 35 hours). If the person's job or business activity has no regular pattern and no fixed number of working hours or days, HMRC will look at the nature of the job in light of the prevailing conditions and practices in that job in that place and then determine whether the job is full-time.

It was held by Lord Justice Moses in the *Davies v HMRC*[35] judicial review hearing that if an individual was to have 'left' the country for the purposes of paragraph 2.2, there was no need for there to be a distinct break.[36] This is clearly beneficial to the taxpayer. It also follows from this case that the individual must leave before the relevant tax year commences. The requirement to be absent for a whole tax year will not be met if the individual leaves part way through the year and then remains away for the entirety of a subsequent tax year.[37]

It is however advisable to establish the intended period of overseas employment from the outset. Although intentions may change over time (either shortening or lengthening the overseas stay) it is helpful to have written proof (letter of employment, amendment of employment contract or new, fixed term, contract of employment) at the time of departure.

The meaning of this phrase 'incidental' was considered in the case of *Robson v Dixon*.[38] The taxpayer was a pilot. He worked for a Dutch airline and flights were mostly from Amsterdam to North and South America. He spent around

32 HMRC 6, paragraph 2.1.
33 Extra Statutory Concession A78.
34 HMRC 6 (paragraph 8.5), as amplified in the Revenue's own Tax Bulletin (February 1993, p 57).
35 [2010] EWCA Civ 83.
36 [2010] EWCA Civ 83 at para 33.
37 [2010] EWCA Civ 83 at para 33.
38 48 TC 527.

60 days in the UK. In addition, he spent some time in the UK when the planes he flew made a stopover in London. The question arose as to whether the duties performed in the UK were merely incidental. It was held by Pennycuick VC that the test of whether duties were incidental was a qualitative rather than quantitative one. In the present case, there was no qualitative difference between what the individual performed in the UK and what he performed outside it. So, his duties in the UK were held not to be merely incidental. Pennycuick VC does allow the taxpayer's appeal with respect to one year in which the individual's duties in the UK were brief and unexpected (he had to land his plane due to fog).[39] The judge's comments indicate that a duty which is either performed in the UK by way of derogation from routine or a one-off performance of a duty could be 'merely incidental'.

HMRC's approach is that if the work the person does in the UK is of the same kind as, or of similar importance to, the work that he does abroad, it will not be regarded as merely incidental unless there is clear evidence that it is ancillary or subordinate to the work abroad.[40] While there is some flexibility in applying this test,[41] attendance in the UK for the purposes of any serious business activities will be regarded as more than merely 'incidental'.

Finally, under the provisions of self-assessment, individuals are required to confirm their residence status on their tax return. HMRC do not now provide formal residence rulings but will instead give guidance on residence in limited circumstances.[42] It is, however, still possible, when leaving the UK, to get a *de facto* residence ruling by completing the Form P85. This form allows repayment claims to be made by a person departing the UK and allows HMRC to issue a 'no tax' coding to a person who continues to be paid in the UK.

Example

Lisle's employer sent him to work in Germany for 16 months. He left the UK on 1 April 2011 and returned on 30 July 2012, spending Christmas 2011 and Easter 2012 in the UK. These visits were for 8 days and 10 days respectively (counting arrival days but ignoring departure days).

Lisle was not resident and not ordinarily resident in the UK from 2 April 2011 to 29 July 2012. However, if he had left the UK on 6 April 2011 he would not have met the conditions above and would have remained resident and ordinarily resident (because his absence would not have covered a complete tax year).

---

39 48 TC 527 at 535.
40 See HMRC 6, paragraph 10.6 et seq.
41 See the Revenue's Tax Bulletin, February 1993, p 57.
42 See the Revenue's Tax Bulletin, June 1997, pp 425–427.

12.15 Employment income

An employee who is resident outside the UK is outside the scope of income tax on all emoluments paid in respect of duties performed by him abroad. Emoluments which are paid in respect of duties performed in the UK other than 'incidental duties' are chargeable to tax under ITEPA 2003, unless an exemption is available under an applicable double tax treaty. In determining whether particular emoluments are payable for 'UK duties' or 'non-UK duties' it is helpful (so as to minimise, if not avoid, later disputes) if the employee has separate employment contracts. If this is not the case, HMRC are entitled to calculate the taxable amount by apportioning the total emoluments in the tax year according to the number of days spent in the UK. If, however, the importance and (in a loose sense) the 'value' of the work performed in the UK is greater than that performed abroad, HMRC will instead assess a greater proportion of the emoluments as attributable to the UK duties. In such circumstances the employee can accept the apportionment or challenge the assessment on the basis that HMRC has misunderstood the particular facts.

Should the employee incur costs of moving to take up the employment abroad and which are reimbursed (as expenses) by the employer, it is possible that such expenses will be charged to tax. The position in a purely UK context is now set out in Chapter 8 (Benefits in Kind) above.[43] If an individual is reimbursed for the expense of moving to a new employment overseas it is arguable that such expenses are attributable to the employment and are not therefore taxable in the UK. This is not however always accepted by HMRC. To ensure that this is the treatment of such expenses the employee should insist that he is reimbursed by the new employer (and not the 'old' one if members of the same organisation) and paid overseas once he has left the UK. Should he be paid in the UK it is open to the employee to seek HMRC's agreement that the payment is in respect of the new overseas employment and thus is not liable to UK tax (e g PAYE).

12.16 Working abroad – the expenses position

A UK resident (and ordinarily resident prior to 6 April 2013) employee who performs the duties of his or her employment wholly outside the UK and who incurs the costs of going abroad at the start of the employment and of coming back to the UK on its end is entitled to a tax deduction for the expenses on the basis that they are necessarily incurred in the performance of such duties.[44] If travel is only partly for such directly work-related purposes, relief is only available in respect of that part.[45] Thus whether the employer meets the cost, or the employee does and is reimbursed, no tax liability arises. The same is

43 At **8.4** (Removal and Relocation Packages).
44 ITEPA 2003, s 341.
45 ITEPA 2003, s 341(5).

true if the employment abroad involves the expense of board and lodging for the employee outside the UK. Equally, if board and lodging is only partly for such a work-related purpose, relief is allowed only for that specific part.[46] If an individual has more than one employment and the duties of one or more of them are performed wholly or partly overseas, he or she gets the same tax treatment for costs of travelling between the employments where either or both places are outside the UK since the relief is attributed to the destination employment.[47] Similarly, if an employee performs the duties of an employment partly outside the UK, payment or reimbursement by the employer of the costs of travelling to and from those duties performed outside the UK will not be taxed as long as each visit to the UK comes after carrying out duties that can only be performed outside the UK, followed by a return trip (out of the UK) to continue the performance of such duties.[48]

Where an individual is employed outside the UK for a continuous period of 60 days or more, the payment or reimbursement by the employer of travelling expenses incurred by the employee's spouse (or children under 18) at the beginning of, or during, that period in visiting the employee will not be charged to tax in his hands. The relief is limited to no more than two journeys in each direction by the same person in any one tax year and does not extend to an[49] accommodation or subsistence expenses of the spouse or children paid for or reimbursed by the employer.

12.17 Termination payments

The basic position on termination is set out in Chapter 10 above. Relevantly in an overseas context, any lump sum payment made on the termination of an employment which is otherwise taxable under section 401 of ITEPA 2003 will entirely escape tax if the terms of section 413(1) are satisfied. Thus relief will be available if the period of employment includes 'foreign service' which amounts to: (a) three-quarters of the whole period of service; or (b) where service has exceeded ten years, the whole of the last ten years; or (c) where service has exceeded 20 years, one-half of that period including any ten of the last 20 years. 'Foreign service' is defined, relevantly, in two ways[50]. First, as employment, the earnings from which are not relevant earnings, or second, employment income taxable as such but with the benefit of the 100% seafarers deduction. If these requirements are met, relief is available in full. If not, the exempt amount, after any other deductions, will be determined by looking at the proportion of foreign service to total service.[51]

46 ITEPA 2003, s 369(1), (2).
47 ITEPA 2003, s 342(1)–(7).
48 ITEPA 2003, s 370(3)–(5).
49 ITEPA 2003, s 371(3)–(7).
50 ITEPA 2003, s 413(2).
51 ITEPA 2003, s 414.

Finally, in this context it should be noted that section 401 is a charging provision in its own right. Thus, as confirmed in *Nichols v Gibson*,[52] a payment can be taxable under section 148 (now 401) without falling into what were (at the time of that case) one of the three Cases of Schedule E. The effect of this is that a termination payment paid to an employee can be taxable in the UK even where he or she has not been resident (or ordinarily resident prior to 6 April 2013) in the UK or some part of the duties of the employment have been performed in the UK. While most people will be excluded from the charge as a result of having 'foreign service' (under section 413 of ITEPA 2003) this may not always be the case. It follows from this that if an employee has spent any significant period working in the UK he or she may need to continue working abroad for up to ten years before being sure of escaping UK tax liability on any termination payment received at the end of the employment.

12.18 UK residents working overseas

Individuals who work outside the UK for short periods but continue to be resident (and ordinarily resident up to 6 April 2013) in the UK from year to year also continue (not surprisingly) to be chargeable to tax on their total worldwide employment income under Chapter 2 of ITEPA 2003.

12.19 THE CAPITAL GAINS TAX POSITION

The capital gains tax treatment of those persons who arrive in, or leave, the UK is complex and outside the scope of this work.

It should, however, be noted that considerable changes were made in the Finance Act 1998, amending the normal rules on 'residence' and 'non- residence'. This should be borne in mind when employees are leaving to work abroad and then returning to the UK. The present position can be stated shortly.

Prior to 1998–99 individuals who were neither resident nor ordinarily resident in the UK were (with immaterial – for these purposes – exceptions) outside the scope of capital gains tax. 'Residence' and 'ordinary residence' were interpreted in the same way as for income tax purposes. A person who was treated as neither resident nor ordinarily resident in the UK from the date of his departure from the UK was not normally changed to tax on gains accruing to him from disposals made after the date of his departure.[53] However, Concession D2 made it clear that an individual who left the UK permanently (or for a fixed period) remained chargeable to capital gains tax in the year of departure in

52 [1996] STC 1008.
53 Revenue ESC D2, in its unamended – pre 16/3/1998 – form.

respect of any gains made on the disposal of assets of a business carried on in the UK through a branch or agency. Similarly, gains which were made in the tax year of return to the UK, whether before or after the date of return, were taxable if the individual had been abroad for less than three years. Where however, a person had neither been resident nor ordinarily resident in the UK in the three years prior to returning to the UK, he was only taxed on gains realised after the return to the UK.

The position now is radically different. By section 10A of the Taxation of Chargeable Gains Act 1992 (TCGA 1992) all gains made by an individual during a period of temporary non-residence in the UK are changed to tax in the UK in the year of return. The period of temporary non-residence is defined in Part 4 of Schedule 45 to the FA 2013 as a period of five complete tax years or less. As will be appreciated, this represents a significant extension of the ambit of UK taxation. An individual working or studying abroad will thus have to stay away from the UK for five full tax years (ie be resident somewhere else) for gains made on the sale of assets to escape capital gains tax. Employees looking to realise gains (eg on shares) whilst abroad will now need to contemplate a considerable stay out of the UK. Prior to 2005–06 this could only be avoided if the employee concerned could rely on the provisions of a suitable double tax treaty to override the new five year rule[54] although this escape route has also now been removed.

The most important 'capital' asset for most employees is their home (otherwise known to HMRC as the 'principal private residence').[55] Notwithstanding the changes made to the rules on residence in 1998, the gain realised on the disposal of an individual's principal private residence is (in general) exempt from capital gains tax. However for both those employed in the UK and those employed abroad the exemption depends upon the period of occupation by the owner. If a home is occupied by the owner throughout the period of ownership, full exemption is available. If not (relevantly for those working abroad) some periods of absence during which the owner did not live in the house are ignored. These include all periods during which the owner worked full-time in an employment or office wholly outside the UK provided that, both before and after those periods, it was the owner's only or main residence and he had no other residence eligible for exemption – eg a holiday home. The last three years of ownership are regarded as a period of owner-occupation in any event.[55a] In addition, the exemption can continue where, after a period of absence, a person does not return to live in the principal residence because his employment contract requires him to work elsewhere.[56] Periods of absence are

54 See TCGA 1992 s 10A(10).
55 See TCGA 1992, s 223.
55a There is a proposal in the Finance Bill 2014 to cut this period to 18 months.
56 Revenue ESC D4.

also ignored by HMRC where a husband and wife are living together[57] and the property is owned by one spouse but the conditions are satisfied by the other.[58]

12.20 ISSUES FOR EMPLOYERS

Many of the most salient points for employers where there is an 'overseas' element (whether coming to the UK or going abroad) will be apparent from the preceding paragraphs of this Chapter. For simplicity these are gathered together here in abbreviated form. For many employers these issues fall into three main categories: determining the status of the employee, analysing the correct treatment of the employment income, and complying with statutory obligations.

12.21 Status of the employee

The first requirement for employers – in any employment situation – is to determine at what point the employee moves into or out of the scope of the UK tax net. For both income tax and capital gains purposes this involves determining questions of 'residence' (and 'ordinary residence' prior to 6 April 2013) – see Chapter 2 above. It may also be necessary to determine whether any change in the employment position could cause a change in an employee's domicile (see Chapter 2). Such questions must be answered – in the first place – by reference to the general legal tests in the UK and abroad. Once this has been done, the double tax position must be verified to see if any relevant double tax treaty (and, specifically the 'tie breaker' clause in Article 4 of many treaties) or double tax relief makes any difference to the position as a matter of general law.

Employers may need to bear in mind the importance of the 1998 and 2005 changes made to the capital gains tax residence rules; employees will have to be reminded that leaving the UK for any period short of five complete tax years is insufficient to break the ties of UK tax liability. Both for income tax and capital gains tax purposes it is important to determine (as far as possible) how long an individual is to be in, or away from, the UK.

12.22 Duties and employment income

Having analysed the status of the employee, it is then necessary to analyse the status of the income received by the employee. Whether employment income is taxable under Chapter 2 of ITEPA 2003 will depend on two further issues –

57 As to which see ITA 2007, s 1011.
58 Revenue ESC D3.

where the duties of the employment are performed (or are to be performed) and where the employee is paid (or is to be paid). This can often turn on whether the employee has (or is to have) more than one contract of employment. For example a separate contract of employment for duties performed overseas will help:

- to establish that the employee is leaving for more than a temporary period abroad;
- to delineate duties which might be regarded as more than merely 'incidental';
- to separate 'UK duties' from 'non-UK duties'; and
- to establish the '100% deduction', now only available to 'seafarers'.

12.23 Compliance

The third (and crucially the main) area of concern specific to employers is the question of tax compliance in situations with an overseas element. This will invariably depend on the answers to the questions identified in the two preceding categories of issues. Although the operation of the PAYE system is specifically considered in Chapter 5 above, employers should specifically bear in mind that:

(1) The collection of tax under the PAYE system has a territorial limit[59] so that no deduction need be made from employment income paid by an employer who has no 'trading presence' in the UK.

(2) Employees who work in and out of the UK during a year can be regarded (by agreement with HMRC) as falling within the PAYE system up to a specified amount or proportion of earnings.[60]

(3) In the case of a payment by an 'intermediary' (eg a non-resident company) by or on behalf of a UK resident employer, there is a PAYE liability on the UK resident unless the non-resident intermediary itself operates the PAYE system.[61]

(4) An employee who is seconded by his employer to work for another person may be paid by his normal employer or an intermediary for his employer (or indeed an intermediary for that other person) outside the scope of PAYE. In such circumstances for PAYE purposes it is the other person (the secondment employer) who is treated as having made the payment.[62]

59 See **5.9** in Chapter 5.
60 ITEPA 2003, s 690(1)–(9).
61 ITEPA 2003, ss 687, 688, 710.
62 ITEPA 2003, ss 689 and 691.

12.24 THE NATIONAL INSURANCE POSITION

The basic structure of the national insurance contribution system and, in particular the territorial scope of what is, in truth a 'tax', is set out in Chapter 6 above.

The 'overseas' element of the operation of the UK national insurance position and its inter-relationship with the social security systems of other countries, inside and outside the EU, is incapable of sensible summary or abridgement and readers are directed to specialist works on the subject.

Two points should, however, be noted. First, it is *vital* to obtain the most up-to-date information since the NIC position changes frequently; discovering that changes have been made can be difficult but a good starting point is the HMRC website (www.hmrc.gov.uk). Second, it should be borne in mind that the requirements to pay national insurance contributions can be looked at in two ways: (1) is the employee *obliged* to pay? (2) Is the employee *entitled* to pay? Some employees may wish to (or even should) continue paying contributions voluntarily even when working outside the UK so as to preserve entitlement to state benefits.

12.25 Non-domiciled persons and the remittance basis

12.26 The basic structure of income tax

Persons who are resident in the UK pay income tax, subject to reliefs and exemptions, on all of their income, wherever it arises in the world and this is known, colloquially, as the arising basis. Certain persons who are not domiciled[63] in the UK, however, benefit from a more beneficial treatment under which they pay tax in the UK on income which arises abroad (so that it does not have a UK source) to the extent that the income is remitted to the UK. Similar rules apply to capital gains which arise abroad. This is known, colloquially, as the remittance basis. Prior to 6 April 2008, and the effective date of the Finance Act 2008, this remittance basis was a very favourable basis upon which to pay tax in the UK and made the UK attractive for overseas visitors and, even, longer term overseas residents.

12.27 The new regime – outline[64]

12.28 Claiming the benefit of the remittance basis

With effect from 6 April 2008, the Finance Act 2008 now requires individuals who are non-UK domiciled (or prior to 6 April 2013, not ordinarily resident in

63 The basic concepts of residence and domicile are dealt with at Chapter 2 above.
64 See FA 2008, Schs 7, 25 and, now, ITA 2007, ss 809A et seq.

the UK) to make a claim, by way of entry on their tax return, for the remittance basis to apply for the particular tax year concerned. It is therefore open to an individual to claim in one year and not in the next; thus in year 2013–14 the remittance basis may apply, in 2014–15 the arising basis and then, again, in 2015–16 the remittance basis.

Guidance as to the new remittance basis and answers to frequently asked questions can be found in HMRC6 and on the HMRC website at www.hmrc.gov.uk/cnr/res-dom-faqs.htm

12.29 The £30,000 'fee'

An individual who wishes to claim the benefit of the remittance basis and who is over the age of 17 in the relevant tax year and has been UK resident[65] in at least seven of the last nine immediately preceding tax years, is required, when claiming the benefit of the new basis, to identify an amount of unremitted foreign income and gains which will be subject to an additional charge.[66] The unremitted income and gains identified by the taxpayer must be part (or all) of the individual's foreign income and gains for the tax year concerned (see the Income Tax Act 2007 (ITA 2007), section 809C) and must be such that the 'relevant tax increase' does not exceed, currently, £30,000. The 'relevant tax increase' is effectively the tax charge arising on the amount of income or gains identified; the amount must therefore be such that, after reliefs and deductions, UK tax of £30,000 is paid. In effect, therefore, there is a 'fee' or charge for the application of the remittance basis of, currently, £30,000. Foreign income and gains, for these purposes, are the sums of foreign employment income, foreign investment income and capital gains which arose to the individual in the tax year concerned.

The effect of identifying such foreign income or gains is that tax is then charged on the income or gains concerned on the arising basis subject to all of the rules relating to other income and gains taxed on that basis.

It is intended that such tax will also be available for credit in other jurisdictions against foreign tax suffered there whether pursuant to double tax treaties between such jurisdictions and the UK or by way of unilateral relief abroad. There remains, however, some doubt as to whether this is universally true since some jurisdictions do not give credit for what is, in substance, a 'voluntary' tax paid in (here) the UK. Potential problems arise in relation to tax in the USA in this regard.

65 Partial years of residence in the UK count for these purposes as do years in which the individual is resident in the UK and also 'Treaty' resident in another country: see HMRC frequently asked questions at www.hmrc.gov.uk/cnr/res-dom-faqs.htm.

66 ITA 2007, ss 809C(1), (2), 809H(2).

In consequence of the arising basis applying to this slice of identified income or gains, such sums can be remitted to the UK without further charge under the remittance basis.

12.30 Failure to identify income or gains

If an individual does not nominate the 'right' amount of income and gains so as to give rise to tax of at least £30,000, then his tax bill is increased accordingly. This means that where the relevant tax increase would otherwise be less than £30,000, the individual is treated by section 809H(4) of ITA 2007 as if he had identified enough income (and not gains) so as to give rise to a £30,000 tax charge. In effect, there is a deemed charge, that charge being to income tax and not capital gains tax.

Example 3

Bruce, a US domiciled but UK resident employee who is liable to tax at 40%, nominates £50,000 of bank interest under section 809H(2), giving a tax increase of £20,000. As this falls short of the £30,000 'fee', section 809H(4) applies so as to produce further nominated income of £25,000 and a further charge to tax of £10,000.[67]

12.31 Small amounts of unremitted income and gains

If an individual has less than £2,000 of unremitted foreign income and gains he can use the remittance basis without making a claim and thus without paying the £30,000 'fee' (see section 809D of ITA 2007). Similarly, if an individual has no UK sourced income or gains in a tax year and no foreign income or gains (of this year or earlier years) are remitted to the UK in the year and the individual has been resident in the UK for not more than six out of the nine immediately preceding tax years, or he was under 18 throughout that year, then, again, the remittance basis applies automatically without a claim (see section 809E).

12.32 The application of the remittance basis

As and when the remittance basis applies the relevant individual is taxed on foreign sourced income (and, in some cases, gains) to the extent that the sums

67 Double tax relief is only due on the income or gains actually nominated under s 809H(2), here income of £50,000 and tax of £20,000 of income tax. If and when the additional income of £25,000 is remitted to the UK, it is taxed on remittance.

concerned (or sums representing them) are received or enjoyed in the UK. What constitutes remittance to the UK is addressed below.

12.33 Personal allowances etc

Further differences relate to the allowances and exemptions available to such persons. In the first category of case (where an individual has to claim the remittance basis and does so), he is then not entitled in that tax year to the personal allowance, blind person's allowance, tax reductions for married couples and civil partners and the annual exempt amount for capital gains tax purposes (section 809G). No such rules operate in the second category of case (where the remittance basis applies without a claim being made – eg in the case of minors). In the third category of case (where the remittance basis could be claimed but is not in a particular year), the individual is taxed in the usual way on the arising basis and such allowances are available in full.

Example

A 22 year-old UK-resident, but non-UK domiciled, individual has £20,000 of earnings under a non-UK employment contract with a non-resident company, wholly for non-UK duties in 2013–14. The earnings are on deposit with a non-UK bank and are his only foreign income or gains for the years 2008–09 onwards. The employee has been UK-resident since 2008-9 and his only UK income for 2013–14 is taxed investment income of £50. If the individual remits all but £1,999 of his 2013–14 non-UK earnings to the UK by 5 April 2014, the remittance basis will apply automatically for 2013–14 under ITA 2007, s 809D. The remitted income of £18,001 will be taxable in the UK under ITEPA 2003, s 22, but the individual can set his personal allowance against it. Alternatively, if the individual does not remit any foreign earnings to the UK in 2013–14, the remittance basis will apply automatically for 2013–14 under ITA 2007 s 809E. The foreign earnings will be taxable if they are ever remitted to the UK (under ITEPA 2003, s 22). The individual can set his personal allowance against his UK taxed investment income.

12.34 What sums are remitted?

Given that the individual must nominate foreign income and gains so as to enjoy the benefit of the remittance basis, what happens when he later remits an amount of income (say) from that nominated income (upon which he has, in effect, paid UK tax) before other unremitted foreign income? In such a case the regime makes provision for rules to determine the order in which sums are deemed to be remitted to the UK. Perhaps not surprisingly, in such a case it is the unremitted income (which is taxable on receipt in the UK) which is deemed to be remitted first so leaving 'offshore' (until last) the income on which UK tax has already been paid (sections 809I, 809J).

Under the terms of section 809J, it is necessary to identify sums of income by reference to a number of prescribed steps:

- Step 1: Find the relevant amount which is the total of the individual's nominated income and gains (in the relevant year and earlier years), and his remittance basis income and gains (in the year and earlier years) remitted to the UK in the relevant tax year.
- Step 2: Find the amount of foreign income and gains for the year, other than the amount nominated under s 809C, in each of a number of different categories of foreign income and gains (eg relevant foreign earnings). If the remittance basis does not apply, treat this sum as zero and move to step 6.
- Step 3: Find the earliest of the listed types of income for which the amount determined under Step 2 is not nil. If that amount does not exceed the relevant amount, treat the individual as having remitted the income and gains within that paragraph for that tax year. Otherwise, treat the individual as having remitted the relevant proportion of each kind of income and gains within that paragraph, the relevant proportion being the relevant amount divided by the amount determined under Step 2 for that paragraph.[68]
- Step 4: Reduce the relevant amount by the amount taken into account under Step 3.
- Step 5: If this reduced relevant amount is not nil, start again at Step 3 but this time at the next earliest paragraph in the list for which the amount determined under Step 2 is not nil.
- Step 6: If the relevant amount as reduced is not nil once Steps 3–5 have been undertaken for all paragraphs for which the amount determined under Step 2 is not nil, start again at Step 2, but read the reference to foreign income and gains for the relevant tax year as those relating to the appropriate tax year which had not been remitted by the beginning of the relevant tax year. The appropriate tax year is the latest tax year which is before the last tax year for which Step 2 has been undertaken and which is a tax year for which the remittance basis applies.

68 It is also necessary to deal with foreign tax suffered on the income concerned. For example, imagine an individual who had £1,000 of foreign dividends from which the source country deducted £100 withholding tax and £1,000 of dividends from another country from which £200 of withholding tax had been deducted. If the individual remits £1,000 it is treated as £500 less £50 of the first dividend, plus £500 less £100 of the second dividend, giving a total of £1,000 less £150 of withholding tax.

12.35 The meaning of remitted

An individual's income or chargeable gains are remitted to the UK if both conditions A and B are met or if either condition C or D is met (section 809L of ITA 2007).

Condition A is that money or other property is brought to, or received or used in, the UK by, or for the benefit of, a relevant person, or a service is provided in the UK to or for the benefit of a *relevant person* (section 809L(2)).

Condition B is that either:

(a) the property, service or consideration for the service is, wholly or in part, the income or chargeable gains;

(b) the property, service or consideration derives, wholly or in part and directly or indirectly, from the income or chargeable gains, and in the case of property or consideration, is property of, or consideration given to, the *relevant person*;

(c) the income or chargeable gains are used outside the UK, directly or indirectly, in respect of a *relevant debt*; or

(d) anything deriving, wholly or in part and directly or indirectly, from the income or chargeable gains is used in respect of a *relevant debt* (section 809L(3)).

Condition C is that *qualifying property* of a *gift recipient*:

(a) is brought to, or received or used in, the UK and is enjoyed by a *relevant person*;

(b) is consideration for a service that is enjoyed in the UK by a *relevant person*; or

(c) is used outside the UK, directly or indirectly, in respect of a *relevant debt* (section 809L(4)).

This condition ensures that it is not possible to escape the effect of conditions A and B by making a gift to a person for that person to bring the subject-matter of the gift to the UK.

Condition D is that property of a person other than a *relevant person*, apart from *qualifying property* of a *gift recipient*:

(a) is brought to, or received or used in, the UK and is enjoyed by a *relevant person*;

(b) is consideration for a service that is enjoyed in the UK by a *relevant person*; or

(c) is used outside the UK, directly or indirectly, in respect of a *relevant debt*,

in circumstances where there is a *connected operation* (section 809L(5)).

For the purposes of these rules, the following definitions apply:

A *relevant person* is (section 809M):

(a) the individual;

(b) the individual's husband or wife;

(c) the individual's civil partner;

(d) a child or grandchild of a person falling with any of paragraphs (a)–(b), if the child or grandchild has not reached the age of 18;

(e) a close company in which a person falling within any other paragraph in this list is a participator;

(f) a company in which any other person falling within this list is a participator and which would be a close company if it were resident in the UK;

(g) the trustees of a settlement of which any person falling within this list is a beneficiary; or

(h) a body connected with such a settlement.

For these purposes, a man and woman living together as husband and wife are treated as if they were husband and wife and two people of the same sex living together as civil partners are treated as if they were civil partners of each other (section 809M(3)).

Qualifying property (see section 809N(7)) in relation to a gift is the property which is the subject matter of the gift, anything that derives, wholly or in part and directly or indirectly, from that property or any other property that is dealt with as described in Condition C (a)–(c) by virtue of an operation relating to the gift of the property to the gift recipient, or with a view to enabling the gift to be made. These references to 'derived' property include property that does not belong to the individual but which he can benefit from by virtue of an interest, right or arrangement.

A *gift recipient* (section 809N(2)) is a person, other than a *relevant person*, to whom the individual makes a gift of money or other property that is income or chargeable gains of the individual, or derives, wholly or in part and directly or indirectly, from such income or gains. Whether a person is a relevant person is determined at the time the gift was made; if the person to whom the gift was made subsequently becomes a relevant person they cease to be a gift recipient (section 809N(3), (4)).

A gift is a disposal for no consideration or for consideration less than the full consideration in money or money's worth that would be given if the disposal were a bargain made at arm's length. Where the gift is a transfer for a consideration less than market value, the gift is the difference between the market value and the actual consideration. The notion of a gift includes the case where the individual retains an interest in the property or an entitlement to benefit from it.

Relevant debt (section 809L(7)) means a debt that relates, wholly or in part and directly or indirectly, to:

(a) money or other property that is brought to, or received or used in, the UK by, or for the benefit of, a *relevant person*;

(b) any service provided in the UK to, or for the benefit of, a *relevant person*;

(c) *qualifying property* of a *gift recipient* that is brought to, or received or used in, the UK and enjoyed by a relevant person;

(d) *qualifying property* of a *gift recipient* that is consideration for a service that is enjoyed in the UK by a *relevant person*;

(e) property of a person other than a *relevant person* in circumstances where there is a *connected operation* under which property or services are brought to, or received or used in, the UK and enjoyed by a *relevant person*;

(f) property of a person other than a *relevant person* where there has been a *connected operation* and which is consideration for a service that is enjoyed in the UK by a *relevant person*.

A *connected operation* (section 809O(3)) is an operation which is effected with reference to, or with a view to enabling or facilitating, a qualifying disposition. A *qualifying disposition* (section 809O(4)) is a disposition made by a relevant person to or for the benefit of a person falling within section 809L(5), of money or other property that derives, wholly or in part and directly or indirectly, from income or chargeable gains of the individual. This does not include a disposition which is or is part of the giving of full consideration for the dealings in Condition D (a)–(c).

Enjoyment of a property or service does not include cases where:

(a) it is enjoyed virtually to the entire exclusion of all relevant persons;

(b) full consideration in money or money's worth is given by a relevant person for the enjoyment;

(c) it is enjoyed by relevant persons in the same way and on the same terms as it might be enjoyed by at least a section of the general public.

In a case where Condition C (a) or (b) or Condition D (a) or (b) apply to the importation or use of property, the income or chargeable gains are regarded as remitted at the time the property or service is first enjoyed by a relevant person by virtue of that importation or use (section 809L(6)).

12.36 The amount remitted

The amount of income or gains remitted is governed by specific rules in section 809P of ITA 2007 as follows:

- If the property or consideration remitted to the UK is the income or chargeable gains, the amount remitted is equal to the amount concerned.
- If the property, service or consideration derives from the income or chargeable gains, the amount remitted is equal to the amount of the income or chargeable gains from which the property, service or consideration derives.
- If the income or chargeable gains are used outside the UK to satisfy a relevant debt, the amount remitted is equal to the amount of income or chargeable gains used in this way.
- If anything deriving from the income or chargeable gains is used outside the UK to satisfy a relevant debt' the amount remitted is equal to the amount of the income or chargeable gains from which what is used derives.
- In cases to which section 809L Condition C relates, the amount remitted is equal to the amount of the relevant income or chargeable gains.
- In cases to which section 809L Condition D relates, the amount remitted is equal to the amount of the relevant income or chargeable gains.
- Provision is also made so that where a debt is only partly in respect of the property or service, if the amount remitted would otherwise be greater, it is limited to the amount the debt would be if it were wholly in respect of the property or service. The reference above to relevant income or chargeable gains in relation to qualifying property of a gift recipient means, broadly, the income or gains of which the property in question consists or consisted, or from which it derives or derived.
- If the amount remitted, together with any amount previously remitted would otherwise exceed the amount of the income or chargeable gains, the amount remitted is limited to the amount which, when taken together with any amount previously remitted, is equal to the amount of the income or chargeable gains.

12.37 Remittances from mixed funds

Remittances will, in practice, often be made from mixed funds, being money (e g in a bank account) which is made up of different sources of income and capital gains from more than one tax year. Provision is made for special rules of allocation to determine whether and to what extent the remittance conditions are met. These rules are found in section 809Q and operate by reference to a number of steps, as follows:

- Step 1: For each of the different categories of foreign income and gains, find the amount of the individual's income and gains for the relevant tax year (the tax year in which the transfer occurs) in the mixed fund immediately before the transfer.
- Step 2: Find the earliest paragraph for which the amount determined under Step 1 is not nil. If that amount does not exceed the amount of the transfer, the transfer is treated as containing the income or gains within that paragraph and for that tax year. Otherwise the transfer is treated as containing the relevant proportion of each kind of income or gains within that paragraph and for that tax year, where the relevant proportion is the amount of the transfer divided by the amount determined under Step 1 for that paragraph.
- Step 3: Treat the amount of the transfer as reduced by the amount taken into account under Step 2.
- Step 4: If the amount of the transfer as reduced under Step 3 is not nil, start again at Step 2 with the next earliest paragraph not previously taken into account for which the amount determined under Step 1 is not nil.
- Step 5: If the amount of the transfer (as reduced under Step 3) is not nil once Steps 2 and 3 have been undertaken in relation to all paragraphs of income for which the amount determined under Step 1 is not nil, start again at Step 1, reading the reference to the relevant tax year as a reference to the tax year immediately before the last tax year for which the Step 1 calculation has been made in relation to the transfer.

Specific consideration should be given to the detailed operation of these rules (and various sub-rules) before attempting to operate section 809Q.

12.38 Other practical rules

Where capital payments relating to items deemed as income or chargeable gains are remitted to the UK before the income or gain to which they relate is treated as arising, they are treated as remitted at the time they are treated as arising or accruing (section 809U).

Money brought into the UK to pay the remittance basis fee of £30,000 is not treated as a remittance if the money comes from untaxed foreign income or gains and is paid direct to HMRC (section 809V(3)). The exemption only applies if the £30,000 is paid in respect of the tax due for a year in which the remittance basis charge has been claimed and is due. The money must be sent direct from an overseas bank account to HMRC and is not paid via a UK bank account. If the payment is repaid by the Revenue, it is treated as a remittance when it is repaid (section 809V(2)).

12.39 Exempt property

Finally, provision is made for certain types of property ('exempt property') to be brought to the UK without triggering a remittance of income or gains. The current categories of such property include the following (see section 809Z):

(a) Property meeting the public access rule (typically works of art or antiques exhibited in museums to the general public for up to two years).

(b) Property for personal use (typically clothes, footwear, jewellery or watches).

(c) Property of any description brought into the UK for the purposes of being repaired in the UK and the exported again once repaired.

(d) Property of any description that is brought to the UK for a temporary period of no more than 275 'countable days' (such days excluding days on which the public access rule is satisfied).

(e) Property of any description if the notional remitted amount is less than £1,000.

Chapter 13

Taxation of Pension Provision

13.1 INTRODUCTION

Most individuals wish to make provision to enable themselves to continue to enjoy a reasonable standard of living on retirement. Many will also wish to provide income or capital sums for their dependants after their deaths.

An employer, realising these desires, is frequently willing to assist them to make provision for their old age and dependants. He may accomplish this in either or both of two ways. First, he may himself pay a pension or lump sum upon the retirement of one of his employees. Second, he may make payments to a third party – such as a trust fund or insurance company – during the employment with a view to that third party providing benefits to the individual on the cessation of his employment.

A number of social advantages follow from provision being made by individuals for their retirement. To promote these advantages, the tax code pursues a fiscal policy which encourages this provision. The legislation achieves this, in essence, by enabling individuals to delay the receipt of income until they retire. This income is invested in a fiscally friendly climate and is then, together with profits therefrom, paid out to the individual on his retirement. Where the conditions are fulfilled, the liability to income tax is delayed until the individual receives the income and profits.

Before the scheme introduced by the Finance Act 2004, effective from what has become known as 'A' day, ie 6 April 2006, the law governing the taxation of occupational pension schemes and personal pension schemes had become particularly complex even by the standards of tax legislation. It was contained in primary and secondary legislation, barnacled over with successive amending provisions and further complicated by a raft of guidance notes issued by what was then the Inland Revenue as to its discretionary practice. In December 2002, the Treasury and Revenue published a consultation document 'Simplifying the taxation of pensions: increased choice and flexibility for all' which proposed modernising the taxation of pension provision by replacing the (then) eight different regimes with one unified regime.

The new regime is intended to introduce clarity, transparency and a reduction in administrative burdens for pension schemes, their members, operators and sponsors – including employers – leading to a simpler and more accessible environment for pension saving.

The purpose of this Chapter is to highlight the important tax issues around retirement provision for the employment specialist. A detailed recitation of the entirety of the fiscal code for 'registered' (ie fiscally advantaged) pension schemes, which occupies over 130 sections and ten schedules of the Finance Act 2004, is beyond the scope of this Book.

Broadly speaking, there are five fiscal reasons for employees or employers to participate in registered pension schemes:[1]

(i) by investing income before tax has been deducted from it, a larger sum is invested and allowed to grow;

(ii) the investment of that larger sum benefits from certain reliefs from income tax and capital gains tax (CGT) that other investments made by an individual do not. This allows the pension fund to build up more quickly. This is the 'friendly fiscal climate' referred to above;

(iii) by delaying the receipt of income until after an individual has ceased to work, income may be moved from a point in time at which the recipient is liable to pay higher rate income tax to a point in time at which he is not;

(iv) so long as the scheme rules so permit, an individual can take up to 25% of the value of his or her pension fund at the time of retirement as a tax free lump sum; and

(v) for an employer, contributions to an employee's pension scheme do not carry with them any liability to pay secondary Class 1 National Insurance Contributions (ie employer's NICs on earnings) and so they are, for that employer, a cheaper way to remunerate employees.

The price of these advantages is predominantly one of a loss of flexibility as to the time at which payments of pension can be made – which is broadly no earlier than retirement – and the nature of the payments which can be made. These restrictions are designed to secure various policy ends amongst which being that the contributions are used for the purpose of providing for the individual in his retirement. This is achieved by placing the pool of contributions beyond his reach until he reaches a certain age or is forced to retire by ill-health. The legislation then limits the individual's ability to deal with the money on his retirement; he may not take in the form of a lump sum more than 25% of

1 These are set out in Finance Act 2004, ss 186–201.

the pool of contributions built up over the years and, generally, must take the remainder in the form of income.

13.2 REGISTERED PENSION SCHEMES

13.3 What is a pension scheme?

The Finance Act 2004 does not specify any particular legal form for a registered pension scheme. Such may be established by, for example, a trust, contract, resolution of a board, etc. This can be seen in the wide language used in the statutory definition of a pension scheme:

> 'A scheme or other arrangements, comprised in one of more instruments or agreements, having or capable of having effect so as to provide benefits to or in respect of persons –
>
> (a) on retirement;
>
> (b) on death;
>
> (c) on having reached a particular age;
>
> (d) on the onset or serious ill-health or incapacity, or
>
> (e) in similar circumstances.'[2]

As is clear from the word 'or', a pension scheme does not have to provide benefits in all of these situations. If it provided benefits on death in service only, it would still fall within the definition of a 'pension scheme'. Only schemes falling within this definition are capable of registration, and it is the status as a *registered* pension scheme which attracts the tax advantages identified above.

13.4 Occupational pension schemes

Relevantly, there is a special category of pension scheme known as an occupational pension scheme which is a:

> 'pension scheme established by an employer or employers and having or capable of having effect so as to provide benefits to or in respect of any or all of the employees of –
>
> (a) that employer or those employers, or
>
> (b) any other employer.'[3]

2 Finance Act 2004, s 150(1).
3 Finance Act 2004, s 150(5).

HMRC's Registered Pension Schemes Manual gives the following examples of arrangements which may comprise occupational pension schemes:

- An employer (or employers) establishing a pension scheme may specify, for example, that the membership is for employees in a group of companies plus self- employed individuals who work with them.
- A representative body that is itself an employer may establish a pension scheme for people who are employees in a particular industry.
- One or more employers within a geographical area may set up a pension scheme for employees of theirs within that geographical area.'[4]

The Finance Act 2004 imposes additional restrictions and conditions on occupational pension schemes. These additional restrictions are considered to be necessary because of the nature of the relationship between the pension scheme and the employer. The legislation is predicated upon there being a greater possibility of abuse in the case of occupational pension schemes, a possibility borne of the fact that the relationship between pension scheme and employer is likely to be closer than that where the scheme was established by a financial institution.

13.5 Registration of a pension scheme

Anyone can establish a pension scheme. However, a pension scheme can only be registered if it is either an occupational pension scheme or has been established by a person with permission under the Financial Services and Markets Act 2000 to establish in the UK a personal pension scheme or stakeholder pension scheme.[5]

An application to register a pension scheme must be made to HMRC on a form they specify and containing the information required by HMRC. Since October 2007, HMRC have required applications for registration to be made electronically.[6] An application must be accompanied by a declaration that, in particular, the instruments or agreements whereby the pension scheme is established do not entitle any person to 'unauthorised payments' (see **13.7** below).

This requirement – that there be no unauthorised payments – is the key limitation to registering pension schemes and so, indirectly, the principal *quid pro quo* for the tax benefits outlined above.

4 See the Registered Pension Schemes Manual (which can be found at www.hmrc.gov.uk) at paragraph 02102020.
5 Finance Act 2004, s 154(1). Discussions as to the registration of pension schemes otherwise than occupation pension schemes are outside the ambit of this book.
6 Pensions Tax Simplification Newsletters 27 of 10 April 2007 and 30 of 12 October 2007.

13.6 What contributions can be made?

Each individual has a lifetime allowance which is the amount of his pension benefits that qualify for the tax privileges from registered pension schemes.

Every time an individual starts to take pension benefits – a 'benefit crystallisation event' as it is termed by the legislation[7] – the cost of providing those benefits (together with the value of any other benefits paid or being paid) will be tested against the lifetime allowance. The scheme administrator will carry out his test before it starts paying benefits. The standard lifetime allowance for the tax year 2013–14 is £1.5 million.

Once the cost of providing all those benefits goes above the lifetime allowance the amount over the lifetime allowance will be taxable at the rate of:

- 25% if the excess is used to provide a pension; or
- 55% if the excess is used to pay a lump sum.[8]

It is the cost of providing the pension that is tested against the lifetime allowance, not the amount of pension received.

There is also an *annual allowance* the effect of which is to limit the amount of tax privileges available on pension savings paid by or in respect of an individual in a tax year.[9] For the tax year 2013–14, the annual allowance is £50,000.[10]

Increases in value of a registered pension scheme in excess of that annual allowance will be subject to tax at 'the appropriate rate'[11] but the amount of that excess is not treated as income.[12]

13.7 Authorised and unauthorised payments

The key requirement for registration of a pension scheme is, as has been set out above, that the instruments or agreements whereby it was established do not entitle any person to any 'unauthorised payments'. This notion of unauthorised payment is described by the legislation[13] as payments falling into one of two descriptions, unauthorised *member* payments and unauthorised *employer* payments.

7 Finance Act 2004, s 216.
8 Finance Act 2004, s 215(2).
9 Finance Act 2004, ss 227 et seq.
10 Finance Act 2004, s 228.
11 Finance Act 2004, s 227(4).
12 Finance Act 2004, s 227(5).
13 Finance Act 2004, s 160(5).

Because of the very valuable tax advantages attaching to registered pension schemes, and the purpose (i e encouraging the provision of retirement income) for which those tax advantages are extended, one would expect the definition of authorised and unauthorised payments to be very carefully drafted. And one's expectations would not be disappointed.

As to employer payments, the structure of the legislation is to define those which are authorised;[14] all others are unauthorised. Authorised employer payments cover such things as certain repayments of surpluses,[15] payments made to the employer in compensation for certain wrongful acts by the employee[16] and certain loans to employers.[17]

As to member payments, again, the structure of the legislation is to define those which are authorised[18] and all others are unauthorised. The categories of authorised payments are as follows:

(i) payments of pensions permitted by the pension rules or the pension death benefit rules;

(ii) payments of lump sums permitted by the lump sum rules or the lump sum death benefit rules;

(iii) recognised transfers;

(iv) scheme administration member payments;

(v) payments pursuant to a pension sharing order or provision; and

(vi) a residual category of other payments of a description prescribed by regulations made by HMRC.

The rules defining each of these categories are lengthy and complex and their precise elucidation is beyond the scope of this book.[19] However, the main categories of authorised payments are a pension paid for life and a lump sum benefit paid when the pension starts.

As to the pension for life, unless the individual is suffering from ill health, the pension must not start before the minimum pension age, that is:

- the employee's 50th birthday (for payments made before 6 April 2010);
- the employee's 55th birthday (for payments made from 6 April 2010).

14 Finance Act 2004, s 175.
15 Finance Act 2004, s 177.
16 Finance Act 2004, s 178.
17 Finance Act 2004, s 179.
18 Finance Act 2004, s 164(1).
19 But the eager student of pension law can find them in Finance Act 2004, ss 164–171.

If benefits are paid before this age they will be unauthorised benefits and will be taxed accordingly.

As to lump sum payments, the tax rules allow a lump sum of up to 25% of the value of the fund providing pension benefits to be paid free of income tax, so long as certain other conditions are also satisfied. So if the value of the pension fund is £100,000, as long as the lump sum you receive is £25,000 or less, it can normally be paid tax-free. However, there are certain preconditions. For example, the lump sum must be paid immediately before the recipient becomes entitled to the pension. If the recipient puts off taking his benefits until his 75th birthday or later, the lump sum payment will not be tax-free. Moreover, the total of the tax-free lump sums received from all pension schemes cannot be more than 25% of the lifetime allowance for the tax year in which the lump sum is received. Again, if the payment exceeds this sum, the excess will be an unauthorised payment and taxed as such.

The taxation of unauthorised payments is set out in sections 208–213 of the Finance Act 2004. Broadly the tax charge in respect of an unauthorised payment to or in respect of an employee falls upon the employee.[20] And, in respect of unauthorised employer payments, again, the charge falls upon the person to or in respect of whom the payment is made.[21] That tax charge is 40% but a surcharge of 15% is also applied where a certain quantum of unauthorised payments is made.[22]

13.8 Relief for member's contributions

The principal relief is relief for member's contributions. An individual who is an active member of a registered pension scheme is entitled to relief in respect of relievable pension contributions paid during a tax year if the individual is a 'relevant UK individual' for that year.[23]

This formulation contains a number of limitations to the circumstances in which relief may be available. However, the important one is the geographical limitation inherent in the phrase 'relevant UK individual'.[24] In order to obtain relief, the individual must have employment income chargeable to income tax or be resident in the UK at some time during the year or be resident in the UK both at some time during the preceding five tax years and when he became a member of the scheme.[25]

20 Save for where the employee is dead, where it falls upon the recipient of that payment.
21 Finance Act 2004, s 208.
22 Finance Act 2004, ss 209 and 210.
23 Finance Act 2004, s 188(1).
24 The definition of which is contained in Finance Act 2004, s 189.
25 Or have general earnings from overseas Crown employment subject to UK tax.

The maximum amount of relief available for member's contributions in a tax year is the individual's 'relevant UK earnings' chargeable to income tax in the year.[26] And his relevant UK earnings are the aggregate of his employment income, income derived from the carrying on of a trade, profession or vocation, income derived from carrying on a UK furnished holiday lettings business and patent income where the individual, alone or jointly, devised the intention the subject of the patent.[27]

Generally, the relief is given by entitling the individual by whom the contribution is paid to deduct and retain out of it a sum equal to income tax on the contribution at the basic rate of income tax for the tax year in which the payment is made.[28] So if he wishes to pay £1,000, he need actually only pay £780. The scheme administrator then recovers that £220 from HMRC. If income tax or capital gains tax at the higher rate or additional rate is chargeable in that tax year, the basic rate limit is increased by the amount of the contribution.[29] This effectively means that the individual only pays income tax at 22% on the amount contributed and this 22% matches, in the example given above, the £220 he is treated as having retained. The net effect is that he does not pay income tax on that £1,000. This relief is known as relief at source.

However, in the case of occupational pension schemes, relief is typically given under what are known as 'net pay arrangements'.[30] Net pay arrangements adopt the simpler mechanism of deducting the amount of the contribution from the individual's employment income from the employment.

13.9 Relief for scheme investments

The Finance Act 2004 also enacts a benign fiscal environment within which investments held for the purposes of registered pension schemes can grow. Both income from such investments[31] and most underwriting commissions applied for the purposes of such schemes[32] are excluded from liability to income tax.[33]

Moreover, gains accruing to a person on a disposal of investments held for the purposes of a registered pension scheme are not chargeable gains for the purposes of capital gains tax.[34]

26 Finance Act 2004, s 190.
27 Finance Act 2004, s 189(2) and (2A).
28 Finance Act 2004, s 192.
29 Finance Act 2004, s 192(4).
30 Finance Act 2004, ss 191(3) and 193.
31 Finance Act 2004, s 186(1)(a).
32 Finance Act 2004, s 186(1)(b).
33 Finance Act 2004, s 186(1).
34 Taxation of Chargeable Gains Act 1992, s 271(1A).

13.10 Relief for employers' contributions

Contributions made by an employer to a registered pension scheme in respect of any individual are generally deductible in calculating the employer's profits chargeable to income tax or corporation tax. This is so even if the contributions are of a capital nature.[35] They are also chargeable in respect of the accounting period in which they are paid,[36] displacing the normal accountancy treatment of such payments which would otherwise obtain. It is worth noting that this may have the effect of delaying the time at which the employer would otherwise be entitled to take a deduction (from, for example, the point in time at which the liability to make the payment arose) as well as accelerating that point in time.

There is provision where an employer makes an exceptionally large contribution in an accounting period, to spread that contribution for tax purposes over two or more accounting periods.[37] The aim is to prevent employers reducing the tax liability on their profits in a good year by making a large contribution to a registered pension scheme in that year. Contributions will be spread where the contribution paid in the current accounting period exceeds 210% of the amount of the contributions paid in the previous accounting period.[38]

Contributions under a registered pension scheme by an employer do not give rise to a liability to income tax on the employee.[39]

13.11 UNREGISTERED PENSION SCHEMES

13.12 Introduction

Prior to the Finance Act 2004, much employer/employee tax planning sought to exploit the fiscal asymmetry which was available in respect of what were then known as 'unapproved' retirement benefits schemes. That asymmetry was essentially this, that the employer could obtain a deduction in its computation of profits for the purposes of calculating its corporation tax liability without their being a corresponding liability to income tax on the part of the employee.[40]

The fiscal authorities needed two attempts to address this asymmetry. Schedule 24 to the Finance Act 2003 removed the employer's deduction in respect of contributions to an 'employee benefit scheme'. However, the draftsman

35 Finance Act 2004, s 196(2)(a).
36 Finance Act 2004, s 196(2)(b).
37 Finance Act 2004, s 197.
38 Finance Act 2004, s 197(1)(b).
39 ITEPA 2003, s 308.
40 It will be recalled that this asymmetry continues to exist in respect of registered pension schemes.

apparently overlooked the fact that, frequently, the deduction was obtained not in respect of the contribution but in respect of a provision in the accounts against the cost of making a contribution which might be now or might be in the future. It followed that there were many instances where that Schedule failed to hit its target.

A further attempt followed in the Finance Act 2004 as part of the wholesale reform of the taxation of retirement benefits provision. Section 246 of that Act applies where the employer's expenses of providing benefits do not consist of making contributions but are shown in the employer's accounts. Unless the benefits give rise to a liability to income tax on receipt, they are not deductible in calculating the employer's profits.[41] Where they are benefits in respect of which a person is, on receipt, chargeable to income tax, the expenses are (if deductible under normal principles) deductible in computing the profits but only in the period in which they are paid.[42] In other words, the deduction is delayed until there is a corresponding liability to income tax.

Section 246 only applies to benefits provided under an employer-financed retirement benefits scheme (or EFRBS). An EFRBS is a scheme to provide 'relevant benefits' to employees which is not a registered pension scheme.[43] The concept of 'relevant benefits', upon which, of course, the notion of EFRBS is parasitic, is discussed below. However, essentially, an EFRBS is any scheme set up by an employer to make financial provision for the retirement or death of employees. The employer may make contributions in advance in order to fund the benefits (a funded scheme) or simply pay benefits on retirement or death (an unfunded scheme). Both such arrangements are, if unregistered, likely to comprise an EFRBS.

13.13 Relevant benefits

The notion of 'relevant benefits' thus determines whether the restriction on deductibility applies. It should be noted that section 246 applies to the 'expenses of providing benefits ... under an EFRBS' but an EFRBS is defined as a 'scheme for the provision of benefits consisting of *or including* relevant benefits'.[44] So the fact that expenses are not of providing relevant benefits does not necessarily mean that they will escape the section 246 restriction on deductibility.[45] If the expenses are expenses of providing benefits under a scheme[46] only some of the

41 Finance Act 2004, s 246(2).
42 Finance Act 2004, s 246(3).
43 ITEPA 2003, s 393A.
44 ITEPA 2003, s 393A.
45 Indeed, if excluded benefits are paid out of an EFRBS, on one reading of Finance Act 2004, s 246 and ITEPA 2003, ss 393A and 393B, no deduction could be obtained in respect of them. However, it is thought unlikely that HMRC would seek to take the point.
46 For the very broad definition of which word, see ITEPA 2003, s 393A(4).

benefits under which are relevant benefits, nevertheless all of those expenses will be subject to the section 246 restriction.[47]

'Relevant benefits' under EFRBS[48] are defined as:

> 'Any lump sum, gratuity or other benefit (including a non-cash benefit) provided (or to be provided) –
>
> (a) on or in anticipation of the retirement of an employee or former employee,
>
> (b) on the death of an employee or former employee,
>
> (c) after the retirement or death of an employee or former employee in connection with past service,
>
> (d) on or in anticipation of, or in connection with, any change in the nature of service of an employee, or
>
> (e) to any person by virtue of a pension sharing order or provision relating to an employee or former employee.'[49]

However, certain benefits are carved out of this definition, including pension income taxed under Part 9 of ITEPA 2003,[50] and such 'excluded benefits' as benefits in respect of ill-health or disablement of an employee during service and benefits in respect of the death by accident of an employee during service.[51] There are also regulations[52] that exclude a number of benefits which were not chargeable to tax when provided by the employer where provision continues after the employment has ceased.

13.14 Payments on retirement

It will not always be easy to tell whether a payment is made on or in anticipation of 'retirement'. The word is not further defined in the Act; judges have resisted filling this lacuna[53]and so it must be given its ordinary, normal meaning. At the extremes, no difficulty is raised. A payment made to an employee on his turning 60 or 65 and giving up work clearly will fall within the definition.

47 The notion of 'relevant benefits' is also important in determining whether a payment received by an employee or ex-employee is chargeable to tax, see **10.2** in Chapter 10.

48 An EFRBS is defined as a scheme 'for the provision of benefits consisting of or including relevant benefits to or in respect of employees or former employees' which is not a registered pension scheme: ITEPA 2003, s 393A.

49 ITEPA 2003, s 393B(1).

50 ITEPA 2003, s 393B(2)(a).

51 ITEPA 2003, s 393B(3). Excluded benefits are likely to escape tax entirely.

52 The Employer-Financed Retirement Benefits (Excluded Benefits for Tax Purposes) Regulations 2007, SI 2007/3536.

53 See, for example, *Johnson v Holleran* [1989] STC 1, per Morritt J at p 6e.

Where, on the other hand, an employee is forced out of employment against his wishes any payment made is likely to be taxed under section 401.

In an attempt to deal with the borderline cases, HMRC have given a number of examples of what would and would not constitute retirement.[54]

(i) A long-service employee leaves to take a senior executive position in another company at the age of 60. The employee has retired.

(ii) A division of the company is sold and the 55 year old manager responsible for running it leaves to take a job with the purchaser. The manager has retired unless the service is being treated as continuous for pension purposes.

(iii) A person in his 50s has a heart attack and is advised by his doctor to leave and seek a less stressful position. If the person were re-employed in an entirely different capacity with the same employer or finds employment with another employer, HMRC would generally accept the member had retired early from the original employment (possibly on ill-health grounds or possibly on normal early retirement grounds – depending on the scheme rules and exact medical advice). But if the ex-gratia payment made is purely consolation for loss of health that results in the premature termination of employment, it would not be regarded as made in connection with retirement.

(iv) An employee aged 35 is involved in an accident and suffers disabilities that make it impossible to continue with the job. A lump sum paid on retirement solely by reason of disability from an accident is not taxable as a benefit from either a non-approved or an employer-financed retirement benefits scheme.

(v) An employee aged 50 leaves to take a job nearer home to be able to nurse her aged parents. Employee has retired.

13.15 Payments in anticipation of retirement

This raises no difficulty over and above that rehearsed in the preceding paragraph. A payment will be made in anticipation of retirement where it is paid *before* the employee retires in anticipation thereof.

It should be noted that the authors are aware that the Revenue have sought to contend that a payment made by an employer to continuing employees in compensation for them giving up some or all of their rights under a pension scheme (typically a defined benefit scheme) is a 'relevant benefit' as being a payment in anticipation of retirement. However, in the authors' opinion, such a contention is clearly wrong.

54 See Employment Income Manual paragraph 15400. It should be noted that the Manual emphasises that this is only guidance and each case will depend on its particular facts.

13.16 Payment on death

The question whether a payment is made on the death of an employee ought not to raise any difficulty.

13.17 Payments after retirement or death in connection with past service

Similarly a payment made *after* retirement or death will be a relevant benefit if it is made 'in connection with past service'. The words 'in connection with' are words of very wide import and 'in connection with past service' is likely to mean no more than it is paid by the employer or someone connected therewith.[54a]

13.18 On or in anticipation of or in connection with any change in the nature of the service

These words subsist as a reminder of a time when it was thought that payments made to an employee on a change in the nature of his service were not otherwise taxable. However, it is now clear that such are in fact employment income[55] and they are now effectively obsolete.

Regulations impose an obligation on the employer to inform HMRC of the coming into operation of an EFRBS on or before 31 January following the tax year during which the scheme came into operation.[56] Those regulations also require an employer to inform HMRC of all benefits provided from an EFRBS by 7 July following the tax year in which the benefits are paid.

13.19 Taxation on receiving relevant benefits

A lump sum payment on the termination of employment may be taxed under any of a number of provisions. First, it may be taxable under section 9 of ITEPA 2003 as earnings from employment. Second, it may be taxable as a payment for a restrictive undertaking under section 225 of ITEPA 2003. Third, it may be taxable as a relevant benefit provided under an EFRBS: section 394 of ITEPA. Each of these provisions will lead – in the case of a simple lump sum payment – to roughly the same tax liability. So, at least for present purposes, it matters not which provision the payment is caught under. However, if it falls within none of these provisions, it may fall to be taxed under the more beneficial section 401 regime. The first and second questions are addressed in

54a See discussion in *Barclays Bank plc v HMRC* [2007] EWCA 442 Arden LJ at [18]–[26].

55 See Chapter 4.

56 The Employer-Financed Retirement Benefits Schemes (Provision of Information) Regulations 2005, SI 2005/3453.

Chapter 10 at **10.3** et seq and Chapter 4 at **4.36** respectively. The purpose of this paragraph is to address the third question.

Before turning to address this question, two preliminary observations must be borne in mind. First, any payment made for redundancy will always be within section 401.[57] Second, a payment made on termination of employment may comprise several different elements, for example accrued wages, a payment in lieu of notice and compensation for loss of office. Each element of the payment must be considered *separately* under the above rules.

13.20 Is there an EFRBS?

The nature of employer-financed retirement benefits schemes has been addressed above.[58] However, it may be useful to repeat the fact that an EFRBS is a scheme for the provision of benefits consisting of or including 'relevant benefits'[59] and references to a 'scheme' include references to a deed, agreement, series of agreements or other arrangements providing for relevant benefits.[60] Therefore if relevant benefits are provided under a contract or agreement to settle a dispute there will clearly be an EFRBS.

13.21 Is there a charge to tax?

There will be a relevant benefit – a term the ambit of which is discussed above – where a 'lump sum, gratuity or other benefit (including a non-cash benefit)' is provided irrespective of the person to whom those benefits are provided. Although, curiously, the legislation appears to tax the recipient of the benefit – who may, depending on the terms of the scheme, be the spouse or child or the employee – rather than the employee.[61] It is, however, likely, given the potential for tax mitigation – by shifting income from a high earner to a low earner – inherent in such a construction that the legislation will be tested before the First-tier Tax Tribunal.

There is a category of benefit carved out from that of relevant benefits, namely, 'excluded benefits', which do not give rise to a charge to tax under Chapter 2 of Part 4I of ITEPA 2003. Excluded benefits are defined,[62] *inter alia*, as benefits in respect of ill-health or disablement of an employee during service and in respect of the death by accident of an employee during service.[63] And such payments will be taxed under section 401, if at all.

57 See **10.5** in Chapter 10.
58 See **13.12**.
59 ITEPA 2003, s 393A(1).
60 ITEPA 2003, s 393A(4).
61 ITEPA 2003, s 394(1).
62 ITEPA 2003, s 393B(3).
63 Together with benefits payable under certain life insurance policies and prescribed by regulations: ITEPA 2003, s 393B(4).

13.22 Application of Part 7A of Chapter 2 ('the disguised remuneration provisions') to EFRBS

Section 394(5) provides that no liability to income tax arises by virtue of any other provision of ITEPA 2003 in respect of a benefit to which Part 6 of Chapter 2 applies, except any liability to income tax on general earnings or on an amount which counts as employment income under Part 7A of Chapter 2.[64] This means that in principle the application of the rules on EFRBS may be displaced by the application of the disguised remuneration provisions.

The Finance Act 2011 introduced a new Part 7A into ITEPA 2003 containing wide-reaching and complex anti-avoidance provisions (commonly referred to as the 'disguised remuneration provisions').

Under Part 7A, a charge to income tax (and liability to national insurance contributions) arises on the value of a 'relevant step' taken by a third party as part of an arrangement which is (wholly or partly) a means of providing recognition or rewards or loans to an employee or a person linked with him. The value of the relevant step counts as employment income of the employee. It is worth noting that the 'relevant step' can take various forms – it can be the earmarking of a sum or money or an asset, a payment of a sum of money or the transfer of an asset, or the act of making an asset available.[65] As a relevant step can include the earmarking of a sum or an asset (without the employee have any immediate right to that sum or asset) it is possible for a charge to tax on employment income to arise before the employee has received anything or become entitled to use any asset.

There are a number of exclusions from Part 7A. Any steps taken by a third party in relation to one of the share schemes recognised in Part 7[66] do not give rise to a charge to tax under Part 7A.[67]

Part 7A takes precedence over the other provisions of the ITEPA 2003[68] so should always be considered first when a third party is involved in delivering any form of valuable consideration to an employee.

It seems to be the case that if sums are put into some sort of EFRBS arrangement for a wide number of beneficiaries, but no further steps are taken, that will not amount to earmarking (HMRC's policy being that there is no earmarking if a particular potential beneficiary is not identified, whether that is correct in law is open to debate).

64 ITEPA 2003, s 394(6).
65 ITEPA 2003, ss 554B–554D.
66 See Chapter 9 (Taxation of Shares and Share Options).
67 ITEPA 2003, ss 554E and 554I–554M.
68 ITEPA 2003, s 554Z6.

13.23 Application of the disguised remuneration provisions to pension income

The disguised remuneration provisions in Part 7A will not apply in respect of pension income. Pension payments will be subject to tax under Part 9, in priority over Part 7A.[69] To the extent that a pension scheme is not excluded under section 554E, it will, however, be liable to Part 7A charges on any new relevant step which constitutes earmarking on or after 6 April 2012, with credit given against the Part 9 charge for earlier Part 7A charges.

69 ITEPA 2003, s 554S.

Index

[all references are to paragraph number]

A Guide to EU Renewable Energy Policy

Comparing Europeanization and Domestic Policy Change in EU Member States

---

Edited by

Israel Solorio

National Autonomous University of Mexico

Helge Jörgens

ISCTE-Instituto Universitário de Lisboa, Portugal

Edward Elgar PUBLISHING

Cheltenham, UK • Northampton, MA, USA

Published by
Edward Elgar Publishing Limited
The Lypiatts
15 Lansdown Road
Cheltenham
Glos GL50 2JA
UK

Edward Elgar Publishing, Inc.
William Pratt House
9 Dewey Court
Northampton
Massachusetts 01060
USA

A catalogue record for this book
is available from the British Library

Library of Congress Control Number: 2016962562

This book is available electronically in the **Elgar**online
Social and Political Science subject collection
DOI 10.4337/9781783471560

MIX
Paper from
responsible sources
FSC® C013056
FSC
www.fsc.org

ISBN 978 1 78347 155 3 (cased)
ISBN 978 1 78347 156 0 (eBook)

Typeset by Columns Design XML Ltd, Reading
Printed and bound in Great Britain by TJ International Ltd, Padstow

Contents

Tables

Contributors

Andrzej Ancygier is Energy Expert at Climate Analytics and Lecturer in Environmental Politics at New York University, USA and Freie Universität in Berlin, Germany.

Mischa Bechberger holds a PhD as a political scientist and has worked for more than ten years in the field of promotion policy for renewable energies.

Pierre Bocquillon is a Lecturer in politics at the University of East Anglia, UK. He works on European politics and the politics of energy and climate change.

Simona Davidescu is a Research Associate at the EU–Asia Institute at ESSCA Angers and Associate Lecturer at the Department of Politics, University of York, UK.

Lorenzo Di Lucia is an Associate Researcher at Imperial College London, UK, working on an integrated approach to the governance of land use and bioenergy systems.

Maria Rosaria Di Nucci is a Senior Researcher at the Environmental Policy Research Centre, Freie Universität Berlin, Germany.

Helene Dyrhauge is an Associate Professor, Institute for Social Sciences and Business at Roskilde University, Denmark.

Gonzalo Escribano is Director of the Energy Programme at Elcano Royal Institute (Madrid), in Spain, and Professor of Economics at the Spanish Open University (UNED).

Aurélien Evrard is a Lecturer in Political Science at Université Sorbonne Nouvelle – Paris 3, France and Research Associate at Sciences Po, Centre d'Études Européennes (CEE), France.

Jenny Fairbrass is Senior Lecturer in Business and Management at the Norwich Business School of the University of East Anglia, UK. Co-convenor of the University Association for Contemporary European Studies Collaborative Research Network (UACES CRN) on the European Energy Policy.

Rosa Fernandez is Senior Lecturer and Programme Leader in Economics at the University of Chester, UK.

Rainer Hinrichs-Rahlwes has a leading role at European Renewable Energies Federation (EREF).

Bernd Hirschl is head of the Department on Sustainable Energy and Climate Protection at the Institute for Ecological Economy Research (IÖW) in Berlin and Professor at the Brandenburg University of Technology Cottbus-Senftenberg, Germany.

Ralitsa Hiteva is a Research Fellow at the Science Policy Research Unit at the University of Sussex, UK and a member of the Sussex Energy Group. Ralitsa works on infrastructure governance and policy, business model innovation and environmental governance.

Thomas Hoppe is Associate Professor within the faculty of Technology, Policy and Management (TPM) at Delft University of Technology, the Netherlands.

Karolina Jankowska is project manager and editor of a daily newsletter on media coverage of energy policy and energy transition by the Sunbeam GmbH in Berlin, Germany. She has also worked as a researcher, scientific advisor, consultant and lecturer. She holds a PhD as a political scientist.

Helge Jörgens is a Visiting Professor at ISCTE-Instituto Universitário de Lisboa, Portugal, and Senior Lecturer in the Department of Political and Social Sciences of the Freie Universität Berlin, Germany.

Tomas Maltby is Lecturer in International Politics in the Department of Political Economy at King's College London, UK.

Dörte Ohlhorst is Deputy Managing Director at the Environmental Policy Research Centre, Freie Universität Berlin, Germany.

Eva Öller is a PhD candidate at the Environmental Policy Research Center, Freie Universität Berlin, Germany.

Daniele Russolillo is Programme Manager of Fondazione per l'Ambiente – Turin School of Local Regulation, Italy, working on sustainable energy policies and economic regulation of local public services.

Israel Solorio is Associate Professor of Public Administration at the National Autonomous University of Mexico. Co-convenor of the University Association for Contemporary European Studies Collaborative Research Network (UACES CRN) on the European Energy Policy.

Ellen van Bueren is Professor of Urban Development Management at Delft University of Technology and Principal Investigator at the Institute for Advanced Metropolitan Solutions (AMS) in Amsterdam, the Netherlands.

Thomas Vogelpohl is a trained political scientist, who works as postdoctoral researcher at the FernUniversität in Hagen, Germany. His key research area is the analysis of environmental, energy and climate policies, with a special focus on German and European biofuels policy.

Foreword

For nearly two decades, culminating in the European Council Conclusions of March 2007, when the 20-20-20 targets were agreed, the European Union (EU) was rightly considered to be a frontrunner and a role model of sustainable energy policies and particularly of renewable energy sources (RES) development and deployment. But only a few years after the enabling legislation of the 20-20-20 package entered into force, the meeting of the European Council on 23 October 2014 was widely described as a turning point. The EU has at the least renounced its position as a leader in global RES development, if not changed from frontrunner to laggard. But it is also true that the Council Conclusions will not stop development of RES in Europe: that is no longer possible, due to immense learning curves and cost decreases in the last few years, and due to the significant contributions of RES to economic growth and to the security of energy supply in Europe. But implementing the 2030 targets will, however, significantly slow down RES development in Europe, while the rest of the world is at the point of starting and accelerating growth of RES, as well as ambitious enabling policies and frameworks. Word is out that Europe might risk losing a flourishing and future-oriented industry. How could this dramatic change happen after only seven years?

It all started – or rather it became obvious – back in the early 1990s. After years of research and development (R&D) programmes, a tipping point seemed to be approaching in the mid-1990s. The European Commission's Green Paper of 1996, the White Paper of 1997, the Campaign for Take-Off starting in 1999, the renewables electricity directive of 2001, the energy performance of buildings directive of 2002 and the biofuels directive of 2003 were major milestones of a focused development of policies for RES. In 1997, EU targets for RES were set for the first time. They were only indicative and not legally binding for the member states. But member states were obliged to set their own national targets, in line with the overall level of ambition of the EU. Despite the voluntary character of the targets the discussions around new technologies were controversial and some claimed they were too expensive and could never provide a relevant contribution to Europe's energy supply and to greenhouse gas (GHG) reduction. These arguments had some impact, particularly because climate change and resulting needs for GHG reduction were considered to be the main drivers for RES. Their economic and job creation potential as well as their crucial role for security of energy supply were not yet in the focus of the European agenda.

Discussions about the future of climate and energy policies in Europe continued. With the two directives for electricity and for biofuels in place, it was obvious that the heating and cooling sector was the missing link. Half of the EU's energy is consumed in this sector, but no relevant policies were in place to introduce RES in the building sector. A new consensus evolved that a heating and cooling directive was needed. A share of 25 per cent RES by 2020 soon emerged as a reasonable target, uniting a majority of the European Parliament and the European RES sector. A wide consensus had developed that enabling policies should be further developed and adapted so that growth of RES could be truly efficient all over Europe. The good reasons for RES had become overwhelming.

RES development was not easy to compare between the different EU member states. Whereas in Germany, due to the very effective and efficient Feed-In Tariffs (FITs), most of the investment in RES was done by private individuals, small and medium-sized companies and farmers, in other countries, for example Spain, the incumbent utilities themselves invested heavily in RES. Consequently, the share of small and decentralized RES is much smaller there than it is in Germany and in Denmark, Austria and some others. Yet other countries, such as the United Kingdom (UK), actually limited the deployment of RES by means of policies from which only large players could benefit and which resulted in much higher costs than FITs. Administrative barriers and the 'not in my back yard' (NIMBY) syndrome added to the unsatisfactory picture.

When 2010 was approaching, it became evident that the degree of target compliance was very different in the different member states. Therefore another lesson evolved from the deficits of the 2010 legislation. It was widely agreed that binding targets together with clear policies and regular monitoring would be more effective than just indicative ones. Although publicly blaming and shaming did have some impact resulting in policy improvements, the lack of penalization was broadly seen as a major obstacle, together with the continued existence of administrative barriers and the absence of a level playing field for RES in distorted energy markets. This is why the introduction of binding national targets for the share of RES in 2020 was high on the RES sector's agenda. In parallel, there was a discussion about whether or not a RES target for the

EU (of 20 per cent in 2020) should be broken down into sectoral targets for electricity, heating and cooling and for transport.

Driven by the positive attitude towards RES all over Europe, in March 2007 the European Council eventually agreed – in the wider context of a climate and energy package – on a binding European 2020 target of at least 20 per cent RES in gross final energy consumption, underpinned by differentiated binding national targets for each member state and a minimum share of at least 10 per cent RES in the transport sector of every member state and the EU as a whole. The agreement was celebrated as a landmark decision for RES development. Enacted in the renewable energy directive (RED) of 2009, which for the first time comprises all three sectors – electricity, heating and cooling, and transport – the trajectory and the policy choices for the EU and for each member state were clearly set. The evaluation of the 27 National Renewable Energy Action Plans (NREAPs), submitted in 2010, indicated that the 20 per cent target may even be exceeded in 2020.

The 2020 climate and energy package included the settlement of a long-discussed question: will the support mechanisms for RES in the EU be harmonized or will it be up to the member states to design their own frameworks, including the right to limit support to domestic production? The consensus between the European Parliament and European Council was explicitly entered into the RED: member states are responsible for reaching their national targets. Therefore they must have the right to design and restrict their national support mechanisms. They may, however, on a voluntary basis cooperate with neighbours and with third countries in order to achieve their targets more effectively or at lower costs. Although it is always useful to learn from good practice elsewhere, this agreement was necessary due to various degrees of market transparency and accessibility in the different member states. Despite the fact that the final provisions of the RED explicitly hold that the member states' right to define their national support schemes must not be affected by any revision of the directive up to 2020, it is not really surprising that this consensus has been disputed from the very beginning: by those who never wanted it, and by those who realized later that effective national support schemes tend to bring in new market players and thus facilitate effective competition with incumbent utilities and their assets.

Since the RED entered into force in 2010, a lot has happened. RES continue to grow in many member states and even more so worldwide. Growth rates of wind and solar photovoltaic (PV) installations in China, for example, have been outpacing European development for the last few years. Onshore wind has experienced smooth but regular cost decreases over the last decade and is more than cost-competitive with new conventional power plants today. Solar PV prices and costs have decreased at unprecedented rates since the coincidental occurrence of the global financial and economic crisis, and massive overcapacities for panel production have slashed costs below grid parity in an increasing number of countries around the world. In recent years, PV, particularly decentralized rooftop installation, has grown much faster than expected and has been outpacing wind power for a few years in several markets, including Germany. The massive growth of PV in recent years and continued growth of wind power over more than a decade has led the energy system towards another tipping point: the need for system change not only in the power grids, but increasingly integrating heating and cooling and transport for mutual balancing. In parallel, energy markets need to be redesigned in order to provide the necessary signals for deployment of variable wind and solar power and of flexibility services including storage, power-to-gas, power-to-heat, grid extension, demand shift and various other requirements of a modern, RES-based sustainable and secure energy system.

On this background, the European Council of October 2014 had planned to take the necessary decisions to pave the way for a safe and sustainable energy supply in Europe until and beyond 2030. In the preparation phase of the Council Conclusions, particularly those stakeholders or member states which are closely linked to the incumbent fossil and nuclear energy system have asked for low levels of ambition, no 2030 targets at all, or for only a GHG reduction target. Allegedly, the GHG-only target would be the most effective way to deliver on GHG reduction by leaving the energy mix – including fossil and nuclear – to the member states. Although this was obviously an attempt to undermine effective growth of RES, the Council Conclusions followed this path. As a result, the Conclusions were not ambitious enough by far to meet the challenges of a sustainable energy system based on RES and in line with the needs of climate protection and safe and affordable energy supply, particularly after the Paris Agreement.

The target level of the 2030 climate and energy framework is disappointing. Forty per cent GHG reduction by 2030 compared to 1990 is not a really meaningful contribution to the target of limiting global warming to a maximum of 2°C compared to pre-industrial times; and even less can it be considered sufficient when it comes to implementing a 1.5° target, as the Paris Agreement is calling for. The 27 per cent targets for RES and for energy efficiency are hardly more than business as usual. Twenty-seven per cent RES by 2030 would translate into reducing the average annual growth rate of renewables to 1.1 per cent from 2020 to 2030 (after more than 6 per cent from 2010 to 2020). Renouncing from binding national targets after 2020 is weakening the implementation of the 2020 targets.

The European Council – though dressed up by ambitious language – has surrendered to the opponents of climate protection. Meaningful reforms of the Emissions Trading System (ETS), which might have provided a small chance to deliver a carbon price that would make investment in fossil fuels unprofitable, were postponed to far beyond 2020. And it was agreed that member states can decide to largely remove their support of RES as long as others fill the gap to deliver the 27 per cent in 2030. This is particularly problematic, because it allows member states to return to coal use or to try building new nuclear power plants, until they eventually find out that it is unaffordable or unsafe enough or both; even more so, since the European Commission has decided to allow state aid for nuclear power in the UK. All this will reduce investment in RES and energy efficiency and thus prevent timely and effective decarbonization of the energy sector. This is why it is extremely important to assure that the post-2020 framework for energy and climate policies in the EU starts with achieving the 2020 targets instead of weakening or reducing them in the upcoming new legislative packages.

Since the October 2014 Council Conclusions, some movement has taken place. The Energy Union Strategy has been further developed, trying to encompass all EU energy policies under this umbrella. And political pressure to change support schemes for renewable electricity from FITs to tendering systems as the new normal has significantly increased. Ignoring negative experiences around the world (cost increases and regulatory uncertainty), the European Commission is trying to enforce tendering and certificates, where FITs and premiums have been very successful. Unfortunately, member states – including Germany – seem to be supporting this U-turn in support policies. A positive aspect of the Energy Union strategy is the objective of tackling the energy market design and transforming it for the benefit of variable RES and a wide range of decentralized RES producers and consumers (prosumers). Successfully agreeing on a market design which favours flexibility, and penalizes inflexibility and carbon emissions, could have a strong positive impact on further progress of the transition towards an RES-based energy system.

This book contains key information for understanding the development of the EU's renewable energy policy, which was – until the 2014 Conclusions of the European Council – among the most ambitious frameworks worldwide for facilitating the transition towards a sustainable energy system. The authors provide key national case studies for understanding how member states, based on their own policy priorities, have shaped the EU framework and the present debates. The book addresses policy development in key member states, with case studies from all major sides of the present debates: long-standing and very recent EU members, northern and southern countries, traditional and new front-runners of RES, notorious nuclear supporters and also coal-addicted countries. The book also tackles interaction between domestic and European levels and the resulting dynamics of policy diffusion across Europe. Finally, an analysis of the external dimension of the EU renewable energy policy is also included.

Rainer Hinrichs-Rahlwes

Preface

The transformation of energy systems towards a greater incorporation of renewable energy sources (RES) is one of the most impressive examples of political and economic change in Europe of the past decades. Since the late 1980s, European Union (EU) member states from north to south and from west to east have dramatically increased the share of RES in their domestic energy mixes. Today, and despite a considerable slowdown since the beginning of the 2010s, the EU is a global leader in renewable energy policy and is widely seen as proof that the necessary transformation towards a carbon-free energy supply is no longer a utopia. But how did this policy change in the EU and its member states come about? Who were the leading actors, what were the underlying causal mechanisms and how did the unique structure of the European multi-level polity contribute to this outcome? These questions stand at the core of the present book. By systematically comparing the development of renewable energy policies in the electricity and transport sectors in ten EU member states from the 1980s to the present day, we seek to shed light on the complex dynamics of RES promotion in the European multi-level system. The comparative analysis is guided by a common analytical framework that conceptualizes policy change in the EU as a mix of bottom-up, top-down and horizontal interactions between a wide range of actors at the European level and in the member states. It is complemented by a view of the external dimension of RES promotion in the EU; that is, the ways in which the EU and its member states have an impact on renewable energy policies in non-EU countries.

The book is the result of a long and collaborative effort. It started in 2011 when Israel Solorio and Mischa Bechberger met in Barcelona and decided to join forces to carry out research on this topic. In March 2013 they started to develop a book proposal on a guide to EU renewable energy policy. In summer 2013 Helge Jörgens joined the book project when Israel came to the Environmental Policy Research Centre (FFU) of the Freie Universität Berlin for a two-year stay as a post-doctoral visiting scholar funded by the Secretary of Science, Technology and Innovation of the Mexico City Government (SECITI).

In the midst of this process, Mischa took up a new job at GIZ (Deutsche Gesellschaft für International Zusammenarbeit) and decided to step back as co-editor of the book. Shortly after, in summer 2015, both Israel and Helge left Berlin. While Israel took up his new position as Associate Professor of Public Administration at the National Autonomous University of Mexico, Helge headed for Lisbon for a two-year sabbatical leave and a position as visiting professor at ISCTE-Instituto Universitário de Lisboa. At the same time, major developments in the field of climate and renewable energy policy occurred – both at the international level (that is, the Paris climate summit in December 2015) and at the EU level (e.g. the 2030 Climate and Energy Framework and the revision of the renewable energy directive) – that had to be included in the analysis. Also, the Brexit decision had to be taken into account, especially considering the relevant role that the United Kingdom has played in shaping this policy. While all this led to a delay in finalizing the manuscript, the timing of its publication could not be any better. At the time this book is published, renewable energy policy in Europe is at a crossroads. The almost unconditional support to electricity from RES (RES-E) as well as to biofuels has given way to a more sceptical view of the associated costs and Europe's chances of 'going it alone' in the transformation of energy systems. Both developments – the EU-wide surge of EU renewable energy policy as well as first signs of their dismantling – are reflected in our analysis. At a crucial moment in time for this policy, this book provides an informed and empirically rich reflection on where we are in renewable energy policy, how we got here, and where to go from here.

This work would not have been possible without the support and engagement of many persons and organizations. Above all, we want to express our gratitude to the authors of the 15 chapters of this book. Their engagement, their patience and especially their willingness to repeatedly revise and update their chapters in what may easily be one of the most dynamic policy domains in EU policymaking were essential for the successful completion of this book. Our thanks also go to the Department of Political and Social Sciences of the Freie Universität Berlin and the FFU who provided Israel Solorio with the infrastructure and working space necessary to conduct this research. In particular, we would like to thank the director of the FFU, Miranda Schreurs, for supporting this project from its very beginning. We thank Oriol Costa, Christian Hey, Kirsten Jörgensen, Kerstin Tews and Severin Fischer for their valuable comments, criticism and contributions. A special thanks goes to the Fritz Thyssen Foundation for providing instrumental support to the authors during the revision process and to the Academic Association for Contemporary European Studies (UACES) and the UACES Collaborative Research Network on the European Energy Policy for helping us keep the chapters up to date.

Cate Mackay, Erica Callery and Mel Eycons did a great job in terms of language editing before the manuscript's final submission. Sofia Fuentes and Carla Covarrubias provided invaluable support with the formatting of the chapters and preparing the final manuscript files. Finally, we want to thank Rachel Downie, Karissa Venne and Alan Sturmer at Edward Elgar Publishing for their continuous support and their great patience as one self-imposed deadline after another was missed.

Helge Jörgens, Israel Solorio and Mischa Bechberger
October 2016

Abbreviations

ABEA	Association of Bulgarian Energy Agencies
ABIEC	Association of Big Industrial Energy Consumers
ACP	African, Caribbean and Pacific
ADEME	French Agency for the Environment and Energy Management
AEEP	Africa–EU Energy Partnership
AIM	Agencia de Informacao de Mocambique (Mozambique National News Agency)
ANRE	Romanian Energy Regulatory Authority
APER	Associazione Produttori di Energia da fonti Rinnovabili
APPA	Asociación de Empresas de Energías Renovables
APRB	Romanian Biofuels Producers' Association
ARBIO	Romanian Association of Biomass and Biogas
BGWEA	Bulgarian Wind Energy Association
BIOTEAM	Biomass Team, Intelligent Energy Europe project, 2013–16
BMF	Federal Ministry of Finance
CA-RES	Concerted Action on the Renewable Energy Sources Directive
CAP	Common Agricultural Policy
CEP	climate and energy package
CGB	General Confederation of Beetroot Producers
CHP	combined heat and power
CIP	Interministerial Committee for Prices
CLER	Comité de Liaison des Energies Renouvelables
CNE	Comisión Nacional de Energía
CO_2	carbon dioxide
COP	Conference of the Parties

CSP	concentrated solar power
CSP	Country Strategy Paper
DG	Directorate General
DG TREN	Directorate General Energy and Transport
DGEMP	Direction Générale de l'Energie et des Matièrs Premièrs
DLR	German Aerospace Centre
EBB	European Biodiesel Board
EC	European Community
EC BREC	Baltic Renewable Energy Centre
EC BREC/ IBMER	Baltic Renewable Energy Centre / Institute for Building, Mechanisation and Electrification of Agriculture
EC BREC IEO	Institute for Renewable Energy
ECCP	European Climate Change Programme
ECJ	European Court of Justice
ECOFIN	Economic and Financial Affairs Council
ECSC	European Coal and Steel Community
ECT	Energy Community Treaty
EDC	electricity distribution company
EDF	Électricité de France
EDF	European Development Fund
EEA	European Environmental Agency
EEC	European Economic Community
EEG	Renewable Energy Sources Act
EIA	environmental impact assessment
ENEL	Ente Nazionale per l'Energia Elettrica
ENGO	environmental non-governmental organization
EP	European Parliament
EPA	Economic Partnership Agreement
EREC	European Renewable Energy Council
EREF	European Renewable Energies Foundation
ERSA	Energy from Renewable Sources Act
ESO	electricity system operator
ETS	Emissions Trading System
EU	European Union

EUEI	European Union Energy Initiative
EUEI-PDF	EU Energy Initiative Partnership Dialogue Facility
Euratom	European Atomic Energy Community
FEE	France Energie Eolienne
FIPs	Feed-In Premiums
FITs	Feed-In Tariffs
FNE	France Nature Environnement
FNSEA	Fédération Nationale des Syndicats d'Exploitants Agricole
FQD	fuel quality directive
GBS	general budget support
GCs	Green Certificates
GD	government decision
GDP	gross domestic product
GHG	greenhouse gas
GMO	genetically modified organism
GO	guarantee of origin
GOVMOZ	Government of Mozambique
GRTN	Gestore Rete Trasmissione Nazionale
GSE	Gestore Sistema Elettrico
GW	gigawatts
GWh	gigawatt hour
ha	hectare
HPP	hydropower plant
IEE	Intelligent Energy Europe
IEM	Internal Energy Market
IFP	Institut Français du Pétrole
ILUC	indirect land use change
Interreg	European Territorial Co-operation
IPCC	Intergovernmental Panel on Climate Change
IPP	independent power producer
ktoe	kilotonnes of oil equivalent
kW	kilowatt
kWh	kilowatt hour

LPG	liquefied petroleum gas
MBSF	Mozambique Biofuel Sustainability Framework
MENA	Middle East and North Africa
MEP	Member of the European Parliament (chapter 2)
MEP	Scheme on Environmental Quality of Electricity Production (chapter 4)
MP	member of parliament
MPCs	Mediterranean Partner Countries
MSP	Mediterranean Solar Plan
Mtoe	million tonnes of oil equivalent
MW	megawatt
MWh	megawatt hour
NAP	National Action Plan
NBPS	National Biofuels Policy and Strategy
NEK	National Electricity Company
NFFO	Non-Fossil Fuel Obligation
NGO	non-governmental organization
NIMBY	not in my back yard
NREAP	National Renewable Energy Action Plan
ODAMOZ	Official Development Assistance to Mozambique database
OMC	Open Method of Coordination
PEN	National Energy Plan
PGE	Polish Energy Group
PJ	petajoule (quadrillion joules)
PPMs	process and production methods
PSD	Social Democratic Party
PSE SA	Polskie Sieci Elektroenergetyczne S.A.
PSL	Polish People's Party
PV	photovoltaic
R&D	research and development
RAC	Réseau Action Climate France
RAESBA	Renewable and Alternative Energy Sources and Biofuels Act

REALISE Forum	Renewable Energy and Liberalisation in Selected Electricity Markets Forum
RECP	Africa–EU Renewable Energy Cooperation Programme
RECS	Renewable Energy Certificate System
RED	renewable energy directive
REFUREC	Renewable Fuels Regulators Club
REO	Rynek Energii Odnawialnej – portal internetowy (Internet portal about the renewable energy market)
RES	renewable energy sources
RES-E	renewable energy sources for electricity
RES-T	renewable energy sources for transport
RO	Renewables Obligation
RTE	Réseau de Transport d'Electricité
RTFO	Renewable Transport Fuel Obligation
RWEA	Romanian Wind Energy Association
SADC	Southern Africa Development Community
SBS	sector budget support
SDE	Sustainable Energy Production
SER	Syndicat des Energies Renouvelables
SEWRC	State Energy and Water Regulatory Commission
SMEs	small and medium-sized enterprises
TFEU	Treaty on the Functioning of the European Union
TGAP	Taxé Générale sur les Activités Polluantes
TGCs	Tradable Green Certificates
TIC	Taxe Intérieure sur la Consommation
TIPP	Taxé Intérieur sur les Produits Pétroliers
TREC	Trans-Mediterranean Renewable Energy Cooperation Network
TSO	Transmission Systems Operator
UfM	Union for the Mediterranean
UK	United Kingdom
UN	United Nations
UNCTAD	United Nations Conference on Trade and Development
USDA	United States Department of Agriculture

WNP	Wirtualny Nowy Przemysł – portal gospodarczy (Internet portal for economy)
WTO	World Trade Organization
WWF	World Wide Fund for Nature
WWII	World War II

PART I

Introduction

1. The EU and the promotion of renewable energy: an analytical framework

Helge Jörgens and Israel Solorio

1.1 WHY THE EU RENEWABLE ENERGY POLICY?

There are several reasons why the promotion of renewable energy sources (RES) has ranked high among the priorities of the European Union (EU) in the field of energy policy, including a broad range of political, economic and environmental factors. Yet perhaps the single most important reason why the EU has become a global forerunner in the promotion of RES relates to the EU's institutional structure and the resulting nature of its energy policy. On the one hand, since a formal competence in the field of energy policy was not given to the EU until the Treaty of Lisbon in 2009 (Morata and Solorio, 2012), for years the European 'policy-makers borrowed legal competence from economic and environmental parts of the EU treaties in order to justify proposing and passing energy measures' (Buchan, 2009, p. 7). In particular, environmental policymaking provided an effective basis for EU programmes and policies in the field of energy policy and a potent channel for increasing the EU's influence on the energy policies of its member states (Tosun and Solorio, 2011). Against this backdrop, RES promotion, together with the promotion of energy efficiency and savings, was an almost natural choice for the EU in order to increase its overall influence in the energy policy field (Morata and Solorio, 2012). On the other hand, since the 1970s, the idea of a 'Green Europe' has gradually turned into one of the normative foundations of the EU (Lenschow and Sprungk, 2010, p. 134). A recent expression of the EU's self-perception as an ecological forerunner is its aspiration to become a global leader in climate change policy (Wurzel and Connelly, 2011). Within this strategy, RES promotion became a flagship component of the EU's energy policy (Knudsen, 2012).

Today, RES promotion continues the important role that energy issues have played throughout the historical process of European integration. However, while the European Coal and Steel Community (ECSC) in 1951 and the European Atomic Energy Community (Euratom) in 1957 were both founding pillars of what is nowadays known as the EU (Matláry, 1997, p. 14), today none of these institutions constitute core elements of the EU's energy policy. The ECSC expired in 2002, whereas Euratom remains as a 'separate legal entity' from that of the European Union (Barnes, 2013, p. 106). Conversely, RES promotion appeared on the agenda back in the 1970s together with efforts of the European Commission to invigorate cooperation in the energy field after the oil crisis (see Chapter 2 by Solorio and Bocquillon on the history of EU renewable energy policy). Ever since then, it has figured prominently on the EU's policy agenda.

But RES promotion, as well as energy policy as a whole, has become increasingly politicized in the EU over the past years (Tosun et al., 2015). In an EU obsessed with recovering the vigour and competitiveness of its economy, RES promotion is persistently being contested, both at the European level and within the member states. The October 2014 European Council's discussions on the climate and energy targets for 2030 were illustrative of this turn. While during the negotiations of the 2009 climate and energy package there was a broad consensus among member states on the need of having binding national targets for RES promotion for 2020, this time the agreement was reduced to a global RES target for the EU as a whole (see Chapter 2 by Solorio and Bocquillon). The EU is generally considered as a world leader on RES promotion. However, for many critics, recent developments concerning the 2030 goals place this position at risk, together with the European 'greenness' (see the Foreword by Hinrichs-Rahlwes).

This book proposes to be a guide for understanding the EU renewable energy policy, understood as the set of policy instruments developed at the European level to promote RES between the member states, including instruments of regional policy, research and development programmes, and market and environmental measures. In particular, we are interested in shedding light on the complex interplay of domestic and European drivers of policy change in the promotion of RES in the fields of electricity (RES-E) and transport (biofuels).[1] How do actors, institutions and policies at the supranational, national and local level affect each other, resulting in a European multi-level regime for the promotion of RES? What role do processes of top-down, bottom-up and horizontal Europeanization play, and how do they interact? Although the policies of RES promotion in the EU have received considerable attention in the literature, in particular by scholars in the fields of European studies, environmental policy and energy policy (e.g. Mez, 2007; Jacobs, 2012; Boasson and Wettestad, 2013), we still lack a thorough understanding of the interplay of policymaking at the European level and in the member states (or even the countries in the EU's neighbourhood).

Against this backdrop, the objective of this book is to present a detailed and updated picture of what the EU renewable energy policy is, how it evolved, and how it interacts with the domestic policies of its member states. The book compares the development of RES policies in ten EU member states (Bulgaria, Denmark, France, Germany, Italy, the Netherlands, Poland, Romania, Spain, and the United Kingdom) as well as in selected non EU countries, and explores how they interact with RES policymaking at the EU level. We apply a common analytical framework that draws on the Europeanization literature as well as on concepts and findings from the literature on policy diffusion, thereby following the 'European' route to the study of national politics and policies (Vink and Graziano, 2007, p. 4). Focusing on the whole EU policy cycle, the chapters in this book aim to understand how member states have shaped the EU's renewable energy policy, how EU policies have affected policymaking at the national level, how policies and instruments adopted at the national level have diffused between member states, and how and why the positions of the member states towards an EU-wide harmonization of renewable energy policies have changed over time. This picture is completed by an analysis of the external dimension of the EU renewable energy policy, for both RES-E and biofuels. In sum, this book aims to provide a comprehensive and multifaceted understanding of the EU renewable energy policy as one of the longest and most ambitious attempts worldwide to facilitate the transition towards a more sustainable energy system.

1.2 RENEWABLE ENERGY AND THE EUROPEANIZATION OF ENERGY POLICY

In order to study renewable energy policy in the EU and to untangle the complex policy process that surrounds it, we draw on the Europeanization framework as our principal analytical tool. Adopting a Europeanization perspective allows us to put emphasis not only on the domestic drivers of national policy change, but also on the (sometimes neglected) role of the EU in RES promotion. It also directs our analytical focus to the 'interactive process' of EU policy-making (Radaelli, 2004), characterized by an interdependent mix of uploading, downloading and cross-loading of policies and programmes between the European and the national levels and across EU member states (Bulmer and Radaelli, 2004; Bache and Jordan, 2006). In order to adequately account for the multiplicity of factors that drive policy change in the European multi-level polity, we distinguish between three types of Europeanization – bottom-up, top-down and horizontal – all of which prove to be relevant in some countries or at some point in time. Thus, by adding a horizontal dimension, our analytical framework goes beyond concepts of Europeanization as a 'two-way process' where 'member state governments both shape European policy outcomes [bottom-up] and adapt to them [top-down]' (Börzel, 2002, pp. 193–194). Horizontal Europeanization – that is, the direct diffusion or transfer of policies from one EU member state to another in the shadow of potential EU-wide harmonization – has received only marginal attention in the Europeanization literature (see, e.g., Bomberg and Peterson, 2000; Liefferink and Jordan, 2004). However, in the energy policy domain, where the EU has only limited competences, we argue that it might play an important role.

The following section presents in more detail the three forms of Europeanization and their relationship to the EU renewable energy policy, and integrates them into the analytical framework that will guide the empirical chapters of the book. Table 1.1 gives an overview of the different types of Europeanization and their underlying causal mechanisms, as well as their potential outcomes.

1.2.1 Bottom-Up Europeanization

Arguably, 'bottom-up' Europeanization is the point where the European policy cycle starts. It describes how policies or institutions are initially formed at the European level (Vink and Graziano, 2007, p. 9); how European norms, rules and practices evolve over time (Börzel, 2002, p. 193). Bottom-up Europeanization focuses on the influence of member states in the formulation of policies at the EU level (Radaelli, 2004). Member state governments are the single most important group of actors in the process of EU policymaking, either directly in the Council of Ministers or indirectly by setting the terms under which power is delegated to the supranational bodies of the EU. Thus, ultimately, it is the member states who decide whether to adopt new EU legislation or not. Accordingly, Bulmer and Radaelli (2004) refer to this kind of Europeanization as 'governance by negotiation', where the member state executives hold a key position in the decision-making process (Börzel, 2002, p. 195).

Table 1.1 Types of Europeanization, causal mechanisms and expected outcomes

Europeanization type	Causal mechanisms	Sources of influence	Expected outcomes
Bottom-up (uploading)	Pace-setting	Strategic capacity for pushing policies linked to national preferences	Minimize the costs or maximize the benefits of EU policies
	Foot-dragging	Power for blocking or weakening policies potentially costly for national interests or at least obtaining side-payments	
	Fence-sitting	Neutral or indifferent stance; building tactical coalitions	
Top-down (downloading)	Prescription of concrete institutional and governance models	Degree of institutional compatibility	Policy change or policy resistance derived from the EU impulse
	Altering the opportunity structure	Resource and power redistribution between domestic actors	
	Promoting changes in the beliefs and expectations	Mobilization of support for domestic reforms	
Horizontal (cross-loading)	Learning	Availability and use of information about existing policies in other EU member states (e.g., best practice)	Cross-national policy convergence in the absence of EU-wide legal harmonization
	Norm-based imitation	Notions about appropriate action in the field of RES policy are shared across EU member states; norm entrepreneurs try to push these ideals	
	Competition (political or economic)	Governments take unilateral action in order to avoid or minimize negative political or economic externalities resulting from other member states' policies	

Sources: Based on Knill and Lehmkuhl (1999, 2002), Börzel (2002) and Busch and Jörgens (2012a).

In processes of bottom-up Europeanization – or, as Börzel (2002) terms it, the 'uploading' of domestic policies and institutions to the EU level – individual member states may become disproportionately influential in the formulation and adoption of EU policies. The mechanism of bottom-up Europeanization has been thoroughly explored in the literature on the role, influence and strategies of environmental forerunner states (Andersen and Liefferink, 1997; Liefferink and Andersen, 1998). In general terms, this literature on leaders (as well as laggards) assumes a rational behaviour on the part of the member states. For example, Börzel (2002) argues that member states' 'responses to Europeanization are shaped, firstly, by their policy preferences and, secondly, by their action capacities' (Börzel, 2002, p. 196). Specific focus has been placed on member states that take on the role of forerunners or pioneers. A forerunner can be defined 'as a member state which is "ahead" of EU environmental policy in the sense of having developed more advanced policies' (Liefferink and Andersen, 1998, p. 256). Liefferink and Andersen consider that one of the main drivers for EU member states to become pioneers in environmental policymaking and subsequently try to upload their ambitious policies to the European level is to avoid competitive disadvantages for their industry (Liefferink and Andersen, 1998, p. 254).

An important attempt to identify the strategies used by environmental pioneers to shape policies at the EU level was made by Liefferink and Andersen (1998, p. 256), who distinguished the roles of pusher by example, defensive forerunner, constructive pusher and opt-outer. Building on this work, Börzel (2002) identified three typical ways in which member states responded to Europeanization. The first strategy, 'pace-setting', is about pushing those policies at the European level that reflect a member state's policy preferences in order to minimize the subsequent implementation costs. For some time, this strategy was used mainly by the classic 'green' member states (Germany, Denmark, the Netherlands, Sweden, Finland and Austria) (Liefferink and Andersen, 1998). The second strategy, 'foot-dragging', consists of blocking or delaying costly policies in an effort to prevent them altogether, or at least to achieve some compensation for the expected implementation costs. Blocking the adoption of stricter EU (environmental) law is often considered to be a 'southern problem' (Börzel, 2000). Finally, with less pronounced policy preferences, member states are likely to take a neutral stance in the European policy process. This third strategy is known as 'fence-sitting' and includes building tactical coalitions with both pace-setters and foot-draggers (Börzel, 2002). All in all, as Tosun et al. (2015) argue, the bottom-up perspective of Europeanization research provides a good explanation for how the EU policymakers' agendas are shaped, namely by (influential) member states and their respective preferences.

1.2.2 Top-Down Europeanization

While bottom-up Europeanization relates to the ways in which EU member states shape European policies, institutions and laws, top-down Europeanization relates to the implementation or the impact of these EU policies at the domestic level of the member states. Given that the adoption and implementation (or non-implementation) of EU directives is easily observable, top-down Europeanization occupies a central place in most of the Europeanization literature. This kind of Europeanization occurs where 'the supranational institutions have a considerable amount of power delegated to them' (Bulmer and Radaelli, 2004, p. 5), and it provides a useful analytical tool to study how Europe and the EU matter (Börzel and Risse, 2000). But, as Caporaso argues, the 'route from Brussels to member states is not a straight line' (Caporaso, 2007, p. 30) as 'the domestic outcomes feed back into the process of Europeanization' (Caporaso, 2007, p. 27). Therefore, in order to understand the domestic change produced by top-down Europeanization, it is necessary to understand how it interacts with a variety of domestic factors.

Knill and Lehmkuhl's (1999) typology of Europeanization mechanisms is a useful guide for understanding the variety of impulses generated by the EU from above. According to the authors, EU policies and programmes create adaptational pressures that span from: (1) the prescription of concrete institutional and governance models; to (2) altering opportunity structures at the domestic level; and (3) promoting changes in the beliefs and expectations of the domestic actors in order to gain support for the reforms promoted by the EU (Knill and Lehmkuhl, 1999, 2002). In this sense, it might be considered that very often a European directive includes more than one of these Europeanization mechanisms.

Most of the top-down Europeanization literature has emphasized the role of the prescription of concrete regulatory or institutional models. Here, the degree of fit or misfit between policies or institutions at the European level and those at the level of individual member states creates adaptational pressures which in turn affect the degree of domestic policy change (Risse et al., 2001, p. 7). Börzel and Risse (2000, p. 5) argue that 'adaptational pressures are generated by the fact that the emerging European polity encompasses structures of authoritative decision-making which might clash with national structures of policy-making'. In this case, whether change at the national level will occur depends on the existence of a prior misfit as the explanatory factor for policy change.

However, empirical evidence suggests that European policies may lead to domestic policy change even in cases of 'complete congruence between European and domestic policy and institutional arrangements' (Knill and Lehmkuhl, 2002, pp. 256–257). Bulmer and Radaelli (2004, p. 9) contend that the misfit or 'goodness of fit' argument 'is valid only under certain conditions', namely, when there is a presence of EU policy templates or models. In fact, the EU renewable energy policy is a case where the misfit is practically non-existent because of a lack of a harmonized support scheme model (see Chapter 2 by Solorio and Bocquillon). Therefore, the challenge in this context is to investigate whether and how Europeanization can be possible even without the misfit element.

The second mechanism identified by Knill and Lehmkuhl, altering domestic opportunity structures, refers primarily to a change in the distribution of power and resources between actor coalitions caused by European policymaking (Knill and Lehmkuhl, 2002, p. 268). Europeanization challenges existing 'institutional equilibria' by strengthening a coalition of domestic actors that supports the reforms intended by the EU (Knill and Lehmkuhl, 1999, p. 2). This mechanism of Europeanization can be deployed either by market-making or by market-correcting policies (Bulmer and Radaelli, 2004, p. 6). In the first case, it is more about policies allowing the entrance of RES into national markets (for example, by removing physical barriers for RES-E such as the connection to the grid). In the second, it is more about improving the competitiveness of RES in the energy markets (for example, by means of financing research and development programmes for RES). The promotion of RES could be considered to be market-correcting as RES are perceived as a means of correcting the negative environmental externalities produced by the EU's energy sector (Knudsen, 2012). Owing to the unfinished liberalization process of the Internal Energy Market (IEM), dominant economic actors within the sector, such as electricity utilities, are also expected to play a key role for the success or failure of policy change regarding RES promotion in the EU (Boasson and Wettestad, 2013, p. 79). Therefore, while the EU renewable energy policy may play an important role in redistributing the power and resources between actor coalitions, the case studies will also analyse the impact of the liberalization of energy markets in the EU on the composition and relative power of the opposing actor coalitions in RES policymaking.

The third mechanism, EU-triggered changes in the beliefs of domestic actors, is the least hierarchical but the most fundamental Europeanization mechanism. This mechanism is about consensus-building, but this time by means of an EU-induced change in the 'cognitive input' of the domestic actors (Knill and Lehmkuhl, 2002, p. 262). It might be complementary to the mechanism of altering opportunity structures at the domestic level, since both are oriented towards building support for domestic reforms. By changing the beliefs and expectations of the domestic actors, Europeanization may, for example, overcome persistent institutional veto points at the national level.

For the national case studies, it is crucial to look at the responses of three key actors to developments at the European level: RES producers, environmental non-governmental organizations (ENGOs) and traditional (and often still dominant) corporations and organizations in the sector such as the big electricity utilities. Given the 'packaging' of the EU renewable energy policy as a 'green' policy (Tosun and Solorio, 2011; Morata and Solorio, 2012), it would be expected that for both cases, RES-E and biofuels, the coalition supporting EU reforms should comprise RES producers and ENGOs (Solorio and Popartan, 2014). Such a coalition would be expected to act as a 'change agent', attempting to persuade other domestic actors to become more supportive of the promotion of RES (Börzel and Risse, 2000, p. 9). Conversely, we would expect traditional dominant actors of the sector such as the big electricity utilities to act as veto players against the changes promoted by or through Brussels.

Ideally, Europeanization would lead to the acceptance of the policy in question, leading to a series of policy changes that, in this case, would facilitate a major penetration of RES into the national electricity and transport sectors. In other words, successful Europeanization should lead to some degree of domestic change towards policy models propagated at the EU level (Börzel and Risse, 2000, p. 10). However, there may be cases where Europeanization does not lead to any changes at all, or can even have the paradoxical effect of national policies becoming less European than before (Radaelli, 2000). The first reaction is known as inertia, while the latter is defined as retrenchment, occurring when there is a widely shared negative perception of EU policies (Börzel and Risse, 2000). In this scenario, Europeanization may trigger domestic opposition to the policy in question. Consequently, one of the core concerns of this book and of the individual case studies is to assess whether or not Europeanization has actually led to the desired policy changes at the domestic level.

1.2.3 Horizontal Europeanization

Horizontal Europeanization refers to the direct diffusion or transfer of policies from one EU member state to another, within and affected by the institutional, political and discursive context of the EU. While bottom-up and top-down Europeanization have been studied for many years, concepts of horizontal Europeanization constitute a more recent strand in the EU literature. Its starting point was an increased scholarly interest in policy areas where the legislative competencies of the EU are limited or where intergovernmental agreement in the Council of Ministers has been difficult or even impossible to achieve. This focus has brought alternative or less direct forms of Europeanization to the front. The EU's Open Method of Coordination (OMC) is the most prominent of these mechanisms of horizontal rather than top-down Europeanization (see, for example, Büchs, 2007; Lodge, 2007; Nedergaard, 2007; Zohlnhöfer and Ostheim, 2007). Although horizontal Europeanization works in the absence of binding supranational law, or in issue areas where the adaptational pressures emanating from the EU are rather limited, it nevertheless may lead to policy change or even to a convergence of domestic policies towards the goals of the EU (Bulmer and Radaelli, 2004). In contrast to the vertical mechanisms of top-down Europeanization, it is based on a decentralized, voluntary and information-based process of horizontal cross-fertilization of ideas and policies between EU member states. It typically results in a process of voluntary convergence towards common policy goals which may be loosely coordinated by European institutions, as in the case of the OMC, but which may just as well emerge from uncoordinated processes of bilateral imitation and learning between member states.

Being relatively new to the Europeanization literature, the concept of horizontal Europeanization builds on a body of empirical research from comparative politics and international relations which shows that growing economic and political interdependence leads national governments to increasingly orient their domestic policy choices towards the previous choices of other governments. These processes, often labelled as processes of 'policy diffusion', 'horizontal policy learning' or 'policy transfer', have received growing attention in recent years (Jörgens et al., 2014; Busch and Jörgens, 2012a, 2012b; Holzinger et al., 2008; Simmons et al., 2008; Bulmer and Padgett, 2005; Simmons and Elkins, 2004). One of the core findings of this literature is that 'the mutual adjustment of autonomous states to each other's policy decisions' (Busch and Jörgens, 2012a, p. 221) often has effects that are very similar to those of binding international agreements or supranational policymaking through EU directives.

Although a policy diffusion perspective has not yet been systematically incorporated into the study of Europeanization processes, there are some preliminary conceptualizations that our analytical framework can draw upon. In a research note published in 2000, Fritz W. Scharpf argued that 'mutual adjustment' between national governments constitutes the 'default mode of Europeanized policy responses to increasing economic interdependence'. 'Here, national governments continue to adopt their own policies nationally, but they do so in response to, or anticipation of, the policy choices of other governments' (Scharpf, 2000, p. 11). Busch and Jörgens (2012b) have substantiated this claim empirically in their study on the diffusion of RES-E policies among EU member states. They find that 'decentralized and voluntary mechanisms of policy coordination can have effects that are very similar to those of centralized policy-making', and argue that processes of top-down Europeanization are often accompanied by less visible processes of bilateral imitation or learning which can best be conceptualized as 'horizontal Europeanization'. In fact, empirical studies show that these processes of decentralized and non-coercive policy diffusion are strongest in 'highly institutionalized contexts like the EU' (Busch and Jörgens, 2012b, p. 81; see also Bulmer and Padgett, 2005). They may occur in the absence of top-down Europeanization, but they may just as well supplement instances of supranational law-making. In the latter case, horizontal Europeanization may manifest itself in a convergence of domestic policies and instruments beyond the concrete goals and measures contained in supranational law.

What are the causal mechanisms underlying processes of policy diffusion? While scholars have identified a large number of potential mechanisms, these can be grouped into three generic categories: (1) (boundedly) rational learning; (2) norm-based imitation; and (3) economic or political competition (Busch and Jörgens, 2012a, pp. 234–235; for a similar categorization see Gilardi, 2012).

Learning occurs when national policymakers search outside national boundaries for effective solutions to domestic problems. The previous policy choices of states which had been confronted with comparable problems may offer valuable clues for their own decisions (Rose, 1991). Especially in complex decision situations, time-pressed policymakers are more likely to adopt policies already carried out somewhere else than to invent completely new programmes (Karch, 2008). Processes of policy learning can be more or less rational. While learning is always based on the belief that the potential benefits of a policy will outweigh its costs – Mossberger and Wolman (2003) refer to this as a form of 'prospective policy evaluation' – the information on which the expected costs and benefits of a policy are calculated is often insufficient or biased. Consequently, policy learning usually is at best 'boundedly' rational (Simmons and Elkins, 2003, p. 282; Weyland, 2007). Learning can be expected to occur mostly with regard to specific policy instruments, for example with regard to the type of instrument used to promote RES. By observing the effectiveness (but also the negative and/or unintended consequences) of an existing support scheme, policymakers can draw conclusions about the probable performance of this instrument in their own country. This mechanism of learning through prospective policy evaluation constitutes one of the main drivers of horizontal Europeanization.

The second category of mechanisms, norm-based imitation, comprises the different ways in which policy innovations are adopted in order for a country to gain national and international legitimacy. Policy innovations which are highly visible and which represent widely recognized values are particularly suited for symbolic imitation (Braun and Gilardi, 2006). In the area of environmental policy, this mechanism has played a central role, for instance, in the worldwide diffusion of ministries of the environment, but also in the spread of sustainable development strategies and the introduction of constitutional clauses on environmental protection (Busch and Jörgens, 2005; on the diffusion of sustainable development strategies, see also Jörgens, 2004). Norm-based imitation also comprises processes of socialization where certain internationally shared norms of appropriate behaviour serve as role models for domestic policymaking (Finnemore and Sikkink, 1998). This process can be expected to occur mainly with regard to the fundamental decision of whether RES should be promoted at all, but also with regard to the level of national RES targets. Norm diffusion can be strengthened when international organizations or transnational actor networks act as norm entrepreneurs by actively trying to persuade governments to adopt certain policies (Keck and Sikkink, 1998).

The third group comprises several mechanisms based on competition. In the case of economic competition, states adopt policies that are already in place elsewhere, with the strategic aim to preserve or improve their international competitiveness. Mostly this competition is conceived as a race to the bottom, where states alternately lower national standards until a common minimum is reached (Holzinger and Knill, 2005). The most recent national debates about 'excessive' RES promotion being a threat to domestic competitiveness could – in the absence of EU-wide harmonization, that is, top-down Europeanization – eventually lead to a race to the bottom in the form of a cross-national dismantling of RES quotas or Feed-In Tariffs (FITs). A second mechanism in this group is political competition. Here states struggle to become pioneers or early adopters of a policy innovation so that they can influence international policy developments in accordance with their domestic regulatory traditions and institutional structures, thereby minimizing future political and economic adjustment costs (Héritier et al., 1996). Often, political regulatory competition triggers action by the EU, leading to legal harmonization based on the policies in place in one or several pioneering member states (bottom-up Europeanization). Thus, the boundaries between the mechanisms of horizontal political competition and bottom-up Europeanization are not always sharp, and their empirical identification depends largely on the outcome; that is, on whether the cross-national leader–follower–laggard dynamics lead to the adoption of policies at the EU-level or not.

In the environmental policy field such processes of diffusion by political competition are found above all in issue areas relevant to the Single European Market (for example, packaging waste laws; see Gehring, 1997; Haverland, 2000). While political competition can be expected to play a role in the early decisions of EU member states to adopt RES policies in the first place, economic competition should occur primarily in times of economic crisis, especially when some forerunners have unilaterally introduced ambitious domestic policies, but attempts of an EU-wide harmonization of these policies have failed.

From the different ways in which horizontal Europeanization may occur in EU renewable energy policy, one seems particularly probable. We expect horizontal Europeanization in the EU renewable energy policy to occur primarily with regard to the design of support schemes. Since the negotiations of the first RES-E directive, the Commission has been pursuing the goal of having a European support scheme for RES-E in line with market-based mechanisms (see Chapter 2 by Solorio and Bocquillon). But (as shown in more detail in Chapter 2) this has been a history of failures for the Commission. The attempt at having a European support scheme was frustrated both during the negotiations of 2001 and again during the discussions of the renewable energy directive (RED) in 2009. In order to compensate for the lack of a European support scheme, the Commission set up a model close to the OMC. As a result, EU renewable energy policy facilitates the conditions for a horizontal Europeanization (Kahles and Müller, 2013). This function has been reinforced with the elaboration of national renewable energy action plans, intended to trigger an information-based process of cross-fertilization of ideas and policies between EU member states. Against this backdrop, Busch and Jörgens (2012b) as well as Jacobs (2012) explain the rapid spread of national FITs among EU member states despite the EU's inability to agree on a specific support scheme as a typical case of horizontal Europeanization. While the biofuels case has not experienced a similar debate on the harmonization of support schemes, it certainly also presents opportunities for analysing the diffusion of support schemes as a process of horizontal Europeanization. An example would be the diffusion of tax exemptions as a mechanism for biofuels promotion among EU member states (Wiesenthal et al., 2009, p. 794). Nevertheless, horizontal Europeanization can also be expected to occur with regard to RES targets (norm-based imitation) and, more recently, with regard to the lowering or dismantling of FITs or RES quotas.

1.3 OUTLINE OF THE BOOK

This book brings together experts from several European countries in an attempt to provide detailed and differentiated insights on the EU renewable energy policy, how it evolved, and its interaction with the domestic policies of its member states (and even beyond the EU). Although all contributors have been invited to adopt the overall analytical framework presented in the previous section, they have also been encouraged to reinforce it with the most suitable theoretical and analytical tools for their respective chapters.

In Chapter 2, Israel Solorio and Pierre Bocquillon trace the chronological evolution of the European structures of governance for RES promotion, including both the RES-E and the RES for transport (RES-T) sectors. By focusing on the historical evolution of the EU renewable energy policy, the authors capture the tensions between the attempts at centralizing renewable energy governance at the EU level (that is, Europeanization), and the preferences of several member states pushing for the renationalization of this policy.

In Chapter 3, Thomas Vogelpohl, Dörte Ohlhorst, Mischa Bechberger and Bernd Hirschl open the series of national case studies by examining the case of Germany as a pioneer in RES promotion. They expound the way in which Germany's interaction with the EU and other member states shows traits of all three types of Europeanization (top-down, bottom-up and horizontal). Importantly, the authors of this case study analyse how the German pioneer role – including its 'Energiewende' – has not always been welcomed in Europe and has sometimes led to conflict and disputes at the European level.

Chapter 4 tests the long-standing perception of the Netherlands as a 'green' member state. By assessing the Dutch behaviour in the context of the EU renewable energy policy and the influence of Europeanization processes – and contrary to what might have been expected from this environmental forerunner – Thomas Hoppe and Ellen van Bueren show that the Netherlands has adopted a laggard role when it comes to RES promotion. Continuing with the cases of 'green' member states, in Chapter 5 Helene Dyrhauge explains Denmark's role as an environmental forerunner by tracking the development of the national energy policy and its influence on EU renewable energy policy (that is, bottom-up Europeanization).

Chapter 6 deals with a very special national case: the United Kingdom (UK). In this chapter, Israel Solorio and Jenny Fairbrass provide an in-depth analysis of the British policy-shaping capacity at the EU level. The authors demonstrate that, in spite of the Brexit debates, the UK has been a key actor in the construction of EU renewable energy policy by means of both bottom-up and horizontal Europeanization, while the national energy policy has been only marginally transformed by European integration.

Chapter 7 tackles the Italian case and its relationship with the EU renewable energy policy. With it, Maria Rosaria Di Nucci and Daniele Russolillo open the series of national case studies dealing with Southern European countries. The authors argue that Italy has neither been influential at the EU level, nor has it complied effectively and in a timely manner with EU policies and institutional pressures. In Chapter 8, Israel Solorio and Rosa Fernandez argue that, beyond the economic cycle, the explanation of the early expansion as well as the recent retrenchment of the Spanish renewable energy policy importantly lies in the interaction between European factors and the domestic scenario. To complement the perspective on the Southern European countries' role, Chapter 9 by Pierre Bocquillon and Aurélien Evrard focuses on the French case. The authors illustrate the limited influence of the European factors in the development of French renewable energy policy and the ambiguous attitude of France at the European level.

The case of Poland is addressed in Chapter 10 by Karolina Jankowska and Andrzej Ancygier, opening the set of case studies dedicated to Eastern European countries. Given that the Polish government has resisted any progress in the European renewable energy policy that could potentially require or cause far-reaching changes to the national status quo (bottom-up Europeanization), this case study is also key for understanding the evolution of the EU renewable energy policy. In Chapter 11, Simona Davidescu shows that the need to adopt the EU *acquis* provided Romania with both an impetus and a straitjacket for reform in the RES sector, resulting in uneven development across the RES-E and biofuels sectors and a variety of structural, procedural and practical barriers to policy implementation. Chapter 12 by Ralitsa Hiteva and Tomas Maltby presents the case study of Bulgaria, a country where the implementation of EU renewable energy policy (that is top-down Europeanization) has been affected by lack of administrative capacity to govern a transition towards a larger share of RES.

In Chapter 13, Gonzalo Escribano tackles Europeanization from a different perspective. He develops the concept of outward Europeanization for referring to the EU efforts to promote RES-E related norms in the neighbourhood and tests it against the development of the Mediterranean Solar Plan in Morocco. Complementing this focus on the external dimension of the EU renewable energy policy, Lorenzo Di Lucia examines in Chapter 14 the external dimension of the EU biofuels policy and its impact in Mozambique. In the closing chapter, Helge Jörgens, Eva Öller and Israel Solorio outline the key findings of the case studies and analyse them in light of the three-sided Europeanization analytical framework presented above.

NOTE

1. In the field of biofuels, it is important to distinguish between first-generation biofuels, which are produced from food crops such as starch, sugar, animal fats and vegetable oil, and second-generation biofuels, which can be manufactured from various types of biomass including, for example, organic waste.

REFERENCES

Andersen, M.S. and D. Liefferink (1997), *European Environmental Policy: The Pioneers*, Manchester: Manchester University Press.

Bache, I and A. Jordan (2006), *The Europeanization of British Politics*, London: Palgrave Macmillan.

Barnes, P. (2013), 'The changing fortunes of nuclear energy in the sustainability discourse', in P. Barnes and T. Hoerber (eds), *Sustainable Development and Governance in Europe: The Evolution of the Discourse on Sustainability*, Abingdon and New York: Routledge, pp. 106–120.

Boasson, E.L. and J. Wettestad (2013), *EU Climate Policy: Industry, Policy Interaction and External Environment*, Farnham and Burlington, VT: Ashgate.

Bomberg, E. and J. Peterson (2000), 'Policy transfer and Europeanization: passing the Heineken test?', Queens Papers on Europeanization, No. 2.

Börzel, T. (2000), 'Why there is no southern problem: on environmental leaders and laggards in the European Union', *Journal of European Public Policy*, 7 (1), 141–162.

Börzel, T. (2002), 'Member State responses to Europeanization', *Journal of Common Market Studies*, 40 (2), 193–214.

Börzel, T. and T. Risse (2000), 'When Europe hits home: Europeanization and domestic change', *European Integration online Papers* (*EIoP*), 4 (15), http://eiop.or.at/eiop/pdf/2000-015.pdf.

Braun, D. and F. Gilardi (2006), 'Taking "Galton's problem" seriously: towards a theory of policy diffusion', *Journal of Theoretical Politics*, 18 (3), 298–322.
Buchan, D. (2009), *Energy and Climate Change: Europe at the Crossroads*, Oxford: Oxford University Press / Oxford Institute for Energy Studies.
Büchs, M. (2007), *New Governance in European Social Policy: The Open Method of Coordination*, Basingstoke: Palgrave Macmillan.
Bulmer, S. and S. Padgett (2005), 'Policy transfer in the European Union: an institutionalist perspective', *British Journal of Political Science*, 35 (1), 103–126.
Bulmer S. and C. Radaelli (2004), 'The Europeanisation of national policy?', Queen's Papers on Europeanisation, No. 1/2004.
Busch, P.-O. and H. Jörgens (2005), 'International patterns of environmental policy change and convergence', *European Environment*, 15 (2), 80–101.
Busch, P.-O. and H. Jörgens (2012a), 'Governance by diffusion: exploring a new mechanism of international policy coordination', in J. Meadowcroft, O. Langhelle and A. Ruud (eds), *Governance, Democracy and Sustainable Development: Moving Beyond the Impasse?*, Cheltenham and Northampton, MA: Edward Elgar Publishing, pp. 221–248.
Busch, P.-O. and H. Jörgens (2012b), 'Europeanization through diffusion? Renewable energy policies and alternative sources for European convergence', in F. Morata and I. Solorio (eds), *European Energy Policy: An Environmental Approach*, Cheltenham and Northampton, MA: Edward Elgar Publishing, pp. 66–84.
Caporaso, J. (2007), 'The three worlds of regional integration theory', in P. Graziano and M.P. Vink (eds), *Europeanization: New Research Agendas*, New York: Palgrave Macmillan, pp. 23–34.
Finnemore, M. and K. Sikkink (1998), 'International norm dynamics and political change', *International Organization*, 52 (4), 887–917.
Gehring, T. (1997), 'Governing in nested institutions: environmental policy in the European Union and the case of packaging waste', *Journal of European Public Policy*, 4 (3), 337–354.
Gilardi, F. (2012), 'Transnational diffusion: norms, ideas, and policies', in W. Carlsnaes, T. Risse and B.A. Simmons (eds), *Handbook of International Relations*, London: Sage, pp. 453–477.
Haverland, M. (2000), 'National adaptation to European integration: the importance of institutional veto points', *Journal of Public Policy*, 20 (1), 83–103.
Héritier, A., C. Knill and S. Mingers (1996), *Ringing the Changes in Europe: Regulatory Competition and the Transformation of the State*, Berlin: De Gruyter.
Holzinger, K., H. Jörgens and C. Knill (2008), 'State of the art – conceptualizing environmental policy convergence', in K. Holzinger, C. Knill and B. Arts (eds), *Environmental Policy Convergence in Europe: The Impact of International Institutions and Trade*, Cambridge: Cambridge University Press, pp. 7–29.
Holzinger, K. and C. Knill (2005), 'Causes and conditions of cross-national policy convergence'. *Journal of European Public Policy*, 12 (5), 775–796.
Jacobs, D. (2012), *Renewable Energy Policy Convergence in the EU*, Farnham: Ashgate.

Jörgens, H. (2004), 'Governance by diffusion – implementing global norms through cross-national imitation and learning', in W.M. Lafferty (ed.), *Governance for Sustainable Development: The Challenge of Adapting Form to Function*, Cheltenham and Northampton, MA: Edward Elgar Publishing, pp. 246–283.

Jörgens, H., A. Lenschow and D. Liefferink (eds) (2014), *Understanding Environmental Policy Convergence: The Power of Words, Rules and Money*, Cambridge: Cambridge University Press.

Kahles, M. and T. Müller (2013), 'Powerful national support systems versus Europe-wide harmonisation – assessment of competing and converging support instruments', in R. Hinrichs-Rahlwes (ed.), *Sustainable Energy Policies for Europe: Towards 100% Renewable Energy*, London: Routledge, pp. 69–79.

Karch, A. (2008), 'Diffusion mechanisms and the policymaking process', paper prepared for presentation at the 2008 Annual Meeting of the American Political Science Association, Boston, MA, 28–31 August.

Keck, M.E. and K. Sikkink (1998), *Activists Beyond Borders: Advocacy Networks in International Politics*, Ithaca, NY: Cornell University Press.

Knill C. and D. Lehmkuhl (1999), 'How Europe matters: different mechanisms of Europeanization', *European Integration online Papers (EIoP)*, 3 (7), http://eiop.or.at/eiop/texte/1999-007a.htm.

Knill, C. and D. Lehmkuhl (2002), 'The national impact of European Union regulatory policy: three Europeanization mechanisms', *European Journal of Political Research*, 41, 255–280.

Knudsen, J. (2012), 'Renewable energy and environmental policy integration: renewable fuel for the European energy policy?', in F. Morata and I. Solorio (eds), *European Energy Policy: An Environmental Approach*, Cheltenham and Northampton, MA: Edward Elgar Publishing, pp. 48–65.

Lenschow, A. and C. Sprungk (2010), 'The myth of a green Europe', *JCMS: Journal of Common Market Studies*, 48, 133–154.

Liefferink, D. and M.S. Andersen (1998), 'Strategies of the green member states in EU environmental policy-making', *Journal of European Public Policy*, 5 (2), 254–270.

Liefferink, D. and A. Jordan (2004), 'Europeanization and policy convergence: a basis for comparative analysis', in A. Jordan and D. Liefferink (eds), *Environmental Policy in Europe: The Europeanization of National Environmental Policy*, London: Routledge, pp. 14–28.

Lodge, M. (2007), 'Comparing non-hierarchical governance in action: the Open Method of Coordination in pensions and information society', *Journal of Common Market Studies*, 45 (2), 343–365.

Matláry, J. (1997), *Energy Policy in the European Union*, New York: St Martin's Press.

Mez, L. (ed.) (2007), *Green Power Markets: Support Schemes, Case Studies and Perspectives*, Brentwood: Multi-Science Publishing.

Morata, F. and I. Solorio (eds) (2012), *European Energy Policy: An Environmental Approach*, Cheltenham and Northampton, MA: Edward Elgar Publishing.

Mossberger, K. and H. Wolman (2003), 'Policy transfer as a form of prospective policy evaluation: challenges and recommendations', *Public Administration Review*, 63 (4), 428–440.

Nedergaard, P. (2007), 'Maximizing policy learning in international committees: an analysis of the European Open Method of Coordination (OMC) committees', *Scandinavian Political Studies*, 30 (4), 521–546.

Radaelli, C.M. (2000), 'Whither Europeanization? Concept stretching and substantive change'. *European Integration online Papers (EIoP)*, 4 (8), http://www.eiop.or.at/eiop/pdf/2000-008.pdf.

Radaelli, C.M. (2004), 'Europeanisation: solution or problem?'. *European Integration online Papers (EIoP)*, 8 (16), http://www.eiop.or.at/eiop/pdf/2004-016.pdf.

Risse, T., M.G. Cowles and J. Caporaso (2001), 'Europeanization and domestic change: introduction', in M.G. Cowles, J. Caporaso and T. Risse (eds), *Transforming Europe: Europeanization and Domestic Change*, Ithaca, NY: Cornell University Press, pp. 1–20.

Rose, R. (1991), 'What is lesson-drawing?', *Journal of Public Policy*, 11 (1), 3–30.

Scharpf, F.W. (2000), 'Notes toward a theory of multilevel governing in Europe', Discussion Paper 00/05, Cologne: MPIfG.

Simmons, B.A., F. Dobbin and G. Garrett (eds) (2008), *The Global Diffusion of Markets and Democracy*, Cambridge: Cambridge University Press.

Simmons, B.A. and Z. Elkins (2003), 'Globalization and policy diffusion: explaining three decades of liberalization', in M. Kahler and D.A. Lake (eds), *Governance in a Global Economy: Political Authority in Transition*, Princeton, NJ: Princeton University Press, pp. 275–304.

Simmons, B.A. and Z. Elkins (2004), 'The globalization of liberalization: policy diffusion in the international political economy', *American Political Science Review*, 98 (1), 171–189.

Solorio, I. and L. Popartan (2014), 'The implementation of the EU biofuels policy in Spain and the UK: a case of contested Europeanization', *Biofuels*, 5 (2), 129–140.

Tosun, J., S. Biesenbender and K. Schulze (eds) (2015), *Energy Policy Making in the EU: Building the Agenda*, London: Springer.

Tosun, J. and I. Solorio (2011), 'Exploring the energy–environment relationship in the EU: perspectives and challenges for theorizing and empirical analysis', in J. Tosun and I. Solorio (eds), *Energy and Environment in Europe: Assessing a Complex Relationship*, *European Integration online Papers (EIoP)*, Special Mini-Issue 1, Vol. 15, http://eiop.or.at/eiop/pdf/2011-007.pdf.

Vink, M.P. and P. Graziano (2007), 'Challenges of a new research agenda', in P. Graziano and M.P. Vink (eds), *Europeanization: New Research Agendas*, Basingstoke: Palgrave, pp. 3–20.

Weyland, K. (2007), *Bounded Rationality and Policy Diffusion: Social Sector Reform in Latin America*, Princeton, NJ: Princeton University Press.

Wiesenthal T., G. Leduc, P. Christidis, B. Schade, L. Pelkmans, L. Govaerts and P. Georgepoulos (2009), 'Biofuel support policies in Europe: lessons learnt for the long way ahead', *Renewable and Sustainable Energy Reviews*, 13 (4), 789–800.

Wurzel, R.K.W. and J. Connelly (eds) (2011), *The European Union as a Leader in International Climate Change Politics*, Abingdon: Routledge.

Zohlnhöfer, R. and T. Ostheim (2007), 'Politiktransfer durch die Europäische Beschäftigungspolitik? Methodische Überlegungen und empirische Analyse des Falls Deutschland', in K. Holzinger, H. Jörgens and C. Knill (eds), *Transfer, Diffusion und Konvergenz von Politiken*, Wiesbaden: VS Verlag für Sozialwissenschaften, pp. 327–347.

2. EU renewable energy policy: a brief overview of its history and evolution

Israel Solorio and Pierre Bocquillon

2.1 INTRODUCTION

The European Union's (EU) renewable energy policy has been in the making for decades. Its early history consisted of small and incremental steps dating back to the 1970s (Nilsson, 2011). From the late 1990s onwards, however, in the wake of the single market agenda and the establishment of an international climate change regime, more significant policy developments were put into motion (Tosun and Solorio, 2011). This chapter retraces the evolution of EU renewable energy policy, from limited sectorial attempts to promote renewable energy sources (RES) to the creation of one of the most comprehensive programmes for supporting RES development worldwide.

The chapter focuses on the historical evolution of the European governance structures for RES promotion, including both the electricity (RES-E) and transport (RES-T) sectors, following a chronological approach. It traces the tension between attempts to centralize renewable energy governance at the EU level and the preferences of several member states for a flexible framework that allows for a wide range of national support policies; these positions being to a large degree determined by different national political and economic contexts for RES promotion (see Reiche and Bechberger, 2004, 2005). The chapter argues that, although the 2009 renewable energy directive (RED) represented a leap forward in terms of the Europeanization of national renewable energy policies, centralization has been only partial and has not gone unchallenged, as shown by the debates on the 2030 RES targets and the subsequent revision of the RED. Section 2.2 presents the early days of EU renewable energy policy, based on soft coordination mechanisms. Section 2.3 focuses on the development of the first concrete measures in the early 2000s (RES-E and biofuels directives), characterized by indicative objectives and a loose regulatory framework. Section 2.4 analyses the consolidation of EU renewable energy policy through the RED, including binding objectives and decentralized national policy frameworks. Section 2.5 shows how the 2030 RES targets have been shaped by conflicting positions in a contest between centralization and re-nationalization, together with a heated debate on the future of biofuels support as part of EU renewable energy policy. Finally, section 2.6 presents some concluding remarks on the evolution of EU renewable energy policy.

2.2 FIRST STEPS: SOFT COORDINATION AND MODEST SUPPORT FOR RESEARCH, DEVELOPMENT AND DEMONSTRATION

At the European level, attempts at promoting RES were made from the late 1970s onwards (Nilsson, 2011). Following the two oil shocks, the Commission of the European Community (EC), the Council of Ministers and the newly established European Council called for research and development (R&D) support for 'new sources of energy' as a way to curb oil dependence and enhance European energy security (Boasson and Wettestad, 2013, p. 79; Hildingsson et al., 2012, p. 19). The EC adopted indicative energy-saving objectives and a programme for the 'rationalisation of the use of energy', including renewable energy research, demonstrations and regional applications (Twidell and Brice, 1992, p. 472). Yet these remained limited in view of member states' reluctance to relinquish their control over energy supplies. During the 1980s the promotion of RES was incorporated into the EU's regional policy. For instance, the VALOREN programme (1986) aimed to develop certain less-favoured regions of the Community by exploiting endogenous energy potential (see Chapter 7 by Di Nucci and Russolillo on Italy). Overall, before the 1990s most large-scale R&D support came from national programmes in a few pioneering EC countries – Germany, the Netherlands and Denmark – and neighbours – Finland and Sweden (Jacobsson and Bergek, 2004; Meyer, 2007; see also Chapter 3 by Vogelpohl et al. on Germany, Chapter 4 by Hoppe and van Bueren on the Netherlands, and Chapter 5 by Dyrhauge on Denmark).

At the beginning of the 1990s climate change moved to the centre of the EU's agenda (Skjaerseth, 1994; Morata and Solorio, 2012). This gave a new impulse to RES promotion, which was reframed as a means of addressing global warming. The JOULE and THERMIE programmes, adopted in 1989 and 1990, respectively, as part of the second Framework

Programme for Research and Technological Development, provided limited support for demonstration activities for non-nuclear energy. More significant was the ALTENER programme, adopted in 1993 in the wake of the Rio Earth Summit (1992) with the objective of reducing carbon dioxide (CO_2) emissions by means of RES promotion. The programme was part of a wider package of energy and climate measures, including the creation of a carbon/energy tax, and aimed to demonstrate EU climate commitments at the international level. However, due to stark opposition from several member states to the carbon/energy tax, the package unravelled (Skjaerseth, 1994). As for the ALTENER decision, this was substantially watered down. The programme was granted less funding than initially planned and contained only indicative objectives: a target of 8 per cent of RES in EU energy consumption by 2005, an objective of tripling RES-E generation, and a target of 5 per cent biofuels by 2005. In its infancy, EU renewable energy support constituted 'soft coordination of research, development and demonstration (R&D) policies' (Hildingsson et al., 2012, p. 21). In parallel, at the national level, several member states shifted from R&D support to more ambitious programmes aiming to support market developments for RES technologies. Denmark (1986), followed by Portugal (1988), Germany (1990), Greece, Luxembourg and Spain (1994), adopted a Feed-In Tariffs (FITs) system to support RES deployment (Busch and Jörgens, 2005, 2012; see also Chapter 3 by Vogelpohl et al. on Germany, Chapter 5 by Dyrhauge on Denmark, and Chapter 8 by Solorio and Fernandez on Spain). Other countries, such as the United Kingdom (UK) (1990), Ireland (1996) and France (1996), opted for tendering schemes as their main support instrument (see Chapter 6 by Solorio and Fairbrass on the UK, and Chapter 9 by Bocquillon and Evrard on France). At this stage, policy developments were mainly national and EU programmes were dwarfed by the more comprehensive and ambitious support schemes of a handful of pioneering countries; chiefly Denmark, Germany and Spain. Early actions at the EU level were nevertheless important in facilitating the conditions for developing national renewable energy policies while setting the basis for future action.

2.3 THE DEVELOPMENT OF EU RENEWABLE ENERGY POLICY: INDICATIVE OBJECTIVES, A LOOSE REGULATORY FRAMEWORK

The release of the 1996 Commission Green Paper on RES (COM, 1996), followed a year later by a White Paper entitled 'Energy for the future:

renewable sources of energy' (COM, 1997), represented a key turning point in the evolution of EU renewable energy policy. The White Paper included an indicative target of 12 per cent RES in EU primary energy consumption by 2010, and listed a set of measures to overcome remaining obstacles to RES development in the sectors of electricity, transport, and heating and cooling (COM, 1997, pp. 14–18). Released in the context of implementing the single market agenda, the two Commission documents emphasized the need to curb barriers to RES trade (Lauber, 2005b). Notably, the White Paper proposed creating a European system of tradable 'renewable energy credits' with the dual aim of fostering RES deployment and preventing 'market distortions' arising from the spread of national support schemes. It was not until a few years later that the Commission came up with legislative proposals, emboldened by new international energy and climate developments.

In 2000 the Commission launched the European Climate Change Programme (ECCP) in order to implement the EU's Kyoto commitments. RES promotion was therefore increasingly framed as a means of achieving EU climate commitments (Morata and Solorio, 2012). In addition, the rise in oil and gas prices, as well as the increasing dependence on fossil fuel imports, fuelled energy security concerns (COM, 2000), to which RES promotion was seen as a response. It was in this context that the Commission proposed the first two EU directives for RES promotion under EU environmental competencies (ex art. 174): one directive for the promotion of renewable electricity (RES-E) and one for biofuels (RES-T) (Tosun and Solorio, 2011). The Council and the Parliament eventually adopted them in 2001 and 2003, respectively.

2.3.1 The Renewable Electricity Directive

Directive 2001/77/EC on the promotion of RES-E was the first EU legislation explicitly oriented towards promoting RES (Reiche and Bechberger, 2004, 2005). It was originally proposed in May 2000, after a bumpy process of consultation with member states, the European Parliament (EP) and stakeholders (Lauber, 2005a, 2005b). Three issues were particularly contested: (1) the definition of RES; (2) the possibility of establishing binding RES targets for member states; and (3) whether or not the directive would contain a harmonized support system (Rowlands, 2005).

Regarding the first issue, several member states pushed successfully for a broad definition, including large hydroelectricity and industrial waste, that would make it easier to achieve their targets. On the second issue, both the Commission and the EP defended the need for mandatory

RES targets for member states. In contrast, the Council considered that the indicative target of 12 per cent was a useful and sufficient guide for national efforts towards RES promotion (Meyer, 2003, p. 666). Member states prevailed, and the targets that were eventually adopted, although relatively ambitious, remained non-binding (Rowlands, 2005, p. 970). Finally, concerning the third issue, a Commission draft leaked in October 1998 called for the harmonization of RES support schemes by establishing a European market for trading in renewable energy certificates (Lauber, 2007; Lauber and Schenner, 2011). The Commission argued that different policy instruments or differences in levels of support could create trade barriers within the liberalized European electricity market and result in unfair competition. However, within the Council the proposal was strongly opposed by both Germany and Spain (see Chapter 3 by Vogelpohl et al., and Chapter 8 by Solorio and Fernandez). During the negotiations, the issue split those market-oriented governments with plans for Tradable Green Certificates (TGCs) markets and those increasingly numerous countries that had successfully implemented FITs (Busch and Jörgens, 2005, 2012; Rowlands, 2005, p. 972).

The final directive dodged the most sensitive issues, resulting in a relatively weak text without mandatory targets for member states and without any harmonization of national support systems (Midttun and Koefoed, 2003, p. 684). The main objective set by the directive was an indicative goal of 22.1 per cent of RES-E in total EU electricity consumption by 2010. The annex of the directive also included national indicative targets, ranging from 5.7 per cent for Luxembourg to 78.1 per cent for Austria, based on countries' 'technological and economic potential'. While there was no European model for supporting RES-E, the Commission was in charge of presenting a report on the experience gained through the application and coexistence of different mechanisms. The directive also intended to tackle issues related to the grid system, requiring member states to take the necessary measures – including the possibility of establishing priority access to the grid – to ensure the transmission and distribution of RES-E.

2.3.2 The Biofuels Directive

Following the RES-E directive model, in November 2001 the European Commission proposed a legislative package for promoting biofuels. The main motivations were threefold: (1) curbing fast-rising transport emissions; (2) reducing EU dependence on imported oil in a context of rising prices and increased geopolitical tensions; and (3) supporting agricultural and farmers' revenues (Di Lucia and Nilsson, 2007; Afionis and Stringer,

2012; Akrill and Kay, 2014, pp. 55–56). As part of this package, the first proposal was a 'taxation directive' allowing for reduced rates of excise duty on biofuels. The second proposal, a 'deployment directive', set targets for developing biofuels in transport. The first one, negotiated under a unanimity rule in the Council, unravelled because of the sensitivity of the taxation issue, and was replaced by the more general directive, 2003/96/EC, restructuring the Community framework for the taxation of energy products (see Chapter 3 by Vogelpohl et al. on Germany, and Chapter 8 by Solorio and Fernandez on Spain). The 'deployment directive', however, was rapidly adopted by the Council and Parliament, under the Treaty's environmental provisions, in May 2003 (Tosun and Solorio, 2011).

Similarly to the RES-E directive, the nature of the targets proved especially controversial. Those countries that had already developed a significant biofuels sector (for example, Austria, Germany, France, Italy, Spain and Sweden), as well as the Commission and the EP, supported binding targets. They were opposed by those countries with a limited agricultural sector and some other more environmentally minded ones, which contested the benefits of biofuels in terms of security of energy supplies or greenhouse gas (GHG) reduction (that is, Denmark, the Netherlands and the UK) (Di Lucia and Nilsson, 2007, pp. 537–540). In the end, the directive only contained indicative targets for reaching a 2 per cent share of biofuels consumption in transport by 2005, rising to 5.75 per cent in 2010. The directive also left member states a large degree of freedom in choosing the most suitable instruments for biofuels promotion. As with the RES-E directive, the final text was therefore a loose framework for what remained a rather decentralized policy.

Although at the time the benefits of biofuels were already being contested, overall there was widespread support in view of the climate change and energy security challenges faced by the EU (Skogstad, 2016, p. 9). The most vocal opponents were the oil industry, which saw biofuels as competitors, environmental advocacy groups such as the World Wide Fund for Nature (WWF), as well as the Greens in the EP. To alleviate concerns, it was agreed that the Commission would report not only on the implementation of the directive but also on the sustainability of biofuel production, starting in 2006 and every two years thereafter.

2.4 CONSOLIDATION OF EU RENEWABLE ENERGY POLICY: BINDING OBJECTIVES AND A DECENTRALIZED NATIONAL POLICY FRAMEWORK

From the mid-2000s onwards, renewable energy policy climbed up the European agenda again, due to a combination of domestic and international factors. A review of the RES-E and biofuels directives showed that the indicative targets lacked teeth (COM, 2007). Only a few countries were on track to achieve their national objectives, while the EU as a whole was lagging behind its targets. In parallel, in a context of rising energy imports and security-of-supply concerns, heightened by the 2006 gas crisis between Ukraine and Russia, the Commission devised a comprehensive EU energy strategy, outlined in the 2006 Green Paper, that stressed the role of RES in climate mitigation and supply security (Morata and Solorio, 2012). Finally, the publication of new scientific evidence on the urgency and economic costs of climate change – from the Stern Review on the economics of climate change to the Intergovernmental Panel on Climate Change's (IPCC) Fourth Assessment Report in 2007 – contributed to creating a favourable context for RES promotion. In December 2007, as media and public attention to climate change was rising, the parties to the Kyoto protocol adopted the 'Bali Roadmap', which set a path towards a post-Kyoto international climate agreement.

It was in this context that the Commission proposed a set of three targets as part of a cross-sectoral climate and energy package, the so-called '20-20-20' targets: a 20 per cent reduction in GHG emissions (expandable to 30 per cent in case of international agreement), a 20 per cent energy saving target and a target of 20 per cent RES in EU final energy consumption. A sub-target of 10 per cent of RES in transport (RES-T) was also included. Although the Commission favoured binding targets, several member states – including the British and French governments – remained reluctant about these for RES (see Chapter 6 by Solorio and Fairbrass on the UK, and Chapter 9 by Bocquillon and Evrard on France). Yet, at a landmark European Council in March 2007, under the leadership of the German Chancellor Angela Merkel (see Chapter 3 by Vogelpohl et al. on Germany), the heads of state and government adopted the 20-20-20 targets. Against the expectations of many, the 20 per cent RES target was made compulsory, while the 10 per cent RES-T target was also made binding but 'subject to production being sustainable' to alleviate concerns about the effects of biofuels on the environment and food production (Bocquillon, 2015, p. 138; European Council, 2007, p. 21).

The conclusions of the European Council provided the impetus and established guidelines for the Commission to draft a raft of new legislation which formed the climate and energy package (CEP). Presented in January 2008, the CEP included a draft directive that distributed the efforts being made to achieve 20 per cent RES in final energy consumption among member states, made the 10 per cent RES-T target compulsory, and established a scheme for ensuring the sustainability of biofuel production. This text was negotiated quickly and adopted by the heads of state and government along with the rest of the package at their December 2008 summit, to demonstrate leadership in light of the climate conference at Copenhagen in 2009 (Morata and Solorio, 2012).

2.4.1 The Return of the Debate on the Harmonization of RES-E Support Schemes

During the negotiations there were relatively circumscribed discussions on the proposed national targets. The European Council's endorsement of the targets gave them strong legitimacy. In addition, and to anticipate critiques, the Commission abandoned its plan of sharing the effort in a 'cost-effective' way based on the RES potential of each member state, which would have been actively contested by various member states. Instead, the Directorate General Energy and Transport (DG TREN) proposed a distribution key founded on economic justice criteria – combining a flat rate of 5.5 per cent with a variable part depending on gross domestic product (GDP) per capita and adjusted to account for the past efforts of 'early starters' – which proved more resilient to criticisms (Howes, 2010; Bocquillon, 2015, p. 139). Yet, member states quasi-unanimously opposed the setting of binding intermediary targets in their National Action Plans (Gullberg, 2013).

Two aspects of the directive were particularly disputed. First, the Commission attempted once again to harmonize national support schemes for RES-E by means of a TGCs scheme in the name of 'cost-effectiveness' and 'flexibility' in achieving the targets (Nilsson et al., 2009; Lauber and Schenner, 2011). However, Germany and Spain, two large member states which had successfully promoted RES through national FITs, fiercely opposed harmonization out of fear that it would endanger their national systems (see Chapter 3 by Vogelpohl et al. on Germany, and Chapter 8 by Solorio and Fernandez on Spain). They had the support of national and European RES industry organizations – notably the European Renewable Energy Council (EREC) and the

European Renewable Energies Federation (EREF) – as well as the EP, whose rapporteur was the experienced Green MEP Claude Turmes. The Commission eventually backed down, proposing a directive that included certificate trading between companies but with possible opt-outs for member states under certain conditions (Fouquet and Johansson, 2008; Toke, 2008, p. 3003). This proposal, intended as a compromise, still faced stiff opposition from several FIT countries, the RES industry and the EP. In the summer of 2008, Germany in cooperation with the UK and Poland – two countries which had implemented tradable certificates at home – proposed a settlement that broke the deadlock (Lauber and Schenner, 2011; Boasson and Wettestad, 2013). It included cooperation and flexibility mechanisms to achieve national targets, but no TGCs scheme.

2.4.2 Managing the Controversy over Biofuels Sustainability

The second major bone of contention was the issue of biofuels' environmental sustainability. From the start, the benefits of biofuels in terms of climate mitigation and energy security were contested. However, the controversy reached new levels in 2008 when food price volatility, largely blamed on the expansion of biofuels and competition between food and fuel crops, caused riots in several countries across the global South, from Egypt to Haiti. In Europe, environmental and development non-governmental organizations (NGOs) seized on these events to challenge the 10 per cent biofuels target, arguing that it was responsible for hunger, land grabs, deforestation and the destruction of ecosystems in developing countries (Pilgrim and Harvey, 2010). New scientific studies were also harnessed to question the benefits of biofuels in terms of GHG emission reductions when the emissions associated with indirect land use change (ILUC) – the displacement of other activities by biofuels production – were taken into account (Fargione et al., 2008; Searchinger et al., 2008).

Responding to concerns over the sustainability of biofuel production, the Commission transformed the 10 per cent biofuel target into a target for all renewable energy sources in transport (for example, electric cars). The Energy and Environment DGs also worked jointly on a scheme establishing 'sustainability criteria' under which biofuels production could be counted towards the achievement of the 10 per cent target, which set criteria in terms of land conservation – excluding highly biodiverse lands or lands with high carbon stocks (such as forests and wetlands) – and GHG reductions, with a minimum GHG emission saving limit. As argued by Levidow (2013) and Palmer (2014), to deflect conflict and depoliticize the issue of biofuels sustainability, the Commission framed it as mainly a GHG emission reduction problem, de facto reducing its scope to a mere technical matter of carbon accounting.

In spite of these moves to deflect conflict, the biofuel target aroused acute debates. On the one hand, the green bloc constituted countries with limited biofuels markets or strong environmental movements, headed by Denmark, Germany, the Netherlands and the UK. These had more ambitious demands concerning the sustainability criteria for biofuels. On the other hand, those countries with significant domestic biofuels production or agricultural potential – such as Austria, France, Poland and Spain – lobbied in favour of the 10 per cent target (Sharman and Holmes, 2010). They opposed certain sustainability criteria that were not favourable to their domestic production, while often supporting rigorous criteria for biofuels imported from third countries (Müngersdorff, 2009). This cleavage was not clear-cut however. Germany, which had a high level of biofuels production, was generally supportive of biofuels under certain conditions, while the Nordic countries wanted criteria loose enough to allow their forestry and peat sectors to be counted as sustainable biofuels. Further, the EP was especially sensitive to the social and environmental impacts of biofuels and wanted to strengthen and extend environmental and social criteria. The French Presidency, which had strong stakes in promoting biofuels, was instrumental in brokering a compromise agreement that maintained the 10 per cent target but included slightly more stringent GHG and other sustainability criteria (see Chapter 9 by Bocquillon and Evrard on France).

2.4.3 The Final Agreement

In 2009, directive 2009/28/EC on promoting the use of RES, also known as the renewable energy directive (RED), amended and repealed both the RES-E and the biofuels (RES-T) directives. It established a common framework for promoting RES, including not only the electricity sector but also transport, and heating and cooling, setting an overall EU RES target of 20 per cent by 2020, as well as mandatory national targets in terms of overall share of RES in gross final consumption of energy. A flat mandatory target of 10 per cent RES for all member states was also included for the transport sector. The implementation of these objectives was left in the hands of national governments, which were required to elaborate National Action Plans including non-binding subsectoral and interim objectives in transport, electricity, and heating and cooling.

For electricity, the directive included mechanisms aimed at providing flexibility and strengthening cooperation between member states.

Although it refrained from harmonizing national support schemes, it introduced the possibility of joint support schemes, joint projects and statistical transfers of RES between member states counting towards the achievement of their national targets (see Howes, 2010 for more details). To facilitate the integration of RES in national energy systems, the directive established that member states should provide for either priority access or guaranteed access to the grid system for electricity produced from RES. The RED also opened the door for RES-E imports from third countries (see Chapter 13 by Escribano on the Mediterranean Solar Plan).

In a context of enduring controversy, the initial plans for the transport sector underwent further changes. The directive established that all types of RES should be taken into account as counting towards the 10 per cent target in transport. In addition, to make the target more acceptable to the EP and easier to achieve for member states, a multiplier was applied to second-generation biofuels – from non-food crops – as well as to electric cars. The directive included sustainability criteria for biofuels as well as mechanisms for calculating their greenhouse gas impact which broadly reflected the Council agreement. To be counted towards the target, biofuels needed to achieve a 35 per cent reduction in GHG emissions, rising to 50 per cent in 2017 (Akrill and Kay, 2014, pp. 65–66; Howes, 2010). In addition, they could not be sourced from highly biodiverse lands, and biofuel operators were required to provide a list of information related to environmental sustainability and social criteria to the Commission. Nevertheless, the highly technical, yet politicized, issue of ILUC was not taken into account in the calculation of GHG savings – despite the insistence of the EP – while other sustainability and social criteria remained vaguely defined. However, the EP obtained reinforcement of the monitoring and reporting requirements from the Commission, starting in 2012 and occurring every two years thereafter (Müngersdorff, 2009).

Overall, the contextual conditions in 2008–2009 were key to maintaining a relatively high level of ambition and commitment to RES promotion at the European level. International climate change negotiations and the EU's aim of presenting itself as a climate leader were decisive in the quick adoption of the 2020 goals and implementing legislation (Wurzel and Connelly, 2011). The sequence resulted in a more Europeanized structure of governance, through binding objectives with a centralized review process, but also the maintenance of decentralized national policy frameworks based on National Action Plans which left member states free to define their RES support schemes (Boasson and Wettestad, 2013; Bürgin, 2015).

2.5 RES PROMOTION AND THE 2030 GOALS: TENSIONS BETWEEN CENTRALIZATION AND RE-NATIONALIZATION OF EU RENEWABLE ENERGY GOVERNANCE

The road to adopting the 2030 targets has been marked by tensions between pressures for harmonization and attempts at re-nationalization. Moreover, the heated debate on the future of biofuels support has endured. These debates have influenced the negotiations over three key reforms of EU renewable energy policy: the 2030 climate and energy framework, the guidelines on state aid for environmental protection and energy 2014–2020, and, last but not least, directive 2015/1513, which amended important parts of the RED related to biofuels promotion.

2.5.1 Between Renationalization and Convergence: RES Support after the Economic Crisis

The need to establish energy and climate targets for the post-2020 period has been driven by the evolution of the international climate change regime, in particular the 2011 Durban agreement to begin negotiations on a new global regime to replace the defunct Kyoto Protocol, to be concluded at the Paris United Nations conference of December 2015. Nevertheless, the setback of the Copenhagen conference in 2009, where participating countries failed to reach an agreement and the EU was sidelined by the United States and China, has dealt a blow to the EU's self-proclaimed leadership in climate change (Wurzel and Connelly, 2011; Skovgaard, 2013). In addition, the financial crisis and its economic and budgetary consequences have fuelled debates about the cost of RES support schemes, which have been blamed for rising electricity prices in several member states (Bürgin, 2015, p. 698; see also country case studies in this volume). Criticisms of the costs of RES support schemes have been further intensified by the rapid fall in the cost of some RES technologies, especially solar photovoltaic, due in part to mass production in China which has driven several European producers out of the market. This context has influenced implementation of the RED and subsequent discussions on the 2030 goals.

Both the European Commission and the Council were divided on the nature of the 2030 framework governance structure. Part of the Commission, including then President Barroso, DG Environment and Climate Commissioner Hedegaard, as well as a faction of DG Energy, were in favour of keeping the established framework based on a general and ambitious EU target combined with national binding objectives. They had the support of the EP and environmental groups, which advocated an RES target of at least 30 per cent. This group especially emphasized the co-benefits of RES in terms of security of supply and jobs (Bürgin, 2015, p. 700). On the other hand, a strong faction of economists in DG Climate Action, as well as Energy Commissioner Oettinger, supported the UK's request for a single GHG reduction target, to be achieved through a reformed emissions trading scheme in a 'cost-effective' and 'technology-neutral' manner (see Chapter 6 by Solorio and Fairbrass). This strategy was congruent with several member states' aims to avoid binding commitments and re-nationalize renewable energy policies.

In January 2014 the European Commission put forward its proposal for a post-2020 climate and energy framework which included a 40 per cent GHG emissions reduction target by 2030 combined with a 27 per cent RES target. Disregarding the results of its own impact assessment, which showed the benefits of an ambitious RES target in terms of job creation and fossil fuel import reduction (COM, 2014a), the Commission settled for a watered-down compromise solution that preserved GHG emissions reduction ambitions at the expense of RES. The compromise consisted of a binding but unimpressive RES target of 'at least 27%' at EU level – only slightly above the business-as-usual scenario – and no mandatory objectives at the national level, in the name of flexibility. This move reflected the personal influence of the Energy Commissioner (Bürgin, 2015) but also, and above all, increasing divisions and reluctance among member states.

The October 2014 European Council, where the 2030 climate and energy framework was finally agreed by the heads of state and government, was held hostage by some member states, such as the UK and France, which were lagging behind their targets and were looking to recover control over their energy mix (EurActiv, 2014; European Council, 2014). The Poland-led Visegrad Group, representing Central European countries, also fought to get maximum flexibility and financial assistance to modernize their energy systems and meet future climate targets (van Renssen, 2014). In the end, an agreement was reached on the 40 per cent GHG emissions reduction target, at the cost of significant concessions such as free allowances for less wealthy member states. The 27 per cent RES target was maintained but without binding national objectives, while an energy efficiency target of at least 27 per cent was purely indicative.

Whereas the 2030 climate and energy framework agreement suggests renationalization of the EU renewable energy policy's governance structure, the guidelines on state aid for environmental protection and energy

2014–2020 (COM, 2014b) reveal a more discreet process of Europeanization of national RES support schemes. After several unsuccessful attempts to harmonize national support schemes through EU legislation, the Commission has adopted a different strategy for folding RES support into the framework of the internal energy market, in a context where governments are concerned with the costs of RES support schemes and their impact on energy prices (Jacobs, 2015). The revised environmental and energy aid guidelines prescribe that FITs are no longer considered permissible state aid and have to be progressively replaced by models that grant more importance to market signals, such as Feed-In Premiums (FIPs) or tradable certificate schemes (Boscheck, 2014; see also Chapter 3 by Vogelpohl et al. on Germany). This has accelerated the convergence of support systems across Europe, with several countries switching to FIPs.

2.5.2 Arrested Development: ILUC and the Backlash against First-Generation Biofuels

Since the adoption of the RED, the debate on biofuels' sustainability has carried on unabated (Solorio and Popartan, 2014). It has focused in particular on ILUC associated with biofuel production and its impact on GHG emissions. ILUC is especially difficult to measure since it requires life cycle assessments of specific biofuel crops and complex modelling of land use change dynamics (Di Lucia et al., 2012, p. 10; see also Chapter 14 by Di Lucia). Inconclusive and disparate pieces of scientific evidence on the scale and intensity of this phenomenon have been harnessed in a political battle between the proponents of biofuels: those countries with significant production, the biofuel industry and farming lobbies; and their critics: oil companies, and environmental and developmental NGOs (Skogstad, 2016, pp. 13–15).

According to the RED, the Commission was expected to produce a report on ILUC in 2010 which gave further evidence of the scientific uncertainty surrounding the issue, while recognizing the potential role of ILUC (COM, 2010). In 2012, responding to its critics and in view of growing evidence of the negative impacts of biofuel production, the Commission proposed a 5 per cent cap – close to current consumption – on the use of first-generation biofuels (for example, biofuels made from food crops), with the aim of limiting competition between fuel and food crops, and to favour the emergence of advanced biofuels. It also suggested taking ILUC into account in the calculation of GHG emissions reductions through the inclusion of an ILUC factor, and setting a 2 per cent sub-target for advanced biofuels. This move was supported by environmental advocacy groups such as Greenpeace, Friends of the Earth and Transport & Environment, as well as by the EP. The Council was divided between countries which pushed for a higher cap (mainly producers such as France, Portugal, Spain and several Central European countries), and those countries which supported the 5 per cent cap (Belgium, Denmark, the Netherlands, the UK and Germany, despite the latter's high levels of production) (Greenpeace, 2013; Skogstad, 2016, p. 18). In the end, the Council settled for a middle-ground position corresponding to a 7 per cent cap, combined with an optional target of 0.5 per cent second-generation biofuels by 2020. Member states will be required to submit information about ILUC, the potential inclusion of which in the calculation of GHG emissions is left to a future review. The EP reluctantly endorsed this compromise in spring 2015, after lengthy negotiations and as a second-best option (EurActiv, 2015).

Biofuels production has stalled, partly as a result of policy uncertainty created by ILUC debates, both at the EU level and in several member states. The economic slump has also contributed to this evolution through the levelling-off of fuel consumption and a collapse in oil prices. The negative image associated with biofuels and their uncertain benefits in terms of GHG emission reductions have curbed the enthusiasm that was apparent in the mid-2000s. In this context the future of the EU's biofuel policy appears especially uncertain.

2.6 CONCLUSION: THE RISE AND FALL OF EU RES POLICY?

European legislation on RES promotion represents a pioneering and ambitious attempt to transform energy systems in the face of the climate change challenge. Although other considerations – such as the harmonization of national support schemes as part of the internal market, or the support to the agriculture sector – have played an important role as well, international climate leadership has been the driving factor in these developments. Both the RES-E and biofuels directives, although lacking teeth – a reflection of member states' divisions and cautious approach – represented the first steps in the establishment of an innovative regulatory framework for RES promotion in the early 2000s. The 2009 RED built on this framework but included binding commitments to overcome the limitations of the previous legislation. The RED also marked a shift towards a more integrated approach to RES promotion, including the three sectors of RES-E, RES-T and heating and cooling. Finally, it partially centralized RES promotion at the EU level by setting mandatory national RES targets and giving the Commission oversight over National Action Plans. Yet, despite the Commission's activism, the directive came short of harmonizing or centralizing support schemes for RES, which remained a national prerogative.

The implementation of the RED has been relatively successful. As of 2015, the European Environmental Agency (2015, p. 10) estimated that the EU as a whole, and no less than 20 member states, were on track to meet their 2020 targets, transport being the sector in which progress has been the slowest. Yet, despite this positive outcome, RES promotion has somewhat lost momentum at EU level as well as in several member states. Since the outbreak of the economic crisis, RES support has faced a particularly unfavourable context, which has been exploited by some governments to reclaim control over their jealously guarded national energy mixes and by incumbent (fossil fuel and nuclear-based) energy industries to roll back renewable energy policy support.

The EU climate and energy targets for 2030 reflect these changing conditions. The RES target of 27 per cent by 2030 is only slightly above the business-as-usual scenario and only secondary to the climate mitigation goals of 40 per cent GHG emissions reductions by 2030. The rejection of mandatory national RES targets suggests a partial but significant renationalization of renewable energy policies, which has not stopped the Commission from seeking harmonization by other means (through its state aid guidelines). This long-standing tension between harmonization and national control can be expected to persist.

As for the promotion of biofuels, it has also been negatively affected by the economic context, but it is the enduring controversy over the sustainability of first-generation technologies that explains slow progress. From 'green bullet' to decarbonize the transport sector – and support agriculture – biofuels have become synonymous with land grabs and unaccounted indirect emissions, in large part as a result of the advocacy work of environmental NGOs. The economic interests of the agri-business lobby and of several governments have prevented a complete roll-back, but it is not incidental that no specific transport target has been proposed for 2030. In this context, it remains to be seen how rising emissions in the transport sector will be addressed in the revised RED.

REFERENCES

Afionis, S. and L.C. Stringer (2012), 'European union leadership in biofuels regulation: Europe as a normative power?', *Journal of Cleaner Production*, 32, 114–123.

Akrill, R. and A. Kay (2014), *The Growth of Biofuels in the 21st Century: Policy Drivers and Market Challenges*, Basingstoke: Palgrave.

Boasson, E.L. and J. Wettestad (2013), *EU Climate Policy: Industry, Policy Interaction and External Environment*, Farnham and Burlington, VT: Ashgate.

Bocquillon, P. (2015), 'Embedded intergovernmentalism: cooperation and conflict in EU energy policy-making', PhD thesis, Cambridge: University of Cambridge.

Boscheck, R. (2014), 'State aid, national energy policy and EU governance', *Intereconomics*, 49 (5), 256–261.

Busch, P.O. and H. Jörgens (2005), 'The international sources of policy convergence: explaining the spread of environmental policy innovations', *Journal of European Public Policy*, 12 (5), 860–884.

Busch, P.O. and H. Jörgens (2012), 'Europeanization through diffusion? Renewable energy policies and alternative sources for European convergence', in I. Solorio and F. Morata (eds), *European Energy Policy: An Environmental Approach*, Cheltenham and Northampton, MA: Edward Elgar Publishing, pp. 66–84.

Bürgin, A. (2015), 'National binding renewable energy targets for 2020, but not for 2030 anymore: why the European Commission developed from a supporter to a brakeman', *Journal of European Public Policy*, 22 (5), 690–707.

COM (1996), 'Energy for the future: renewable sources of energy. Green Paper for a Community Strategy and Action Plan', Communication from the Commission. Brussels, COM (96) 576 final, 20.11.1996.

COM (1997), 'Energy for the future: renewable sources of energy. White Paper for a Community Strategy and Action Plan', Communication from the Commission. Brussels, COM (97) 599 final, 26.11.1997.

COM (2000), 'Green paper: towards a European strategy for the security of energy', Brussels, COM (2000) 779 final, 29.10.2000.

COM (2007), 'Report on the progress made in the use of biofuels and other renewable fuels in the Member States on the European Union', Brussels, 10.01.2007.

COM (2010), 'Report from the Commission on indirect land use change related to biofuels and bioliquids', Brussels, COM (2010) 811 final, 22.12.2010.

COM (2014a), Impact Assessment accompanying the Communication 'A policy framework for climate and energy in the period from 2020 up to 2030', Brussels, SWD (2014) 15 final, 22.1.2014

COM (2014b), 'Guidelines on state aid for environmental protection and energy 2014–2020', *Official Journal of the European Union*, 2014/C 200/01, 28 June.

Di Lucia, L., S. Ahlgren and K. Ericsson (2012), 'The dilemma of indirect land-use changes in EU biofuel policy: an empirical study of policy-making in the context of scientific uncertainty', *Environmental Science and Policy*, 16, 9–19.

Di Lucia, L. and L.J. Nilsson (2007), 'Transport biofuels in the European Union: the state of play', *Transport Policy*, 14, 533–543.

EurActiv (2014), 'EU leaders adopt "flexible" energy and climate targets for 2030', 24 October, accessed on 15 July 2016 at https://www.euractiv.com/section/sustainable-dev/news/eu-leaders-adopt-flexible-energy-and-climate-targets-for-2030/.

EurActiv (2015), 'Lawmakers agree to limit food-based biofuels', 14 April, accessed on 15 July 2016 at https://www.euractiv.com/section/sustainable-dev/news/lawmakers-agree-to-limit-food-based-biofuels/.

European Council (2007), 'Presidency conclusions', Brussels, 8–9 March.

European Council (2014),'European Council conclusions', Brussels, 23–24 October.

European Environmental Agency (EEA) (2015), 'Trends and projections in Europe 2015: tracking progress towards Europe's climate and energy targets', Luxembourg, EEA Report no. 4/2015.

Fargione, J., J. Hill, D. Tilman, S. Polasky and P. Hawthorne (2008),'Land clearing and the biofuel carbon debt', *Science*, 319, 1235–1238.

Fouquet, D. and T. Johansson (2008), 'European renewable energy policy at crossroads – focus on electricity support mechanisms', *Energy Policy*, 36 (2008), 4079–4092.

Greenpeace (2013), 'Biofuels: EU Energy Ministers must choose right path for the world's climate & food security', accessed on 15 July 2016 at http://www.greenpeace.org/eu-unit/Global/eu-unit/reports-briefings/2013/20131209%20Joint%20NGO%20Biofuels%20Media%20Advisory.pdf.

Gullberg, A.T. (2013), 'Pressure or information? Lobbying for binding renewable energy targets in the European Union', *Review of Policy Research*, 30 (6), 611–628.

Hildingsson R., J. Stripple and A. Jordan (2012), 'Governing renewable energy in the EU: confronting a governance dilemma', *European Political Science*, 11, 18–30.

Howes, T. (2010), 'The EU's new renewable energy directive (2009/28/EC)', in S. Oberthür and M. Pallemaerts (eds), *The New Climate Policies of the European Union: Internal Legislation and Climate Diplomacy*, Brussels: VUB Press, pp. 117–150.

Jacobs, D. (2015), 'Designing financing mechanisms for electricity from renewable energy sources: the role of the European Commission as an agenda shaper', in J. Tosun, S. Biesenbender and K. Schulze (eds), *Energy Policy Making in the EU. Building the Agenda*, London: Springer, pp. 107–128.

Jacobsson, S. and A. Bergek (2004), 'Transforming the energy sector: the evolution of technological systems in renewable energy technology', *Industrial and Corporate Change*, 13 (5), 815–849.

Lauber, V. (2005a), 'Renewable at the level of the European Union', in D. Reiche (ed.), *Handbook of Renewable Energies in the European Union*, Frankfurt: Peter Lang, pp. 39–53.

Lauber, V. (2005b), 'European Union policy towards renewables', in V. Lauber (ed.), *Switching to Renewable Power: A Framework for the 21st Century*, London: Earthscan, pp. 203–216.

Lauber, V. (2007), 'The politics of the European Union policy on support schemes for electricity from renewable energy sources, 2007', in L. Mez (ed.), *Green Power Markets: Support Schemes, Case Studies and Perspectives*, Brentwood: Multi-Science Publishing, pp. 9–29.

Lauber, V. and E. Schenner (2011), 'The struggle over support schemes for renewable electricity in the European Union: a discursive-institutionalist analysis', *Environmental Politics*, 20 (4), 508–527.

Levidow, L. (2013), 'EU criteria for sustainable biofuels: accounting for carbon, depoliticizing plunder', *Geoforum*, 44, 211–223.

Meyer, N.I. (2003), 'European schemes for promoting renewables in liberalized markets'. *Energy Policy*, 31, 665–676.

Meyer, N.I. (2007), 'Learning from wind energy policy in the EU: lessons from Denmark, Sweden and Spain', *European Environment*, 17 (5), 347–362.

Midttun, A. and A.L. Koefoed (2003), 'Greening of electricity in Europe: challenges and developments', *Energy Policy*, 31, 677–687.

Morata, F. and I. Solorio (eds) (2012), *European Energy Policy: An Environmental Approach*, Cheltenham and Northampton, MA: Edward Elgar Publishing.

Müngersdorff, M. (2009), 'Evaluating EU decision-making processes: a case study on the "Renewable Energy in Transport Target" and the "Sustainability Criteria for Biofuel Production" in the context of the EU's climate and energy package', Stockholm Environment Institute, Working Paper.

Nilsson, M. (2011), 'EU renewable energy policy: mixed emotions towards harmonization', in V.L. Birchfield and J.S. Duffield (eds), *Towards a Common European Union Energy Policy: Problems, Progress and Prospects*, New York: Palgrave, pp. 113–130.

Nilsson, M., L.J. Nilsson and K. Ericsson (2009), 'The rise and fall of GO trading in European renewable energy policy: the role of advocacy and policy framing', *Energy Policy*, 37, 4454–4462.

Palmer, J.R. (2014), 'Biofuels and the politics of land-use change: tracing the interactions of discourse and place in European policy making', *Environment and Planning*, 46, 337–352.

Pilgrim, S. and M. Harvey (2010), 'Battles over biofuels in Europe: NGOs and the politics of markets', *Sociological Research Online*, 15(3), 4, accessed 15 August 2016 at http://www.socresonline.org.uk/15/3/4.html.

Reiche, D. and M. Bechberger (2004), 'Policy differences in the promotion of renewable energies in the EU member states', *Energy Policy*, 32, 843–849.

Reiche, D. and M. Bechberger (2005), 'Renewable energies in the EU – member states in comparison', in D. Reiche (ed.), *Handbook of Renewable Energies in the European Union*, Frankfurt: Peter Lang, pp. 19–37.

Rowlands, I.H. (2005), 'The European directive on renewable electricity: conflicts and compromises', *Energy Policy*, 33, 965–974.

Searchinger, T., R. Heimlich, R.A. Houghton, F. Dong, A. Elobeid, J. Fabiosa, S. Tokgoz, D. Hayes and T.-H. Yu (2008), 'Use of US croplands for biofuels increases greenhouse gases through emissions from land-use change', *Science*, 319, 1238–1240.

Sharman, A. and J. Holmes (2010),'Evidence-based policy or policy-based evidence gathering? Biofuels, the EU and the 10% target', *Environmental Policy and Governance*, 20 (5), 309–321.

Skjaerseth, J. (1994), 'The climate policy of the EC: too hot to handle', *Journal of Common Market Studies*, 32 (1), 25–42.

Skogstad, G. (2016), 'Policy feedback and self-reinforcing and self-undermining processes in EU biofuels policy', *Journal of European Public Policy*, 24 (1), 1–21.

Skovgaard, J. (2013),'The limits of entrapment: the negotiations on EU reduction targets, 2007–2011', *Journal of Common Market Studies*, 51, 1141–1157.

Solorio, I. and L. Popartan (2014),'The implementation of the EU biofuels policy in Spain and the UK: a case of contested Europeanization', *Biofuels*, 5 (2), 129–140.

Toke, D. (2008), 'The EU renewable directive – what is the fuss about trading?', *Energy Policy*, 36, 3001–3008.

Tosun, J. and I. Solorio (2011), 'Exploring the energy–environment relationship in the EU: perspectives and challenges for theorizing and empirical analysis', *European Integration online Papers (EIoP)*, Special Mini-Issue 1, Vol. 15, http://eiop.or.at/eiop/texte/2011-007a.htm.

Twidell, J. and J. Brice (1992),'Strategies for implementing renewable energy: lessons from Europe', *Energy Policy*, 20 (5), 464–479.

van Renssen, S. (2014), 'The EU's great 2030 energy and climate compromise', *Energy Post*, 24 October, accessed on 15 July 2016 at http://www.energypost.eu/eus-great-2030-energy-climate-compromise/.

Wurzel, R. and J. Connelly (2011), *The EU as a Leader in International Climate Change Politics*, New York: Routledge.

PART II

National case studies

3. German renewable energy policy: independent pioneering versus creeping Europeanization?

Thomas Vogelpohl, Dörte Ohlhorst, Mischa Bechberger and Bernd Hirschl

3.1 INTRODUCTION

The German 'Energiewende' is perceived throughout the world as a demanding transformation approach towards an energy system with a high share of renewable energy sources (RES). With first attempts starting in the early 1970s, and with more intense efforts as of the early 1990s, innovative domestic policies have been adopted to increase the share of RES, with relative success both in the RES for electricity (RES-E) and the renewable energy sources for transport (RES-T) sector. However, these pioneer RES policies were not only welcomed in Europe, but also led to conflicts and disputes at the European Union (EU) level.

Therefore, this chapter asks how the vertical and horizontal interactions between Germany and both the EU and other member states can be appraised. Did Germany push its pioneer policy at the EU level? Or did it block or weaken policies at the EU level which did not fit the domestic policy? Did Germany promote its pioneer policy in other member states? Or did the EU or other countries undermine this pioneering role? Did the EU prescribe or otherwise promote opposing policy models? Which mechanisms and strategies were at play in these contexts? And, last but not least, what are the differences between RES-E and RES-T policy with regard to the German case? To answer these questions, we will build on the analytical framework of Europeanization, according to which these vertical and horizontal interactions can be classified into three types of Europeanization: bottom-up (uploading), top-down (downloading), and horizontal (cross-loading), each of them associated with specific mechanisms and strategies (see Chapter 1 by Jörgens and Solorio).

In the following sections, we will expound that Germany's interaction with the EU and other member states shows traits of all three types of Europeanization, but is mainly characterized by its pioneering position in RES promotion. Due to this, Germany's provision emphasized horizontal Europeanization (cross-loading) for at least a decade, particularly in the RES-E sector. Simultaneously, Germany shaped European policy in a foot-dragging way: it influenced the design of European law in order to keep room for manoeuvre at the national level. Thus, Germany was for a long time able to safeguard its RES policies against harmonization efforts by the European Commission. Recently, however, Germany has been jeopardizing its pioneer position, and top-down Europeanization is increasingly affecting its domestic RES policies in both the RES-E and the RES-T sector.

3.2 ANALYTICAL UNDERPINNINGS AND METHODS

Germany is often considered a pioneer or forerunner in EU renewable energy policy (Jänicke, 2011; Jacobsson and Lauber, 2006; Solorio et al., 2014; Mez, 2009). But what does being a pioneer country mean in terms of the abovementioned types of Europeanization? Environmental policy pioneering can be related to two types of Europeanization: uploading and cross-loading. Uploading – specifically the mechanism of pacesetting – represents a rather offensive strategy. It implies that the pioneering country actively uploads its domestic pioneer policy to the supranational level. This presupposes the strategic capacity for pushing policies in line with domestic preferences at the EU level (see Chapter 1 by Jörgens and Solorio). Thus, a question of pivotal importance is whether a pioneering country has this capacity; and, in the case that it does, how does it use this capacity strategically? In the case that it uses it sensibly and successfully, a pioneering country can avoid or minimize downloading costs potentially triggered by differing EU-wide legal harmonization efforts. Instead, other member states would be forced to adopt the policy of the pioneering country, which implies costs to the former and a competitive edge to the latter. As Liefferink and Andersen (1998) suppose, this strategy can be expected to be pursued by a classic 'green' member state like Germany.

However, uploading (in the sense of pacesetting) is not the only strategy pursuable by environmental policy pioneer countries. Cross-loading represents an alternative pioneering strategy. It implies that pioneering countries – confronted with the impossibility of uploading national policies – act as norm entrepreneurs which function 'as (intellectual) leaders under conditions of uncertainty. Their solutions for general environmental problems are adopted by other countries' (Jänicke, 2005, p. 129), thereby providing 'a stimulus to rethink established policies and to cause changes in beliefs concerning what is feasible' (Andersen and Liefferink, 1997, p. 4). Furthermore, cross-loading is a way to avoid or minimize negative political or economic externalities. In the context of the EU multi-level system, however, cross loading of pioneer policies has to be accompanied by the uploading strategy of foot-dragging; that is, avoiding legal harmonization at the supranational level which would compromise the pioneer policy. Therefore, strategic activities of the cross loading country not only have to be focused on fellow countries, but also on the supranational level, where a policy framework needs to be promoted which gives member states enough leeway to adopt and implement the pioneer policy.

Thus, pioneering in environmental policy in the EU implies a certain Europeanization strategy: either the uploading, pacesetting one, or the alternative cross-loading, norm-entrepreneurial one that has to be accompanied by foot-dragging at the supranational level. Recent developments, however, hint at Germany's loss of a pioneering role in the area of renewable energy policy. Along with this supposition the question arises as to whether Germany is also being affected by EU policy. Top-down Europeanization, particularly in the case of EU renewable energy policy, does not necessarily take the form of concrete policies or institutional models which are prescribed in a legally binding manner by the EU. There are also less obvious forms of top-down Europeanization which take effect via the alteration of opportunity structures. They can be triggered by a change in the distribution of power and resources between actor coalitions at the domestic level caused by European policymaking. They can also be initiated via changes in the belief systems and expectations of actors at the domestic level which are triggered by 'cognitive input' from the EU level (see Chapter 1 by Jörgens and Solorio).

This conceptual framework of Europeanization equips us with the analytical tools necessary to answer the questions raised in the introduction. Methodologically, this analysis is based on comprehensive secondary literature on the German RES-E and RES-T policies supported by the analysis of primary policy documents. These documents include drafts of laws and regulations, minutes of parliamentary plenary and committee meetings, reports of hearings and conferences, statements and studies commissioned by the actors involved, press releases, and so on. These documents were qualitatively analysed in order to extract the positions of the actors involved and the interactions between the national and the EU level. In cases where relevant information could not be obtained from the literature analysis, where open questions needed to be clarified, or where preliminary results needed to be validated, these analyses were complemented by individual interviews with experts deeply involved in the relevant policy processes.

3.3 RES-E POLICY IN GERMANY AND ITS REPERCUSSIONS AT THE EU LEVEL

3.3.1 Early RES-E Policy in Germany

The promotion of RES-E in Germany took its first steps after the first oil price crisis in 1973. Until the late 1980s however this promotion consisted only of smaller incentive programmes for wind and solar energy. This changed in 1990, when the Electricity Feed-In Act was passed. It was one of the first laws in Europe obliging public energy utilities to purchase and remunerate RES-E on a yearly fixed basis.[1]

During the 1990s, not only the RES-E support policy, but also the general legal framework for the energy sector was important for the promotion of RES-E in Germany. Several governments had unsuccessfully tried to introduce more competition in the energy market, but failed over many years due to the resistance of powerful advocacy coalitions, dominated by energy companies (Monstadt, 2004). However, directive 96/92/EC requested a liberalization of the electricity market and thus exerted pressure on member states to take action. The directive was eventually implemented in Germany in 1998 by the first amendment to the Energy Industry Act. Thus, the liberalization process in Germany was characterized by a downloading process, or more specifically by the EU using the mechanism of prescribing a liberalized governance model. Germany downloaded the EU strategy of liberalization. German lobby groups welcomed the directive: they expected both more competition and lower prices from a market reform (industrial lobby groups, parts of the government, cartel office), and more leeway towards greening and decentralizing the electricity supply (Green Party, environmental associations, new market players) (Hirschl, 2008, pp. 144–149). The directive explicitly allowed priority schemes for RES.

Despite this regulatory clarity a heated policy debate regarding RES-E support schemes took place between the European Commission and different actors which gave the start signal for the negotiation process of the RES-E directive. On the one hand, the Commission considered

Feed-In Tariffs (FITs) to be distortive state aid, and strove for harmonization based on a Europe-wide green certificate system (Busch and Jörgens, 2012, p. 75). The energy industry lobbied both at national and EU level to promote quota models. On the other hand, the Environment Commissioner, member states such as Germany and Spain (see Chapter 8 by Solorio and Fernandez), as well as large parts of the renewable lobby, advocated FITs. The European Parliament as well as the European Council promoted subsidiarity and maintenance of the member states' scope for action (Hirschl, 2008, pp. 299–306). In Germany, the debates started in the mid-1990s, when RES-E expansion successes were already achieved in wind and hydropower. Because of this development, German power utilities and energy organizations tried to exploit European regulation for their interests: they called the European Court of Justice (via the Kiel Regional Court) in 1998 to take action against the Electricity Feed-In Act as they considered it state aid; the ensuing court proceedings (*Preussen Elektra vs. Schleswag*) extended over a period of three years.

Meanwhile, Directorate General (DG) Competition exerted pressure on the German government and requested the abolition of the compensation scheme of the Electricity Feed-In Act (Jacobsson and Lauber, 2006, p. 265). The German government thereupon proposed a reduction of feed-in rates in 1997, which was welcomed by the ministry in charge of this matter, the German Ministry of Economic Affairs. As a result, German actors, particularly the wind energy association, sought supporters at the European level and set up a European lobby organization (the European Renewable Energies Foundation, EREF) in 1999, with the aim of trying to avoid EU harmonization (foot-dragging). On the national level, a broad and unprecedented social alliance ('tailwind campaign' 1997) for RES was formed, including different social groups such as associations, environmental groups, trade unions and churches (Jacobsson and Lauber, 2006, p. 265; Bruns et al., 2011, p. 370).

German policies for RES support were further strengthened with the new Red–Green coalition which had taken office in 1998 and had committed to the preservation of the German model of FITs (Hirschl, 2008, pp. 257–279). The new German government took over the European Council Presidency in 1999 and thus gained more influence on the Council of Energy Ministers. In this context the German Federal Ministry of Economic Affairs campaigned for the preservation of national support schemes. Moreover, the Treaty of Amsterdam came into force in 1999, strengthening the European Parliament and the principle of subsidiarity.

In the middle of the negotiation process of the RES-E directive, the Renewable Energy Sources Act (EEG) was adopted in 2000, replacing the Electricity Feed-In Act, and established a new, pioneering support policy with improved investment security for generators: while under the Electricity Feed-In Act compensation rates were expressed as percentages of average customer tariffs, the new rates were fixed for 20 years. A key regulatory element of the EEG was the distribution of costs from RES-E compensation across all power grid operators on a pro rata basis, calculated on the ratio of RES-E in nationwide electricity sales (Bechberger and Reiche, 2004; Mez, 2009, pp. 386–387).

When the German EEG was adopted in April 2000, the 2001 European RES-E directive was still not in place. However, due to the premature resignation of the European Commission in 1999 and the related personal and jurisdictional change, a more pragmatic course was taken in the discussion of support schemes (Hirschl, 2008). Thus, Germany was successful in advocating for national scope of action in an uploading, foot-dragging sense.

3.3.2 2001–2006: Autonomous Support Schemes and FITs Diffusion Despite Resistance

The 2001 RES-E directive eventually presented by the European Commission did not prescribe a harmonized support scheme but obliged member states to create suitable instruments which would help to attain concerted, yet non-binding national targets (see Chapter 2 by Solorio and Bocquillon). A few months before, in March 2001, the Advocate General of the European Court of Justice (ECJ) eventually pronounced its decision in the *Preussen Elektra vs. Schleswag* case, finding that the Electricity Feed-in Act did not constitute impermissible state aid. One year later, DG Competition withdrew its initial objections to the Electricity Feed-In Act and the EEG, also due to the fact that the EEG of 2000 responded to earlier European Commission criticism by setting fixed remuneration rates differentiated according to technology, by setting time limits for the support, establishing degressive compensation for new installations, and by defining a biannual monitoring and revision process with the aim of preventing overcompensation (Lauber, 2001; Jacobsson and Lauber, 2006).

Neither the 2001 RES-E directive nor the proclamation of the ECJ caused any further adaptational pressure on Germany. Limited misfit was the result of an uploading or, more specifically, a foot-dragging process. Both provided a legal backing for the German EEG and its remuneration system in terms of European law (Oschmann and Sösemann, 2007, p. 2). This resolution of legal uncertainties led to a wind power boom and photovoltaic (PV) breakthrough in Germany (Bruns et al., 2011). However, coal and nuclear interests fought the law with renewed vigour, amplified by the German Ministry of Economic Affairs.

Germany's support scheme served as a model for other countries and thus provided for horizontal Europeanization by learning and imitation processes. In 2007, 19 of the 27 member states had adopted FITs as a central support instrument because it turned out to be an effective means to promote RES-E (AEE, 2012). Their horizontal diffusion was triggered by cross-national observation, information and communication of the regulatory reform (Busch and Jörgens, 2012). The role of Germany as a forerunner and norm entrepreneur was supplemented by an active cross-loading strategy in order to defend negative externalities resulting from the policies of other member states. During the Renewables Conference 2004 in Bonn, German and Spanish participants founded the Feed-In Cooperation, a governmentally driven, best-practice exchange platform with the aim to establish political support and diffusion of FIT models throughout Europe (Hirschl, 2008, p. 382). This strategy proved to be successful. The European Commission in 2005 concluded that national feed-in systems are typically more effective and efficient than quota systems (Bechberger and Reiche, 2007, p. 34). Formally, the European Commission therefore favoured 'coordination rather than harmonization' (COM, 2005a).

3.3.3 2007–2014: Ambitious RES-E Targets Threatened by Instrumental Shift

However, the debate about harmonization and the argument against FITs continued. The trade with guarantee-of-origin certificates for RES-E as well as the idea of a harmonized European quota system, based on the United Kingdom (UK) model (see Chapter 6 by Solorio and Fairbrass), were the most controversial aspects of the draft version of the new renewable energy directive (RED) presented in early 2008. Large energy utilities and actors pursuing a market-liberal policy in the European Commission supported this policy. In reaction to the draft, an opposition was formed, particularly made up of countries with established support schemes, the European Renewable Energies Foundation (EREF), the European Renewable Energy Council (EREC) and various environmental groups. This coalition of actors feared that FITs schemes would have been undermined due to the prescription of trade in certificates of origin, as provided in the European Commission proposal.

In coalition with Spain (see Chapter 8 by Solorio and Fernandez), Germany became active as a defensive forerunner in an uploading, foot-dragging sense. Both states took a strong stance in defending FITs-based approaches during the formulation phase of the 2009 RED (Solorio et al., 2014). At a meeting of the International Feed-in Cooperation in spring 2008, German government representatives explained that they were not willing to accept harmonization of support systems in the directive, because this would undermine the viability of Germany's successful feed-in system and similar systems in other countries. Instead they suggested introducing flexibility mechanisms for those member states which insisted they were unable to achieve the targets of the future directive domestically. The German statement was supported not only by Spain, but also by Slovenia, Latvia, Denmark and other member states (Hinrich-Rahlwes, 2013, p. 33). Moreover, two letters influenced the process. The German Environmental Minister and the Spanish Minister of Industry addressed a joint letter to the European Commission opposing a European-wide tradable green certificate scheme (Bechberger, 2009, p. 700). In addition, in an open letter to the European Commission, EREC criticized the mandatory trading mechanism since it would lead to harmonization and jeopardize the most successful national support schemes (EREC, 2008).

Eventually, Germany's foot-dragging strategy proved to be successful: the content of the 2009 RED implicitly fostered the German support policy. The directive was part of a comprehensive climate and energy package which substantially strengthened the European legal framework for RES (Lafferty and Ruud, 2008; Morata and Solorio, 2012) and resulted in growing support for FITs (SRU, 2011, p. 161). Despite different individual objectives of the member states and their autonomy to choose distinct implementation instruments, the 2009 RED set the stage for de facto convergence of member state RES-E subsidy policies (Hildingson et al., 2010, p. 115).

After the Fukushima incident in 2011, Germany raised its domestic ambitions for a sustainable energy supply. It adopted a (renewed) nuclear phase-out plan and set up an ethics commission which strengthened the necessity of a coherent and effective strategy towards a sustainable energy supply with a high share of RES. Nonetheless, the controversy surrounding numerous details of the national energy transition strategy continued (Geden and Fischer, 2014, p. 26). In the context of the financial and economic crisis in Europe a competitiveness discourse became stronger in Germany, which focused on the pace of RES-E expansion and the respective costs of RES-E promotion (Bundesregierung, 2013, p. 50).

In December 2013, the European Commission reinforced its commitment to regulatory harmonization and opened an investigation into the

German EEG of 2012, specifically on the support for energy-intensive companies benefiting from a reduced renewables surcharge (Oxera, 2014; COM, 2013). The revised Environmental and Energy Aid Guidelines presented in 2014 prescribed a concrete governance model: they declared that after a transitional phase, and with the exception of small installations, FITs would no longer be permissible state aid, but tendering procedures or tradable certificates would have to be introduced instead (Boscheck, 2014).

Subsequently, the new German federal government (a grand coalition) presented a revised EEG in 2014, which included several restrictive rulings to (supposedly) better control the expansion of RES-E in Germany and the related cost development: limited annual maximum extension corridors for the main RES-E technologies (wind, PV, biomass), a burden on self-generated and consumed RES-E with the EEG surcharge, a mandatory use of self-marketing from 2016 onwards and the gradual introduction of a tender system. By 2017, the level of RES remuneration will be determined by a competitive price building mechanism via auctions. The German government provided a fundamental instrumental shift from its former FITs model to a volume-based auction system[2] (Zengerling, 2014, p. 1; Tews, 2014).

As regards the instrumental design, the revised EEG can at first glance be regarded as a case of top-down, prescribing Europeanization. In the political debate the impression arose that this development did not take place due to national considerations, but that it is strongly dictated by European state aid rules as the European Commission prescribes an obligation to gradually introduce auctions. But it is not clear whether the guidelines actually require opting out of the FITs (Münchmeyer et al., 2014). However, they were a welcome argument for the German government to opt out of FITs in the longer term.

The European Council decision of 2014 on a future 2030 climate and energy package strongly lacks ambition for all three 2030 EU targets (greenhouse gases, RES and energy efficiency), lacks national binding RES targets, and includes only indicative efficiency targets (see Chapter 2 by Solorio and Bocquillon). This step backwards in the ambitiousness of European climate protection policy is likely to lead to top-down Europeanization of the emission reduction targets set as part of the German Energiewende. In view of this and as a defensive forerunner, Germany should have stepped up its uploading efforts at the EU level (Geden and Fischer, 2014; Solorio et al., 2014). As the German government did not take such an approach regarding the recent 2030 framework for climate and energy policies, it can be summarized that it failed to act as a pioneer at the European level in the sense of uploading or cross-loading its ambitious policy.

3.4 RES-T POLICY IN GERMANY AND ITS REPERCUSSIONS AT THE EU LEVEL

3.4.1 Tax Exemptions in Close Interaction with the EU Biofuels Directive

In the context of rising oil prices and growing agricultural surpluses in the 1980s, biofuels appeared on the German agenda as a potential solution to both problems. However, they remained a niche product until the end of the 1990s, developing more as a side effect particularly of agricultural policies on the EU level than through explicit promotion. The situation, however, changed as of the early 2000s. The Red–Green coalition elected in 1998 increasingly supported RES, particularly for electricity generation, and wanted to extend this support to the transport sector (Beneking, 2011, pp. 55–59).

At the EU level, at the same time, commitments under the Kyoto Protocol were – next to increasing oil independence and supporting domestic agriculture – another motivation for more biofuels support. This led to the proposal of a biofuels directive of November 2001 which suggested biofuel targets for 2005 and 2010 and admixtures of biofuels to fossil fuels. This proposal was accompanied by a proposed amendment of the mineral oil excise tax directive (92/81/EEC) which included an allowance for member states to exempt biofuels from excise taxation by up to 50 percent (COM, 2001). In Germany, however, most biofuels were fully exempt. In order to maintain this domestic regulation, the German Red–Green government pushed for an amendment of the mineral oil tax law that introduced a 100 percent tax exemption for all biofuels, in full awareness of the non-conformity with the aforementioned European Commission proposals.

If adopted this way, the German government would have had to safeguard its new biofuels policy vis-à-vis the EU. Thus, shortly after the German mineral oil tax law was officially amended in a way that established the 100 percent tax exemption for biofuels in early June 2002 (Beneking, 2011, pp. 59–62), the coalition parties decided to work towards the abolition of the proposed amendment of the mineral oil excise tax regulations at the EU level which would have limited tax exemptions to 50 percent (Deutscher Bundestag, 2002). In terms of bottom-up Europeanization mechanisms, Germany's strategy can best be described as foot-dragging: Germany tried to prevent restrictive mineral oil excise tax legislation which would have led to adaptational costs. To this end, Germany mainly used its blocking power in the Economic and Financial Affairs Council (ECOFIN), and succeeded rapidly. The amendment of the mineral oil excise tax directive which would have limited the possibility for tax exemptions was scrapped in the ECOFIN Council of 20 June 2002 (Schmitz, 2003, p. 220).

Simultaneously, Germany strategically pushed for a total repeal of both the proposed amendment and the mineral oil excise tax directive as a whole. Instead, it supported the reanimation of the energy taxation directive which was first proposed in 1997 (and had been pending ever since) and the integration of the regulation of biofuels excise taxes into this directive; which was so decided in the same ECOFIN Council of 20 June 2002 mentioned above (Beneking, 2011, pp. 62–63). Thus, the issue of biofuels taxation was shifted to another policy arena, which gave Germany more time and space to push for a biofuels taxation regulation. Eventually, the amended legislative proposal of the energy taxation directive of April 2003 included the possibility for member states to completely exempt biofuels from excise taxes (Beneking, 2011).

The biofuels directive was eventually adopted in May 2003. It included only non-binding targets and gave member states leeway regarding the respective instruments, including the possibility of full excise tax exemptions as allowed for by the energy taxation directive which was finally adopted in October 2003 (see Chapter 2 by Solorio and Bocquillon). This way, there were hardly any adaptational costs on the part of Germany. However, the energy taxation directive included a regulation that requires member states making use of tax exemptions for biofuels to annually report on raw material price developments from 2004 on, in order to justify tax breaks and avoid overcompensation. In effect, Germany had to include an overcompensation clause in its biofuel tax regulation. This proved to be very meaningful in the years to come. Thus, slight traces of top-down Europeanization can be identified here, since the EU prescribed this concrete governance model of avoiding overcompensation and making tax exemptions contingent on price developments; which was, however, in a similar form already included in the German regulation on biofuels tax exemptions adopted in 2002.

The German government was able to shape the EU biofuels directive by applying a two-tiered strategy: in anticipation of the looming EU directive, Germany hurried ahead domestically. Simultaneously, Germany made sure that the parts of the proposal not conforming to the new German biofuels policy were scrapped and – by helping to amend the energy taxation directive accordingly – that member states were able to fully exempt biofuels from excise taxes.

Besides this foot-dragging strategy, German biofuels policy was also diffused horizontally: in the years 2004–2006 tax exemptions were introduced in more than ten member states (Vogelpohl, 2011), which might not have happened if tax exemptions had been limited by the biofuels directive. Thus, a cross-loading of tax exemption models for biofuels took place in the EU (since these models diffused in absence of EU-wide legal harmonization), which may at least partly have been inspired by the successful German model.[3] However, the effect of Germany's pioneer biofuels policy should not be overestimated. As Vogelpohl (2011) shows, the EU biofuels directive had a key impact on the diffusion of biofuels policies in the EU, since it committed member states to substantially support biofuels. The number of instruments available to do so, however, was limited. Tax exemptions were actually the only major biofuels support policy instrument in force in EU member states, most notably and successfully in Germany. Therefore, other member states may have imitated the (not only) German model of tax exemptions as a sort of best-practice example for supporting biofuels. The Europeanization mechanism of horizontal learning might apply, since information on an existing policy instrument was available and might have been used by other member states. Nonetheless, the spread of tax exemptions for biofuels in Europe was not actively promoted by Germany. If German tax exemptions for biofuels had a cross-loading effect at all, it was unintentional, since Germany did very little to inspire or persuade other member states to implement similar tax exemptions. Germany did not act much as a norm entrepreneur in this case.

3.4.2 Policy Change in Anticipation of the RED

In 2005, the federal Ministry of Finance (BMF) submitted the first report on tax exemptions for biofuels, which pointed to a substantial loss of tax revenue because of the dynamic development of the German biofuels market. The BMF therefore proposed to 'modestly' charge taxes on biodiesel to avoid overcompensation (BMF, 2005). The proponents of a tax on biodiesel further gained influence after the federal election in Germany in autumn 2005, which led to a change of government from the Red–Green to a grand coalition. In July 2006, a gradual introduction of taxes on biodiesel was eventually adopted (Beneking, 2011, pp. 73–78). Furthermore, a quota for biofuels was introduced in October 2006, which was intended to accompany the lowering of tax breaks for biofuels in order not to jeopardize the overall consumption of biofuels and the targets stipulated by the EU biofuels directive (Beneking, 2011, pp. 78–79). Ever since, companies which place fuel on the market have been forced to sell a certain share of biofuel, which rose to 6.25 percent in 2014.[4] At first glance, these changes in German biofuels policy were adopted without close interactions with the EU level. However, EU subsidy regulations were an argument in the debates about introducing excise taxes on biodiesel. The changes were presented as unavoidable because of the aforementioned overcompensation prescriptions of the EU energy taxation directive (Deutscher Bundestag, 2006).

At the EU level, the non-binding target of 2 percent for 2005 established in the biofuels directive was not achieved (COM, 2006).[5] Therefore, the EU needed a strategy to overcome the biofuels inertia. In the biomass action plan (COM, 2005b) and the biofuels strategy (COM, 2006) the European Commission obviously hinted at its preference for quota systems instead of tax exemptions. Thus the 2006 changes in German biofuels policy were plausibly influenced by the EU. The German policy changes also took place in anticipation of the forthcoming revision of the EU's biofuels policy. This Europeanization effect can be described as a mixture of two top-down mechanisms: a prescription of concrete institutional and governance models through the EU energy taxation directive, and the promotion of changes in the beliefs and expectations through its preference for biofuel obligations. However, it has to be stated that the biofuels policy change in Germany in 2006 mainly emanated from the domestic level. EU influence was supportive of this change, but remained auxiliary.

Simultaneously, German actors tried to seize this opportunity to shape the future EU biofuels policy by promoting the introduction of a mandatory target, sustainability criteria and a certification system. When the biofuel quota was adopted in Germany in 2006 – before the legislative process at the EU level started in 2008 – it was from the outset planned to be tied to sustainability criteria. In 2007, the German government drafted an ordinance that specified these criteria and how compliance with them could be proved (Bundesregierung, 2007). This ordinance, however, was submitted for notification to the Commission, which was just about to start the legislative process of the RED (BMWi and BMU, 2007, pp. 49–50). Thus, the Commission postponed the notification of the German biofuels sustainability ordinance for the time being and went on to develop its own sustainability regulations, which were then to be transposed into national law by the member states. These EU sustainability regulations for biofuels presented in the directive proposal of January 2008 (COM, 2008; issued only a few weeks after the German draft ordinance) and finally adopted in the RED in 2009, however, were very similar to those the German government had drafted in 2007 (Beneking, 2011, p. 96).[6]

Thus, by having been – next to the Netherlands and the UK (see Chapter 4 by Hoppe and van Bueren, and Chapter 6 by Solorio and Fairbrass) – a forerunner and norm entrepreneur in this respect, Germany was able to upload parts of its domestic biofuel policy to the EU level by offering the blueprint for sustainability criteria and certification. In turn, the implementation costs of transposing the EU system into national systems were almost nonexistent. These elements of bottom-up Europeanization can best be described as pacesetting. Consequently, in September 2009, only a few weeks after the RED was adopted, Germany transposed it into national law and was again able to present itself as the European model student in this context.

The regulation of sustainability is also the area where elements of horizontal Europeanization can be found. Germany was active in cross-loading its blueprint sustainability regulation and its implementation in the context of initiatives such as the Renewable Fuels Regulators Club (REFUREC), a pan-European informal network of governmental institutions responsible for regulating biofuels, and Concerted Action on the Renewable Energy Sources Directive (CA-RES), a dialogue between national authorities responsible for the implementation of the RED, in which participating countries exchange experience and best practices and develop common approaches.

However, Germany's cross-loading in this context should again not be overestimated since the cross-national convergence of sustainability regulations for biofuels in Europe did not occur in the absence of EU-wide legal harmonization. In fact, ever since the adoption of the RED, the EU has set the tone for biofuels policy in Europe, and leeway for autonomous decisions at the domestic level is considerably restricted. The main issues that have been discussed concerning the EU biofuels policy in recent years – their (contested) sustainability and, consequentially, whether to expand the sustainability criteria and/or to lower the binding sectoral target for biofuels or not – are therefore both regulated and decided on at the supranational level through the RED.

3.5 COMPARATIVE ANALYSIS AND CONCLUSION

Comparing the evolution of German RES-E and RES-T policy and its interactions with the EU level, one can see several similarities, but also some interesting differences. As regards the similarities, Germany in both cases largely autonomously adopted a pioneering role in promoting RES and was, over a long time period, essentially able to safeguard the routes taken against interference or harmonization efforts from the European level. Thus, both cases are, in general, similar as regards the Europeanization mechanism, which can best be described as foot-dragging. More than uploading the pioneer policy at the supranational level in the sense of pacesetting, Germany managed to fend off EU-wide harmonization against its own domestic policy approach with the goal of avoiding potential adaptational costs.[7]Although much more intentional in the case of RES-E than in the case of RES-T, this strategy of foot-dragging at the supranational level in both cases has been accompanied by processes of horizontal Europeanization, for example a cross-loading of the German national pioneer policy to other EU member states (in the absence of EU-wide legal harmonization). Despite these similarities, clear differences between the two cases can also be identified as regards their mechanisms and extent of horizontal Europeanization: the German model of RES-E promotion via fixed FITs has been much more commonly adopted in other EU member states than the German model of RES-T promotion via tax exemption. Thus, the pioneering and cross-loading role of Germany as a norm entrepreneur was significantly stronger in RES-E policy than in RES-T policy.

Another important difference between the cases concerns the continuity of the policies. Whereas FITs for RES-E were successfully defended by their advocates against the attacks by proponents of a quota system up to 2014, tax exemptions for biofuels were abandoned in favour of a quota system in 2006 under the pressure of the mineral oil and automotive industries and the German Ministry of Finance. In both cases, however, the European Commission has expressed a preference for quota systems. In the case of biofuels, the advocacy coalition for quotas was strong enough to successfully promote them as the superior instrument to reach higher biofuel shares in a cost-effective way. In the case of RES-E, resistance powers in favour of FITs were, until very recently, strong enough to defend this incentive instrument. Thus, whether the European Commission's preference materializes in Germany or not, strongly depends on domestic factors such as the resistance powers of opposing coalitions.[8]

Despite these differences, new analogies can be observed as well. Very recently the EU regained influential power over German RES-E policy as well, and a new convergence is becoming apparent. As shown in section 3.3, the new EU state aid guidelines were used as a pretext for a shift in the support scheme in the latest EEG revision of 2014. Whereas in RES-T policy competencies have gradually shifted from the domestic to the EU level since the mid-2000s, German RES-E policy seems to have developed in a similar direction only very recently.

To come back to the question of whether Germany can be considered as a pioneer regarding its renewable energy policy, we can conclude that it at least was a pioneer, both in the RES-E and in the RES-T sector. It is conspicuous, however, that in both cases the German government eventually adapted its policies to EU pressures. Admittedly, these pressures have to be put into perspective, since domestic factors, such as the stance of the Ministry of Finance and the Ministry of Economic Affairs or the increasingly politicized impact of costs, certainly still played a major role. Nonetheless, it is striking that Germany, despite having been a forerunner in renewable energy policy and an important veto player in the sense of foot-dragging at the supranational level, at least partly has been Europeanized from the top down. Thus, top-down Europeanization seems to be stronger than appears at first sight, even in areas such as renewable energy policy where EU competencies have emerged relatively late and also only gradually, as in 'least-likely cases' of top-down Europeanization such as Germany.

While recognizing that an integrated European approach is required, this is at the same time associated with significant risks since European climate and energy policy seems to be losing its dynamic; a situation in dire need of a pioneer able to motivate hesitant states towards adoption of an ambitious policy. Even though it might seem unlikely in the light of the most recent policy decisions, it would also be desirable from a European perspective if Germany were to restart its efforts to pursue ambitious domestic energy transition policy, thereby possibly resuming its pioneering role and its successful approach of simultaneously foot-dragging on the supranational and cross-loading on the horizontal level.

NOTES

1. Except for the wind energy sector, however, the individual tariffs were not sufficient for other RES-E to reach market entry.
2. According to first analyses of these important changes, clear risks arise of missing the national RES goal for 2020 as fixed within the EU 2009 RES directive (Nitsch, 2014, p. 11), of reduced value chain effects and job losses (Hirschl et al., 2014, p. 26.; Zengerling, 2014, p. 17; Geiserand von OppenRechtsanwälte, 2014, p. 3).
3. The introduction of the comprehensive tax exemption triggered a 'biofuel boom' in Germany from 2004 to 2007, when the share of biofuels in the total transport fuel market rose from 1.8 percent to 7.4 percent.
4. These policy changes had considerable effects on the German biofuels market. In stark contrast to the previous development, the overall share of biofuels in the German fuels market shrank for the first time in decades (from 7.4 percent in 2007 to 6.0 percent in

2008). Ever since, the sales of biofuels have been almost entirely dependent on the quota level (Vogelpohl, 2014).
5. Germany, in this context, was the European model student, having exceeded the target by a large margin.
6. In both cases, sustainability criteria are related to greenhouse gas emissions savings, a ban of raw materials from certain areas (such as land with high biodiversity value or protected areas) and certain agro-environmental practices ('cross-compliance' and 'good agricultural practice'). Also in both cases, proof of compliance with these criteria is to be achieved via certification systems recognized by state authorities. For a closer comparison see sections 1 and 2 of the German draft ordinance (Bundesregierung, 2007) and articles 17 and 18 of the RED directive.
7. With the notable exception of the 'upload' of the system of sustainability criteria and certification for biofuels.
8. In the cases at hand, the design of the domestic support scheme played an important role. Whereas tax exemptions for biofuels directly burden the state budget, FITs for RES-E pass on the costs directly to consumers, just as quotas do in the case of RES-T. Therefore, the German federal Ministry of Finance was a major opponent of tax exemptions for biofuels – and thereby an important supporter of the European Commission's preference for quota systems – whereas it was more or less neutral in the case of FITs for RES-E.

REFERENCES

AEE (Agentur für Erneuerbare Energien) (2012), 'Feed-in tariffs guarantee successful expansion of renewable energy'. *Renews Kompakt*, 22 June.

Andersen, M.S. and D. Liefferink (1997), 'Introduction: the impact of the pioneers on EU environmental policy', in M.S. Andersen and D. Liefferink (eds), *European Environmental Policy: The Pioneers*, Manchester: Manchester University Press, pp. 1–39.

Bechberger, M. (2009), *Erneuerbare Energien in Spanien. Restriktionen und Erfolgsbedingungen,* Stuttgart: Ibidem-Verlag.

Bechberger, M. and D. Reiche (2004), 'Renewable energy policy in Germany: pioneering and exemplary regulations', *Energy for Sustainable Development*, 8(1), 25–35.

Bechberger, M. and D. Reiche (2007), 'Diffusion of renewable feed-in tariffs in the EU-28: an instrumental contribution for the dissemination of renewable energies', in L. Mez (ed.), *Green Power Markets: Support Schemes, Case Studies and Perspectives* Brentwood: Multi-Science Publishing, pp. 31–50.

Beneking, A. (2011), 'Genese und Wandel der deutschen Biokraftstoffpolitik. Eine akteurszentriertePolicy-Analyse der Förderung biogener Kraftstoffe in Deutschland. Fair Fuels?', Working Paper 3. Institut für ökologische Wirtschaftsforschung, Berlin.

BMF (German Federal MinistryofFinance) (2005), 'Bericht zur Steuerbegünstigung für Biokraft- und Bioheizstoffe', Bundestagsdrucksache 15/5816. Deutscher Bundestag, Berlin.

BMWi (German Federal Ministry of the Environment, Nature Conservation and Nuclear Safety) and BMU (German Federal Ministry of Economics and Technology) (2007), *Bericht zur Umsetzung der in der Kabinettsklausurin Meseberg beschlossenen Eckpunkte für ein Integriertes Energie- und Klimaprogramm*, Berlin, BMU/BMWi, 23–24 August.

Boscheck, R. (2014), 'State aid, national energy policy and EU governance', *Intereconomics*, 49 (5), 256–261.

Bruns, E., D. Ohlhorst, B. Wenzel and J. Köppel (2011), *Renewable Energies in Germany's Electricity Market. A Biography of the Innovation Process*, Dordrecht: Springer.

Bundesregierung (2007), 'Verordnung über Anforderungen an eine nachhaltige Erzeugung vonBiomasse zur Verwendung als Biokraftstoff (Biomasse-Nachhaltigkeitsverordnung – BioNachV)', Entwurf vom 5 December, Berlin.

Bundesregierung (2013), 'Deutschlands Zukunft gestalten – Koalitionsvertrag zwischen CDU, CSU und SPD', 18, Legislaturperiode.

Busch, P.O. and H. Jörgens (2012), 'Governance by diffusion: exploring a new mechanism of international policy coordination', in J. Meadowcroft, O. Langhelle, A. Ruud (eds), *Governance, Democracy and Sustainable Development: Moving Beyond the Impasse?*, Cheltenham and Northampton, MA: Edward Elgar Publishing, pp. 221–248.

COM (2001), 'Communication on alternative fuels for road transportation and on a set of measures to promote the use of biofuels', COM(2001) 547 final. Brussels: CEC.

COM (2005a), 'Annex to the Communication from the Commission: The support for electricity from renewable energy sources – Impact assessment; Commission staff working document', COM(2005) 627 final, SEC(2005) 1571, Brussels, 7 December.

COM (2005b), 'Biomass action plan', COM(2005) 628 final, Brussels: CEC.

COM (2006), 'An EU strategy for biofuels', COM(2006)', 34 final, Brussels: CEC.

COM (2008), 'Proposal for a directive on the promotion of the use of energy from renewable sources', COM(2008) 19 final, Brussels: CEC.

COM (2013), 'State aid: Commission opens in-depth inquiry into support for energy-intensive companies benefitting from a reduced renewables surcharge', Press Release, 18 December.

Deutscher Bundestag (2002), 'Beschlussempfehlung und Bericht des Ausschusses für Umwelt, Naturschutz und Reaktorsicherheit (16. Ausschuss) zu der Unterrichtung durch die Bundesregierung', Drucksache 14/8428 Nr. 2.13. Drucksache 14/9615, Berlin: Deutscher Bundestag.

Deutscher Bundestag (2006), 'Bericht des Finanzausschusses (7. Ausschuss) zu dem Gesetzentwurf der Bundesregierung', Drucksachen 16/1172, 16/1347, Drucksache 16/2061, Berlin: Deutscher Bundestag.

EREC (2008), 'European renewable energy industry cannot support current Commission plans on the framework directive for renewable energies', 14 January.

Geden, O. and S. Fischer (2014), 'Moving targets: negotiations on the EU's energy and climate policy objectives for the post-2020 period and implications for the German energy transition', SWP Research Paper 3, Berlin, March.

Geiser and von Oppen Rechtsanwälte (2014), *Wesentliche verfassungsrechtliche Angriffspunkte einer EEG-Umlage auf Solarstrom für den Eigenverbrauch*, Berlin.

Hildingson, R., J. Stripple and A. Jordan (2010), 'Renewable energies: a continuing balancing act?', in A. Jordan, D. Huitema, H. van Asselt, T. Rayner and F. Berkhout (eds), *Climate Change Policy in the European Union: Confronting the Dilemmas of Mitigation and Adaptation?*, Cambridge: Cambridge University Press, pp. 103–124.

Hinrich-Rahlwes, R (2013), *Sustainable Energy Policy for Europe – Towards 100% Renewable Energy*, Leiden: CRC Press/Balkema.

Hirschl, B. (2008), *Erneuerbare Energien-Politik – Eine Multi-Level Policy-Analyse mit Fokus auf den deutschen Strommarkt*, Wiesbaden: VS Verlag für Sozialwissenschaften.

Hirschl, B., K. Heinbachand and S. Salecki (2014), 'Auswirkungen des Referentenentwurfs zum EEG 2014 auf Wertschöpfung und Beschäftigung durch EE bis 2020. Institut für Ökologische Wirtschaftsforschung (IÖW) Berlin – Kurzstudie im Auftrag von Greenpeace Deutschland', Hamburg, April.

Jacobsson, S. and V. Lauber (2006), 'The politics and policy of energy system transformation – explaining the German diffusion of renewable energy technology', *Energy Policy*, 34 (3), 256–276.

Jänicke, M. (2005), 'Trend-setters in environmental policy: the character and role of pioneer countries', *European Environment*,15 (2), 129–142.

Jänicke, M. (2011), 'German climate change policy: political and economic leadership', in R.W. Wurzel and J. Connelly (eds), *The European Union as Leader in International Climate Change Politics*, London and New York: Routledge.

Lafferty, W.M. and A. Ruud (2008), 'Introduction: promoting green electricity in Europe: the challenge of integrating contextual factors', in W.M. Lafferty and A. Ruud (eds), *Promoting Sustainable Electricity in Europe: Challenging the Path Dependence of Dominant Energy Systems*, Cheltenham and Northampton, MA: Edward Elgar Publishing, pp. 1–44.

Lauber, V. (2001), 'Regulierung von Preisen und Beihilfen für Elektrizität aus erneuerbaren Energieträgern durch die Europäische Union', *Zeitschrift für Neues Energierecht*,5 (1), 35–43.

Liefferink, D. and M.S. Andersen (1998), 'Strategies of the green member states in EU environmental policy-making', *Journal of European Public Policy*, 5 (2), 254 –270.

Mez, L. (2009), 'Renewables in electricity generation: Germany as pioneer?', in B. Eberlein and B. Doern (eds), *Governing the Energy Challenge: Canada and Germany in a Multi-Level Regional and Global Context*, Toronto: University of Toronto Press, pp. 371–395.

Monstadt, J. (2004), *Die Modernisierung der Stromversorgung. Regionale Energie- und Klimapolitik im Liberalisierungs- und Privatisierungsprozess*, Wiesbaden: Verlag für Sozialwissenschaften.

Morata, F. and I. Solorio (2012), *European Energy Policy: An Environmental Approach*, Cheltenham and Northampton, MA: Edward Elgar Publishing.

Münchmeyer, H., M. Kahles and F. Pause (2014), 'Erfordert das europäische Beihilferecht die Einführung von Ausschreibungsverfahren im EEG?', Würzburger Berichte zum Umweltenergierecht Nr. 5, 16 July.

Nitsch, J. (2014), 'Szenarien der deutschen Energieversorgung vor dem Hintergrund der Vereinbrungen der Großen Koalition', Kurzexpertise für den Bundesverband Erneuerbare Energien e.V.

Oschmann, V. and F. Sösemann (2007), 'Erneuerbare Energien im deutschen und europäischen Recht – Ein Überblick', *Zeitschrift für Umweltrecht (ZUR)*, 18 (1), 1–8.

Oxera (2014), 'Agenda – Running out of power? Commission moderates state aid reforms for energy, April 2014', accessed on 8 November 2014 at www.oxera.com/Latest-Thinking/Agenda/2014/Running-out-of-power-Commission-moderates-state-ai.aspx.

Schmitz, N. (2003), *Bioethanol in Deutschland. FNR-Schriftenreihe Nachwachsende Rohstoffe*, Nachwachsende Rohstoffe Vol. 21, Münster: Landwirtschaftsverlag.

Solorio, I., E. Öllerand and H. Jörgens (2014), 'The German energy transition in the context of the EU renewable energy policy', in A. Brunnengräber, M.R. Di Nucci (eds), *Im Hürdenlauf zur Energiewende*, Wiesbaden: Springer, pp. 189–200.

SRU (German Advisory Council on the Environment) (2011), 'Pathways towards a 100% renewable electricity system', Special Report, Berlin.

Tews, K. (2014), 'Europeanization of energy and climate policy: new trends and their implications for the German energy transition process', FFU-report 03-2014, Berlin: Environmental Policy Research Center.

Vogelpohl, T. (2011), 'Konvergenzdynamiken in der europäischen Biokraftstoffpolitik – Internationale Institutionen als Motor der Politikangleichung? Fair Fuels?', Working Paper 2, Berlin: IÖW.

Vogelpohl, T. (2014), '"Das ist Wettbewerb. Und das ist normaler Strukturwandel." Die Neoliberalisierung der deutschen Biokraftstoffpolitik', in B. Hirschl, K. Dietz (eds), *Biokraftstoffe zwischen Sackgasse und Energiewende*, München: Oekom, pp. 15–39.

Zengerling, C. (2014), 'Kurzgutachten im Auftrag von Greenpeace e.V. – Rechtliche Bewertung einzelner Regelungen des Referentenentwurfs (EEG RefE) im Rahmen der Verbändeanhörung zur EEG-Novelle 2014', Hamburg, 4 March.

4. From frontrunner to laggard: the Netherlands and Europeanization in the cases of RES-E and biofuel stimulation

Thomas Hoppe and Ellen van Bueren

4.1 INTRODUCTION

The Netherlands has long cherished its reputation of compliance with European Union (EU) policies and directives, often playing an initiating role (Van der Heijden et al., 2014). In the 1990s the Netherlands was famous for its integrated environmental policy, which aimed to address causes in addition to effects. However, the progressive environmental policies of the 1990s were replaced by restrictive policies of right-wing government coalitions, which came into power after 2001 (with the exception of the rather progressive 2007–10 coalition). By 2013 the Netherlands had become a laggard in environmental policy, scoring 42nd position on the Climate Change Performance Index 2015, just ahead of the United States (position 44) and China (position 45), leading only Estonia (position 46) of all EU member states (Burck et al., 2014). Moreover, facts and figures on the share of renewable energy sources (RES) for electricity (RES-E) and the share of biofuels as RES for transport (RES-T) were disappointing compared to the EU ambitions as reflected in the RES-E and biofuels directives and the achievements of other member states.

In this chapter we reflect on how this occurred, set against Europeanization processes. The main research question in this chapter therefore is: how did Europeanization processes – in particular bottom-up processes leading to harmonization of national policies, top-down processes of domestic transposition and implementation of EU policies, and horizontal processes of bilateral policy transfer and diffusion – shape the development of Dutch renewable energy policy, and how did this in turn affect EU renewable energy policymaking?

Section 4.2 presents the main analytical concepts and methods used. Section 4.3 presents the RES-E case, and section 4.4 the biofuels case. Each of the cases starts with a general introduction, followed by a description of the period before and after the establishment of the EU directive and the relevant Europeanization processes. Finally, in section 4.5 the Europeanization processes are compared and assessed to address which of the Europeanization processes affected the formulation of domestic and EU policies and the selection of policy instruments.

4.2 ANALYTICAL UNDERPINNINGS AND METHODS

4.2.1 Models of Europeanization

Based on Börzel and Risse's work, Europeanization is defined as the processes and mechanisms by which European policymaking may lead to change at the domestic level (Börzel and Risse, 2000, p. 3). In this chapter we focus on three models of Europeanization: top-down Europeanization, bottom-up Europeanization and horizontal Europeanization (see Chapter 1 by Jörgens and Solorio).

Top-down Europeanization addresses the adoption and implementation of EU directives in member states' domestic policies. This model is characterized by a three-step process (Caporaso, 2007), starting with the EU generating some sort of impulse for domestic change (for example, the EU renewable energy policy). Subsequently, this leads to adaptation pressure, which is mediated by domestic factors, finally producing an outcome at the national level. Besides changing domestic policy from the top down, it is of interest to analyse whether EU directives have helped to change the 'rules of the game' in favour of RES in national energy policies. Another key element of the impact of the EU renewable energy policy is the influence it has had on the positions of the different national actors in the energy sector. Bottom-up Europeanization is used by member states (such as the Netherlands) to 'maximize the benefits and minimize the costs of European policies' (Börzel, 2002, p. 96). They can try to 'upload' policies to the European level, attempting to influence EU policymaking to protect national interests. The horizontal Europeanization model is based on a decentralized, voluntary, information-based process of cross-fertilization of ideas and policies between EU member states. This process of voluntary convergence towards common policy goals may be loosely coordinated by European institutions, but it may just as well emerge from uncoordinated processes of bilateral imitation and learning between member states. The concept of horizontal

Europeanization draws from a body of empirical research into comparative politics and international relations, which shows that growing economic and political interdependence leads national governments to increasingly orient their domestic policy choices towards the previous choices of other governments. These processes, often labelled processes of 'policy diffusion', 'horizontal policy learning' or 'policy transfer', have received increasing attention in recent years (Jörgens et al., 2014; Busch and Jörgens, 2012a, 2012b; Simmons et al., 2008; Bulmer and Padgett, 2005; Simmons and Elkins, 2004).

4.2.2 Methods

Data collection relied mostly on secondary sources, such as academic journal articles, book chapters, conference papers, records (fiches) of EU discussions, reports (by central government agencies, non-governmental organizations and advisory committees involved in policy-making processes at the EU level), and online multimedia. When key information could not be retrieved from secondary sources, experts were contacted (from central government, advisory committees involved in policymaking processes at EU level, and at universities). Data were analysed in an argumentative interpretive manner. The research design used in this study concerned a comparative analysis of two case studies: green electricity (RES-E) (2001/77/EC; 2009/28/EC), and biofuels (2003/96/EC; 2009/28/EC; 2009/30/EC).

4.3 GREEN ELECTRICITY (RES-E) CASE STUDY

4.3.1 The Period Prior to the 2001 RES-E Directive

The Dutch electricity system is best described as a fossil-based thermal system, dominated by inexpensive natural gas and coal as main production sources. Energy infrastructures, technologies, regulations and 'innate' user preferences resemble this dominant natural gas system, with big utilities in the lead. The national electricity grid system is well developed and among the most reliable in Europe. Thanks to many good cross-border connections, the high-voltage grid is well integrated into the European transmission network (Arentsen, 2009). Since the 1970s, following the oil crises, multiple RES-E technologies have been developed and adopted, notably wind power, solar power and bioenergy. By 1990 RES accounted for 1 per cent of total electricity consumption in the

Netherlands. In 2001 (when the RES-E directive 2001/77/EC was implemented) this had risen 2.98 per cent, climbing to 9.98 per cent by 2014 (11.79 billion kilowatt hours, kWh). Since 2013 the share of RES in electricity consumption (10.39 per cent) had declined slightly. Domestically produced RES-E mostly derives from wind (4.92 per cent) and biomass sources (4.31 per cent) (CBS et al., 2016). Large-scale uptake of wind energy has been stimulated by central government since the 1990s, but has had a difficult history, as state policies were poorly designed, omitting local communities from the policymaking processes, which led to substantial problems in the implementation stages. In the 1990s, less than half of the targeted 1,000 megawatt (MW) goal was actually established (Hofman, 2005). To a great extent this was due to a neglect of social and cultural factors in policymaking and implementation (Wolsink, 1996; Arentsen, 2009). Regarding electricity from biomass conversion, the two methods most used are waste incineration plants and co-firing of biomass streams in electricity generation plants (Hofman, 2005). The use of biomass matches very well with the existing electricity infrastructure and power relationships between the key actors in the sector. Moreover, waste as a renewable resource contributes to the business case of coal-firing plants, and co-firing of biomass is considered a much cheaper option than switching to natural gas to meet carbon dioxide (CO_2) emissions standards (Verbong and Geels, 2007).

Europeanization first began to play a role in the 1990s. Following the 1992 Maastricht Treaty, the European Commission decided to push for the liberalization of the energy markets (Verbong and Geels, 2007; see also Chapter 2 by Solorio and Bocquillon). The Netherlands became one of the forerunners in this process and Europeanization was much more focused on this process than on the upcoming RES-E directive. In anticipation of two new electricity Acts, privatizing and liberalizing the electricity market and opening it up to distribution firms, distribution companies had become much more customer-oriented. This also favoured the marketing of RES-E (Hofman, 2005). Following the 1995 Third National Energy White Paper with an ambition of 10 per cent of RES in 2020, several government policies were launched to promote the use of (the more expensive) RES-E, such as the green certificates granting fiscal and marketing advantages to users (Dinica and Arentsen, 2003), and voluntary agreements between central government and the energy distribution sector on targets for green electricity sales. The targets were, however, never met (Van Rooijen and Van Wees, 2006).

Furthermore, regulatory changes were made. In 2001, the market for green electricity was liberalized, well in advance of the market for carbon-based electricity (which was not liberalized until 2004). To support the competition of RES-E with non-RES-E, central government introduced an energy tax from which customers of green electricity were exempted (Van Rooijen and Van Wees, 2006). However, the instrument had a negative side effect. Domestic RES-E production capacity could not supply the steeply rising demand for green electricity. Foreign RES-E was eligible and domestic production could not compete with the cheap RES-E produced in power stations that had already been written off in other European countries (Agterbosch et al., 2007). This was partly due to the well-established cross-border grid connections, which facilitated the import of green electricity (Verbong and Geels, 2007).

By 2001, despite the policy efforts, less than 3 per cent of total Dutch electricity consumption originated from RES. An important explanation for the slow uptake of RES-E can be found in the prolonged, massive resistance of the Dutch electricity sector to the introduction of RES-E (Hofman and Marquart, 2001). With the active support of the Ministry of Economic Affairs, the sector had long focused on large-scale, centrally produced fossil and nuclear power. Moreover, environmental policies focused on the reduction of energy consumption. In summary, the decentralized production models of RES-E matched poorly with the energy sector's structure, organization and ambitions (Arentsen, 2009).

4.3.2 The 2001 RES-E Directive and its Impact

The Netherlands played a rather active and progressive role in the negotiations in the run-up to the establishment of the 2001/77/EC RES-E directive (Rowlands, 2005). Compared to national policy goals, the directive represented a reduction of the share of RES-E in total domestic electricity consumption. National policy was designed (following the 1995 Third National Energy White Paper) to achieve approximately 17 per cent RES-E in total electricity consumption by 2020 (Ministerie van Economische Zaken, 1995), whereas the directive's goal was to achieve 9 per cent by 2010. The 2001 RES-E target was therefore not considered a problem, particularly because the text of the directive recognized several types of waste as biomass, so the directive was not considered a threat in the Netherlands, with its rapidly increasing capacity from co-firing and combined heat and power (CHP) plants (which allowed for co-firing and the incineration of vast amounts of biomass 'waste' streams). During the negotiations, however, the Netherlands did push for adoption of additional waste streams in the directive's definition of RES. This (when proposed by the European Commission) was contested by the European Parliament. In terms of Europeanization it is fair to state that the Dutch national government considered the RES-E target allocated by the EU to be fair, and held to this goal during negotiations with the EU. At the same time, however, the Netherlands actively engaged in EU discussions to amend the directive to protect national interests, in particular those of the domestic energy and waste sectors. Hence, bottom-up Europeanization occurred to some extent. The top policy priorities for the Netherlands, though, remained establishing security of supply, a liberalized energy sector, and increasing energy saving efficiency.

Following the implementation of the 2001 RES-E directive, the 1998 National Electricity Act was amended twice to facilitate its implementation. The first amendment concerned the establishment of mechanisms supporting national energy production from RES. A switch was made from (expensive and ineffective) demand-oriented policies to supply-oriented ones (Arentsen and De Bruijn, 2005; Van Rooijen and Van Wees, 2006). A second amendment followed in 2004, replacing 'green certificates' with 'guarantees of origin'. Besides regulations, key policy instruments that were used following implementation of the 2001 directive concerned a covenant (between national government and energy-supplying companies) to cut CO_2 emissions by 3 million tonnes via co-firing of biomass in electricity generating plants, subsidy schemes (promoting investment in local RES-E production) and tax exemptions. National government also fiscally supported the importation of RES-E. Moreover, the Dutch national government had already liberalized the RES-E market in 2001, whereas the market for 'grey' electricity was only liberalized in 2004 (Kenniscentrum InfoMil, 2014). While demand creation for RES-E was relatively successful in the Netherlands, the creation of a (domestic) supply was less successful. RES-E was bought cheaply from (already written off) RES-E producers in other EU member states, which already had progressive supply-driven policies for RES-E production. As a consequence, there was an uneven playing field between Dutch RES-E suppliers and those in other EU member states. In order to stem the tide and to harmonize with other EU member states, the Dutch government decided to implement Feed-In Tariffs (FITs) (Agterbosch et al., 2004). This can be viewed as a giving in to pressure by peer member states, and hence as a form of horizontal Europeanization.

In 2002 a FIT was introduced in the form of a scheme to support domestic production of RES-E (MEP: the grant scheme on Environmental Quality of Electricity Production). This provided entrepreneurs with a fixed compensation (per kWh) for domestically produced RES-E with a guarantee for ten years (Agterbosch et al., 2004). The MEP scheme came into force in the summer of 2003.

However, the MEP subsidy scheme was terminated three years later, in August 2006. The scheme had been very popular, but was open-ended and therefore very expensive. The government coalition claimed that in the absence of the scheme the RES-E goals would also be achieved by 2010, and decided to end the subsidy scheme prematurely (Kern and Smith, 2008). In hindsight the scheme was judged to have 'succumbed to its own success' (Koppejan and Van Est, 2011, p. 33). The sudden abolition of the MEP scheme, with the reduction of investment risks as one of its central aims, led many potential investors to distrust Dutch central government. As a consequence RES-E production growth slowed dramatically. The abolishment of the MEP scheme contributed to the poor reputation of Dutch renewable energy policies. They were considered opaque, confusing and lacking in long-term security, due to the numerous policy instruments and the many changes in the details of these policies (Agnolucci, 2007; Arentsen et al., 2007). By 2006 the share of RES-E in total domestic electricity production was 6.5 per cent (Arentsen, 2009), and RES-E and RES in general had not become (national) electricity policy priorities (Kern and Smith, 2008). In sum, the contribution of the RES-E directive to domestic RES-E policy had been relatively small, as there was little EU pressure on the Netherlands, and only few domestic policies were actually changed by it.

4.3.3 The 2009 RED and its Impact

During the negotiations in the run-up to the third EU energy package and the 2009/28/EC renewable energy directive (RED), the Netherlands was involved in a different way than during the negotiations on the 2001 RES-E directive. EU pressure was considered more serious, and a defensive bottom-up Europeanization approach was taken to protect the interests of the Dutch electricity sector. Although the Netherlands supported the EU 2030 goals and the development of a broader institutional framework (for example, greater collaboration between EU member states and greater harmonization), it did stress the importance of subsidiarity and the comparative cost advantages of energy production (not surprisingly emphasizing the importance of natural gas, and trying to get this issue explicitly on the EU policy agenda). Responsibilities were considered to be organized best at national level and with stakeholders (Netbeheer Nederland, 2009). The Dutch RES objective was to achieve a 16 per cent RES share of total energy consumption by 2020. Not much later, this goal was renegotiated to 14 per cent in 2020; the 16 per cent target was to be attained by 2023.

Following the announcement of the 2009 EU RED, the Netherlands, in common with other EU member states, formulated a National Action Plan (NAP). This, however, was to a great extent based on previous Dutch (environmental and energy) programmes emphasizing clean energy, energy savings and renewable energy (in Dutch: *'Schoon en Zuinig'*; *'Nieuwe Energie voor Klimaat'*), which had already been adopted in 2007 by the Dutch government, in part as a response to a revived attention to climate change. The main policy instrument of the NAP concerned a support scheme for sustainable energy production (SDE: the operating grant Encouraging Sustainable Energy Production), which used a FIT to support the production of renewable energy, including RES-E, heat and biogas. The SDE scheme basically replaced the already abolished MEP scheme.

To a great extent the NAP actions prolonged national programme policies, contributing to deregulation and the lowering of entrepreneurs' administrative costs, which was in line with the right-wing character of successive central government coalitions. Although the SDE scheme and its successors were launched with great expectations, they were considered to be only slightly effective in encouraging the large-scale domestic uptake of RES-E technology. Moreover, the national government's RES-E support policies met with substantial criticism and experienced difficulties during implementation; in particular, lack of local support for the planning of wind parks – something the country had already experienced in the 1990s (Wolsink, 1996) – and many economic, regulatory and social barriers blocking wide-scale uptake of biogas installations (Hoppe and Sanders, 2014). By 2016 progress in national policy implementation was not on track to attain the country's assigned contribution to the EU's 20-20-20 goals (ECN et al., 2016).

Besides central government being subjected to EU directives (top-down Europeanization) and policy trends diffusing from other member states (for example, FITs; horizontal Europeanization), decentralized governments also experienced forms of Europeanization. Provincial governments adopted policies originating from other regional government member states; for example, the Dutch Province of Overijssel adopted a competition programme to spur RES-E production by local communities based on best practices in Germany and Denmark (Warbroek and Hoppe, 2017; see also Chapter 3 by Vogelpohl et al., and Chapter 5 by Dyrhauge). And local government public officials and civil servants participated in excursions to best-practice, low-carbon communities in other member states, to learn about policies and management strategies that worked and that they could potentially adopt themselves; for example, lessons from the best-practice low-carbon community of Saerbeck in Germany, which attracted 'local energy policy tourists' from all over the world (Hoppe et al., 2015). This form of horizontal Europeanization has undoubtedly contributed to a great number of local governments and provinces adopting progressive policy agendas promoting RES-E. In turn, this has contributed to local capacity building, in particular in relation to the establishment of many low-carbon citizens' initiatives throughout the Netherlands. Between 2007 and 2011, more than 300 citizen-led energy co-operatives were established (Oteman et al., 2014). Some of them started to collaborate with peers from other EU member states in EU programme-funded projects, such as Interreg and Horizon 2020, which in turn led to some form of (horizontal and top-down) Europeanization.

In summary, there are three important explanations for the complicated relation between the Netherlands and Europeanization in the field of RES-E. The first is that in terms of Europeanization, the Dutch focus was much more oriented towards complying with the electricity directives aimed at market liberalization than on complying with the RES-E. This relates to a second reason, that in Dutch electricity policy, energy saving and energy efficiency were for a long time preferred to the production and consumption of RES-E: policy goals that were strongly supported by incumbents in the energy sector, and 'locked in' by the natural gas lobby, which has a strong influence in the Dutch energy system. A third reason is that renewable energy policy, including the development of support mechanisms to achieve the RES-E targets, has been subjected to the strong political volatility in the Netherlands since 2001. In terms of 'uploading', the Netherlands can be characterized as a fence-sitter, not particularly interested (any longer) in setting the agenda for RES-E, while making sure that the ambitions of the directives remain modest and within reach. In terms of 'downloading', some important regulatory amendments were passed to comply with the directives. Moreover, broad national regulatory frameworks were already in place to facilitate the smooth implementation of EU directives. In terms of horizontal Europeanization, the Netherlands has been at the receiving end, adopting policies such as the FITs at state level, but also adopting other policies and best practices at regional and local government levels. Finally, we can state that the EU directives did not much influence the 'level playing field' of the electricity sector, as the incumbent actors (centralized energy producers and grid operators) did not experience any loss of influence, nor of power.

4.4 BIOFUELS CASE STUDY

4.4.1 The Period Prior to the 2003 Biofuels Directive

Just like RES-E, the development of biofuel markets in the Netherlands has proved rather problematic. Since the 2003 EU biofuels directive (2003/30/EC) was issued, biofuels have gained a great deal of attention. However, despite policy schemes, tax exemptions and several experiments, the development of biofuel markets in the Netherlands has remained rather limited as compared to other EU member states such as Germany and France (see Van der Laak et al., 2007; see also Chapter 3 by Vogelpohl et al., and Chapter 9 by Bocquillon and Evrard). Biofuels have been consumed in the Netherlands since 2005, notably in the transport sector. Biofuels demand basically stopped growing after a steep take-off in the period 2005–07 (from 0 to 13 PJ/yr). However, in 2012, still only 13 PJ of biofuels were consumed in the domestic transport sector. In 2012, 5 per cent of energy consumed in the sector stemmed from RES, and more than 90 per cent of those renewable sources were processed into biofuels (Planbureau voor de Leefomgeving et al., 2014).

The European Commission has been supporting biofuels through research and development (R&D) projects for more than two decades, aiming to create a new market for biofuel crops for the declining agricultural sector (Van der Laak et al., 2007). In addition, the EU proposed to support biofuels with generic tax exemptions (Suurs and Hekkert, 2009). Since the early 1990s small entrepreneurial experiments were organized with policy support and finance from the EU and Dutch regional governments. Although the initial experiments were technically successful, economic returns were disappointing. A major limitation was the scarcity of land to grow biofuel crops (i.e. 'first generation biomass'; LEI, 2005). Nevertheless, domestic developments continued, driven by the preparation of biofuel-related EU policies (Hillman et al., 2008). During the late 1990s, first-generation biofuels were criticized by scientists, engineers and environmental non-governmental organizations (NGOs) for being too expensive, even in comparison to the alternative of co-firing them in generating plants, and with only a very modest environmental performance. Central government refrained from action, mainly because it was internally divided on the alleged benefits and drawbacks of first-generation and second-generation biofuels, with different ministries and groups of stakeholders involved (Suurs and Hekkert, 2009). As a consequence, market parties did not undertake much action to spur further biofuel development. In 1998, following the EU White

Book, the political attention to climate change led to a window of opportunity for the development of biofuels, which were seen as an important way to lower greenhouse gas (GHG) emissions. A policy support programme on low CO_2 content gases and fuels was issued in 1998 (GAVE: the National Programme for the Assessment and Support of Gaseous and Liquid CO_2-Neutral Energy Carriers) (Suurs and Hekkert, 2009). The programme assessed multiple biofuel options and prioritized second-generation biofuels with a high potential for CO_2 emissions reduction. In addition, the programme targeted innovations in fuel production, improved supply chain collaboration, and set up a demonstration project (Hillman et al., 2008). At the time, Dutch central government was not in favour of a progressive biofuels policy, and neither was public opinion. Advocates of biofuels policy were more commonly found in industry, where biofuels were seen as an important international growth market (Koppejan and Van Est, 2011).

4.4.2 The 2003 Biofuels Directive and its Impact

During the negotiations running up to the biofuels directive the Netherlands did not actively push to lower the 5.75 per cent biofuels consumption target (to be achieved in 2010). It just complied with the indicative, non-binding target that applied to all member states. Nonetheless, the Netherlands was in favour of supporting second-generation biofuels. The 2003 biofuels directive implied that there would be less attention (by policymakers and investors) to second-generation as compared to first-generation biomass. Policy would focus on the latter, which was considered attractive to countries with large agricultural crop cultivation sectors such as Germany and France (but not the Netherlands) (Suurs and Hekkert, 2009; see also Chapter 3 by Vogelpohl et al., and Chapter 9 by Bocquillon and Evrard).

In a 2004 White Paper on Transport Emissions, the Dutch national government expressed its preference to delay implementation in favour of second-generation biofuels, which were expected to be more efficient in terms of carbon emissions reduction and costs (Rijkswaterstaat, 2014). The 2007 target of a 2 per cent share of RES in the transport (RES-T) sector (and 5.75 per cent in 2010), as stated in the biofuels directive, would therefore not be met. By 2005 the EU warned the Netherlands (and 19 other member states) that (national) implementation of the 2003 EU directive was behind schedule, and that national government should intensify its efforts to attain the 2 per cent target. Besides pressure from the EU, the national government's biofuels policy was also criticized in the Netherlands. The national parliament and the industry argued that the national biofuels policy in the Netherlands was 'insufficient and lacking ambition' (Koppejan and Van Est, 2011, pp. 36–37).

A generic tax exemption (excise duty) was temporarily issued in 2006, while the sector lobbied for a long-term tax exemption at EU level. In 2007 the temporary exemption was replaced by a regulation that made it mandatory for gasoline and diesel distributors to blend a minimum percentage (2 per cent) of biofuels into diesel or petrol, favouring first-generation biofuels which were definitely needed to comply with the EU targets ('*Besluit biobrandstoffen wegverkeer*' in Dutch) (Koppejan and Van Est, 2011). Distributors of petrol and diesel could produce and sell biofuels themselves, but were also allowed to meet the target by purchasing biofuels produced by others. In the latter case, administrative trading of biofuels took place by issuing so-called 'bio-tickets' (RVO.nl, 2014a). The 2003 EU biofuels directive gave the domestic market an impetus, and regional entrepreneurs started to implement plans for the construction of small biofuel plants. Besides central government, a few regional governments also embraced biofuels, in particular for lowering GHG emissions, and for regional economic interests (Van der Laak et al., 2007).

Meanwhile, the Dutch government did not abandon second-generation biofuels. From 2006 to 2014, a €60 million R&D programme was available for the development of second-generation biofuels. At the time, first-generation biofuels were merely considered a stepping stone towards future use of second-generation biofuels (Suurs and Hekkert, 2009). From 2006 to 2008, criticism of the distributive and environmental effects of first-generation biofuels revived. Rather than using first-generation 'edible' oil crops, biofuels were to be produced from local green waste streams, hence second-generation biofuels. National government also succeeded in getting concerns on first-generation biofuels on the policy agenda, as expressed in the 2004 White Paper on Transport Emissions. This led to a system of sustainability criteria incorporating CO_2 reduction potential and land use effects of particular biofuel chains, a system which at a later stage would also be adopted by the EU in the RED and the Fuel Quality Directive (in which the sustainability criteria for biofuels would even be lower than those in the Netherlands) (Koppejan and Van Est, 2011). The idea was that information on biofuel quality would be presented to end-consumers via a certification system.

Following a political debate in the national parliament ('Motie Spies'; Kamerstukken II, 2007/08, 31 200 XI, nr. 38), a call was made to intensify the use of second-generation biofuels under the co-blending policy by increasing the weight of second- (and third-) generation biofuels (also on the condition that at least a 35 per cent reduction in GHG emissions would be established) as compared to first-generation biofuels. This led to the development of the so-called 'double count' scheme, which was later implemented in 2009 (*'Regeling dubbeltelling'* in Dutch) (Tweede Kamer, 2008). The 'double count' meant that second-generation biofuels with high environmental performance – including a CO_2 emission reduction of at least 35 per cent – were assigned a higher weight in biofuel registration (RVO.nl, 2014a). During the development of the national double count scheme the Minister of the Environment pushed for progressive standardization at EU level (pushing for higher standards than 35 per cent GHG emissions reduction). At the same time, the European Commission was also preparing a 'double counting' scheme. The Dutch Minister pushed for stricter sustainability criteria in this scheme and strongly supported harmonization on the issue. She succeeded, and the EU later tried to spread the instrument to other EU member states. The 'double count' case illustrates the 'uploading' of a Dutch policy initiative to the EU level (although at the time the EU was also making preparations regarding the instrument).

Due to criticism of the alleged sustainability quality of (first-generation) biofuels and the national implementation of the double count scheme, a calculation was made that resulted in a lowering of the national target of 5.75 per cent (the 2003 EU directive target) to 4.00 per cent in 2009 (Staatsblad van het Koninkrijk der Nederlanden, 2009). Implementation of the so-called 'double count' scheme, however, proved to be a rather effective incentive that led to the early adoption of waste-derived biofuels. By 2012 almost 25 per cent of the total Dutch biofuels market was based on wastes and residues, a substantially higher figure than in most other member states (NEa, 2012; Van Grinsven and Kampman, 2013). Moreover, 'double counting' of biofuels (notably in biodiesel produced from wastes and residues, such as used frying fat) accounted for nearly 70 per cent of RES-T consumption (Planbureau voor de Leefomgeving et al., 2014). Later, the scheme was subject to criticism, in particular by the committee advising the Dutch national government on EU biofuels policy (the 'Corbey Committee', named after the Dutch delegate in EU biofuels policymaking).

4.4.3 The 2009 RED and FQD and their Impact

In pursuing the adoption and harmonization of the double count scheme, the Netherlands played an active role in the negotiations running up to the 2009 RED (2009/28/EC) and fuel quality directive (FQD) (2009/30/EC). It actively stressed the importance of sustainability (indirect land use change, ILUC; and the FQD) criteria in biofuels certification systems and policy. The sustainability criteria in the RED were considered a 'direct result of Dutch efforts in the negotiations' (Koppejan and Van Est, 2011, p. 38).

Implementation of the RED and FQD meant that the national biofuels regulations (2007) were replaced. Regulatory enforcement was assigned to the Dutch Emission Authority. The RED and FQD (as administrative policy schemes) were attached to the Dutch Environmental Policy Act. The RED basically continued the blending goals: 4.25 per cent by 2011, 4.5 per cent by 2012, 5 per cent by 2013 and 5.5 per cent by 2014. Moreover, biofuels sold by fuel providers were to meet European sustainability standards, which were to be verified by independent auditors. Besides fuels, fuel providers were also allowed to account for biogas and green electricity, to which different weights applied (RVO.nl, 2014b). By 2020 a 6 per cent reduction in GHG emissions was to be achieved, mainly via biofuels (NVDB, 2014). The use of 'bio-tickets' was maintained (RVO.nl, 2014b).

In the years after issuing the RED and the FQD, the Dutch national government actively engaged in EU debates on biofuels in order to resolve uncertainties regarding certification, reporting, and ILUC standards (Commissie Duurzaamheidsvraagstukken Biomassa, 2010). Other issues were: not to increase the target for co-blending of biofuels in transport fuels; to make current policies and certification systems stricter in the use of the ILUC criteria; to await the results of the 2014 evaluation of the 2009 EU directives (instead of formulating a progressive domestic biofuel policy); and to continue supporting second-generation biofuels use (Commissie Duurzaamheidsvraagstukken Biomassa, 2012). Hence, the Netherlands remained actively involved in EU discussions on biofuels, trying to modify EU policies.

In summary, the 2003 EU biofuels directive spurred the development of the biofuels market in the Netherlands for nearly four years. At the time, a national debate on sustainability criteria for biofuels ensued, which led to the development and implementation of a progressive 'double counting' scheme in support of second-generation biofuels. In addition, this initiative was even successfully 'uploaded' to the EU. The Netherlands would remain actively involved in EU discussions on the environmental quality and sustainability of biofuels, and succeed in getting sustainability criteria in the RED. Compared to the 2003 biofuels directive, the implementation of the 2009 RED and FQD was much less effective. Basically, no market development (in terms of volume growth) in the Netherlands was established in the period following implementation of the two directives. To a great extent this related to uncertainties in how (the formulation of) EU policy would have an impact on the domestic biofuels market. As a consequence, the Netherlands adopted a 'wait and see' strategy in EU discussions, but did continue efforts at EU level to support the adoption of measures in favour of second-generation biofuels.

4.5 CONCLUSION

The two cases show that Dutch renewable energy policies have been far from consistent over the past two decades. RES-E and biofuels were not priorities in Dutch energy policies, which focused on market liberalization, security of energy supply, and energy savings. Negotiations with the EU on the targets to be achieved mostly aimed to minimize the impact on the Dutch stakeholders in the energy and waste sectors. Despite the regulatory changes resulting from the directives, there has been no redistribution of resources or power among the key stakeholders in the energy domain. In both cases, all three forms of Europeanization were observed, although some (i.e. top-down and bottom-up Europeanization) were more commonly encountered than others (i.e. horizontal Europeanization). Table 4.1 summarizes the Europeanization mechanisms that were observed in the RES-E and biofuels cases.

Top-down Europeanization was observed in both the RES-E and biofuels cases following the issue of directives. Typically, national implementation of the directives led to amendments in national regulatory frameworks and the development of support schemes. It can be argued that in terms of instrumentation, EU directives on biofuels introduced novel instruments to the Netherlands; whereas this was less so in the case of RES-E, where policy frameworks were already in place, and adapted to smooth the implementation of EU directives.

Horizontal Europeanization was identified in the development of the support mechanisms contributing to the targets set in the directives. In the case of RES-E, the overwhelming evidence of the success of FITs as implemented in other member states (and the uneven playing field this produced) eventually convinced the Dutch government to follow this strategy. Also citizens and firms, often referring to Germany, pointed out that such an incentive was indispensable to the adoption of RES-E. In the case of biofuels, the horizontal influence was less explicitly present, mainly because views and potential for (first-generation) biofuels production differed from other EU member states, in particular Germany and France.

Table 4.1 Observed Europeanization mechanisms in the RES-E and biofuels cases

Europeanization mechanism	RES-E case	Biofuels case
Top-down	Regulatory amendments made following implementation of the 2001 and 2009 Directives. However, national policies were to a great extent already aligned to the two directives (arguably to smooth implementation of the EU directives).	Regulatory changes made following implementation of the 2003 and 2009 Directives. Uncertainties regarding implementation path of 2009 directives.
Horizontal	Diffusion of FITs from other member states (MSs) and adoption in national policy (MEP, SDE schemes). Diffusion of regional and local government policies from other MSs to Dutch peers (e.g., best practices, competition schemes).	None*
Bottom-up	'Uploading' of policy and attempts to adapt the directive during the negotiations of the 2001 RES-E directive. Lowering of the national RES target during and after the 2009 RES directive negotiations with the EU (stressing subsidiarity).	'Uploading' of progressive incentives (i.e., the 'double counting' scheme) to spur adoption of second-generation biofuels. Pushing for strict regulation and certification of ILUC and FQD criterions.

Note: * The authors could not find evidence to support the claim that horizontal Europeanization took place regarding biofuels policy.

Bottom-up Europeanization took place in two ways. Firstly, the Netherlands (in the role of a proactive green member state) pushed for and succeeded in 'uploading' policies and standards to the EU. This was observed in both the RES-E and the biofuels case studies. Secondly, the Netherlands tried and succeeded in lowering targets that had been allocated to the country by the EU. In the case of biofuels this was related to the successful implementation (and even 'uploading') of a scheme that used a novel calculation method supporting second-generation biofuels (a goal that was already explicitly supported by the Netherlands in the EU discussion of biofuels). Bottom-up Europeanization also took place to modify EU directives (definitions and textual changes) so as to protect the interests of national industries.

In summary, the domestic biofuels market seems much more sensitive to vertical Europeanization than the domestic RES-E market. Given our mixed findings on the effects of the EU directives we assessed, and the influence of horizontal cross-national EU influences, we tend to agree with Busch and Jörgens's claim that 'the mutual adjustment of autonomous states to each other's policy decisions often has effects that are very similar to those of binding international agreements or supranational policy-making through EU-directives' (Busch and Jörgens, 2012a, p. 221), in the Dutch RES-E case. However, there is little evidence to support this claim vis-à-vis the Dutch biofuels case.

REFERENCES

Agnolucci, P. (2007), 'Renewable electricity policies in the Netherlands', *Renewable Energy*, 32, 868–883.

Agterbosch, S., P. Glasbergen and W. Vermeulen (2007), 'Social barriers in wind power implementation in the Netherlands: perceptions of wind power entrepreneurs and local civil servants of institutional and social conditions in realizing wind power projects', *Renewable and Sustainable Energy Reviews*, 11 (6), 1025–1055.

Agterbosch, S., W. Vermeulen, and P. Glasbergen (2004), 'Implementation of wind energy in the Netherlands: the importance of the social-institutional setting', *Energy Policy*, 32(18), 2049–2066.

Arentsen, M.J. (2009), 'The Netherlands: muddling through in the Dutch delta', in W. Lafferty and A. Ruud (eds), *Promoting Sustainable Electricity in Europe: Challenging the Path Dependence of Dominant Energy Systems*, Cheltenham and Northampton, MA Edward Elgar Publishing, pp. 45–72.

Arentsen, M., M. Bechberger, M-R. Di Nucci, A. Midttun, C. Casale and A. Klemenc (2007), 'REALISE-Forum; Renewable energy and liberalization in selected electricity markets-forum', EU Intelligent Energy Europe, CSTM-SR, 318, Enschede: University of Twente, CSTM, Freie Universität Berlin, Norwegian School of Management, CESI RICERA, and Slovenski E-Forum, https://ec.europa.eu/energy/intelligent/projects/en/projects/realise-forum.

Arentsen, M. and T. de Bruijn (2005), 'National room to manoeuvre: the Dutch position in EU energy policies', in F. Wijen, K. Zoeteman and J. Pieters (eds), *A Handbook of Globalization and Environmental Policy: National Government Interventions in a Global Arena*, Cheltenham and Northampton, MA: Edward Elgar Publishing, pp. 417–434.

Börzel, T. (2002), 'Member State responses to Europeanization', *Journal of Common Market Studies*, 40 (2), 193–214.

Börzel, T. and T. Risse (2000), 'When Europe hits home: Europeanization and domestic change', *European Integration online Papers* (*EIoP*), 4 (15), https://papers.ssrn.com/sol3/papers.cfm?abstract_id=302768.

Bulmer, S. and S. Padgett (2005), 'Policy transfer in the European Union: an institutionalist perspective', *British Journal of Political Science*, 35 (1), 103–126.

Burck, J., F. Marten and C. Bals (2014), *Climate Change Performance Index 2015*, Bonn and Berlin: German Watch and CAN, accessed on 3 December 2014 at https://germanwatch.org/en/9472.

Busch, P.-O. and H. Jörgens (2012a), 'Governance by diffusion: exploring a new mechanism of international policy coordination', in J. Meadowcroft, O. Langhelle and A. Ruud (eds), *Governance, Democracy and Sustainable Development: Moving Beyond the Impasse?*, Cheltenham and Northampton, MA: Edward Elgar Publishing, pp. 221–248.

Busch, P.-O. and H. Jörgens (2012b), 'Europeanization through diffusion? Renewable energy policies and alternative sources for European convergence', in F. Morata and I. Solorio (eds), *European Energy Policy: An Environmental Approach*, Cheltenham and Northampton, MA: Edward Elgar Publishing, pp. 66–84.

Caporaso, J. (2007), 'The three worlds of regional integration theory', in P. Graziano and M. Vink (eds), *Europeanization: New Research Agendas*, New York: Palgrave Macmillan, pp. 23–34.

CBS, PBL and Wageningen UR (2016), 'Hernieuwbare elektriciteit, 1990–2014 (indicator 0517, versie 27, 3 februari 2016)', CBS, The Hague; Planbureau voor de Leefomgeving, The Hague/Bilthoven en Wageningen UR, Wageningen, accessed on 22 March 2016 at http://www.compendiumvoordeleefomgeving.nl/indicatoren/nl0517-hernieuwbare-elektriciteit.html?i=6-38.

Commissie Duurzaamheidsvraagstukken Biomassa (2010), 'Aanbevelingen over certificering en rapportage in het kader van de EU-richtlijn Hernieuwbare Energie', Utrecht: Rijksdienst voor Ondernemend Nederland.

Commissie Duurzaamheidsvraagstukken Biomassa (2012), 'De duurzaamheidssteiger; Stappen vooruit in het biobrandstoffenbeleid', Utrecht: Rijksdienst voor Ondernemend Nederland.

Dinica, V. and M.J. Arentsen (2003), 'Green certificate trading in the Netherlands in the prospect of the European electricity market', *Energy Policy*, 21, 609–620.

ECN, PBL, CBS and RVO.nl (2016), 'Nationale Energieverkenning 2015', Petten/Amsterdam, The Hague, Utrecht, accessed on 24 March 2016 at http://www.cbs.nl/NR/rdonlyres/C0F1D74C-1EB1-4E3B-9A46-ECA28ABFED7E/0/2015nationaleenergieverkenning.pdf.

Hillman, K.M., R.A.A. Suurs, M.P. Hekkert and A. Björn Sandén (2008), 'Cumulative causation in biofuels development: a critical comparison of the Netherlands and Sweden', *Technology Analysis and Strategic Management*, 20 (5), 593–612.

Hofman, P.S. (2005), 'Innovation and institutional change: the transition to a sustainable electricity system', Dissertation, Enschede: University of Twente.
Hofman, P.S. and E.E. Marquart (2001), *Electricity in Flux: Sociotechnical change in the Dutch electricity system 1970–2000*, Bilthoven: Dutch National Programme on Global Air Pollution and Climate Change.
Hoppe, T., A. Graf, B. Warbroek, I. Lammers and I. Lepping (2015), 'Local governments supporting local energy initiatives: lessons from the best practices of Saerbeck (Germany) and Lochem (The Netherlands)', *Sustainability*, 7 (2), 1900–1931.
Hoppe, T. and M.P.T. Sanders (2014), 'Agricultural green gas demonstration projects in the Netherlands: a stakeholder analysis', *Environmental Engineering and Management Journal*, 13 (12), 3083–3096.
Jörgens, H., A. Lenschow and D. Liefferink (eds) (2014), *Understanding Environmental Policy Convergence: The Power of Words, Rules and Money*, Cambridge: Cambridge University Press.
Kamerstukken II, 2007/08, 31 200 XI, nr. 38 ('Motie Spies').
Kenniscentrum InfoMil (2014), 'Handboek EU-milieubeleid en Nederland; Uitvoering en effecten in de praktijk', The Hague: InfoMil, accessed on 22 March 2016 at http://www.infomil.nl/onderwerpen/integrale/handboek-eu/klimaatverandering/elektriciteit/uitvoering-effecten/.
Kern, F. and A. Smith (2008), 'Restructuring energy systems for sustainability? Energy transition policy in the Netherlands', *Energy Policy*, 36, 4093–4103.
Koppejan, D. and R. Van Est (2011), 'Bio-economiebeleid: Inspirerend maar niet sturend', in D. Stemerding and R. van est (eds), *Naar de kern van de bio-economie: De duurzame beloftes van biomassa in perspectief*, The Hague: Rathenau Instituut, pp. 31–48.
LEI (2005), *Beschikbaarheid koolzaad voor biodiesel*, Wageningen, The Hague: Landbouw Economisch Instituut.
Ministerie van Economische Zaken (1995), *Derde energienota*, The Hague: SDU.
NEa (2012), *Naleving jaarverplichting 2011 hernieuwbare energie vervoer en verplichting brandstoffen luchtverontreiniging*, The Hague: Nederlandse Emissieautoriteit (Nea).
Netbeheer Nederland (2009), 'Net voor de toekomst; een verkenning', Arnhem: Netbeheer Nederland, http://www.netbeheernederland.nl/Content/Files/373_320008-Rapport%20Net%20voor%20de%20Toekomst.pdf.
NVDB (2014), 'De stimulering van betere biobrandstoffen door het stellen van een scherp CO2-doel', Position paper van de Nederlandse Vereniging voor Duurzame Biobrandstoffen (NVDB), The Hague: NVDB.
Oteman, M., M. Wiering and J.K. Helderman (2014), 'The institutional space of community initiatives for renewable energy: a comparative case study of the Netherlands, Germany and Denmark', *Energy, Sustainability and Society*, 4 (1), 11.
Planbureau voor de Leefomgeving, CBS and Wageningen UR (2014), *Verbruik van hernieuwbare energie 1990–2013*, accessed on 14 September 2014 at http://www.compendiumvoordeleefomgeving.nl/indicatoren/nl0385-Verbruik-van-hernieuwbare-energie.html?i=9-53.

Rijkswaterstaat (2014), *Handboek EU-milieubeleid in Nederland, Uitvoering en effecten in de praktijk*, Kenniscentrum Infomil, accessed on 29 June 2016 at http://www.infomil.nl/onderwerpen/integrale/handboek-eu/klimaatverandering/biobrandstoffen/uitvoering-effecten/.

Rowlands, I. H. (2005), 'The European directive on renewable electricity: conflicts and compromises', *Energy Policy*, 33 (8), 965–974.

RVO.nl (2014a), 'Nederlands Beleid Biobrandstoffen 2006–2010', accessed on 12 September 2014 at http://www.rvo.nl/onderwerpen/duurzaam-ondernemen/duurzame-energie-opwekken/gave/beleid-biobrandstoffen/nl-beleid-2006-2010.

RVO.nl (2014b), 'Nederlands Beleid Biobrandstoffen', accessed on 12 September 2014 at http://www.rvo.nl/onderwerpen/duurzaam-ondernemen/duurzame-energie-opwekken/gave/beleid-biobrandstoffen.

Simmons, B.A., F. Dobbin and G. Garrett (eds) (2008), *The Global Diffusion of Markets and Democracy*, Cambridge: Cambridge University Press.

Simmons, B.A. and Z. Elkins (2004), 'The globalization of liberalization: policy diffusion in the international political economy', *American Political Science Review*, 98 (1), 171–189.

Staatsblad van het Koninkrijk der Nederlanden (2009), 'Besluit van 6 mei 2009 tot wijziging van het Besluit biobrandstoffen wegverkeer 2007 (verlaging percentages toe te voegen biobrandstoffen)', Jaargang 2009, STB12401. ISSN 0920 – 2064, Sdu Uitgevers. 's-Gravenhage 2009.

Suurs, R.A.A. and M.P. Hekkert (2009), 'Competition between first and second generation technologies: lessons from the formation of a biofuels innovation sytems in the Netherlands', *Energy*, 34, 669–679.

Tweede Kamer (2008), Vergaderjaar 2007–2008, 31 200 XI en 22 112, nr. 99. (Regeling dubbeltelling).

Van der Heijden, J., E. ten Heuvelhof, B. Broekhans, S. van der Arend, E. van Bueren, C. Harteveld and T. van Ruijven (2014), 'Contrasting stories on overcoming governance challenges: the implementation of the EU Water Framework Directive in the Netherlands', *Local Environment*, 19 (3), 318–333.

Van der Laak, W.W.M., R.P.J.M. Raven and G.P.J. Verbong (2007), 'Strategic niche management for biofuels: Analysing past experiments for developing new biofuel policies', *Energy Policy*, 35, 3213–3225.

Van Grinsven, A. and B. Kampman (2013), *Ranking Dutch Oil Companies on Biofuels*, Publication code 13 4786 09, Delft: CE.

Van Rooijen, N.M. and M.T. van Wees (2006), 'Green electricity policies in the Netherlands: an analysis of policy decisions', *Energy Policy*, 34, 60–71.

Verbong, G. and F. Geels (2007), 'The ongoing energy transition: lessons from a socio-technical, multi-level analysis of the Dutch electricity system (1960–2004)', *Energy Policy*, 35 (2), 1025–1037.

Warbroek, W.D.B. and T. Hoppe (2017), 'Modes of governance and policy of decentralized governments supporting local low-carbon energy initiatives; exploring the cases of the Dutch regions of Overijssel and Fryslân', *Sustainability*, 9 (1), 75.

Wolsink, M. (1996), 'Dutch wind power policy: Stagnating implementation of renewables', *Energy Policy*, 24 (12), 1079–1088.

5. Denmark: a wind-powered forerunner

Helene Dyrhauge

5.1 INTRODUCTION

Danish renewable energy policy is a story of how civil society was able to push for wind power instead of nuclear energy and how one central politician was able to shape Danish environmental and energy policy, which has led to Denmark becoming a forerunner in terms of renewable energy sources (RES) promotion. The story begins in the 1970s, when the oil crisis fuelled the pressure on the government to reduce its dependency on fossil fuels. Initially the government wanted to invest in nuclear power but pressure from grass-roots movements and universities together with wind power entrepreneurs changed the policy direction towards RES. The strong resistance against nuclear energy and the advocacy coalition (Sabatier, 1998) promoting wind power influenced the normative basis of Danish energy policy. The main policy shifts in Danish energy policy happened in the late 1970s and early 1980s, and today wind power has become an important energy source. Vestas, one of the world leading wind turbine producers, is Danish, and has been influential in investing and developing wind turbines from the initial smaller ones to the big offshore wind parks. Overall, RES and technology sectors have become important for the Danish economy, which has influenced its policy orientation at the EU and international levels.

The 2009 renewable energy directive (RED) requires Denmark to increase the share of RES from 17 per cent in 2005 to 30 per cent in 2020; only five other member states have higher targets (Latvia, Austria, Portugal, Finland and Sweden). The 2013 progress report shows that Denmark is on course to meet its targets (COM, 2013). Indeed, Denmark is seen as a forerunner, which has established some of the highest RES standards and targets in the European Union (EU). Crucially, the literature suggests that Denmark traditionally has adopted a defensive position on environmental policies where it has either tried to anticipate the

European Commission's policy initiatives or actively defended its domestic policies and standards in European Council negotiations (Liefferink and Andersen, 1998; Andersen, 1998). In other words, Denmark's position as an environmental forerunner has put it ahead of EU policy development, where Denmark generally has tried to push for stronger environmental policy instruments. This chapter explains how Denmark has become an environmental forerunner by tracking Danish energy policy development from the 1970s, when Denmark relied on imported fossil fuels, until today, when Denmark has become energy self-sufficient, due to North Sea oil and to progressive adoption of RES, most notably wind power. This chapter argues that there has been limited Europeanization. Instead domestic advocacy coalitions and individual politicians have been the main drivers in the development of Danish renewable energy policies.

The chapter starts by outlining the analytical framework, explaining how domestic advocacy coalitions are important for understanding bottom-up Europeanization. Section 5.2 outlines the analytical framework, detailing the role of domestic advocacy coalitions in fostering the Danish forerunner position in Europeanization of RES. Section 5.3 details the development of RES in Denmark from the 1970s onwards and explains how specific norm entrepreneurs have been able to influence the Danish political system, especially how RES have become institutionalized within the public administrative system. Section 5.4 turns towards the EU and analyses Denmark's RES policies in relation to development at EU level, especially focusing on the 2009 RED and liberalization of the Danish electricity market, which were closely connected. Section 5.5 explains how the focus on RES for electricity (RES-E) has been at the expense of a national policy on biofuels. The final section draws conclusions on the extent to which Denmark's position as forerunner has led to domestic policy changes due to domestic factors or due to the EU.

5.2 EUROPEANIZATION AND FORERUNNER POSITION

Research on Europeanization attempts to explain a reorientation of national policies in relation to EU policy developments; this can range from domestic policy reform to subtle adjustments of existing public administrative procedures. However, not all changes in domestic policies are due to Europeanization. Forerunners, like Denmark, tend to introduce stronger environmental policy protection before the EU, due to either national domestic interests or pressure from domestic actors, in the form of specific advocacy coalitions. A forerunner or pace-setter will try to upload its policy preferences to the EU level (see Chapter 1 by Jörgens and Solorio), thus a forerunner is presumed to be a strategic actor which protects its own national interests. This leads to bottom-up Europeanization. However, it can be difficult to maintain a forerunner position over time and a member state can lose its forerunner position either due to changes at the domestic level or because other member states become forerunners (Wurzel et al., 2013). Nevertheless, a forerunner has established comprehensive public administrative structures which facilitate and promote high environmental standards.

An environmental forerunner establishes strong norms and cultures, which become institutionalized throughout the political system. These norms have often developed due to domestic factors, especially pressure from domestic actors and grass-roots movements. As such it can be viewed as a bottom-up process. Specifically, '[a] "forerunner" is defined as a Member State which is "ahead" of EU environmental policy in the sense of having developed more advanced policies with higher level of protection' (Liefferink and Andersen, 1998, p. 256). A forerunner can adopt different strategies, either trying to push by example, or defending its domestic environmental standards at international level. A defensive forerunner is concerned that EU legislation will have a negative impact on domestic environmental standards, yet it is less concerned about finding EU-level solutions. In general, forerunners 'wish to maintain the freedom to develop and implement their own national policies. European policies are welcome so long as they promote domestic policy goals' and do not 'constrain the autonomy of a Member State to set stricter standards' (Börzel, 2002, p. 203). Thus, a defensive forerunner is likely to veto a proposal, or not implement legislation, if it does not fit with domestic standards. Denmark has traditionally been seen as a defensive forerunner, where it has both pushed the EU for stronger environmental protection and also defended its policies (Andersen and Liefferink, 1998; Andersen, 1998). A forerunner is less affected by EU policy development compared to a laggard member state because a forerunner has institutionalized environmental norms and environmental protection at the domestic level, which makes it easier to implement EU legislation there.

A forerunner is often seen as a pioneer, which is a country with a first-mover advantage, yet a pioneer will not necessarily become a forerunner, just as a laggard can become a forerunner. A state's environmental position is therefore not static, but depends on both domestic and external factors. These factors are dependent upon a successful advocacy coalition which is able to facilitate policy change. For example, 'a necessary condition for becoming a pioneer [and forerunner] is a high capacity for environmental policy-making. This encompasses the institutional, economic and informational opportunities and the relative strengths of the green advocacy coalition in the country' (Jänicke, 2005, p. 140). According to Jänicke (2005, p. 136), a successful advocacy coalition consists of traditional environmental supporters who work with industry modernizers to achieve stronger environmental policies. Indeed the advocacy coalition framework 'explicitly argues that most coalitions will include not only interest group leaders, but also agency officials, legislators from multiple levels of government, applied researchers, and perhaps even a few journalists'. Similarly, the advocacy coalition framework 'assumes that policy core beliefs are the fundamental "glue" of coalitions because they represent basic normative and empirical commitments within the domain for specialization of policy élites' (Sabatier, 1998, p. 103). These domestic green advocacy coalitions change over time, but for forerunners, the green norms and ideals will have been institutionalized in their public administration, which in turn influences how member states respond to EU policy developments and often results in limited domestic changes due to European policies.

5.3 THE DEVELOPMENT OF DANISH RENEWABLE ENERGY POLICY

5.3.1 Civil Society's Protest and Influence on Government's Energy Plans

Danish environmental protection and advocacy towards RES pre-dates the 1970s oil crisis. In 1969 the first nature protection law (Naturfredningsloven) was adopted and a group of activists gatecrashed an academic conference on nuclear energy to announce that they were establishing an alternative energy plan focusing on RES. The event led to the creation of the environmental grass-roots movement NOAH (today the Danish arm of Friends of the Earth) (Kampmann, 1996). By the time of the oil crisis (1973–74), Denmark had already created some environmental institutions, such as the environmental ministry, and civil society groups were beginning to oppose nuclear energy. NOAH was instrumental in promoting an alternative vision to nuclear energy, and it became one of the most influential grass-roots movements in recent Danish history, organizing demonstrations and lobbying successive governments, in addition to working with researchers at different universities. Several Danish protest songs have become national symbols of the grass-roots movements in their fight against nuclear power. In particular, the opposition to the Swedish nuclear power plant, Barsebäk, across the Øresund from Copenhagen, was important for the protest movements. Many people were concerned about the implications of having a nuclear power plant so close to the Danish capital.

The first national energy plan was published in 1976, which prescribed that nuclear energy should provide 23 per cent of total energy consumption by 1995, and thereby replace the dependence on imported fossil fuels (Blegaa et al., 1977, p. 87). Although the 1976 national energy plan saw nuclear energy as important for the Danish energy mix, later in 1976 the government postponed the introduction of nuclear energy. However, the formal nuclear energy plans were only abandoned in 1985, by which time there was no support for nuclear energy and the protest movements had won the political discussion. From the 1970s onwards, civil society together with independent research from universities, mainly the Danish Technological University, and industrial entrepreneurs (wind power) had put pressure on successive governments to focus on RES instead of nuclear energy. This opposition against nuclear energy must be seen in relation to the national opposition towards the Barsebäk nuclear power plant, which started operating in 1977. The groups which opposed nuclear energy focused on the implications of accidents, disposal of nuclear waste, and also the potential risk of terrorists and dictators gaining access to uranium (Meyer, 2000, p. 86).

As an alternative to the 1976 national energy plan, researchers from the Risø Institute[1] together with civil society, including NOAH, created an alternative energy plan (Hvelplund, 2005, p. 89). The 1976 alternative energy plan aimed to prioritize RES technologies, which at the time were not commercially viable. The plan also emphasized improvements of energy conversion systems (Blegaa et al., 1977). Wind and solar energy were part of the 1976 official energy plan, but the government was unsure of the viability of these technologies, and especially whether they would be commercially available by the late 1980s (Handelsministeriet, 1976). Thus, RES did not have a big role in the 1976 energy plan. However, wind power was important, and by the mid-1970s industrial entrepreneurs and researchers at the Risø Institute had built small wind turbines. In 1979 the government introduced subsidies as incentives for individual persons or a small cooperative to buy wind turbines and install these in the local community, and in 1981 the first wind map was published (Meyer, 2007). Initially the subsidies were 30 per cent of investment, but over time the subsidies were gradually reduced and finally phased out in 1989 (Auken, 2002, p. 153); subsidies were later reintroduced and have continued to be important for the growth in wind turbine parks. By 1989 the wind power industry had started to mature (Madsen, 2000, p. 163). Overall, wind power has become part of Danish industrial policy and has become an export sector; by 2001 it had 'supplied 50 per cent of the world's wind turbine capacity' and had become 'the third largest export industry' in Denmark (Midttun, 2001, p. 94).

Overall the public debate during the 1970s and early 1980s was influenced by researchers from the universities, especially the Risø Institute, and other independent organizations such as NOAH (Hvelplund, 2005). The idea of RES promotion was eventually adopted by successive governments. The Danish government environmental strategy paper from 1988, 'Vores Fælles Fremtid' (Our Common Future) (Verdenskommissionen, 1988) was a direct response to the Brundtland report and indeed used the same title, where sustainability had to be integrated into the Danish political and administrative system (Statsministeriet, 1988, p. 6). RES represented 4 per cent of total energy consumption in 1987, and they were an integral part of the restructuring of energy production with the aim of reducing pollution (Statsministeriet, 1988, p. 106). Interestingly the strategy paper does not mention the EU. The implementation of the Single European Act, especially the chapter on environment, had been problematic for Denmark because Danish politicians were concerned that EU legislation would have a negative effect on Denmark's high environmental standards. This debate clearly demonstrates the Danish defensive forerunner position and concerns about how EU legislation affects Denmark's own environmental standards.

Overall, the 1970s were characterized by strong civil society groups, which together represented an advocacy coalition; and their opposition against nuclear energy and promotion of RES, especially wind power, was eventually adopted by Danish governments. The 1980s national energy plans focused on RES and energy efficiency. Simultaneously the environmental debate started to become more professionalized, with academics and industry becoming more influential, whereas the grassroots movements almost disappeared (Læssøe, 2007, p. 236). Moreover, the 1980s saw a green majority in the parliament, where the social liberals who were in a coalition government with the conservatives and liberals often created a green majority with the social democrats and two socialist parties (Andersen, 1998, p. 265). The green majority in the parliament pushed the coalition government towards stronger environmental protection. The social liberals eventually left government and in 1993 became part of a social democratic-led coalition government.

5.3.2 The Reign of Svend Auken (Minister for Environment and Energy, 1993–2001)

The 1993 general election led to a change in government from a conservative–liberal coalition to a social democratic–social liberal coalition government. The change in government had important implications for Denmark's position as an environmental forerunner. Firstly, Prime Minister Poul Nyrup Rasmussen (social democratic) appointed Svend Auken as Minister for the Ministry of Environment and Energy. Svend Auken was a strong advocate of more environmental protection. He believed that Denmark had to take a leading position on the environment, nationally, internationally and at EU level, whilst he also recognized that Denmark could learn from other countries (Auken, 1996, p. 11). Secondly, Poul Nyrup Rasmussen merged the Environment ministry and the Energy ministry. To ensure complete integration of the two ministries, the administrative structures were changed to emphasize a more environmental ethos (Auken, 1996). This administrative integration of the two ministries created a synergy between the two policy fields which often have contradictory policy goals. The Ministry of Environment and Energy represented innovative political leadership, where it developed a strong and often innovative central administration (Hvelplund, 2005, p. 88).

At EU level Denmark was one of the greenest member states; as a strong defensive forerunner Denmark focused on 'developing and maintaining strict national politics' and its approach 'was combined with an uncompromising approach in Brussels', where Denmark adopted a pusher-by-example strategy to defend its forerunner position (Liefferink and Andersen, 1998, p. 267). Simultaneously, Svend Auken took a more active role in EU environmental policymaking compared to earlier when Denmark was more concerned about protecting its own higher environmental standards instead of developing EU environmental policy. This is evident in the 1985 Danish veto on a proposal for a regulation on car emissions, whilst Denmark also had a poor implementation record (Andersen, 1998). Moreover, Svend Auken made sure that the European Environmental Agency was located in Copenhagen. Thus, the national norms and policy preferences regarding RES and the environment became stronger during the Auken period and became more institutionalized in the public administrative system and the Danish approach to RES.

5.3.3 From Defensive Forerunner to Climate Change Sceptic and Back Again

The new millennium brought changes to Danish environment and energy policy. The general election in 2001 led to a change in government from the social democratic-led coalition government to a liberal–conservative coalition government (2001–09) led by Anders Fogh Rasmussen. The new Prime Minister, Anders Fogh Rasmussen, separated the Ministry for Environment and Energy to create two independent ministries. Initially, Anders Fogh Rasmussen was very sceptical towards the climate change agenda, and as part of his reform of the national advisory bodies he set up the Environmental Assessment Institute, which was headed by the climate sceptic Bjørn Lomborg.

The creation of the Environmental Assessment Institute signalled a deliberate departure from previous Danish environmental policy priorities, creating more liberal norms and leading to weaker sustainability. For example, the new government halted support for wind power and cancelled three planned offshore wind parks (Ryland, 2010, p. 81). Anders Fogh Rasmussen later revised his position on climate change and in 2008 Denmark became more active and started to invest in new wind turbine parks again (Sovacool, 2013, p. 835). However, the Danish government in 2007 had already started to invest in new wind turbine parks again. In the meantime, the de-prioritization of wind power influenced the Danish wind turbine sector, which had started to focus on exporting its knowledge and products (Energistyrelsen, 2011). The new export-orientated strategy generated growth both in terms of employment and in terms of the economic power of the sector. The increased economic power of the sector influenced the government's position at EU level, where the Danish government began to use more economic arguments to support RES, especially the potential for innovation and industrial development (Knudsen, 2012, p. 55). This also supported the more liberal economic policies pursued by the Anders Fogh Rasmussen government.

5.4 THE DANISH ENERGY REFORM AND IMPLEMENTATION OF THE RES-E DIRECTIVES

5.4.1 The Danish Energy Reform

EU energy market opening started in the mid-1990s. Whilst the process aimed to create competition and a single market for electricity, it fed into the increased focus on RES and several EU directives were adopted in parallel. The liberalization required changes to the Danish electricity sector, including changes to administrative structures, where independent agencies had to be created in order to ensure fair competition.

The Danish electricity sector has traditionally been a decentralized one, in which local small independent power plants have been controlled by the municipalities. Today many co-fired local power plants are fuelled by biomass, mainly from waste and wood. Crucially the power plants continue to provide both electricity and heating to the local communities. The decentralized energy system also extended to infrastructure, where a connection between the east and west energy grids was only established in 2005 (Sovacool, 2013, p. 835). As Table 5.1 shows, there has been an increase in the use of biomass, which in 2012 accounted for 11.8 per cent of domestic electricity production, whilst wind power accounted for 30 per cent (Energistyrelsen, 2012, p. 12). According to Hvelplund (2005, p. 86) the growth in biomass and waste has reached saturation point, which only leaves room for more growth for wind power and possible new technologies such as photovoltaic (PV) and wave power plants. Indeed, Table 5.1 shows that there has been a limited increase in biomass compared to wind power, which has increased substantially since 2005, when the government again started to support investment in new wind turbine parks.

Table 5.1 Electricity from RES in Denmark (%)

	1994	2000	2003	2005	2009	2010	2011	2012
RES-E share in total	5.3	15.9	22.9	27.4	28.9	34.8	40.7	43.1
Solar energy	0.0	0.0	0.0	0.0	0.0	0.0	0.0	0.3
Wind power	3.4	12.1	15.8	18.5	19.3	21.9	28.0	29.8
Hydropower	0.1	0.1	0.1	0.1	0.1	0.1	0.0	0.1
Biomass	1.5	3.1	6.3	8.1	8.5	11.9	11.6	11.8
Straw/hay	0.2	0.5	2.1	2.4	1.9	3.1	2.2	1.8
Wood	0.4	0.7	1.8	2.9	3.8	6.2	6.6	7.5
Biodegradable waste	0.9	1.9	2.3	2.8	2.8	2.6	2.7	2.6
Biogas	0.3	0.6	0.8	0.8	1.0	1.0	1.0	1.1

Source: Energistyrelsen (2012, p. 12).

The 1996 electricity reform was mainly due to a decision by the national competition authority and happened before the EU electricity market opening started; this anticipation of EU policy developments brought Denmark into compliance with subsequent EU legislation and Denmark did not have to make further reforms (Jakobsen, 2010, p. 898). Nonetheless, Danish politicians, including Svend Auken, did not support the liberalization (Olsen, 2006, p. 10); and compared to the other Nordic countries, with which Denmark worked closely on electricity issues, Denmark lagged behind (Midttun, 2001, p. 93). The Danish approach to electricity production favours a democratic planned economy, which engages the local community and the sector-specific stakeholders (Midttun, 2001; Knudsen, 2012). Indeed, the Danish political system is characterized by corporatism, where 'interest groups play a key role in policy formulation and implementation in general and in EU matters in particular' (Bursens, 2002, p. 183). Similar to most political reforms in Denmark, the agreement on Danish electricity reform was made by the Poul Nyrup Rasmussen coalition government and the opposition (liberals and conservative). Agreements between the government and the opposition ensure that the next government does not reverse the reform, thereby creating a more legitimate reform process.

Whilst the 1996 reform was caused by domestic factors it also feeds into the general assumption of Denmark as a good compliance member state. Similarly, the early implementation follows Denmark's pattern of implementation and anticipated EU environmental requirements ahead of EU policy developments. This can also be seen in the 1999 Danish Energy Reform Act which included a Danish carbon dioxide (CO_2) trading scheme, which should be seen as part of Denmark's international commitment to the Kyoto targets of reducing CO_2 emissions (Regeringen, 1999). Support schemes have been an important element of the Danish commitment to RES, starting in the late 1970s where individuals were given financial support to erect wind turbines in their local area. Nevertheless, various governments have periodically stopped financial support for new wind turbine parks, which has led to stagnation in the level of energy from wind turbines. Thus governmental support for investment in new wind turbine parks is important.

The alignment between energy liberalization and environmental concerns, in other words RES-E, supports the Danish integrated approach to energy and environmental policy (Midttun, 2001, p. 99). In 1999, the Danish government (led by Poul Nyrup Rasmussen, 1993–2001) assumed that 'the EU Commission preferred more market-oriented support systems, and would seek further harmonization of national support systems to this end. This has turned out to be a premature decision, given that the

EU Commission has postponed the harmonization of support schemes' (Meyer, 2007, p. 353; see also Chapter 2 by Solorio and Bocquillon). Instead the agreement between the new government (led by Anders Fogh Rasmussen) and the opposition postponed the introduction of an RES-E certificate until it was possible to establish a common market at EU level (Regeringen, 2002).

5.4.2 The Danish Positions on RES-E Directives

The first RES-E directive from 2001 was adopted whilst Svend Auken was minister, and Denmark committed itself to an indicative RES-E target of 29 per cent by 2010. During the European Council negotiations only Denmark, and later Germany, supported binding targets (Lauber, 2002, p. 30); the other member states preferred indicative targets, whilst both the European Parliament and the European Commission wanted binding targets for RES (Rowlands, 2005, p. 970). Moreover, the member states were divided on a number of issues including the definition of RES (Rowlands, 2005, pp. 967–968), and this intra-organizational division influenced the final 2001 RES-E directive. In general, a split European Council often leads to a weak policy outcome as the Parliament will not be able to push for a stronger directive.

In 2008 the European Commission published its climate and energy package, which included a proposal for a revision of the 2001 RES-E directive. Again, Denmark wanted stronger and more ambitious targets compared to those published by the European Commission, and the Danish government did not support using the financial crisis as an excuse to water down the proposals, including the 2009 RED, as some other member states wanted (Udenrigsministeriet, 2008a, 2008b). Moreover, the Danish government wanted a quick decision-making process, and a policy outcome which would strengthen the EU's environmental leadership and show the world that the EU is an environmental forerunner (Europaudvalget, 2008, p. 49). The EU adopted mandatory national targets for the revised 2009 RED, thereby making it a stronger policy instrument. The 2009 RED commits Denmark to a share of 30 per cent of RES in gross final energy consumption by 2020 (2009 RED). Svend Auken would have liked to have seen a 50 per cent target, and for Denmark to become the first CO_2-neutral country (Ryland, 2010, p. 83). Sweden is the only member state which has such a high target for 2020.

Crucially the stronger 2009 RED strengthened the EU's position as an environmental leader. However, its position was challenged during the 15th session of the Conference of the Parties to the United Nations Framework Convention on Climate Change (known as COP15), which was hosted by Denmark in December 2009. Here Denmark wanted to showcase its environmental leadership and set ambitious targets for the negotiations, yet a mixture of domestic and external factors made it impossible for the participating countries to reach an agreement and thereby replace the Kyoto agreement (Parker et al., 2012). Overall, the COP15 was seen as a failure.

In 2014, the Danish government supported the European Commission's 2030 climate change targets, and wanted a slightly more ambitious binding target of 40 per cent CO_2 emissions reduction, at least 30 per cent energy efficiency and at least 30 per cent RES (Øyen, 2014). Yet Prime Minister Helle Thorning-Schmidt (social democrats) recognized the difficult situation and diverging national preferences, which made it difficult to reach an agreement in the Council (Øyen, 2014). Indeed, it had been difficult to reach an agreement on the EU's 2030 climate and energy change package in the European Commission, where the then Commissioner for Climate Change Connie Hedegaard and the Commissioner for Energy Günther Oettinger had disagreed up until the publication of the proposal in January 2014. After the Council meeting in October 2014, Prime Minister Helle Thorning-Schmidt said she was satisfied with the result, especially given the major differences between the 28 member states, and that the agreement would prepare the EU for the COP21 negotiations in Paris in December 2015 (Albrechtsen, 2014). Overall, the Danish position in the European Council represents environmental pragmatism, where it is more important to reach a less ambitious agreement than to push for ambitious targets which do not result in an agreement. This pragmatism is also evident in the Danish presidency of the EU (January–July 2012), where a key priority for the presidency was to successfully finish the negotiations of the EU Energy Efficiency Plan as part of the European Commission's roadmap to a low carbon economy, which included a proposal for a directive on Energy Efficiency. Prior to the Danish presidency, the Danish government had stopped pushing its own policy preferences and instead started to focus on finding compromises which would enable a Council agreement. Whilst the final energy efficiency directive was less ambitious compared to the European Commission's initial proposal, the final result was still ambitious given the diverging national preferences in the Council (Petersen and Enghave, 2015). This result-oriented negotiation strategy by the Danish presidency, where it is more important to reach agreements even though they might be less ambitious compared to Danish preferences, is not new. Danish presidencies tend to be ambitious and results-orientated. This can be seen in the 2002 presidency when Denmark successfully concluded the 2004 enlargement agreement and 2002 climate and energy package.

5.4.3 Danish Implementation of RES Directives

The Danish target for the share of RES in total energy production was set prior to both the 2001 RES-E and the 2009 RED, as part of political agreements between the government and opposition on the 2000 and 2008 national energy plans. These targets were uploaded to the EU level as the European Commission accepted the targets set by the Danish government, which has resulted in a continual increase in RES. Also, more importantly, the RES-E directives did not require Denmark to implement policy change as the administrative system was able to absorb the new EU legislation. More specifically, the 2009 RED did not require legal changes (Udenrigsministeriet, 2008a) and the implementation of the 2009 RED was an administrative process.

In general, Danish implementation of EU legislation is predominately administrative changes to existing national law, and the main issue is to identify where to insert these amendments (Basse, 2011, p. 26). The use of executive orders 'implies that the minister and their administration are responsible for the implementation but the Danish parliament is not involved as legislative power' (Martinsen, 2014, p. 195). Moreover, the implementation of EU directives is often technical. Consequently, Danish politicians are rarely involved in implementation. Instead this is determined by civil servants in the relevant ministries, who have developed a culture of coordination to ensure that the appropriate stakeholders, both internal and external, are involved in the implementation process. However, EU liberalization, for example of the energy sector, requires administrative and structural changes as new independent agencies have to be established. This requires political involvement from the Danish parliament.

The Danish public administration of RES has become institutionalized and the institutional capacity of the public administration is formed by the Danish forerunner position, where Denmark has had higher standards and goals compared to the EU. Indeed, the policy initiatives in the RES plan will ensure that Denmark reaches a leading position before 2020 (Basse, 2011, p. 33). Due to Denmark's commitment to being a forerunner, EU legislation and policy priorities have had a limited impact on Danish renewable energy policy.

5.5 FOOT-DRAGGER: DANISH BIOFUEL POLICY

Compared to RES-E there is no advocacy coalition to support biofuel for transport; instead the domestic actors (industries, non-governmental organizations and researchers) are divided on the issues. Similarly, there is no political consensus and Danish politicians are also divided (Øyen, 2014). The Danish political debate reflects the EU and global debate about the impact of biofuels on food prices and land usage (Afionis and Stringer, 2012; Mol, 2010), especially as most biofuels are imported from other parts of the world, most notably Brazil. Instead, the Danish government believes that the use of biomass for the production of heat and electricity reduces CO_2 emissions much more than biofuels for transport (Energistyrelsen, 2006). Critical environmental voices believe biofuels for transport, most notably first-generation biofuels, are not economically or environmentally feasible, and instead they want to increase environmental standards for new cars.

Moreover, the Danish biofuels targets in the biofuels directive are low, especially compared to its high targets in RES-E. In 2005, the European Commission sent a letter of notification to Denmark regarding the implementation of the biofuels directive, in which the Commission stated that the Danish zero targets for use of biofuels for transport was unacceptable, and requested that Denmark set a national target. Consequently, the Danish government decided to use 60 million kroner (€7.9 million) to invest in biofuels, mainly for public transport and vehicles used by the public sector (Transportministeriet, 2005). This late and weak response to the Commission's letter regarding implementation should not be seen as Danish resistance towards stronger environmental protection; instead, this policy position ties into the existing policy path which emphasizes RES in heat and electricity production. Thus the Danish foot-dragging (see Chapter 1 by Jörgens and Solorio for a conceptual discussion) reflects the complexity of the biofuels discourse, especially in relation to food prices and actual reductions in CO_2 emissions. Denmark prefers to strengthen its existing policy path by investing in electrical cars, although the infrastructure for recharging is still lacking. In the 2013 energy agreement between the government and opposition, they decided to promote the development of gas, hydrogen and electrical cars, including establishing infrastructure for these types of vehicles (Klima og Energiministeriet, 2013, p. 13). The development of a policy for alternative fuels for transport is only just emerging in Denmark. Crucially, the lack of an advocacy coalition and the contested discussion about the benefit of biofuels for transport is affecting the policy field.

5.6 CONCLUSION: DENMARK, A CONTINUED FORERUNNER

The three core elements in the Danish environmental energy plan since the 1970s have been to increase energy efficiency, increase the RES share of total energy production and reduce reliance on imported fossil fuels. Moreover, Denmark has adopted taxes on energy fuels, electricity and carbon, which aim to promote continued energy efficiency, whilst simultaneously providing financial support to projects which promote RES-E production, especially wind power. Consequently, Denmark has become a forerunner in RES-E and environmental policies, which precisely aim to increase the share of RES, increase energy efficiency, and reduce emissions and reliance on imported fossil fuels. The position of forerunner originates from a domestic advocacy coalition, which has grown from environmental groups into big export-oriented companies. Simultaneously there has been political support for RES-E and these norms have become institutionalized in the public administration. These strong domestic actors have been the main drivers pushing Denmark towards stronger renewable energy policy. As such, there has been limited Europeanization as Denmark has been ahead of EU legislation and has had more ambitious policy goals.

The emphasis on wind power and co-fired power plants has been at the expense of biofuels. Compared to RES-E there is no national advocacy coalition to promote biofuels and the lack of consensus on the benefits of first-generation biofuels has influenced Danish policy developments, especially as the politicians themselves have been divided. Also the general biofuel debate is fragmented at all levels from domestic and EU through to the global level. This lack of an advocacy coalition in biofuels and a fragmented policy field has clearly influenced Danish biofuel policy. It is therefore not surprising that Denmark, as an environmental forerunner, is continuing to prioritize wind power, in which it has established a presence and in which there is less debate about the environmental benefits. Despite the more sceptical perspective on the environment in the first Anders Fogh Rasmussen government, there was a continued political commitment to protect Denmark's forerunner position, where it traditionally has acted as a defensive forerunner at EU level, often pushing for stronger environmental policy instruments. The Helle Thorning-Schmidt government appears to have become more pragmatic in its position in the European Council, preferring to find solutions instead of vetoing policy initiatives. However, more research is needed to determine the Danish negotiation position over time in relation to RES, especially which factors foster a defensive forerunner position.

Finally, the continued commitment to RES promotion is evident in the latest domestic targets where Denmark has to reduce greenhouse gas emissions by 40 per cent by 2020. By 2035, Danish electricity and heating have to be based on RES; and by 2050 all energy, including the transport sectors, must be based on RES (Regeringen, 2013, p. 7). This continued forerunner position is due not only to ideological beliefs but also to the increased economic importance of the renewable energy sector, in particular the wind turbine industry, which has become a world leader and an important export.

NOTE

1. The Risø Research Institute is part of the Danish Technological University and also the only place in Denmark with a nuclear reactor, which was used for research purposes. Some researchers at the Institute supported the introduction of nuclear energy. The nuclear reactor has now been decommissioned.

REFERENCES

Afionis, S. and L.C. Stringer (2012), 'European Union leadership in biofuels regulations: Europe as a normative power?', *Journal of Cleaner Production*, 32, 114–123.

Albrechtsen, R. (2014), 'EU chefer vedtager klimamål', *Altinget*, 24 October, accessed on 6 February 2015 at http://www.altinget.dk/artikel/eu-chefer-vedtager-klimamaal.

Andersen, M.S. (1998), 'Denmark: the shadow of green majority', in M.S. Andersen and D. Liefferink (eds), *European Environmental Policy: The Pioneers*, Manchester: Manchester University Press, pp. 251–286.

Andersen, M.S. and D. Liefferink (1998), 'Introduction: the impact of the pioneers on European environmental policy', in M.S. Andersen and D. Liefferink (eds), *European Environmental Policy: The Pioneers*, Manchester: Manchester University Press, pp. 1–39.

Auken, S. (1996), 'Forord af Miljø- og Energiminister Svend Auken', in Miljø- og Energiministeriet 1971–96: Undfangelse, Udvikling og Udblik. Miljø- og Energiministeriet.

Auken, S. (2002), 'Answers in the wind: How Denmark became a world pioneer in wind power', *Flecher Forum of World Affairs*, 26 (1), 149–157.

Basse, E.M. (2011), 'Vedvarende energi – de lovgivningsmæssige rammebetingelser', København, Jurist- og Økonomforbundets Forlag.

Blegaa, S., L. Josephsen, N.I. Meyer and B. Sørensen (1977), 'Alternative Danish energy planning', *Energy Policy*, 5 (2), 87–94.

Börzel, T. (2002), 'Member State responses to Europeanization', *Journal of Common Market Studies*, 40 (2), 193–214.
Bursens, P. (2002), 'Why Denmark and Belgium have different implementation records: on transposition laggards and leaders in the EU', *Scandinavian Political Studies*, 24 (2), 173–195.
COM (2013), 'Commission staff working document accompanying the document report from the Commission to the European Parliament and the Council: renewable energy progress report', SWD (2013) 102 final, 27 March.
Energistyrelsen (2006), 'Energipolitisk redegørelse 2006: Transport og energiministerens redegørelse i henhold til Lov om energipolitiske foranstaltninger', 18 April, ENS J.Nr. 030199-300007-0031.
Energistyrelsen (2011), 'Notat: vinmølleindustrien som historisk flagskib', 24 Maj, j.nr. Ref. PCJ/HW/FGN.
Energistyrelsen (2012), Energistatistik 2012. Copenhagen: Energistyrelsen.
Europaudvalget (2008), 'Offentligt referat fra Europaudvalgets møde 22/2-08', Folketinget.
Handelsministeriet (1976), 'Dansk energipolitik 1976', May, accessed on 1 May 2014 at http://www.ens.dk/sites/ens.dk/files/dokumenter/publikationer/downloads/dansk_energipolitik_1976.pdf.
Hvelplund, F. (2005), 'Denmark', in D. Reiche, M. Bechberger, S. Körner and U. Laumanns (eds), *Handbook of Renewable Energies in the European Union: Case Studies of the EU-15 States*, Frankfurt a. M.: Peter Lang AG, pp. 83–101.
Jakobsen, M.L.F. (2010), 'Untangling the impact of Europeanization and globalization: a systematic analysis of two Danish reforms', *Journal of European Public Policy*, 17 (6), 891–908.
Jänicke, M. (2005), 'Trendsetters in environmental policy: the character and role of pioneer countries', *European Environment*, 15, 129–142.
Kampmann, J. (1996), 'Oprettelsen af ministeriet for forureningsbekæmpelse – senere Miljøministeriet', in D. Rehling (ed.), *Miljø- og Energiministeriet 1971–96: Undfangelse, Udvikling og Udblik*, Copenhagen: Miljø- og Energiministeriet, pp. 15–23.
Klima- Energi og Bygningsministeriet (2013), 'Energipolitisk redegørelse 2013: Klima- Energi og Bygningsministerens redegørelse til Folketinger om energipolitikken', 24 April.
Knudsen, J.K. (2012), 'Renewable energy and environmental policy integration: renewable fuel for the European energy policy?', in F. Morata and I. Solorio (eds), *European Energy Policy: An Environmental Approach*, Cheltenham and Northampton, MA: Edward Elgar Publishing, pp. 48–65.
Lauber, V. (2002), 'Renewable energy at the EU level', in D. Reiche (ed.), *Handbook of Renewable Energies in the European Union: Case Studies of all Member States*, Frankfurt a.M.: Peter Lang, pp. 39–54.
Liefferink, D. and M.S. Andersen (1998), 'Strategies of the "green" member states in EU environmental policy-making', *Journal of European Public Policy*, 5 (2), 254–270.
Læssøe, J. (2007), 'Participation and sustainable development: the post-ecologist transformation of citizen involvement in Denmark', *Environmental Politics*, 16 (2), 231–250.

Madsen, B.T. (2000), 'Den Industrielle Udvikling', in E. Beuse, J. Boldt, P. Maegaard, N.I. Meyer, J. Windeleff and I. Østergaard (eds), *Vedvarende energi i Danmark: En krønike om 25 opvækstsår 1976–2000*, Copenhagen: OVEs Forlag, pp. 149–166.
Martinsen, D.S. (2014), 'Public administration, civil servants and implementation', in M. Marcussen, L. Miles and A. Wivel (eds), *Denmark and the European Union*, London: Routledge, pp. 189–202.
Meyer, N.I. (2000), 'VE-udviklingen I Danmark – oversigt over et spændende og broget forløb', in E. Beuse, J. Boldt, P. Maegaard, N.I. Meyer, J. Windeleff and I. Østergaard (eds), *Vedvarende energi i Danmark: En krønike om 25 opvækstsår 1976–2000*, Copenhagen: OVEs Forlag, pp. 75–111.
Meyer, N.I. (2007), 'Learning from wind energy policy in the EU: lessons from Denmark, Sweden and Spain', *European Environment*, 17, 347–362.
Midtun, A. (2001), 'Deregulated energy markets and the environment: the Nordic experience', *Environmental Politics*, 10 (2), 90–114.
Mol, A.P.J. (2010), 'Environmental authorities and biofuel controversies', *Environmental Politics*, 19 (1), 61–79.
Olsen, O.J. (2006), 'Konkurrence på det danske elmarked efter reformen i 1999', AKF working paper, 3 January 2006.
Øyen, M. (2014), 'Thorning nedtoner forventninger til EU's nye klimamål', *Altinget*, 23 October, accessed on 6 February 2015 at http://www.altinget.dk/eu/artikel/thorning-nedtoner-forventninger-til-eus-nye-klimamaal.
Parker, C.F., C. Karlsson, M. Hjerpe and B.O. Linnér (2012), 'Fragmented climate change leadership: making sense of the ambiguous outcome of COP-15', *Environmental Politics*, 21 (2), 268–286.
Petersen, P.S. and S.M. Enghave (2015), 'Kold luft i brandvarme forhandlinger – en analyse af de intra- og interorganisatoriske forhandlinger af EU's energieffektivitetsdirektiv', MA dissertation, Institute for Society and Globalisation, Roskilde University.
Regeringen (Poul Nyrup Rasmussen) (1999), 'Elreformen: Aftale mellem regeringen, Venstre, det Konservative Folkeparti, Socialistisk Folkeparti og Kristeligt Folkeparti om en lovreform for elsektoren', 3 March.
Regeringen (Anders Fogh Rasmussen) (2002), 'Aftale mellem Regeringen, Socialdemokratiet', Socialistisk Folkeparty, Det Radikale Venstre og Kristeligt Folkeparti om udskydelse af VE-marked, 19 June.
Regeringen (Helle Thorning-Schmidt) (2013), 'Regeringens klimaplan: På vej mod et samfund uden drivhusgasser', August.
Rowlands, I.H. (2005), 'The European directive on renewable electricity: conflicts and compromises', *Energy Policy*, 33, 965–974.
Ryland, E. (2010), 'Danish wind power policy: domestic and international forces' *Environmental Politics*, 19 (1), 80–85.
Sabatier, P.A. (1998), 'The advocacy coalition framework: revisions and relevance for Europe', *Journal of European Public Policy*, 5 (1), 98–130.
Sovacool, B. (2013), 'Energy policymaking in Denmark: implications for global energy security and sustainability' *Energy Policy*, 61, 829–839.
Statsministeriet (1988), *Regeringens handlingsplan for miljø og udvikling*, København: Statens Informationstjeneste.

Transportministeriet (2005), 'Biobrændstof i transport-sektoren', Nyheder, 14 November, accessed on 29 September 2014 at http://www.trm.dk/da/nyheder/2005/biobr%C3%A6ndstof+i+transport_sektoren/.

Udenrigsministeriet (2008a), 'Redegørelse til Folketinget for Rådsmøde (Transport, Telekommunikation og Energi) den 28. februar 2008 – Energidelen', Journal nr. 400. C.2-0, kontor EUR, 11 March.

Udenrigsministeriet (2008b), 'Redegørelse for rådsmøde (energi) den 10 October 2008', Journal nr. 400.C.2-0, kontor EUR, 29 October.

Verdenskommissionen (1988), 'Vores Fælles Fremtid', Copenhagen: FN-forbundet and Mellemfolkeligt Samvirke.

Wurzel, R.K.W., A.R. Zito and A.J. Jordan (2013), *Environmental Governance in Europe: A Comparative Analysis of New Policy Instruments*, Cheltenham and Northampton, MA: Edward Elgar Publishing.

6. The UK and EU renewable energy policy: the relentless British policy-shaper

Israel Solorio and Jenny Fairbrass

6.1 INTRODUCTION

Ever since the United Kingdom (UK) joined the European Communities in 1973, the British reputation has been that of an 'awkward partner' (George, 1990). This reputation has remained through time and gained renewed relevance after the Brexit decision, where in a referendum held in June 2016, 52 per cent of British voters manifested a desire to leave the European Union (EU). Perhaps one of the best examples of the troubled relationship between the UK and its European partners is the development of the EU's energy and climate policies. Francis McGowan (2011) defined the British role in EU energy policy as a shift from being an awkward partner to an active protagonist, while Tim Rayner and Andrew Jordan (2011) described the UK's engagement with EU climate change policy as 'rather paradoxical': a leader in global and European negotiations but a laggard in the implementation of these agreements domestically.

When joining the EU in the 1970s the UK struggled with the European method of governance (Jordan, 2000). The response to this challenge on the part of British policymakers was to actually transform European structures and ways of doing things. Initially, the UK was reluctant about the EU's energy and climate policies. British negotiators blocked any attempt at an EU energy policy during the 1970s in order to jealously protect the North Sea oil and gas reserves, and they did the same with the first attempts to develop a common European response to climate change by hindering the adoption of a carbon tax in the 1990s (McGowan, 2011, p. 203). However, soon after, the UK became a policy-shaper in a more proactive way. So much so that some authors argue that the EU's energy and climate policies have evolved at a 'British tempo' (Ciambra and Solorio, 2015), being critically shaped by the UK (Cass, 2007).

This chapter tests the well-established idea of Britain as an awkward partner using the case of renewable energy sources (RES) promotion in the EU; a policy that not long ago was considered a cornerstone of EU climate and energy policies (Tosun and Solorio, 2011). To do so, it employs the Europeanization analytical framework outlined in Chapter 1 of this book. This chapter pays special attention to the bottom-up dimension of Europeanization, arguing that the UK has been able to effectively 'upload' its national interest to the EU level. This is thanks to a strategy that has consisted of sometimes adopting the role of a pace-setter, sometimes performing a foot-dragger role, and sometimes acting as a fence-sitter when necessary (see Chapter 1 by Jörgens and Solorio). The overall result has been a role for Britain as a relentless policy-shaper of EU renewable energy policy.

The chapter is structured as follows. Section 6.2 details the analytical framework to be employed. Section 6.3 analyses how the UK has shaped the EU's policy oriented to the promotion of RES for electricity (RES-E), while section 6.4 tackles the case of RES for transport (RES-T). Ultimately, section 6.5 assesses the UK's role in shaping EU renewable energy policy, the strategies displayed across the different negotiation processes and how those negotiating positions have been affected by top-down and horizontal Europeanization processes.

6.2 ANALYTICAL UNDERPINNING: THE BRITISH CAPACITY FOR SHAPING AND TAKING EU POLICIES

For years, Europeanization studies were mostly concerned with the impact of the EU on its member states (that is, top-down Europeanization). For example, Andrew Jordan (2000) gave an account of the way in which British environmental policy was transformed by the EU. This merely top-down approach dominated Europeanization studies until authors such as Tanja Börzel (2002) started signalling the need to link the top-down and bottom-up dimensions of Europeanization. Specifically, she centred attention 'on the ways in which Member States governments both shape European policy outcomes and adapt to them' (Börzel, 2002, p. 194). Thus, Europeanization began to be understood as a cycle where downloading and uploading processes were different sides of the same coin. With increasing sophistication in Europeanization studies, however,

Börzel's two-way process approach has given way to the notion of 'circular Europeanization', 'which also includes European integration and its influence at the national level, which in turn influences European integration anew' (Saurugger, 2014, p. 184). Importantly, this novel approach not only incorporates the variable of time but additionally establishes a framework where horizontal Europeanization processes can also take place (see Chapter 1 by Jörgens and Solorio).

The circular approach has allowed us to overcome some of the limits of linear Europeanization models (Saurugger, 2014). However, the fact is that our understanding of Europeanization processes still relies upon previously developed analytical tools and concepts. This is the case for member states' methods of influencing EU policies, still based on Börzel's typology of pace-setting, foot-dragging and fence-sitting strategies (see Chapter 1 by Jörgens and Solorio). In this regard, while pace-setting 'involves the active shaping of European policies according to domestic preferences', foot-dragging 'aims at stopping or at least containing the attempts of other Member States to upload their domestic policies to the European level' (Börzel, 2002, pp. 197–203). The former strategy is typically adopted by 'green' member states – acting as environmental leaders, pioneers or forerunners (Liefferink and Andersen, 1998) – while the latter pertains more to latecomers, as the UK can be considered in terms of RES development (Dinica, 2002).

Fence-sitting suggests a rather ambivalent strategy, where member states 'build changing coalitions with pace-setters and foot-draggers' (Börzel, 2002, p. 206), depending on the issue under discussion and the most convenient position for the national interest. Normally, the fence-sitter does not have a strong vested interest in the policy in question. Andersen and Liefferink (1997) argue that the UK usually adopts this strategy in environmental issues. Therefore, the proposed explanation is relevant to this case in the sense that fence-sitters adopt this strategy, given that they 'may miscalculate the costs involved in downloading a European policy or do not give much importance to the issue' (Börzel, 2002, p. 207). Also, they 'may prefer to avoid costly European policies simply by not implementing them' (Börzel, 2002, p. 208). Accordingly, it is expected that fence-sitters – like foot-draggers – will have a rather disappointing implementation record.

Equipped with the analytical tool-kit presented above, this chapter develops a causal process-tracing aimed at disentangling the UK's capacity to 'upload' its national preferences in the making of EU renewable energy policy. Given the adopted circular approach, a particular challenge to this chapter is to understand how British strategy has been affected across time by both top-down and horizontal Europeanization processes. This research is primarily based on a documental analysis using both primary and secondary sources, including parliamentary debates, official documents from the UK government, scientific reports and documents from EU institutions, as well as journal articles and newspaper notes on the subject.

6.3 BRITAIN AND RES-E DEVELOPMENT IN EUROPE: THE INFLUENTIAL ROLE OF A LATECOMER

6.3.1 Background: The UK as a Latecomer in RES-E Promotion

The existence of a national programme to support RES research and development (R&D) in the UK dates back to 1975 (Brown, 1993). During the time of the oil shocks that marked Europe's national energy policies, Britain was at the forefront of research in RES technologies and was starting to develop domestic manufacturing capabilities (Jackson, 2000). Nevertheless, the upheaval in the energy markets – a product of the oil crises – rapidly changed the priorities of the UK government towards developing North Sea oil and gas (Surrey, 1990). National policymakers then considered RES development irrelevant (Reiche and Bechberger, 2004, p. 844) and the British position on RES technologies was severely affected by budget cuts in the government's R&D spending (Jackson, 2000). Of course, this shift in the support for RES was only one part of major changes in national energy policy in line with overall economic policy, at the time led by the Conservatives and characterized by a privatization–liberalization drive (Matláry, 1997, p. 29). The UK became a 'first-mover' in the implementation of a model that transformed energy policies across Europe (Padgett, 2003, p. 231) and which was the gateway for a major role for EU institutions in energy policy (Eising, 2002). However, as far as RES is concerned, privatization failed to attract private capital for its development (Connor, 2003).

From 1990, the UK had a specific programme for the promotion of RES-E: the so-called Non-Fossil Fuel Obligation (NFFO). By means of this instrument, generators of non-fossil-fuel-based plants received a premium price from electricity companies (Mitchell, 1995). However, the 'NFFO was primarily set up as a means to subsidise nuclear generation, which had proved too difficult to privatise' (Mitchell and Connor, 2004, p. 1936). Dieter Helm argues that the inclusion of RES-E within the NFFO was based on the consideration that the 'non-fossil' label would be better received than the less acceptable 'nuclear' one (Helm, 2003,

p. 350). Once the door was opened, however, it was impossible to impede support for RES-E (Mitchell and Connor, 2004, p. 1936) and it began to be a recipient of the NFFO (for a review of the evolution of the NFFO see Mitchell, 1995). Still, in 1999 the percentage of consumed electricity from RES barely reached 2.8 per cent (UK Parliament, 2001). In the end, even though the NFFO was a lesson-learning experience for the British government, its failure meant that the UK became a European latecomer in RES-E promotion.

6.3.2 The RES-E Directive: The Unexpected British Pace-Setter

In 1997 the Labour Party returned to government, undertaking numerous policy reviews, 'so that changes to energy (and renewable energy) were slow' (Mitchell and Connor, 2004, p. 1938). It was in this context of limited RES-E development and a policy in transition that the UK faced the discussions on the RES-E directive (see Chapter 2 by Solorio and Bocquillon). Just as Britain's liberal ideas gained traction within the EU institutions, so the British position also improved in the course of this negotiation process. After the liberalization of the European electricity markets started in 1996, early proposals emanating from the European Commission considered market instruments to be the best way to reorganize the RES-E sector in the EU (Lauber, 2005). In a report that preceded the 1998 draft directive, the Commission considered that, at some stage, transition towards a RES-E support model based on trade and competition would be inevitable (Busch and Jörgens, 2012, p. 79).

Against this background, the road to the 2001 RES-E directive can be best characterized as the rise and (temporary) fall of the Commission's ambitions to harmonize the European support schemes based on Tradable Green Certificates (TGCs). This model was perceived as more compatible with the internal market rules against the less market-friendly Feed-In Tariffs (FITs) model (Rowlands, 2005, p. 971; Lauber and Schenner, 2011, p. 517). Bearing in mind that the Commission's liberal approach was UK-inspired (Ciambra and Solorio, 2015), and given that at the time of the negotiations British policymakers were already pursuing a TGCs system at the domestic level (Rowlands, 2005, p. 972), the UK's role – at least concerning this part of the debate – can be considered as that of an unexpected pace-setter. The fact that harmonization did not prevail in the final directive can only be explained by the resistance of member states such as Germany and Spain (see Chapter 3 by Vogelpohl et al. on Germany, and Chapter 8 by Solorio and Fernandez on Spain). The British latecomer acted as a pace-setter, while the German pioneer performed a foot-dragger role; their roles were inverted during the RES-E directive negotiations. However, this process was the basis for the diffusion of the TGC model across Europe, that is, horizontal Europeanization (Busch and Jörgens, 2005, p. 878). In the UK, the Renewables Obligation (RO), a system based on green certificates, started operating in April 2002 (Mitchell and Connor, 2004).

Another aspect of the directive in which the UK role was decisive concerns the definition of RES. A key concern for British policymakers was the fact that the Commission's original proposal excluded electricity generated from the incineration of municipal waste and landfill gas (UK Parliament, 2000), sources that were considerably developed under the NFFO (Mitchell and Connor, 2004). During the Council negotiations, the positions of Italy, the Netherlands and the UK were key to broadening the definition of RES (Rowlands, 2005, p. 968). In the end, the UK national objective included within the RES-E directive was the same as that which the British government had been using as a baseline since Labour regained power: 10 per cent of electricity to be produced from RES by 2010 (House of Lords, 2004, p. 14).

Bearing in mind that this directive lacked an EU model for support systems, considering the broadened RES definition which was included, and given that 'the Commission was put under pressure by virtually all ministers in the Council to make the targets indicative' (Rowlands, 2005, p. 970), the overall result was a directive that placed limited adaptation pressure on the UK. Still, the objective of 10 per cent RES-E in national electricity consumption by 2010 represented a huge challenge for Britain (House of Lords, 2004) which was finally not met: the UK failed to achieve the 2010 RES-E goals (COM, 2013, p. 4).

6.3.3 The UK and the RED: Midway between Pace-Setter and Fence-Sitter

The negotiation process for the renewable energy directive (RED), which was adopted in 2009 (see Chapter 2 by Solorio and Bocquillon), was considerably guided by the UK from very early on in its conception. To start with, the integration between the EU's energy and climate policies was only possible thanks to the role played by former Prime Minister Tony Blair (in office 1997–2007). He used the British presidency of the European Council in 2005 in order to put forward a proposal for expanding the EU's competences on energy (Solorio et al., 2013, pp. 96–98). The policy initiatives that emerged from this process eventually led to the 2009 EU climate and energy package, to which the RED pertains (Morata and Solorio, 2012). Importantly, this U-turn by the UK was motivated by the depletion of North Sea reserves, which 'required a radical rethink' of British energy policy (Helm, 2007). Britain was largely responsible for the reactivation of broader EU climate and energy policies but it was a long way – and one which was not always UK-led – from endorsing the 20-20-20 targets set by the European Council in March 2007 to adopting the RED in its final form. In fact, the UK's support for EU-wide climate and energy targets was a surprise, and is said to have gone against the Tony Blair administration's recommendations (Bocquillon, 2015, p. 138).

In 2006, the Commission began pushing the debate forward with the goal of shaping the idea of an EU strategy for sustainable, competitive and secure energy, including new legislation on RES (COM, 2006) (for an explanation of this process, see Tosun and Solorio, 2011). In spite of the fact that its own evaluation report on support schemes published in December 2005 'contradicted several theoretical arguments' in favour of TGCs, considering them less cost-efficient and less effective at deploying RES-E than the FITs model (Lauber and Schenner, 2011, p. 519), the Commission's 2008 directive proposal kept the idea of a harmonized European support system based on TGCs (see Chapter 3 on Germany by Vogelpohl et al.).

The UK government actively lobbied the Commission to back trade in RES during 2007. Therefore, some analysts have called the Commission's hard line on this pro-market stance the 'British disease' (Toke, 2008, p. 3003). Allegedly, the intense push from Britain was based on the consideration that, otherwise, electricity prices would dramatically increase if the UK was forced to meet the national binding targets for RES by 2020 (Fouquet, 2007). Protests from important RES-E producers such as Germany and Spain (see Chapter 3 on Germany by Vogelpohl et al., and Chapter 8 by Solorio and Fernandez on Spain), together with concerns about industrial competitiveness (in a context of economic crisis), gave way to a more pragmatic stance on the part of the Commission, to rising opposition against a harmonized European support system based on TGCs, and, eventually, to trading in RES enthusiasts – including the UK – to dismiss the harmonization idea in favour of a consensus among member states (Nilsson, 2011, p. 123). In 2008, the UK, together with Germany and Poland (see Chapter 3 on Germany by Vogelpohl et al., and Chapter 10 by Jankowska and Ancygier on Poland), presented a joint proposal to the Council that discarded TGCs 'while introducing instruments for "non-trading flexibility"' (Lauber and Schenner, 2011, p. 520). The coalition proposed three optional flexibility mechanisms which were to be finally included within the RED: statistical transfers of RES guarantees of origin between member states, joint projects for the development of RES, and the possibility of setting up joint support schemes between member states (Bocquillon, 2015, p. 144). On support schemes, the UK began the negotiations as a pace-setter but finished as a fence-sitter by building a tactical coalition that overcame the impasse at the Council.

Bearing in mind that the UK has no strong vested interest in the RES-E sector, its broadly proactive role in the negotiations leading to the RED appears rather paradoxical (McGowan, 2011, p. 205). However, everything makes more sense if we consider that the 'British position has essentially been to advocate the replication of the British market approach in Europe' (Helm, 2007, p. 8). Moreover, British officials were trapped by their own climate change leadership discourse and, when leaked documents showed that the UK negotiators were opposed to binding national targets, social pressure forced the British government to reaffirm 'the government's commitment with the overall policy' (McGowan, 2011, p. 205; for the original leak see *Guardian*, 2007).

Under the RED, Britain has to meet 15 per cent of its national overall energy consumption with RES by 2020. Several reforms to Britain's renewable energy policy can only be understood in the framework of EU policies, for example the RO revision[1] (see Wood and Dow, 2011) and the introduction of FITs[2] to encourage the development of a range of small-scale RES technologies (see Toke, 2007). Still, in 2015 the Commission considered that the UK needed to assess whether its existing policies were sufficient to meet the RES targets (COM, 2015, p. 4). While it is hard to argue against the fact that 'EU directives have also provided significant shape to UK energy policy' (Pollitt, 2010, p. 2), it is clear that the UK has moulded EU renewable energy policy in a way that has considerably reduced adaptation pressure at the domestic level and granted leeway for maintaining national energy policy priorities.

The role of Britain as an awkward partner in RES-E promotion, characterized as performing as a relentless policy-shaper but a laggard concerning implementation, was deepened during the negotiations for the 2030 targets during 2013–14. Given the revival of nuclear energy in the UK, and considering the discovered shale gas potential, British officials pushed for a single target for greenhouse gases (GHGs) emissions reduction with the intention of giving flexibility to member states in terms of compliance (Bürgin, 2015, p. 699). In the end, Britain's position was crucial in making the 27 per cent target for RES not binding at the national level (EurActiv, 2014). Shaping the 2030 goals in such a way that they prioritize GHG emissions reductions and sideline the relevance of RES targets is one of the most recent legacies from the awkward partner in EU renewable energy policy before the Brexit decision.

6.4 THE UK AND BIOFUELS POLICY: THE LEADING LAGGARD

6.4.1 The Instrumental Laggard and the Biofuels Directive

Before the EU started promoting biofuels, their production and consumption were insignificant in the UK. As in the case of RES-E, the existence of oil resources limited the national policy framework for promoting market demand and the development of a biofuels industry (Eikeland, 2006, p. 26). Britain's biofuels policy has been a direct response to EU pressures. National biofuels production only started in 2002 in the case of biodiesel, and in 2005 for bioethanol (Bomb et al., 2007, p. 2261). Against this background, and given that initially the Commission intended to set mandatory biofuels targets with 'an obligation on Member States to ensure that as from 2005 a minimum share of transport fuel sold on their territory consists of biofuels' (Jansen, 2003, p. 29), it is easy to understand why the UK was one of the toughest opponents of the biofuels directive initial proposal. Predictably, Britain adopted the role of a foot-dragger during the entire negotiation process between 2002 and 2003 (Solorio and Popartan, 2014, p. 134).

Two issues were specially contested by British negotiators. On the one hand, the UK government was reluctant about mandatory biofuels objectives (UK Parliament, 2002a). A generalized rejection from part of the Council of the binding nature of targets forced the Commission to give way to a less restrictive directive (see Chapter 2 by Solorio and Bocquillon). On the other hand, the Commission's recommendation about the introduction of a selective tax based on the environmental performance of biofuels was dismissed by British officials under the argument that the 'UK strongly withholds the right to take decisions on taxation policy and is opposed to any action not consistent with this principle' (UK Parliament, 2002a). Britain's negotiation position was in favour of allowing member states to give tax incentives for biofuels, but against the details of the initial proposal (UK Parliament, 2002b). Arguably, the UK's role was instrumental in shaping the common position text with the adoption of indicative targets and the reformulation of the biofuels taxation policy (Solorio and Popartan, 2014, p. 134).

The adoption of this directive originated an intense domestic debate on the convenience of promoting biofuels. Yet, the fact is that in terms of public policy the only tangible step initially taken by the British government was the establishment of fuel duty incentives, adopted from July 2002 (Berti and Levidow, 2014, p. 138). The rest of the measures can even be seen as anecdotal, such as sponsoring research and development or information provision. This is so much so that, in 2003, Parliament's Environment, Food and Rural Affairs Committee accused the British government of adopting an 'ambivalent attitude' towards biofuels policy (House of Commons, 2003). It was only in 2007, after an intense domestic debate (see Solorio and Popartan, 2014), that the UK government adopted the Renewable Transport Fuel Obligation (RTFO) in order to further implement the biofuels directive. Its adoption arrived rather late and, ultimately, the UK failed to meet the 2010 biofuels target: 5.75 per cent of commercialized fuels (COM, 2013, p. 4). Interestingly, in advance of the EU RED, in 2008 the UK adopted a carbon and sustainability reporting scheme in order to monitor GHG emissions savings and the sustainability of biofuels (Chalmers and Archer, 2011). In this way the UK, a country once known as the 'dirty man of Europe', paradoxically became a European pioneer in the certification of biofuels sustainability.

6.4.2 The UK and the Future of the EU Biofuels Policy: Ecologist for Convenience?

The British negotiation position before the RED was directly determined by the implementation of the biofuels directive. With only an embryonic industry and not enough time to reform agricultural policy in order to allow the planting of crops for biofuels production, raw material imports became the most viable solution for reaching the biofuels objective. Against this backdrop, and considering that the domestic debate was highly determined by climate change concerns, environmental internal opposition to biofuels sprang up (Solorio and Popartan, 2014, p. 134).

In 2007, as part of the national debate on the RTFO and the convenience of supporting biofuels, the most influential environmental non-governmental organizations – including Greenpeace, Friends of the Earth, Oxfam and the World Wide Fund for Nature (WWF) – united in a powerful media campaign in order to 'put pressure on the UK government to implement rigorous sustainability criteria (including minimum greenhouse gas savings) as part of the RTFO' (Pilgrim and Harvey, 2010). Concerns about biofuels sustainability were fuelled by the March 2007 agreement of the European Council on a 10 per cent biofuel target by 2020 (Berti and Levidow, 2014, p. 139). Bearing in mind the doubts about biofuel sustainability, even institutional bodies such as Parliament's Environmental Audit Committee called for a moratorium on biofuels in 2008 (Solorio and Popartan, 2014). Given these intra-institutional divisions, and considering the wider public controversy, the UK government commissioned an expert revision of biofuel policy (Berti and Levidow, 2014, p. 140). The result of the government review, the so-called 'Gallagher Review', concluded: 'Biofuels can only contribute GHG savings from transport if significant emissions from land-use change are avoided and appropriate production technologies are employed' (RFA, 2008). Taking into consideration the Gallagher Review's results, the UK government decided to slow down the rate of increase in the obligation level to 3.5 per cent for 2010; began looking for alternatives to meet the 2020 target, widening the products eligible under the RTFO to include biobutanol; and made the environmental effects of biofuel production a central issue in the discussion of future biofuel targets (Solorio and Popartan, 2014, p. 135; see also *Guardian*, 2008).

Importantly, the Gallagher Review not only affected the conditions for deploying biofuels at the domestic level but also markedly influenced the RED discussions on the environmental and ecological impact of biofuels (Müngersdorff, 2009, p. 36). In many aspects the UK government's hands were tied during the discussions of the RED, so the 2020 target was subjected to a precondition of the availability of second-generation biofuels by British negotiators (Berti and Levidow, 2014, p. 142). As Müngersdorff argues, '[t]he UK played the maybe most ambiguous role in the whole policymaking process, trying to tighten the regulations of the Renewables Directive wherever possible and thus making most targets, including those in the biofuel sector, very difficult to achieve' (Müngersdorff, 2009, p. 29). Britain's role was so ambivalent that, while pushing strongly for the consideration of indirect land-use changes under the RED (see Di Lucia et al., 2012), at the same time it fought any consideration of social criteria which might compromise World Trade Organization rules (Müngersdorff, 2009, p. 37). Concerning the negotiations of RED's RES-T component, Britain behaved as a fence-sitter to its maximum possible expression, far away from the position of green member states such as Germany or Denmark (see Chapter 3 on Germany by Vogelpohl et al., and Chapter 5 on Denmark by Dyrhauge).

Paradoxically, the Commission's 2013 report on the 2020 RES targets pointed out the fact that five member states dominated biofuels production and consumption in the EU: France, Germany, Italy, Spain and the UK (COM, 2013, p. 10). However, while biofuels consumption continues to grow domestically (especially for the case of biodiesel[3]), the fact is that the UK is still a long way behind the directive target of 10 per cent of renewable energy sources for transport (RES-T) (EurObserv'ER, 2015, p. 8). Therefore, it is no surprise that, as part of the British negotiation position for revised RES-T targets towards 2020 in 2013, the UK defended double-counting from advanced biofuels as a formula to make achieving the 10 per cent target for 2020 easier (Greenpeace, 2013).

6.5 COMPARATIVE ANALYSIS AND CONCLUSIONS

Given that until recently the UK's national energy policy was determined by the possession of North Sea oil and gas reserves, RES promotion was sidelined and subjected to market preferences for decades. It was only thanks to EU pressure that the UK started promoting both RES-E and RES-T (that is, top-down Europeanization). However, this development has been constrained, given the combination of the UK's capacity to actively shape EU renewable energy policy in a way that has considerably reduced adaptation pressures, and the British preference for avoiding greater adaptation costs by implementing EU policies in a superficial or partial manner. Overall, while the UK stands as a successful shaper of EU renewable energy policy, its implementation record and the achieving of its RES goals are rather weak (closer to what can be expected from a fence-sitter or a foot-dragger). As far as the British case is concerned, looking at the interrelationship between the top-down and bottom-up dimensions of Europeanization is useful for understanding how policy change has been hindered both at the EU level and at the domestic level in the UK.

In terms of bottom-up Europeanization, the main focus of this chapter, in both the RES-E and RES-T cases the UK has steadily attempted to debilitate EU policies. However, the main difference between them is that the Commission's market-oriented approach towards the promotion of RES-E gave the UK a central role during the negotiation processes. This was so much so that, in spite of the fact that the UK is not a leader in RES-E promotion, it acted as a pace-setter during the RES-E directive and the RED negotiations (at least concerning the debate on support models). Not surprisingly, the British position on RES-T has been closer to that of a traditional foot-dragger. However, it is revealing that the UK has taken a pragmatic stance through its recurrent fence-sitting strategy, building changing coalitions with pace-setters and foot-draggers depending on the most convenient option for the national interest. This happened during the RED negotiations concerning the debates on support schemes for RES-E and during the debates on biofuels sustainability criteria.

Across time, the UK's positions on the different negotiation processes have been affected by both top-down and horizontal Europeanization processes. The most evident case of the former is the way in which the British position during the negotiations for the RES-T component of the

RED was affected by domestic (negative) reactions following the implementation of the biofuels directive. For the latter, the clearest example is the support given by the UK to the TGCs model just at the time when the Commission was pushing for the homogenization of European support systems during the RES-E directive negotiation, soon afterwards adopting the RO. Horizontal Europeanization has also been present in the adoption of instruments for domestic biofuels promotion (first with tax exemptions and then with consumption obligations). However, it is important to remark that, given the fact that the UK does not have a strong vested interest in RES promotion – for either RES-E or biofuels – the adoption of a certain policy instrument has influenced but not determined the British negotiating position. In this sense, it is important to remark that these observations on the interrelationship between the different Europeanization processes, and between them and the British negotiating position, have only been possible thanks to the adopted circular Europeanization approach.

All in all, this chapter has made the case for the British playing the role of an 'awkward partner' which has been able to significantly shape EU renewable energy policy according to national interests, but has been incapable of meeting its domestic commitments on RES promotion. After successfully subordinating RES promotion in the EU to climate change mitigation goals, the UK has opted to abandon the 'European boat'. The British legacy is a EU renewable energy policy weakened in terms of objectives and renationalized in terms of governance (see Chapter 2 by Solorio and Bocquillon). Finally, it is important to note that this chapter has contributed to the understanding of the complex relationship between the UK and the EU in terms of RES promotion. However, two central elements remain to be elucidated. On the one hand, the top-down impact of Europeanization has still to be further unravelled. Considering the Brexit decision, it is important to shed light on what the actual EU legacy for the UK's (renewable) energy policy has been. On the other hand, while this research has showed how the UK has shaped the EU renewable energy policy according to national preferences, it remains to be further explained how these preferences are formed and what are the particular interests behind the positions defended by the UK at the EU level.

NOTES

1. The RO is the main support mechanism for the deployment of large-scale RES-E projects in the UK.
2. FITs in the UK were announced in 2008 but implemented only at the end of 2010.

3. The consumption of biodiesel rose sharply, from 766 million litres in 2013 to 955 million litres in 2014. In contrast, bioethanol remained practically static: 819 million litres in 2013 compared to 812 million litres in 2014 (EurObserv'ER, 2015, p. 7).

REFERENCES

Andersen, M.S. and D. Liefferink (eds) (1997), *European Environmental Policy: The Pioneers*, Manchester: Manchester University Press.

Berti, P. and L. Levidow (2014), 'Fuelling expectations: a policy-promise lock-in of UK biofuel policy', *Energy Policy*, 66 (2014) 135–143.

Bocquillon, P. (2015), 'Embedded intergovernmentalism: cooperation and conflict in EU energy policy-making', PhD thesis, Cambridge: University of Cambridge.

Bomb, C., K. McCormick, E. Deurwaarder and T. Kaberger (2007), 'Biofuels for transport in Europe: lessons from Germany and the UK', *Energy Policy*, 35 (4), 2256–2267.

Börzel, T. (2002), 'Member State responses to Europeanization', *Journal of Common Market Studies*, 40 (2), 193–214.

Brown, A. (1993), 'The UK renewable energy programme', *Renewable Energy*, 3 (2–3), 279–288.

Busch, P.-O. and H. Jörgens (2005), 'The international sources of policy convergence: explaining the spread of environmental policy innovations', *Journal of European Public Policy*, 12, 860–884.

Busch, P.-O. and H. Jörgens (2012), 'Europeanization through diffusion? Renewable energy policies and alternative sources for European convergence', in F. Morata and I. Solorio (eds), *European Energy Policy: An Environmental Approach*, Cheltenham and Northampton, MA: Edward Elgar Publishing, pp. 66–84.

Bürgin, A. (2015), 'National binding renewable energy targets for 2020, but not for 2030 anymore: why the European Commission developed from a supporter to a brakeman', *Journal of European Public Policy*, 22 (5), 690–707.

Cass, L.R. (2007) 'The indispensable awkward partner: the United Kingdom in European climate policy', in P.G. Harris (ed.), *Europe and Global Climate Change: Politics, Foreign Policy and Regional Cooperation*, Cheltenham and Northampton, MA: Edward Elgar Publishing, pp. 63–86.

Chalmers, J. and G. Archer (2011), 'Development of a sustainability reporting scheme for biofuels: a UK case study', *Energy Policy*, 39 (10), 5682–5689.

Ciambra, A. and I. Solorio (2015), 'The liberalization of the Internal Energy Market: is the EU dancing at a British tempo?', in J. Tosun, S. Biesenbender and K. Schulze (eds), *Energy Policy Making in the EU: Building the Agenda*, London: Springer, pp. 147–165.

COM (2006), 'Green Paper: A European strategy for sustainable, competitive and secure energy', 08/03/06, COM(2006) 105 final, http://eur-lex.europa.eu/legal-content/EN/TXT/HTML/?uri=URISERV:l27062&from=EN.

COM (2013), 'Renewable energy progress report', Brussels, 27/03/2013, COM(2013) 175 final, http://eur-lex.europa.eu/legal-content/EN/TXT/PDF/?uri=CELEX:52013DC0175&from=EN.

COM (2015), 'State of the Energy Union', 18/11/2015, COM(2015) 572 final, http://eur-lex.europa.eu/resource.html?uri=cellar:ebdf266c-8eab-11e5-983e-01aa75ed71a1.0008.02/DOC_1&format=PDF.

Connor, P.M. (2003), 'UK renewable energy policy: a review', *Renewable and Sustainable Energy Reviews*, 7 (1), 65–82.

Di Lucia, L., A. Ahlgren and K. Ericsson (2012), 'The dilemma of indirect land-use changes in EU biofuel policy – an empirical study of policy-making in the context of scientific uncertainty', *Environmental Science and Policy*, 16, 9–19.

Dinica, V. (2002), 'Policies for renewable energy support in the United Kingdom', in D. Reiche (ed.), *Handbook of Renewable Energies in the European Union*, Frankfurt: Peter Lang, pp. 295–311.

Eikeland, P. (2006), 'Biofuels – the new oil for petroleum industry?', FNI report 15/2005, Lysaker, Norway: Fridtjof Nansen Institute.

Eising, R. (2002), 'Policy learning in embedded negotiations: explaining EU electricity liberalization', *International Organization*, 56, 85–120.

EurActiv (2014), 'EU leaders adopt "flexible" energy and climate targets for 2030', 24 October, accessed on 15 July 2016 at http://www.euractiv.com/section/sustainable-dev/news/eu-leaders-adopt-flexible-energy-and-climate-targets-for-2030/.

EurObserv'ER (2015), 'Biofuels Barometer', accessed on 15 July 2016 at http://www.eurobserv-er.org/biofuels-barometer-2015/.

Fouquet, D. (2007), 'Prices for renewable energies in Europe: Feed in Tariffs versus quota system – a comparison', European Renewable Energies Federation (EREF), Brussels.

George, S. (1990), *An Awkward Partner: Britain in the European Community*, Oxford: Oxford University Press.

Greenpeace (2013), 'Biofuels: EU Energy Ministers must choose right path for the world's climate & food security', accessed on 15 July 2016 at http://www.greenpeace.org/eu-unit/Global/eu-unit/reports-briefings/2013/20131209%20Joint%20NGO%20Biofuels%20Media%20Advisory.pdf.

Guardian (2007), 'Revealed: cover-up plan on energy target', 13 August.

Guardian (2008), 'Kelly orders biofuels review', 21 February, https://www.theguardian.com/environment/2008/feb/21/biofuels.transport.

Helm, D. (2003), *Energy, the State and the Market: British Energy Policy since 1979*, Oxford: Oxford University Press.

Helm, D. (2007), 'British energy policy', University of Oxford, 15 August, accessed at http://dieterhelm.co.uk.

House of Commons (2003), *Biofuels, Seventeenth Report of Session, 2002–2003, Volume I*, House of Commons, Environment, Food and Rural Affairs Committee, London: Stationery Office.

House of Lords (2004), 'Renewable energy: practicalities', Volume I: Report, HL Paper 126-I.

Jackson, T. (2000), 'Renewable energy sources', Centre for Environmental Strategy, University of Surrey, CES Working Paper 07/00.

Jansen, J.C. (2003), 'Policy support for renewable energy in the European Union: a review of the regulatory framework and suggestions for adjustment', ECN Report, http://www.ecn.nl/docs/library/report/2003/c03113.pdf.

Jordan, A. (2000), 'The Europeanisation of UK environmental policy, 1970–2000: a departamental perspective', School of Environmental Science, University of East Anglia, Working Paper 11/00.

Lauber, V. (2005), 'Renewable energy at the level of the European Union', in D. Reiche (ed.), *Handbook of Renewable Energies in the European Union*, Frankfurt: Peter Lang, pp. 39–53.

Lauber, V. and E. Schenner (2011), 'The struggle over support schemes for renewable electricity in the European Union: a discursive-institutionalist analysis', *Environmental Politics*, 20 (4), 508–527.

Liefferink, D. and M.S. Andersen (1998), 'Strategies of the green member states in EU environmental policy-making', *Journal of European Public Policy*, 5 (2), 254–270.

Matláry, J. (1997), *Energy Policy in the European Union*, New York: St Martin's Press.

McGowan, F. (2011), 'The UK and EU energy policy: from awkward partner to active protagonist?', in V.L. Birchfield and J.S. Duffield (eds), *Toward a Common European Union Energy Policy*, New York: Palgrave Macmillan, pp. 187–213.

Mitchell, C. (1995), 'The renewables NFFO: a review', *Energy Policy*, 23 (12), 1077–1091.

Mitchell, C. and P. Connor (2004), 'Renewable energy policy in the UK 1990–2003', *Energy Policy*, 32 (17), 1935–1947.

Morata, F. and I. Solorio (eds) (2012), *European Energy Policy: An Environmental Approach*, Cheltenham and Northampton, MA: Edward Elgar Publishing.

Müngersdorff, M. (2009), 'Evaluating EU decision-making processes', Stockholm Environment Institute, Working Paper.

Nilsson, M. (2011), 'EU renewable electricity policy: mixed emotions toward harmonization', in V.L. Birchfield and J.S. Duffield (eds), *Toward a Common European Union Energy Policy*, New York: Palgrave Macmillan, pp. 113–130.

Padgett, S. (2003), 'Between synthesis and emulation: EU policy transfer in the power sector', *Journal of European Public Policy*, 10 (2), 227–245.

Pilgrim, S. and M. Harvey (2010), 'Battles over biofuels in Europe: NGOs and the politics of markets', *Sociological Research Online*, 15 (3), 4, accessed on 15 August 2016 at http://www.socresonline.org.uk/15/3/4.html.

Pollitt, M.G. (2010), 'UK renewable energy policy since privatisation', EPRG Working Paper, No. 1002, Electricity Policy Research Group, Cambridge University, January.

Rayner, T. and A. Jordan (2011), 'The United Kingdom: a paradoxical leader?', in R.K.W. Wurzel and J. Connelly (eds), *The European Union as a Leader in International Climate Change Politics*, New York: Routledge, pp. 95–111.

Reiche, D. and M. Bechberger (2004), 'Policy differences in the promotion of renewable energies in the EU member states', *Energy Policy*, 32, 843–849.

RFA (2008), 'The Gallagher Review of the indirect effects of biofuels production', London.

Rowlands, I.H. (2005), 'The European directive on renewable electricity: conflicts and compromises', *Energy Policy*, 33, 965–974.

Saurugger, S. (2014), 'Europeanisation in times of crisis', *Political Studies Review*, 12 (2), 181–192.
Solorio, I., M. Bechberger and L. Popartan (2013), 'The European energy policy and its "green dimension": discursive hegemony and policy variations in the greening of energy policy', in P. Barnes and T. Hoeber (eds), *Sustainable Development and Governance in Europe: The Evolution of Discourse*, London: Routledge, pp. 91–105.
Solorio, I. and L. Popartan (2014), 'The implementation of the EU biofuels policy in Spain and the UK: a case of contested Europeanization', *Biofuels*, 5 (2), 129–140.
Surrey, J. (1990), 'Beyond the single market and EC energy issues', *Energy Policy*, 18 (1), 42–54.
Toke, D. (2007), 'Making the UK Renewable Programme FITTER', World Future Council.
Toke, D. (2008), 'The EU renewables directive – what is the fuss about trading?', *Energy Policy*, 36, 2991–2998.
Tosun, J. and I. Solorio (eds) (2011), 'Exploring the energy–environment relationship in the EU: perspectives and challenges for theorizing and empirical analysis', in J. Tosun and I. Solorio (eds), *Energy and Environment in Europe: Assessing a Complex Relationship*, *European Integration online Papers* (*EIoP*), Special Mini-Issue 1, Vol. 15. https://eiop.or.at/eiop/pdf/2011-007.pdf.
UK Parliament (2000), 'Select Committee on European Union Sixth Report', 7 November, http://www.publications.parliament.uk/pa/ld200001/ldselect/ldeucom/15/1599.htm.
UK Parliament (2001), 'Select Committee on Environmental Audit Memoranda, Appendix 9', January, http://www.publications.parliament.uk/pa/cm200001/cmselect/cmenvaud/334/334m13.htm.
UK Parliament (2002a), 'Biofuels for Transport: (15500/01), Select Committee on European Union Forty-Ninth Report', http://www.publications.parliament.uk/pa/ld200203/ldselect/ldeucom/196/19616.htm.
UK Parliament (2002b), 'Promotion of the Use of Biofuels in Road Transport, Select Committee on European Scrutiny Nineteenth Report', 22 February. http://www.publications.parliament.uk/pa/cm200102/cmselect/cmeuleg/152-xix/15205.htm.
Wood, G. and S. Dow (2011), 'What lessons have been learned in reforming the Renewables Obligation? An analysis of internal and external failures in UK renewable energy policy', *Energy Policy*, 39 (5), 2228–2244.

7. The fuzzy Europeanization of the Italian renewable energy policy: the paradox of meeting targets without strategic capacity

Maria Rosaria Di Nucci and Daniele Russolillo

7.1 INTRODUCTION

In Italy, until the middle of the 1990s (roughly corresponding to the period of the political system known as '*prima repubblica*', before the radical change in constellation of the political parties) the national '*raison*' and economic interests prevailed over European institutional pressures and developments. Even the strategic decisions of the nationalized energy utilities were arranged by the dominant political party coalitions (Prontera, 2010, p. 497). A shift from the domestic rationale was first sparked by European Union (EU) regional and cohesion policies, where Europeanization promoted an alteration of the domestic opportunity structure through the allocation and administration of the cohesion and structural funds (Zerbinati, 2004; Brunazzo, 2010). Then followed the case of competition policy, where the realization of the internal energy market and the subsequent liberalization of the energy markets fostered a significant transformation of the Italian energy system and policy.

A cursory review of the academic literature reveals that there are hardly any analyses of the Europeanization of Italian energy policy, let alone renewable energy policy. Most of the literature addressing the Italian case concerning the development of renewable energy sources (RES) focuses on the efficiency of supporting instruments, but barely on the EU impact on national energy politics and policies. This chapter attempts to partly fill this gap. It concentrates on the policy and regulatory framework and incentives in the fields of renewable energy sources for electricity (RES-E) and renewable energy sources for transportation (RES-T), and analyses the changes in national policy induced by Europeanization processes (both top-down and horizontal).

The chapter is structured as follows. Section 7.2 sketches the analytical framework whilst section 7.3 discusses the major features of the RES-E policy development and argues for a Europeanization of the Italian electricity policy via regional and competition policy. Section 7.4 illustrates the current status of biofuels policy and shows that Europeanization has been only partially beneficial to the sector. Finally, section 7.5 provides a comparative analysis and draws conclusions on whether the Europeanization approach represents an appropriate heuristic tool to explain the evolution of Italian RES incentives and policy.

7.2 ANALYTICAL UNDERPINNING AND METHODS

Europeanization of Italian renewable energy policy can be considered partly as an outcome of EU competition (liberalization of the energy markets) and regional policy (especially structural policy and cohesion policy) encompassing institutional actors at the central level as well as institutions such as regions, provinces and municipalities. Aspects relevant to Europeanization of the cohesion policy have been highlighted by, amongst others, Graziano (2010), who focused on the policies of the late 1990s and early 2000s and argued that Italy witnessed a high degree of misfit between domestic and EU institutions. The regulations of the structural funds and the implications of Europeanization for local government in Italy were investigated by Zerbinati (2004) and Brunazzo (2010).

With regard to the Europeanization of Italian energy policy via competition policy, Prontera (2010) argues against the 'goodness of fit' approach (see Chapter 1 by Jörgens and Solorio) and considers such logic to be inadequate to explain policy change and policy development in the Italian electricity sector. He integrates the 'goodness of fit' framework with an analysis of the degree of institutionalization of national policies. Accordingly, in order to understand and evaluate Europeanization mechanisms, it is necessary to analyse the conditions and preconditions under which European policies interact with already existing national policies, and strengthen or weaken them. This chapter assumes that it is important to analyse the role of mediating factors such as national actors and institutions. In the same way, 'institutional misfit' affecting changes in institutions and institutional powers can also offer a useful angle, especially concerning the analysis of the devolution of regulatory competences to the regional level.

Europeanization in Italian RES policies is characterized by a continuous calibration between national distinctness, various pressures to adapt, and processes of mediation and response. Top-down Europeanization offers a major point of departure for the analysis. However, evidence for other types of Europeanization can also be expected, that is, a limited bottom-up and a notable horizontal Europeanization. As for top-down and bottom-up Europeanization, the focus of this chapter is on whether and how EU policy and domestic policy influenced each other, as well as on investigating the degree of convergence, 'bad mixture' or co-evolution between European and domestic policies. This chapter also investigates whether the successes and failures of previous or parallel experiences in other European countries, especially regarding the evolution of the RES-E promotion instruments, ended up triggering the decision to adopt similar policies in Italy, and whether and how domestic stakeholder groups insisted on their position or promoted change (for example, horizontal Europeanization).

Empirical evidence to support the analysis in the RES-E field was derived from the project REALISE Forum,[1] which provides insights on the preferences and positions of the most relevant Italian stakeholders in the selection and implementation of instruments to support RES-E (Casale, 2006; Casale et al., 2007). Apart from academic literature, official documents and statistics, drafts of laws, minutes of committee meetings, reports of hearings and conferences, press releases and websites as well as online journals were important sources for the analysis of stakeholders' positions. These sources were supplemented by the reports of EU collaborative projects financed under the Intelligent Energy Europe (IEE) programme, which dealt with the assessment of the incentive mechanisms for RES-E.[2] For the case of biofuels, interviews with industrial actors and stakeholders were conducted in the framework of the IEE project BIOTEAM.

7.3 THE DEVELOPMENT OF RES-E IN ITALY

The evolution of RES-E in Italy is characterized by a discontinuous, incoherent energy, technology and industrial policy inhibiting the development of a national RES industry (Di Nucci, 2007). Nonetheless, in the last decade, there has been a sustained growth of RES. At the end of 2013, RES-E contributed around 40 per cent of the total installed power capacity in Italy and 37 per cent of the total gross electricity production (Terna, 2015). One of the grounds for such a steady growth is the rather generous incentive policy until 2014. The Italian support system is very complex and differentiates according to size and technologies, ranging from Tradable Green Certificates (TGCs) to various forms of Feed-In Tariffs (FITs) and fiscal incentives. Moreover, RES-E is supported at a national level as well as by regions, provinces and local authorities.

7.3.1 Early RES-E Development[3]

RES, notably hydroelectric and geothermal power, contributed substantially to the Italian electricity balance until the early 1960s. Afterwards, due to the cheap oil prices and a powerful petroleum lobby, hydroelectric power was substituted by oil-fired plants and Italy became heavily dependent on imported oil. Following the oil crisis in 1973, the diversification of the energy balance mainly occurred through substitution of oil with natural gas. After the oil crisis of 1979, the National Energy Plan (PEN), released in 1980 and revised in 1981, also included RES. In 1982, a piece of legislation (law 308/1982) set targets and financial incentives for RES as well as energy efficiency. It restricted the monopoly of ENEL, the state-owned electricity company (established in 1962 as Ente Nazionale per l'Energia Elettrica), by permitting generation up to 3 megawatts (MW) by independent power producers (IPPs) and enabled the delegation of some decisions concerning RES matters to regional governments. Additionally, various national research and development (R&D) programmes provided support for the development of RES technologies and for the realization of pilot and demonstration plants.

In the aftermath of the Chernobyl disaster in 1986 and following the referendum in 1987 to phase out nuclear power, the PEN of 1988 also indicated targets for the development of RES by the year 2000. Law 9/91 regulated authorizations to build hydropower plants and increased the liberalization threshold for RES plants from 3 MW to 25 MW. In the 1990s, the main instrument for RES development was, however, directive 6/92 of the Interministerial Committee for Prices (CIP), issued to comply with law 9/91. By establishing premium prices for electricity generated by RES plants connected to the national grid, setting rules for the production of electricity through independent power producers, and introducing an obligation that allowed third parties to feed electricity into the grid, the directive dramatically changed the incentive policy for RES-E production. This scheme continued to be in use until 1995. Because the system was considered too costly, in 1996 the procedure was suspended and only projects already authorized could be implemented. A major setback of the CIP/92 system was its failure to become a specific instrument for RES (Lorenzoni, 2003). In fact, roughly 70 per cent of the total contribution was devoted to cogeneration and waste-to-energy, favouring large national electric and industrial groups (Di Nucci, 2005, p. 203).

7.3.2 The Role of the EU Regional and Liberalization Policies

The role of regional and cohesion policy

Italian regions have competencies for economic development, but their capacity for policy action remains limited, and central government still plays an important role in regional development issues. In the last decades, however, the role of the regions has been strengthened, especially through a progressive devolution of competences, but also as a result of EU regional policy. Against this background, it is not surprising that the first stage of sustained expansion of wind power occurred at a time in which the transfer of powers from the central state to the regions took place, especially in matters concerning governance of the territory and energy planning. Regions started to grant capital cost subsidies, promoting the setting-up of competitive RES-E plants in addition to the available incentive mechanisms.

The implementation of the structural funds triggered a reorganization of the necessary administrative structures to implement regional development programmes and to coordinate partnerships of public and private actors as part of the programme management. These funds provoked an alteration of the opportunity structure of domestic actors and a strengthening of institutional capacity and efficiency of public administrations. Between 1987 and 1992, a large number of EU programmes enabled local governments to access EU funds. In the energy field, the VALOREN programme and the Interreg programme also played an important role. Although this participation represented a challenge to the regional institutions, which had limited expertise in implementing industrial policy, the activities of regional policymakers and actors encouraged European cooperation in the RES field. Changes were initially driven by pressure to adapt, but in a second stage learning and horizontal diffusion of EU best practices activated a capacity-building which included not only strategic planning capabilities, but also the political self-confidence necessary to promote at EU level positions and activities in line with national preferences (Brunazzo, 2010).

Moreover, the Europeanization of Italian regional policies promoted an increased participation of Italy in EU decision-making processes in this area, especially due to a stronger engagement of regional representatives in Brussels.[4] Italy managed not only to formulate a national position on the regulation of structural funds, but also to promote national interests during the relevant negotiation phases (Brunazzo and Piattoni, 2004, p. 170).[5] Thus, the participation of Italian regional actors in the definition of the EU cohesion and structural policy constitutes an interesting case, showing a timid shift from a top-down to a bottom-up approach, or, as Brunazzo (2010, p. 2) puts it, from the role of a 'policy-taker' to that of a 'policy-shaper'.

The role of competition policy

The starting conditions in the Italian electricity sector showed no 'goodness of fit' with respect to the liberalization promoted by the EU. The reform was based on competition and market liberalization, factors that were both incongruent with pre-existent Italian policy characterized by strong state intervention and dirigisme. In the middle of the 1990s, Italy took a neoliberal stand concerning its energy market and embarked on a far-reaching liberalization and deregulation reform. The liberalization of the domestic electricity sector was triggered by the pressure to transpose the EU liberalization directives, which was perceived by domestic actors as the opportunity to start a reform and put an end to direct state participation. At the same time, the crisis of the party system that had shaped the national energy policy in the previous decade 'disadvantaged the traditional players in electricity policy making and provoked a change in the structure of relationships in the policy field' (Prontera, 2010, p. 499).

The domestic debate on liberalization had already been strongly influenced in 1994–95 by the ongoing debate in the EU, especially in the United Kingdom (UK) (see Chapter 6 by Solorio and Fairbrass). The Italian reform took place in a political context characterized by great instability and loss of influence of traditional state actors. Paraphrasing Radaelli (2004), Europe represented the 'solution' to legitimate the willingness to reform and to change the underlying policy paradigm from state intervention to competition. Italy's electricity market underwent a steady process of liberalization with a restructuring process that lasted years and witnessed adjustments and novel developments regarding market rules, new market actors and institutions.[6] The national debate on reform was characterized by an improbable consensus among a wide range of actors on the necessity to transpose the EU directive into domestic legislation that embraced conservative as well as leftist parties, while only the trade unions opposed the reform. The centre-leftist Prodi (1996–98) and the following D'Alema (1998–2000) governments catalysed an 'implicit' coalition of interest that in a relatively short time achieved a radical unbundling of the national electricity monopolist ENEL.

In 1999 the Bersani Decree transposed directive 96/92/EC and acted as a 'framework law' for restructuring the Italian electricity sector. It also brought about radical changes for RES development. Among other elements, the decree established TGCs and RES obligations (quotas) for electricity producers and importers, and introduced priority dispatching for RES-E as well as funds for specific incentives for RES-E to be managed by regional authorities, according to a tender mechanism. A reason for the adoption of the TGC system is that the EU, in a first unofficial draft of the RES-E directive of October 1998, had already expressed preference for a support model based on quota systems (Arentsen et al., 2007, p. 4). This hampered the ambitions of some Italian RES stakeholders for a further adjustment of the previous CIP 6/92 FIT. The previous system was labelled in the political debate as a distorting, dirigistic instrument.

In the liberalization process of the Italian electricity market there can be found top-down Europeanization, but at the same time also elements of learning (for example, horizontal Europeanization). The fact that other countries had also abandoned FITs schemes (Denmark; see Chapter 5 by Dyrhauge), and that in the UK, a country that had served Italy as a model for the liberalization of the energy sector, a Renewables Obligation (RO) certificate scheme was going to be introduced (see Chapter 6 by Solorio and Fairbrass), may have been a strong motivation. The introduction of the quotas and TGCs was triggered by the anticipation that the national policies would be harmonized and that quotas and TGCs would be the dominant instruments. This choice was reinforced by the expectations that a market-oriented type of support would be more compatible with the internal electricity market.

7.3.3 The Implementation of the 2001 RES-E Directive: Progressive Adaptation to EU Policy Change and Changing Stakeholder Positions

During the negotiation of the 2001 RES-E directive, Italian officials saw the EU policy as an opportunity to reinforce domestic electricity policy. Even actors that traditionally were against major changes in the electricity field (for example, the ex-monopolist ENEL and the trade unions) did not challenge the principles of the directive. The transformation took place in a voluntary, non-coercive way and the decision-makers were eager to gain a new role. This applies in particular to the new actors established by the liberalization reform, and the role played by the newly established transmission system operator Gestore Rete Trasmissione Nazionale (GRTN). As the Italian issuing body responsible for the certification of generation plants and for issuing the guarantee of origin (GO), GRTN had a representative on the board of the European Association of Issuing Bodies and was actively engaged in the development of the Renewable Energy Certificate System (RECS) initiative which started a voluntary market for trading in 2002.

The RES-E directive was transposed into national legislation by decree 387/2003 in December 2003. Italy adopted an indicative target of 22 per cent for RES-E by 2010. It strengthened and widened the previously existing instruments and rulings, coordinating and defining procedures and lead times for the authorization of plants and connection to the grid. The mandatory quota and TGC scheme was regulated in detail by subsequent laws in 2005. However, several provisions to be transposed needed further implementing actions, most of which were taken subsequently in 2005 – for example, FITs for photovoltaic (PV) or the new Decree on TGC – or even later in 2006 and 2007.[7] Whereas the Ministry of the Environment remained largely apathetic, the energy policy of the conservative Berlusconi government was dominated by the industry-friendly stance of the Ministry of Industry that finally presented a rather controversial decree to be followed by law 239/2004 (the so-called Marzano law) allowing faster permitting procedures.

An important milestone opening the national debate and leading to a revision of the Italian incentive system was the release in December 2005 of the first evaluation report of the European Commission on RES-E support (COM, 2005), followed by a second report a year later (COM, 2007). The evaluation showed that the FITs system had become by far the dominant support model in Europe, and its performance in terms of effectiveness and cost efficiency was compelling. For the European Commission, harmonization was no longer a short-term objective and the focus of policy moved from harmonization and one predominant EU-wide mechanism to co-existence of mechanisms, and supranational and regional coordination (Arentsen et al., 2007; Toke, 2008).

A progressive shift of positions and viewpoints of Italian stakeholders and decision-makers took place, a typical case of adaptation to EU pressures. But at the same time there were also unmistakable signs of horizontal Europeanization mechanisms and change of policy through policy diffusion and imitation. In this regard, the additional support system based on FITs introduced for PV in October 2005 counteracted some of the shortcomings of the TGCs model and introduced a technology-oriented model based on premium FITs, as in Spain (see Chapter 8 by Solorio and Fernandez), thus following the trend of FITs diffusion in the EU (Busch and Jörgens, 2012). This move was supported by the major RES stakeholders. In this context, a new ministerial decree of February 2006 rendered the previous conditions of July 2005 (granting FITs to PV plants over 20 years) even more favourable (higher ceilings to the overall capacity of funded projects). Legislative decree 152/2006 extended the availability of the quota/TGCs scheme from eight to 12 years. At the end of 2007, the Italian government introduced some new provisions for RES-E, and small generators had the choice between selling their TGCs and opting for FITs. A survey of the REALISE Forum project reveals that in 2006 Italian stakeholders having experience with both the FITs and the quota/TGCs system, on average assessed the FITs support system as more effective and fairer with respect to the various RES technologies than the quota/TGCs system.

Government officials learnt from the experience of other countries and started considering the success in the expansion of RES mostly as a result of the support policies, for example FITs. Horizontal Europeanization started affecting changes in the preferences and position of domestic actors. A wide range of Italian institutional and economic actors found it beneficial to support a policy change towards similar lines as successful countries in RES promotion (for example Germany and Spain). The FITs system was perceived as less complicated and stakeholders showed willingness to change support scheme.[8]

7.3.4 Italy and the Climate and Energy Package: The Push for GO Trading

Within the Energy Council, in 2007 Italy opposed the introduction of binding RES-E targets. However, dissent also grew about the indicative target. The Italian Ministry of Economic Development, which was in charge of the transposition of the RES-E directive, supported RES-E trading, and the Commission seemed to look sympathetically at the possible addition of imported RES-E for achieving national targets, provided that any possible 'double-counting' could be avoided. Italy pursued the voluntary certification of RES-E plants. The GRTN recognized the GO issued in other EU countries and engaged at EU level not only for issuing the GO for disclosure, but also for the voluntary market and for target counting. The aim was to use certification in the case of imported energy for the exemption of green certificate and quota systems. In September 2008 the Italian government published an assessment carried out with the support of several ministries, following a consultation with industry, which found that the maximum theoretical potential for RES-E in Italy would be around 21 million tonnes of oil equivalent (Mtoe) and that consequently the goal of 17 per cent was difficult to reach. Against this background, RES-E trade and imported certified

RES-E represented a means to reach the indicative target with less domestic RES-E generation. Moreover, the inclusion of national binding targets into the 2009 RED was perceived by political and industrial stakeholders as too big a challenge, and an imposition to modify the energy mix.[9]

It could be claimed that in that period there was an attempt to push for standardized GO, disclosure, redemption and labelling of RES-E. Stakeholders such as the transmission system operator and Gestore Sistema Elettrico (GSE), later replacing part of the activities of GRTN, favoured the establishment of a common framework of rules ensuring fair access of RES-E to the market and the electrical system, and also got involved in various EU initiatives and projects. Italy, however, was not able to achieve any success in the EU negotiations.

The legislative decree of March 2011 transposed the 2009 RED (opening the way to RES 'target flexibility') into national law, also regulating statistical transfers and joint projects. The target flexibility (share to fill the gap between the 2020 RES target and the domestic RES deployment) was designated to be 0.8 per cent (1.1 Mtoe) of the gross final energy demand to be met through flexible cooperation mechanisms. The law however stated that cooperation should be enhanced only in the case that the interim target for 2016 could not be achieved (MSE, 2013).

The law aimed to 'to strengthen and rationalize' the RES support system and to reach the double objective of increasing RES-E in line with European objectives, and reducing subsidies.[10] The level and procedures for the extension of the FITs system, however, were not considered and important details for a new incentive system were postponed to subsequent legislation to be enacted within 12 months after approval of the law. The debate that surrounded the law was characterized by a diversity of positions, but all stakeholders were in favour of reintroducing a FITs system, even though RES-E producers received lower incentives than those enjoyed through the TGCs scheme. One of the reasons was that banks were more willing to finance projects when the tariff is guaranteed over time. In this regard, the law stated that for wind farms starting operations after 2012 the TGCs system should be replaced by FITs. Wind farms operational by 2012 should continue to receive TGCs until 2015 before being absorbed into the FIT system (O'Brian, 2011).

In compliance with the 2009 RED, incentives for PV originally expected to run from 2011 to 2013 were possible only for plants connecting to the grid by the end of May 2013. The sudden change in the support scheme provoked the strong protest of the Renewable Energy Producers Association (Associazione Produttori di Energia da fonti

Rinnovabili, APER), the organization representing more than 400 Italian RES-E producers, which asked the then Energy Commissioner Oettinger to put pressure on the Italian government.[11] Although there was a clear aim to reach the 2020 targets, the large number of laws and decrees issued to comply with the directive did not seem to possess the necessary strategic orientation. According to APER, this would condemn Italy to the role of 'follower' in a 'double-speed' Europe.[12] The successive ministerial decree of July 2012 introduced the so-called Fifth Energy Incentives Plan for RES-E plants other than PV.

Under the following Monti government, in March 2013, the Ministry of Economic Development released the final version of the 2020 National Energy Strategy (MSE, 2013). The report indicates that the future electricity mix has to rely on natural gas and RES-E and sets more ambitious targets than in the National Renewable Energy Action Plan (NREAP) (a share of RES-E of 35–38 per cent, above the target of 26 per cent and the RES share in the gross final energy consumption of 19–20 per cent). This adjustment was the obvious consequence following the massive deployment of PV plants in 2010 and 2011. The so-called 'Destinazione Italia' decree of December 2013 amended the regulatory framework for RES plants and biofuel targets.

In recent years the incentives system underwent a drastic restructuring in line with other EU countries. In the recent plans to put a limit on solar incentives under the new PV support scheme, and in the attempts to scrap incentives from 2017, elements of imitation (horizontal Europeanization) can be found, since the annual limit on installed PV capacity is in line with the activities in other European countries such as Spain (see Chapter 8 by Solorio and Fernandez).

7.3.5 Progressive Change of Position Prior to the Climate and Energy Package 2030

The Italian position in terms of targets has changed enormously in recent years. Whilst in 2009 there was still a large consensus about keeping lower targets for greenhouse gas (GHG) emissions and RES, this position gradually changed in the following years. On the eve of the negotiation on the 2030 climate and energy package, a coordination group led by the Advisor for European Affairs of the Cabinet and a meeting of various ministers (Environment, European Policies, Economic Development) was established in 2013. In the period preceding the Italian presidency in the second semester of 2014, the government tried to show engagement in sustainability and climate protection issues and joined the league of the 'green' European countries. This attitude is somehow surprising, especially considering that in September 2013 Italy was involved in an infringement procedure regarding the transposition of the 2009 RED. However, there are clear signs of 'Europeanized' positions of Italian officials. During the Brussels summit of EU leaders of October 2014 to agree on targets to reduce GHG emissions and increase RES and energy efficiency, Italy favoured setting the binding target for RES at 27 per cent (EurActiv, 2014). The Italian Ministry of Environment was amongst the 'Green Growth' group ministers who issued a joint statement on 18 December 2014 calling for early action to strengthen the EU emissions trading scheme and introduce legislation to reach Europe's GHG emissions commitment of at least a 40 per cent reduction domestically. The signatories recognized 'the important role of renewable energy, energy efficiency and other safe and sustainable low carbon technologies in meeting the EU 2030 targets and broader EU energy policy objectives cost-effectively, and welcome the planned review of the energy efficiency target by 2020'.

7.4 THE DEVELOPMENT OF BIOFUELS IN THE TRANSPORT SECTOR IN ITALY

7.4.1 The Beginnings of the Biofuel Policy in Italy

Production of biofuels in Italy started in 1993 with NOVAOL in Livorno, the first biodiesel facility in Europe. The main push came from the early concept of green chemical industry defined by the leading Italian group Montedison. This concept had a twofold objective: create new growth opportunities for the Italian chemical sector, and try to cover the need for cleaner fuels to fight local pollution. A similar trend was taking place in the same years in France and Germany (see Chapter 9 by Bocquillon and Evrard, and Chapter 3 by Vogelpohl et al.), the other two forerunners in Europe, and the industrial sector association, the European Biodiesel Board (EBB), was founded, building upon the contacts between the industrial representatives in these three countries (Interview 1). The industrial achievement of NOVAOL was preceded and accompanied by an efficient lobby activity that instigated the establishment in the mid-1990s of the first national tax exemption scheme for biodiesel supplied to final users. The industrial biodiesel achievement at the end of the 1990s can be seen as the outcome of the strong interest of the farming lobby to contribute to the mitigation of climate change and expand the growth possibilities of the agricultural production (Rocchietta, 2002).

7.4.2 Italy and the Biofuels Directive

The early phase of implementation

During the negotiations leading up to the adoption of the biofuels directive, Italy was in favour of setting binding targets for biofuels at the EU level. Taking into account industry support for biodiesel, this position is not surprising and follows the positions of France and Germany (Rocchietta, 2002). At the beginning of 2003, the main Italian industrial associations involved in transportation fuels concluded a relevant agreement for a structural cooperation on biofuels (Staffetta Quotidiana, 2003a). A few months after the entry into force of the biofuels directive during the Italian EU presidency, Industry Minister Marzano highlighted the need to reduce asymmetries in energy issues in Europe, among other things in energy taxations and fiscal incentives for biofuels (Staffetta Quotidiana, 2003b).

The second and third Berlusconi governments in place from mid-2001 to mid-2006 were in charge of transposing and implementing the biofuels directive in the transport sector. It was transposed only two years after adoption through the legislative decree 128/2005 and the reference target to be achieved by the end of 2005 was set at 1 per cent, half the target of 2 per cent suggested by the biofuels directive. Moreover, annex II of article 8 of the legislative decree 128/2005 specifically stated that the less ambitious biofuels targets for Italy had to be understood in the framework of the 'limited national production potential of biofuels' on national territory. It could be claimed that industrial capabilities and technology were available and fully adequate to support a biodiesel pathway, but problems arose in relation to the primary energy (for example, biomass cultivated on national territory), especially in conjunction with the food/feed issue and the fight of the environmental lobbies against first generation biofuels.

In 2005 the government launched a fiscal policy which envisaged a quota system for producers eligible to receive annual excise exemptions (tax relief). The official implementation reports sent by the member states to the Commission (MSE, 2007) include the specific quota as well as the injection into the grid, fiscal deductions, and so on. This tax relief can be considered an example of modest horizontal Europeanization, even though the presence of more binding targets and more structured tax reliefs in other member states did not prompt a similar outcome in Italy.

The role of RED and the situation in Italy between 2009 and 2013: what kind of Europeanization?

With regard to RES-T in the RED of 2009, Italy has taken a rather passive stance, demonstrated for example by the postponement of the adoption of sustainability criteria for biofuels until the publication of the ministerial decree of 2012 (Ministero dell'Ambiente, 2012). These criteria were criticized by industrial operators for not providing a stable and calculable legal framework, as had been requested by the business sector (Confindustria, 2011). The domestic policy was not particularly affected by the mandatory targets, but in 2013 operational tasks were transferred from the Ministry of the Environment to the Ministry of Economic Development.

The analysis of consumption data shows a patchy and uneven trend of demand in the sector, with a decrease of consumption in 2012 compared to 2011 mainly due to the effect of the economic crisis and the uncertainties around the European legislation (EurObserv'ER, 2013, 2014). The strong difference between the production capacity and the actual production tells a story of overinvestment in the biodiesel sector that is common in the EU. In 2012, the average ratio in EU-27 between actual production and production capacity was 48 per cent, well above the share of 12 per cent achieved in Italy (EurObserv'ER, 2013; MSE, 2012). Biodiesel demand was met progressively through imports from countries using incentives to export the product or feedstock, for example soybeans from the United States or Argentina (Cocchi, 2011; Di Mario et al., 2011). In 2011, the breakdown of renewable fuel consumption in the EU-27 was in energy terms 80:20 in favour of biodiesel, whereas in Italy at the same time the ratio was 92:8, showing a relatively small importance of bioethanol in the Italian transport sector (EurObserv'ER, 2013). Despite this relatively minor interest, the Italian Mossi & Ghisolfi Group launched the pre-commercial operation for the world's first second-generation bioethanol plant, based in north-west Italy.

The discussion above reveals that Europeanization (both top-down and horizontal) has been rather weak in the Italian biofuel sector. The low degree of adaptational pressures might explain the negative trend on domestic biofuel policy. This, in turn, was made structurally worse by the effects of the financial crisis on fuel consumption and by some cultural and socio-economic issues and indirect land-use change debate, as well as the intrinsic difficulty of assessing the sustainability of such a pathway (Rocchietta, 2014; BIOTEAM, 2014). Moreover, the aforementioned transfer of energy competences to the regions and the EU regional policy were not able to generate effective actions by regional governments in the biofuel sector (Interview 1), as in the case of the wind energy sector, for example.

RES-T in Italy towards the 2030 targets

At the end of 2013, law decree n.145 of December 2013 limited the national consumption obligation for biofuels in energy terms to 4.5 per cent. Nevertheless, at the end of 2014, at the end of the Italian EU presidency, new targets were set by the Italian government, with binding targets for 2022 ensuring the RED target of a 10 per cent share of RES-T in total fuel consumption by 2020 (MSE, 2014). With respect to biomethane, Italy is still a laggard when compared to Germany (see Chapter 3 by Vogelpohl et al.). In fact, the decree issued at the end of 2013 lacked a full regulatory framework for biomethane, still to be defined by the national energy regulatory authority, and this caused strong discontent among industrial operators (*Quale Energia*, 2014).

With regard to the discussions about the indirect land use change (ILUC) directive, the Italian position has been in favour of the decoupling of bioenergy pathways and food cultivation, and in fact the agreement of December 2014 of the EU Energy Council on the ILUC directive was led by the Italian EU presidency (EurActiv, 2014). As for the discussion of the 2030 package, the Italian position was cautious from the very beginning, putting on the table the need for a deep regulatory impact analysis (Governo Italiano, 2014).

7.5 COMPARATIVE ANALYSIS OF RES-E AND BIOFUELS, AND CONCLUDING REMARKS

The reconstruction of the Europeanization process in Italian RES policies has shown, on the one hand, that the impact of EU policy has led to varying degrees of domestic policy change, and that some national actors have managed to exploit the adaptational pressures deriving from Europeanization to enhance a reform of the Italian energy and regional policy. On the other hand, it has illustrated that Italy has hardly been able to gain a presence in Brussels, at least during the crucial phases of decision-making, as in the case of the target flexibility. Undeniably, Europeanization influenced Italian policy-making and affected changes in objectives as well in the regulatory framework and support system for RES-E and, partly, RES-T. The path followed, however, has not generated a coherent policy which could provide adequate responses to the EU policies.

Paradoxically, Italy had already managed to achieve the targets envisaged by the 2009 RED.[13] The RES share of gross final consumption reached 11.5 per cent in 2011, 2.9 per cent above the intermediate target of 8.6 per cent set by the RED. According to recent data (Eurostat, 2016) Italy reached a RES-E share of 17.1 per cent in 2014 (achieving the national RED target six years prior to the deadline). In the RES-T sector Italy is also on track to achieve the target of 10 per cent by 2020 (MSE, 2014). However, achieving EU targets makes Italy neither a forerunner nor a case of best practice in the transposition of EU directives. Rather, this achievement demonstrates that it is possible to attain EU targets even without attempting to upload policies linked to national policy preferences, or by transposing EU legislation in a timely way.

Except for the formal transposition of EU directives into national law, Europeanization in the Italian RES sector was relatively weak and occurred mostly through horizontal mechanisms. Horizontal Europeanization in the biofuels sector could be observed in setting up the trading scheme and the national voluntary scheme for sustainability certification. In the RES-E sector similar processes could be observed with regard to market-based certificate trading systems such as TGCs.

As far as horizontal Europeanization is concerned, it appears that in the 2000s and later a wide range of Italian institutional and economic actors found it beneficial to adjust to EU pressures and to support a policy change along similar lines as those of successful countries, especially in the promotion of RES-E, such as Germany and Spain; and, on a minor note, in the promotion of biofuels, such as France and Germany (see Chapter 9 by Bocquillon and Evrard, and Chapter 3 by Vogelpohl et al.). In general, whilst for the RES-E case it can be claimed that the successes or failures of previous or parallel experiences in other European countries ended up prompting the decision to adopt similar policies, and domestic stakeholder groups moved from their original position and promoted change, this aspect of horizontal Europeanization was much weaker in the case of RES-T for biomethane and only partially worked for the biodiesel sector. Against this background, we can talk about policy change triggered by a combination of 'spontaneous' policy diffusion for RES-E, as well as of pressures coming from an unusually compact domestic coalition of interests pushing for reform.

In conclusion, the case of Italy underlines that EU renewable energy policy can provide a model around which to redesign a domestic policy, but that for this to take place actors able to exploit adaptational pressures or willing to learn from best-practice cases are indispensable. Italy did not succeed in being influential and complying effectively and in a timely manner with EU policies and institutional pressures, with resulting technical and political hitches in the design of an effective energy policy.

NOTES

1. Renewable Energy and Liberalisation in Selected Electricity Markets Forum (REALISE Forum), coordinated by the Freie Universität Berlin and supported by the European Commission under the Intelligent Energy Europe Programme (2005–07).
2. The major results of these projects can be found on the Intelligent Energy Europe-EACI website, http://www.eaci-projects.eu/iee/page/Page.jsp?op=home.
3. This section draws on Di Nucci (2007).
4. This view has also been expressed by regional representatives in Brussels during interviews, for example with Simona Costa of Casa Liguria.
5. The state of progress for the 2007–13 EU budget programming shows that Italy has used just 40 per cent of its share of EU regional funds (EurActiv Italy). In the period 2014–20, Italy will receive about €29 billion of EU funds for regional projects, to be matched by an equivalent amount from its own budget.
6. For details on the liberalization of the electricity market, see Polo and Scarpa (2003) and Di Nucci (2004).
7. Further legislative decrees implementing the EU directive raised the initial RES obligation of 2 per cent by 0.35 per cent per year for 2004–06, and further increases of the minimum obligation quota were adopted for the periods 2007–09 and 2010–12.
8. The Italian quota/TGC scheme could be considered as a 'mixed type' scheme as the TGC market price was not set by the free play of demand and supply only, but was regulated in order to provide investors with adequate revenues, at least in the short term. These characteristics render a shift to a full FIT system easier than in countries with a fully market-based TGC scheme.
9. See also the interview of Gatta, the then chairman of the Italian Association of Electricity Enterprises (Assoelettrica) in EurActiv (2008).
10. This is a quote from an Italian government statement reported on the webpage of the Law Library of Congress: 'Italy: Renewable Energy Law Adopted', accessed on 27 April 2014 at http://www.loc.gov/lawweb/servlet/lloc_news?disp3_l205402587_text.
11. See http://www.aper.it/public/sitoaper/FontiRinnovabili/pAper/2011/18_04_11APER_Oettinger.pdf.
12. The European Commissioner sent a letter to the then Minister for Economic Development and requested to increase efforts to transpose the Directive 2009/28/EE and to set up 'a clear, stable and predictable support scheme for the solar energy sector and ensure stability for investors' (http://in.reuters.com/article/2011/04/18/us-italy-renewables-oettinger-idINTRE73H44720110418).
13. Data from national monitoring system SIMERI, last accessed on 15 January 2015 at http://approfondimenti.gse.it/approfondimenti/Simeri/Monitoraggio/Pagine/C1.aspx.

REFERENCES

Arentsen, M., M. Bechberger, M.R. Di Nucci and L. Mez (2007), 'Stakeholder dynamics in European support of renewable electricity production', in L. Mez (ed.), *Green Power Markets*, Brentwood: Multi-Science Publishing, pp. 51–70.

BIOTEAM (2014), 'Harmonized bioenergy pathway sustainability assessment framework', http://www.sustainable-biomass.eu/.

Brunazzo, M. (2010), 'From policy-taker to policy-shaper: the Europeanization of Italian cohesion policy', *World Political Science Review*, 6 (1), 1–28.

Brunazzo, M. and S. Piattoni (2004), 'Negotiating the regulation of the structural funds: Italian actors in EU regional policy-making', *Modern Italy*, 9 (2), 159–172.

Busch, P.-O. and H. Jörgens (2012), 'Governance by diffusion: exploring a new mechanism of international policy coordination', in J. Meadowcroft, O. Langhelle and A. Ruud (eds), *Governance, Democracy and Sustainable Development: Moving Beyond the Impasse?*, Cheltenham and Northampton, MA: Edward Elgar Publishing, pp. 221–248.

Casale, C. (2006), 'Country Report from Italy on production of electricity from renewable energy sources and relevant support schemes', Berlin, Report of the IEE-Project Realise-Forum.

Casale, C., M.R Di Nucci and L. Salvaderi (2007), 'Sistemi di incentivazione delle rinnovabili in Europa. Il progetto REALISE: caratteristiche e finalità raggiunte', *Pianeta Terra 14*, (2007), 44–49.

Cocchi, M. (2011), 'IEA Bioenergy Task 40 – Country Profile Italy 2011', http://www.bioenergytrade.org/downloads/iea-task-40-country-report-2011-italy.pdf.

COM (2005), 'The support of electricity from renewable resources', COM (2005) 627 final, Brussels, {SEC(2005) 1571}, Brussels.

COM (2007), 'Communication from the Commission to the Council and the European Parliament, Green Paper follow-up action – Report on progress in renewable electricity', COM (2006) 849 final,{SEC(2007) 12}, Brussels.

Confindustria (2011), 'Audizione al Senato sullo schema di D.lgs. recante attuazione della direttiva 2009/28/CE', http://www.senato.it/documenti/repository/commissioni/comm10/documenti_acquisiti/AG%20302/2011_02_02%20-%20Confindustria.pdf.

Di Mario, F., G. Braccio, V. Pignatelli, N. Colonna and F. Zimbardi (2011), 'Biomasse ed Energia – quaderno ENEA', http://www.enea.it/it/enea_informa/documenti/quaderni-energia/biomasse.pdf.

Di Nucci, M.R. (2004), 'The liberalization of the Italian energy market: Part I: The structure and framework of the electricity system', *EnergiewirtschaftlicheTagesfragen1/2*, 101–108.

Di Nucci, M.R. (2005), 'Italy', in D. Reiche (ed.), *Handbook of Renewable Energies in the European Union*, Frankfurt: Peter Lang.

Di Nucci, M.R. (2007), 'The role of renewables in the Italian energy policy: the development of green power', in L. Mez (ed.), *Green Power Markets*, Brentwood: Multi-Science Publishing, pp. 311–334.

EurActiv (2008), 'Italian renewables target "unreachable"', 7 February, accessed on 8 December 2014 at http://www.euractiv.com/energy/gatta-italian-renewables-target-unreachable/article-170176.

EurActiv (2014), 'Energia: De Vincenti, ok ministri Ue a direttiva Iluc', Press Release, accessed on 20 February 2015 at http://www.euractiv.it/it/news/ambiente-energia/10456-energia-de-vincenti-ok-ministri-ue-a-direttiva-iluc.html.

EurObserv'ER (2013), *Biofuels Barometer*, accessed on 30 April 2014 at http://www.eurobserv-er.org/pdf/baro216_en.asp.

EurObserv'ER (2014), *Biofuels Barometer*, accessed on 8 January 2015 at http://www.eurobserv-er.org/pdf/baro222_en.asp.
Eurostat (2016), 'Energy from renewable sources', accessed on 26 February 2016 at http://ec.europa.eu/eurostat/statistics-explained/index.php/Energy_from_renewable_sources.
Governo Italiano (2014), 'Preparazione della posizione italiana sul pacchetto clima-energia 2030 della Commissione Europea', press release accessed on 20 February 2015 at http://www.governo.it/Presidenza/Comunicati/dettaglio.asp?d=74541.
Graziano, P. (2010), 'From local partnerships to regional spaces for politics? Europeanization and EU cohesion policy in southern Italy'. *Regional and Federal Studies*, 20 (3), 315–333.
Lorenzoni, A. (2003), 'The Italian Green Certificates market between uncertainty and opportunities', *Energy Policy*, 31 (1), 33–42.
Ministero dell'Ambiente (2012), 'Decreto Ministeriale 23 gennaio 2012 Sistema nazionale di certificazione di sostenibilità dei biocarburanti e dei bioliquidi'.
MSE (Ministero per lo Sviluppo Economico) (2007), 'Implementation report of the Directive 2003/30/CE', accessed on 30 April 2014 at https://ec.europa.eu/energy/sites/ener/files/documents/member_states_reports_directive_2003_30_ec_2007.zip.
MSE (Ministero per lo Sviluppo Economico) (2012), 'National energy balance 2012', accessed on 2 February 2014 at http://dgerm.sviluppoeconomico.gov.it/dgerm/ben/ben_2012_rev1.pdf.
MSE (Ministero per lo Sviluppo Economico) (2013), 'Italy's National Energy Strategy: for a more competitive and sustainable energy', Rome, March, accessed at http://www.encharter.org/fileadmin/user_upload/Energy_policies_and_legislation/Italy_2013_National_Energy_Strategy_ENG.pdf.
MSE (Ministero per lo Sviluppo Economico) (2014), 'Decree 10 October 2014. Aggiornamento delle condizioni, dei criteri e delle modalita' di attuazione dell'obbligo di immissione in consumo di biocarburanti compresi quelli avanzati'.
O'Brian, H. (2011), 'Italy: the Italian government has approved a new renewable energy law', *Windpower Monthly*, March, accessed on 27 April 2014 at http://www.windpowermonthly.com/article/1058414/italy-leaves-detail-fit-legislation.
Polo, M. and C. Scarpa (2003), 'The liberalization of energy markets in Europe and Italy', Innocenzo Gasparini Institute for Economic Research.
Prontera, A. (2010), 'Europeanization, institutionalization and policy change in French and Italian electricity policy', *Journal of Comparative Policy Analysis: Research and Practice*, 12 (5), 491–507.
Quale Energia (2014), 'Biometano. Coordinamento Fonti Rinnovabili ed Efficienza Energetica: i ritardi dell'Autorità aggravano la crisi del settore', 24 September, http://www.qualenergia.it/articoli/20140924-biometano-free-i-ritardi-della-autority-aggravano-la-crisi-del-settore.
Radaelli, C. (2004), 'Europeanization: solution or problem?', *European Integration online Papers (EIoP)*, 8 (16), accessed on 22 April 2014 at http://eiop.or.at/eiop/texte/2004-016a.htm.

Rocchietta, C. (2002), 'Keynote speech of C. Rocchietta, President of EBB', Asstra workshop, available in the archive of Staffetta Quotidiana, 15 June.
Rocchietta, C. (2014), 'Italian and European perspectives for the biofuel sector – Proceedings of Agroenergia'. workshop in Tortona, 13 February 2014.
Staffetta Quotidiana (2003a), *Accordo Assopetroli-Assobiodiesel*, 4 February.
Staffetta Quotidiana (2003b), *La UE si prepara al semestre di presidenza italiano*, 24 May.
Terna (2015), *Dati statistici sull'energia elettrica in Italia 2014*. www.terna.it.
Toke, D. (2008), 'The EU Renewables Directive – what is the fuss about trading?', *Energy Policy*, 36, 3001–3008.
Zerbinati, S. (2004), 'Europeanization and EU funding in Italy and England: a comparative local perspective', *Journal of European Public Policy*, 11 (6), 1000–1019.

Interview

Interview 1: Claudio Rocchietta, former CEO of NOVAOL and founder and first president of EBB. Telephone interviews: February 2014, January 2015.

8. Spain and renewable energy promotion: Europeanization upside down

Israel Solorio and Rosa Fernandez

8.1 INTRODUCTION

It is hard to speak about renewable energy sources (RES) in Spain without alluding to the role the European Union (EU) has played in its promotion at the national level, in the case of both RES for electricity (RES-E) and biofuels. Since its accession in 1986, Spain has benefited from EU regional funds, complementing the early attempts of RES promotion at the national level with European-funded development projects. The later liberalization of energy markets in the EU deeply impacted on the national energy policy, also affecting the perspectives for RES deployment. Both are examples of a top-down relationship between the EU and Spain. As the EU renewable energy policy was taking shape, though, Spain emerged as a decisive actor for the negotiations of the early legislation on the subject (the 2001 RES-E directive and the 2003 biofuels directive), uploading some elements of its policy while blocking others that would have represented considerable adaptation costs (that is, bottom-up Europeanization). However, many things have changed since then in Spain, affecting the conditions for RES development and, consequently, the Spanish position towards EU policy. On the one hand, Europeanization has notably influenced the domestic scenario, with mixed results in terms of policy change. On the other, economic crisis shifted the political priorities for the national government, with cutbacks greatly affecting the support for RES at the national level despite the EU's reinforced regulatory framework.

Once considered a European example of successful policies for RES promotion, post-crisis Spain is in the spotlight for having reversed its policy: slashing subsidies, radically changing the regulatory framework since 2008 and therefore affecting the investment environment. The dismantling of the national renewable energy policy reached such a degree that in 2015 the European Commission warned that the Spanish 'need to assess whether their policies and tools are sufficient and effective in meeting their renewable energy objectives' (COM, 2015a, p. 5). The negative performance of Spain in terms of the implementation of EU legislation might be seen as simply a collateral effect of the financial crisis, if not for the key influence that Europeanization had in this process, both in good times and in bad. To put it simply, Spain – and its renewable energy policy – is a case study representative of the complex interrelationship between the developments at the European and the national level, and the unanticipated outcomes of policy change and resistance that Europeanization produces in member states.

This chapter argues that, beyond the economic cycle, the explanation for the expansion and retrenchment of the Spanish renewable energy policy lies, importantly, in the interaction between European factors and the domestic scenario. Drawing on the Europeanization literature, it focuses on the following questions: how did Europeanization, in spite of the limited adaptational pressure, stimulate policy change at the national level? What has been the Spanish role in shaping the EU renewable energy policy, and how and why has this role changed over time? The remainder of this chapter is organized as follows. Section 8.2 further elaborates on the Europeanization framework. Particular attention is paid to explaining the Europeanization potential without a significant degree of misfit, and to the concept of 'circular Europeanization'. Section 8.3 presents the case of RES-E in Spain, while section 8.4 develops the case of biofuels. Section 8.5 carries out a comparative analysis on the Europeanization in both sectors, including the dynamics of policy change and resistance.

8.2 ANALYTICAL UNDERPINNINGS AND METHODS: EUROPEANIZATION AS A PROCESS

Europeanization literature is fundamentally about policy change (see Exadaktylos and Radaelli, 2012; Coman, 2014). But as Europeanization literature has reached its maturity, the understanding about the multiple paths in which policy change takes place has become more complex. The early trend of Europeanization studies put the focus on the EU's transformative power by means of the adaptational pressure placed on member states (Risse et al., 2001, p. 7), where the – top-down – Europeanization 'pressure is a function of the degree of fit (misfit) or congruence (incongruence) between "Europe" and the domestic level'

(Caporaso, 2007, p. 29). However, the empirical evidence suggested that misfit might not always occur, so Bulmer and Radaelli (2004, p. 9) argued that the 'goodness of fit' argument is 'valid only under certain conditions'; namely, when there is a presence of EU policy templates or models. The difference between approaches is not minor, considering that the less strict the policy is, the more space there is for domestic actors – as mediating factors or intervening variables – to influence the adaptation process.

Additionally, another debate emerged in parallel concerning national reactions to European integration (that is, bottom-up Europeanization). While early understandings defined bottom-up Europeanization as the part of the process where member states' negotiation strategies are designed to 'maximize the benefits and minimize the costs of European policies' (Börzel, 2002, p. 196), most recent arguments establish that 'Europeanization can only be a useful tool ... if it takes into account the effects of feedback stemming from domestic resistance to change' (Saurugger, 2014, p. 182). This critique has led to the notion of circular Europeanization, in which 'incremental Europeanization gives rise to contention which in turn can lead to actors demanding either increased or decreased supranational governance' (Coman, 2014, p. 3). This argument is in line with the notion of Europeanization as 'usage' (Woll and Jacquot, 2010; see Chapter 9 by Bocquillon and Evrad for its application to the French case), which places a stronger emphasis on the role of domestic actors and their reaction to EU policies.

Departing from this revisionist perspective concerning the feedback loops in the EU policymaking and considering that the different types of Europeanization posited in Chapter 1 (by Jörgens and Solorio) can occur within the circular Europeanization (that is, top-down, bottom-up and horizontal Europeanization), this chapter tracks the complex interrelationship between the developments at the European and the national level in Spain since the emergence of the 2001 RES-E directive and 2003 biofuels directive, until the negotiation and adoption of the 2030 RES targets. Given the Spanish forerunner position in RES promotion and the flexible nature of the EU renewable energy policy (see Chapter 2 by Solorio and Bocquillon), a particular analytical challenge for this chapter is to investigate how Europeanization was possible without the misfit element. It is for that reason that we pay particular attention to the alteration of domestic opportunity structures and the changes in the beliefs and expectations of domestic actors as potential explanatory factors for how the EU promoted policy change in Spain (see Knill and Lehmkuhl, 1999). In line with the circular Europeanization trend that focuses on 'how the norm developed at the EU level has been influenced by domestic debates, positions and power games between actors' (Saurugger, 2014, p. 184), a central aspect for this chapter is to explore whether Europeanization has facilitated the emergence of a 'winning coalition' supporting the introduction of new rules in favour of RES, or whether it has provoked the emergence of 'veto points' at the national level that have later reacted either in favour of or against more supranational governance in this policy area.

In methodological terms, this chapter adopts not a linear but circular approach to Europeanization. Hence, it looks at the 'European integration and its influence at the national level, which in turn influences European integration anew' (Saurugger, 2014, p. 184). The interdependence between X – representing the EU – and Y – representing the national level – adds its own complexity to the study of EU policymaking (Radaelli, 2012, p. 10), aggravated by the existence of domestic actors playing the role of intervening variables; both for the national adaptation to EU pressures and for shaping national positions during the negotiations at the EU level. This methodological complexity is tackled by means of a process tracing that allows us to gain a clearer picture of the causal path followed by Europeanization as a circular process of policy change and resistance. This longitudinal analysis is based on a research project carried out between 2008 and 2013 on the impact of the EU renewable energy policy on Spain. In the framework of this project, semi-structured interviews were conducted with civil servants, business representatives and environmental non-governmental organizations (ENGOs). The information gathered from those interviews was complemented with a document analysis from both primary and secondary sources, an inquiry that has been updated for the purpose of this chapter.

8.3 RES-E IN SPAIN: THE POWER OF BELIEF AND THE COUNTER-POWER OF VETO POINTS

8.3.1 Background

The Spanish renewable energy policy started in the early 1970s. By then Spain had a high level of dependence upon imported energy resources (Dinica and Bechberger, 2005, p. 264), and as a reaction to the 1970s oil crises, the Spanish government took specific steps towards the development of RES-E, mostly in the area of research and demonstration projects. The first piece of national legislation that considered a support scheme for RES-E was issued already in 1980, with law 82/1980 on energy conservation. The accession to the EU in 1986 allowed a flow of economic resources that strengthened the incipient Spanish policy renewable energy policy. This context facilitated a favourable starting point to Spain concerning RES promotion in comparison with other European countries (Reiche and Bechberger, 2004, p. 844). By 1990 the Spanish share of RES in gross inland consumption was already at 6.7 per cent, the seventh highest of the EU-15.

During the 1990s the domestic opportunity structure for RES promotion was importantly affected by the liberalization of the EU energy markets, which meant for Spain the adaptation of its electricity sector to the market rules. In this context, a special regime for RES-E production was defined, which was the basis for the Spanish Feed-In Tariffs (FITs) support scheme[1] in 1994 (Dinica and Bechberger, 2005, p. 263). By that time the EU renewable energy policy was in the making and Spain, as a European forerunner, was an influential actor during its formation (Interview 1). In 1994 the Spanish government hosted the 'Madrid Declaration', the initial step towards the White Paper as the landmark piece of the EU renewable energy policy (see Chapter 2 by Solorio and Bocquillon). But Spain also demonstrated that it was a pacesetter during the negotiations at the European level, pushing strongly for the 12 per cent of RES that was finally adopted in the White Paper – subsequently followed by the RES-E and biofuels directives – (Interview 2); and it was a 'good student' in the implementation of the European agreements. Soon after the launching of the RES White Paper (November 1997), Spain published a piece of legislation[2] that detailed issues such as the support scheme for RES-E, and the 1999 Plan for the Promotion of Renewable Energy picked up the 12 per cent RES objective by 2010 (Solorio, 2011, p. 111).

8.3.2 The First RES-E Directive: No Misfit, but Something Changed (2001–07)

During the negotiations of the 2001 RES-E directive, the Spanish role as pacesetter was hindered by the Commission's enthusiasm for the harmonization of national support schemes in the form of tradable certificates, according to the idea that this fitted better into the internal energy market. Together, Spain and Germany defended the member states' freedom to choose their own support system for RES-E (Interview 3). Their positions were backed by the success of their respective FITs in wind energy promotion (Meyer, 2003, p. 668). From then on, both countries engaged in a cooperation process that facilitated the diffusion of FITs across the EU (that is, horizontal Europeanization) (see also Chapter 3 by Vogelpohl et al. on the German case). Facing the opposition of two of the largest RES-E producers in the EU, the Commission called off the idea of harmonizing support schemes and favoured coordination instead (Rowlands, 2005, p. 971). With no relevant misfit in terms of support schemes, and having already adopted measures for further RES-E promotion, the 2001 RES-E directive meant no significant adaptational costs for Spain.

When the directive came into effect, most of the requirements included were already in place in the Spanish legislation. The first Spanish report on the implementation of this directive made reference to measures adopted back in 1997 and 1998. With no misfit having place, Europeanization came thanks to a change in the beliefs and expectations of domestic actors and to a favourable domestic opportunity structure that favored RES-E expansion. To start with, the 2001 directive further encouraged domestic support for RES-E. Governmental sources interviewed affirmed that the EU policy brought confidence and security to the Spanish market on the path being taken (Interview 4). The RES-E producers defined the change in such terms that, during the first years following the implementation of this directive, it was politically incorrect not to support RES (Interview 1). Europeanization changed the beliefs and expectations of domestic actors concerning RES-E, creating 'an atmosphere of enthusiasm' for investment (Dinica and Bechberger, 2005, p. 267). In this context, a coalition of national actors emerged supporting the changes promoted by Brussels, with RES producers and the ENGOs being particularly active.

The change in the beliefs and expectations of domestic actors came together with a domestic opportunity structure – already Europeanized thanks to the liberalization of energy markets and the flow of EU economic resources to Spain – that favoured RES-E expansion in Spain. Apart from the fact that RES-E production via the special regime linked to FITs maintained a rising trajectory, the growing electricity demand that at the time existed in Spain – a product of economic growth[3] – facilitated the entrance of RES-E into the market (Interview 3). RES-E took care of the deficit in electricity coverage in Spain without any opposition from traditional energy producers (Interview 5). The domestic opportunity structure, combined with the change in beliefs and expectations, was positive for RES-E expansion. This was demonstrated by the fact that even big electricity utilities diversified their investment portfolio, participating in RES-E development (Interview 6).

Progressively, RES-E expansion began altering the Spanish electricity market and, as a consequence, the domestic opportunity structure as well. Driven by grid management concerns about 'the impact of a relatively high (and increasing) share of wind generation on grid stability' (del Río,

2008, p. 2924), several elements of the Spanish FITs were modified in 2004 by means of a royal decree.[4] As Jacobs explains, the '2004 amendment established the dual remuneration system, comprising the fixed tariff payment option and the market sales option' (Jacobs, 2012, p. 79). The official position argued that this change was oriented towards a better fit of RES-E into the electricity market (Interview 3). RES-E producers considered it hasty to push producers under a special regime to compete in the market, under similar conditions, with production under the ordinary regime (APPA, 2004), but the fact is that RES-E continued its rising trajectory. In 2006 over 19 per cent of the electricity consumed in Spain came from RES. As RES-E expansion kept its pace, tensions within the Spanish electricity market started to emerge. In spite of the fact that by 2006 RES-E was still considered to be a strategic sector of the Spanish economy, it is fair to say that by then the implementation of the EU directive had started to raise contention. RES-E had been progressively displacing traditional sources of energy from the electricity mix, and competitors started looking at the advantages given to RES-E producers – the product of the RES-E directive implementation – with suspicion. Consensus over RES-E was over and, paradoxically, it was as a result of the changes brought by EU legislation (that is, top-down Europeanization). A new adjustment to the Spanish FITs was implemented in 2007 that, although it reaffirmed priority access to the grid for RES-E, also opened the door for a periodical revision of the tariffs received by producers under the special regime.[5]

8.3.3 The Renewed Directive and the RES-E Policy Collapse in Spain (2008–onwards)

In terms of Spanish interests, the negotiations of the renewable energy directive (RED), which was meant to replace the 2001 RES-E directive, started off on the wrong foot. From 2007, the pro-traders lobby – supporting a European scheme based on tradable certificates – started putting pressure on the European level (Nilsson et al., 2009, p. 4457). As a result, in early January 2008 the circulating versions of the proposal were favourable to this position (Toke, 2008, p. 3003). Again, Spain and Germany defended the FITs (EurActiv, 2008). In an attempt to accommodate the positions of both countries, a Commission proposal 'introduced an opt-out clause that would allow member states to not participate in the proposed … scheme' (Nilsson et al., 2009, p. 4458). In a letter sent to the former Energy Commissioner Piebalgs, the Spanish and German governments argued that '[a] European trading regime, even if combined with a temporary phasing-in or opt-out clause, is not acceptable' (EurActiv, 2008). Furthermore, the letter stated that the harmonization based on tradable certificates 'will put a very successful development of renewables at risk' (Taylor, 2008).

With two of the largest RES-E producers against harmonization of support systems, the 'Commission decided to give way in the face of such protests' (Toke, 2008, p. 3003). Once again, the final proposal excluded any sort of harmonization. Interestingly, in spite of having a domestic industry on the rise, the Spanish role during the negotiations was limited to protecting its own environment and hampering the adoption of a European scheme to support RES-E based on tradable certificates that would have meant significant adaptation costs (that is, a bottom-up Europeanization foot-dragging strategy). This defensive position can only be explained by considering the tensions that the implementation of the RES-E directive had provoked within the Spanish electricity market, which were aggravated with the economic crisis, forcing the Spanish government to change position towards RES-E at both the national and the European level.

With the economic crisis in 2007–08, electricity demand fell dramatically. As a result, RES-E gained a major share of the national electricity consumption thanks to the preferential access to the grid required by EU legislation. Conversely, the participation of nuclear, carbon, fuel gas, and gas via combined-cycle plants significantly decreased (REE, 2009, p. 10). This shift in the consumption patterns was perceived as a threat by the Spanish main electricity utilities, which still had vested interests in traditional sources of energy (Dunham, 2014). In response, the main Spanish electricity utilities such as Endesa and Gas Natural started blaming RES-E – and the FITs – for the tariff deficit,[6] using this argument to justify exorbitant increases in the price of electricity in a context where the crisis was hitting Spaniards hard (Andreu, 2014).

Electricity utilities adopted a 'veto' position against RES-E that, given its traditional tight links with the Spanish government, was translated into substantial changes in the national legislation. Making use of the arguments for the need to tackle the tariff deficit, and for the importance of giving stability to the electricity market, the national government gradually dismantled the Spanish renewable energy policy, resulting in the stagnation of the RES-E sector. First, in 2010 the government approved retroactive cutbacks to functioning RES-E plants, especially affecting the wind, solar thermoelectric and photovoltaic-based projects.[7] Later, in 2012, the government froze support to new RES-E plants, a measure that affected already functioning plants.[8] Amid the criticism from the RES sector, a reform of the electricity sector was approved in

2013 which critically affected the conditions for electricity production under the special regime. The general consensus from both RES-E producers and ENGOs was that the government's reform changed the rules of the game in favour of the big utilities and the traditional sources of energy (Greenpeace, 2013a).

With all the above-presented elements in mind, it is not a surprise that Spain did not push for ambitious RES goals during the negotiations of the 2030 EU climate and energy package in late 2014. Instead, together with Portugal, Spain pushed for 'a binding obligation for member states to make 15% of their national generation capacity available to other EU nations' (EurActiv, 2014), a proposal that was oriented towards selling the RES-E surplus to France. However, Spain and Portugal failed to become pacesetters in interconnection, and the most they obtained was a commitment that 'the Commission will take "urgent measures" to ensure at least 10% electricity connection capacity in those countries currently below that' (Van Renssen, 2014).

The latest stab at the once successful Spanish FITs was the royal decree 413/2014. The new austerity-driven economic regime, which also affected already functioning plants, changed the conditions under which investments were originally made and transformed the design of FITs: whereas formerly it was linked to the amount of electricity produced, the new support system depends on the installed plant's power capacity. Only this change in the rules of the game can explain the difficulties that the national RES-E industry faces in spite of the fact that in 2015 RES-E was the main contributor to the national electricity mix, with a 36.9 per cent share (REE, 2015). In fact, RES-E producers have argued that 'Spain is in danger of missing its 2020 renewable energy target because of its inadequate subsidy regime' (ENDS EUROPE, 2016). Against this background, compliance with the RED, and specifically with the national target of 20 per cent of RES for 2020, appears to be the only solution for RES-E producers to maintain the gains made. In fact, Spanish RES-E producers and ENGOs have been continually denouncing the dismantling of the Spanish renewable energy policy to the European Court of Justice and the European Commission. To top it all, in October 2015 Spain approved the royal decree 900/2015 – internationally known as the 'sun tax' – which regulates administrative, technical and economic conditions of energy supply for self-consumption and, among other things, prohibits the association of consumers, and charges for the support that the system provides to self-consumers/producers.

8.4 BIOFUELS IN SPAIN: THE DARKNESS OF A 'GREEN' POLICY

8.4.1 Spain as Pacesetter of the Biofuels Directive

Differently to the RES-E development, it is only possible to trace back national regulation for biofuels promotion in Spain to the late 1990s. In the framework of the liberalization of national energy markets, law 34/1998 was adopted in order to change the regulation of the hydrocarbons sector. Interestingly, this instrument not only established a definition of biofuels, but also set national targets for domestic consumption towards 2010. The Spanish commitment to biofuels promotion was stressed again two years later with the royal decree 6/2000, which created a commission for the study of biofuels use. Its report proposed a set of measures to support biofuels, including tax exemptions (APPA, 2005a, p. 55). In response, in 2002, Spain adopted a total tax exemption for biofuels, valid until the end of 2012.

Even without the same years of experience promoting biofuels as other European forerunners (see Chapter 3 by Vogelpohl et al. on Germany, and Chapter 9 by Bocquillon and Evrard on France), Spain again appeared during the negotiations of the 2003 biofuels directive as a pacesetter (that is, bottom-up Europeanization). To start with, Spain played a crucial role in maintaining the medium-term target of biofuels for 2010 included within the directive, which was opposed by some member states (Interview 2). But most important were the negotiation skills displayed during the Spanish presidency of the Council in the first semester of 2002. As part of the bloc of member states having past experience in using partial or total exemptions from fuel taxes for biofuels promotion (Wiesenthal et al., 2009, p. 793), achieving the adoption of the biofuels taxation directive was part of the Spanish presidency's objectives (Maldonado García-Verdugo, 2002, p. 9). Indeed, the political agreement over the energy taxation directive – including biofuels taxation – was reached in Madrid during the Economic and Financial Affairs Council (ECOFIN) of June 2002 thanks to Spain's brokering skills (ICE, 2002). However, this directive was enacted in 2003 at the same time as the biofuels directive. Wiesenthal et al. explained Spain's adopted role in terms of the mix between 'high interest in consumption with a high potential for feedstock production' (Wiesenthal et al., 2009, p. 793).

It was probably unintended, but Spanish experience in biofuels promotion was also a driver behind the diffusion of tax exemptions across

Europe (that is, horizontal Europeanization). Following the adoption of the biofuels directive between 2004 and 2006, tax exemptions were introduced in several member states as an instrument to comply with the targets set by the directive (see Chapter 3 by Vogelpohl et al. on Germany). Considering that member states 'with a high penetration of biofuels have, or have had, a favourable tax regime in place, e.g. Germany (until the end of 2006), France, Sweden, and Spain' (Wiesenthal et al., 2009, p. 794), the Spanish role in this process should not be underestimated.

Given Spain's forerunner position in biofuels promotion and the Spanish influence during the negotiation phase, the EU biofuels directive produced a limited adaptational pressure at the domestic level (Solorio and Popartan, 2014, p. 133). An institutional inertia followed the first years of the directive's implementation in Spain. To give an example, the first implementation report presented the tax exemption adopted back in 2002 as one of the main instruments for pursuing the biofuels target. Interestingly, differently to the biofuels definition included within the European legislation, royal decree 1700/2003 transposing both biofuels directives considered only bioethanol and biodiesel for the purpose of biofuels promotion (APPA, 2005a, p. 58). No major changes were presented during the first years of implementation of this directive in Spain. It was not until 2006 that Spain regulated the use of biofuels by means of royal decree 61/2006, which established the 5.75 per cent objective for the commercialization of biofuels to be achieved by 2010, and established the blending limits (maximum 5 per cent for bioethanol, and specific labelling for cases where bioethanol composition exceeded 5 per cent of the mixture). Strikingly, it was not until 2006 that Spain was notified by the European Commission that the existing tax exemption was compatible with the EU state aid rules (COM, 2006a, p. 7).

In 2000 there were no functioning biofuels plants in the national territory, but by 2004 Spain was already a leader in bioethanol production, also with positive results in biodiesel (Shnepf, 2006). While these figures illustrate the impact of the EU biofuels policy in Spain, it has to be said that by 2005 national biofuels consumption barely reached 1 per cent of the total fuel consumption, failing to reach the 2 per cent interim target contemplated in the directive (APPA, 2005a, p. 38). As a result, the main demand from biofuels producers was to have a national plan for biofuels consumption in order to achieve the 5.75 per cent objective by 2010 (APPA, 2005b). This demand for a national plan promoting consumption by domestic biofuel producers also derived from the pressure they were under because of the fact that until 2006 oil companies and car producers did not show an interest in biofuels and, as a result, 'most of the national production was exported' (Di Lucia and Kronsell, 2010, p. 557). Additionally, since the implementation of the biofuels directive there has been a growing gap between domestic production and consumption, which was only aggravated by the fact that the pressure triggered by Europeanization opened the Spanish market for imported biofuels. Given that most of the third-country producers were already being subsidized at home, Spanish biofuels producers were facing unfair competition from outside the EU.

As a result, after years of institutional inertia and a lack of visible reactions from national actors that characterized the first years of implementation of the biofuels directive, this policy became more politicized and contested. On the one hand, the growth of the national biofuels industry, together with the prospect of a stronger regulatory EU framework, forced oil companies and car producers to get involved in this policy. At the same time, ENGOs started raising concerns about the sustainability of first-generation biofuels. On the other, the national biofuels industry, making use of the need to comply with EU targets, started pressing for a stronger national policy for biofuels promotion. Europeanization gave rise to contention – especially from ENGOs, but also from oil producers – while at the same time improving the domestic opportunity structure for the emergence of a national biofuels industry that, some years before, had been difficult to imagine.

8.4.2 Policy Change and Policy Resistance in Biofuels Policy (2007–onwards)

In 2006, the European Commission launched the EU Strategy for Biofuels, proposing the use of biofuel obligations and encouraging 'Member States to give favourable treatment to second-generation biofuels in biofuels obligations' (COM, 2006b, p. 7). Given the European Commission's push, considering the need to boost national biofuel consumption and having in mind the opposition of the oil operators, Spanish biofuel producers urged the national government to approve a quota for biofuels of no less than 5.83 per cent by 2010 (APPA, 2007). In spite of the fact that the Industry Ministry presented the draft bill in July 2007, it took until October 2008 for it to be enacted. After more than one year of complaints from the biofuels industry, Spain adopted a quota for biofuels which significantly changed the rules of the game for biofuels promotion.

In general terms, order ITC/2877/2008 brought the Spanish biofuels policy closer to the European guidelines. Not only did it mean the establishment of a biofuels quota as proposed by the European Commission two years earlier, but it also broadened the definition of biofuels exactly in line with the EU directive (including, for example, biogas and biomethanol). The mandatory targets were in line with the biofuels industry demand: 1.9 per cent by 2008, 3.4 per cent by 2009, and 5.83 per cent by 2010. Importantly, the target referred to market quotas, establishing the energy content for each type of biofuel. While the national biofuels industry declared itself ready to contribute to reaching these targets, it also warned against the fact that unfair competition from outside the EU might jeopardize the benefits of the obligation (*Renewable Energy Magazine*, 2008). In fact, the first report on the implementation of the biofuels quota showed uneven results for the national industry (CNE, 2011). In 2009 the national production of biodiesel covered 69.12 per cent of the domestic consumption, compared to 12.48 per cent that came from Argentina; and the domestic production of bioethanol supplied 67.24 per cent of the domestic consumption, compared to 18.24 per cent produced in Brazil and 6.55 per cent from France. To put these figures into perspective, in 2009 the annual sales of biodiesel were 79.63 per cent of the total commercialized biofuel (1,169,626 m^3), compared to 20.37 per cent represented by bioethanol sales (299,158 m^3). However, in terms of raw materials the figures were not that positive for national producers.

With a growing biofuels market, the Spanish ENGOs became more actively involved in campaigns against first-generation biofuels. The interviews with ENGOs' members confirmed their opposition to this policy. For example, a Friends of the Earth Spain campaigner argued that biomass is not the only renewable source of energy that can be used in the transport sector (Interview 7), while a Greenpeace biofuels campaign representative raised the issue of the traceability of feedstocks (Interview 8). The more the national biofuels policy became Europeanized, the more resistance it found in environmental groups; too much for a policy that was meant to alleviate climate change and procure environmental protection. In this regard, the 2009 renewed directive[9] brought to Spain sustainability elements that precisely attempted to tackle the concerns raised by the ENGOs. In 2011, two years after the adoption of the RED, Spain adopted royal decree 1597/2011 that regulated the sustainability criteria of biofuels and the double-counting for certain biofuels. Nevertheless, Spanish ENGOs have continued campaigning against biofuels and have warned that Spain might emit up to 9 million tonnes of carbon dioxide (CO_2) in meeting the 2020 objectives for RES in the transport sector, considering the indirect land use change (ILUC) (Bowyer, 2011). As a matter of fact, Spanish ENGOs had pronounced against the specific target for RES in the transport sector since the negotiations of the RED, under the consideration that Spain was not in a position to meet this target in a sustainable way (Greenpeace, 2008). Their estimation is that Spain will increase biofuel consumption from 2008 to 2020 to 2635 kilotonnes of oil equivalent (ktoe) – 255 ktoe in bioethanol usage and 2380 ktoe in biodiesel (Bowyer, 2011, p. 11).

Despite this resistance, ENGOs have not been the main obstacle that the national biofuels industry has faced, as complexities related to the fuels market also became important. In 2010 a dramatic increase in biofuels imports was reported in Spain, with only 54.56 of the national consumption produced domestically. In response, the domestic biofuels industry began pressing for measures to protect national biofuels from the non-EU unfair competition. In 2012, order IET/822/2012 was adopted governing the allocation of biodiesel production, a measure understood as a way to establish limits to imports. Nevertheless, in order to avoid a penalty from the World Trade Organization (WTO), Spain modified this with ministerial order OM/IET/2736/2012, eliminating the prohibition of non-EU biodiesel. Another demand from the national biofuels industry was the transposition of the fuel quality directive (FQD), representing a substantial change in the blend limits for biofuels (for biodiesel, incrementing the maximum limit to 7 per cent of the mixture; and 10 per cent for bioethanol) (APPA, 2010). This option faced strong resistance from the automobile sector under technical considerations; at the same time, the oil industry blamed the car fleet in Spain as the main obstacle to increasing national biofuels demand (EuropaPress, 2010). In the end, however, the transposition of the FQD in Spain meant the increase of blending limits as demanded by the domestic biofuels industry.[10]

Coupled with the debates about the future of the EU biofuels policy (see Chapter 2 by Solorio and Bocquillon), the Spanish biofuels policy has also faced a dismantling process, although not as deep as in the case of RES-E. With the crisis hitting the Spanish economy hard, the Spanish government reduced the biofuels targets for 2013 from 6.5 to 4.1 per cent. For the Spanish biofuels industry, this equated to the death of the sector, considering the non-EU unfair competition that domestic producers had been dealing with for years (*El Pais*, 2012). Additionally, given that the total tax exemption for biofuels was valid only until the end of 2012, the taxation system was reformed, maintaining a special treatment for biofuels but eliminating the total tax exemption.[11] Last but not least, in 2015 the Spanish government significantly reformed the national biofuels policy by means of royal decree 1085/2015, changing the mid-term targets again (5 per cent for 2017, 6 per cent for 2018, 7 per cent for 2019, and 8.5 per cent for 2020), excluding the differentiated targets for biodiesel and bioethanol that had been implemented since 2008, and modifying the implementation of the sustainability criteria in order to favour first-generation biofuels.

The Spanish government's enthusiasm for biofuels has been motivated by the important need to give a push to the agricultural sector and boost new industries. In that sense, Spain has used the EU biofuels policy in order to protect the national interest, becoming at times a pacesetter at the European level. However, as the EU policy shifted toward a more sustainable path for biofuels promotion, Spain appeared as an environmental laggard. For example, in December 2013 during the negotiations of the EU biofuels policy reform, Spain promoted the least restrictive cap on the amount of first-generation biofuels – together with Poland, Hungary, Slovakia, Romania and the Czech Republic – pushing for a limit of 8 per cent, or even to remove any limits on land-based biofuels (Greenpeace, 2013b). Likewise, in 2015 Spain was formally asked to ensure the correct implementation of the RED. The Commission drew attention to the fact that, contrary to what is foreseen by the directive, 'Spanish law suspends the application of sustainability criteria in Spain for the achievement of the target in transport' (COM, 2015b).[12] In fact, the EurObserver 2015 report on biofuels consumption in the EU, in spite of placing Spain as the fifth-largest European consumer (below only France, Germany, the United Kingdom and Italy), posits Spain's failure to implement the legal framework to certify its biofuel consumption as its main challenge to meet the RED objectives for 2020 (EurObserv'ER, 2015, p. 7).

8.5 COMPARATIVE ANALYSIS AND CONCLUDING REMARKS

The Spanish case is illustrative of how Europeanization can actually produce changes at the domestic level without the existence of the misfit factor. In the case of RES-E, the change in the beliefs and expectations of domestic actors produced by Europeanization is fundamental for understanding the emergence of Spain as a European champion in RES-E production. In this context, the role of the alteration of the domestic opportunity produced by Europeanization seems at first glance comparatively minor. However, to understand the size of the impact of this second Europeanization mechanism one should consider that it was Europeanized even before the arrival of the RES-E directive, thanks to related EU policies such as the liberalization of the energy markets and the regional policy. Together, the change in the beliefs and expectations of domestic actors and the altered domestic opportunity structures explain the early impact of Europeanization in favour of RES-E production in Spain between approximately 2001 and 2007. On the other hand, the biofuels case shows a major role of the alteration of domestic opportunity structures as a Europeanization mechanism in the emergence of the national biofuels industry. In fact, the need to comply with the EU targets in this sector has been constantly used by the national industry as a bargaining leverage to obtain favourable regulatory changes. However, it has to be said that, given the nature of the fuels market, the misfit has been more present in this last case (for example with the changes produced by the FQD in the blending limits for fuels).

In spite of their different starting points, RES-E and biofuels have arrived at the same stagnation point in Spain, mainly due to the opposition to full implementation of EU regulations by domestic lobby groups, limiting the results of the top-down Europeanization process. While in both cases Europeanization has given rise to contention (that is, Europeanization upside-down), the main difference is that for the RES-E case the veto power that emerged (that is, electricity utilities) has been powerful enough to push the national government to limit the transformation of the Spanish electricity market by means of dismantling the national FIT scheme. This change in the position of the national government towards RES-E has been contested by RES-E producers and ENGOs, which have kept pressing for more supranational governance in order to boost a renewables-based energy transition in Spain. On the contrary, the opposition to the EU biofuels policy has been more diverse (including actors such as ENGOs, oil producers and the automobile industry) and, consequently, less effective to take down the national policy of biofuels promotion. However, the economic crisis together with the failure in the design of the EU biofuels policy has pushed this sector as well to a stagnation point.

Overall, the use of the concept of circular Europeanization has allowed us to reach important theoretical and empirical conclusions. In this way, looking at the effects of top-down Europeanization (stemming from policy change to resistance) has been fundamental for understanding the changing national attitude towards the EU renewable energy policy during the subsequent European negotiations. This calls for not only paying attention to the entire – Europeanization – policy cycle in order to understand the dynamics of policy change and resistance, but also taking a closer look at the role of domestic actors as intervening variables, both for the national adaptation to EU pressures and for shaping national positions during the negotiations at the EU level. On the empirical side, this comparative exercise has demonstrated that, despite the fact that both policies – RES-E and biofuels – are part of the EU renewable energy policy, their reception as environmental policies has been radically different. This has meant that, while for RES-E promotion the coalition between producers and ENGOs has been central to contest the dismantling of the national FIT scheme, ENGOs have been one of the main opponents to the deployment of first-generation biofuels in Spain. Notably, this apparently contradictory reaction from national actors points to the problems of the EU renewable energy policy design.

NOTES

1. The Special Regime was adopted through law 40/1994 on the planning of the national electrical system (commonly known as the 'LOSEN Law') and further explained by means of royal decree 2366/1994.
2. Law 54/1997 on the electricity sector.
3. The continuous increase in energy consumption linked to economic activity and growth is in itself an indication of the failure to decouple energy consumption from economic activity, with very limited progress on energy intensity.
4. Royal decree 436/2004.
5. Royal decree 661/2007 regulating the production activity under the special regime.
6. The tariff deficit is the imbalance between regulated costs and revenues of the electricity system. It began accumulating in 2001, reaching €26 billion in 2012, and a record €29 billion in 2013.
7. These measures included: royal decree 1565/2010 regulating and modifying certain aspects related to the production of RES-E based on the special regime, royal decree 1614/2010 establishing cutbacks to wind and solar thermoelectric energy, and law 14/2010 establishing urgent measures to correct the tariff deficit, applying retroactive cutbacks to functioning photovoltaic plants.
8. See royal decree/law 1/2012 which suspended the retribution to new RES-E plants under the special regime.
9. The 10 per cent of RES in the transport sector was incorporated in the national legislation by means of law 2/2012 2020 for a sustainable economy.
10. The transposition of the FQD was made in September 2010 by means of royal decree 1088/2010.
11. See law 15/2012 on fiscal measures for energy sustainability.
12. The Commission also referred to the fact that the Spanish law treats sustainable biofuels and raw materials of different geographical origins differently, in an unjustified manner.

REFERENCES

Andreu, J. (2014), 'The shocking price of Spanish electricity', *El País*, 1 January, accessed on 17 November 2014 at http://elpais.com/elpais/2014/01/01/inenglish/1388590410_230748.html.

APPA (2004), 'APPA ante el nuevo Decreto de Retribución del Régimen Especial', 31 March, accessed on 15 July 2016 at http://www.appa.es/descargas/prensa/notasprensa/11notasb-10.htm.

APPA (2005a), 'Una Estrategia de Biocarburantes para España (2005–2010)', June, accessed on 15 July 2016 at http://www.appa.es/descargas/Estrategia_Biocarbur_APPA.pdf.

APPA (2005b), 'La producción de combustibles limpios sólo llegará al 0,8%, según un estudio de APPA', 17 March, accessed on 15 July 2016 at http://appa.es/descargas/prensa/notasprensa/11notasa-3.htm.

APPA (2007), 'APPA reclama al Gobierno la aprobación urgente de las obligaciones separadas e idénticas de uso del bioetanol y del biodiésel ya previstas en el proyecto de Orden Ministerial', 27 December, accessed on 15 July 2016 at http://www.appa.es/descargas/prensa/NotaprensaAPPAOrdenoblibioCarburantes_dic%2007.pdf.

APPA (2010), 'El 75% de las plantas españolas de biodiésel están paradas, mientras una avalancha de importaciones argentinas inunda el mercado', 8 July, accessed on 15 July 2016 at http://www.appa.es/descargas/Biocarburantes-Situacion_Biocarburantes_Espana-Julio2010.pdf.

Bowyer, C. (2011), 'Anticipated indirect land use change associated with expanded use of biofuels and bioliquids in the EU', Institute for European Environmental Policy, March, accessed on 15 July 2016 at http://www.foeeurope.org/sites/default/files/publications/iluc_report_november20101.pdf.

Börzel, T.A. (2002), 'Member State responses to Europeanization', *JCMS: Journal of Common Market Studies*, 40 (2), 193–214.

Bulmer, S. and C. Radaelli (2004), 'The Europeanization of national policy?', *Queen's Papers on Europeanization,* 1/2004, accessed July 2016 at http://www.ceses.cuni.cz/CESES-141-version1-2_2__Radaelli_europeanization_of_national_policy.pdf.

Caporaso, J. (2007), 'The three worlds of regional integration theory', in P. Graziano and M.P. Vink (eds), *Europeanization: New Research Agendas*, New York: Palgrave Macmillan, pp. 23–34.

CNE (2011), 'Informe anual sobre el uso de biocarburantes correspondiente al ejercicio 2009', 3 February, accessed on 15 July 2016 at https://www.cnmc.es/Portals/0/Ficheros/Energia/Informes/PA012_09.pdf.

COM (2006a), 'Exención del impuesto especial sobre los biocarburantes' accessed on 15 July 2016 at http://ec.europa.eu/competition/state_aid/cases/172365/172365_583304_39_2.pdf.

COM (2006b), 'An EU strategy for biofuels', accessed on 15 July 2016 at http://eur-lex.europa.eu/legal-content/EN/TXT/PDF/?uri=CELEX:52006DC0034&from=ES.

COM (2015a), 'Renewable energy progress report', accessed on 15 July 2016 at http://eur-lex.europa.eu/resource.html?uri=cellar:4f8722ce-1347-11e5-8817-01aa75ed71a1.0001.02/DOC_1&format=PDF.

COM (2015b), 'March 2015: Energy: SPAIN asked to correctly apply the Renewable Energy Directive', accessed on 15 July 2015 at https://ec.europa.eu/energy/en/march-2015-energy-spain-asked-correctly-apply-renewable-energy-directive.

Coman, R. (2014), '*Concordia Discors* from cumulative Europeanization to deeper integration', in R. Coman, T. Kostera and L. Tomini (eds), *Europeanization and European Integration. From Incremental to Structural Change*, Basingstoke: Palgrave Macmillan, pp. 1–11.

Del Río, P. (2008), 'Ten years of renewable electricity policies in Spain: an analysis of successive feed-in tariff reforms', *Energy Policy*, 36 (8), 2917–2929.

Di Lucia, L. and A. Kronsell (2010), 'The willing, the unwilling and the unable – explaining implementation of the EU Biofuels Directive', *Journal of European Public Policy*, 17 (4), 545–563.

Dinica, V. and M. Bechberger (2005), 'Renewable energy policies in Spain', in D. Reiche (ed.), *Handbook of Renewable Energy Policies in the European Union – Case Studies of All Member States*, Frankfurt am Main: Peter Lang Publishing Group, pp. 263–277.

Dunham, A. (2014), 'Energy giants out to kill off Spain's solar sector', *Local*, 21 March, accessed on 17 November 2014 at http://www.thelocal.es/20140321/sun-tax-talk.

El País (2012), 'La producción nacional de biodiésel se desploma', 22 March, accessed on 15 July 2016 at http://elpais.com/elpais/2012/03/20/motor/1332246036_957442.html.

ENDS EUROPE (2016), 'Wind industry slams new Spanish system', 21 January, accessed on 15 March 2016 at http://www.endseurope.com/article/45005/wind-industry-slams-new-spanish-system.

EurActiv (2008), 'Industry, governments criticise renewables trading plan', 16 January, accessed on 15 July 2016 at http://www.euractiv.com/section/sustainable-dev/news/industry-governments-criticise-renewables-trading-plan/.

EurActiv (2014), 'EU leaders adopt "flexible" energy and climate targets for 2030', 24 October, accessed on 15 July 2016 at http://www.euractiv.com/section/sustainable-dev/news/eu-leaders-adopt-flexible-energy-and-climate-targets-for-2030/.

EurObserv'ER (2015), *Biofuels Barometer*, accessed on 15 July 2016 at http://www.eurobserv-er.org/biofuels-barometer-2015/.

EuropaPress (2010), 'La industria petrolera advierte de la imposibilidad de cumplir los objetivos de biocarburantes de APPA', 28 September, accessed on 15 July 2016 at http://www.europapress.es/economia/energia-00341/noticia-economia-energia-industria-petrolera-advierte-imposibilidad-cumplir-objetivos-biocarburantes-appa-20100928113542.html.

Exadaktylos, T. and C. Radaelli (2012), *Research Design in European Studies: Establishing Causality in Europeanization*, Basingstoke: Palgrave Macmillan.

Greenpeace (2008), 'Posición de Greenpeace sobre los criterios de sostenibilidad de los biocombustibles', accessed on 15 July 2016 at http://www.greenpeace.org/espana/Global/espana/report/other/posici-n-de-greenpeace-sobre-b.pdf.

Greenpeace (2013a), 'Iberdrola, empresa enemiga de las renovables', accessed on 15 July 2016 at http://www.greenpeace.org/espana/Global/espana/report/cambio_climatico/Iberdrola%20empresa%20enemiga%20de%20las%20renovables.pdf.

Greenpeace (2013b), 'Biofuels: EU energy ministers must choose right path for the world's climate & food security', accessed on 15 July 2016 at http://www.greenpeace.org/eu-unit/Global/eu-unit/reports-briefings/2013/20131209%20Joint%20NGO%20Biofuels%20Media%20Advisory.pdf.

ICE (2002), 'Balance Económico de la Presidencia Española de la Union Europea', accessed on 15 July 2016 at http://www.revistasice.com/CachePDF/BICE_2736_03-37__F5B84BF22693B667CCD805975D4A282C.pdf.

Jacobs, D. (2012), *Renewable Energy Policy Convergence in the EU*, Farnham: Ashgate.

Knill, C. and D. Lehmkuhl (1999), 'How Europe matters: different mechanisms of Europeanization', *European Integration online Papers* (*EIoP*), 3 (7), accessed on 15 July 2016 at http://eiop.or.at/eiop/texte/1999-007a.htm.

Maldonado García-Verdugo, Ascensión (2002), 'Memoria de la Presidencia Española de la Unión Europea', accessed on 15 July 2016 at http://www.ief.es/documentos/recursos/publicaciones/revistas/cron_trib/articulo_105_documentos UE.pdf.

Meyer, N.I. (2003), 'European schemes for promoting renewables in liberalized markets', *Energy Policy*, 31 (7), 665–676.

Nilsson, M., L.J. Nilsson and K. Ericsson (2009), 'The rise and fall of GO trading in European renewable energy policy: the role of advocacy and policy framing', *Energy Policy*, 37 (11), 4454–4462.

Radaelli, C. (2012), 'Europeanization: the challenge of establishing causality', in T. Exadaktylos and C. Radaelli (eds), *Research Design in European Studies: Establishing Causality in Europeanization*, Basingstoke: Palgrave Macmillan, pp. 1–16.

REE (2009), 'El Sistema eléctrico español 2009', accessed on 15 July 2016 at http://ree.es/sites/default/files/downloadable/inf_sis_elec_ree_2009.pdf.

REE (2015), 'El Sistema eléctrico español 2015', accessed on 15 July 2016 at http://www.ree.es/sites/default/files/downloadable/inf_sis_elec_ree_2015.pdf.

Reiche, D. and M. Bechberger (2004), 'Policy differences in the promotion of renewable energies in the EU member states', *Energy Policy*, 32 (7), 843–849.

Renewable Energy Mazagine (2008), 'La aprobación definitiva de la obligación de biocarburantes satisface al sector', accessed on 15 July 2016 at http://www.renewableenergymagazine.com/article/la-aprobacion-definitiva-de-la-obligacion-de.

Risse, T., M.G. Cowles and J. Caporaso (2001), 'Europeanization and domestic change: introduction', in M.G. Cowles, J. Caporaso and T. Risse (eds), *Transforming Europe: Europeanization and Domestic Change*, Ithaca, NY: Cornell University Press, pp. 1–20.

Rowlands, I.H. (2005), 'The European directive on renewable electricity: conflicts and compromises', *Energy Policy*, 33 (8), 965–974.

Saurugger, S. (2014), 'Europeanisation in times of crisis', *Political Studies Review*, 12 (2), 181–192.

Schnepf, R. (2006), 'European Union biofuels policy and agriculture: an overview', CRS Report for Congress, accessed on 15 July 2016 at research.policyarchive.org/4344.pdf.

Solorio, I. (2011), 'La europeización de la política energética en España: ¿qué sendero para las renovables?', *Revista Española de Ciencia Política*, 26, 105–123.

Solorio, I. and L. Popartan (2014), 'The implementation of the EU biofuels policy in Spain and the UK: a case of contested Europeanization', *Biofuels*, 5 (2), 129–140.

Taylor, P. (2008), 'Germany and Spain warn EU on renewables plan', Reuters, 15 January, accessed on 15 July 2016 at http://www.reuters.com/article/environment-energy-eu-renewables-dc-idUSL1513207220080115.
Toke, D. (2008), 'The EU Renewable Directive – what is the fuss about trading?', *Energy Policy*, 36 (8), 3001–3008.
Van Renssen, S. (2014), 'The EU's great 2030 energy and climate compromise', *Energy Post*, 24 October, accessed on 15 July 2016 at http://www.energypost.eu/eus-great-2030-energy-climate-compromise/.
Wiesenthal T., G. Leduc, P. Christidis, B. Schade, L. Pelkmans, L. Govaerts and P. Georgepoulos (2009), 'Biofuel support policies in Europe: lessons learnt for the long way ahead', *Renewable and Sustainable Energy Reviews*, 13 (4), 789–800.
Woll, C. and S. Jacquot (2010), 'Using Europe: strategic action in multi-level politics', *Comparative European Politics*, 8 (1), 110–126.

Interviews

Interview 1, with a founding member of a Spanish renewable energy association (APPA), July 2010, Madrid.
Interview 2, with a representative of a Spanish renewable energy association (APPA), July 2010, Madrid.
Interview 3, with a Spanish official, National Energy Commission, July 2010, Madrid.
Interview 4, with a Spanish official, State Secretariat for Climate Change, July 2010, Madrid.
Interview 5, with a representative of a Spanish coal industry association (Carbunion), July 2010, Madrid.
Interview 6, with the director of the Spanish Energy Club, July 2010, Madrid.
Interview 7, with a Friends of the Earth Spain campaigner, July 2010, Madrid.
Interview 8, with a Greenpeace Spain campaigner, July 2010, Madrid.

9. Complying with, resisting or using Europe? Explaining the uneven and diffuse Europeanization of French renewable electricity and biofuels policies

Pierre Bocquillon and Aurélien Evrard

9.1 INTRODUCTION

Despite a considerable potential and the establishment of a Feed-In Tariffs (FITs) system in 2000, France has failed to stimulate the large-scale deployment of renewable energy sources for electricity (RES-E). It has tended to follow rather than trigger European developments and its implementation record appears rather mixed. The promotion of biofuels has been more successful, especially following the adoption of a biofuels obligation in 2005, but was largely motivated by domestic concerns over agriculture rather than European commitments. Overall, the role of European factors in the development of French renewable energy policy looks blurry, to say the least. At the European level, the ambiguous attitude of France on RES-E, which has alternated between foot-dragging and occasional leadership, mirrors internal divisions and hesitations. On biofuels, the country has acted more consistently as a pusher however.

In the academic literature, there is a shortage of in-depth research analysing French renewable energy policy, especially in comparison with other more advanced member states such as Denmark, Germany or Spain (but see Evrard, 2013; Szarka, 2007a). Studies looking at the growing impact of European processes on French renewable energy policy are especially lacking. To fill this gap, this chapter applies the conceptualization of Europeanization presented in Chapter 1 to the French case, with the aim of disentangling the role of European and national factors in the development of new measures such as the FIT system and biofuels obligation. The chapter also strives to specify the country's role in shaping European Union (EU) renewable energy policy. Finally, this research aims to explain both the differential impact of European dynamics, as well as the uneven influence of France in the fields of biofuels promotion and RES-E at the EU level.

The next section briefly presents the framework of the chapter, which, building on the mechanisms of Europeanization identified in Chapter 1, introduces an actor-centred sociological approach to the practices and 'usages of Europe'. Sections 9.3 and 9.4 present in turn the two sub-case studies on RES-E and biofuels promotion. Applying – and reflecting upon – our theoretical framework, the last section compares the two cases and draws some general conclusions.

9.2 ANALYTICAL UNDERPINNING AND METHODS: AN ACTOR-CENTRED SOCIOLOGICAL APPROACH TO EUROPEANIZATION

Three particular models of Europeanization are the focus of this book: the 'top-down', the 'bottom-up' and the 'horizontal' models. The first emphasizes adaptational pressures generated by the EU; the second focuses on member states' ability to shape European policies; and the third stresses diffusion processes, policy transfer and mutual adjustments between member states (see Chapter 1 by Jörgens and Solorio). These three routes to Europeanization should be regarded as complementary. Participation in European processes – through negotiations or through the implementation of European laws – can for instance stimulate exchange of ideas between national actors, and foster international comparisons and imports of best practices across borders, thus contributing to horizontal Europeanization. Reciprocally, convergence between member states facilitates agreement at the European level and reinforces adaptational pressures.

The Europeanization literature, in both its vertical and horizontal versions, tends to overemphasize structural aspects – economic structures, institutions, ideas – at the risk of losing sight of the actors' role. In the top-down model of Europeanization, domestic actors often come into play as mere 'mediating factors' or 'intermediary variables', and often with little distinction between different types of actors. Similarly, the transfer and diffusion literature emphasizes institutional isomorphisms (see Chapter 1 by Jörgens and Solorio), but tends to overlook the role of actors' strategies and responses. Conversely, we assume that focusing on actors' behaviours and strategies, be they individual or collective, helps the analysis not only of the direct impact of the EU but also of processes of adaptation, mutual adjustment and avoidance. Domestic actors implement, resist and sometimes subvert European constraints. They are not only passive receivers of European norms; they can also use them as resources for their own purposes.

Especially useful in this perspective is an approach in terms of 'usages of Europe' (Woll and Jacquot, 2010). This actor-centred approach to Europeanization helps to shift the emphasis towards mechanisms of appropriation of European processes. Actors can use Europe in varied ways, sometimes contradictory, depending on their preferences, values and strategies. Woll and Jacquot distinguish between three different usages. The 'strategic usage' refers to the direct use of EU legal, institutional and budgetary resources to achieve certain purposely defined goals. The 'legitimating usage' of Europe corresponds to the use of European arguments and narratives to justify certain positions and measures. Finally, the 'cognitive usage' represents the use of European referents to frame and debate certain issues at the national level. While the legitimating usage is essentially instrumental and motivated by individual gains, the cognitive usage is more oriented towards problem-solving and deliberation. Focusing on actors and their usages is especially useful to complement the 'three routes' approach since it can help us to specify the interplay between top-down, bottom-up and horizontal dynamics.

The empirical part of this chapter is based on two complementary research projects. The first one, conducted between 2005 and 2010, looks at French renewable energy policy in a comparative perspective (Evrard, 2013). The second one, started in 2010, focuses on European energy and climate change policymaking and the role of France therein. By bringing together these two research projects, we aim to shed light on the interplay between the national and European levels, over an extended period of time of nearly ten years. Both studies rely on qualitative research designs, comparative case studies and process tracing. In the framework of these two projects, as well as more specifically for this chapter, semi-structured interviews were conducted with civil servants, business representatives and non-governmental organization (NGO) executives in both France and Brussels. These interviews, complementing document analysis, enabled us to better grasp the perceptions, motivations and influence of the different actors involved in the French renewable energy sector.

9.3 PROMOTING RENEWABLES IN A NUCLEARIZED ENERGY SYSTEM: THE EUROPEANIZATION OF RES-E POLICY

The French attitude towards RES-E promotion represents a paradox. The country enjoys very favourable geographical conditions and its potential is one of the best in Europe for the production of wind and solar power (Reiche and Bechberger, 2004). However, as regards the deployment of RES-E compared with other EU member states, France has often been considered a laggard. This reflects its difficulty in implementing strong support policies and in catching up with European pioneers. In 2015, 76 per cent of the country's total electricity production came from nuclear energy (RTE, 2016, p. 13); only 19 per cent came from renewable energy sources (RES), mainly from large hydropower (11 per cent) and wind power (4 per cent). Moreover, the share of RES-E has remained stable overall for the past quarter-century. This situation contrasts with the rapid development of RES-E generation in other countries such as Denmark, Germany or Spain in the same period.

The main explanation for this apparent paradox lies in the historical and structural specificities of the French electricity sector. It has been dominated by Électricité de France (EDF), a public monopoly created through a 1946 nationalization law, even following the progressive liberalization of the sector in the 2000s. The centralization of both production and decision-making processes in the post-war period fitted into a 'Colbertist tradition' favouring state-led industrial policies based on large centralized programmes (Finon, 1996). Often described as 'a state within the state', EDF was at the centre of a closed policy network also including the administration, notably the Ministry of Industry and its General Directorate for Energy and Raw Materials (Direction Générale de l'Energie et des Matières Premières, DGEMP). It was dominated by technocratic elites, particularly the engineers from Corps des Mines. Influenced by the preferences of these elites as well as by the legacy of Charles De Gaulle, which was marked by the promotion of national independence and development of nuclear technologies for military purpose, electricity policy was firmly oriented towards centralized production and nuclear power in the wake of the first oil shock of 1973 (Hecht, 2009). In this context only large hydropower, which had developed long before nuclear energy, could find a place in the national electricity mix. The promotion of other RES such as solar or wind power, which were associated with the anti-nuclear movement, faced strong resistance from the electricity sector's dominant actors (Evrard, 2013).

The development of policies to promote RES-E at the European level, as well as in other European countries, played an important role in altering – but not overthrowing – the national status quo.

9.3.1 Early Developments: Horizontal Europeanization by Default

Up to the 1990s, despite pioneering research and development (R&D) projects (on solar energy in particular) the French renewable energy sector was not getting strong political and financial support. As a result, European programmes – such as the JOULE, THERMIE and ALTENER schemes – played a significant role in financing and fostering research (see Chapter 2 by Solorio and Bocquillon). They offered experts and scholars opportunities to carry out their research, helped researchers to take part in European networks, and stimulated exchanges of best practices and benchmarking. Through their participation in international meetings, the wind sector's small and dispersed actors became aware of the existence of strong associations in Denmark and decided to create one on the same model, France Energie Eolienne (FEE) (Interview 1). This represents a clear instance of horizontal Europeanization, driven by learning processes in research and organizational practices. Renewable energy actors made both an instrumental and cognitive usage of 'Europe' that helped them to build up their position.

From the 1990s onwards, the influence of the EU over the French electricity sector became stronger, notably in the context of the liberalization of European electricity markets (Eising and Jabko, 2001). It is also during this period that the idea emerged that France was lagging behind its European partners in terms of RES promotion. This is notably visible in public documents, as illustrated by the Brosse report:

> Large industrialized countries have made considerable efforts to develop renewable energies in the last two or three years. France is falling behind. Our country should not stay away from this general movement. The EEC [European Economic Community] itself intends to develop an active policy in this matter. One does not see how France could stay isolated in Europe and why it would do so. (Brosse, 1992, p. 44)

In this period, the dominant political and economic actors of the electricity sector were influenced by the pressure to 'catch up' with other countries, as well as by the growing importance of environmental issues. EDF proceeded to a timid shift in its discourse and behaviour. The utility adopted a strategy of opening up to public opinion, announced that it would not oppose decentralized energy technologies any more, and even started developing an interest in RES-E (Interview 2). In 1996 it entered into a partnership agreement with ADEME – the French Agency for the Environment and Energy Management – and the Ministry of Industry to launch the 'Eole 2005' tender scheme, which aimed for the installation of between 250 megawatts (MW) and 500 MW of new wind power capacity within ten years. This evolution can be interpreted as characteristic of a process of horizontal Europeanization, driven mainly by economic competition with EU partners and adaptation to global and European environmental norms.

However, the implementation of the Eole programme faced important difficulties and the results remained very limited in terms of wind power deployment (Nadai, 2007; Szarka, 2007b). Besides, the role of European factors in this evolution should not be overestimated. Several domestic factors also contributed to the renewed interest in RES-E promotion, for instance the professionalization of the 'renewable lobby' or the participation of the Greens in the Plural Left Coalition from 1997 onwards (Evrard, 2013).

9.3.2 Catching up with 'Europe': Interactions between the 2000 Electricity Bill and the 2001 RES-E Directive

In 2000 France adopted a new electricity bill, also known as the law on the modernization and development of the public service in electricity, which introduced for the first time a FIT system for RES-E (article 10). The policymaking process leading to the adoption of this law, which represented a turning point for French RES-E policy, highlights the interaction between EU and domestic policies.

The first factor of change was related to the process of liberalization of electricity markets engaged at the European level. Four years after its adoption in 1996, directive 96/92/EC on common rules for the internal market in electricity was finally transposed into French national law through the 2000 electricity bill. The attendant debates opened a window of opportunity for renewable energy proponents to upgrade support to RES-E. In the 1990s, renewable energy actors had got organized and had reinforced their policy influence, notably through the creation of the Syndicat des Energies Renouvelables (SER). An advocacy coalition emerged including renewable energy associations (such as the SER and FEE), environmental NGOs and the Green Party (Les Verts). This coalition benefited from an especially favourable political context, since Les Verts had got into power as part of a left-wing coalition with the Socialist Party. In addition, the debates on a RES-E directive that were taking place at the same time in Brussels also contributed to create a favourable context for RES promotion. As a result, the coalition managed to include RES promotion on the agenda of energy sector reforms.

Processes of horizontal Europeanization were decisive in shaping the content of the French electricity bill. In anticipation of the energy debate, Socialist Prime Minister Lionel Jospin had commissioned a survey of the RES situation in France and Europe, to give a new impulse to this sector. In 2000 Yves Cochet, a prominent Green member of parliament and vice-president of the National Assembly, presented an influential report that advocated the establishment of a FIT system modelled on the pioneering German scheme (Cochet, 2000). The subsequent adoption of the FIT scheme reflected a combination of policy learning and economic competition, notably with Germany (Szarka, 2007b, pp. 323–324; see also Chapter 3 by Volgelpohl et al.).

The negotiations on the RES-E directive, concluded in 2001, provided France with an opportunity to upload its preferences to the European level.[1] Yet, during the negotiations France acted as fence-sitter, engaging in changing coalitions only to limit the costs of implementation. Concerning the definition of RES, France sided with the group of countries that pushed successfully for the inclusion of large hydropower. This was a matter of national interest given the structure of its energy mix. As regards objectives, the government accepted a quite ambitious indicative target of 21 per cent electricity produced from RES in national consumption by 2010; to be compared to the 15 per cent share already reached in 1997. Because of both the timing of the 2000 French presidency and participation of the Green Party in the government, it was impossible for French negotiators to overtly oppose the target proposed by the Commission. Yet experts in the administration perceived it as 'senseless' and impossible to reach (Interview 4). Finally, France was not strongly involved in the debate on policy instrument harmonization. Since it was in the process of adopting a FIT system at home, it nonetheless supported the FIT coalition (Rowlands, 2005, p. 972).

The implementation of the RES-E directive is interesting for its usage by domestic actors. Even though national targets were not mandatory, RES-E proponents made a 'discursive use' of the directive, arguing for the necessity to adopt new measures to reach national objectives. According to one of them, 'European acts are mostly useful to show that we won't be able to reach the targets we set up' (Interview 3). The large number of press articles published in the following years that insist on France's backwardness, suggests that these entrepreneurs were successful in instilling this idea in public opinion. However, neither the FIT nor the European commitments were sufficient to trigger a reorganization of the sector and an RES-E 'rush'. Progress was notably hampered by low FITs, complex planning procedures and lack of grid connections (Szarka, 2007b, pp. 326–327). Still, there are signs that the European context had an influence. The 2005 energy law introduced spatial planning for wind power on the Danish and German models, while the wind FIT was stepped up in 2006. As for the decision of Prime Minister de Villepin to double the solar photovoltaic (PV) FIT in 2006, it was justified as much by the need to strengthen public support to an emerging industry as by European commitments (Debourdeau, 2011).

9.3.3 The 2009 Directive: Occasional Climate Leader but Implementation Laggard

When RES promotion was put back on the European agenda by the Commission in January 2007 (see Chapter 2 by Solorio and Bocquillon), the French government adopted a rather cautious approach reflecting the limited progress made at home in recent years. France was indeed clearly lagging behind its 21 per cent indicative RES-E target.[2] At the February Energy Council, the French government acted as a foot-dragger. It supported an objective of 20 per cent RES in EU final energy consumption by 2020, but opposed binding targets. This position reflected the stance of major actors such as EDF and AREVA, which defended the French nuclear industry (Interview 10). However, French reticence was won over during the March European Council when German Chancellor Angela Merkel, who was presiding over the debates, managed to convince its most reluctant counterparts including President Chirac to agree on a binding RES target, in a context of intense pressure for climate action (see Chapter 3 by Vogelpohl et al.).

The position of France evolved from foot-dragging to circumstantial leadership following the election of President Sarkozy in May 2007. Under pressure from former TV presenter and green activist Nicolas Hulot during his campaign, Nicolas Sarkozy had signed an 'ecological pact' and committed to set in motion an innovative national consultation process on environmental issues, the 'Grenelle de l'environnement' (Whiteside et al., 2010). As France was to hold the EU Council presidency in the second half of 2008, the climate and energy package became the symbol of its domestic environmental commitments at the European level. It was also seen as a means for international prestige and influence in the context of ongoing international negotiations on a post-Kyoto agreement. The French government made clear early on that the adoption of the package would be one of its top priorities. This strategy shaped its position on the draft renewable energy directive

(RED). France accepted without major opposition the mandatory objective of 23 per cent RES in national energy consumption by 2020, a target considered ambitious in view of the slow progress achieved in recent years.[3]

In the debate over policy instruments, the French position was also ambivalent. Unlike Germany or Spain, and despite a clear preference for FITs, France did not display strong opposition to the Tradable Green Certificates (TGCs) scheme originally proposed by the Commission. The reasons are twofold. Firstly, as the incumbent Council Presidency, the French government wanted to keep a low profile, so as not to antagonize other member states, appearing as an 'honest broker', and reaching an agreement by the end of its term (Interview 9). Secondly, France did not have strong vested interests as it had not massively invested in the industrial development of RES-E technologies. Yet the government wanted to keep control over renewable energy policy instruments, mainly as a matter of national sovereignty.[4] Therefore, it welcomed the compromise solution put forward by Germany, the United Kingdom and Poland in June 2008, which proposed flexibility mechanisms – statistical transfers, joint projects and joint support schemes – as an alternative to a fully fledged TGCs market (see Chapter 3 by Vogelpohl et al; Chapter 6 by Solorio and Fairbrass; and Chapter 10 by Jankowska and Ancygier). Overall, the position of France on the RED oscillated between circumstantial leadership on the climate package's policy objectives and fence-sitting as regards specific measures.

If the climate and energy package negotiations were largely considered a French success, implementation has proven difficult and controversial. During the consultation process conducted in 2008–09 as part of the 'Grenelle de l'environnement', most actors accepted European commitments. Again, one of the main arguments used to justify RES-E promotion was the need to 'catch up', that is, to develop new policies to meet demanding European targets (top-down Europeanization); and compete with more advanced European partners such as Denmark, Germany and Spain (horizontal Europeanization). The first law to emerge from this consultation, the 'Grenelle 1' law (2009), was consensual and confirmed the 23 per cent target. By contrast the follow-up 'Grenelle 2' law, adopted in July 2010 and which contained more detailed measures, was fiercely debated. It required the Superior Council for Energy to monitor progress towards the European target. It also established sector-specific measures. In the wind sector, for instance, it set the objective of 500 new wind turbines per year to bring up total capacities to 19 gigawatts (GW) in 2020. However, the accompanying regulatory measures were denounced by the SER, RES-E industries and environmental associations as the 'death of wind energy' for setting additional administrative constraints for new projects (Evrard, 2012).

From 2009, support for RES-E aroused criticisms and resistance, in a context of economic turmoil and uncertainty over the future of the international climate change regime. In 2010, the high level of the solar PV FIT was made responsible for a speculative bubble and rising electricity prices, and criticized for favouring technology imports over national industry support. Following a moratorium, the PV FIT was substantially decreased and its gradual reduction made steeper (Debourdeau, 2011). The wind sector was also the object of a polemic. In 2008, the association Vent de colère ('wind of anger'), a federation of more than 200 small associations opposed to the development of wind turbines, brought the French state before the Conseil d'Etat, the highest administrative jurisdiction, for having failed to notify the Commission of the wind FIT as required in EU state aid rules. In March 2012, the Conseil d'Etat sought a legal opinion from the Court of Justice of the EU, which ruled in December 2013 that the wind FIT was a state aid. In the meantime, France notified the Commission regarding the FIT, which judged in March 2014 that it was compatible with EU state aid rules (Collet, 2014). This case created strong uncertainty in the sector and slowed down the development of several projects (Bezat, 2013). This episode illustrates the ambivalent effects of European rules, which can either stimulate or slow down RES progression, depending on the way they are used by domestic actors.

In this context, the share of RES in final energy consumption has grown slowly in recent years, reaching 13.4 per cent in 2012 and 14.3 per cent in 2014. In its review of progress towards EU energy and climate targets, the European Environmental Agency noted that France, along with five other member states, was below its indicative 2011 interim RES target (EEA, 2013, p. 11). That same year RES-E represented 16.5 per cent of France's gross final consumption, slightly over the indicative interim objective of 16 per cent indicated in the National Action Plan (NAP). A study coordinated by Ecofys for the European Commission noted fair progress in policy developments, notably an adequate revision of the FITs, which have been made more progressive; and the start of open tenders for large wind farms and solar plants. However, the report also deplored the lack of clear and transparent administrative procedures to guarantee RES-E access to the grid (Ecofys, 2012, p. 112). Efforts will need to be stepped up to reach the ambitious objective of 23 per cent RES-E in 2020 included in the NAP. In fact, it already appears clear in the French administration that it will be difficult for the country to meet its 2020 RES-E target (Interview 9).

As a result, in the debate on new energy and climate targets for 2030, the French government adopted an even more reserved position than during the 2007–08 negotiations. It strongly supported the Commission proposal for a binding target of 40 per cent greenhouse gas (GHG) emissions reduction by 2030, which was seen as favourable to its nuclear industry and was strongly symbolic in the perspective of the high-profile Paris climate conference of December 2015. On the other hand, French authorities favoured the 27 per cent RES target proposed by the Commission in January 2014 over the more ambitious 30 per cent target backed by the European Parliament. The European Council eventually adopted the former in October 2014. More discreetly, France was also part of the group of countries arguing against further binding national targets (Lindgaard, 2014). Yet, at the national level, the 'law on the energy transition' adopted by the Parliament in July 2015 contains an objective of 32 per cent RES in energy consumption by 2030 (and 40 per cent of electricity production). The law also introduces a system of Feed-In Premiums for large facilities from January 2016, in parallel to the existing FIT system. This instrument, which was considered as more in line with the Commission's guidelines on state aid rules of April 2014, was also inspired by the German and British models (Fabrégat, 2015; EurObserv'ER, 2015a, pp. 6–7). These recent developments therefore confirm the interplay between vertical and horizontal dynamics of Europeanization in the case of French renewable electricity.

9.4 GREENING SUPPORT TO AGRICULTURE? THE EUROPEANIZATION OF FRENCH BIOFUELS POLICY

In contrast to the RES-E sector, France is a forerunner in biofuels promotion. It has established itself as EU's top biofuels consumer (EurObserv'ER, 2015b, p. 54), and is also the first country in Europe in terms of land surfaces used for biofuels production (6 per cent). It has developed a small production of ethanol, mainly from sugarbeet and cereals, and is the first European producer and consumer of biodiesel, mostly from rapeseed. This reflects a long-standing promotion of diesel-based transportation.

The weight of its agriculture sector largely explains France's positive attitude towards EU biofuels policy. The French farming lobby, represented by its powerful federation, the Fédération Nationale des Syndicats d'Exploitants Agricole (FNSEA), and by specialized associations such as the General Confederation of Beetroot Producers (CGB), is very influential and has strong connections to the state, notably through the Ministry of Agriculture, which have proven decisive in shaping the country's position towards the Common Agricultural Policy (CAP). The promotion of biofuels at the European level has been perceived as a 'golden opportunity' to maintain indirect subsidies to intensive agriculture and to soften the impact of CAP reforms (Szarka, 2006, p. 634).

9.4.1 Early Developments: A New Market for Agriculture

From the 1990s onwards, the CAP has progressively shifted from a productivist and protectionist orientation towards the promotion of more economically and environmentally sustainable farming practices. The 1992 CAP reform obliged farms to set aside part of their land to control for the overproduction of cereals. In France the state tried to compensate for this loss in revenues for farmers by granting tax exemptions for the production of non-food production on set-aside lands (Cour des Comptes, 2012, pp. 47–49). Since 1992, biofuels have benefited from rebates from the national tax on petroleum products (Taxe Intérieur sur les Produits Pétroliers, TIPP[5]), which aimed to offset the 'additional cost' of biofuels compared to traditional fuels.[6] Thanks to this voluntaristic fiscal policy, France emerged as a European pioneer. The French government thus creatively responded to CAP reforms, using change in EU regulations on agriculture strategically to favour the development of biofuels.

France consistently acted as a pusher on biofuels, trying to upload its preferences at the European level. It was one of the main supporters of a 1992 Commission proposal setting a framework for reduced rates of excise duty for motor fuels from agricultural origins. In this period, the French biofuels support policy had come under scrutiny from the Commission and European Court of Justice for its discriminatory nature toward non-national producers. Consequently, France was keen on having a European framework in place that would ensure legal certainty for biofuels promotion and favour the emergence of a European market for its production. However, the proposal faced strong opposition and was finally withdrawn by the Commission in 1998.[7]

9.4.2 The 2003 Biofuels Directive: Incentive or Convenient Justification?

Despite this initial setback, France carried on pushing for strong EU support. In 2001 the Commission proposed a directive on the promotion of biofuels as part of its European Climate Change Programme (see

Chapter 2 by Solorio and Bocquillon). It originally intended to propose mandatory targets for the share of biofuels in transport, rising from 2 per cent in 2005 to 5.75 per cent in 2010. France, which had already developed a small domestic production, supported mandatory objectives, along with other main producers and consumers: Austria, Germany, Italy, Spain and Sweden (Di Lucia and Nilsson, 2007, p. 540; see also Chapter 3 by Vogelpohl et al.; Chapter 7 by Di Nucci and Russolillo; Chapter 8 by Solorio and Fernandez). But a large front of opposition questioned the benefits of biofuels in terms of both environmental protection and security of supply. In the end, the final directive adopted in 2003 included only indicative targets.

In 2004, in the context of a national consultation process on energy, Prime Minister Jean-Pierre Raffarin unveiled an ambitious programme, the Plan Biocarburant, to foster the production and use of biofuels. Three main rationales were invoked: support to agriculture, energy independence, and GHG emissions reductions. It was clear however that the government's main motivation was to support agriculture. European objectives were restated as justification for the programme (legitimating usage), but the Plan Biocarburant put forward targets that were even more ambitious than those endorsed at the European level. In the 2005 energy bill, the objective of 5.75 per cent biofuels was moved forward from 2010 to 2008, and a new objective of 7 per cent was set for 2010, as well as a 10 per cent indicative target for 2015. The targets were coupled with a biofuels obligation.[8] This new fiscal instrument had been pushed by Members of Parliament coming from areas with important agricultural production, notably beetroot producing regions (Interview 11).

The new biofuels policy created tensions with environmentalists, who denounced the impact of intensive agriculture; with the refinery industry, which was already experiencing overcapacities in petrol production; as well as with the car industry (Szarka, 2006, p. 634). In its 2006 progress report on the implementation of directive 2003/30/CE, the Commission noted that France was lagging behind its 2 per cent indicative interim objective for 2005 (COM, 2007, p. 7). Yet, the biofuels obligation provided strong incentives and, after an initial period of adaptation, the biofuels share in transport skyrocketed. Thanks to strong domestic policies and a favourable European environment, France reached its 5.75 per cent European target as early as 2008, in line with its national plan and two years before the deadline set by directive.

9.4.3 The RED: Uploading National Ambitions and Managing Criticisms

Despite growing concerns about its environmental and social impacts, French support for biofuels production has remained strong at EU level. In its 2007 energy and climate change review, the Commission proposed a 10 per cent target for RES for transport (RES-T) by 2020, officially to reduce carbon emissions in the transport sector and enhance security of supply. The Directorate General for Agriculture also pushed the target as a means to favour the development of the biofuels markets for European agriculture (Sharman and Holmes, 2010, p. 314). The 2006 sugar regime reform had led to a drastic reduction in guaranteed sugar prices and to the opening of EU markets, creating a need for compensation for EU sugar production. It is thus no surprise that the French farming lobby, notably beetroot producers, were fervent advocates of the RES-T target. In a context of rising attention for climate issues, the target was eventually made binding at the March 2007 European summit, under German leadership and with the backing of the French government.

During the RED negotiations, the RES-T objective was particularly controversial, with an increasing number of environmental NGOs and academic studies pointing more and more vocally to the environmental and social impacts of biofuels production, as well as to potential competition with food production. With the sudden rise in food crop prices in summer 2008, which led to protests in several countries of the global South, public awareness increased sharply. As the polemic inflated at home, the French government set up a working group composed of members of the Ministry of Ecology, ADEME and the Institut Français du Pétrole (IFP) – a national research centre on oil and energy – to assess the economic and environmental impact of 'first-generation' biofuels based on food crops.[9]

At the European level, France defended the interests of its farming lobby (Ricard, 2008). The French position was also shaped by the strong political push to get an agreement on the package during its presidency. The French authorities carefully steered the negotiations to avoid any direct challenge to the 10 per cent target, which could have led to the unravelling of the whole package. During thorny negotiations on the definition of sustainable criteria for biofuels production, French representatives supported criteria which would put foreign countries at a disadvantage – notably through stricter environmental and social requirements – while opposing those that could affect domestic production (Interview 7). To get a deal, French officials were especially prone to make concessions, albeit to the detriment of the RED's environmental integrity. In negotiations with the European Parliament, the French presidency opposed the inclusion of indirect land use change (ILUC) in the calculation of GHG emissions reduction targets, stressing the absence of reliable methodology (Müngersdorff, 2009, p. 41).

Since the entry into force of the RED, French biofuels have continued their progression, albeit at a slower pace. The 7 per cent target was reached in 2012, two years after the deadline set in the national programme (Cour des Comptes, 2012). Since then, the biofuels share has flattened off. No further target has been adopted, and the 10 per cent national indicative objective for 2015 was abandoned. According to the 2012 review of implementation of the RED, France was falling short of meeting its interim objectives, especially in terms of ethanol use. Although the French biofuels obligation is generally considered adequate, the country adopted its sustainability scheme only in late 2011, after being summoned by the Commission, and despite the Grenelle's commitments, it has failed to adopt further measures (Ecofys, 2012, pp. 53, 147). Progress has notably been hampered by enduring concerns over the negative impact of first-generation biofuels on food prices, land use and the environment (ADEME, 2012). Since 2008, French environment and development NGOs, notably France Nature Environnement (FNE) and the Réseau Action Climat France (RAC), have become increasingly active and have established themselves as a real counterforce (Interview 11). In addition, debates between the Ministry of Finance and the Ministry of Agriculture on the level of tax exemptions have sharpened in a context of austerity and budget constraints.[10]

European debates on new measures to alleviate the harmful effects of first-generation biofuels and favour the development of second-generation technologies have also contributed to curb the government's enthusiasm. Since 2012, the Council of the EU and European Parliament have been embroiled in difficult negotiations on the establishment of a cap on first-generation biofuels to achieve the 10 per cent target. In contrast with the more ambitious positions of the Commission and European Parliament who defended a 5 per cent cap, the French government argued, in line with the position of the Council of the EU, for a 7 per cent cap, which represents business as usual in the existing national framework (Interview 11). It was also reserved about the establishment of a specific target for second-generation biofuels deployment by 2020, preferring to maintain the status quo. The position defended by France and the Council eventually prevailed and was ratified by the European Parliament in spring 2015. At the national level, the 'law on the energy transition' adopted in summer 2015 reiterates the European objective of a 10 per cent share of renewable energy in transport by 2020, but also set an objective of 15 per cent RES in final consumption in transport by 2030.

9.5 COMPARATIVE ANALYSIS AND CONCLUDING REMARKS: DIFFERENTIATED IMPACTS AND USES OF EUROPE

The French case is particularly interesting for studying Europeanization given the striking discrepancy between RES-E and RES-T policies. Looking at bottom-up Europeanization, the country's reserved attitude towards RES-E promotion contrasts with its positive approach to biofuels promotion. From the start, France has been a forerunner and 'pusher' on biofuels. Not only did French public authorities support high targets at the European level, but they also endorsed more ambitious ones at the national level. It is only in recent years that environmental concerns over first-generation biofuels and fiscal constraints have hampered further developments. The situation appears quite different for RES-E, a sector in which France can be considered a fence-sitter. The country has acted mainly in a reactive fashion, adopting new targets and instruments in order to catch up with its European commitments and with more advanced partners. The leadership it has occasionally displayed, notably during the negotiations on the 2009 climate and energy package, has more to do with the prestige associated with international climate negotiations than with long-term commitments.

As this chapter shows, top-down processes of Europeanization also differ across the two sectors, reflecting the weight of national economic and political structures. The EU RES-E policy challenges core elements of the French electricity sector. The traditions of centralism, state interventionism and primacy of nuclear power do not fit with EU support for decentralized energy production. Conversely, EU biofuels policy is more in line with the national agricultural tradition and represents an opportunity to support French farming. Successful top-down Europeanization largely depends on the preferences of national interest groups and their ability to facilitate or hinder the implementation of EU commitments. In both sectors, influential actors have defended salient economic stakes: EDF and the nuclear lobby in the case of RES-E; the FNSEA and the farming lobby for biofuels. Yet European processes have also contributed to shaping these interests by influencing opportunity structures and issue-framing. For instance, European commitments have encouraged EDF and Alstom to invest in RES, including large offshore wind projects, in order not to be left out of a European-wide process. This, in turn, has changed the perception of RES in the administration, which now appears as a more 'serious' and large-scale industrial policy (Interview 8). Similarly, European debates on ILUC have fuelled environmental NGOs' activism and pushed the administration and politicians to a more cautious attitude regarding biofuels promotion.

Europeanization is not only vertical but also horizontal. European partners, Germany in particular, have provided a model that has influenced policy developments in France. The French FIT was directly inspired by the German support system (see Chapter 3 by Vogelpohl et al.). As is the case with vertical Europeanization, the success of horizontal processes depends on the domestic context. The German model was imported by a coalition of actors in a favourable moment, marked by the participation of the Green Party in the government. The examples of Denmark, Germany and Spain have been used repeatedly by the RES-E advocacy coalition to promote further measures, framed as a way to catch up with more advanced European neighbours. As regards biofuels promotion, processes of horizontal Europeanization are less evident.

As should be clear from these two case studies, domestic actors are not mere recipients of European processes; they also contribute to shaping them. They can make use of Europe in different ways, depending on their specific interests and ideas. It is thus no surprise if the effects of Europe can at times appear ambivalent. For instance, the French renewable energy coalition made a 'legitimating usage' of European commitments and 'cognitive usage' of EU scientific resources in order to promote RES-E. Conversely, the anti-wind lobby has been able to make 'strategic use' of European law with the opposite goal. It resorted to EU state aid rules to contest the FIT system for wind power. In the biofuels sector, French authorities have strategically used EU biofuels policies as a way to compensate farmers for CAP reforms and justify national policies. But the environmental lobby has also been able to exploit European debates on ILUC to gain influence in the domestic policy process. Overall, well-established and powerful national actors, such as EDF and the farming lobby, have been especially efficient in shaping, using and resisting European processes. Nevertheless, the recourse to European references and legislation has been a key factor in empowering less-established actors such as the pro- and anti-renewable lobbies, or environmental NGOs.

From a theoretical perspective, this chapter makes the case for an actor-centred perspective on Europeanization that articulates structural conditions with the agency of individual and collective actors. Europeanization is clearly not an automatic process and the domestic level is more than a passive filter of European processes. European and national politics often interact in complex ways, both vertically and horizontally. Europeanization cannot be fully understood without looking at the way different domestic actors make use of European resources and opportunities, or resist European constraints, depending on their own positions. Such an approach could help go beyond the classic leader/laggard classification and draw a more detailed picture of the differentiated influence of Europe on national polities.

NOTES

1. The country was in an especially favourable position since the new directive was supposed to be adopted during the French presidency, in the second half of the year 2000.
2. France was one of the 15 EU countries which missed its indicative target in 2010 (COM, 2013, p. 4).
3. In the administration, the 23 per cent target was not perceived as favourable but was endorsed due to the strong political push of the presidency.
4. The administration was generally hostile to a trading system and wanted to preserve the FIT, perceived as more efficient in promoting renewable energy technologies and manageable at the national level (Interviews 5 and 7).
5. The TIPP was replaced by the National Consumption Tax on Energy Products (Taxe Intérieure sur la Consommation, TIC) in 2002.
6. These partial tax rebates are differentiated depending on biofuel type. To limit the losses in revenues for the state, the amount of biofuels eligible to tax reductions is restricted through quotas and licences.
7. Although the Commission finally approved a revised scheme in 1997, the European Court of Justice (ECJ) ruled that it was incompatible with state aid rules (2000). The French scheme was eventually authorized through a Council decision in 2002, along with similar schemes in Denmark, Italy and the Netherlands.
8. From 2005 onwards, transport fuel distributors were exempted from a General Tax on Polluting Activities (Taxe Générale sur les Activités Polluantes, TGAP), either partially or totally, depending on the achievement of a biofuels incorporation annual target rising to 7 per cent in 2010. In 2014, the objectives of incorporation were 7 and 7.7 per cent, respectively, for bioethanol and biodiesel.
9. The final report, released in April 2010, presented a largely positive assessment of the environmental impact of biofuels (EurActiv, 2009). However, both its methodology and conclusions were harshly criticized by environmental NGOs, leading to the commissioning of a second report on ILUC.
10. The definition of tax exemption rates has traditionally created tensions between the Ministry of Agriculture, which wants more favourable rebates, and the Ministry of Finance, which wants to limit tax losses. In this enduring dispute, the Ministry of Environment has usually acted as a mediator (Interview 11).

REFERENCES

ADEME (2012), 'Retrospective analysis of the interaction between the development of biofuels in France, changes in French and world markets (agricultural production, processed products and coproducts) and changes in land use', Final report, March.

Bezat, J.-M. (2013), 'Le développement de l'éolien terrestre est de nouveau menacé par l'Europe', *Le Monde*, 20 December, accessed on 10 November 2014 at http://www.lemonde.fr/economie/article/2013/12/20/le-developpement-de-l-eolien-terrestre-est-de-nouveau-menace-par-bruxelles_4337977_3234.html.

Brosse, C. (1992), 'Rapport sur les énergies renouvelables', Paris, 24 December.

Cochet, Y. (2000), 'Rapport au Premier ministre: Stratégie et moyens de développement de l'efficacité énergétique et des sources d'énergie renouvelables en France', Paris, December.

Collet, P. (2014), 'Eolien: l'exécutif européen valide (pour l'instant) le tarif d'achat français', *Actu-Environnement.com*, 27 March, accessed on 7 November 2014 at http://www.actu-environnement.com/ae/news/tarif-achat-eolien-aide-etat-validation-commission-europeenne-21203.php4.

COM (2007), 'Biofuel progress report: report on the progress made in the use of biofuels and other renewable fuels in the Member States of the European Union', COM (2007) 845 final, Brussels, 10 January.

COM (2013), 'Renewable energy progress report', COM (2013) 175 final, Brussels, 27 March.

Cour des Comptes (2012), 'La politique d'aide aux biocarburants', Public report on the evaluation of public policies, Paris, January.

Debourdeau, A. (2011), 'De la "solution" au "problème": la problématisation de l'obligation d'achat de l'énergie solaire photovoltaïque en France et en Allemagne', *Politix*, 95 (3), 103–127.

Di Lucia, L. and L.J. Nilsson (2007), 'Transport biofuels in the European Union: the state of play', *Transport Policy*, 14, 533–543.

Ecofys (2012), 'Renewable energy progress and biofuels sustainability', Report for the European Commission, coord. by Ecofys, Brussels, September.

EEA (European Environmental Agency) (2013), 'Trends and projections in Europe 2013: tracking progress towards Europe's climate and energy targets until 2020', EEA Report no. 10/2013, Copenhagen, 9 October.

Eising, R. and N. Jabko (2001), 'Moving targets: national interests and electricity liberalization in the European Union', *Comparative Political Studies*, 34 (7), 742–767.

EurActiv (2009), 'L'Ademe publie son rapport sur les agrocarburants en catimini', 12 October, accessed on 7 November 2014 at http://www.euractiv.fr/energie-environnement/tagenergie20100208ademe-publie-son-rapport-sur-agro carburants-en-catimini_51382-2059.html.

EurObserv'ER (2015a), 'Le Baromètre 2015 des Energies Renouvelables Electriques en France', 6th edition, Paris.

EurObserv'ER (2015b), 'The state of renewable energies in Europe', 15th Eurobserv'ER Report, 2015 edition, Paris.

Evrard, A. (2012), 'Les effets du Grenelle de l'environnement: le secteur des énergies renouvelables', in D. Boy, M. Brugidou, C. Halpern and P. Lascoumes (eds), *Le Grenelle de l'Environnement: Acteurs, Discours, Effets*, Paris: Armand Colin, pp. 273–292.

Evrard, A. (2013), *Contre Vents et Marées: Politiques des Energies Renouvelables en Europe*, Paris: Presses de Sciences Po.
Fabrégat, S. (2015), 'Energies renouvelables: le gouvernement fait évoluer le complement de rémunération', *Actu-Environnement.com*, 27 May, accessed on 15 July 2015 at http://www.actu-environnement.com/ae/news/mecanisme-soutien-energies-renouvelables-prime-tarif-achat-24581.php4.
Finon, D. (1996), 'French energy policy: the effectiveness and limitations of Colbertism', in F. McGowan (ed.), *European Energy Policies in a Changing Environment*, Heidelberg: Springer, pp. 21–56.
Hecht, G. (2009), *The Radiance of France: Nuclear Power and National Identity After World War II*, 2nd edition, Cambridge, MA: MIT Press.
Lindgaard, J. (2014), 'A Bruxelles, la France agit contre les énergies renouvelables', *Mediapart*, 23 January.
Müngersdorff, M. (2009), 'Evaluating EU decision-making processes: a case study on the "renewable energy in transport target" and the "sustainability criteria for biofuel production" in the context of the EU's climate and energy package', Stockholm Environment Institute, Working Paper, June.
Nadai, A. (2007), 'Planning, siting and the local acceptance of wind power: some lessons from the French case', *Energy Policy,* 35 (5), 2715–2726.
Reiche, D. and M. Bechberger (2004), 'Policy differences in the promotion of renewable energies in the EU member states', *Energy Policy*, 32 (7), 843–849.
Ricard, P. (2008), 'Les Etats européens divisés au sujet des agrocarburants', *Le Monde*, 8 May, accessed on 7 November 2014 at http://www.lemonde.fr/planete/article/2008/05/08/les-etats-europeens-divises-au-sujet-des-agro carburants_1042455_3244.html.
Rowlands, I.H. (2005), 'The European directive on renewable electricity: conflicts and compromises', *Energy Policy*, 33, 965–974.
RTE (2016), 'Bilan électrique 2015', Annual report of the Réseaux de Transport d'Electricité.
Sharman, A. and J. Holmes (2010), 'Evidence-based policy or policy-based evidence gathering? Biofuels, the EU and the 10% target', *Environmental Policy and Governance*, 20, 309–321.
Szarka, J. (2006), 'From inadvertent to reluctant pioneer? Climate strategies and policy style in France', *Climate Policies*, 5 (6), 627–638.
Szarka, J. (2007a), *Wind Power in Europe: Politics, Business and Society*, Basingstoke: Palgrave.
Szarka, J. (2007b), 'Why there is no wind rush in France?', *European Environment,* 17, 321–333.
Whiteside, K.H, D. Boy and D. Bourg (2010), 'France's "Grenelle de l'environnement": openings and closures in ecological democracy', *Environmental Politics,* 19 (3), 449–467.
Woll, C. and S. Jacquot (2010), 'Using Europe: strategic action in multi-level politics', *Comparative European Politics*, 8 (1), 110–142.

Interviews

Interview 1, with a representative of a French renewable energy association, Comité de Liaison des Energies Renouvelables (CLER), 7 November 2005, Paris.

Interview 2, with a former EDF executive, 4 December 2007, Paris.

Interview 3, with a founding member of the French Wind Energy Association (FEE), 4 December 2007, Paris.

Interview 4, with a French energy official, Direction Générale de l'Energie et des Matièrs Premièrs (DGEMP), Ministry of Industry, 4 March 2008, Paris.

Interview 5, with a French energy official, Ministry for Ecology (DGEC), 27 April 2010, Brussels.

Interview 6, with a French official, Permanent Representation of France, 13 February 2012, Brussels.

Interview 7, with a European Commission official, DG Environment, 28 November 2010, Brussels.

Interview 8, with a European Commission official, DG Energy, 13 November 2012, Brussels.

Interview 9, with a French official, former Deputy Director for renewable energy and former member of the Cabinet of the Minister for Ecology, 24 January 2014, phone interview.

Interview 10, with a former Energy Attaché, Permanent Representation of France and Policy Director at EPIA, 26 February 2014, phone interview.

Interview 11, with a French official, former Director for refinery and biofuels, Director for oil industry and new products, Ministry for Ecology, 11 April 2014, Paris.

10. Poland at the renewable energy policy crossroads: an incongruent Europeanization?

Karolina Jankowska and Andrzej Ancygier

10.1 INTRODUCTION

At the European level, Poland is well known for its opposition to climate change policy measures aiming at reducing carbon dioxide (CO_2) emissions, including development of renewable energy sources (RES). Generally, the country is depicted as a foot-dragger with some entrepreneurial skills developed more recently to shape European policy according to its preferences (Jankowska, 2011, Jankowska, 2017). At the domestic level, Poland behaves generally as a laggard when it comes to the implementation of European Union (EU) renewable energy policy. This label applies especially to the electricity sector, where close links between the government and state-owned energy enterprises hinder the development of RES for electricity (RES-E). In the transport sector, the Polish government was much more welcoming in adopting ambitious European biofuels targets. However, Poland's willingness to replace fossil fuels by renewable energy sources for transport (RES-T) was limited exclusively to first-generation biofuels, which could potentially create many new jobs in the Polish farming sector. Generally, the Polish government has resisted any progress in the European renewable energy policy that could potentially require or cause far-reaching changes to the status quo at the national level and/or be costly for national interests (be it by successful blocking of EU policies, or weakening of EU policies). This chapter deals with the complex relationship between Poland and EU renewable energy policy.

There exist already some analyses of policy change in the field of renewable energy policy in Poland and the role of the EU in this, as well as of interactions between Polish and European renewable energy policy (see, e.g., Podrygała, 2008; Jankowska, 2011, 2012; Ancygier, 2013).

However, they focus exclusively on the electricity sector. A systematic analysis of Europeanization of the transport sector with regard to biofuel promotion in Poland is lacking. Also, the impact of the EU on RES-E and biofuel promotion in Poland in comparison has not been studied so far. This chapter aims to fill these gaps. In particular, it tries to explain how and why different domestic actors have shaped Poland's position towards European renewable energy policy (bottom-up Europeanization) as well as how these actors were affected by those policies adopted in Brussels (top-down Europeanization). Moreover, it investigates how and why these multi-level interactions and impacts have changed over time.

The next section presents the analytical framework of the chapter, which combines Europeanization with the advocacy coalition framework and the policy monopoly concept. In sections 10.3 and 10.4 case studies on renewable electricity and biofuels promotion in Poland are analysed and explained based on this framework. The last section compares the two cases, draws some general conclusions and explains how the applied analytical framework helps in analysing the Europeanization process with regard to EU renewable energy policy.

10.2 ANALYTICAL UNDERPINNING AND METHODS: EUROPEANIZATION IN A MULTI-LEVEL SYSTEM

In general terms, this chapter relies on the Europeanization framework outlined in Chapter 1 by Jörgens and Solorio. However, in order to identify the causal factors behind what we call Poland's 'incongruent' Europeanization, this chapter combines Europeanization with the advocacy coalition framework (e.g., Sabatier, 2007, pp. 189–220) and the policy monopoly concept (e.g., Baumgartner and Jones, 2009). From this analytical perspective, interactions between the European and the domestic level are not straightforward, but steadily disturbed and influenced by diverse (intervening) factors such as long- and short-term constraints and resources of (dominant) advocacy coalitions (or policy monopolies), their policy beliefs, as well as domestic opportunity structures (see more in Sabatier, 2007, pp. 189–220; Jankowska, 2012, pp. 45–53).

Special attention is paid to the concept of policy monopoly, which may favour or constrain the reformist attempts of advocates proposing changes to the status quo and be a potential favouring factor or obstacle to policy change at the EU or domestic level. It may thereby lead either to accepting, weakening or blocking change at the EU level or to a (partial) Europeanization, a 'superficial' (formal, without actually reaching the goals) Europeanization or a failure of Europeanization at the domestic level. Its two most important characteristics are as follows: 'First, a definable institutional structure is responsible for policymaking, and that structure limits access to the policy process. Second, a powerful supporting idea is associated with the institution' (Baumgartner and Jones, 2009, p. 7). Those who are able to define the issue on the agenda (through a favourable policy-making structure; polity) in line with their policy beliefs have a dominant position during the later policy formulation and implementation process (politics), be it on the national or EU level. These factors are helpful in analysing both the role of Poland in the formulation of EU renewable energy policy as well as the impact of the EU and other member states on the Polish renewable energy policy.

The authors have written this chapter based on their own analysis and research projects on RES policy in Poland. Those projects deal with the impact of the EU and other member states on Polish RES-E policy and the Polish role in its formulation at the EU level (Jankowska, 2011, 2012, 2017; Ancygier, 2013). Further analysis of the most current developments in this field as well as analysis of the impact of the EU and member states on biofuel promotion in Poland and the Polish role in the formulation of EU biofuel policy have been conducted specifically for this chapter. All the studies and analyses mentioned rely on qualitative research designs, content analysis and process tracing. The authors analysed primary and secondary material and diverse statistical data sources. For the above-mentioned research projects the authors conducted semi-structured interviews with business representatives, members of diverse non-governmental organizations (NGOs), researchers and civil servants in Poland.

10.3 THE EUROPEANIZATION OF RES-E POLICY IN POLAND

10.3.1 General Background of the Power Sector in Poland

In 2013, over 87 per cent of electricity produced in Poland came from coal (Polskie Sieci Elektroenergetyczne, 2014), mainly hard coal. In order to understand the role of the hard coal industry in Poland nowadays we need to look especially at the last decades. The domestic coal industry has been developing since the seventeenth century (first documented mining in Upper Silesia) and established itself as a strategic element of Polish industry and economy, guaranteeing energy security based on domestic resources, creating jobs and contributing to economic growth especially after World War II (WWII). This development has led to a path-dependency in Poland's energy policy. It continuously reinforces a status quo in this field that can be defined as the maintenance of a conventional system based on fossil fuels and/or nuclear power, centralized production facilities, and non-flexible consumption patterns (e.g., Jankowska, 2012).

During the communist period this status quo was strengthened by nationalization and centralization, creating a strong economic and political interdependence between the state and the electricity sector. This interdependence persisted after the collapse of communism in 1989 (Jankowska, 2012). After 1989, the Polish power sector was reformed and reorganized several times, taking into account major challenges resulting from Poland's accession to the EU and competition in the internal European electricity market. Some of these reforms, such as the introduction of unbundling as well as the third-party access principle (as required by directive 2003/54/EC), have had a positive impact on RES-E development in Poland, allowing the emergence of new actors, such as renewable energy enterprises (top-down Europeanization). Others, such as the horizontal consolidation process started in 2005, followed by the vertical consolidation one year later, had the aim of creating few, but powerful, conventional energy companies, similar to Western European structures (horizontal Europeanization). They have, however, strongly limited the market access of small and medium-sized renewable energy enterprises.

Although privatization programmes do exist, the Polish state retains the right to maintain major shares in the four biggest energy companies, especially in Polish Energy Group (PGE) and Tauron, which together dominate more than 60 per cent of the electricity market. All of Poland's freely elected governments since 1989 have feared losing state control of the power sector, and each has tried to maintain a strong economic and political interdependence. They have also paid great attention to the interests of coal miners represented by large and influential trade unions.

The Ministry of Treasury defending the interests of the state-owned power companies has become one of the major features of the existing policy monopoly, playing a crucial role in shaping Polish energy policy with regard to the power sector. The main goal of Poland's policy in this sector has been to keep the dominant position of PGE on the market, not only by defending the role of coal as the major source of energy in Poland but also by planning to build two nuclear power plants by 2030 (Ancygier and Caspar, 2014). Also, production of shale gas, which the Minister of Environment Maciej Grabowski declared to be his main priority (WNP, 2013), is high on the government's agenda. The general background of the Polish power market as described here constrains enormously the capacity of RES-E advocates to take an active role and to increase the degree of political and institutional compatibility with EU RES-E policy. However, since at least 1989, Poland has made some important steps towards RES-E development.

10.3.2 EU Accession and the 2001 RES-E Directive: Turning Points in Policy Formulation, 'Superficial' Europeanization

During the late 1980s and beginning of the 1990s, Poland did not have any coherent vision or strategy for the development of RES-E (Jankowska, 2012, pp. 204–212, 315). Although between 1993 and 1999 there existed a Feed-In Tariff (FIT) scheme, only the smallest installations up to 5 megawatts (MW) received this support. This situation slowly started to change in the mid-1990s, when the European Commission began to influence indirectly the policy process in the field of RES-E in Poland. During that time a coalition of RES-E advocates (RES-E producers, their associations, and so on) also emerged and has since then been playing a growing role in the policy process.

As far back as 1994, parallel to the beginning of the EU accession process, the European Commission set up a renewable energy research institute in Poland called EC BREC, the Baltic Renewable Energy Centre (Podrygała, 2008, p. 72). Although EC BREC (later EC BREC/IBMER, the Institute for Building, Mechanisation and Electrification of Agriculture; and EC BREC IEO, the Institute for Renewable Energy) became a part of the Polish Ministry of Agriculture in 1997 (it became independent in 2001), it has become the most important and influential RES-E advocate in Poland, and it was this institute which managed to put RES-E on the political agenda. In November 1997, it organized the first nationwide conference on the topic 'Development of Renewable Energy in Poland' which involved RES-E industry representatives and researchers. During the conference demands for the support of RES-E were formulated for the first time (Podrygała, 2008, p. 72). EC BREC was also involved in the preparation and adoption of the parliamentary resolution on the growth of RES adopted in July 1999, in the preparation and adoption of the Development Strategy for the Renewable Energy Sector (Strategia rozwoju energetyki odnawialnej) (Ministry of Environment, 2000) as well as in the preparation of the draft of the first standalone renewable energy law in Poland, a draft which was ultimately not adopted. It can therefore be stated that the EU co-initiated the debate concerning RES-E development in Poland in the 1990s and supported capacity-building and policy formulation in this area by promoting changes in the beliefs and expectations of domestic actors and altering the domestic opportunity structure (that is, top-down Europeanization).

The Development Strategy for the Renewable Energy Sector (hereafter: the Strategy), adopted by the Polish parliament in 2001, paved the way for EU accession and implementation of the 2001 RES-E directive. Although adopted a month earlier than the directive, the Strategy included direct references to the draft directive (Podrygała, 2008, p. 76). Shortly after the adoption of the Strategy, the Ministry of Economy developed an ordinance based on this that introduced a quota obligation in Poland (Jankowska, 2011, p. 167). This can be seen as an example of horizontal Europeanization on the one hand, because during that time more countries chose this support scheme. On the other hand, it is an example of top-down Europeanization because since the publication of the White Paper on the European energy policy in 1995, which initiated the debate on RES-E policy harmonization in the EU, the European Commission had begun to favour this instrument in communicating its view to member states (Busch and Jörgens, 2012, p. 75).

The target set in the ordinance for electricity suppliers amounted to 7.5 per cent for RES-E in 2010 (Jankowska, 2011, p. 167). It was included in the EU accession treaty and subsequently also in the RES-E directive. Determining the Polish RES-E target happened without much resistance as EU accession had been of the highest priority for all Polish governments since 1989 (Jankowska, 2011, p. 173; Jankowska, 2017, p. 150). Although the Polish Minister of Economy, responsible for the EU accession negotiations in the field of energy and the negotiations on the RES-E directive, tried to lower the target which was initially introduced by his predecessor, he was not able to assert himself against the European Commission (Podrygała, 2008, p. 84). This is an example of the strong impact of adaptational pressure from the EU accession process and the implementation of the *acquis* on Polish RES-E policy (that is, conditionality).

However, the Strategy was not only supposed to set targets for the share of RES in Poland. It obligated the government of the following legislative period to adopt a separate renewable energy law. Among other things, it called for the introduction of a support scheme for RES-E based on certificates, competition and tendering. In 2001, the EC BREC/IBMER was commissioned by the government to prepare a draft of the RES law. The proposed draft was a solid basis to meet the Polish 2010 RES-E target. After the government reorganization in 2004, the Minister of Environment changed and blocked the adoption of the EC BREC/IBMER proposal in the Cabinet. The new director of the ministry's

Instruments for Environmental Protection department had previously worked for the state's grid operator PSE SA, and therefore had close connections to the conventional power industry (political interdependence) (Grużewski, 2004). He strongly criticized the EC BREC/IBMER draft law and prepared an alternative proposal intended to limit support for RES-E. During the consultation process for the law, only representatives of the conventional energy industry were invited to participate, which is a clear example of an institutional structure limiting access to the policy process, a core characteristic of policy monopoly. Finally, however, the Cabinet did not adopt the proposal of the Ministry of Environment, because it would have failed to meet the Strategy and EU obligations. Only the energy law (Sejm, 1997) was amended in 2005 by introducing Tradable Green Certificates (TGCs) to support RES-E development. A separate renewable energy law was not adopted in Poland until 2015.

However, the support scheme put in place in 2005 did not include many of the incentives that had been initially proposed by RES-E advocates in the draft law prepared by EC BREC/IBMER. For instance, it did not set different certificate prices for different RES technologies and fixed only the bottom price of a certificate, which did not provide enough investment security and financial incentives for RES-E producers. Moreover, it included support for large hydropower plants whose repayment terms had been already completed for a long time, as well as biomass co-firing in inefficient coal plants which reduced the price of TGCs on the market, reducing incentives for other, small-scale, private and decentralized RES technologies. Consequently, the adopted policy measures were, in the opinion of many experts (e.g., Podrygała, 2008, pp. 53, 85–86; Jankowska, 2012, pp. 283–284; Ancygier, 2013, pp. 310–313), insufficient for achieving the 2001 RES-E directive target. In fact, Poland did not achieve it by 2010.

Limited policy change derived from EU accession and the 2001 RES-E directive was caused to a significant extent by the existence of a long-standing policy monopoly. On the other hand, without EU adaptational pressure even such a limited policy change as the amendment of the energy law would probably not have occurred in Poland in the RES-E policy field. But still, this was only a formal implementation of the RES-E directive which Poland could dare to undertake due to the lack of serious consequences (for example, financial penalties) of not meeting of the RES-E target. The Europeanization of RES-E policy in Poland at this stage was merely 'superficial'.

10.3.3 The 2009 Directive: Foot-Dragging in Negotiations, Superficial Implementation

Shortly after the European Commission presented a draft of the renewed directive, Poland criticized the national target for 2020 and proposed a lower one (11 per cent, or eventually 13 per cent of gross energy consumption). Nevertheless, it finally approved the Commission's proposal (Jankowska, 2012, p. 281). This can be seen as a mild foot-dragging strategy. Indeed, during the negotiations of the EU 2009 climate and energy package, Poland was decidedly more concerned with its other parts, especially the revision of the EU Emissions Trading System (ETS), than with the draft proposal of the renewable energy directive (RED). Therefore, the national discussion about the energy and climate package also almost completely ignored the RES policy issues, whereas the existing policy monopoly concentrated its strengths and resources on fighting the ETS Directive. Another reason for the mild foot-dragging could be the rather long-term target for 2020 as set in the RED proposal, whereas the ETS directive proposal concerned a short-term period and would have a direct impact from 2013 (Jankowska, 2011; Jankowska, 2012, pp. 281–282).

The change in the political and public understanding of the role of RES-E in the national electricity mix could also have influenced the position of Polish negotiators at the EU level. The question in the political discussion and the public eye has since then no longer been whether RES-E should be developed, but how the development should be carried out. A crucial element of change was top-down Europeanization by means of changing expectations and beliefs of domestic actors. Europeanization contributed to increasing knowledge and thus understanding and acceptance of the RES-E policy among politicians and society (Jankowska, 2012).

Once Poland won the battle over the revision of the EU ETS directive in 2009, the existing policy monopoly has undertaken attempts to weaken the implementation of the 2009 RED at the national level by allowing only moderate alterations in the existing system which would not reduce their economic and political advantages. The National Renewable Energy Action Plan for RES which Poland adopted in December 2010, six months later than required in the 2009 RED, includes measures which may involve the domestic conventional power industry in the development of RES-E in Poland. According to the plan, Poland would achieve its EU goal through the development of wind energy, biomass co-firing and the building of one additional large hydropower plant with 100 MW capacity (Jankowska, 2012, p. 319). Such investments can only be financed and conducted by the huge companies of the conventional power sector. What is more, the government amended the existing energy law in July 2013, introducing a support mechanism for small scale RES-E technologies up to 40 kilowatts (kW) of installed capacity (so-called micro-scale installations) based on a FIT scheme. However, according to the amendment, the produced RES-E could be sold for only 80 per cent of the average electricity price from the last year. This element has been criticized as being too little to encourage investments, and as advantageous, again, merely for the domestic conventional energy companies.

In April 2014 the government sent to the parliament the long-expected separate renewable energy law, which was adopted by the lower chamber of the Polish parliament (Sejm) in January 2015. Against the will of the government the majority of the members of parliament added an amendment which introduced differentiated FITs for RES units with installed capacity below 10 kW. However, the level of the tariffs was significantly reduced during the debate over the renewable energy law in the Senat, the upper chamber of the Polish parliament. And the situation for larger installations looks much worse. The introduced capacity and price caps in the auctioning process are believed to block RES-E development and seem to be beneficial only for the conventional energy companies.

Although the share of RES in final energy consumption increased to over 11.45 per cent in 2014, almost 77 per cent of it was coming from the co-firing of biomass in coal-fired power plants (Central Statistical Office of Poland, 2015, pp. 2–3). Since biomass co-firing in those power plants wears them out faster, mostly old, inefficient plants are used for this purpose, even though it cannot be considered as a contribution to fulfilling the 2009 RED target (Jankowska, 2012, p. 313). With many coal-fired power plants planned to be switched off due to the air pollution obligations resulting from the industrial emissions directive (WNP, 2014), a lack of stable and predictable incentives for RES, and a slowdown of investments in new wind energy power plants, it remains questionable whether Poland will be able to fulfil its 2020 target. The implementation of the RED is therefore an example of a 'superficial' Europeanization of Polish RES-E policy.

This had a negative impact on Poland's willingness to adopt binding RES targets for 2030. In 2012, the Polish Ministry of Environment stated clearly that it will veto any such targets if proposed by the European Commission (REO, 2012). This may have been one of the main reasons why there was no agreement on a binding 2030 RES target during the meeting of the Council in October 2014, despite strong German support (BMWi, 2014). Thus, it can also be referred to as an example of

'Polonization' of the European energy and climate policy (Ancygier, 2013, p. 385), and a clear example of a foot-dragging strategy, which was this time not merely 'mild'.

10.4 THE EUROPEANIZATION OF BIOFUEL POLICY IN POLAND

10.4.1 Before EU Membership: Enthusiasm for Biofuels and Legislative Chaos

Similarly to the electricity sector, Poland is also heavily reliant on fossil fuels in the transport sector. Due to stable oil deliveries from the Soviet Union, no trend towards alternative fuels existed until the mid-1990s. When in 1994 the government introduced tax exemptions for biofuels, the measure was not motivated by European environmental policy or fossil fuel dependency but by the attempt to provide farmers with an additional source of income (Gwiazdowicz, 1994). Reducing excise taxes turned out to be very successful and led to an increase in biofuels production. But due to budget constraints it was decreasing annually and therefore made a long-term investment in production facilities difficult. As a result, the share of biofuels in the transport sector decreased from 1.72 per cent in 1997 to 0.78 per cent in 2000 (Sejm, 2003b, p. 2).

The EU began to have an impact on Polish biofuels policy in the early 2000s when it published two important documents: the Green Paper 'Towards a European strategy for the security of energy supply', which suggested introducing a target of a 7 per cent biofuels share in the transport sector by 2010 and 20 per cent by 2020 (COM, 2001a, p. 43); and a draft of the biofuels directive in November 2001, which included a target of 5.75 per cent for alternative fuels in the transport sector by 2010 (COM, 2001b; see Chapter 2 by Solorio and Bocquillon). In response to European legislation and differently from the situation in the electricity sector, domestic actors in Poland relatively quickly created a strong coalition supporting the development of biofuels and thus the implementation of EU legislation in this area (policy taking). But the main reason was not a decrease of the CO_2 emissions from the transport sector but – like in some other countries (e.g. France, see Chapter 9 by Bocquillon and Evrard) – the potential of biofuels to create new jobs in the agriculture sector. With over 8 million people fully or partly employed in the agriculture sector in Poland in 1998 (Stankiewicz, 2000, p. 34), increasing the standard of living for farmers also had great political importance. Some journalists and experts even called Poland the 'Kuwait of Europe' and expressed the hope that the huge overcapacity of Polish agriculture could be used to power European cars after Polish EU accession (Weiss, 2002). But to fulfil all these hopes, more coherent biofuels legislation was necessary.

In July 2002 three separate drafts of a biofuels law were submitted to the Polish parliament. The first was drafted by the government (Sejm, 2002c), the second by a group of members of parliament (MPs) from the opposition party Civic Platform (Sejm, 2002a), and the third by MPs from the Eurosceptic opposition party Samoobrona (Self Defence), which was popular especially among farmers (Sejm, 2002b). Whereas the first two drafts were very similar and included an ambitious target of 5 per cent for the share of biofuels in the transport sector by 2006, according to the proposal of the Eurosceptic Self Defence party this target was to be reached two years later in 2008 mainly by using domestic resources for biofuels production. Based on all three projects, a compromise proposal, which still included the requirement to use exclusively domestic resources, was adopted by the parliament. In the end, however, the biofuels law was vetoed by the President, who argued that car drivers could not be forced to use fuels which might be harmful to the engines of their cars, and that limiting access of foreign products to the Polish market would contradict European law (Sejm, 2003a).

In April 2003, shortly after the President's veto, the government sent another draft of the biofuels law to the parliament. Its content was strongly influenced by stakeholders from the farming sector. In December 2003 they organized themselves into the National Chamber of Biofuels with the goal of defending the interests of the Polish companies which were developing the biofuels sector (Wojciechowska, 2004). Also the opposition Polish People's Party (PSL), which targeted farmers as their main electorate, expressed the intention to introduce measures that would increase the share of biocomponents in the transport sector. With the well-organized biofuels advocates and strong support for biofuels in the government, a policy monopoly emerged which aimed at making biofuels development beneficial for the Polish agricultural sector. A way to achieve this goal was to force oil companies to increase the share of biocomponents that they were supposed to mix with the fuels they sold, a measure that met the opposition of the Lotos Group, the biggest state-owned oil company in Poland (Pańczyszyn, 2009). Despite this opposition, the law included a 4 per cent target for the share of biofuels in 2004; twice as high as the one discussed in Brussels for 2005. The reason for this high level of ambition was the hope that after joining the EU Poland would already have the resources and the infrastructure to produce biofuels which could then be exported to other EU countries (Aumiller, 2003).

As it happened, this ambitious target turned out to be unrealistic. When the biofuels law entered into force in January 2004, there was not enough capacity to allow the fulfilment of the 4 per cent target for the share of biofuels in the transport sector using domestic resources. Therefore, the government decided to lower the target in a separate ordinance to 1.6 per cent by September 2004 and 2.4 per cent by the end of the year, to give domestic actors more time to develop necessary production capacity (Council of Ministers, 2004b). The situation of the biofuels sector worsened further after the Constitutional Court declared the already signed biofuels law as unconstitutional due to the fact that it did not allow consumers to choose between regular fuels and fuels including biocomponents. The court also criticized those elements of the law which obliged distributors of fuels to include a certain share of biocomponents and thus, according to the court, it ran contrary to the spirit of the free market. The court further argued that although Poland was obliged to implement European legislation, the indicative target mentioned in the biofuels directive did not justify such 'radical' measures (Constitutional Court, 2004).

In this regard it can be stated that the prospect of accession had a strong impact on Polish biofuels even before Poland became a member of the EU. Although some measures promoting biofuels did already exist in the 1990s, it was the implementation of the EU's biofuels directive that invigorated the discussion about biofuels in Poland and led to the creation of a coalition supporting this source of energy. At the same time, however, one can notice an instrumentalization of EU policy to achieve goals different from those which had led to the formulation of the 2003 biofuels directive. Although the directive mentioned the possibility of 'creating new opportunities for sustainable rural development', there was no explicit mention of the potential for job creation. This has become the main goal of Polish biofuels policy, however, and has had important repercussions for the Europeanization of Polish biofuels policy in subsequent years.

10.4.2 Poland in the EU: Delayed Implementation of the European Biofuels Legislation

The legislative insecurity caused first by the President's veto in 2003 and the Constitutional Court's judgment a year later had a negative impact on investments in biofuels. The situation improved slightly after the introduction of excise exemption on 1 May 2004; coincidentally, the first day of Poland's membership of the EU (Council of Ministers, 2004a). Nonetheless, the 2003 biofuels directive still had not been fully implemented into Polish law, and the share of biofuels Poland was expected to reach in 2005 was only 0.5 per cent instead of the 2.0 per cent included in the directive (Wiśniewski, 2005). This led the European Commission to issue a letter of formal notice to Poland for failing to submit its national report as expected (COM, 2005).

As a result of the pressure from Brussels, implementation of the 2003 biofuels directive was among the tasks mentioned in the 'Polish Energy Policy until 2025', adopted in 2005. The draft of the new law, which was supposed to transpose the biofuels directive, this time included a much more realistic goal for biofuels development as it simply referred to the EU's indicative target of 5.75 per cent (Ministry of Economy, 2005). As in the case of the formulation of previous drafts of the biofuels law, the National Chamber of Biofuels played an important role this time as well, and actively contributed to the early draft of the law (Pańczyszyn, 2006).

In the end, the biofuels law entered into force on 1 January 2007. Its final version included a number of elements which contributed to rapid development of biofuels in Poland in the subsequent years. Among other things, it significantly reduced the bureaucratic barriers for farmers producing biofuels for their own needs. But especially important was the introduction of national indicative targets for the minimum share of biocomponents which should be added to the fuels traded or consumed. The targets were to be defined by the Council of Ministers every three years for the next six years (Sejm, 2006). An ordinance specifying these targets was issued a year later. It included not only the 5.75 per cent target for the share of biofuels by 2010 introduced in the 2003 biofuels directive, but also a much more ambitious target of 7.10 per cent for the share of biofuels by 2013 (Council of Ministers, 2007).

As a result, the consumption of biofuels in Poland increased from 1 per cent in 2005 to 6.3 per cent in 2010. It was the third-highest result in the EU, after Austria and Sweden, and almost twice as high as the EU-28 average (Eurostat, 2014). But the desired effects of the biofuels development in the form of additional jobs and sources of income for farmers did not materialize. Due to the reduction of tax exemptions on biofuels and the possibility of importing cheaper biocomponents from South American and Asian countries, the situation of the biofuels industry in Poland worsened significantly and most of the capacity was not used. In 2010 only 18 per cent of bioethanol consumed in Poland had been produced domestically (Krzemiński, 2013).

The implementation of the 2003 biofuels directive in Poland turned out to be very inefficient. Not only did Poland fail to transpose it on time, which led to a formal 'letter of notice' from the European Commission, but also, with most of the biofuels coming from abroad, the domestic goal of job creation was not achieved. The main reason for the partial failure of top-down Europeanization was the attempt to use European biofuels policy to create new jobs quickly while ignoring the need to provide investors with a stable, long-term legal framework for the development of biofuels domestically.

10.4.3 Changing Winds from Brussels and Opposition from Poland

In the meantime, first-generation biofuels lost their popularity at the European level. The main reasons were their potential contribution to an increase in food prices, and in some cases a less positive than expected reduction of the CO_2 emissions (Oxfam, 2012). During the negotiations of the energy and climate package in 2008 Poland did not take any clear position on the role of biofuels and – differently from the overall RES goal – was seemingly satisfied with the 10 per cent goal suggested by the Commission. At the same time, however, the government and the National Biofuels Association were strongly opposed to replacing first-generation by second-generation biofuels, which would not have such a beneficial effect on farmers growing rapeseed. As a result, these associations have been calling for an implementation of the 2009 RED in a way which would on one hand tighten the sustainability criteria, and thus limit the import of biofuels from outside of Europe, while at the same time also limit the possibility to replace biofuels by other alternatives (Stępień, 2012).

The Polish government failed to implement the 2009 RED with regard to biofuels until the Commission began to threaten sanctions. Only in 2014, almost four years after the deadline, the biofuels law from 2006 was amended to fulfil the requirements of the directive in respect to sustainability standards (Sejm, 2014). Before, in 2013, the government adopted an ordinance with the national indicative targets for the years 2013–2018. According to this target, the increase in the share of biofuels was to slow down, but still should have been much higher than at the EU level on average (Council of Ministers, 2013).

As a result, the Polish targets for first-generation biofuels were much higher than those proposed by the Commission in its draft of the so-called ILUC directive (see Chapter 2 by Solorio and Bocquillon). The latter would limit the share of the first-generation biofuels to 5 per cent within the 10 per cent 2020 RES-T target of the 2009 RED (COM, 2012). During a vote on the Commission's proposal, 47 out of 50 members of the European Parliament from Poland voted against it. Also, during voting in the Council, Poland formed part of the blocking majority, thus making adoption of the ILUC directive in the form suggested by the Commission impossible. Only in mid-2014 did Poland accept the new version of a significantly watered-down directive. In this way Poland defended the policies and targets it introduced as a result of EU impact, a situation difficult to imagine in the case of the electricity sector. Consequently, a top-down Europeanization of the biofuels policy in the initial years of Polish EU membership led to a bottom-up uploading of measures defending the continuation of the use of first-generation biofuels in the EU.

10.5 COMPARATIVE ANALYSIS OF RES-E AND BIOFUEL CASES AND CONCLUSIONS

In the analysed case studies, the different mechanisms of Europeanization manifest themselves in quite different and ambiguous ways. Although Poland has often tried to weaken (foot-dragging) RES-E targets at the EU level (bottom-up Europeanization), only in the case of 2030 RES target adopted in 2014 has it had enough political power, entrepreneurial skill and interest to shape European policy according to its preferences. Until then, Poland had attributed lower meaning and impact to those European RES-E targets than to other measures such as, first and foremost, the EU ETS.

Differently from RES-E, biofuels targets were readily agreed upon (policy taking) even though legislative chaos and a lack of necessary infrastructure made their achievement initially very difficult. The EU's move towards second-generation biofuels led to Poland's opposition and increased activity at the European level in shaping the biofuels policy. The bottom-up Europeanization with regard to RES-E is therefore an example of a foot-dragging strategy, generally mild and unsuccessful, with the only exception of the 2030 RES target. In contrast, in the case of biofuels, the Polish foot-dragging tactic of defending ambitious goals concerning development of first-generation biofuels was more successful and led to delay in the adoption of the ILUC directive until its new version, with higher targets for first-generation biofuels, was adopted in June 2014.

Concerning horizontal Europeanization, clear examples could be mainly found only in the RES-E case. They show that Poland has been eager to adopt policies, best practices and norms shared by the majority of member states when they have suited its own preferences, such as consolidation of the energy industry and introduction of quota obligations and TGCs. As more member states have begun to introduce FITs, Poland has not followed this trend (with the recent exception of a FIT for the micro-scale installations).

Ambiguities could also be observed with regard to the impact of the European renewable energy policy on national RES-E and biofuels policy (top-down Europeanization). Although the EU supported domestic RES-E advocates by setting the legal framework as well as by promoting changes in the beliefs and expectations of domestic actors, and altering the opportunity structure, the policy outcomes have been weakly compatible with EU policy, guaranteeing at best only its formal implementation, without any deeper compliance by changing the status quo of Polish energy policy ('superficial' Europeanization). On the other hand, the Polish government and domestic actors embraced the targets of the 2003 biofuels directive. Despite some delay, a separate biofuels law was adopted in 2006, which enabled Poland to reach its target much earlier than by 2010, although in a very inefficient way (partial Europeanization). The main reason was the attempt to use European biofuels policy to quickly create new jobs in the farming sector while ignoring the need to provide domestic investors with a stable, long-term legal framework. More serious problems began when the EU started introducing sustainability criteria for biofuels and promoting second- and third-generation biofuels.

Reasons for this incongruent Europeanization in the RES-E and RES-T fields have mainly been different resources, belief systems (or issue definitions), and opportunity structures of their dominant advocacy coalitions (or policy monopolies): as opposition to RES-E on the one hand and as biofuels advocacy on the other. It shows clearly that Europeanization is not a single and separate force of influence, but a process that is itself interfered with by many diverse factors in a multi-level system, that only altogether may help to understand the policy change.

In the power sector, the mentioned mechanisms of Europeanization have been caused by the unwillingness and inability to abandon Poland's state-owned, centralized and coal-based power industry structures and arrangements. Although the understanding of the role of RES-E in the political and public debate has changed enormously since at least 1989, policy-makers have almost always been acting more in the interest of the representatives of the conventional power industry than in that of the RES-E industry and consumers. The conventional power sector is still more powerful and better organized than the emerging RES-E advocates. There has been a strong economic and political interdependence between the state and the conventional power industry. All of these are reasons for the continuing existence of a policy monopoly in the Polish power sector. And this policy monopoly allows for only moderate alterations in the existing system which would not reduce its economic and political advantages. Therefore, all RES-E policies introduced in Poland have been designed in ways that do not affect the role of the conventional power industry, or at least try to minimize these changes.

For the biofuels case, EU membership has offered a window of opportunity to develop the agricultural sector and provide farmers with additional income. Differently from the power sector, in this case a policy monopoly of the biofuels industry has developed. The actors opposed to an ambitious biofuels policy were few and – as turned out to be decisive – did not enjoy strong support on behalf of the government. At the same time biofuels advocates, as opposed to RES-E advocates, managed to organize themselves and present a common position towards policy changes. Although the National Biofuels Chamber has not always been successful in influencing Polish biofuels policy, for example when it failed to prevent the reduction of tax exemptions for biocomponents, it managed to influence the policy-making process which led to the adoption of the biofuels law. But, despite using arguments about the beneficial impact of biofuels on climate protection, their introduction in Poland has always been much more about jobs than about the environment. The much smaller potential of second-generation biofuels in comparison to first-generation biofuels for job creation in the agricultural sector led Poland to oppose their stronger promotion at the EU level and domestically.

REFERENCES

Ancygier, A. (2013), *Misfit of Interests instead of the "Goodness of Fit"? Implementation of European Directives 2001/77/EC and 2009/28/EC in Poland*, Hamburg: Verlag Dr. Kovac.

Ancygier, A. and O. Caspar (2014), 'Der Mythos der übermächtigen Kohlelobby. Warum Polen energiepolitisch anders ist und wie Deutschland damit umgehen sollte', *IPG-Journal*, Juli, accessed on 4 August 2015 at http://www.ipg-journal.de/rubriken/nachhaltigkeit-energie-und-klimapolitik/artikel/der-mythos-der-uebermaechtigen-kohlelobby-520/.

Aumiller, A. (2003), 'Co może przerwać chocholi taniec wokół ustawy o biopaliwach?', *Czysta Energia*, 8/2003, accessed on 4 August 2015 at http://www.e-czytelnia.abrys.pl/czysta-energia/2003-8-89/poselskim-okiem-544/co-moze-przerwac-chocholi-taniec-wokol-ustawy-o-biopaliwach-2997.

Baumgartner, F.R. and B.D. Jones (2009), *Agendas and Instability in American Politics*, Chicago, IL, USA and London, UK: University of Chicago Press.

BMWi (2014), 'Der klima- und energiepolitische EU-Rahmen bis 2030 im Informationsportal Erneuerbare Energien', accessed on 4 August 2015 at http://www.erneuerbare-energien.de/EE/Redaktion/DE/Standardartikel/eu_klima_und_energierahmen.html.

Busch, P. and H. Jörgens (2012), 'Europeanization through diffusion? Renewable energy policies and alternative sources for European convergence', in F. Morata and I. Solorio (eds), *European Energy Policy: An Environmental Approach*, Cheltenham, UK and Northampton, MA, USA: Edward Elgar Publishing, pp. 66–84.

Central Statistical Office of Poland (2015), 'Energia ze źródeł odnawialnych w 2014 r.' (information note), 18 December, accessed on 23 February 2017 at http://stat.gov.pl/obszary-tematyczne/srodowisko-energia/energia/energia-ze-zrodel-odnawialnych-w-2014-roku,3,9.html.

COM (2001a), 'Green Paper. Towards a European strategy for the security of energy supply', accessed on 4 August 2015 at http://ec.europa.eu/energy/green-paper-energy-supply/doc/green_paper_energy_supply_en.pdf.

COM (2001b), 'Proposal for a directive of the European Parliament and of the Council on the promotion of the use of biofuels for transport', COM (2001) 547 final, accessed on 4 August 2015 at http://eur-lex.europa.eu/legal-content/EN/TXT/PDF/?uri=CELEX:52001DC0547&from=EN.

COM (2005), 'The European Commission notifies Member States on delays in implementing European legislation on biofuels', Press Release IP/05/318, accessed on 11 February 2017 at http://europa.eu/rapid/press-release_IP-05-318_en.htm.

COM (2012), 'Proposal for a Directive of the European Parliament and of the Council amending Directive 98/70/EC relating to the quality of petrol and diesel fuels and amending Directive 2009/28/EC on the promotion of the use of energy from renewable sources', COM (2012) 595 final, accessed on 24 February 2017 at http://eur-lex.europa.eu/LexUriServ/LexUriServ.do?uri=COM:2012:0595:FIN:En:PDF.

Constitutional Court (2004), 'Wyrok Trybunału Konstytucyjnego z dnia 21 kwietnia 2004 r. sygn. akt K 33/03', *Dziennik Ustaw*, nr 109. poz. 1160, accessed on 11 February 2017 at http://www.dziennikustaw.gov.pl/du/2004/s/109/1160/1.

Council of Ministers (2004a), 'Rozporządzenie Ministra Finansów z dnia 26 kwietnia 2004 r. w sprawie zwolnień od podatku akcyzowego', *Dziennik Ustaw*, nr 97. poz. 966, accessed on 4 August 2015 at http://isap.sejm.gov.pl/DetailsServlet?id=WDU20040030016.

Council of Ministers (2004b), 'Rozporządzenie Rady Ministrów z dnia 10 stycznia 2004 r. w sprawie minimalnej ilości biokomponentów wprowadzanych do obrotu w paliwach ciekłych lub biopaliwach ciekłych w 2004 r', *Dziennik Ustaw*, nr 3. poz. 16, accessed on 4 August 2015 at http://isap.sejm.gov.pl/DetailsServlet?id=WDU20040970966.

Council of Ministers (2007), 'Rozporządzenie Rady Ministrów z dnia 15 czerwca 2007 r. w sprawie Narodowych Celów Wskaźnikowych na lata 2008–2013', *Dziennik Ustaw*, nr 110. poz. 757, accessed on 4 August 2015 at http://isap.sejm.gov.pl/DetailsServlet?id=WDU20071100757.

Council of Ministers (2013), 'Rozporządzenie Rady Ministrów z dnia 23 lipca 2013 r. w sprawie Narodowych Celów Wskaźnikowych na lata 2013–2018', *Dziennik Ustaw*, nr 2013. poz. 918, accessed on 4 August 2015 at http://isap.sejm.gov.pl/DetailsServlet?id=WDU20130000918.

Eurostat (2014), 'Share of renewable energy in fuel consumption of transport', accessed on 4 August 2015 at http://epp.eurostat.ec.europa.eu/tgm/table.do?tab=table&init=1&plugin=1&language=en&pcode=tsdcc340.

Grużewski, D. (2004), 'Energetyczna unia personalna', *Czysta Energia*, 4 (32), accessed on 4 August 2015 at http://e-czytelnia.abrys.pl/czysta-energia/2004-4-116/prawo-990/wokol-ustawy-czy-jest-8222-energetyczna-unia-personalna-3605.

Gwiazdowicz, M. (1994), 'Biopaliwo szansą dla polskiego rolnictwa i środowiska', *Kancelaria Sejmu. Biuro Studiów i Ekspertyz*, accessed on 4 August 2015 at http://biurose.sejm.gov.pl/teksty_pdf_94/i-229.pdf.

Jankowska, K. (2011), 'Poland's climate change policy struggle: greening the East?', in R.K.W. Wurzel and J. Connelly (eds), *The European Union as a Leader in International Climate Change Politics*, London, UK and New York, NY, USA: Routledge Taylor & Francis Group, pp. 163–178.

Jankowska, K. (2012), *Die Kräfte des Wandels. Die Wandlung Polens von einer auf Kohle basierenden zu einer an erneuerbaren Energien orientierten Gesellschaft*, accessed on 12 August 2014 at Dissertations online FU Berlin: http://www.diss.fu-berlin.de/diss/receive/FUDISS_thesis_000000037268.

Jankowska, K. (2017), 'Poland's clash over energy and climate policy: Green economy or grey status quo?', in R.K.W. Wurzel, J. Connelly and D. Liefferink (eds.), *The European Union in International Climate Change Politics: Still Taking a lead?*, London, UK and New York, NY, USA: Routledge

Krzemiński, J. (2013), 'UE ogranicza wsparcie dla biopaliw, Polska nie', *Obserwatorfinansowy.pl*, 30 September, accessed on 4 August 2015 at http://www.obserwatorfinansowy.pl/forma/rotator/ue-ogranicza-wsparcie-dla-biopaliw-polska-nie/.

Ministry of Economy (2005), 'Polityka Energetyczna Polski do 2025 roku', accessed on 4 August 2015 at http://www.oze.bpp.lublin.pl/dokumenty/kraj_meryt/pol_energ.pdf.

Ministry of Environment (2000), 'Strategia rozwoju energetyki odnawialnej', accessed on 4 August 2015 at http://www.pga.org.pl/prawo/strategia-OZE.pdf.

Oxfam (2012), 'The hunger grains', *Oxfam Briefing Paper* 161, 17 September, accessed on 4 August 2015 at http://www.oxfam.org/en/eu/research/hunger-grains.

Pańczyszyn, T. (2006), 'Nowelizacja ustawy o biokomponentach', *Czysta Energia*, 6/2006, accessed on 4 August 2015 at https://e-czytelnia.abrys.pl/czysta-energia/2006-6-229/forum-2433/nowelizacja-ustawy-o-biokomponentach-6273.

Pańczyszyn, T. (2009), 'Stanowisko Koalicji na Rzecz Biopaliw', *Czysta Energia*, 5/2009, accessed on 4 August 2015 at http://e-czytelnia.abrys.pl/czysta-energia/2009-5-411/forum-4104/stanowisko-koalicji-na-rzecz-biopaliw-9854.

Podrygała, I. (2008), *Erneuerbare Energien im polnischen Stromsektor. Analyse der Entstehung und Ausgestaltung der Instrumente zur Förderung der Stromerzeugung aus erneuerbaren Energien*, Stuttgart: Ibidem-Verlag.

Polskie Siecie Elektroenergetyczne S.A. (PSE SA) (2014), 'Miesięczne raporty z funkcjonowania Krajowego Systemu Elektroenergetycznego i Rynku Bilansującego (Dane operatywne)', accessed on 4 August 2015 at http://www.pse.pl/index.php?modul=8&y=2013&m=12&id_rap=212.

REO (2012), 'UE: Polska przeciw celowi 30 proc. zielonej energii do 2030 r.', 19 June, accessed on 4 August 2015 at http://www.reo.pl/ue-polska-przeciw-celowi-30-proc-zielonej-energii-do-2030-r.

Sabatier, Paul, A. (ed.) (2007), *Theories of the Policy Process*, Boulder, CO: Westview Press.

Sejm (1997), 'Prawo energetyczne z dnia 10 kwietnia 1997', *Dziennik Ustaw*, nr 54 poz. 348, accessed on 2 August 2015 at http://isap.sejm.gov.pl/DetailsServlet?id=WDU19970540348.

Sejm (2002a), 'Poselski projekt ustawy o biopaliwach', *Druk 860*, accessed on 4 August 2015 at http://orka.sejm.gov.pl/Druki4ka.nsf/($vAllByUnid)/2266025E797EDCB8C1256C2F00292641/$file/860.pdf.

Sejm (2002b), 'Poselski projekt ustawy o organizacji rynku eko-paliw płynnych i ich składników', Druk 859, accessed on 4 August 2015 at http://orka.sejm.gov.pl/Druki4ka.nsf/($vAllByUnid)/032FC5B1CC620E65C1256C2F00292603/$file/859.pdf.

Sejm (2002c), 'Rządowy projekt ustawy o organizacji rynku eko-paliw ciekłych oraz eko-komponentów do ich produkcji', *Druk 760*, accessed on 4 August 2015 at http://orka.sejm.gov.pl/Druki4ka.nsf/wgdruku/760/$file/760.pdf.

Sejm (2003a), 'Wniosek prezydenta o ponowne rozpatrzenie przez Sejm ustawy z dnia 19 grudnia 2002 r. o organizacji rynku biopaliw ciekłych oraz biokomponentów do ich produkcji', *Druk 1261*, accessed on 4 August 2015 at http://orka.sejm.gov.pl/Druki4ka.nsf/wgdruku/1261/$file/1261.pdf.

Sejm (2003b), 'Uzasadnienie do projektu ustawy o biokomponentach stosowanych w paliwach ciekłych i biopaliwach ciekłych', *Druk 1479*, accessed on 4 August 2015 at http://orka.sejm.gov.pl/Druki4ka.nsf/wgdruku/1479/$file/1479.pdf.

Sejm (2006), 'Ustawa z dnia 25 sierpnia 2006 r. o biokomponentach i biopaliwach ciekłych', *Dziennik Ustaw*, nr. 169. poz. 1199, accessed on 4 August 2015 at http://isap.sejm.gov.pl/DetailsServlet?id=WDU20061691199.

Sejm (2014), 'Ustawa z dnia 21 marca 2014 r. o zmianie ustawy o biokomponentach i biopaliwach ciekłych oraz niektórych innych ustaw', *Dziennik Ustaw*, poz. 457, accessed on 4 August 2015 at http://isap.sejm.gov.pl/DetailsServlet?id=WDU20140000457.

Stankiewicz, D. (2000), 'Sytuacja ekonomiczna mieszkańców wsi', *Informacja BSE* nr. 737, accessed on 4 August 2015 at http://biurose.sejm.gov.pl/teksty_pdf_00/i-737.pdf.

Stępień, A. (2012), 'Priorytety KIB na 2012 r. – déjà vu?', *Czysta Energia*, 5/2012, accessed on 4 August 2015 at http://e-czytelnia.abrys.pl/czysta-energia/2012-5-611/forum-6967/priorytety-kib-na-2012-r-deja-vu-14698.

Weiss, W. (2002), 'Polska drugim Kuwejtem', *Czysta Energia*, 4/2002, accessed on 4 August 2015 at http://e-czytelnia.abrys.pl/przeglad-komunalny/2002-4-4/forum-3277/polska-drugim-kuwejtem-292.

Wiśniewski, G. (2005), 'Wizja rozwoju biopaliw transportowych w Unii Europejskiej', *Czysta Energia*, 8/2008, accessed on 4 August 2015 at https://e-czytelnia.abrys.pl/czysta-energia/2005-8-187/prawo-1021/wizja-rozwoju-biopaliw-transportowych-w-unii-europejskiej-5174.
WNP (2013), 'Maciej Grabowski nowym ministrem środowiska', *wnp.pl*, accessed on 20 November 2013 at http://energetyka.wnp.pl/maciej-grabowski-nowym-ministrem-srodowiska,211794_1_0_0.html.
WNP (2014), 'Nowe zagrożenia dla elektrowni węglowych', *wnp.pl*, accessed on 7 August 2014 at http://energetyka.wnp.pl/nowe-zagrozenia-dla-elektrowni-weglowych,231783_1_0_0.html.
Wojciechowska, U. (2004), 'Tylko biopaliwa płynne', *Czysta Energia*, 2/2004, accessed on 6 August 2015 at http://e-czytelnia.abrys.pl/czysta-energia/2004-2-123/wywiad-miesiaca-819/tylko-biopaliwa-plynne-3799.

11. The Europeanization of renewable energy policy in Romania

Simona Davidescu

11.1 INTRODUCTION

The development of a renewable energy policy in Romania is at first glance a success story of significant growth in just a few years, going against its perceived 'laggard' reputation (Noutcheva and Bechev, 2008). This chapter looks at how European Union (EU) directives in this sector have been transposed in Romania, altering the opportunity structure for domestic actors and international business interests. However, results were uneven across sectors and a variety of structural, procedural and practical barriers to policy implementation still persist. Furthermore, the promotion of renewable energy sources (RES) has been contested during the last few years and has been associated with the economic crisis, high energy prices and political turf wars. Despite this, the authorities declared on 1 January 2014 that Romania's 2020 target of 24 per cent RES in the energy mix had already been reached (Ionascu, 2014).

The literature on renewable energy in Romania has grown greatly in recent years, following renewed interest in this policy area at the domestic level from policymakers, businesses and the voluntary sector (*Diplomat*, 2011, 2013), coupled with the effects of restructuring the power generation sector in Romania (Haar and Marinescu, 2011; Diaconu et al., 2009). Although largely descriptive, the literature assesses the potential (Dinica, 2003) and recent growth of the RES sector in Romania (Colesca and Ciocoiu, 2013), as well as the instruments for promoting RES-E (Dinica, 2003; *Diplomat*, 2011, 2013) and limits or obstacles to RES-E (Dinica, 2003; Budusan, 2011). This chapter addresses a gap in the literature regarding the impact of EU regulation in the field of renewable energy before and after Romania's EU accession in January 2007. In doing so, it reveals the limits of the EU's influence when targets are within reach and domestic policymakers face significant opposing coalitions, in the context of an economic crisis.

The focus is on RES for electricity (RES-E) policy and on biomass or biofuels as an example of RES for transport (RES-T). The research questions addressed here are: what was the EU's policy impact in these two fields of renewable energy policy? Were the domestic changes generated by conditionality conducive to sustainable compliance after accession? The preliminary argument in this chapter is that support for RES-E and RES-T in Romania is another example of 'shallow Europeanization' (Goetz, 2005), following mainly a top-down dynamic, and overall weak sustainability, based on declaratory commitment to principles, while the main object of policies is economic growth (Baker, 2006, pp. 30–33). Although changes generated by conditionality have empowered a set of actors, the overall climate is one of limited implementation. Despite a range of barriers, investment in RES-E (particularly wind and solar) reached unexpected levels and contributed to Romania attaining its 2020 target early, while significantly lagging behind its targets for RES-T. The main explanation put forward is related to the set of instruments used, in particular financial incentives, different barriers to implementation and the availability of cheaper external solutions (imports) in the case of RES-T.

The following section looks at the analytical framework and research methods used, while section 11.3 and section 11.4 trace the legislative process of RES-E and RES-T support schemes, respectively, with their many amendments and barriers to implementation in practice. The chapter concludes with a comparative view of the RES-E and RES-T sectors and a reflection on their overall sustainability in Romania.

11.2 ANALYTICAL UNDERPINNING AND METHODS

The chapter uses the Europeanization framework as detailed in Chapter 1 (by Jörgens and Solorio), with the main expectation being that the Europeanization of RES-E and RES-T in Romania will be largely top-down, following on from the need to comply with EU rules. Rationalist institutionalism accounts of the EU's domestic impact and 'logic of consequences' look at how 'the EU changes the opportunity structure for utility-maximizing domestic actors' (Sedelmeier, 2011, p. 11). Despite the change in the opportunity structure and a sudden and substantive growth in investment in RES more generally, a significant 'institutional misfit' and a range of barriers to implementation in practice suggest that the legacies of the communist and post-communist periods are important in understanding adjustment costs. Using historical institutionalism, this chapter takes into account how the different historical legacies (including geography, institutional setting, culture, economic and social conditions) impact on aspects of democratization (Pop-Eleches, 2007). These legacies explain the limits to Europeanization and its 'shallow' nature in the case of Romania.

Post-accession, the main questions raised in the literature on Europeanization have been related to the sustainability of formal institutions and possible policy reversals (Sedelmeier, 2011, p. 25). It is mainly to this literature on compliance that the chapter makes a contribution, looking in detail at implementation beyond the formal legal transposition of EU directives, including legislative amendments, non-compliance, creative compliance and policy reversal.

Furthermore, the chapter looks at the extent to which there is evidence of bottom-up Europeanization in terms of Romania's ability to influence policy decisions at the EU level after its entry in 2007. The initial position adopted by Romania has been one of fence-sitting, a neutral stance marked by less-pronounced policy preferences, constrained action capacity and reliance on coalition building depending on the issue involved (Börzel, 2002, p. 207). Fence-sitters such as Romania would prefer to avoid costly European policies 'simply by not implementing them rather than raising opposition in the decision-making process' (Börzel, 2002, p. 208). The relationship between Romania and the Visegrád 4 countries, as well as examples of lesson-drawing from other member states such as Spain and the United Kingdom, show only limited and occasional evidence of horizontal Europeanization.

This chapter employs text- and document-based analysis in the study of political institutions, using a qualitative research design and legislative process tracing. The chapter looks at a range of primary sources: documents and policies from Romania and the EU level, interviews with stakeholders published in the media, information from official websites of institutions involved in the policymaking process and other relevant stakeholders.

11.3 THE EUROPEANIZATION OF RES-E POLICY IN ROMANIA

11.3.1 The Appeal of Large Hydro and the 'Lost Decade' of the 1990s

The development of RES-E has been hailed as one of the few positive legacies of the communist regime in Romania, with hydropower being overwhelmingly preferred. From the 1960s to the late 1980s all major rivers had large hydropower plants in place, providing an additional energy source to the dominant coal and gas (Dinica, 2003, p. 149). In the 1980s, other types of RES-E started to be financed from the state budget, in particular small hydro and wind plants, using largely domestic technology, but suffering from 'overcentralized management', 'severe technology import restrictions' and the distorting practice of keeping fossil fuel prices low, especially coal (Pencea, 1993, p. 137).

The early 1990s saw some continuation of previous practices in terms of reliance on cheap fossil fuels, and even the large hydro sector suffered from a shortage of funding in the context of transition. Small hydro plants and wind farms under construction or in need of refurbishment were being abandoned or slowly privatized (Pencea, 1993). Overall, the liberalization, privatization and restructuring of the energy sector was almost non-existent in this period, following a view that 'utilities in the energy sector should remain integrated and property of the state' (Constantinescu, 2013). A change in government in 1996 gave top priority to Romania's late effort to join the EU in the first accession wave, by starting liberalization in this sector and addressing transparency and functionality,[1] while the state still retained the majority stake in all types of energy generation (*Diplomat*, 2011).

By 1998 it was clear that Romania and Bulgaria (see Chapter 12 by Hiteva and Maltby) would only join the EU in a second accession wave, resulting in some of the reform efforts taking a back seat, especially with regard to the privatization of the energy sector and the liberalization of energy prices (Haar and Marinescu, 2011). This is consistent with the findings of the literature on Europeanization in the candidate countries, in that the 'EU's policy impact depended on a credible membership incentive' (Sedelmeier, 2011, p. 22).

11.3.2 The Accession Negotiations and Romania's Entry in the European Union (2002–07)

Further reforms in the electricity sector can be linked to the start of the EU accession negotiations on the energy chapter, from March 2002–04. Diaconu et al. (2009, p. 117) note that 'from the very beginning, Romania accepted the entire Community *acquis* in the electricity sector and did not foresee any problems in fully applying it upon the accession'. The transposition of the *acquis* was done largely in a top-down manner, addressing the policy misfit in the first instance. The government usually issued emergency government decisions (GDs)[2] that entered into immediate effect, to be adopted by parliament without much debate at a later date. Further legislative changes were needed for implementation: developing action and implementation plans and amendments to keep up with changes at the EU level.

The pre-accession period was dominated by top-down Europeanization: Romania's sustained efforts to formally adopt and transpose the *acquis* at a fast pace. Romania transposed the RES-E directive through emergency procedure in GD 443/2003, setting a target of 30 per cent of national gross electrical energy consumption from RES-E by 2010, to include large hydro, at a time when other RES investment was negligible. A further GD 1892/2004 introduced gradual mandatory quotas for RES-E until 2010 and a new instrument to promote investment: Green Certificates (GCs).[3] Data from 2008 included in the National Renewable Energy Action Plan showed that out of a total production of RES-E of 16 918 GWh (gigawatt hour) (100 per cent), large hydro represented 95.4 per cent, hydro between 1 and 10 MW (megawatts) or 3.9 per cent, hydro less than 1 MW or 0.6 per cent, and wind 0.1 per cent (NREAP, 2010, p. 21). A further GD 958/2005 introduced minimum and maximum values for GC and effectively created a centralized market, dominated by hydroelectric power (*Diplomat*, 2013). Despite this initial supporting legislation, there were limited investments in RES-E, as loans were difficult to secure because of significant upfront costs, high risk and limited reward of one certificate per megawatt hour (MWh) (Mediafax, 2011). At this pace, Romania was heading for a possible infringement of its commitments for the RES-E targets after accession.

11.3.3 The Post-Accession Period: Changing Pace

While the previous period was a case of top-down Europeanization, a first test of Romania's capacity to upload its own preferences (that is, bottom-up Europeanization) came soon after the 2007 accession, with the negotiations of the EU climate and energy package. The position for these negotiations was based on the first Energy Strategy of Romania (2007–20) and prior domestic legislation in this area. The draft strategy was discussed in early 2007 by a committee of politicians from across the political spectrum and reviewed by the EU Energy Commissioner, Andris Piebalgs, in a visit to Romania (Wall Street Romania, 2007). The agreed target of 24 per cent of RES-E from gross domestic consumption was criticized by the domestic media as unrealistic[4] (*Income Magazine*, 2010), but the authorities were trapped by their prior conflated predictions and commitments and did not object to the Commission's proposal.

Romania has used effectively the opposition of other new member states led by Poland (see Chapter 10 by Jankowska and Ancygier), and joined a common position at a meeting in Gdansk between leaders of the Eastern member states and the French President Sarkozy (due to France holding the Council presidency at the time), on minimizing the costs of reducing carbon emissions and a more flexible application of the climate and energy package (Evenimentul Zilei, 2008). This 'fence-sitting' approach of building tactical coalitions with foot-draggers such as the Visegrád 4 countries (Börzel, 2002, p. 194) has proved beneficial for subsequent negotiations in the European Council. The result of negotiations on the 2020 climate and energy package was portrayed by both President Traian Băsescu and Prime Minister Călin Popescu Tăriceanu as a success and in the national interest, and the side-payments obtained were the simplification of procedures to access EU funding and the highest percentage of EU funding for Romania's contribution to reducing greenhouse gas (GHG) emissions from 1990 levels (Financiarul, 2008).

At the domestic level, change in the level of investment in RES-E was prompted by a separate parliamentary initiative. This broke with the pattern of decision-making by emergency legislation and was met with opposition from the government. The parliamentary initiative led by the opposition (B.536/2007[5]) – eight members of parliament from the Social Democratic Party (PSD) as well as national minority groups – preceded the negotiations at the EU level of the climate and energy package. It drew on some examples from member states such as Germany (see Chapter 3 by Vogelpohl et al.), Denmark (see Chapter 5 by Dyrhauge) and Spain (see Chapter 8 by Solorio and Fernandez), as models to follow in stimulating investment in RES-E, rather than borrowing specific policy instruments (B.536/2007, Expunere de Motive).

This shows that pro-RES actors were benefiting from an altered opportunity structure, and were able to draw on compliance data from across the EU (OPTRES, 2007). The Tăriceanu government opposed the draft on the grounds that the previous GD 1892/2004 was in compliance with EU directives, and the proposed legislation could only be valid for a maximum of two years before it would have to be substantially amended to comply with the new EU climate and energy package under negotiation (B.536/2007, Punct de Vedere). Despite these reservations, law 220/2008[6] passed with ease through both chambers of the Romanian parliament after being debated in four different committees. The media portrayed this result as the victory of business interest groups, which effectively lobbied members of the Chamber of Deputies and the Senate (Gellner, 2013).

One of the main provisions of law 220/2008 was to differentiate the GCs in terms of the type of technology: one for hydropower, two for wind, three for biomass and four for solar energy. Moreover, investment was encouraged by other incentives: the value of GCs was raised, the duration of the scheme varied according to how new the equipment was, tax exemptions were applied,[7] mandatory annual quotas of green energy were set, and there was a guaranteed priority access to the electrical energy transportation and distribution network. Overall, the legislative framework for the support of RES-E was considered 'one of the most generous in the EU' (*Diplomat*, 2013). The scheme sent a clear positive signal to investors and the number of new projects soared over the next few years, up to €3 billion by 2013 with a further commitment to double this figure over the following years[8] (*Diplomat*, 2013). The surge in RES-E projects highlighted capacity problems for grid connection (guaranteed by law 220/2008): demand was reported to outgrow the transport capacity of the national grid by a factor of four, making major investments necessary in the near future (Burchett, 2011).

However, the government decided to use delay tactics: action and implementation plans did not follow to operationalize the new legislation and the European Commission was not notified of the scheme on the grounds of state aid. Law 220/2008 was not implemented even a couple of years later, when it started to be amended. In order to transpose the renewable energy directive (RED), an amendment (law 139/2010) passed through parliament with ease, despite a large number of changes (mainly clarifications) to almost every article. A further amendment a year later was deemed necessary 'in order ... to obtain as soon as possible the approval of the [support] scheme by the European Commission' (GD 88/2011, Nota de Fundamentare). An informal dialogue on this issue between Romanian authorities and the European Commission (2009–11) comprised letters containing 47 clarification questions (Pirvoiu, 2011a). By 2011, the European Commission considered that provisions of law 220/2008 did not constitute state aid, and that support in the aggregate did not result in overcompensation (COM, 2011, p. 15). This finally gave the green light for the implementation of law 220/2008 via an emergency decision (GD 88/2011). It was a year later that parliament passed it into law with some additional clarifications (law 134/2012). The support scheme in this form lasted until 2013, when new amendments were proposed to drastically limit its remit and applicability.

This long delay in implementation raised significant concerns for investors that had already secured loans with stringent conditions and made investment plans (Pirvoiu, 2013). Despite this, the effects of the support legislation in practice were a surge in investment, particularly from foreign businesses (while local technology and investors could only marginally compete); a development of the market in legal services; and a boost for the development of wind and solar energy. By December 2013, projects of 2503 MW from wind energy, 1155 MW from solar energy, 65 MW from biomass and 530 MW from small hydro had been installed (*Diplomat*, 2013). Lobby groups representing a wide set of interests were set up, such as the Romanian Wind Energy Association,[9] which benefited from direct lobbying of the European Commission's Directorate General (DG) Energy as well as DG Environment (RWEA, 2013).

The controversy surrounding policy implementation had obscured the deeper institutional misfit, which became apparent after 2011. As the RES-E sector was growing, there was a need for a designated central institution for energy, but its set-up took until 2014. The restructuring of the Ministry of Economy in 2012 saw the allocation of a Department for Energy, with specific attributions for 'realizing the national conditions for the implementation of the energy-climate change package' (MECBE, 2012, p. 81). While the Romanian Ministry of Environment had been involved in negotiations in the Council of Ministers for the climate and energy package, in terms of policy implementation its role was limited to the climate change part of the package. Throughout 2013 there had been a clear move towards the creation of a 'mini-ministry' by the head of the Department for Energy, Constantin Niță (PSD), which included relocating to a separate building and gathering all staff with any energy-related skills or experience (around 250 of the MECBE's 700 members of staff), predominantly those who were specialists in 'conventional' energy (Pirvoiu, 2013). By March 2014, Constantin Niță took over the position of Minister of Economy and a new portfolio was put in place for a Delegated Minister for Energy, Răzvan-Eugen Nicolescu, a former attaché to the EU on energy issues.

The institutional reforms were necessary not only at the central level, but also at the local level: dealing with a cumbersome permit system and limited numbers of specialized staff to investigate the impact of proposed projects. A study from 2012 found excessive bureaucracy and corruption to be the main barriers to RES-E (a total of approximately 100 approvals and permits were necessary for the launch of a project), together with a lack of financing (Terra Mileniul III, 2012). Furthermore, projects were often approved without proper examination of their environmental impact, particularly at the local level. Environmental groups had consistently opposed specific wind, biomass and small hydro projects that had received approval for construction in protected natural areas, blaming local authorities for corrupt practices and a deliberate breach of existing legislation (Terra Mileniul III, 2012). These concerns were overshadowed by mounting opposition to RES-E after 2012, led by emerging powerful veto players, which made the government change direction towards the 'dismantling' of the support scheme, invoking the economic crisis.

11.3.4 Coping with the Economic Crisis

Throughout 2012–13, the country's leading industrial lobby started to mobilize more effectively, blaming the RES-E support scheme for a significant increase in electricity prices. New technology, increased competition in the electricity market and the generous GC support system were driving up prices for consumers (*Diplomat*, 2013). Furthermore, the effects of the economic crisis led to a decrease in consumption levels for electricity, significant loss of jobs and cuts in levels of public expenditure. The lock-in effect of EU accession meant that the government could not continue its practice of writing off debts for big industrial consumers, one of the legacies of the communist regime continued in the post-communist period, coupled with keeping the price of electricity low (UN, 2001). The Association of Big Industrial Energy Consumers (ABIEC) emerged in this period as a powerful veto player, considering that its members alone consumed around 10 per cent of the total domestic energy production (Pirvoiu, 2014b). It was joined by trade unions from the industry sector as well as concerned citizens, who protested in front of government buildings (Cartel Alfa[10], 13 April 2014; Pirvoiu, 2013).

The government and the Romanian Energy Regulatory Authority (ANRE) responded by amending law 220/2008 further (GD 57/2013), including the suspension of Green Certificates until 2017, a provision allowing the government to change the support scheme at any point in the calendar year, and setting a limit to the amount of electricity certified through GCs per annum. The announcement of this new change to the legislation led to a market freeze: 'There were no more signings of contracts with turbine producers, no more projects were sold, no more loans were granted' (*Diplomat*, 2014).

Numerous complaints from RES-E investors and environmental non-governmental organizations (ENGOs) were sent directly to the European Commission, expressing concern about the planned modifications to the RES-E support scheme (Pirvoiu, 2014a). After several informal contacts, the European Commission recommended the start by Romanian authorities of a formal pre-notification process. This was used by other domestic actors, such as President Traian Băsescu, as a weapon in his ongoing conflict with the head of the government, Victor Ponta, by refusing to promulgate GD 57/2013, sending it for re-examination in both chambers of parliament and to the Constitutional Court[11] (Pirvoiu, 2014a).

In January 2014, ANRE officially declared that Romania had already reached its 2020 target of 24 per cent RES-E of the gross final energy consumption, as part of its commitments under the 2009 RED (Ionascu,

2014). Following this announcement, ABIEC lobbied for further concessions and ArcelorMittal threatened the government with a move out of Europe (Bărbulescu, 2013). In response, the Ponta government proposed further legislation to exempt big energy consumers from supplementary taxes on energy (Pirvoiu, 2014b), waiting for the results of an EU-level debate on 'Draft guidelines on environmental and energy state aid for 2014–20' before sending a formal notification to the European Commission.

The impact of the economic crisis has pushed Romanian authorities not only to devise new policy amendments to protect heavy industry, but also to support this more actively in a bottom-up approach at the EU level. For negotiations on the 2030 climate and energy package, Romania has continued to build coalitions with fellow Visegrád 4+ members (Joint Statement, 2014). The Joint Statement did not support binding targets, calling for a solidarity mechanism and compensatory measures for lower-income member states. It questioned the impact of the package on the competitiveness of the industry, invoking the economic crisis, coupled with raising energy prices for domestic consumers and the Ukraine crisis's impact on energy security (Joint Statement, 2014).

There is some limited evidence of horizontal Europeanization following the logic of economic competition, as the government linked the last policy amendments of 2013–14 to the economic crisis and the unpopular increase in electricity prices, using examples of other member states dismantling their support schemes, particularly Spain (Sisea, 2013; see also Chapter 8 by Solorio and Fernandez). Furthermore, Prime Minister Victor Ponta considered that it was worth learning lessons on energy policy from Poland (see Chapter 10 by Jankowska and Ancygier), as stated during an official visit in 2013 (Bodeanu, 2013).

Overall, the picture of RES-E support in Romania is illustrative of the type of policies and strategies Romania came up with over the last decade: one of mixed signals, from overwhelming legislative support to backtracking and reversals of decisions, but the lock-in effect of EU legislation created the conditions for the emergence of RES-E supporters and ultimately the reaching of assumed targets.

11.4 BIOFUELS AND RES-T PROMOTION IN ROMANIA

By contrast, the promotion of biofuels in the transport sector in Romania has been a case of failure to reach targets, with a large deviation in RES-T targets from its National Renewable Energy Action Plan

(NREAP) ambition, of 4 per cent biofuels, compared with the 5.75 per cent target by 2010 (ECOFYS, 2012, p. 48). This was due to a range of barriers to implementation specific to this sector and the availability of external solutions, mainly cheap imports of biofuels. Unlike the RES-E case, there had been almost no prior investment in the use of biofuels for the transport sector before the first related legislation was introduced in mid-2000. This has been again mainly a case of top-down Europeanization, prompted by the need to comply with the *acquis* before the EU accession in 2007. The main mechanism for Europeanization has been the adoption of existing EU policy prescriptions, as prompted by conditionality and the proximity of accession.

The path to policy transposition for the biofuels directive was via emergency decree (GD 1844/2005), followed by a clarification amendment (GD 456/2007). The initial targets set in GD 1844/2005 were a 2 per cent mix of biofuels by the accession date of 2007, and 5.75 per cent by 2010. The Ministry of Economy and Commerce was the central institution in charge of monitoring, implementation, information and reporting to the European Commission. This policy was not subject to debate during Romania's negotiations on the energy chapter (2002–04), as it was not considered problematic because of its voluntary targets, hence the later transposition. By 2006 members of the Romanian negotiating team from the Ministry for European Integration considered that Romania would not be able to reach the 2 per cent target before the EU accession in January 2007 (Chiriac and Vasilache, 2006).

The first amendment of the legislation in 2007 signalled some of the problems for this area: GD 456/2007 set sanctions[12] and placed the burden on 'economic operators' for the introduction of the fuel mix on the market. These specifications were designed to address in practice the deliberate non-compliance of the main domestic fuel producers (Petrom and OMV), which were waiting for financial incentives and legislative clarifications before making any investments (Chiriac and Vasilache, 2006). A first set of incentives entered into effect at the start of 2007 through a new fiscal code that eliminated excises for biofuels (Chiriac and Vasilache, 2006). This was short-lived: in 2008 and again in 2011,[13] the Ministry of Finance reinstated excises, blaming the EU for changes in price (Budusan, 2011). Romanian authorities had limited interest in using a wider range of instruments (beyond subsidies or tax cuts) for biofuels promotion and for learning from abroad. This is consistent with the short-termism of government policies which characterized the transition period, and a lack of political agreement on the direction of a longer-term energy strategy which would not be subject to reversibility (Matei, 2014).

Law 220/2008 contributed to the promotion of biomass more generally by allocating three green certificates per MWh produced. Most of the investment has been concentrated on solid biomass for electricity and heating, rather than the transport sector. However, the existing legislative framework has altered the domestic opportunity structure and prompted the emergence of a range of entrepreneurs from both the business sector and the political elite. The initial reaction of business investors after the transposition of the biofuels directive and law 220/2008 was slow, and spearheaded again – as in the case of RES-E – by a handful of foreign investors, mainly from Portugal and Germany,[14] followed by the United States (Angheluta, 2012). Domestic-only businesses were more limited, with a few factories under construction in Vaslui and Zimnicea. The first association promoting the interests of domestic producers, the Romanian Biofuels Producers' Association (APRB), was set up in 2007; while a more visible Romanian Association of Biomass and Biogas (ARBIO) was established in 2012. By 2014 ARBIO had 45 members and started a more sustained public awareness campaign, with supporters from core ministries and parliament (Hoza, 2014). Some of the biggest landowners in Romania[15] were also investing in bioethanol refineries and were reputed to have been the behind-the-scenes supporters of a similar support scheme for biofuels as that for RES-E (Pirvoiu, 2011b).

At the end of 2010, a parliamentary legislative initiative from the House of Deputies was proposed for the promotion of biofuels for transport (CD 388/2011),[16] stipulating a shorter period for reaching the 10 per cent target, by 2015, and the elimination of excises for biofuels. The supporters from both the opposition and government parties battled against the government, and it took until the end of 2013 for the proposal to be finally rejected by the Chamber of Deputies. The explanation for the failure of this initiative was that by this time the full effect of the economic crisis was being felt, coupled with the backlash against the RES-E support scheme, and a further rise in fuel prices would have been an unpalatable option for most members of parliament (*Pilot Magazin*, 2011).

Further revision of legislation by the government via GD 829/2010 was linked for the first time to meeting commitments under the Kyoto Protocol (ratified by law 3/2001) and the 10 per cent biofuels target of the 2009 RED (GD 829/2010, Nota de Fundamentare[17]). The Tăriceanu government's position was one of fence-sitting in the negotiation of this target: building coalitions with neighbouring countries on specific issues, while accepting the Commission's target proposals in exchange for concessions on EU financial aid: for biofuels specifically, the side-payment was making the automobile industry eligible for European Investment Bank loans (Financiarul, 2008).

Another amendment followed only a year later (GD 935/2011) and was designed to set staggered annual quotas[18] for reaching the 10 per cent mix in 2020 for petrol and 7 per cent by 2015 for diesel. Furthermore, clear criteria for sustainability in the sourcing of biofuels were set, specifying that these apply for biofuels of domestic, EU or other provenance. The amendment came in direct response to the existing practice of most conventional fuel producers and distributors of using imported biofuels (Budusan, 2011).

This legislation was supplemented by some general strategic policy documents, such as energy strategies[19] and a specific Biomass Master Plan (Ministry of Economy, 2010). Based on estimates and national strategic documents, the government believed targets could be reached if the 'significant potential' of 'biomass'[20] was fully exploited (Ministry of Economy, 2010), but these followed optimistic assumptions of sustained economic growth without any further instruments for the promotion of biofuels, beyond recommending institutional coordination and further strategies at the regional level, as well as making full use of EU funding (Ministry of Economy, 2010, p. 17). The lack of suitable projects that would use EU funding was linked to Romania's general absorption problems (Katsarova, 2013), but also to a range of barriers specific to this area, coupled crucially with the availability of cheap biofuels from imports, while domestic crops were exported in unprocessed form (Budusan, 2011).

Some of the main barriers to the use of domestic crops for biofuels were related to infrastructure problems that can be linked to the legacies of the early transition period: the small size of farms (an average of 2 hectares), the differing amounts of feedstock between areas and the poor quality of the roads in rural areas which can become impassable in winter (*Diplomat*, 2011). This was coupled with the difficulty of securing funding for projects (Ministry of Economy, 2010, p. 5), due to much larger start-up investments (in costly technology, and the need for irrigation, transportation and storage capacity), leading to higher production costs in the short run (Budusan, 2011). The requirements of banks could potentially be insurmountable, for example with regards to land ownership or inflexible development plans that did not leave room for the unpredictability of a drought (*Diplomat*, 2013). Contracts that would ensure supply were difficult to set up, because of the ageing farming population's distrust of this level of long-term commitment, the lack of cooperation between small producers and the lack of a system for collecting agricultural waste (Budusan, 2011). This was coupled with a range of administrative barriers including obtaining the necessary permits and approvals from too many institutions,[21] while at the local level, the scarcity of financial resources for the administration was coupled with a lack of long-term planning and information (Miron, 2014).

Finally, there were some practical obstacles to the consumption of biofuels: a large pool of older vehicles that could not use biofuels, and a reluctance on the part of the public to even try a higher percentage mix (Budusan, 2011). Furthermore, there was also mounting opposition from environmental groups to specific projects. This was the case for agricultural crops grown in protected natural areas, prompting awareness of the link between biofuels and food scarcity, as well as the increased use of genetically modified organisms (GMOs) for biofuel crops and rampant deforestation, fuelled by corruption and unsustainable practices (Terra Mileniul III, 2013).

In the current context of the economic crisis, there is little indication of a solution to address this wide range of legislative, administrative, structural, practical and environmental obstacles, in the absence of adequate instruments and incentives for the promotion of biofuels. While the focus on biomass is mainly on continued use for heating and RES-E (particularly co-generation), rather than transport (Ministry of Economy, 2010), at least at a declaratory level, there is widespread political support for biofuels, with 'biomass' being named a top priority for the next Energy Strategy of Romania (Matei, 2014).

11.5 CONCLUSIONS

The cases of RES-E and RES-T promotion in Romania were illustrative of the limits to Europeanization and the importance of domestic political developments. In both cases it was EU policies which prompted change in the beginning, and which were subsequently linked to an economic rationale for attracting foreign investment (RES-E) and tapping into otherwise wasted domestic potential, consistent with rationalist institutionalism accounts. While the targets for RES-E were already reached in January 2014, despite delays in implementation and policy retrenchment, Romania is lagging well behind its RES-T targets and looks to continue doing so for the foreseeable future. The reasons for this discrepancy were a mixture of structural constraints, legacies of the communist and early transition periods and wider processes of transformation (including liberalization, restructuring and land restitution), as well as timing and economic considerations.

Fast transposition of EU directives and a generous support scheme allowed RES-E investment to increase beyond expectations after 2008, leading by 2013 to a backlash from veto players and policy retrenchment.

Romania has experienced significant delays in implementation, as a way of dealing with the economic crisis. Domestic-level commentators blamed the start–stop and reverse strategy of the government on political short-termism and lack of vision (*Diplomat*, 2013), reflected in the institutional misfit and 'stickiness' of previous institutional structures and administrative practices, which were often a barrier to sustainable development more generally (Davidescu, 2013). The incentive systems for the promotion of renewables in RES-E and RES-T had very different effects, often unintended or miscalculated by policymakers, despite both cases being characterized by a need to reach ambitious targets. This was because policy implementation has been a constant struggle, and politically motivated. Historical institutionalism has been particularly relevant in showcasing the importance of legacies for understanding the barriers to policy implementation, despite early transposition of EU directives.

The impact of the support scheme for RES-E has been far-reaching for the entire energy sector and consumers, hence electorally costly; while the responsibility for reaching RES-T targets was passed on to economic operators, the penalties for non-compliance have been low and the effects on fuel price rises have been less dramatic. The set of actors promoting RES-E and RES-T differed greatly in terms of legislative input and the level of financial investment. While RES-E promotion has highlighted the political, institutional and physical limits to implementation, the promotion of RES-T added to these structural limits, which were too costly to address in the short term.

However, this chapter has shown that the need to adopt the EU *acquis* has provided both the impetus and a straitjacket for reform, resulting in shallow institutionalization and some innovative ways of bending the rules. New actors have emerged on the scene and coalitions of supporters and detractors of RES-E and RES-T development are here to stay. At a declaratory level and in the development of strategy documents, biomass is still a key priority area for the Romanian government and tipped for significant investment in the future. In practice, however, the discrepancy between legislative commitments, targets, incentive systems and investment levels in the RES-E and RES-T sectors seems wider than ever.

NOTES

1. The liberalization measures included the breaking of monopolies and the creation of an electricity market. The supporting institutions were a state-level national energy authority (RENEL), the Romanian Energy Regulatory Authority (ANRE), the Competition Commission (Haar and Marinescu, 2011, p. 2248) and the electricity market operator (OPCOM).

2. '*Hotarare de Guvern*' (HG) or '*Ordonanta de Urgenta*' (OU) were the main legal terms used, here translated and abbreviated as 'government decision' (GD).
3. Defined as 'a quantity of 1MWh of electrical energy produced from renewable energy sources', regardless of the technology.
4. The media noted that out of all the other member states, Romania's 24 per cent target 'had the smallest percentage of growth' and did not take into account the steady domestic increase in electricity consumption and the fact that estimates in strategy documents were often based on limited information and overoptimistic projections, 'attracting smiles in Brussels' (*Income Magazine*, 2010).
5. Legislative process tracing for initiative B.536/2007, accessed on 10 August 2014 at http://www.cameradeputatilor.ro/pls/proiecte/upl_pck.home.
6. Law no. 220/2008 on Establishing the Promotion System for the Production of Energy from Renewable Sources, Romanian government, http://www.cameradeputatilor.ro/pls/proiecte/upl_pck.home.
7. This involved 'a guarantee of maximum 50 percent of the value of the medium or long term loans or tax and fee exemptions or discounts for reinvested profit, for three years from the commissioning of the investment' (law 220/2008).
8. This commitment is now under threat as a result of recent changes in legislation (GD 57/2013).
9. The Romanian Wind Energy Association (RWEA) is an umbrella organization founded in 2008, bringing together energy producers, turbine manufacturers, construction, transportation, insurance, accountancy, environmental consultancy, law firms and even banks (RWEA, 2013).
10. Open Letter to the Romanian Government from the National Trade Confederation Cartel Alfa, the Federation of Steel Industry Union Metarom, the National Federation of Trade Unions Solidaritatea, Metal and the Federation of Unions in the Metalurgical Industry, in consensus with industry owners.
11. This was rejected by the Constitutional Court on the grounds that although the European Commission had not been formally notified, this did not result in a breach of national constitutional law.
12. The fines established were, however, minimal: between 7500 lei and 150 000 lei (GD 456/2007).
13. After a brief period in which excises for biofuels were again reduced, compared with those for regular petrol and diesel (Budusan, 2011).
14. The Portuguese Martifer group and the German group MAN Ferrostaal.
15. Adrian Porumboiu and Ioan Niculae were cited as the main producers of rape crops and processed bioethanol in the country (Pirvoiu, 2011b).
16. Chamber of Deputies, 388/07.06.2011, 'Legislative project regarding the promotion and use of biofuels and other renewable fuels for transport', accessed on 10 August 2014 at http://www.cameradeputatilor.ro/pls/proiecte/upl_pck.home.
17. Legislative process tracing GD 829/2010, accessed on 10 August 2014 at http://www.cameradeputatilor.ro/pls/proiecte/upl_pck.home
18. An increase of 1–2 per cent every two years, to alleviate the burden on economic operators (GD 935/2011).
19. Romania's energy strategy for 2007–20 (approved through GD 1069/2007), revised for 2011–20. A new energy strategy is under way, with an initial overview released in early December 2014 and launch of public consultations in spring 2015.
20. The term 'biomass' is consistently preferred by Romanian authorities as a generic word covering energy used for electricity generation, as well as heating and transportation. Biomass is already used in proportions of 84.6 per cent for heating; and biogas (0.1 per cent) for co-generation (Ministry of Economy, 2010).
21. The Ministry of Agriculture and Rural Development; the Ministry of Regional Development and Public Administration; the Ministry of Transport; the Ministry of Environment and Climate Change; the Delegated Ministry for Waters, Forests and Fisheries; and the Delegated Ministry for Energy.

REFERENCES

Angheluta, Gelu (2012) 'Biocombustibilii – Solutia viitorului' (Biofuels – a solution for the future), *Journal of Romanian Agriculture*, 28 (June), accessed on 10 October 2014 at http://agricultura-ro.ucoz.ro/news/biocombustibilii_solutia_viitorului/2012-06-28-122.

Baker, S. (2006), *Sustainable Development*, London: Routledge.

Bărbulescu, Ovidiu (2013), 'Ce a cerut Mittal Guvernului: Amanarea unor obligatii, exceptari de taxe, retele electrice', *Mediafax*, accessed on 10 October 2014 at http://www.mediafax.ro/economic/exclusiv-ce-a-cerut-mittal-guvernului-amanarea-unor-obligatii-exceptari-de-taxe-retele-electrice-11123815.

Bodeanu, T. (2013), 'Ponta: "Daca nu luam masuri in privinta preturilor la energie, ajungem un muzeu al omenirii"', *Ziare*, accessed on 15 October 2013 at http://www.ziare.com/victor-ponta/premier/ponta-daca-nu-luam-masuri-in-privinta-preturilor-la-energie-ajungem-un-muzeu-al-omenirii-1239138.

Börzel, T. (2002), 'Member State responses to Europeanization', *Journal of Common Market Studies*, 40 (2), 193–214.

Budusan, I. (2011), 'De ce a esuat industria de biocombustibili in Romania', *Manager*, accessed on 22 April 2014 at http://www.manager.ro/articole/analize/analiza-de-ce-a-esuat-industria-de-biocombustibili-in-romania-11761.html.

Burchett, K. (2011), 'Romania faces major power infrastructure investment requirements', *HIS Global Insight Daily Analysis*.

Cartel Alfa (2014), 'Suprataxarea energiei electrice si gazelor determina dezindustrializarea Romaniei', Open Letter to the Romanian Government, accessed on 10 October 2014 at http://www.google.co.uk/url?sa=t&rct=j&q=&esrc=s&frm=1&source=web&cd=2&ved=0CCoQFjAB&url=http%3A%2F%2Fwww.cartel-alfa.ro%2FDocs%2F20140312Scrisoare%2520GUVERN.doc&ei=zphgVPq_E-bP7QaE04HgDQ&usg=AFQjCNG6E-jLcR0-tRU9AgI6PzkPseZeUw&sig2=oR9jv8Znm6dFYeTWxXDq2w&bvm=bv.79189006,d.ZGU.

Chiriac, M. and A. Vasilache (2006), 'Biocarburantii – o tinta ratata momentan de Romania', *HotNews*, accessed on 10 November 2013 at http://www.hotnews.ro/stiri-arhiva-1151709-biocarburantii-tinta-ratata-momentan-romania.htm.

Colesca, S.E. and C.N. Ciocoiu (2013), 'An overview of the Romanian renewable energy sector', *Renewable and Sustainable Energy Reviews*, 24, 149–158.

COM (2011), 'Green certificates for promoting electricity from renewable sources', SA. 33134 2011/N – RO, Brussels, 13 July, accessed on 15 April 2014 at http://ec.europa.eu/competition/state_aid/cases/240906/240906_1239907_192_2.pdf.

Constantinescu, J. (2013), 'Reforma in energia electrica: Ce s-a vrut, ce-a iesit si cum ar trebui sa arate', accessed on 20 May 2014 at http://cursdeguvernare.ro/despre-reforma-in-energia-electrica-ce-s-a-vrut-si-ce-a-iesit-i-cum-ar-trebui-sa-arate-o-reforma-prietenoasa-pentru-economie-si-consumator.html.

Davidescu, S. (2013), 'The sustainable development discourse in post-Communist Central and Eastern Europe: the case of Romania', in P.M. Barnes and T. Hoerber (eds), *Sustainable Development and Governance in Europe:*

The Evolution of the Discourse on Sustainability, London: Routledge, pp. 163–176.

Diaconu, O., G. Oprescu and R. Pittman (2009), 'Electricity reform in Romania', *Utilities Policy*, 17, 114–124.

Dinica, V. (2003), 'Romania', in Danyel Reiche (ed.), *Handbook of Renewable Energies in the European Union II: Case Studies of all Accession States*, Frankfurt: Peter Lang, pp. 149–162.

Diplomat (2011), *Romanian Renewable Energy Overview*, accessed on 16 June 2014 at www.energyguide.ro.

Diplomat (2013), *Romanian Renewable Energy Overview*, accessed on 15 March 2014 at www.energyguide.ro.

Diplomat (2014), 'The painful cycle of change', 2 February 2014, accessed 20 May 2014 at http://www.thediplomat.ro/articol.php?id=4648.

ECOFYS (2012), 'Renewable energy progress and biofuels sustainability', Report for the European Commission, ENER/C1/463-2022-Lot2, accessed on 10 October 2014 at http://ec.europa.eu/energy/renewables/reports/reports_en.htm.

Evenimentul Zilei (2008), 'Romania negociaza pachetul energie-clima', 6 December, accessed on 12 October 2014 at http://www.evz.ro/romania-negociaza-pachetul-energie-clima-831256.html.

Financiarul (2008), 'Băsescu şi Tăriceanu, mulţumiţi de rezultatele Consiliului European de iarnă', accessed on 10 December 2012 at http://www.financiarul.ro/2008/12/12/basescu-si-tariceanu-multumiti-de-rezultatele-consiliului-european-de-iarna/.

Gellner, Adrian (2013), 'A confrontation between lobbyists, round two', in *Diplomat* (ed.), *Romanian Renewable Energy Overview*, accessed on 15 March 2014 at www.energyguide.ro.

Goetz, K.H. (2005), 'The new member states and the EU: responding to Europe', in S. Bulmer and C. Lequesne, *The Member States of the European Union*, Oxford: Oxford University Press, pp. 254–280.

Haar, L.N. and N. Marinescu (2011), 'Energy policy and European utilities strategy: lessons from the liberalization and privatization of the energy sector in Romania', *Energy Policy*, 39, 2245–2255.

Hoza, N.V. (2014), 'Inaugurarea ARBIO. Biomasa si biogazul sunt o prioritate pentru Romania. Acum ne trebuie o strategie nationala', *EnergieLive*, 26 June, accessed on 5 July 2014 at http://energielive.ro/inaugurarea-arbio.

Income Magazine (2010), 'Obiectivele ambitioase pentru reducerea emissiilor de CO2 sunt nerealiste', 6 April, accessed on 10 October 2014 at http://incomemagazine.ro/articles/obiectivele-ambitioase-pentru-reducerea-emisiilor-de-co2-sunt-nerealiste.

Ionascu, D. (2014), 'Emil Calotă, vicepreşedinte ANRE: Producţia de energie din surse regenerabile ar putea creşte cu circa 60% în acest an, până la 10 TWh', *Adevărul*, 24 March, accessed on 5 October 2014 at http://adevarul.ro/economie/stiri-economice/emil-calota-vicepresedinte-anre-productia-energie-surse-regenerabile-putea-creste-circa-60-an1_533058a00d133766a8305220/index.html.

Joint Statement (2014), 'The 21st Meeting of the Ministers of Environment of the Visegrad Group Countries, the Republic of Bulgaria and Romania',

Bratislava, Slovakia, 30 September, accessed on 10 October 2014 at www.visegradgroup.eu.

Katsarova, I. (2013), 'The (low) absorption of EU Structural Funds', Library of the European Parliament, accessed on 10 November 2013 at http://www.europarl.europa.eu/eplibrary/The-low-absorption-of-EU-Structural-Funds.pdf.

Matei, C. (2014), 'Strategia energetică a României 2014–2035, finalizată în toamna acestui an, estimează Karoly Borbely', *Agerpres*, 10 May, accessed on 10 October 2014 at http://www.agerpres.ro/externe/2014/06/10/strategia-energetica-a-romaniei-2014-2035-finalizata-in-toamna-acestui-an-estimeaza-karoly-borbely-15-01-29.

MECBE (Ministry of Economy, Commerce and Business Environment) (2012), 'Ordin 2580, regarding the rules for the organization and functioning of the Ministry of Economy, Commerce and Business Environment', 28 November, accessed on 10 October 2014 at http://www.minind.ro/ROF_MECMA_28112012.pdf.

Mediafax News Brief Service (2011), 'Foreign investors ask Romania for quicker legislation updates', 23 March, www.mediafax.ro.

Ministry of Economy (2010), 'Master Plan Biomasa pentru Romania', drafted with NL Agency, Netherlands and ENERO Romania, accessed on 15 April 2007 at http://www.minind.ro/biomasa/Plan_de_Actiune_pentru_Biomasa.pdf.

Miron, R. (2014), 'The socioeconomic impacts of local energy programmes: a case study of Avrig, Romania', *Management of Environmental Quality: An International Journal*, 25 (3), 352–360.

Noutcheva, G. and D. Bechev (2008), 'The successful laggards: Bulgaria and Romania's accession to the EU', *East European Politics and Societies*, 22 (1), 114–144.

NREAP (National Renewable Energy Action Plan) (2010), Romania, Bucharest, accessed on 15 April 2014 at http://www.ebb-eu.org/legis/ActionPlanDirective2009_28/national_renewable_energy_action_plan_romania_en.pdf

OPTRES (2007), 'Assessment and optimization of renewable energy support schemes in the European electricity market', Final Report, Intelligent Energy Europe with the support of the European Commission, accessed 20 October 2014 at http://ec.europa.eu/energy/renewables/studies/doc/renewables/2007_02_optres.pdf.

Pencea, D. (1993), 'Renewable energy development in Romania', *Renewable Energy*, 3 (2–3), 137–139.

Pilot Magazin (2011), 'De ce ne-a scumpit Boc benzina', 2 March, accessed on 10 October 2014 at http://pilotmagazin.ro/2011/03/de-ce-ne-a-scumpit-boc-benzina/.

Pirvoiu, C. (2011a), 'Dupa o intarziere de peste doi ani, Ministerul Economiei a reusit sa elaboreze normele de aplicare a Legii privind promovarea energiei regenerabile', *Hotnews*, 19 January, accessed on 15 June 2014 at http://economie.hotnews.ro/stiri-energie-8220822-dupa-intarziere-peste-doi-ani-ministerul-economiei-reusit-elaboreze-normele-aplicare-legii-privind-promovarea-energiei-regenerabile.htm.

Pirvoiu, C. (2011b), 'Miza pe energie: PSD si PDL isi unesc fortele in Parlament pentru a adopta doua proiecte care incalca legislatia nationala si comunitara',

HotNews, 17 November, accessed on 15 June 2014 at http://m.hotnews.ro/stire/10722473.

Pirvoiu, C. (2013), 'Retrospectiva sectorului energetic 2013', *HotNews*, 30 December, accessed on 15 June 2014 at http://economie.hotnews.ro/stiri-energie-16312755-retrospectiva-sectorul-energetic-2013-supraimpozitari-scandaluri-coruptie-proteste-proiecte-esuate-implementarea-managementului-profesionist-privatizari.htm.

Pirvoiu, C. (2014a), 'Disputa premier-presedinte pe tema certificatelor verzi', *Hotnews*, 12 March, accessed on 15 June 2014 at http://economie.hotnews.ro/stiri-energie-16803120-razboiul-premier-presedinte-tema-certificatelor-verzi-ponta-spune-presedintele-are-interesul-creasca-preturile-energie-purtatorul-cuvant-presedintiei-afirma-ponta-dezinformeaza.htm.

Pirvoiu, C. (2014b), 'Proiect de Hotarare de Guvern privind ajutoare de stat pentru companii industriale', *HotNews*, 17 April, accessed on 15 June 2014 at http://economie.hotnews.ro/stiri-energie-17059151-proiect-hotarare-guvern-privind-ajutoare-stat-pentru-companii-industriale-marii-consumatori-energie-vor-exceptati-plata-pana-85-din-certificatele-verzi.htm.

Pop-Eleches, G. (2007), 'Historical legacies and post-communist regime change', *Journal of Politics*, 69 (4), 908–926.

RWEA (2013), 'Despre RWEA', accessed on 15 May 2014 at http://rwea.ro/despre-noi/despre-rwea/.

Sedelmeier, U. (2011), 'Europeanization in new member and candidate states', *Living Reviews in European Governance*, 6 (1), accessed on 15 June 2015 at http://www.europeangovernance-livingreviews.org/Articles/lreg-2006-3/.

Sisea, C. (2013), 'Energia regenerabila, sacrificata pe fondul crizei si al alegerilor', *Ziare*, 7 February, accessed on 15 June 2013 at http://www.ziare.com/mediu/energie-regenerabila/energia-regenerabila-sacrificata-pe-fondul-crizei-si-al-alegerilor-1219136.

Terra Mileniul III (2012), 'Bariere in dezvoltarea proiectelor de energie din surse regenerabile', 19 March, accessed on 15 June 2015 at http://terramileniultrei.ro/bariere-in-dezvotarea-proiectelor-de-energie-din-surse-regenerabile/.

Terra Mileniul III (2013), 'E timpul sa decidem: alimente pentru oameni sau pentru masini?', Open letter to EU Energy Ministers, 12 November, accessed on 20 May 2014 at http://terramileniultrei.ro/noutati-terra-mileniul-trei/e-timpul-sa-decidem-alimente-pentru-oameni-sau-pentru-masini/.

UN (2001), *Environmental Performance Review: Romania*, United Nations Economic Commission for Europe, Committee on Environmental Policy, New York: UN Publications.

Wall Street Romania (2007), 'Liviu Voinea: Atingerea unui numitor comun la strategia energetica va fi dificila', 30 January, accessed on 12 December 2014 at http://www.wall-street.ro/articol/Economie/24835/Liviu-Voinea-Atingerea-unui-numitor-comun-la-strategia-energetica-va-fi-dificila.html#Scene_1.

12. Hitting the target but missing the point: failing and succeeding in the Bulgarian renewable energy sector

Ralitsa Hiteva and Tomas Maltby

12.1 INTRODUCTION

Despite reaching its European Union (EU) 2020 target of 16 per cent renewable energy sources for electricity (RES-E) by 2012, and achieving 19 per cent by 2013 (Eurostat, 2014a), domestic support for renewable energy sources (RES) in Bulgaria has been steadily declining, while numerous retroactive measures have left RES capacities stranded and many projects in limbo. On the other hand, Bulgaria is facing a significant reduction in its electricity production by 2030 with the closure of coal power plants and its nuclear power plant. Furthermore, as one of the newest members of the EU, Bulgaria has had access to a wide range of funding for renewable projects. The questions this chapter addresses are: what factors have driven the development and subsequent stagnation of the Bulgarian RES sector, and why does Bulgaria seem to be a reluctant overachiever? This chapter traces the development of RES in Bulgaria from the 1960s until 2015, paying particular attention to the role of EU policy in shaping Bulgaria's RES sector and policy. To this end the chapter aims to explain national policy change in two areas: the promotion of RES-E, and biofuels in the transport sector, in the context of Europeanization mechanisms. The main research question is to what extent do Europeanization mechanisms – the result of EU accession for Bulgaria in 2007, and pre-accession conditionality – explain the growth and stagnation of the RES market. Section 12.2 outlines the analytical framework for the research, section 12.3 considers the RES-E case study, and section 12.4 examines biofuels. In conclusion (section 12.5) it is argued that top-down Europeanization was a highly influential process in determining renewable sector developments. However, instead of acting as a catalyst for the growth of a sustainable RES industry, EU pressure resulted only in a temporary change in investment opportunities, failing to effect long-term change in the beliefs and expectations of key domestic actors in the energy sector.

12.2 ANALYTICAL UNDERPINNING AND METHODS

The dynamic changes to the Bulgarian RES since 2005 have been affected by a mixture of top-down and bottom-up mechanisms of Europeanization, the influence of which has changed over time. Europeanization in terms of the top-down pressure from the EU to develop national renewable energy policy has been a process which proved influential in acting as a stimulus for the RES electricity industry in Bulgaria between 2001 and 2011, alongside decreasing technology costs (Parsons Brinckerhoff, 2012). However, Europeanization pressures exerted far less influence on the biofuels sector. EU pressure has been mediated through the material conditions of the Bulgarian energy infrastructure, the veto power of traditional dominant actors and a patchwork regulatory framework in the energy market.

The Europeanization framework used here refers to Radaelli's (2004) interactive and interdependent means of EU policymaking consisting of processes of construction, diffusion and institutionalization of the array of formal and informal mechanisms and practices defined by EU policy processes, and translated in the context of member states. Knill and Lehmkuhl's (1999, p. 2) typology of Europeanization mechanisms argues that adaptation pressure on member states stems from three mechanisms: the prescription of 'an institutional model', altering 'the opportunity structure and domestic actor constellations' and also (over time) changing beliefs and expectations of domestic actors in order to rally support for EU policies (see also Chapter 1 by Jörgens and Solorio). We examine the extent of policy change or policy resistance in Bulgaria derived from the EU impulse on the basis of the degree of institutional compatibility, the degree of resource and power redistribution between domestic actors, and the degree of support mobilization for domestic reforms (Knill and Lehmkuhl, 1999, p. 3).

Whilst Europeanization is conceived as a two-way process (Börzel, 2002), the process of bottom-up Europeanization – the uploading of Bulgarian preferences in renewable energy policy – has been less prominent, due to limits of administrative capacity and long-term strategic planning, and active resistance from national actors. Thus, renewable energy policy can be defined by fence-sitting, foot-dragging and delaying the implementation and operationalization of EU RES-E policies.

There is limited evidence of Bulgaria adopting national policies in response to, or anticipation of the policy choices of other governments – key mechanisms of horizontal Europeanization. This is partly because, both politically and in terms of energy, Russia (and its investment in Bulgarian nuclear energy) is still very influential in Bulgaria (Maltby, 2015). Another reason is that the role of Bulgaria as an exporter of electricity to neighbouring countries such as Greece and Turkey has been declining in recent years. Although Bulgaria is one of several countries in the EU which have lowered and removed Feed-In Tariffs (FITs) and RES quotas, it has cited concerns about national energy security in doing so. The data utilized for this research focus on secondary literature and primary data in the form of EU and Bulgarian government laws, policies and objectives, as well as elite interviews.

12.3 RES-E IN BULGARIA

12.3.1 RES-E in Pre-Accession Bulgaria

Electrification of the whole country, which started in 1950 and was completed in 1970, was described as 'the golden age of Bulgarian electrification' by Tchalakov et al. (2013, p. 132), and was in line with the Soviet model of accelerated electrification by building large and powerful electric power stations. By the mid-1950s the total installed capacity of electricity in the country was significant: 900 megawatts (MW). Driven by industrialization and urbanization demand the Bulgarian electricity system continued to grow until 1989, and Bulgaria became a regional energy hub. Mid- and large-size hydropower plants were developed particularly to stabilize the energy system and balance lignite coal power plant production, where the low yield of lignite coal used in thermal power plants precluded meeting variations in electricity demand (Tchalakov et al., 2013). Following the decline in industrial production during the transition to a market economy, Bulgaria became a major exporter of electricity in the early 1990s because of a large electricity surplus.

During this period the energy sector underwent a series of structural, managerial and material changes, the most significant of which was privatization. One of the prerequisites of Bulgaria's 2007 EU accession was the unbundling of the country's electricity sector. The 1999 EU Electricity Liberalization directive required the Bulgarian government to carry out a series of key changes to the electricity market: market liberalization, providing private companies with access to transmission networks, unbundling (including the setting up of a Transmission Systems Operator, TSO), and establishing procedures for commissioning new generation capacity (Ganev, 2009; SEWRC, 2010). However, the EU's transformative effect on the Bulgarian energy sector started even before Bulgaria applied for EU membership in 1997 (Vachudova, 2005), with the signing of an Association Agreement with the EU (Cameron, 2007), and through 'linkages' and 'leverages' between Bulgaria and the EU (Way and Levitsky, 2007).

In the 1990s and early 2000s Bulgaria introduced changes to the energy sector motivated by more stringent environmental policy, mainly to address air and water pollution. Bulgaria's application to the EU led to a working group on environmental issues, to review EU legal instruments and ensure conformity with EU directives and regulations (United Nations, 2000, p. 3), with an Environmental Protection Act in 1997 followed by a 1998 regulation specifying an Environmental Impact Assessment which conformed with EU law (United Nations, 2000, pp. 3–5).

This period of change introduced a larger number of stakeholders such as private electricity distribution companies (EDCs) in the energy sector, in conjunction with the loss of control by the state over some parts of the energy infrastructure networks. However, the state managed to retain strategic parts of the electricity infrastructure through the establishment of parastatal companies such as the National Electricity Company (NEK). During this first stage of Europeanization, as a non-member state Bulgaria had limited input into the negotiation of the first RES-E directive (directive 2001/77/EC) and, at the same time, the importance of electricity in the energy mix of Bulgaria increased significantly.

12.3.2 A Period of Intense Top-Down Europeanization (2001–10)

The period between 2001 and 2007 was a period of intense top-down Europeanization. It involved preparing the national legislation for EU accession and aligning the ongoing processes of privatization and liberalization of the Bulgarian energy sector with EU standards and requirements. The national indicative target for 2010, set by directive 2001/77/EC, was for an 11 per cent share of electricity from RES in the gross domestic consumption of electricity. To bolster the renewable energy market in the country, the 2003 Law on Energy provided preferential prices for RES electricity (Bulgarian Government, 2003, article 33), without mandatory purchase contracts. With no previous legislation focused on incentivizing RES in Bulgaria, two national programmes were introduced to facilitate the implementation of the EU directives. A RES

National Long-Term Programme for 2005–15 set out the need for the accelerated installation of RES and was supplemented by a National Short-Term Programme in 2007 (Bulgarian Government, 2008a, pp. 10–11).

However, a combination of high technology prices (for solar panels and wind turbines), and a lack of history of state support for the renewable industry resulted in negligible growth in RES-E in Bulgaria before 2007, with zero solar installations, and only 1.7 kilotonnes of oil equivalent (ktoe) of solar photovoltaic (PV) energy (Eurostat, 2014b). Those interested in developing renewable projects were few and far between, and were waiting for Bulgaria's accession to the EU and stronger incentive packages (Interviews 1 and 2).

The 2007 Renewable and Alternative Energy Sources and Biofuels Act (RAESBA) was a turning point for renewable investment in Bulgaria and a significant step forward in the process of Europeanization of the Bulgarian RES sector, with national policy reflecting EU pressure. The Act provided long-term contracts of 12 years for existing RES producers and those who started production by the end of 2010, with the exception of large hydro (above 10 MW) (Bulgarian Government, 2007), and 'obligatory and priority connection of each producer of electric energy from RES … to the closest distribution or transmission enterprise', and for the State Energy and Water Regulatory Commission (SEWRC), to set prices annually (Bulgarian Government, 2007, article 21).

While the RAESBA offered a comprehensive set of incentives for developing wind and solar power in Bulgaria, it did not match the available free grid capacity, and was not strategically planned by the government, for example through phased availability. The national transmission system lacked the necessary capacity to accommodate a rapid increase in intermittent renewable sources such as wind and solar power (COM,[1] 2013, p. 27). Financial and regulatory incentives were undermined by the lack of technical capacity of the electricity grid. The Bulgarian government was criticized at the EU and the national level for failing to introduce clear mechanisms regarding connections to the electricity grid, and for not providing the necessary regulation of market players, which had forced Bulgarian EDCs to stop connecting RES-E producers to the grid (contrary to the law's mandate) (Kirov, 2012; Hiteva, 2013).

The 2008 Bulgarian Energy Strategy supported the Commission's proposal of a 16 per cent RES target by 2020, noting that Bulgaria 'is expected to provide the lowest additional increase (6.6 percent) as compared to the other member states' (Bulgarian Government, 2008a, p. 7). However, this was still an ambitious task, with varying degrees of complexity depending on the speed and type of RES to be introduced into the energy mix. Despite zero installations for solar PV until 2009 in Bulgaria, the Strategy recognized that the 'biggest technical potential' was related to this technology (Bulgarian Government, 2008a, p. 8), but anticipated that only hydro, wind and biomass would contribute significantly to new RES by 2020 (Bulgarian Government, 2008a, p. 70).

The RAESBA was then amended in late 2008, extending geothermal and solar energy contracts from 12 to 25 years, and wind contracts from 12 to 15 years (Bulgarian Government, 2008c), to provide additional incentives. These further strengthened the domestic opportunity structure for RES-E producers. Support levels increased, and obligatory purchase of electricity was introduced (Bulgarian Government, 2008c). This amendment proved successful in stimulating accelerated development of the RES-E sector in Bulgaria. The lengthened contract terms were combined with guaranteed purchase of all produced renewable electricity and connection of newly installed renewable capacity to the national grid free of charge for generators, but at the expense of the EDCs and transmission companies (EREC, 2009).

Using Knill and Lehmkuhl's (1999) typology of Europeanization mechanisms, apart from the prescription of concrete institutional and governance models, such as the introduction of the independent electricity regulator SEWRC, the unbundling of the electricity transmission and distribution infrastructure and the separation of the electricity system operator (ESO) and the NEK, the EU RES directives also went a long way to alter Bulgaria's opportunity structure. This was achieved through market-making (as per Bulmer and Radaelli, 2004, p. 6), with the RAESBA allowing the entrance of RES into national markets by providing zero-cost connection to the grid for RES producers. These top-down Europeanization mechanisms led to a change in the distribution of resources between actors, with the NEK and EDCs now responsible for connecting ever growing RES capacities to the national grid.

Between 2007 and 2011 there was no cap or adequate oversight of how many renewable projects were being planned and built. There was a sixfold increase in onshore wind power between 2008 and 2010; and an exponential growth in the solar PV market, from 1.3 ktoe to 117 ktoe between 2010 and 2013 (Eurostat, 2014b). It is important to note that this was not planned or predicted growth, and was directly linked to EU pressures. The limited engagement of the Bulgarian government with effective long-term strategic planning, coupled with rapidly decreasing PV costs and financial and technical (grid) capacity provided an obstacle. The infrastructure of the Bulgarian electricity network required significant investment (Hiteva, 2013; Ganev, 2009). The cost of connecting these new RES installations to the grid threatened the EDCs' and NEK's financial stability. Between 2009 and 2011 there were significant delays in approving connections to the national grid, while some applications (predominantly for new wind and solar capacity over 5 MW) were stopped altogether without official explanation (Hiteva, 2013).

Powerful and embedded energy sector actors – the EDCs and NEK – resisted the top-down Europeanization of the Bulgarian RES sector by refusing to implement the national policy. The resistance to EU-driven domestic legislation had longer-term effects on national RES policy. To a large extent this could be accredited to the failure of EU RES policy to trigger changes in the beliefs of the domestic actors, an important mechanism of top-down Europeanization identified by Knill and Lehmkuhl (1999). Many of the RES developers and lobbyists for RES in Bulgaria were not domestic actors, but international companies and investors which faced many barriers to influencing changes in the beliefs and routines of domestic actors. Furthermore, the electricity market structure allowed the NEK's refusal to implement national law and connect new RES-E capacities to remain hidden from the public and investors, as EDCs were the official interface for applications for connection and their refusals. In fact, EDCs could not accept connection applications that were refused by the NEK. Entrenched institutional veto points – the NEK, ESO and the national regulator SEWRC – limited the extent of more fundamental transition in the energy sector.

12.3.3 A Period of Resistance to Top-Down and Nascent Bottom-Up Europeanization (2011–15)

Despite a degree of foot-dragging in the implementation of EU RES and climate change policies in the previous period, such as partial transposition of EU legislation and failure to operationalize key tools such as national registers for carbon emissions certificates, occasions of resistance to top-down Europeanization became more prolific after 2011, with the introduction of a series of retroactive measures in RES-E. Contrary to Börzel's (2002) conceptualization of bottom-up Europeanization, the limits to Bulgaria's influence were shaped primarily by its limited action capacities, rather than policy preferences. Partly because of political instability, policy preferences have not been well defined in connection to renewable energy and climate change policies.

The 2011 Energy Strategy recognized the 'unduly high public costs' of 'existing promotion mechanisms for the development of RES', but also that 'over-performance of the target will enable the country to sell the surplus … [through] statistical transfers to other EU states' (Bulgarian

Government, 2011a, p. 20). However, reduced demand from traditional export markets such as Greece, Macedonia and Turkey because of the economic crisis (Iwanov and Arndt, 2013), and Greece's predicted 2020 RES-E target surplus, weakened the RES-E export market. In the same month, the Bulgarian parliament adopted the Energy from Renewable Sources Act (ERSA), which replaced the 2008 RAESBA (Bulgarian Government, 2011b). The rationale of the Bulgarian government was to remedy the fact that 'too many investors have expressed intentions to construct wind and solar farms which go beyond the capacity of the energy system' (NREAP, 2011, p. 18).

The ERSA introduced a set of retroactive measures reducing the duration of purchase contracts from 25 years to 20 years for geothermal and solar, and from 15 to 12 years for wind (Bulgarian Government, 2011a, article 31). These retroactive measures constituted a form of direct resistance to EU RES-E objectives, and the process of top-down Europeanization. They were spurred on by the strong coalition between the regulator SEWRC, ESO, the NEK and the Bulgarian parliament, to protect the financial and political stability of the NEK and the existing electricity regime. Although the retroactive measures prompted penalties and the official expression of concern by the EU, these were largely ignored. Lobbying attempts on behalf of the wind and solar industry sought support from the EU, but fell on deaf ears with the Bulgarian government and society (Hiteva, 2013). The period of favourable market conditions for RES-E prompted by top-down Europeanization was too brief to build a strong coalition in support of RES.

However, the retroactive measures proved insufficient to prevent continued exponential growth in the solar PV market in the immediate short term. The government had failed to foresee this. Objectives set in 2011 for solar PV installations by 2020 had by 2012 been met, and tripled (NREAP, 2011; Eurostat, 2014b). With the introduction of the ERSA and its subsequent revisions the Bulgarian government was gradually becoming more experienced and confident in developing its national interests vis-à-vis those of the EU RES and climate change agenda. Despite pressure from the EU – for example, the visit of the European Commissioner for Climate Action – the Bulgarian government continued to adjust its national legislation (with more than five amendments in three years) to bridge the gap between EU targets and the capacity of national electricity infrastructure (Interviews 2 and 3). Domestic policy resistance had increased in the period 2011–12, and the effects of this change were soon clear.

These changes contributed to a situation of 'high investment insecurity' (Ecofys, 2013, pp. 108–109). Changes in national legislation removed the guarantee of the price formation and required a connection fee in advance of construction, which increased the associated risks for renewable projects. This led to the stranding of installed renewable capacity and reduced investment in wind and solar projects.

Despite this resistance the growth of solar PV, which began only in 2010, and wind which began in 2006, led to Bulgaria reaching its EU 2020 target of 16 per cent RES-E by 2012, achieving 19 per cent by 2013 (Eurostat, 2014a). Bulgaria's RES-E legal obligations were fulfilled eight years ahead of the government's planned trajectory for RES-E installations, set out just a year before, in 2011 (NREAP, 2011). The main catalyst for the initial growth was top-down Europeanization, in the form of the mandatory EU target. This led directly to changes to the 2007 energy law, and the 2008 amendments producing an extensive set of incentives for RES development. Combined with rapidly decreasing technology costs for solar PV, these resulted in exponential growth. The cost of solar PV declined by over 50 per cent between 2010 and May 2012 (Parsons Brinckerhoff, 2012). However, despite the success in achieving the RES-E target, public support for wind and solar power started to decrease as it was associated with higher electricity prices, and government incentives were reduced through a series of retroactive measures and actions.

Policy resistance also took the form of reduction in network prices paid for existing renewable projects in June 2012, by 34–54 per cent for PV and 22–23 per cent for wind (BGWEA, 2013b). The regulator announced that there was no grid capacity to connect new RES plants, initially until June 2013, which was then extended until July 2014 (BGWEA, 2013a), and then 2015 (SEWRC, 2015). At the end of March 2014, the ESO announced that limits in technical capacity meant that 'the maximum working power will be limited with 60 percent (for RES-E producers) connected to the transmission and distribution grids' (BGWEA, 2014, p. 2). Meanwhile, since 2011 the NEK had increasingly curtailed renewable generation, quoting concerns over the reliable operation of the grid and/or the security of supply (BGWEA, 2013a; Capital, 2013).

The regulator also introduced a temporary tax upon renewable energy producers that came into force in September 2012, a grid access fee that was declared illegal in June 2013 (Jirous, 2014). A similar tax on revenues was also introduced in February 2014, and infringement procedures were launched against the Bulgarian government for failure to fully transpose the renewable energy directive (RED) by December 2010 (COM, 2014, pp. 34–36).

The Bulgarian government struggled to stabilize the regulatory regime for RES-E, and after the ERSA was introduced in 2011 there were several bills to amend and supplement it, in order to deal with the large number of preliminary and final grid-connection contracts. Retroactive measures are considered one of the worst signals for renewable investors, with the potential to stifle future market development (Hiteva, 2013). By 2013, Bulgaria was rated as one of the least attractive countries in the EU for investment in RES (Ernst & Young, 2014, p. 16). Although EU RES directives prompted the introduction of national legislation which successfully incentivized the introduction of new capacities of wind and solar power in Bulgaria, government support including legislation was reversed once the RES target was achieved, showing a restrained commitment by the government for more growth of the domestic RES sector and for adhering to more than minimum EU objectives.

The hydropower sector in Bulgaria between 2000 and 2015 was considerably more stable, although it also underwent a change. Hydropower has been intensively developed in the country in the past 50–60 years. Large-scale hydropower is still the main source of renewable electricity in Bulgaria (EREC, 2009) and large hydropower plants (HPPs) retained their role as the main balancing and regulating capacities in the national electricity system (Hristozov, 2012). There are still plans and projects for new large HPPs; however, since mid-2011 new regulatory conditions with more unfavourable prices were introduced (NEK, 2011), decreasing the predicted installation of capacity (SEWRC, 2013). Since 2012, there has also been resistance to small hydropower plants, predominantly through local, regional and international organizations such as the World Wide Fund for Nature (WWF), on environmental grounds (Maltzeva, 2013).

Overall, EU legislation did not have a significant (either negative or positive) impact on the rates of installation of hydropower in the country. While the parastatal NEK justified a handful of larger hydro project plans with the need to balance the introduction of more intermittent RES such as wind and solar, the freeze of RES-E since 2013 suggests that this reasoning lacks credibility.

The impact of the economic crisis from 2007 onward, rapidly increasing RES-E support costs and a failure to increase regulated electricity prices had a significant effect on the RES sector in Bulgaria. Braun argues that the general position of Bulgaria during negotiations of the 2030 climate and energy package was of cynicism within the government about the potential for the country to benefit from ecological modernization (Braun, 2014, p. 143). In 2014, the government stated that it:

> generally supports efforts to reach an agreement on the new climate and energy policy framework ... In the course of negotiations, strict respect for national circumstances and capabilities is essential, particularly in relation to low income Member States. Reaching an agreement on the new, more ambitious goals of the framework should not put at risk the economic development of Member States or result in the European economy becoming less competitive. (Bulgarian Government, 2014)

This statement reflects a lack of ambition for developing the national RES-E sector beyond EU requirements, and a failure of the spirit of the EU RES directives to 'take' in Bulgaria. Bulgaria's lack of enthusiasm for the 2030 climate and energy package is also due to the fact that the country did not benefit as much as expected from the selling of carbon emissions credits, due to long delays with accreditation and developing a national registry for projects, while some constructed projects were stopped because the EU trading scheme provides a smaller allocation of credits than that of mechanisms under the Kyoto Protocol (Capital, 2009).

12.4 BIOFUELS IN BULGARIA

Bulgaria also has substantial potential for generating power from biofuels, including from biomass. About 90 per cent of Bulgaria's land is arable, agricultural or forested land (Todorova, 2011, p. 3). The country also has a history of biodiesel production, since 2001 (CRES, 2008). A Commission report in 2003 highlighted Bulgaria's potential to produce biofuels made from sugar beet and wheat (bioethanol) and sunflower (biodiesel) (COM, 2003, p. 11). However, the 2003 Energy Law made no reference to biofuels or transport (Bulgarian Government, 2003), and RES-T was calculated at 0 per cent in 2005 (Bulgarian Government, 2011a, p. 11), and 0.4 per cent in the same year by Eurostat (Eurostat, 2014b).

Top-down Europeanization in the case of biofuels was superficial. The 2007 Law on Renewable and Alternative Energy Sources and Biofuels made frequent reference to biofuels and transport, although the mechanisms for achieving the target were vague, and largely restricted to the setting of national indicative targets (Bulgarian Government, 2007). The adoption of concrete institutional and governance models prescribed by the EU was limited to the introduction of the 2007 National Long-term Programme for the Promotion of the Use of Biofuels for Transport 2008–2020, which set a national indicative target for 2010 of a 5.75 per cent share of biofuels in the consumption of petrol and diesel fuels in the transport sector. This followed the 2003 EU biofuels and renewables for transport directive (Bulgarian Government, 2011a, p. 10). This was a direct response to EU pressure associated with accession conditionality. Its impact, though, was limited, and Kondili and Kaldellis argue that before 2007 there was little progress on using biofuels in transport because of 'the serious deficit of infrastructure and mentality in general for biofuel promotion (tests, standards, investments, etc.) as well as the lack of clear government policy and any relevant legislation make the development of the domestic market difficult' (Kondili and Kaldellis, 2007, p. 2148).

The national target and long-term programme failed to significantly alter the domestic opportunity structure for biofuels and promote changes in the beliefs and expectations of domestic actors such as the Ministry of Transport, the Ministry of Economy, Energy and Tourism, the Ministry of Agriculture and RES producers. The majority of biofuel plants until 2007 were producing ethanol for the alcohol industry rather than bioethanol for transport (Capital, 2012). There had been a reasonably comprehensive downloading of EU biofuels policy objectives and legislation on paper but not in practice, as legislation was not complemented with the mechanisms at the national level to implement EU objectives until 2012.

There was no detailed programme in the 2008 Bulgarian Energy Strategy draft for how the binding RES-T 10 per cent target was to be achieved, apart from 'doubling the quantity' (Bulgarian Government, 2008a, p. 66). The 2008 National Long-Term Programme to Encourage the Use of Biomass 2008–2020 reiterated an indicative target of 5.75 per cent for 2010 and 2 per cent in 2008 (Bulgarian Government, 2008b, p. 23). Yet Eurostat figures show that by 2008 the figure was only a quarter of that predicted, at 0.5 per cent (Eurostat, 2014b).

There have been significant discrepancies in the RES-T in Bulgaria reported by the government. In 2008 the Bulgarian government reported that RES-T was 0 per cent in 2005 (Bulgarian Government, 2008b). By 2010 this 2005 figure had increased to 1.12 per cent (NREAP, 2010), and was estimated to reach 7.8 per cent by 2020 (NREAP, 2010, p. 26). However, this was short of the EU mandatory target of 10 per cent, and the government resubmitted its National Renewable Energy Action Plan (NREAP) in 2011. This resubmission claimed that the 2020 target would be met and exceeded, although it also reported that the 2005 figure had been miscalculated and was actually 0.1 per cent, not 1.12 per cent (NREAP, 2011, p. 28). This indicates the extent of the lack of capability of the Bulgarian government in the translation of EU directives into national implementation on one hand, and monitoring and reporting on the other.

RES-T reached 1 per cent in 2010, a considerable underachievement relative to the 5.75 per cent indicative target. In 2012 the figure had dropped to 0.3 per cent (Eurostat, 2014b),[2] with the government facing a significant challenge to reach the indicative target of 8 per cent by 2015, and the mandatory target of 10 per cent by 2020 (Bulgarian Government, 2008b, p. 28). Bulgaria's RES-T progress had been extremely limited, and this was acknowledged by the 2011 Energy Strategy (Bulgarian Government, 2011a, p. 21). This resistance can be accredited to the failure to transpose EU legislation; the lack of accredited laboratories for monitoring and control of the quality and content of biofuel mixes; and a failure to monitor implementation of investment programmes by biofuel producers and importers. The Bulgarian government adopted several measures to remedy the situation, including the introduction of a requirement of transport fuel producers to add biofuel to their products in the 2011 ERSA (Bulgarian Government, 2011b), enforcing administrative measures and increasing financial sanctions for non-compliance (Zhivkova, 2010).

On paper the ERSA paved the way for a dramatic improvement in RES-T in the country; however, the requirement for transport fuel producers to add biofuel to their products was delayed until 2012 to allow time for industry adjustment (Bulgarian Government, 2013, p. 32).[3] Once this postponement expired in June 2012, petrol engines required 2 per cent bioethanol, and this gradually crept up to 7 per cent in the first quarter of 2015 (Bulgarian Government, 2013, pp. 31–32). As a direct result of bringing national legislation into compliance with the EU directive, RES-T figures demonstrated a dramatic turnaround, rising from 0.3 per cent in 2012 (the second-lowest in the EU) to 5.6 per cent in 2013, ahead of the EU average (Eurostat, 2015). There was a related significant growth in biogasoline and biodiesel (Eurostat, 2014b), prompted by the transposition of EU legislation; a further increase in administrative and financial sanctions for importers, distributers and suppliers; and the resolution of EU imposed restrictions on the production of local plants.

The biofuels sector is also emerging as a site for bottom-up and horizontal Europeanization in Bulgaria, through the activities of a new group of actors in the country: energy agencies. The development of small and medium-sized biofuel projects at local level has been steadily increasing since 2010. This is largely due to the introduction of individual targets for municipalities for the development of RES projects, a requirement for the development of short-term and long-term plans for sustainable energy production, and the rapid growth of local energy agencies in the country since the mid-2000s (Hiteva, 2013; Interview 4).

The objective of energy agencies is to facilitate energy savings and carbon dioxide emissions reductions at local and regional level, and often they are almost entirely or substantially funded through EU programmes. They provide institutional support to local authorities in meeting their individual targets, including national energy efficiency targets, Covenant of Mayors' targets, and any local sustainability and climate change objectives they may have (Interview 4).

Most importantly, energy agencies are able to tailor their work closely to the needs of a specific municipality and/or region. Most energy agencies in Bulgaria are directly plugged into EU RES agendas, which are disseminated horizontally through municipal networks such as the Covenant of Mayors, because they rely on EU funding for their existence and project work (Davis, 2005). Many energy agencies in Bulgaria have recently focused specifically on the domestic and regional development of biomass, for example through setting up an EU RES league programme, which mimics a football league with two divisions – one for biomass and one for PV projects – where municipalities compete among themselves on the basis of most installed capacity per capita. Municipalities at the top of the national league table go on to compete with municipalities from other member states. The Association of Bulgarian Energy Agencies (ABEA) has started another EU-led initiative called BioRegions, which created for the first time a biomass action plan in Europe (Interview 4).

Energy agencies have been successful in drumming up support for biofuel projects only locally because they still lack support from, and connection with, a wider range of actors in the energy sector, such as government agencies and the regulator. However, energy agencies do play a key role in processes of horizontal Europeanization (cross-loading) through being embedded in networks of learning, geared towards sharing information and best practices between municipalities, energy agencies and local biofuel producers. This allows local authorities to gain access to and learn directly from existing policies in other EU member states. Energy agencies are extremely active in interacting with EU institutions through a 'systematic dialogue' and an 'enhanced' opportunity to express their views via European and national associations of regional and local authorities (Carmichael, 2005; Heinelt and Niederhafner, 2008). Furthermore, some energy agencies such as the Plovdiv Energy Agency are recognized as official partners of the European Commission and as such can directly feed back to the Commission. The value of local energy agencies for the EU and its institutions comes from their roles as knowledge holders, implementation 'watchdogs' and legitimacy vehicles for EU policy (Heinelt and Niederhafner, 2008, p. 183). However, measuring the extent of impact that these energy agencies have had through the process of bottom-up Europeanization requires further research.

12.5 CONCLUSION

It is clear from the case study of Bulgaria that top-down Europeanization was a highly influential process in the development of the wind, solar and biofuels sectors in the country. There are however key differences between the RES-E and RES-T sectors. The EU RES directives led to the introduction of two new types of RES in the country: wind and solar power. However, from July 2013 the national regulator SEWRC permitted only the connection of small-scale wind and solar installations (SEWRC, 2013), and from February 2015 there was an end to RES-E new installation support (SEWRC, 2015).

EU pressure led to dramatic growth in the sector until approximately 2013, and on the surface this appears to be a significant success story. However, with RES-E targets now having been exceeded, financial obstacles and technical limitations of the national grid have undermined short-term RES-E growth. Fluctuating FITs and inconsistency regarding support for different RES technologies have created a volatile investment climate. Instead of acting as a catalyst for the growth of a sustainable RES-E industry, and contributing to an ongoing transition towards a decarbonized energy sector, it appears as though the prescription of concrete institutional and governance models by the EU led to an adherence to the minimum requirements of EU legislation. This did in the short term alter the opportunity structure to an extent, incentivizing RES-E actors which could take advantage of a temporarily attractive investment climate. However, there is little evidence yet to suggest a more substantial change in the beliefs and expectations of key domestic actors which have operated as institutional veto points, in part because of a lack of technical and financial capacity to implement requisite changes in the energy sector.

There is, then, a high level of uncertainly regarding the future of the RES-E industry in Bulgaria, and whilst this has not manifested itself in an attempt to actively shape or resist renewable energy policy, there is a passive resistance to developing RES-E beyond the minimum required. Since EU accession, Bulgarian governments have struggled to synchronize the Bulgarian legislation and governance processes with those of the EU; to learn how to identify the national position and defend it at EU level; to learn how to implement EU legislation; and balance an

EU-led agenda and national interests (Hiteva, 2013; Hiteva and Maltby, 2014). Key to the research questions here, there has been little evidence to suggest that since EU accession in 2007, Bulgaria has shaped or attempted to shape EU policy. As a small newcomer to the EU, Bulgaria is an EU energy policy-taker rather than policy-shaper, and has been slow to contribute to the development of EU energy legislation in line with its national interests.

As seen from the discussion, the development of the RES sector has been affected by lack of administrative capacity to govern a transition towards a larger share of RES in Bulgaria. This is illustrated as much by the lack of coordinated strategy for the implementation of the EU RES directives throughout the whole RES supply chain, as by the frequent number of changes in national RES legislation, which translates into lack of regulatory stability. The reasons for the absence of administrative capacity are manifold and encompass structural issues related to state capture, staff retention, circulation of personnel between government ministries and the private energy sector, and an understaffed regulator (see Hiteva and Maltby, 2014 for more details).

Despite the role of technology price decreases, particularly solar PV, without the implementation of national FITs and other incentives that followed the transposition of EU legislation it is unlikely that Bulgaria would have experienced the rapid growth since 2009 of its RES-E sector. It is thus clear that the motivating logic for national legislation and regulatory framework in RES-E is tied inextricably to EU policy. Yet, there was a failure at the national level to put in place a regulatory framework robust and flexible enough to deal with the challenges of rapid growth in the sector. There was a comprehensive downloading of EU renewable regulations in terms of their transposition into national law. However, provisions were not put in place to adjust quickly to decreasing technology costs; combined with insufficiently developed infrastructure and financial barriers this has led to stagnation.

A recent increase in the emphasis on biofuels support was necessary but overdue, and again appears to be a direct result of EU legislation. A mechanism of top-down Europeanization led to the development of national legislation that has been implemented since 2012. Whilst the EU directive was transposed later, by 2013 Bulgaria was one of the leading member states with regards to RES-T. A nascent process of bottom-up and horizontal Europeanization in Bulgaria has also emerged in the case of RES-T, through the work of energy agencies and municipalities, sometimes leading to municipalities committing to higher targets than their individual targets set by the government. In 2015 this trend was limited to a handful of municipalities and was therefore unlikely to lead to policy change towards higher targets for biofuels than those introduced by the EU.

NOTES

1. Hereafter referred to as 'the Commission'.
2. Though it is important to note that 'the renewable energy consumption shown in the transport sector only includes electricity, because the legislation laying down the requirements for compliance with the sustainability criteria was adopted later. If the consumption of biofuels (biodiesel and bioethanol) had been taken into account, the share of renewable energy in the gross final energy consumption achieved in 2012 would have been approximately 1 % higher' (Bulgarian Government, 2013, p. 8).
3. 'Due to the rise in the prices of petroleum-derived fuels for the transport sector in 2011 and the need to mitigate the negative impact of this development on citizens' (Bulgarian Government, 2013, p. 32).

REFERENCES

BGWEA (2013a), 'BGWEA says continued curtailments of wind and solar are unjustified and in violation of Bulgarian laws', News Release, 26 April.

BGWEA (2013b), 'FiT Review, Bulgarian Wind Energy Association', July, http://bgwea.org.server14.host.bg/Materials/DKEVR/FIT_2013/BGWEA_FiT_Review_July_2013_Final_EN.pdf.

BGWEA (2014), 'Ongoing curtailments of RES production', 14 April.

Börzel, T. (2002), 'Member State responses to Europeanization', *Journal of Common Market Studies,* 40 (2), 193–214.

Braun, M. (2014), *Europeanization of Environmental Policy in the New Europe*, Farnham: Ashgate.

Bulgarian Government (2003), 'Law on energy' State Gazette nr. 107 of 9 December 2003, http://www.erranet.org/index.php?name=OE-eLibrary&file=download&id=2946.

Bulgarian Government (2007), 'Law on Renewable and Alternative Energy Sources and Biofuels', State Gazette nr. 49 of 19 June 2007, http://faolex.fao.org/docs/texts/bul82573.doc.

Bulgarian Government (2008a), 'Bulgarian Energy Strategy by 2020 draft version', November, https://www.google.co.uk/url?sa=t&rct=j&q=&esrc=s&source=web&cd=2&cad=rja&uact=8&ved=0CC0QFjAB&url=http%3A%2F%2Fwww.strategy.bg%2FFileHandler.ashx%3FfileId%3D1436&ei=xOFgVOf_PI7fsAT3r4DYCw&usg=AFQjCNEiuCC_uKPQSESyvvYhCHrJVe8cLw&sig2=8KsB-SgLNMdEdaTvgizyEQ&bvm=bv.79189006,d.cWc.

Bulgarian Government (2008b), 'National long-term programme to encourage the use of biomass 2008–2020', http://www.strategy.bg/FileHandler.ashx?fileId=1422

Bulgarian Government (2008c), 'Renewable and Alternative Energy Sources and Biofuels Act – Prom. SG. 49/19.06.2007, amended SG. 98/14.11.2008, into force since 14.11.2008'.

Bulgarian Government (2011a), 'Bulgarian Energy Strategy 2020', http://www.mi.government.bg/files/useruploads/files/epsp/23_energy_strategy2020%D0%95ng_.pdf.

Bulgarian Government (2011b), 'Energy from Renewable Sources Act', State Gazette No 35/03.05.2011, Effective 03.05.2011 http://www.mi.government.bg/library/index/download/lang/en/fileId/167.

Bulgarian Government (2013), 'Second National Report on Bulgaria's progress in the promotion and use of energy from renewable sources', Ministry of Economy and Energy, December, http://extra.energies-renouvelables.org/policy/report/Article_22_Bulgaria_report_EN.pdf.

Bulgarian Government (2014), 'A draft position of Bulgaria for participation in the meeting of the General Affairs Council', 20 October 2014, http://www.government.bg/cgi-bin/e-cms/vis/vis.pl?s=001&p=0234&n=534&g=.

Bulmer S. and C. Radaelli (2004), 'The Europeanisation of national policy?', Queen's Papers on Europeanisation, No 1/2004.

Cameron, D. (2007), 'Post-communist democracy: the impact of the European Union', *Post-Soviet Affairs*, 23 (3), 185–217.

Capital (2009), 'Какви квоти, какви 20 млн. Евро. Три години Екоминистерството блокира проекта за завод за биодизел на "Астра Биоплант"' (No quotas nor 20 mln. Euro. Three years of blocking the plan for biodiesel plant "Astra Bioplant" by the Ministry of Environment)', Business, Companies, Capital, 16 October, at http://www.capital.bg/biznes/kompanii/2009/10/16/800965_kakvi_kvoti_kakvi_20_mln_evro.

Capital (2012), 'Трудното възкръсване на биогоривата' (Laboured resurrection for biofuels), 27 May, http://www.capital.bg/biznes/kompanii/2012/05/27/1834656_trudnoto_vuzkrusvane_na_biogorivata/?sp=1#storystart.

Capital (2013), 'Critical switch off, politics and economy', 5 April, p. 4.

Carmichael, L. (2005), 'Cities in multi-level governance of the European Union', in M. Haus, H. Heinelt and M. Stewart (eds), *Urban Governance and Democracy. Leadership and Community Involvement*, London: Routledge, pp. 129–148.

COM (2003), 'Biomass availability in Europe', December, http://ec.europa.eu/energy/res/sectors/doc/bioenergy/cres_final_report_annex.pdf.

COM (2013), 'European Commission guidance for the design of renewables support schemes', SWD(2013) 439 final, 5 November, http://ec.europa.eu/energy/gas_electricity/doc/com_2013_public_intervention_swd04_en.pdf.

COM (2014), 'Electricity tariff deficit: temporary or permanent problem in the EU?', October, http://ec.europa.eu/economy_finance/publications/economic_paper/2014/pdf/ecp534_en.pdf.

CRES (2008), '2008 National Report on biodiesel in Bulgaria, EIE- 05- 113, biodiesel chains', ESD Bulgaria, at http://www.cres.gr/biodiesel/downloads/reports/Bulgaria_National_Report.pdf.

Davis, A. (2005), 'Local action for climate change: transnational networks and the Irish experience', *Local Environment*, 10 (1), 21-40.

Ecofys (2013), 'Renewable energy progress and biofuels sustainability', report for the European Commission, submission September 2012, Tender Number: ENER/C1/463-2011-Lot2, http://ec.europa.eu/energy/renewables/reports/doc/2013_renewable_energy_progress.pdf.

EREC (2009), 'Renewable energy policy review Bulgaria', European Renewable Energy Council, http://www.erec.org/fileadmin/erec_docs/Projcet_Documents/RES2020/BULGARIA_RES_Policy_Review__09_Final.pdf.

Ernst & Young (2014), 'Renewable energy country attractiveness index', Issue 40, February, http://www.ey.com/Publication/vwLUAssets/RECAI_40_-_February_2014/$FILE/EY_RECAI%2040_Feb%202014.pdf.

Eurostat (2014a), 'Share of renewable energy in gross final energy consumption', t2020_31, 11 December 2014, http://ec.europa.eu/eurostat/tgm/table.do?tab=table&init=1&language=en&pcode=t2020_31&plugin=1.

Eurostat (2014b), 'Primary production of renewable energy by type', ten00081, http://epp.eurostat.ec.europa.eu/tgm/refreshTableAction.do?tab=table&plugin=1&pcode=ten00081&language=en.

Eurostat (2015), 'Share of renewable energy in fuel consumption of transport', Code: tsdcc340, 9 March, http://appsso.eurostat.ec.europa.eu/nui/submitViewTableAction.do;jsessionid=IjiyKFbOifGI5lpXRixM4xuXv–4zmCNmnOdrsV2YF1BDeVaDsjK!929634355.

Ganev, P. (2009), 'Bulgarian electricity market restructuring', *Utilities Policy*, 17, 65–75.

Heinelt, H. and S. Niederhafner (2008), 'Cities and organized interest intermediation in the EU multi-level system', *European Urban and Regional Studies*, 15 (2), 173–187.

Hiteva, R. (2013), 'Geographies of energy governance – negotiating low-carbon infrastructure in the European Union', DPhil thesis submitted to the University of Manchester, Faculty of Humanities.

Hiteva, R. and T. Maltby (2014), 'Standing in the way by standing in the middle: the case of state-owned natural gas intermediaries in Bulgaria', *Geoforum*, 54, 120–131.

Hristozov, M. (2012), 'Ролята на ВЕЦ и ПАВЕЦ в управлението на енергийния баланс' (The role of HPP and PSHPP in balancing the energy mix), *Energy Review*, 3 (June), http://energy-review.bg/energy-statii.aspx?br=71&rub=728&id=270.

Iwanov, I. and M. Arndt (2013), 'Енергетиката в България: състояние и перспективи' (Bulgaria's energy: now and in the future), Country Report, Konrad-Adenauer-Stiftung e.V., http://www.kas.de/wf/doc/kas_35548-1522-11-30.pdf?130930103735.

Jirous, F. (2014), 'Electricity: promotion in Bulgaria', European Commission, 10 July, http://www.res-legal.eu/search-by-country/bulgaria/tools-list/c/bulgaria/s/res-e/t/promotion/sum/112/lpid/111/page.pdf?out=pdf.

Kirov, V. (2012), 'Public funding for green energy in a context of crisis: country report (Bulgaria)', December, http://www.etui.org/content/download/11365/96105/file/6_Country+report+Bulgaria.pdf.

Knill, C. and D. Lehmkuhl (1999), 'How Europe matters: different mechanisms of Europeanization', *European Integration online Papers (EIOP)*, 3 (7), http://eiop.or.at/eiop/texte/1999-007a.htm.

Kondili, E.M. and J.K. Kaldellis (2007), 'Biofuel implementation in East Europe: current status and future prospects', *Renewable and Sustainable Energy Reviews*, 11 (9), 2137–2151.

Maltby, T. (2015), 'Between amity, enmity and Europeanisation: EU energy security policy and the example of Bulgaria's Russian energy dependence', *Europe-Asia Studies*, 67 (5), 809–830.

Maltzeva, M. (2013), 'Малките ВЕЦ по реките нанасят тежки и необратими вреди на естествените речни екосистеми' (Small scale HPPs along rivers cause significant and irreversible damage to natural river ecosystems), Начало/Био, 23 September, at http://www.greentech.bg/archives/45717.

NEK (Natsionalna Elektricheska Kompania) (2011), 'Annual Report 2011', at http://www.nek.bg/cgi?d=1000.

NREAP (2010), 'National Renewable Energy Action Plan Bulgaria', Bulgarian Government, http://www.buildup.eu/sites/default/files/content/national_renewable_energy_action_plan_bulgaria_en.pdf.

NREAP (2011), 'National Renewable Energy Action Plan Bulgaria', Bulgarian Government, http://pvtrin.eu/assets/media/PDF/EU_POLICIES/National%20Renewable%20Energy%20Action%20Plan/203.pdf.

Parsons Brinckerhoff (2012), 'Solar PV cost update', May, https://www.gov.uk/government/uploads/system/uploads/attachment_data/file/43083/5381-solar-pv-cost-update.pdf.

Radaelli, C. (2004), 'Europeanisation: solution or problem?', *European Integration online Papers* (*EIoP*), 8 (16), 6 October, http://eiop.or.at/eiop/texte/2004-016a.htm.

SEWRC (State Energy and Water Regulatory Commission) (2010), 2009 'Annual report to the European Commission', accessed on 16 July 2011 at http://dker.bg/PDOCS/rep_sewrc_10_en.pdf.

SEWRC (State Energy and Water Regulatory Commission) (2013), 'РЕШЕНИЕ [DECISION] № ЕМ-02', 28 June, http://www.dker.bg/files/DOWNLOAD/res_em-02_13.pdf.

SEWRC (State Energy and Water Regulatory Commission) (2015), 'РЕШЕНИЕ [DECISION] № Ц – 1', 28 January, http://www.dker.bg/docsbg.php?d=3&subD=114

Tchalakov, I., T. Mitev and I. Hristov (2013), 'Bulgarian power relations: the making of a Balkan power hub', in P. Hogselius, A. Hommels, A. Kaijser and E. van der Vleuten (eds), *The Making of Europe's Critical Infrastructure*, Croydon: Palgrave Macmillan, pp. 131–156.

Todorova, T. (2011), 'Bulgaria's big energy challenge: opportunities and barriers to investment in renewable energy', Sustainable Markets Group, accessed on 27 January 2014 at http://pubs.iied.org/pdfs/G03223.pdf.

United Nations (2000), 'Environmental performance reviews: Bulgaria second review', Environmental Performance Reviews Series No. 11, http://www.unece.org/fileadmin/DAM/env/epr/epr_studies/bulgaria.pdf.

Vachudova, M.A. (2005), *Europe Undivided: Democracy, Leverage and Integration After Communism*, Oxford: Oxford University Press.

Way, L.A and S. Levitsky (2007), 'Linkage, leverage, and the post-communist divide', *East European Politics and Societies*, 21 (1), 48–66.

Zhivkova, V. (2010), 'Biofuels – alternative to the traditional fuels in transport', Известия – издание на Икономически университет – Варна, EconLit – Q420, pp. 43–53.

Interviews

Interview 1, RES investor and lobbyist A, Hiteva, personal communication, Varna, 8 March 2011.
Interview 2, senior government expert, Hiteva, personal communication, Sofia, 16 March 2011.
Interview 3, RES investor and lobbyist B, Hiteva, personal communication, Sofia, 9 May 2011.
Interview 4, senior regional energy agency expert, Hiteva, personal communication, Plovdiv, 20 May 2011.

PART III

External dimension

13. RES in the hood and the shrinking Mediterranean Solar Plan

Gonzalo Escribano

13.1 INTRODUCTION

At the beginning of the twenty-first century, renewable energy sources (RES) became one of the hallmarks of the European Union's (EU) energy policy. Concern about pollution and climate change since the 1980s raised public awareness and placed environmental objectives high on the European political agenda (Morata and Solorio, 2012). The promotion of RES, together with other low carbon technologies (nuclear, and carbon capture and storage) and energy efficiency measures, emerged as one of the energy policy responses to address the above-mentioned environmental preferences. The European Commission's initial emphasis on RES was supported by several member states and their industries, helping to situate the EU as a world pioneer in the sector. The European RES industry positioned itself at the technological forefront; European grid and utilities operators are among the most experienced in integrating RES in the energy system; and member states' regulatory frameworks usually served as international benchmarks. All these elements resulted in an increasing contribution from RES to the EU's energy mix and the setting of more ambitious targets at the European level.

The EU has also attempted to promote RES abroad. However, apart from some country exceptions, the contribution of RES has remained marginal in the European neighbourhood, and its benefits are very unevenly distributed. Even biofuel, a commoditized RES, lacks a truly functioning international market (see Chapter 14 by Di Lucia). Furthermore, the contribution of RES to economic and human development in those countries remains largely unexplored. European investments in RES have been concentrated in developed or emerging markets (mainly the EU itself and the United States). The EU's RES imports are mostly limited to biofuels and electricity from RES (RES-E) from Norway and, occasionally, from Morocco. This static and almost closed picture started to change at the turn of the century with the advent of technological development. New transmission and solar technologies inspired the vision for an integrated Euro-Mediterranean RES market, which would allow countries on the southern shore of the Mediterranean to export RES-E. Industrial initiatives such as Desertec and the European-led Mediterranean Solar Plan (MSP) tried to offer an industrial, economic and institutional foundation. Finally, directive 2009/28 on RES explicitly contemplates RES-E imports from third countries.[1] Both pieces of the EU's energy *acquis* constitute a clear strategy of outward Europeanization differentiated for the Mediterranean and for the RES sector (Escribano, 2012).

Then the financial crisis came, biasing the EU's energy trinity of sustainability, security and competitiveness towards the competitiveness. RES support schemes have been reduced, and the EU risks becoming a pioneer unable to exert leadership at the expense of newcomers such as the United States (US) or China. The perception that RES is too much an energy soft power when compared with the hard narrative of US unconventional resources has decreased the appeal of RES in the European neighbourhood. To paraphrase Robert Kagan, fossil fuels are from Mars while RES come from Venus (Escribano, 2013). And the appeal of the EU's renewable energy model (if such a model exists) in its vicinity has also been shrinking quite fast. The Desertec initiative has been abandoned, and the MSP was blocked at the end of 2013 by the opposition of Spain on the grounds of a lack of interconnections with France, and the harsh realities stemming from the radical reform of the Spanish RES-E sector (see Chapter 8 by Solorio and Fernandez).

This chapter analyses two interlinked energy policy instruments put forward by the EU to promote RES-E in its neighbourhood – directive 2009/28 and the MSP – their impact on economic development in Mediterranean Partner Countries (MPCs), and how RES-E imports affect the EU's energy security. Section 13.2 builds upon previous research using outward Europeanization as a framework for analysis of RES-E promotion in the European neighbourhood. Section 13.3 offers a brief overview of the MSP and directive 2009/28 as examples of outward Europeanization in RES-E. Section 13.4 is devoted to the weaknesses of the current MSP approach as a driver for economic development in MPCs, briefly discussing under which conditions its developmental impact would be maximized. In this regard, it addresses gaps in outward Europeanization such as a lack of focus on the domestic conditions, unclear impact on local political economy (winners and losers) and, most importantly, the lack of inclusiveness regarding expectations of third countries (considering almost exclusively governmental and elite preferences). Then, the chapter shows that successful outward Europeanization facilitating international RES-E flows would increase energy security both in MPCs and in the EU. The last section concludes with some final remarks on the need to revamp the MSP to fit it to the new economic, political and regulatory realities that have emerged since its inception, pointing to some key elements of a sustainable ecosystem for outward Europeanization of RES-E in the Mediterranean.

13.2 ARE RES FROM VENUS?

The European Commission seems to have found a strategy to hedge markets and geopolitics through the Europeanization of energy corridors transporting energy towards the EU. The distinction between outward and inward Europeanization is very clear in the energy domain: inward Europeanization is the classical process by which EU member states achieve energy integration (see Chapter 1 by Jörgens and Solorio, and Chapter 2 by Solorio and Bocquillon), while outward Europeanization refers to promoting norms conducive to, let us say, RES-E promotion in the neighbourhood (Escribano, 2011, 2012). The idea is to extend the EU's energy *acquis* to its neighbouring countries, in order to achieve a pan-European energy community, which would include MPCs. The European Commission's 2006 Green Paper explicitly proposed an area of common regulation in the EU and its vicinity, reinforcing provisions aimed at expanding the market in the energy sector via agreements with third countries (COM, 2006). The document 'An energy policy for Europe' highlighted the importance of creating strategic energy partnerships with producing countries, which should be based on the EU's energy regulations and policies (COM, 2007).

The third legislative energy package's provisions concerning the unbundling of production, transport and distribution also include third producer countries. In principle, the EU offered third party access to third countries' companies on a reciprocal basis. Until recently, the reciprocity clause, dubbed the 'Gazprom clause' (which in the Mediterranean could be termed the 'Sonatrach clause' after the Algerian national oil and gas company), stated that a foreign energy company can only buy energy assets in an EU country when it offers the same possibility to EU companies for acquiring such assets at home. The relaxation of the reciprocity clause within the EU in the third legislative package has also led to its relaxation concerning third countries. In the heated discussions that finally led to the approval of the third legislative package, Germany pushed strongly for a more flexible reciprocity clause, which allows for a better management of its close energy relations with Russia (see Chapter 3 by Vogelpohl et al.). The final clause was relaxed in the sense that instead of ownership unbundling (which was no longer obliged by EU reciprocity provisions) a political bilateral agreement between a member state and a non-EU country would suffice to authorize a non-EU energy company, such as Gazprom or Sonatrach, to acquire transmission or distribution assets in the EU (Escribano, 2010).

The outward Europeanization strategy was even clearer regarding the inception of the Energy Community Treaty (ECT) for South-East Europe. The treaty consists of applying EU conventions to the Balkan region and coordinating interconnections (IEA, 2008). The energy security component aims mostly to secure the potential energy corridor coming from Russia, Central Asia and the Middle East, reaching the eastern Mediterranean through Turkey and then heading towards European markets via the Balkans. The European Commission is considering extending the ECT to the southern rim of the Mediterranean, in order to secure a normative and physical Mediterranean Energy Ring that would allow the integration of Euro-Mediterranean energy systems.

The outward Europeanization strategy of exporting EU energy regulations to MPCs, as a means to both modernize the MPCs energy sector and secure energy supplies, is however plagued with difficulties. Its most obvious limitation is that it is difficult to Europeanize MPCs' energy markets when inward Europeanization or integration within the EU itself is progressing only slowly (Escribano et al., 2012). A clearer example is that sometimes it seems easier to the European Commission to propose a trans-Caspian pipeline towards Turkmenistan than to build electricity interconnections across the Pyrenees.

Yet interconnections are the backbone of RES-E promotion within the EU, because only a well-interconnected energy market can profit from the scale and comparative advantages of European RES resources. Physical inward Europeanization is needed to attain the modest 27 per cent target for 2030, set in the climate and energy package by the European Council meeting of 23–24 October 2014. But physical inward Europeanization is even more necessary to reach the more ambitious targets of the EU's 2050 Roadmap, which entails almost full decarbonization of the electricity sector. However, the Iberian push to set a 15 per cent interconnection target for 2030 was not successful, and there are few hopes that the 10 per cent interconnection target for 2020 will be reached from the exiguous current 3 per cent interconnection rate between Spain and France (see Chapter 8 by Solorio and Fernandez, and Chapter 9 by Bocquillon and Evrard).

The challenge to integrate RES, particularly RES-E, into the Euro-Mediterranean energy space seems to focus only on the narrow, normative outward Europeanization path so beloved to the EU in its relations with its neighbours (Buchan, 2011; Escribano, 2010). The idea is that each neighbour would gain differentiated access to the EU's RES market according to its compliance with EU's norms. This market access incentive would anchor RES-related policies and promote its deployment in the European neighbourhood. In the following, this chapter will test the outward Europeanization approach with the case of the MSP.

13.3 EUROPEANIZING RES-E IN THE MEDITERRANEAN: DIRECTIVE 2009/28 AND THE MSP

Transnational RES-E deployment is a complex issue because it requires support schemes that are costly and difficult to implement, both technically and politically. Member states only support nationally produced RES-E, and one of the goals of directive 2009/28 is the facilitation of cross-border RES-E support without necessarily affecting national support systems. In order to do so, it introduces cooperation mechanisms among member states. As already explained in Chapter 2 of this volume, the flexibility measures contemplated by the directive include statistical transfers, joint projects and also joint support mechanisms. Statistical transfers refer to the exchange of Green Certificates. For instance, the Green Certificates generated by solar energy in Southern Europe (if they exceed the respective national objectives) can be accounted for in the objectives of a northern EU member state.

For RES-E imported from third countries, the conditions are not so flexible. They do not include statistical transfers: only physical electricity transfers can be accounted for in member states' RES targets. A member state can implement joint projects with third countries, including in its national objectives the RES-E imported from the third country and consumed within the EU. In the absence of existing (but projected) operative interconnections, the member state can include in its national objectives the amount of RES-E that has been agreed to that end with the third country until the needed infrastructures are in place. There is no obstacle to implement joint support systems for joint projects with third countries. The only limitation, which also applies to intra-EU projects, is that in order to be computed in the national objectives, the imported RES-E cannot benefit from support schemes in the third country, with the significant exception of investment support for the construction of installations.

In fact, even if the directive excludes statistical transfers with third countries, de facto it offers them the opportunity to include statistical transfers by joining the ECT. As the directive clearly states, the contracting parties of the ECT can benefit from the same flexibility measures as EU member states, if it is so decided. This is an open possibility for MPCs to enter the club of statistical transfers, widening the opportunities of RES-E deployment in the region to those countries Europeanizing their energy norms. Few Mediterranean countries outside Europe are nowadays ready to adhere to the ECT, perhaps with the exceptions of Turkey, Israel and Morocco.

Joining the ECT implies adoption of the EU energy *acquis*, a difficult move in a region characterized by lack of competition and state-owned energy companies, some of which have significant hydrocarbon reserves, for example in Algeria, Libya and Egypt. In this regard, the functionalist implications of the ECT in Southwestern Europe are more limited for North African countries, which cannot be compared to the Balkans or Turkey (Renner, 2009). However, convergence towards the RES-related *acquis* could be easier compared with conventional energies, to the extent that it does not threaten significant vested interests and is more prone to institutional innovation due to its incipient weight in energy systems.

In 2011, the European Commission (COM, 2011) issued a communication entitled 'The EU energy policy: engaging with partners beyond our borders'. The communication is clearly an outward Europeanization strategy, including the exchange of information among member states on external energy policy. It also opened the possibility for the European Commission of negotiating mandates to build infrastructure networks with third countries, for example the Council mandate authorizing the European Commission to negotiate an agreement to establish a legal framework with Azerbaijan and Turkmenistan on a trans-Caspian pipeline system. The European Commission noted that a similar approach could be taken to establish a framework to provide legal security and political support to import RES-E from the southern Mediterranean. Both projects were also taken up among the priorities in external infrastructures.

The main proposal relevant to this chapter suggested the possibility of an 'EU–Southern Mediterranean Energy Partnership', initially focused on electricity and RES-E market development. In this regard, the European Commission recognized the need to improve the conditions offered for joint projects with third countries under article 9 of directive 2009/28. Thus, the European Commission assumed that the uncertainty surrounding the MSP did not do justice to what was probably the second most important energy project outside Europe (with or without a formal mandate) after the southern energy corridor to Central Asia. Finally, another new feature was the integration of development cooperation policy and external energy policy intended to fight energy poverty and climate change through development cooperation in RES and energy efficiency.

Under directive 2009/28's institutional design for RES-E flows with third countries, the MSP proposed a road map to catalyse investment, industrial development and regulatory innovation to foster RES-E deployment in the southern neighbourhood. Its goal is to deploy 20 gigawatts (GW) of installed RES-E capacity in the Mediterranean region by 2020, along with the necessary transmission capacities and cross-border interconnections, as well as fostering energy efficiency measures. The 2008 Paris Declaration that gave birth to the Union for the Mediterranean (UfM) stated that 'market development as well as research and development of all alternative sources of energy are … a major priority in efforts towards assuring sustainable development'. Despite the precision about the MSP, the sense of the Declaration calls for the mobilization of all alternative energies, including wind.

Its inclusion in the UfM came out of the French–German bargaining that led to the Paris Declaration, but its origins can be traced back to the Trans-Mediterranean Renewable Energy Cooperation Network (TREC), a partnership created in 2003 between the Club of Rome, the Hamburg Climate Protection Foundation and the National Energy Research Centre of Jordan. Together with the German Aerospace Centre (DLR), the TREC developed the Desertec project, an EU–Middle East and North Africa (MENA) initiative based upon thermo-solar energy (Carafa, 2011). With the support of the Greens and German industry, the German government supported the Desertec initiative in its 2007 presidency of the EU. A few months later the Desertec (2007) *White Book* was presented at the European Parliament, and began to receive increasing support in Brussels. At that time, French President Nicolas Sarkozy was proposing his Mediterranean Union, facing strong opposition from Germany. Finally the Mediterranean Union was watered down to the UfM, which included the MSP as its flagship project but not all the institutional capabilities proposed by the French government. Instead it added six areas for UfM projects to the Euro-Mediterranean *acquis*: the MSP itself, transport corridors, water, small and medium-sized enterprises (SMEs) promotion, a Euro-Mediterranean College, and civil and (only recently) social affairs.

Tasked with the development of the projects, the UfM's Secretariat plays a central role in the institutional network. The delay in its operative constitution, and then the resignation of its Secretary Generals, has not allowed it thus far to stimulate the process. This was coupled with the financial crisis, which dried up financial markets and decreased enthusiasm for RES. The Arab Spring further distorted the institutional landscape and, more importantly, signalled the lack of adequacy of EU Mediterranean policy tools to deal with its consequences. The failure of the Desertec initiative and, finally, the Spanish opposition to the implementation of the MSP has led it to the brink of decline.[2]

Spain blocked the MSP Roadmap for two main reasons which illustrates the 'original sin' of RES-E's outward Europeanization: not practising at home what it preaches in its neighbourhood. Firstly, the Spanish government complained that before building new interconnections with North Africa (Spain has two electricity interconnectors with Morocco and two gas pipelines with Algeria) the EU should work on attaining the 10 per cent interconnection target for 2020 between France and Spain (in June 2015, this was barely 3 per cent), which acts as a protectionist entry barrier for Spanish RES into France and the rest of Europe. Secondly, due to this, Spain's RES-E installed capacity was simply too large, given the reduction of national energy demand prospects. Finally, given the lack of a uniform and consistent RES-E support scheme across the EU financed at least partially by the European budget, RES costs remain too high for a Spanish economy suffering from the burden of high budget deficits and competitiveness erosion due to high electricity prices (see Chapter 8 by Solorio and Fernandez). This is even more the case if we talk of new RES-E imports without the possibility of exports attached.

13.4 RES-E PROMOTION IN THE MEDITERRANEAN: A DRIVER FOR THE DEVELOPMENT OF WHOM?

But aside from financial and institutional problems (governance of the MSP, the role of the European Commission and the UfM Secretariat, member states' opposition, and decreased political tolerance to subsidize RES-E), the MSP has failed to provide a credible and recognizable framework mainly because it has not been able to take MPCs' preferences into account. These preferences consist of profiting from their structural comparative advantages (insolation or wind, abundant space and labour force) and building dynamic ones such as industrial clusters, innovative regulation and technical skills. This section is devoted to the weaknesses of the current MSP approach as a driver for economic development in MPCs.

Directive 2009/28 provides the framework for the integration of RES-E into the Euro-Mediterranean region and the functioning of the MSP. However, the MSP should also reach the UfM's objectives inherited from the Barcelona process of achieving a shared space of peace and prosperity.[3] This was reiterated by the Joint Communication from the European Commission and the High Representative stating the necessity for a 'Partnership for democracy and prosperity with the Southern Mediterranean',[4] which includes RES deployment as a channel for Euro-Mediterranean cooperation.

While the MSP has generated a lot of attention, little has been said about its human development impact for the European neighbourhood. A well-designed MSP should be conceived as a driver for economic development for MPCs in at least five aspects:

1. To provide part of the energy required by MPCs' economic growth.
2. To contribute to the supply of the modern energy services required by economic development.
3. Contributing to eradicate energy poverty.
4. To use solar and wind energy resources to generate new economic activities, new jobs and new incomes.
5. To provide technical cooperation, training and technology transfers in order for MPCs to be able to reap the benefits of RES deployment.

All these elements taken together constitute a consistent cooperation programme for sustainable Euro-Mediterranean energy development. Energy development consists of increasing the provision and use of energy services, and is a key driver of economic development. Energy development also determines the manner in which energy is generated and used, and has a direct impact on sustainable development. It is important to highlight that such a comprehensive programme would constitute the first occasion when energy is conceived as an instrument of economic development in the Mediterranean. The question is whether the MSP has the potential to become a driver for MPCs' development, or can instead be better considered as an EU-centric project aimed at achieving its own environmental objectives together with the promotion of European industries and engineering firms. The answer is that it depends upon the conditions under which RES deployment is implemented.

A study on the impact of RES deployment in Morocco can help to illustrate the complex policy choices involved in the process (de Arce et al., 2012). The general conclusion is that RES-E deployment entails significant economic opportunities for Morocco in terms of gross domestic product (GDP) and employment. In the proposed scenarios, the figures for economic impact on GDP vary from 1.17 per cent to 1.9 per cent at the end of the period (2040), with employment figures for full-time equivalent direct and indirect impact on the economy between 267 000 and 482 000 jobs. It shows that policy decisions regarding exports and improving local capacities are crucial in order to profit as much as possible from the opportunities that RES-E offers to Morocco. The best economic performance is attained with exports (be they virtual or physical) based upon improved local capacities.

The above results are similar to the those obtained by other researchers. Mahía et al. (2014) show that the concentrated solar power (CSP) industry in Morocco is viable under certain conditions, principally the removal of policy-related barriers, and increased legislative and administrative support. Without such measures, current installed CSP capacity in the region does not reach the critical level to become economically viable. Calzadilla et al. (2014) find that an integrated Euro-Mediterranean power system based on RES will be economically viable. However, the costs and benefits for both regions depend on the type of strategy adopted to finance power plants, the development of electricity costs for the different technologies, and on international climate policy. Brand and Zingerle's (2011) simulations point out that optimizing RES-E goals can decrease overall energy system costs. Indeed, the opportunities for European companies have also been analysed in the economic literature (Vallentin and Viebahn, 2010).

All this points to the fact that in order to maximize economic gains, MPCs need to participate more fully in the industrial dimension of the initiative. This means improving their absorption capacity at the industrial level, integrating the RES sector in a comprehensive industrial policy, upgrading infrastructures and regulation. For the EU, it is important to highlight the significance of supporting the country's absorption capacity through technical cooperation programmes, including activities such as training, twinning, scientific exchanges or networking, at every level related to RES deployment.

The Moroccan case clearly illustrates the case for approaching the MSP as a comprehensive sustainable development strategy. In designing regulatory, trading and financing schemes, the focus should be on MPCs' development (Escribano and San Martín, 2012). If the benefits are not to be captured by EU companies and their MPC partners, several measures should be adopted. One of them is the focus on alleviating energy poverty in rural households, which has a positive impact on sustainability and human development. This calls for supporting individual decentralized photovoltaic (PV) systems, but also delivering modern energy services not necessarily related with RES; for instance, liquefied petroleum gas (LPG) and other modern fuels. Another prerequisite is supporting the training of Moroccan manpower to attract investments. However, training should not be exclusively provided for the purposes of maintenance; an activity which generates fewer jobs and added value. A meaningful participation in the construction and operation phases should be attained in the medium term. At the same time the EU should establish a long-term mechanism for promoting technology transfers and for enhancing local innovation capabilities. Without such measures, the developmental impact of introducing technologies such as CSP in countries such as Morocco could be minimal.

Without such prerequisites in mind, the whole discussion on the MSP risks deviating from its main objective. As a project included in the UfM, it should aim for the creation of a shared prosperity area in the Euro-Mediterranean region. This could only be achieved by accompanying MPCs' reform efforts and strengthening their economic opportunities, such as RES-E exports. Southern Mediterranean countries have shown their interest in RES but have also clearly pointed out the kind of European support they require: investment, training and technology transfers. Without the upgrading of MPCs' institutions, human capital and rural energy poverty situations, the MSP risks being reduced to an EU strategy to achieve its own environmental objectives together with promoting European RES-E industries, energy companies and engineering firms. This scenario would add very little to the development within MPCs and therefore should neither be defended nor pursued as a development strategy. In principle it can be thought that this poses no problem for the EU, but this is a short-sighted vision insofar as it does not consider matching MPCs' preferences as a prerequisite for the MSP to succeed.

13.5 RES-E AND RISK IN THE NEIGHBOURHOOD[5]

Together with economic difficulties, societies being tired of paying subsidies to renewables on the northern shore of the Mediterranean and a lack of fit with preferences on the southern shore, RES-E deployment in the southern neighbourhood has been hampered by misperceptions regarding energy security. Obviously, domestic RES deployment contributes to the improvement of energy security indicators related to geographic diversification and energy dependence, reducing vulnerability by diversifying energy sources and origins. However, this picture becomes less clear if RES are deployed beyond national boundaries, such as importing RES-E from North Africa (or Brazilian biofuels). International RES trade flows may affect the level of risk perceived by consumer countries compared to a system where RES are located within national borders. The EU's renewable energy policy aims at promoting both sustainability and energy security by substituting polluting and imported energy sources. This section argues that international RES-E flows do not necessarily harm European energy security, but rather the opposite.

The energy security implications of international RES-E flows can be analysed through the risk–cost framework of portfolio choice theory and its applications to energy.[6] Assuming that electricity from solar origin generated in North Africa is added to the available energy portfolio of the EU under the same risk conditions prevailing in the EU (same return–cost variability), this technology happens to yield higher returns in North Africa thanks to higher insolation levels. The efficient risk–cost frontier is then pushed upwards. Thus, the returns of the EU energy portfolio without including solar energy from North Africa are lower than in the case where the solar contribution is also considered. With the same set of preferences, the equilibrium shifts from a new portfolio with lower risk and cost levels. Depending on preferences regarding risk-aversion, the level of risk could be reduced further.

By contrast, if lowering the expected cost is accompanied by an increase in risk levels, the equilibrium will not achieve any improvement in the cost–risk trade-off. There is also a worst-case scenario in which the integration of non-EU RES resources into the EU energy system outpaces cost reduction with higher risk levels. This scenario leads to the issue of risks inherent to the nature of extra-EU RES corridors. A frequent claim is that transnational RES-E corridors suffer from the same geopolitical weaknesses that call for a reduction of imported fossil fuels in the national energy mix: being dependent upon foreign resources. However, this argument is not supported by careful economic analysis.

If access to international RES-E corridors implies further diversification of geographical origins or energy sources, or both, the vulnerability of a country can actually decrease for a given energy dependence ratio (Aslani et al., 2012). With new resources and/or technologies from new exporting countries, diversification increases and vulnerability decreases, even if the RES-E corridors came from the same countries from which conventional energies are already imported. For instance, importing solar electricity from Algeria into the EU does increase both diversification and dependence for both the EU (supply) and Algeria (demand). From a portfolio perspective, however, the diversification of sources does actually reduce vulnerability.

The nature of RES-E also limits their capacity to serve as a driver for power politics. RES used for electricity generation cannot be stored as easily or as long as fossil fuels. Furthermore, storage costs would definitively be much higher with current storage technologies. Therefore, a North African country could not interrupt its RES-E supply to the EU without simply wasting the resource, at least in the short term. In the longer run, redirecting RES-E supply towards domestic markets would require transmission investments and, equally importantly, in addition to the loss of revenues, it would increase the cost of domestic electricity above politically acceptable levels in these countries.

Presumably, the main risk dimension to be addressed in the European neighbourhood is regulatory risk, which ultimately embodies a wider array of socio-political and institutional risks (this regulatory risk is far from being confined to non-EU countries, as recently seen in Germany and Spain; see Chapter 3 by Vogelpohl et al., and Chapter 8 by Solorio and Fernandez). RES returns depend on regulatory schemes, and expected returns are linked to the credibility of these schemes in the long run. Without a credible and enforceable regulatory and institutional framework, an RES-producing country can try to raise the tariffs at which it sells electricity to its clients. Nevertheless, as explained in the above paragraph, the alternatives would be limited by small market power.

However, the relevant point here is that the shift in the risk–cost-efficient frontier can only occur in an institutional framework that delivers similar levels of regulatory risk and property rights to the levels prevailing in the importing region. In the specific case of Europe, this fact leads to the question of whether the energy security of the EU's RES corridors depends upon its Europeanization, as described in a previous section. This led to the regulatory challenges implied by the integration of North African RES (wind and solar) into the European electricity system.

Directive 2009/28 introduces the institutional framework to reduce regulatory risks, allowing the upward shift of the risk–cost-efficient frontier to lower risk–cost combinations. However, to align regulatory risks with those risks prevailing in the EU, normative convergence towards the EU *acquis* in the field of RES-E would also be needed. Without some degree of normative convergence, these joint projects and support mechanisms can fail to become operational. Issues such as the interoperability of electricity systems, support mechanism control, grid access, transparency in public procurement, authorizations and certifications, among many others, require a minimum degree of normative harmonization, at both the regulatory and the technical level. In short, these elements call for the Europeanization of Mediterranean energy corridors.

In fact, for the purpose of integrating RES-E in the EU energy space, a rigid and complete implementation of the EU energy *acquis* is most likely not required. On the contrary, the MSP illustrates the case of a more restricted, differentiated convergence over a relatively fringe issue (RES versus the more sensitive issue for energy actors and lobbyists of conventional energies). This differentiation has a normative and a geographical dimension, with eventual joint projects and support schemes being implemented with different third countries under diverse agreed normative convergence conditions.

In this regard, the MSP can be understood as an attempt to design an institutional model for the integration of non-EU RES corridors into the EU energy market (Escribano and San Martín, 2012). It is an institutional and market approach, but it can be projected geographically in a differentiated manner. If well designed, it could leave both producers and consumers better off in terms of combinations of costs and risk. The regulatory dimension of the RES corridor, which could be described as a normative corridor, is key to evaluate the contribution of RES to EU – and North African – energy security.

13.6 CONCLUSIONS: REVAMPING THE MEDITERRANEAN SOLAR PLAN

The financial crisis has had a deep impact on the public appetite for RES-E support schemes. The EU risks paying the costs of being a pioneer of RES-E deployment without gaining the benefits of becoming a leader, not only within Europe, but also in its neighbourhood. The abandonment of the Desertec initiative and the blocking of the MSP should be framed in the transformation of the European RES-E sector. This chapter, firstly, has tried to show that the Europeanization of RES-E sector in the neighbourhood is not only about export norms, technology and market designs. MPCs' preferences regarding energy development and capacity building should be taken more seriously for a sustainable cooperative framework to emerge.

Secondly, the chapter has argued that RES-E deployment in the neighbourhood can actually increase European energy security, provided that some levelling of regulatory risk happens through sustainable Europeanization. This regulatory aspect is key for a credible comeback of the MSP and eventual new RES projects in the European neighbourhood.

Its design may well have suffered from a premature obsolescence in regulatory terms. Support schemes such as Feed-In Tariffs (FITs) and quotas with Tradable Green Certificates (TGCs), which have dominated RES regulatory mechanisms, are being increasingly challenged by the experience of emerging RES producers. For instance, Brazil, Chile and Mexico now use auctions, trying to limit RES deployment to areas with high load factors (high wind speeds or high insolation hours) that allow prices to be reached that are close to those of conventional energies (grid parity). While energy scholars have traditionally dismissed auctions, there are new elements showing that under an appropriate design they can open an innovative regulatory path in RES support (Del Río and Linares, 2014). In this regard, a revamping of the MSP that includes these new regulatory developments, and its relation to the energy risk–cost trade-off, seems urgent.

The chapter also suggests that the political and regulatory design of the MSP may already be obsolete. Both aspects call for a reconsideration of the characteristics of the Plan, which will be difficult to isolate from the shortcomings of the European internal electricity market. The European economic crisis will eventually end, and energy demand will grow again. When that time comes, RES deployment in the neighbourhood may be seen as a viable way to diversify European energy corridors from Russian supplies. But perhaps it would be too late to build a coherent and integrated Euro-Mediterranean RES ring. The reconsideration of the role of RES in the neighbourhood, and of the neighbourhood in the European energy system, requires a similar rethinking of the role of the MSP in paving the way to integrate neighbours' RES in the European energy market.

Finally, regarding the outward Europeanization analytical framework, the chapter has shown, firstly, that inward and outward processes of Europeanization are deeply entrenched, in terms of norms and physical infrastructure, and that outward cannot be done without inward. It is quite disturbing to watch the EU promoting a Mediterranean electricity ring while being unable to complete its own internal network. RES can constitute a source of soft energy power, but inward and outward Europeanization should be pursued in a more consistent manner, at home and abroad. Secondly, the chapter shows that partners' preferences should be integrated more fully and in a more inclusive manner, namely regarding energy development and modernization. When approaching this from an industrial policy perspective, it should be clear that without technology transfers, delocalization of industrial processes and more local value-added creation, few spillovers will be created. It is not by creating another subcommittee at the MSP UfM Extended Technical

Committee that the value chain is going to be altered. Lastly, normative outward Europeanization can close the risk gap that is ultimately inhibiting private investment in the RES-E sector across the Mediterranean neighbourhood. Through anchoring regulation and offering credible commitments, this could significantly improve the cost–risk trade-off, and therefore energy security for consumers and producers, north and south of the Mediterranean.

ACKNOWLEDGEMENTS

The author would like to thank Meliyara Consuegra for her research assistance and helpful collaboration in writing this chapter.

NOTES

1. Article 9, directive 2009/28/EC of 23 April 2009 on the promotion of the use of energy from renewable sources. *Official Journal of the European Union*, L 140/16.
2. 14 On October 2014, after a meeting in Rome, Desertec announced that only three of its 19 existing shareholders had decided to stay: Saudi Arabia's ACWA Power, Germany's RWE and China's State Grid. This does not seem the right kind (nor the number) of partners to promote outward Europeanization.
3. The Barcelona Process was launched by the EU in 1995 to compensate the Eastern enlargement process that started after the fall of the Berlin Wall. It was intended to build an area of shared peace and prosperity in three ways: economic cooperation and free trade, political dialogue, and cultural dialogue.
4. March 8, COM (2011) 200 final.
5. This section summarizes the arguments developed in Escribano et al. (2013), which contains a more detailed and formal approach. On this debate see also Komendantova et al. (2011) and Komendantova et al. (2012), Cooper and Sovacool (2013), Kost et al. (2011), Lilliestam and Ellenbeck (2011) and Smith Stegen et al. (2012).
6. There is a vast literature which develops such an approach. See for instance Awerbuch and Berger (2003), Awerbuch et al. (2006), Bar-Lev and Katz (1976), Bazilian and Roques (2008), and Varian (1993).

REFERENCES

Aslani, A., E. Antila and K.V. Wong (2012), 'Comparative analysis of energy security in the Nordic countries: the role of renewable energy resources in diversification', *Journal of Renewable and Sustainable Energy*, 4 (6), 062701.

Awerbuch, S. and M. Berger (2003), 'Diversity and security in the EU: Applying portfolio theory to EU electricity planning and policy-making', Report no. EET/2003/03, International Energy Agency, Paris: IEA/OECD, Paris.

Awerbuch, S., A. Stirling, J.C. Jansen and L.W.M. Beurskens (2006), 'Portfolio and diversity analysis of energy technologies using full-spectrum risk measures', in D. Bodde and K. Leggio (eds), *Understanding and Managing Business Risk in the Electric Sector*, London, UK: Elsevier, pp. 202–222.

Bar-Lev, D. and S. Katz (1976), 'A portfolio approach to fossil fuel procurement in the electric utility industry', *Journal of Finance*, 31 (3), 933–947.

Bazilian, M. and F. Roques (eds) (2008), *Analytical Methods for Energy Diversity and Security. Portfolio Optimization in the Energy Sector: A Tribute to the Work of Dr Shimon Awerbuch*, Oxford, UK and Amsterdam, the Netherlands: Elsevier.

Brand, B. and J. Zingerle (2011), 'The renewable energy targets of the Maghreb countries: Impact on electricity supply and conventional power markets', *Energy Policy*, 39 (8), 4411–4419.

Buchan, D. (2011), 'Expanding the European dimension in energy policy: the Commission's latest initiatives', SP No. 23, Oxford Institute for Energy Studies.

Calzadilla, A., M. Wiebelt, J. Blohmke and G. Klepper (2014), 'Desert power 2050: Regional and sectoral impacts of renewable electricity production in Europe, the Middle East and North Africa', Kiel Working Paper No. 1891.

Carafa, L. (2011), 'The Mediterranean Solar Plan through the prism of external governance', accessed on 7 February at http://www.euromesco.net/images/papers/papersiemed5.pdf.

COM (2006), 'Energy Green Paper. European strategy for sustainable competitive and secure energy', COM 105 final.

COM (2007), 'An energy policy for Europe', COM 1 final.

COM (2011), 'On security of energy supply and international cooperation – The EU energy policy: engaging with partners beyond our borders', 539 final.

Cooper, C. and C.B. Sovacool (2013), 'Miracle or mirage? The promise and peril of desert energy part 1', *Renewable Energy*, 50, 628–636.

De Arce, R., R. Mahía, E. Medina and G. Escribano (2012), 'A simulation of the economic impact of renewable energy development in Morocco', *Energy Policy*, 46, 335–345.

Del Río, P. and P. Linares (2014), 'Back to the future? Rethinking auctions for renewable electricity support', *Renewable and Sustainable Energy Reviews*, 35, 42–56.

Desertec (2007), *Clean Power from Deserts The DESERTEC Concept for Energy, Water and Climate Security, White Book*, Hamburg: Trans-Mediterranean Renewable Energy Cooperation – TREC.

Escribano, G. (2010), 'Convergence towards differentiation: the case of Mediterranean energy corridors', *Mediterranean Politics*, 15 (2), 211–229.

Escribano, G. (2011), 'Markets or geo-politics? The Europeanization of Euro-Mediterranean energy corridors', *Journal of Energy Sector Management*, 5 (1), 39–59.

Escribano, G. (2012), 'A new strategy: the Europeanization of energy corridors to the EU', in J.M. Marín, J. García-Verdugo and G. Escribano (eds), *Energy Security for the EU in the 21st Century: Markets, Geopolitics and Corridors*, New York, NY, USA and Abingdon, UK: Routledge, pp. 276–296.

Escribano, G. (2013), 'Shifting towards what? Europe and the rise of unconventional energy', *Entelequia*, 15, 153–167.

Escribano, G., R. Mahía and R. de Arce (2012), 'The Europeanization of EU member states' energy security policies: convergence patterns', in J.M. Marín, J. García-Verdugo and G. Escribano (eds), *Energy Security for the EU in the 21st Century: Markets, Geopolitics and Corridors*, New York, NY, USA and Abingdon, UK: Routledge, pp. 210–231.

Escribano, G., J.M. Marín-Quemada and E. San Martín González (2013), 'RES and risk: renewable energy's contribution to energy security. A portfolio-based approach', *Renewable and Sustainable Energy Reviews*, 26, 549–559.

Escribano, G. and E. San Martín (2012), 'Morocco, the European energy policy and the Mediterranean Solar Plan', in F. Morata and I. Solorio (eds), *European Energy Policy: An Environmental Approach*, Cheltenham, UK and Northampton, MA, USA: Edward Elgar Publishing, pp. 193–210.

IEA (International Energy Agency) (2008), *Energy in the Western Balkans: The Path to Reform and Reconstruction*, Paris, France: International Energy Agency.

Komendantova, N., A. Patt, L. Barras and A. Battaglini (2012), 'Perception of risks in renewable energy projects: the case of concentrated solar power in North Africa', *Energy Policy*, 40, 103–109.

Komendantova, N., A. Patt and K. Williges (2011), 'Solar power investment in North Africa: reducing perceived risks', *Renewable and Sustainable Energy Reviews*, 15, 4829–4835.

Kost, C., B. Pfluger, W. Eichhammer and M. Ragwitz (2011), 'Fruitful symbiosis: why an export bundled with wind energy is the most feasible option for North African concentrated solar power', *Energy Policy*, 39, 7136–7145.

Lilliestam, J. and S. Ellenbeck (2011), 'Energy security and renewable electricity trade – will Desertec make Europe vulnerable to the energy weapon?', *Energy Policy*, 39, 3380–3391.

Mahía, R., R. de Arce and E. Medina (2014), 'Assessing the future of a CSP industry in Morocco', *Energy Policy*, 69, 586–597.

Morata, F. and I. Solorio (eds) (2012), *European Energy Policy: An Environmental Approach*, Cheltenham, UK and Northampton, MA, USA: Edward Elgar Publishing.

Renner, S. (2009), 'The energy community of Southeast Europe: a neo-functionalist project of regional integration', *European Integration online Papers (EIoP)*, available at http://eiop.or.at/eiop/pdf/2009-001.pdf.

Smith Stegen, K., P. Gilmartin and J. Calucci (2012), 'Terrorists versus the sun: Desertec in North Africa as a case study for assessing risks to energy infrastructure', *Risk Management*, 14, 3–26.

Vallentin, D. and P. Viebahn (2010), 'Economic opportunities resulting from a global deployment of concentrated solar power (CSP) technologies – the example of German technology providers', *Energy Policy*, 38 (8), 4467–4478.

Varian, H. (1993), 'A portfolio of Nobel laureates: Markowitz, Miller and Sharpe', *Journal of Economic Perspectives*, 7 (1), 159–169.

14. External governance and Europeanization beyond borders: EU biofuel policies in Mozambique

Lorenzo Di Lucia

14.1 INTRODUCTION

In the past decade the European Union (EU) has intensively promoted and regulated transport biofuels. Since 2003, following the adoption of the first biofuels directive, EU member states have adopted support policies which have resulted in a rapid expansion of the sector. Between 2004 and 2013 the share of biofuels in the EU motor fuel market grew from 0.7 per cent (COM, 2007) to 4.7 per cent (EurObserv'ER, 2014). In spite of this expansion, the EU remained substantially self-sufficient until 2007 when imports started to surge (USDA, 2014). In 2012 they accounted for nearly one-third of the EU biofuels market (COM, 2012a). At the same time as imports grew, biofuels became the object of an intense debate following the publication of two controversial studies (Searchinger et al., 2008; Fargione et al., 2008). Based on these and the numerous studies which followed, critical concerns were raised over the desirability of biofuels due to the risk of competition with food supply, land clearing and resulting loss of habitat and increased carbon emissions (Pimentel et al., 2009; Fargione et al., 2008). Of particular attention was the deployment of large-scale biofuels programmes in the EU and United States which, through the mechanisms of indirect land use change (ILUC) and market competition, could generate negative impacts in distant regions and, in particular, developing countries (Banse et al., 2008).

In this context, the capacity of the EU to limit the risk of negative impacts in geographically distant regions has become a key point of contention in the debate about transport biofuels. Environmental non-governmental organizations (ENGOs) and other sceptical stakeholders argued that without a proper system to ensure sustainable production of biofuels within and outside the EU, policy support for these technologies should be discontinued (Pilgrim and Harvey, 2010). In response to this, EU policymakers introduced within the 2008 renewable energy directive (RED) a certification scheme to ensure sustainable production of all biofuels consumed in the EU. However, the capacity of this policy instrument to achieve such an ambitious goal is challenged by the lack of EU jurisdiction to enforce compliance in third countries and the limited scope of the selected certification criteria (Di Lucia, 2010).

Against this background, I argue in this chapter that the capacity of the EU to ensure that an expansion of the biofuels sector does not generate unacceptable socio-ecological impacts in developing countries is a necessary condition for biofuels to remain on the post-2020 political agenda in the EU. Therefore, the aim of this chapter is to evaluate the influence exercised by the EU on national systems in countries and regions beyond EU borders and neighbouring countries. The analysis does not attempt to explain why third countries adopt certain policies, or choose to produce biofuels in compliance with EU-inspired sustainability requirements, but seeks to answer two key questions:

1. What mechanisms have been employed by the EU to export to third countries its rules and values relating to sustainable biofuels?
2. To what extent have EU rules and values relating to sustainable biofuels been adopted in domestic policy and applied in practice in third countries?

To answer these questions and to advance the aim of this chapter, I employ an analytical approach derived from the literature of external governance (Lavenex and Schimmelfennig, 2009; Lavenex, 2004) in which scholars have evaluated the means and results of the EU's influence on countries which cannot become, or are not interested in becoming, EU member states.

Mozambique, a less developed country with biofuels ambitions and large production and export potentials, is selected as an empirical case for this study. Mozambique represents a group of tropical developing countries which show weak institutional frameworks for environmental and social protection and, at the same time, high potential to benefit from deploying a domestic biofuels sector. In shedding some light on the case of Mozambique, this chapter seeks to contribute to the understanding of the potentials and challenges of the EU biofuels governance in developing countries.

The study relies primarily on written sources, including scientific and grey literature published on the topic, and interviews with involved actors. Interviews with officials of the Mozambican government (Ministry of Energy and Ministry of Agriculture) and the delegation of the European Commission in Maputo were carried out in 2007 and 2014. These interviews allow a deeper understanding of EU and Mozambican biofuels-related initiatives in the period under analysis.

In the remainder of the chapter, section 14.2 describes the framework employed in the analysis and the theoretical bases upon which it is built. Section 14.3 illustrates EU rules and values relating to sustainable biofuels, while section 14.4 provides an overview of the Mozambican biofuel sector. The results of the analysis of EU external governance in Mozambique are presented in section 14.5, with attention to policy adoption and application in domestic practice. The chapter ends with section 14.6, in which the results of the analysis are discussed and a set of conclusions put forward.

14.2 THE STUDY OF EU EXTERNAL GOVERNANCE AND EUROPEANIZATION BEYOND EU BORDERS

Traditionally, the study of Europeanization has been largely confined to the impact of European integration and governance on the member states of the EU (see, e.g., Knill, 2005; Börzel and Risse, 2003; Knill and Lehmkuhl, 2002; see also Chapter 1 by Jörgens and Solorio). More recently the attention of scholars interested in Europeanization has also included the impact of the EU on neighbouring countries applying for membership (Sedelmeier, 2006; Schimmelfennig and Sedelmeier, 2004; Grabbe, 2003; see also Chapter 13 by Escribano) However, much less attention has been paid to the impacts in countries that are not interested, or have no chance of joining the EU (Knill and Tosun, 2009; Schimmelfennig, 2009).

Emerging scholarly literature on EU external governance explores whether there is an expansion of the regulatory and organizational boundaries of the EU short of enlargement (Lavenex and Schimmelfennig, 2009; Bauer et al., 2007; Lavenex, 2004). The framework developed within this literature to analyse Europeanization both within and beyond EU boundaries emphasizes the relevance of three ideal modes of governance: hierarchy, networks and markets.[1] In a nutshell, hierarchical governance is seen as a form of steering based on formal and precise rules that are non-negotiable and legally binding as well as enforceable upon actors (Lavenex and Schimmelfennig, 2009). Europeanization through hierarchy, or by compliance (Bauer et al., 2007), is thus a coercive mechanism whereby legally binding rules are implemented by national governments to avoid sanctions. Network governance is a broader category in which change is the result of coordination efforts, voluntary negotiations and bargaining, or the unilateral transfer of policies based on processes of imitation or learning. This mode of governance, similar to what Bauer et al. (2007) describe as communication, is marked by an institutionalized infrastructure for the exchange of information and policy learning (Knill and Tosun, 2009). The rationality of this mode is to secure and increase the legitimacy of particular models, through deliberative processes, co-ownership and interaction (Schimmelfennig and Sedelmeier, 2004). Finally, market governance is the third major mode of governance in this framework. Here, change is the result of competition between formally autonomous actors. The adoption and application of EU rules take place in non-member states on a voluntary basis and the potential impacts foremost depend on the interest of actors in accessing the EU market (Lavenex and Schimmelfennig, 2009).

The analytical framework applied in this study relies largely on the framework developed by external governance scholars. In the framework, hierarchical governance is assessed by examining international agreements concluded between the European Commission and the government of Mozambique addressing the sustainability of biofuels. The legal obligations introduced in these international agreements are evidence of hierarchical modes of external governance. Network governance is examined by evaluating the extent and quality of intergovernmental and transnational processes of collaboration and communication between the European Commission and the government of Mozambique in activities linked to the sustainable production of biofuels. Mozambique might adopt and apply EU rules and values if they are seen as appropriate in light of its own values and priorities. It is assumed that this can be triggered by providing an institutionalized structure for communication and policy learning either through intergovernmental interactions, or through transnational processes (Schimmelfennig and Sedelmeier, 2005, pp. 11–12, 18). Finally, market governance is assessed by examining EU policies that change the opportunity structure of actors interested in participating in the EU market.

Although these three modes of governance are heuristic devices which cannot fully represent the complexity of the empirical reality where governance modes often work simultaneously, this framework can be used to characterize a set of EU policy initiatives suitable for exporting

EU rules and values to Mozambique. However, before being able to do this we need to identify EU rules and values on sustainable biofuels. Finally, the influence of EU external governance in Mozambique is examined by assessing policy adoption and domestic practice in Mozambique. Policy adoption is evaluated by identifying cases of matching content between EU rules and values and Mozambique's domestic policy, and conducting a counterfactual analysis of such cases to establish whether the matching content is unlikely to be the result of EU (biofuels) governance. Domestic practice is evaluated by examining the biofuel sector in Mozambique in terms of production, consumption and trade volumes.

14.3 EU RULES AND VALUES ON SUSTAINABLE BIOFUELS

In order to be able to assess the influence of the EU in Mozambique, it is necessary to identify EU rules and values relating to sustainable biofuels. A limitation of this approach is the assumption that common EU values exist, while it is in fact more likely that a wide range of positions exists among actors in the EU. This is addressed by considering as EU rules and values those expressed in official documents by EU institutions (the European Commission, the European Parliament and the Council of the EU).

The sustainability of transport biofuels has become a contested issue among EU institutions only in recent years (Solorio and Popartan, 2014). The RED contains the most accurate account of EU institutions' rules and values on the sustainability of biofuels. Firstly, it establishes a set of mandatory requirements for biofuel producers and distributors (article 17, paragraphs 2–5). These requirements include: (1) a minimum reduction of greenhouse gas (GHG) emissions of 35 per cent (50–60 per cent by 2018) compared to fossil-based fuels; and (2) a ban on the use of feedstock produced from land of high carbon or biodiversity value. For the purpose of this study, these requirements are considered EU rules.

Furthermore, the RED introduces monitoring requirements upon the European Commission and national governments (article 17, paragraph 7; and article 23). These cover both socio-economic issues, namely impact on food security and food prices, respect of land-use rights and compliance with internationally accepted labour standards; and environmental issues, including local impacts on biodiversity, air, soil and water. In this study these issues are considered EU values because, although seen as important by EU institutions, they do not create obligations upon economic actors.

14.4 AN OVERVIEW OF BIOFUEL DEVELOPMENTS IN MOZAMBIQUE

Located in the eastern part of southern Africa, Mozambique is one of the fastest-growing economies in the region, but still one of the poorest countries in the world, with approximately 80 per cent of the population employed in the agricultural sector (UNCTAD, 2012). The country has relatively little experience with biofuels, but is considered a promising region due to the relative abundance of land and water resources, favourable climatic conditions and low population density (Econergy, 2008). According to government estimates, only about 10 per cent of Mozambique's 36 million hectares (ha) of potential agricultural land are currently under cultivation, while 7 million ha are 'available for allocation to land-based economic activities, including biofuels' (Econergy, 2008).

The Mozambican government has promoted the development of a national biofuels industry since 2004, attracting local and foreign investors interested in developing large tracts of land to produce biofuels feedstock. However, shortly after the first large-scale biofuels project (PROCANA) was approved in October 2007 (Schut et al., 2010), the land authorization process was placed on hold until May 2008 due to the high volume of large-scale land requests.[2] The process was reopened only after an agro-ecological land zoning exercise identified areas suitable for biofuels development (Schut et al., 2010). The surge of biofuels investments slowed after 2012 due to the financial crisis, which resulted in a drastic reduction of funds for many of the proposed investments (Atanassov, 2013). However, by the end of 2013 a total of 18 projects (six ethanol projects based on cassava, sugar-cane or sorghum feedstock; and 12 biodiesel projects based on jatropha) were authorized to operate in the country. A combination of financial difficulties, bureaucratic red tape and conflict over land with local communities resulted in delays and small production volumes (Atanassov, 2013).

Despite the slow rate of implementation, Mozambique is recognized for having the most progressive biofuels legislation amongst its neighbours. In 2009, the government adopted a National Biofuels Policy and Strategy (NBPS) to guide the development of the sector (GOVMOZ, 2009). The policy emphasizes the importance of biofuels in contributing to reduced dependency on imported fuels, energy supply diversification, promotion of sustainable rural development and environmental protection, and improved national trade balance, as well as food and energy security. A key component of the NBPS is the definition of an appropriate decision-making system for land use, based on the results of two land zoning exercises.

Another major component of the country's regulatory framework for biofuels is the Mozambique Biofuel Sustainability Framework (MBSF). Finalized in 2012, but still awaiting official approval (Schut et al., 2014), the framework consists of seven core principles and 15 criteria to be upheld by all producers to ensure economic, social and environmental sustainability (NLAgency and Wegeningen University, 2012).

14.5 EU EXTERNAL GOVERNANCE AND THE MOZAMBICAN BIOFUELS SECTOR

This section evaluates the instruments and models of governance employed by the EU to influence Mozambique and assesses the results obtained in terms of policy adoption and application domestically.

14.5.1 Instruments and Modes of EU External Governance

Policy instruments potentially suitable for the exporting of EU rules and values to Mozambique are identified by reviewing EU (internal and external) policies, programmes and initiatives in the fields of energy, aid and development, and trade. The evaluation of each instrument highlights the mode of governance employed and the level of application in the period from 2007 to 2013 (Table 14.1).

Within the energy field, there are a number of initiatives that may be fitting for the export of EU rules and values to Mozambique. The RED, certainly the most important EU initiative on sustainable biofuels, provides two instruments to advance compliance with EU rules. The first, illustrated in article 18.1, relies on changes to the domestic opportunity structure via market access and trade incentives. This instrument, applied since 2010, employs a market mode of governance to promote voluntary compliance among economic actors interested in accessing the EU market. The second instrument (article 18.4) consists of the international agreements concluded between the European Commission and the governments of third countries. Once adopted and implemented these agreements may demonstrate compliance with the RED certification scheme – that is, EU rules – for all the biofuel produced in the third country. This instrument employs a hierarchical mode of governance

Table 14.1 Policy instruments and modes of EU external governance applicable in Mozambique

Field	Policy initiative	Policy instrument	Governance mode	Applied
Energy	Renewable energy directive (internal policy)	Art. 18.1 – Certification of sustainable biofuel. Only certified biofuels receive policy support in the EU.	Market	Yes
		Art. 18.4 – International agreements. Biofuels produced in countries signatory of these agreements comply with the requirements of the RED.	Hierarchy	No
	Africa–EU Energy Partnership	The Africa–EU Renewable Energy Cooperation Programme (RECP) promotes activities to: (1) enhance industrial and business cooperation between the two continents; (2) improve policy and regulatory frameworks for renewable energy in Africa; (3) deploy renewable energy; and (4) educate energy professionals in Africa (AEEP, 2010).	Network	No
	EU Energy Initiative	The ACP–EU Energy Facility is a co-financing instrument which supports projects aiming to increase and improve access to modern, affordable and sustainable energy services for the rural poor in African countries (COM, 2012b).	Network	No
		The EUEI Partnership Dialogue Facility (EUEI-PDF) is a flexible instrument for the development of policies and strategies that contribute to improved access to affordable and sustainable energy services in Africa (EUEI, 2012).	Network	No
	International technical cooperation	EU–Brazil–Mozambique trilateral technical cooperation for bioenergy provides technical assistance for the deployment of bioenergy in Mozambique.	Network	No

Table 14.1 (continued)

Field	Policy initiative	Policy instrument	Governance mode	Applied
Aid and development	EU–Mozambique development cooperation	European Development Fund (EDF) is the main instrument for EU aid for development cooperation in ACP countries.	Network	No
Trade	Economic Partnership Agreement	EU–SADC Economic Partnership Agreements are trade and development agreements negotiated between the EU and SADC region to promote trade and integration of SADC countries into the world economy.	Market	No

since the agreements become mandatory after ratification. However, in the period under analysis, the European Commission did not conclude any agreement under article 18.4, or enter into negotiations with third countries.

In addition to the RED, other energy-related initiatives offer the opportunity to influence Mozambique. In particular, the Africa–EU Energy Partnership (AEEP) is a long-term framework for structured political dialogue and cooperation on energy issues with the aim of increasing the provision of reliable and sustainable energy services on both continents, enhancing access to modern energy services and expanding RES and energy efficiency in Africa (AEEP, 2010). With regard to biofuels, the AEEP invites African and EU authorities to develop programmes and projects for the deployment of sustainable biofuels to advance economic development and social progress in African countries (AEEP, 2010). An important instrument to achieve the aims of the AEEP is the Africa–EU Renewable Energy Cooperation Programme (RECP). The RECP implements and coordinates activities which could be used to promote sustainable biofuels in Mozambique, in accordance with EU rules and values. RECP activities employ a network mode of governance, since projects rely on collaboration and coordination among European and African donors and actors. However, there is no evidence in the RECP project database of activities in the field of biofuels or bioenergy in Mozambique (RECP, 2014).

Another important external policy initiative in the field of energy is the EU Energy Initiative (EUEI) (EUEI, 2012). Established in 2002, the EUEI aims broadly at poverty eradication and sustainable development through two key initiatives: the ACP (Africa, Caribbean and Pacific)–EU Energy Facility and the EU Energy Initiative Partnership Dialogue

Facility (EUEI-PDF). The ACP–EU Energy Facility's goals are to increase energy access in poor areas by deploying RES and promoting energy efficiency, and to improve governance in the energy sector at regional, national and local levels (COM, 2012b). The Facility's projects are typically proposed and conducted in collaboration with local partners. Reliance on collaboration and communication among local and international partners means that these projects employ a network mode of governance. However, although potentially suitable for funding projects that promote sustainable biofuels, none of the projects funded in Mozambique addressed biofuels or bioenergy.[3] Another instrument active within the EUEI is the EUEI-PDF. Created in 2004, the EUEI-PDF is a flexible instrument used to promote collaboration between European and African partners in the field of renewable energy. Among the projects implemented in Mozambique,[4] the Biomass Energy Strategy in Mozambique (BEST) project (2012–13) aimed to contribute to the design and implementation of a national Biomass Energy Strategy (Eco-Consult, 2012). Although offering opportunities to introduce EU-inspired rules about sustainable biofuels in the Mozambican Biomass Energy Strategy, the project's focus was limited to solid biomass and charcoal (Eco-Consult, 2012).

A different type of initiative in the field of energy takes the form of technical cooperation programmes with developing countries (UNCTAD, 2009). The EU–Brazil–Mozambique trilateral technical cooperation for bioenergy, signed in 2010, is a specific initiative for technical cooperation on bioenergy and biofuels, which aims at providing Mozambique with technical expertise from Brazil and the EU (AIM, 2010). Cooperation activities under the agreement offer suitable means for the export of EU rules and values to Mozambique. The agreement relies on a network mode of governance, since activities are typically conducted and designed in collaborations between Mozambican, EU and Brazilian parties. However, in the period under analysis the agreement produced only one feasibility study on sustainable bioenergy production in Mozambique (Cabral, 2014), with the European Commission not actively involved in the related activities (Interview 1).

In addition to the energy field, the field of aid and development offers opportunities for the EU to influence the Mozambican biofuels sector.[5] Mozambique is highly dependent on international assistance and the EU (European Commission and member states) accounts for a large share of development assistance to the country. The European Commission is responsible for the implementation, operation and delivery of EU development aid to Mozambique within the framework of the European Commission–Mozambique Country Strategy Paper (CSP) financed through the European Development Fund (EDF). Between 2008 and 2013, about half of the funds allocated in the 10th EDF were directed to general budget support (GBS) and 30 per cent to sector budget support (SBS) which covers, in particular, infrastructure, health, agriculture and rural development (COM-GOVMOZ, 2007). The aid and development work funded through the EDF relies largely on a network mode of governance, in which the European Commission collaborates with Mozambican actors to implement the actions outlined in the CSP. However, although biofuels are explicitly mentioned in the 2008–13 CSP, no projects addressing the biofuel sector were supported via the 10th EDF in Mozambique (ODAMOZ, 2014; Interview 1).

Finally, the policy field of international trade also offers opportunities to influence biofuel developments in Mozambique, since the EU is a major trade partner of the African country (COM, 2014b). Under the 'Everything But Arms' arrangement, Mozambique has enjoyed duty-free and quota-free access to the EU market for all goods (except arms) since 2001. By limiting free market access to those biofuels that were in compliance with EU sustainability rules and values – that is, applying a market mode of governance – the EU could influence the Mozambican biofuels sector. However, the duty-free access granted to Mozambique, which was renegotiated in 2009 as part of the interim Economic Partnership Agreement (EPA) concluded between the EU and Southern Africa Development Community (SADC) countries, did not establish special trade and market access conditions for biofuels (EU Council, 2009).

In summary, the analysis shows that in the period between 2007 and 2013 the EU favoured a market mode of external governance to influence the sustainability of the biofuel sector in Mozambique. Network and hierarchical modes of governance were not exploited, in spite of an extensive range of opportunities in the fields of aid and development, and energy.

14.5.2 Results of EU External Governance

The results of EU external governance in Mozambique are assessed here by examining both the level of adoption of EU rules and values into domestic policy and programmes and the level of application in domestic practice. Adoption is evaluated in terms of the two primary components of Mozambique's biofuels policy framework: the National Biofuels Policy and Strategy (NBPS) and Mozambique Biofuel Sustainability Framework (MBSF), both illustrated in section 14.4.

With regard to the NBPS, the results show that as a strategic policy document for the development of the biofuels sector in the country, the

NBPS does not directly introduce standards or monitoring systems to address environmental impacts. It broadly states that its execution should promote a positive environmental impact and that any negative impact should be mitigated. However, the NBPS requires the establishment of a biofuels sustainability framework, and elevates as key priorities the need to ensure sufficient food production and access to land. Furthermore, it specifically highlights the climate benefits of biofuels in terms of GHG emissions reductions, although only in connection with financing opportunities through the Clean Development Mechanism. As a result, the content of the NBPS can be considered as partly matching EU values, primarily because of the reference to a sustainability framework and the strong concern with the impact on food security and land use.

In the case of the MBSF, the analysis shows limited matching between the content of EU rules and values and the majority of the principles of the MBSF (Table 14.2). This level of content mismatch can be interpreted as a substantial lack of agreement between EU and Mozambican policymakers about concerns related to biofuel expansion. However, three Principles (1, 5 and 7) show matching content.

- Principle 1 (legality) requires biofuels projects to comply with all applicable domestic laws, regulations and legal procedures including: (1) environmental laws, in particular, related to environmental impact assessment (EIA) (law 20/1997; decree 45/2004), water use (law 16/1991; ministerial order 7/2010), pollutants discharge (decree 18/2004); and (2) laws regulating land use (law 19/1997 and decree 66/1998), human rights protection (Constitution of the Republic of Mozambique; International Human Rights Law acceded by Mozambique) and labour (law 23/2007). The analysis shows that although Principle 1 does not match EU rules, it matches EU values to a large extent due to its concern with biodiversity, local environments, human rights, labour conditions and land use. However, the influence of EU external governance can be questioned. Most of these Mozambican laws and regulations were adopted before biofuels became an important issue in the EU, and/or in compliance with international law ratified by the country before the surge in the debate on biofuels.
- Principle 5 (food security) requires biofuels operations to define a plan to avoid negative impact on the local availability and access to staple foods. This principle matches EU values on food security. However, the influence of EU external governance is, once again, questionable. The interviews with government officials confirm that

food security has been a key concern of the government since at least the end of the civil war in 1992 (Interview 2).

- Principle 7 (environmental protection) requires biofuels operations to demonstrate that biofuels provide reduced GHG emissions compared to fossil fuels. This Principle matches EU rules on GHG emissions reductions, even though it does not adopt the same minimum saving thresholds established in the RED. There is evidence that the matching content is to some extent linked to the EU's biofuels external governance. While in 2007 climate protection was not an important issue for the Mozambican government (Interview 2), Principle 7 contains a verifier that obliges domestic biofuels operators to use an internationally recognized calculation method to demonstrate GHG emissions reductions. The use of a recognized calculation method is a condition for export to the EU market. This suggests that EU governance influenced policy adoption in Mozambique. Moreover, Principle 7 matches EU values when it requires operators to demonstrate evidence of an EIA and actions to minimize negative impact on soil, air, water and biodiversity. However, the matching does not appear to be a consequence of EU external governance, since the EIA regulation and, more generally, concerns with the environmental impact pre-exist the surge in biofuels in Mozambique and apply to a broad range of projects.

Table 14.2 Matching content between Mozambique's policy and EU rules and values of sustainable biofuels

Principle	EU rules	EU values
Legality	No	Yes
Social responsibility	n/a	n/a
Energy security	n/a	n/a
Economic and financial sustainability	n/a	n/a
Food security	n/a	Yes
Industrial and agricultural productivity	n/a	n/a
Environmental protection	Yes (GHG emissions)	Yes

A second component of the assessment is the evaluation of the level of application of EU rules and values in domestic practice. Domestic practice, examined in terms of the volumes of biofuels produced, consumed and traded in compliance with EU rules and values, is an indicator of EU influence on economic actors in Mozambique. However, the domestic biofuels sector was characterized in the period under analysis by very limited production volumes. Although a large area of nearly 210 000 ha was authorized by the government for feedstock cultivation (Table 14.3), only 2–3 per cent of that area was effectively cultivated for the production of biofuels feedstock in 2013 (Atanassov, 2013). The resulting production volumes were negligible, with only two companies supplying biofuels to the domestic market. Cleanstar Mozambique produced 3500 tonnes of ethanol for the domestic cooking fuel market, while NIQEL supplied 152 tonnes of jatropha biodiesel (Locke and Henley, 2013). At the same time, their production was not certified as employing schemes recognized by the European Commission (Atanassov, 2013). As a consequence of the low production volumes, the government decided to postpone the enforcement of the national consumption targets adopted in 2011 (decree 58/2011) when the wave of investments in biofuels projects convinced the government that a flourishing domestic sector was at hand. The sector did not develop as its proponents had expected, due to a combination of factors including a lack of financial capital following the global financial crisis, delays in the authorization processes and conflicts over land rights (Atanassov, 2013).

Table 14.3 Overview of biofuel projects in Mozambique for the year 2013

	Ethanol	Biodiesel	Total
Projects authorized	6	12	18
Projects implemented	3	10	13
Total area authorized (ha)	97 530	111 797	209 327
Area cultivated (ha)	2 080	4 030	6 110
Biofuel production (t/y)	3 500	152	3 652
Planned biofuel production (t/y)	422 000	89 412	511 412

Source: Atanassov (2013).

Under these circumstances, production, consumption and trade volumes are not the most appropriate indicators of the influence of EU external governance in Mozambique. On the one hand, no production of biofuels certified in compliance with EU rules and values could be interpreted as demonstrating the limited impact of EU governance. On the other hand, the small volumes produced could be interpreted as evidence of negligible impact in violation of EU rules and values. Yet this latter interpretation overlooks the fact that land that was assigned to biofuels companies was often converted, causing deforestation. This appears to be incompatible with EU rules and values. Under the current conditions an assessment of land-use changes would be more appropriate. However, the lack of reliable data makes this evaluation impractical at this time.

14.6 DISCUSSION AND CONCLUSIONS

The aim of this chapter is to evaluate the influence of EU external governance on the development of the biofuels sector in Mozambique in relation to the sustainable production of biofuels. The findings of the analysis show that between 2007 and 2013 the EU sought to influence the biofuels sector in Mozambique, primarily by employing market governance and the instruments offered by the RED. The most evident results of this governance strategy can be seen in the level of adoption of EU rules and values in domestic biofuels policies. There is evidence of matching content between EU rules on GHG emissions savings and values related to biodiversity, the local environment, labour conditions, food security and land use rights, and Mozambican policies. However, except for the case of GHG emissions savings, the matching content appears to be independent of EU (biofuel) external governance. This is not necessarily bad news, since there is little scope for influence in cases that show no or little mismatch between EU and domestic policy. However, the findings of the analysis are less encouraging with regard to the practical application of EU rules and values in domestic practice. In the period under analysis, none of the biofuels produced in Mozambique were certified in compliance with EU rules and values. Furthermore, although comprehensive data about the land-use changes associated with biofuels investments are lacking, anecdotal evidence suggests that biofuels projects caused negative land-use changes in Mozambique (see, e.g., Nhantumbo and Salomão, 2010; Borras et al., 2011). Biofuels projects in conjunction with other activities such as mining, forestry and tourism further exacerbate competition for land, water and other resources. Important advances have been made on the assessment and modelling of land-use changes caused by biofuels expansion (Ahlgren and Di Lucia, 2014). However, many developing countries still lack the data needed to feed these models. The rapid evolution of the biofuels sector in many countries, and the growing interest in land acquisitions for agricultural purposes, call for further research and continued monitoring of developments in this field.

The case of EU (biofuels) external governance in Mozambique bears important lessons for EU renewable energy policy. Although the necessity to ensure sustainable production of the biofuels consumed in the EU has been widely recognized, the capacity to effectively influence production in developing countries in accordance with EU priorities remains a major challenge. This chapter puts forward some evidence in support of the idea that such influence is indeed possible. Three sets of potentials deserve attention. Firstly, the EU is an attractive market for producers in developing countries. Many developing countries enjoy duty-free EU market access for their produce. This opens up important trade opportunities, and with them the possibility for the EU to influence product- and non-product-related process and production methods (PPMs) by making the signature of trade agreements conditional on third countries' respect for certain market, environmental or human rights norms (Lavenex, 2014). In the case of Mozambique, where biofuels producers enjoy duty-free access to the EU market, 65 per cent of the projects currently active consider the EU to be their major market for export (Atanassov, 2013). Secondly, the EU has established numerous cooperation frameworks which could be used to address issues related to the sustainability of biofuels in developing countries. In the case of Mozambique, the AEEP and the EUEI offer established policy and institutional frameworks which, together with the European Commission aid and development work in Mozambique, could promote projects and activities in cooperation with local actors. Finally, the European Commission has the competence to conclude bilateral agreements with countries producing biofuels and feedstock for the EU market. Introduced by the RED in 2009 but never employed by the European Commission, this instrument offers the possibility to take a broader, more holistic approach to fulfilling EU sustainability requirements, which is particularly relevant for developing countries (Westberg and Johnson, 2013). This instrument can be used to simultaneously expand the scope of the RED certification scheme and overcome the limitation of a lack of EU enforcement power in third countries.

The results of this study also provide insights into some of the challenges and limits of EU external governance. Firstly, in the case of sustainable biofuels the EU has not been able to coordinate efforts effectively in different policy fields. In agreement with previous studies from other policy fields, for example in energy (Tosun and Solorio, 2011; Selianko and Lenschow, 2015; Nilsson et al., 2012) and aid and development (Carbone, 2008), the EU also suffers from weak policy coherence when it comes to biofuels. EU energy, trade and development policies and activities were not coordinated to advance the goal of sustainable biofuels production in Mozambique. The interviews revealed that within the European Commission there were no detailed instructions and procedures regarding the coordination of development goals and policies and biofuels-related activities (Interview 1). Related to this lies a second major challenge for EU external (biofuels) governance: the limited use of the instruments available within the realm of EU external energy and development policy.[6] As discussed above, external energy and development policy can provide the framework to promote sustainable biofuels systems in developing countries such as Mozambique, where biofuels can significantly contribute to development objectives, economic development and poverty reduction. However, EU policymakers have for too long viewed biofuels as an internal policy issue, in spite of the growing concern with the extraterritorial impacts of biofuels on the natural environment. This view should change. In agreement with the EU biofuels strategy presented in 2006 (COM, 2006), biofuels should not only be a means of climate protection, energy security and rural development in the EU but also, and more importantly, a motor for development and poverty reduction in developing countries.

The EU has been widely described as an environmental champion and normative power. Yet the track record of its action beyond its borders remains disappointing overall (Afionis and Stringer, 2012; Adelle and Jordan, 2009). This chapter confirms these conclusions, but also suggests that there is a wealth of opportunities for the EU to contribute to the development of a sustainable biofuels sector in developing countries. Current EU biofuels policy, which focuses on fulfilling an internal consumption target through certified biofuels alone, cannot be expected to achieve this (AETS, 2013). However, the European Commission seems convinced that more of the same will address the problems, and thus proposes stricter certification requirements (see, for example, the latest European Commission proposal to address ILUC: COM, 2012c). The results of this study suggest that a more coordinated use of the available modes of external governance is likely to yield more positive outcomes. In particular, further involvement of developing countries through the use of the instruments of network governance (for example, within the frameworks of the AEEP and EUEI) and hierarchical governance (for example, bilateral agreements excluding the RED) would go a long way, especially in countries such as Mozambique which have shown real interest in developing a sustainable biofuel sector, and made significant investments in the policy and institutional frameworks needed for that purpose. The study of the synergetic coordination of the instruments of network, hierarchical and market governance remains a key challenge for future research in the field of EU biofuel external governance.

NOTES

1. The notion of governance, understood as a broad term which encompasses all the purposeful mechanisms and measures aimed at steering social systems (Jagers and Stripple, 2003), is employed to describe the process of rules expansion beyond formal EU membership.
2. According to the Constitution, all natural resources in Mozambique, including land, belong to the state. Land can be leased following procedures regulated by the land law (19/1997).
3. See the projects database of the Facility (COM, 2014a).
4. See the projects database of the EUEI (EUEI, 2014).
5. Initiatives in the fields of energy and development often overlap due to the importance of energy to socio-economic development; for example, the AEEP and the EUEI are energy initiatives with clear development objectives.
6. This does not refer to EU member states, such as the Netherlands and Germany, which actively engaged in development activities in Mozambique, offering financial and technical cooperation in the field of sustainable biofuels (Interview 1).

REFERENCES

Adelle, C. and A. Jordan (2009), 'The European Union and the "external" dimension of sustainable development', in F. Biermann, B. Siebenhuner and A. Schreyogg (eds), *International Organizations in Global Environmental Governance*, New York: Routledge, pp. 111–132.

AEEP (2010), 'Africa–EU Energy Partnership Road Map', accessed on 19 October 2014 at http://www.africa-eu-partnership.org/sites/default/files/documents/aeep_road_map_en_1.pdf.

AETS (2013), 'Assessing the impact of biofuels production on developing countries from the point of view of Policy Coherence for Development – Final Report', accessed on 21 October 2014 at https://ec.europa.eu/europeaid/sites/devco/files/study-impact-assesment-biofuels-production-on-development-pcd-201302_en_2.pdf.

Afionis, S. and I.C. Stringer (2012), 'European Union leadership in biofuels regulation: Europe as a normative power?', *Journal of Cleaner Production*, 32, 114–123.

Ahlgren, S. and L. Di Lucia (2014), 'Indirect land use changes of biofuel production – a review of modelling efforts and policy developments in the European Union', *Biotechnology for Biofuels*, 7 (1), 35.

AIM (2010), 'Mozambique, Brazil and EU cooperate on biofuels', accessed on 7 August 2014 at http://allafrica.com/stories/201007161071.html.

Atanassov, B. (2013), 'The status of biofuels projects in Mozambique, Overseas Development Institute', accessed on 28 August 2014 at http://www.odi.org/sites/odi.org.uk/files/odi-assets/publications-opinion-files/8799.pdf.

Banse, M., H. Van Meijl, A. Tabeau and G. Woltjer (2008), 'Will EU biofuel policies affect global agricultural markets?', *European Review of Agricultural Economics*, 35 (2), 117–141.

Bauer, M.W., C. Knill and D. Pitschel (2007), 'Differential Europeanization in Eastern Europe: the impact of diverse EU regulatory governance patterns', *Journal of European Integration*, 29, 405–423.

Borras Jr, S., M.D. Fig and S.M. Suárez (2011), 'The politics of agrofuels and mega-land and water deals: insights from the ProCana case, Mozambique', *Review of African Political Economy*, 38 (128), 215–234.

Börzel, T.A. and T. Risse (2003), 'Conceptualizing the domestic impact of Europe', in K. Featherstone and C. Radaelli (eds), *The Politics of Europeanization*, Oxford: Oxford University Press, pp. 57–80.

Cabral, L. (2014), 'The EU-Brazil partnership on development: a lukewarm affair', ESPO Policy Brief, 10.

Carbone, M. (2008), 'Mission impossible: the European Union and Policy Coherence for Development', *European Integration*, 30 (3), 323–342.

Di Lucia, L. (2010), 'External governance and the EU policy for sustainable biofuels, the case of Mozambique', *Energy Policy*, 38, 7395–7403.

COM (2006), 'An EU strategy for biofuels. Communication from the Commission', COM 34 final, Brussels.

COM (2007), 'Biofuel progress report. Report on the progress made in the use of biofuels and other renewable fuels in the Member States of the European Union', COM 845 final, Brussels.

COM (2012a), 'Impact assessment accompanying the proposal for a Directive amending Directive 98/70/EC and Directive 2009/28/EC', Commission staff working document, SWA 343 final, Brussels, European Commission.

COM (2012b), 'The ACP-EU Energy Facility', accessed on 20 October 2014 at https://ec.europa.eu/europeaid/sites/devco/files/publication-acp-eu-energy-facility-ec-2012_en.pdf.

COM (2012c), 'Proposal for a Directive of the European Parliament and of the Council amending Directive 98/70/EC and Directive 2009/28/EC', COM 595 final, Brussels.

COM (2014a), 'ACP-EU Energy Facility Projects Database', accessed on 12 November 2014 at http://database.energyfacilitymonitoring.eu/acpeu/PublicProjectOverview.xhtml.

COM (2014b), 'Trade between the EU and Mozambique: statistics', accessed on 10 October 2014 at http://trade.ec.europa.eu/doclib/docs/2006/september/tradoc_113422.pdf.

COM-GOVMOZ (2007), 'Country Strategy Paper (CSP) and National Indicative Programme', accessed on 9 August 2014 at http://ec.europa.eu/europeaid/sites/devco/files/csp-nip-mozambique-2008-2013_en.pdf.

ECO-Consult (2012), 'Mozambique biomass energy strategy', accessed on 24 October 2014 at http://www.euei-pdf.org/sites/default/files/files/field_pblctn_file/EUEI%20PDF_Mozambique_BEST_Final%20Report_Dec2012.pdf.

Econergy (2008), 'Mozambique biofuels assessment, final report to the Ministry of Agriculture and Ministry of Energy', Maputo: Mozambique.

EU Council (2009), 'Council decision on the signature and provisional application of the interim Agreement with a view to an EPA between the European

Community and the SADC states', 14062/08, accessed on 18 October 2014 at www.eeas.europa.eu/delegations/mozambique/eu_mozambique/trade_relation/economic_partnership_agreement/index_en.htm.
EUEI (2012), 'The EU Energy Initiative Partnership Dialogue Facility', accessed on 11 October 2014 at http://euei-pdf.org/sites/default/files/files/field_pblctn_file/EUEI%20PDF_Factsheet_May%202012_EN.pdf.
EUEI (2014), 'EUEI-PDF projects', accessed on 12 October 2014 at http://euei-pdf.org/euei-pdf-and-recp-projects.
EurObserv'ER (2014), 'Biofuels Barometer', Systèmes solaires, accessed on 10 October 2014 at http://www.energies-renouvelables.org/observ-er/stat_baro/observ/baro222_en.pdf.
Fargione, J., J. Hill, D. Tilman, S. Polasky and P. Hawthorne (2008), 'Land clearing and the biofuel carbon debt', *Science*, 319, 1235–1238.
GOVMOZ (2009), 'Biofuel policy and strategy' (Política e estratégia de biocombustíveis), Resolution 22/2009, Maputo.
Grabbe, H. (2003), 'Europeanization goes east: power and uncertainty in the EU accession process', *Politics of Europeanization*, 27, 303–329.
Jagers, S.C. and J. Stripple (2003), 'Climate govenance beyond the state', *Global Governance*, 9, 385.
Knill, C. (2005), 'Introduction: cross-national policy convergence: concepts, approaches and explanatory factors', *Journal of European Public Policy*, 12, 764–774.
Knill, C. and D. Lehmkuhl (2002), 'The national impact of European Union regulatory policy: three Europeanization mechanisms', *European Journal of Political Research*, 41, 255–280.
Knill, C. and J. Tosun (2009), 'Hierarchy, networks, or markets: how does the EU shape environmental policy adoptions within and beyond its borders?', *Journal of European Public Policy*, 16, 873–894.
Lavenex, S. (2004), 'EU external governance in "wider Europe"', *Journal of European Public Policy*, 11, 680–700.
Lavenex, S. (2014), 'The power of functionalist extension: how EU rules travel', *Journal of European Public Policy*, 21 (6), 885–903.
Lavenex, S. and F. Schimmelfennig (2009), 'EU rules beyond EU borders: theorizing external governance in European politics', *Journal of European Public Policy*, 16, 791–812.
Locke, A. and G. Henley (2013), 'Scoping report on biofuels projects in five developing countries', Overseas Development Institute, accessed on 27 September 2014 at http://www.epure.org/sites/default/files/publication/8394.pdf.
Nhantumbo, I. and A. Salomão (2010), 'Biofuels, land access and rural livelihoods in Mozambique', London: IIED.
Nilsson, M., T. Zamparutti, J.E. Petersen, B. Nykvist, P. Rudberg and J. Mcguinn (2012), 'Understanding policy coherence: analytical framework and examples of sector–environment policy interactions in the EU', *Environmental Policy and Governance*, 22 (6), 395–423.
NLAgency and Wageningen University (2012), 'Operationalization and implementation of the Biofuel Sustainability Framework for Mozambique', accessed on 2 September 2016 at http://english.rvo.nl/sites/default/files/2014/

03/Operationaliziog%20Biofuel%20Sustainability%20Framework%20in%20 Mozambique%20-%20sept%202012.pdf.

ODAMOZ (2014), 'Official Development Assistance to Mozambique database', accessed on 9 November 2014 at www.odamoz.org.mz.

Pilgrim, S. and M. Harvey (2010), 'Battles over biofuels in Europe: NGOs and the politics of markets', *Sociological Research Online*, 15 (3), 4.

Pimentel, D., A. Marklein, M.A. Toth, M.N. Karpoff, G.S. Paul, R. Mccormack, J. Kyriazis and T. Krueger (2009), 'Food versus biofuels: environmental and economic costs', *Human Ecology*, 37 (1), 1–12.

RECP (2014), 'RECP project database', accessed on 12 November 2014 at www.africa-eu-renewables.org/index.php?lang=eng&page=116.

Schimmelfennig, F. (2009), 'Europeanization beyond Europe', Living Reviews in European Governance, accessed on 15 October 2014 at http://european governance.livingreviews.org/Articles/lreg-2009-3/download/lreg-2009-3Color.pdf.

Schimmelfennig, F. and U. Sedelmeier (2004), 'Governance by conditionality: EU rule transfer to the candidate countries of Central and Eastern Europe', *Journal of European Public Policy*, 11, 661–679.

Schimmelfennig, F. and U. Sedelmeier (2005), 'Conceptualizing the Europeanization of Central and Eastern Europe', in F. Schimmelfennig and U. Sedelmeier (eds), *The Europeanization of Central and Eastern Europe*, Ithaca: Cornell University Press, pp. 1–28.

Schut, M., M. Slingerland and A. Locke (2010), 'Biofuel developments in Mozambique: update and analysis of policy, potential and reality', *Energy Policy,* 38, 5151–5165.

Schut, M.N., C. Soares, G. van de Ven and M. Slingerland (2014), 'Multi-actor governance of sustainable biofuels in developing countries: the case of Mozambique', *Energy Policy,* 65, 631–643.

Searchinger, T., R. Heimlich, R.A. Houghton, F. Dong, A Elobeid, J. Fabiosa, S. Tokgoz, D. Hayes and T.-H. Yu (2008), 'Use of US croplands for biofuels increases greenhouse gases through emissions from land-use change', *Science*, 319, 1238–1240.

Sedelmeier, U. (2006), 'Europeanisation in new member and candidate states', *Living Reviews in European Governance*, 1 (3), 14.

Selianko, I. and A. Lenschow (2015), 'Energy policy coherence from an intra-institutional perspective: Energy security and environmental policy coordination within the European Commission', *European Integration online Papers* (*EIoP*), 19 (1), http://eiop.or.at/eiop/pdf/2015-002.pdf.

Solorio, I. and L. Popartan (2014), 'The implementation of the EU biofuels policy in Spain and the UK: a case of contested Europeanization', *Biofuels*, 5 (2), 129–140.

Tosun, J. and I. Solorio (2011), 'Exploring the energy–environment relationship in the EU: perspectives and challenges for theorizing and empirical analysis', in J. Tosun and I. Solorio (eds), *Energy and Environment in Europe: Assessing a Complex Relationship*, *European Integration online Papers* (*EIoP*), Special Mini-Issue 1, Vol. 15, https://eiop.or.at/eiop/pdf/2011-007.pdf.

UNCTAD (2009), 'South–South and triangular cooperation in the biofuels sector: the African experience', Report prepared for the Multi-year Expert

Meeting on International Cooperation: South–South Cooperation and Regional Integration, accessed on 20 September 2014 at http://unctad.org/en/docs/ciimem2crp2_en.pdf.

UNCTAD (2012), 'The least developed countries report 2012', Conference on Trade and Development, Geneva.

USDA (2014), 'EU Biofuel Annual 2014', GAIN report NL4025, The Hague.

Westberg, C.J. and F.X. Johnson (2013), 'The path not yet taken: Bilateral agreements to promote sustainable biofuels under the EU Renewable Energy Directive', Stockholm Environmental Institute, 41.

Interviews

Interview 1, European Commission 2014, A. Tome De Freitas, European External Action Service – Maputo, telephone, September.

Interview 2, Ministry of Energy and Ministry of Agriculture 2007, M. Mataveia, Ministry of Energy of Mozambique, Maputo, September; and A. Locke, Centre for Agricultural Development (CEPAGRI), Ministry of Agriculture of Mozambique, Maputo, September.

PART IV

Conclusions

15. Conclusions: patterns of Europeanization and policy change in the renewable energy policy domain

Helge Jörgens, Eva Öller and Israel Solorio

15.1 INTRODUCTION

The great transformation of the energy systems of the European Union (EU) and its member states towards a greater incorporation of renewable energy sources (RES) that started in the late 1970s has come to a crossroads. After a slow start, the 1990s and most of the 2000s have witnessed a rapid increase in policies and programmes aimed to promote the production and consumption of energy from RES, both at the level of EU member states and at the European level. These policies have resulted in an equally rapid growth of the share of RES in national and European energy mixes. However, since the late 2000s, the speed of transformation has slowed down considerably and instances of policy dismantling are becoming more frequent.

The preceding chapters analysed this development from a member state perspective. Drawing on this rich empirical and analytical background, this concluding chapter adopts a comparative perspective in order to identify more general patterns of Europeanization and policy change in the renewable energy policy domain over the past decades. In the next section, important steps in the Europeanization of RES-E policies in EU member states are examined. Reference points that help to make the diverse national actions comparable are the major legislative or programmatic decisions taken at the EU level; that is, the RES-E directive of 2001, the renewable energy directive (RED) of 2009 and the 2030 climate and energy framework of 2014. Section 15.3 then compares Europeanization processes in the field of biofuels. Here, the major reference points around which Europeanization dynamics are observed are the biofuels directive of 2003 and again the RED of 2009. The external dimension of RES Europeanization is addressed briefly in section 15.4 while section 15.5 addresses differences between the two policy domains – RES-E and biofuels – in an attempt to explain why the promotion of RES-E has generally been more successful and more sustainable than the promotion of biofuels. Finally, section 15.6 rounds up the analysis by taking an independent and comparative look at the role of two major groups of non-state actors – utilities and environmental NGOs (ENGOs) – and their power, preferences and strategic choices in the RES-E and biofuels sectors.

15.2 PATTERNS OF EUROPEANIZATION IN RES-E POLICY

15.2.1 Europeanization Dynamics Related to the 2001 RES-E Directive

The first EU legislation explicitly designed to promote RES was the renewable electricity directive of 2001 (RES-E directive). Its development dates back to a first Commission Green Paper on RES published in 1996 (see Chapter 2 by Solorio and Bocquillon). Which countries were influential in the design of the directive? And how did it impact on the RES-E policies of EU member states? Table 15.1 summarizes the major Europeanization dynamics related to the negotiation and implementation of the RES-E directive.

First of all, and somewhat surprisingly, our cases show that the RES-E directive had only a limited direct (top-down) impact on national policies to promote RES-E. Instead, top-down Europeanization in the first phase of European RES-E policy occurred indirectly rather than directly. In most countries, it was the EU-driven liberalization of the electricity markets rather than the RES-E directive that triggered the most important national policy changes. It did so by significantly changing domestic opportunity structures. On the economic side it removed structural and institutional barriers to market entry for (potential) producers of RES-E. On the political side, it set the course for domestic policies and programs aimed at gradually and incrementally increasing the share of RES-E in domestic energy production and consumption without raising the opposition of powerful 'natural' opponents such as the big power utilities. As Table 15.1 shows, indirect top-down Europeanization through the liberalization of electricity markets constitutes a major Europeanization dynamic both in old and highly industrialized member states such as Germany (Chapter 3 by Vogelpohl et al.), the Netherlands (Chapter 4 by

Table 15.1 Major Europeanization dynamics with regard to the 2001 RES-E directive

Type of Europeanization	Country	Aims and mechanisms
Top-down	Germany	Indirect Europeanization through EU liberalization policy
	Netherlands	Indirect Europeanization through EU liberalization policy rather than RES-E directive
	Italy	Indirect Europeanization through structural funds and EU liberalization policy
	Spain	Indirect Europeanization through structural funds and EU liberalization policy; change of actors' beliefs and expectations
	France	Indirect Europeanization through EU liberalization policy and weak adaptational pressure from RES-E directive
	Poland	Indirect Europeanization through EU liberalization policy; partial change of actors' beliefs through creation of EU RES research centre in Poland; 'superficial' implementation of RES-E directive
	Romania	Indirect Europeanization through EU liberalization policy; direct Europeanization through transposition of EU *acquis*
	Bulgaria	Indirect Europeanization through EU liberalization policy; direct Europeanization through transposition of EU *acquis*
Bottom-up	Germany	Foot-dragger, concerned that EU-wide harmonization might rule out the national Feed-In Tariffs (FITs) scheme
	Netherlands	Incorporate domestic interests in directive (RES-E from waste and biomass)
	Denmark	Defensive forerunner, concerned that EU-wide harmonization might water-down national policies
	United Kingdom	Pacesetter, pushing hard for harmonization of national support schemes based on Tradable Green Certificates (TGCs); defensive forerunner with regard to RES definition
	Spain	Pacesetter with regard to RES-E targets, foot-dragger with regard to a harmonized support scheme
	France	Strategic fence-sitter, concerned with keeping implementation costs of RES-E directive as low as possible
Horizontal	Germany	German FITs served as model for other countries' support schemes
	Netherlands	Introduce FITs in order to strengthen domestic RES-E producers vis-à-vis their counterparts in other EU member states
	Denmark	Pioneer in RES-E development which served as abstract model for other countries
	Italy	Shift from a FITs scheme to a TGCs scheme following the United Kingdom example
	Spain	Early adopter of FITs which served as model for other countries
	France	Peer pressure and cross-national policy learning led to the adoption of a tender scheme for wind power in 1996 and a FIT in 2000
	Poland	Choice of quota-based support scheme influenced by other member states

Hoppe and van Bueren), France (Chapter 9 by Bocquillon and Evrard) and Italy (Chapter 7 by Di Nucci and Russolillo), and newer EU members such as Spain (Chapter 8 by Solorio and Fernandez), Poland (Chapter 10 by Jankowska and Ancygier) and Bulgaria (Chapter 12 by Hiteva and Maltby). Hoppe and van Bueren's (Chapter 4) observation that in the 1990s 'the Netherlands became one of the forerunners in [the liberalization of energy markets] and Europeanization was much more focused on this process than on the upcoming RES-E directive' characterizes the RES-E priorities of many EU member states at this time.

In addition to the liberalization of electricity markets, EU structural funds also had some impact. Initially, European programmes such as JOULE, THERMIE and ALTENER played a significant role in fostering research at the domestic level. The promotion of RES-E was also incorporated in the EU's regional and competition policy. For instance, the Valoren programme strengthened structurally disadvantaged regions to trigger RES-E development and EU liberalization policies sparked a far-reaching rearrangement of energy systems and markets (see, e.g., Chapter 8 by Solorio and Fernandez on Spain, and Chapter 9 by Bocquillon and Evrard on France). Similarly, in Chapter 7, Di Nucci and Russolillo show that in Italy from the late 1980s the European structural and investment funds strengthened local governments' expertise in the RES-E field and provided funding for investments. The role of regional policy and structural funds was predominantly a capacity-building one, creating or strengthening actors in favour of RES-E promotion.

Interestingly, and contrary to what has been observed in much of the literature on national compliance with EU directives, our case studies show top-down Europeanization to be strongest before – and not after – a European directive was adopted. For example, in Italy, the Bersani decree of 1999 introduced an ambitious support scheme for RES-E based on mandatory quotas, Tradable Green Certificates (TGCs) and priority access to the grid for RES-E that replaced previous Feed-In Tariffs (FITs). A key driver for the change in RES-E policy was the publication in October 1998 of a first unofficial draft of the EU's 2001 RES-E directive. In this draft the European Commission expressed its strong preference for a support model based on quota systems (see Chapter 2 by Solorio and Bocquillon). As Di Nucci and Russolillo argue in Chapter 7, it was this (rather remote) possibility of an EU-wide harmonization towards a system based on RES-E quotas and TGCs, and the resulting threat that support schemes based on FITs might cease to be in compliance with EU law, that triggered the Italian policy change. In France, the negotiations of the EU RES-E directive built momentum for the inclusion of RES-E promotion in the Electricity Bill of 2000 (Chapter 9 by Bocquillon and Evrard).

Direct top-down Europeanization – that is, the implementation of institutional and governance prescriptions regarding the definition, goals and instruments of RES-E promotion – occurred mainly in new member states through the obligation to transpose the entire *acquis communautaire* as a prerequisite for accession to the EU. Both in Romania (Chapter 11 by Davidescu) and Bulgaria (Chapter 12 by Hiteva and Maltby) this mechanism, together with the indirect impact of market liberalization, played an important role in the first stages of RES-E promotion. In contrast, bottom-up Europeanization was driven by older member states that at the same time were forerunners in RES-E promotion and already had elaborate support schemes in place. Their main rationale during the negotiation of the directive was to protect national interests, both economic and political. For example, countries that had a functioning RES-E support scheme based on FITs in place prior to the adoption of the directive tried hard to avoid any EU-wide harmonization of support schemes. The reason was that the European Commission had pronounced a clear preference for more market-oriented support schemes based on TGCs and chances were high that any harmonization of national instruments would follow this model. Thus, rather than trying to upload their domestic system to the European level, countries such as Germany (Chapter 3), Denmark (Chapter 5) and Spain (Chapter 8) opted for the more secure strategy of negative coordination by simply trying to veto any kind of harmonization of support schemes. In contrast, the United Kingdom (UK) (Chapter 6), which was in favour of TGCs schemes, pushed hard but unsuccessfully for an EU-wide harmonization. Other national interests that shaped individual strategies of bottom-up Europeanization related to the definition of RES-E – for example the Dutch attempt to extend it to electricity from waste and biomass incineration (Chapter 4) – or the level of ambition of RES-E targets (Chapter 8 by Solorio and Fernandez on Spain).

Whereas bottom-up Europeanization was dominated by domestic economic and political concerns and characterized by strategies of foot-dragging and negative coordination, it was processes of horizontal Europeanization that positively influenced the instrumental design of many domestic RES-E policies. By setting a concrete and widely visible example for an effective support scheme, the pioneers and proponents of FITs – Denmark, Germany and Spain – were able to influence the shape of RES-E policies in other member states. The observation of Vogelpohl et al. (Chapter 3) that 'Germany's support scheme served as a model for other countries and thus provided for horizontal Europeanization by learning and imitation processes' characterizes not only the first phase of European RES-E policy, but also the second phase that centred around the negotiation and implementation of the 2009 RED (see Table 15.2). However, our cases also show that horizontal Europeanization is not a unidirectional process and that its potential for the cross-national harmonization of policies is limited. At the same time that the FIT system spread to countries such as Italy (Chapter 7), Poland (Chapter 10) took inspiration from the UK and adopted support schemes based on quotas and TGCs. Thus, rather than harmonizing national support schemes, horizontal Europeanization resulted in a continuous oscillation of support schemes between the more environmentally effective FITs and the more economically efficient TGCs or Feed-in Premiums (FIPs).

15.2.2 Europeanization Dynamics Related to the 2009 Renewable Energy Directive

The second major legislative step in EU RES promotion occurred in 2009 with the adoption of the RED. It established an integrated framework RES promotion, not only for the electricity sector but also for transport and heating and cooling. It set an overall EU RES target of 20 per cent by 2020 as well as mandatory national RES targets, but refrained from harmonizing support schemes, and the breakdown of national RES targets into specific targets for RES-E and other types of RES was left to the member states (see Chapter 2 by Solorio and Bocquillon).

Table 15.2 summarizes the main Europeanization dynamics with regard to the negotiation and implementation of the RED. Again, direct top-down Europeanization plays an important role in only a relatively small number of countries, namely Italy and France as well as the new member states Poland, Romania and Bulgaria. The main reason was that – apart from the mandatory national RES targets that were perceived as a great challenge, for example in Italy and France – the directive created only very limited direct adaptational pressure in the member states.

Consequently, the 2009 RED had its biggest impact on those member states that joined the EU after 2004. In other words, the classical mechanism of top-down Europeanization, the direct prescription of institutional or governance models, has been strongest in countries that only recently joined the EU. This can be explained by the fact that accession countries were under special scrutiny to comply with entire body of EU secondary law (including those laws that were still in the making). Even in the case of relatively vague programmes such as the RED (and also the previous RES-E directive), which lacked concrete instrumental prescriptions and specific mandatory RES-E targets and

Table 15.2 Major Europeanization dynamics with regard to the 2009 renewable energy directive (RES-E)

Type of Europeanization	Country	Aims and mechanisms
Top-down	Italy	Reluctant compliance with RED targets
	France	Compliance with the RED goals
	Poland	Incomplete ('superficial') implementation
	Romania	Reluctant compliance with RED
	Bulgaria	Direct Europeanization through fast, but uncoordinated, implementation of EU directives
Bottom-up	Netherlands	Foot-dragger, protecting interests of Dutch electricity sector
	Denmark	Pacesetter with regard to mandatory national targets
	United Kingdom	From pacesetter to coalition-builder with regard to a harmonization of support schemes
	Spain	Foot-dragger regarding an EU-wide harmonization of support schemes; fence-sitter with regard to RES-E targets
	Germany	Foot-dragger regarding an EU-wide harmonization of support schemes; pacesetter with regard to RES-E targets
	France	From foot-dragger with regard to RES-E targets to 'circumstantial' coalition-builder
	Poland	Foot-dragger with regard to RES-E targets
	Romania	Fence-sitting and building tactical coalitions with foot-draggers regarding RES-E targets
Horizontal	Netherlands	Cross-national diffusion of best practice at the subnational level (e.g., from German to Dutch provinces)
	United Kingdom	British TGCs serves as model support scheme for various EU member states
	Italy	Adoption of a FIT in addition to existing TGCs scheme, following the example of Spain and Germany
	Germany	German FITs served as model for other countries' support schemes

therefore did not lead to strong adaptational pressures, accession countries needed to actively demonstrate that they had transposed the directive, and how they had done so. Against this backdrop, Hiteva and Maltby (Chapter 12) characterize Bulgaria's accession to the EU as a 'period of intense top-down Europeanization' as it 'involved preparing the national legislation for EU accession'.

As in the previous period, policy change both at the European level and in the member states was strongly affected by processes of bottom-up Europeanization. With regard to the harmonization of national support schemes, once again a coalition of foot-draggers led by Germany and Spain successfully vetoed a shift towards a common EU-wide approach (Chapters 3 and 8). At the same time, the level of ambition of national RES targets as well as their breakdown into specific sub-targets for the different types of RES was highly controversial. For the first time, new member states that had entered the EU in the first and second round of eastern enlargement undertook serious attempts to upload their domestic policy preferences to the EU level (for Poland, see Chapter 10 by Jankowska and Ancygier; for Romania, see Chapter 11 by Davidescu). Interestingly, the conflicts over support schemes and targets were attenuated and compromise was made possible in part because some member states – such as the UK (see Chapter 6 by Solorio and Fairbrass) and France (Chapter 9 by Bocquillon and Evrard) – changed their negotiation strategy from one based on national preferences to one of coalition-building.

With regard to horizontal Europeanization, this second phase of EU RES-E development was characterized by the parallel diffusion of two types of support schemes: the FITs where Germany continued to be the European role model and TGCs, with the UK being the main point of reference for domestic adoptions. For example, Di Nucci and Russolillo (Chapter 7) observe that the successful cross-national diffusion of FITs led Italy in 2005 to adopt a support scheme for photovoltaics based on FITs although a support scheme based on TGCs was the dominant instrument at the time.

Moreover, the Italian case shows that horizontal Europeanization occurs not only at the level of support schemes, but also at the level of specific settings. An example is the cross-national transfer of limits for installed photovoltaic (PV) capacity. For Italy, Di Nucci and Russolillo observe that annual limits on installed PV capacity introduced in the mid-2010s were 'in line with the activities in other European countries such as Spain'.

Finally, in cases where policy development at the national level is blocked or stays behind the expectation of domestic proponents, the horizontal diffusion of ambitious policies may shift to the subnational level. An example is the Netherlands, where proactive local governments drew inspiration for ambitious RES-E programmes from their counterparts in Germany (see Chapter 4 by Hoppe and van Bueren).

15.2.3 Europeanization Dynamics Related to the Negotiation and Adoption of the 2030 Climate and Energy Framework

The most recent step in the development of the EU RES-E policy was the adoption of the EU's 2030 climate and energy framework and a revision of the guidelines on state aid for environmental protection and energy, both in 2014 (see Chapter 2 by Solorio and Bocquillon). The Europeanization dynamics that evolved around these policy changes are summarized in Table 15.3. Although at the time of writing, in October 2016, it is still too early to assess the dynamics of top-down Europeanization resulting from these decisions, there are indications that indirect Europeanization may once again play a major role in shaping future national RES-E policies. After various unsuccessful attempts to harmonize national RES-E support schemes towards a concrete governance model – a strategy that could be described as 'positive coordination' (Kassim, 2001) – the European Commission and member state governments have started to apply a logic of 'negative coordination' to reach a greater uniformity of national RES-E policies. Rather than directly prescribing a concrete governance model, the new strategy of negative coordination focuses on indirectly reducing the range of permissible alternatives. The periodic revision of the guidelines on state aid for environmental protection provided an opportunity to change the rules for state aid in such a way that FIT-based support schemes would no longer be permissible. Similar to the liberalization of electricity markets since the mid-1990s, the modified state aid rules changed the opportunity structure for domestic actors in the RES-E policy domain. Member state governments as well as a wide range of domestic actors could now oppose environmentally effective FITs without automatically damaging their environmental image. The fact that Germany used this opportunity to opt out of its FIT that had increasingly been contested domestically in 2014 (Chapter 3 by Vogelpohl et al.) shows the potential of this indirect form of top-down Europeanization for harmonizing domestic RES-E support schemes.

With regard to bottom-up Europeanization it is striking that, in the aftermath of the economic and financial crises, economic concerns with high electricity prices, costly infrastructure investments and the competitiveness of domestic industries have become dominant motives for many countries to actively oppose ambitious RES-E targets and to push for greenhouse gas (GHG) emissions reduction targets that leave greater leeway for other forms of reducing carbon emissions such as increasing the share of nuclear power. At the same time, the former pacesetters have gradually shifted towards a strategy of fence-sitting (Germany and Spain) or coalition-building (Denmark).

The reasons for this shift are manifold, but various case studies draw a picture of self-defeating success of RES promotion that was aggravated by the economic and financial crises. For example, in Bulgaria, within a short period of time, an ambitious system of relatively high FITs with a long duration and combined with cost-free and guaranteed grid access was established in order to achieve the EU RES target as well as national RES-E targets. However, this development, driven by fast and relatively hierarchical Europeanization, resulted in a problematic gap between an overly successful incentive mechanism for RES-E generation and a domestic grid infrastructure that was insufficient to accommodate the rapidly growing share of RES-E. The consequence was a partial non-implementation and subsequent dismantling of the RES-E support scheme, both of which became possible because the successful compliance with the EU's RES-E targets had not been accompanied by an equally successful alteration of the beliefs and expectations of key actors at the national level. As Hiteva and Maltby (Chapter 12) write: 'The period of favourable market conditions for RES-E prompted by top-down Europeanization was too brief to build a strong coalition in support of RES'.

In a similar vein, Davidescu (Chapter 11) characterizes the Europeanization of RES policies in Romania as 'shallow', meaning that a fast and very effective transposition of EU directives was later counteracted by 'non-compliance, creative compliance and policy reversal'. Especially in the post-accession period after 2007, changed opportunity structures had strengthened the proponents of an ambitious support scheme for 'new' RES-E – that is, wind and solar power – resulting in the parliamentary adoption of law 220/2008 on the promotion of energy production from RES that significantly strengthened the previous Green Certificate system. However, neither the grid capacity nor the political system's regulatory capacity were able to cope with the rapid growth in RES-E generation triggered by the new support scheme. As in the Bulgarian case, a dynamic Europeanization triggered by relatively ambitious EU targets, a political system concerned with the flawless transposition of the EU's *acquis*, and the emergence of new and beneficial opportunity structures for RES proponents, led to a steep increase in RES-E production that overstrained the existing grid infrastructure and raised electricity prices. However, with the onset of the economic and financial crisis, RES-E opponents gained the upper hand, leading to a partial dismantling of the RES-E support schemes.

The financial and budgetary strains caused by a successful promotion of RES-E are by no means restricted to the less affluent members of the EU. A pioneer with respect to the dismantling of FITs was the Netherlands, which abolished its successful support scheme in 2006, only three years after it came into force. As in the case of Bulgaria and Romania, the main reason was that the support scheme had threatened to become very costly and lacked support in a sector that had traditionally 'focused on large-scale, centrally produced fossil and nuclear power' (see Chapter 4 by Hoppe and van Bueren). A similar development can be observed with regard to Spain, where its very successful FIT underwent a stepwise dismantling in the aftermath of the economic and financial crisis of 2007–08 (Chapter 8 by Solorio and Fernandez). With regard to France, Bocquillon and Evrard (Chapter 9) observe that 'In 2010, the high level of the solar PV FIT was made responsible for a speculative bubble and rising electricity prices, and criticized for favouring technology imports over national industry support. Following a moratorium, the PV FIT was substantially decreased and its gradual reduction made steeper'.

Table 15.3 Major Europeanization dynamics with regard to the 2030 climate and energy framework

Type of Europeanization	Country	Aims and mechanisms
Top-down	Germany	Indirect Europeanization through EU state aid rules, pre-emptive phasing out of FITs
Bottom-up	Poland	Foot-dragger vetoing binding national RES targets
	Germany	Fence-sitter, giving up resistance against a greater harmonization of support schemes
	Denmark	From pacesetter regarding target ambition to compromise-builder
	United Kingdom	Pacesetter for GHG emissions reduction targets, foot-dragger regarding binding national RES targets
	Italy	Cautious pacesetter supporting the proposed GHG and RES targets
	Spain	Fence-sitter due to strong domestic opposition against RES-E policy and dismantling of the national FITs scheme
	France	Pacesetter for GHG targets, foot-dragger regarding ambitious national RES targets
	Romania	Joint foot-dragging with other Central and Eastern European countries regarding ambitious targets, pushing for side-payments or compensatory measures
	Bulgaria	Fence-sitting due to limited capacity for action
Horizontal	France	Adoption of a feed-in-premium for large facilities, inspired by German and British support schemes
	Romania	Legitimization of dismantling of national RES-E support scheme by referring to similar developments in other member states

Finally, horizontal Europeanization also continues to play a role in this third phase of European RES-E development. On the one hand, the modelling of a French Feed-In Premium for large facilities based on the

British and the new German support schemes (see Chapter 9 by Bocquillon and Evrard) indicates a possible EU-wide diffusion of this instrument in the coming years. In any case, the comparative analysis of RES-E policies suggests that a combination of indirect top-down Europeanization (that is, the ban of FIT support schemes through the EU guidelines for state aid) and horizontal Europeanization (that is, the crystallization of best practice within the range of permissible support schemes through processes of cross-national diffusion) might lead to a greater de facto harmonization of national support schemes than has been achieved so far.

15.2.4 Summary: Europeanization Dynamics in the RES-E Sector

Our analysis of the Europeanization of national RES-E policies is in line with findings of the broader Europeanization literature, and adds some new insights. At first glance the cross-country comparison reveals patterns that – at least to some extent – resemble the traditional leader–laggard dynamics of environmental policymaking in the EU and its member states. However, the picture becomes considerably more complex if we differentiate between the overall RES policy targets and the concrete instruments used to reach these targets. While, with regard to policy targets, most of the 'green' member states have opted for a strategy of pacesetting, trying to upload ambitious national targets to the EU level, these same countries, with regard to policy instruments, have refrained from trying to upload their domestic support schemes to the EU level. Instead, they adopted a strategy of foot-dragging by actively fighting any attempt of an EU-wide harmonization of instruments for RES promotion (see Chapter 3 by Vogelpohl et al. on Germany, Chapter 5 by Dyrhauge on Denmark, and Chapter 8 by Solorio and Fernandez on Spain). The reason why these countries refrained from trying to upload their preferred policy design lies in the European Commission's clearly articulated preference for market-oriented support schemes. Against this background, a strategy of negative coordination aimed at vetoing any kind of harmonization appeared to be a safer option than pushing for harmonization and running the risk that a pro-TGCs coalition backed by the European Commission prevailed. Thus, our cases point to a surprisingly strong influence of the European Commission in a policy domain characterized by intergovernmental rather than supranational logics of policymaking.

A second and still widely unexplored finding of the RES-E case studies in this book relates to the directedness of Europeanization processes. Implicitly, much of the Europeanization literature regards policy development in the European multi-level polity as a one-way street where regulations in place in a few forerunner countries first spread to other EU member states and then become harmonized across the EU, while being continuously ratcheted up throughout this process. The first decade and a half of RES-E promotion matches this pattern. The Spanish example is a case in point (see Chapter 8 by Solorio and Fernandez): early domestic initiatives to support RES-E triggered by the oil crises of the 1970s were strengthened by the EU-driven liberalization of the electricity sector and the resulting structural changes. Spain, in turn, began pushing for ambitious targets in the negotiations leading to the 2001 RES-E directive. Once the directive was adopted, it transformed the beliefs and expectations of domestic actors in such a way that for several years it seemed 'politically incorrect' not to support RES. Horizontally, the Spanish FIT support scheme – together with the German one – was imitated by various other EU member states. The resulting boost in RES-E generation across the EU, finally, increased momentum for more ambitious and mandatory targets in the 2009 RED directive.

However, as described above, in the wake of the global economic downturn that started in 2007, we observe an increasing opposition to the most effective support schemes, in particular to systems based on high FITs and/or long-term priority access of RES-E to the grid; and a slow, but steady, dismantling of national and even European support schemes. Interestingly, this dismantling of RES-E support schemes seems to follow a similar sequence of Europeanization mechanisms as the previous strengthening and harmonization of RES-E policies. It began with instances of horizontal Europeanization, that is, some 'pioneer' countries starting to suspend, weaken, or abolish their support schemes and others subsequently imitating this behaviour; for example, when the Romanian government points to Spain and Poland in order to legitimize the dismantling of its own RES-E support policy (see Chapter 11 by Davidescu). Then, a combination of bottom-up and top-down Europeanization set in, where an increasing number of countries attempted to upload their preferences for less ambitious (or less specific) policy targets to the European level. Interestingly, our cases show that this uploading of reduced levels of environmental ambition may be accompanied by a strategic downloading of restrictive interpretations of EU rules provided by the European Commission. This has been the case, for example, with Germany, which – pressured by rapidly growing domestic opposition against its FIT and rising electricity prices – readily welcomed the revision of the EU guidelines on state aid for environmental protection and energy to legitimize a partial dismantling of its FIT. As Vogelpohl et al. write: the EU guidelines on state aid 'were a welcome argument for the German government to opt out of FITs in the longer term' (Chapter 3). In other words, while in phases of 'upwards' Europeanization, member states explicitly state their domestic policy preferences, 'downwards' Europeanization is characterized by 'blame-shifting' and subterfuge.

A third noteworthy finding of our study relates to the mechanism of horizontal Europeanization. There is no consensus in the Europeanization literature as to whether the horizontal transfer of policies between EU member states should be referred to as Europeanization or not. However, the comparative analysis of the Europeanization of national RES policies in this book makes a strong argument for taking horizontal diffusion processes seriously and conceiving of them as a distinct mechanism of horizontal Europeanization.

Strong support for this argument comes from Germany, the country in our sample that relied most strongly on horizontal Europeanization (see Chapter 3 by Vogelpohl et al.). By being a pioneer and pusher-by-example in RES-E promotion (and to a lesser degree also in the field of biofuels), Germany, since 1990, successfully managed to cross-load its domestic policy for RES-E promotion to other EU member states while at the same time refraining from trying to upload it to the European level (see above). In doing so, Germany wanted to avoid the watering-down of its ambitious FIT-based support scheme in the course of the EU decision-making and harmonization process. Nevertheless, this strategy had repercussions at the EU level as the European Commission, some member states, and domestic and European industrial lobby groups critically eyed the spread of FITs across the EU (by 2007, more than two-thirds of the EU member states had adopted FITs as their main RES-E support scheme). Thus, the horizontal transfer of the German model showed at least two typical traits of Europeanization: first, it resulted in a partial convergence of national RES-E support policies across EU member states; and second, it showed a spillover effect at the EU level in that opponents of FITs started to lobby for an EU-wide harmonization towards a more market-oriented support scheme based on RES-E quotas and TGCs.

As a consequence, Germany could not simply rely on the horizontal diffusion of its domestic support scheme and ignore developments at the EU level. In order to continue its path and for other member states to be able to adopt similar FIT-based support schemes, Germany had to make sure that any future European policy framework left enough leeway for member states to follow the German example. During the negotiations of both the 2001 RES-E directive and the 2009 RED, Germany successfully forged alliances with other member states to veto the top-down prescription of a certificate-based support scheme. Against this backdrop, Vogelpohl et al. conclude (in Chapter 3) that any strategy of 'crossloading of pioneer policies has to be accompanied by the uploading strategy of foot dragging; that is, avoiding legal harmonization at the supranational level which would compromise the pioneer policy'.

15.3 PATTERNS OF EUROPEANIZATION IN BIOFUELS POLICY

With regard to the promotion of biofuels, Europeanization has generally set in later and has been less dynamic than in the RES-E domain. This section describes how Europeanization processes have shaped biofuels policy in the EU and its member states, whereas a more detailed explanation of the differential impact of Europeanization in the RES-E and the biofuels sector is given in section 15.5.

15.3.1 Europeanization Dynamics Related to the Negotiation and Implementation of the 2003 Biofuels Directive

As in the RES-E case, direct top-down Europeanization played only a limited role in the shaping of member states' biofuels policies. By 2003, when the EU biofuels directive entered into force, most EU member states already had their own support schemes in place so that adaptational pressures resulting from the directive's modest targets were generally low. An exception was the UK where, due to the exploration of North Sea oil, the production and consumption of biofuels had been insignificant. Consequently, the UK adopted a role of a foot-dragger during the entire negotiation process and was very reluctant to transpose and implement the directive once it was adopted (Chapter 6 by Solorio and Fairbrass). Another country that opposed the directive and was reluctant to comply after it was adopted was the Netherlands. Here, as Hoppe and van Bueren observe in Chapter 4, the constraining factor was 'the scarcity of land to grow biofuel crops'.

The main reason why top-down Europeanization played hardly any role in the first phase of biofuels policy was that in the course of negotiations the directive had been considerably watered down through processes of bottom-up Europeanization. In particular, the targets that member states finally agreed upon were neither ambitious nor mandatory (see Chapter 2 by Bocquillon and Solorio). In addition, a proposed support scheme, based on reduced rates of excise tax on biofuels, was dropped in the second draft of the directive. The dynamics of bottom-up Europeanization summarized in Table 15.4 reflect these debates.

Table 15.4 Major Europeanization dynamics with regard to the 2003 biofuels directive

Type of Europeanization	Country	Aims and mechanisms
Top-down	Netherlands	Reluctant compliance with biofuels directive
	United Kingdom	Reluctant compliance with biofuels directive
	Poland	Slow compliance with biofuels directive, attempt to reinterpret original EU goals to serve divergent national interests
	Romania	Direct Europeanization through transposition of EU *acquis*
	Bulgaria	'Superficial' Europeanization due to limited domestic administrative capacities
Bottom-up	Denmark	Foot-dragger due to contradicting domestic RES priorities
	United Kingdom	Foot-dragger with regard to mandatory targets and an environmental fuel tax
	Italy	Pacesetter with regard to EU targets in line with domestic industry preferences
	Spain	Pacesetter for biofuels targets and green energy taxation
	France	Pacesetter for ambitious and mandatory biofuels targets
	Germany	Pacesetter with regard to overall goal of biofuels promotion, foot-dragger with regard to restrictive mineral oil excise tax legislation
Horizontal	Spain	Model for the diffusion of tax exemptions for biofuels as a means of implementing the biofuels directive
	Germany	Model for the diffusion of tax exemptions for biofuels as a means of implementing the biofuels directive

However, in addition to targets and instruments, a more essential question emerged, that later on became the dominant controversy in biofuels promotion: serious doubts as to the overall sustainability of biofuels. The dynamics of bottom-up Europeanization in the first and, especially, in the second phase of biofuels promotion (see section 15.3.2 below) reflect this. In the run-up to the 2003 biofuels directive, Denmark already opposed ambitious biofuels policies and targets because it perceived them to be environmentally unsustainable (see Chapter 5 by Dyrhauge). At that time, however, countries such as Denmark, Germany, France and Italy backed biofuels policy as a golden opportunity to support their domestic agricultural sectors (see Chapter 3 by Vogelpohl et al., Chapter 7 by Di Nucci and Russolillo, and Chapter 9 by Bocquillon and Evrard).

Finally, horizontal Europeanization played only a minor role in this period. Here, the most important development related to the horizontal diffusion of tax exemptions for biofuels as an instrument to support the production and consumption of biofuels. Interestingly, this process where various member states voluntarily modelled their support schemes on the German and Spanish examples turned, to some extent, into a functional equivalent to the top-down prescription of support schemes that had previously failed.

15.3.2 Europeanization Dynamics Related to the Negotiation and Implementation of the 2009 Renewable Energy Directive

In the second phase of EU biofuels policy, top-down Europeanization again played only a minor role. Again, the relative vagueness of the directive, combined with the fact that most countries had continued to develop their domestic biofuels policies, strongly limited the adaptational pressures that emerged from the directive. As a result it was mainly countries such as Italy that, due to domestic factors, had difficulties in developing a coherent national policy (see Chapter 7 by Di Nucci and Russolillo); or a country such as Poland that did not regard biofuels promotion as an environmental policy, but rather as an agricultural policy (Chapter 10 by Jankowska and Ancygier), that only late and reluctantly complied with the directive.

The dominant issues in biofuels promotion since the mid-2000s were, firstly, the potential impact of biofuels promotion in the EU on food prices and food security in developing countries; and secondly, the question of whether biofuels can be produced in a sustainable way. These doubts apply in particular to first-generation biofuels. Consequently, from the mid-2000s onwards, bottom-up Europeanization mainly centred around the inclusion and design of sustainability criteria and the shift from first-generation to second-generation biofuels. While the Netherlands (Chapter 4 by Hoppe and van Bueren), Germany (Chapter 3 by Vogelpohl et al.) and France (Chapter 9 by Bocquillon and Evrard) acted as pacesetters, Poland wanted to maintain the policy support for first-generation biofuels, as it opened a window of opportunity to invest in the agricultural industry and create jobs in the farming sector (see Chapter 10 by Jankowska and Ancygier). Overall, as will be argued in more detail in section 15.5, the doubts about the ecological sustainability of biofuels and their impact on global food security have shifted the debate from a technical or instrumental one to a moral or ethical one. This shift towards a debate over first principles, where 'value conflicts are more important than instrumental considerations of policy design' (Knill, 2013, p. 309), has stifled policy development both at the EU level and domestically. Consequently, horizontal Europeanization has played a rather negligible role in EU biofuels policy since 2009, being most important in the cross-national spread of German sustainability criteria in the run-up to the RED (Chapter 3 by Vogelpohl et al.).

Table 15.5 Major Europeanization dynamics with regard to the 2009 renewable energy directive (biofuels)

Type of Europeanization	Country	Aims and mechanisms
Top-down	Netherlands	Reluctant compliance ('wait-and-see' strategy)
	Italy	Reluctant and incoherent ad hoc compliance
	Spain	Compliance with EU biofuels targets and sustainability criteria
	Poland	Reluctant and late implementation
Bottom-up	Netherlands	Pacesetter for sustainability criteria and a 'double count' for 2nd and 3rd generation biofuels
	Denmark	Foot-dragger due to incompatibility with Danish RES policies and priorities
	United Kingdom	Fence-sitter due to domestic public debate
	France	Pacesetter with regard to biofuels targets and sustainability criteria in accordance with domestic interests
	Poland	Foot-dragger opposing strong sustainability criteria and 2nd generation biofuels
	Germany	Pacesetter with regard to sustainability criteria
	Romania	Fence-sitting and coalition-building in order to achieve compensation
Horizontal	Germany	Model for sustainability criteria for other countries

15.4 EU RES POLICY BEYOND BORDERS

Europeanization studies usually focus on the EU's impact on its member states. In recent years, this focus has been complemented by studies looking at the EU's attempt to transfer its policies and institutions to countries beyond its borders. Chapter 13 by Escribano on the Mediterranean Solar Plan, and Chapter 14 by Di Lucia on the external EU biofuels policy in Mozambique, focus on the ways in which ambitious EU RES-E and renewable energy sources for transport (RES-T) policies exert influence on the domestic energy policies of neighbouring and developing countries. As these examples highlight, concepts of 'outward Europeanization' are still in their infancy and, similar to horizontal Europeanization, build on a body of literature on 'policy diffusion', 'policy transfer' and 'external governance' (Börzel and Risse, 2012; Delreux and Van Den Brande, 2013). The findings of the empirical sections do not substantially differ across the two cases, reflecting the failure of the EU to develop a strategy to influence domestic RES production beyond its borders.

While Germany is recognized as an active leader facilitating the worldwide diffusion of RES and has gained followers for its FIT support scheme around the world, the EU seems to experience problems with establishing a comprehensive leadership strategy in the RES-E sector. This is somewhat surprising given that RES-E deployment across the Mediterranean neighbourhood would actually increase the EU's energy security and help to diversify its energy corridors from Russian supplies, as Escribano shows based on the examples of the Mediterranean Solar Plan (Chapter 13).

Looking at the biofuels case, the EU's capacity to develop a system that ensures the sustainable production of biofuels in developing countries is the crucial issue. Most of the chapters in this book emphasized the rise of critical voices such as ENGOs and other sceptical stakeholders that started to campaign against policy support for biofuels due to the risk of negative impacts in countries beyond EU borders. In this context, concerns about the sustainability of biofuels were expressed in terms of food security, land clearing and their carbon dioxide (CO_2) balance. Yet, the development of the EU's capacity to effectively influence production in developing countries in accordance with EU priorities remains a major challenge, but will probably be a 'necessary condition for biofuels to remain on the post-2020 political agenda in the EU' (see Chapter 14 by Di Lucia).

While our cases are by no means representative, and external EU governance in the RES policy domain has not been the key focus of our study, the analysis suggests that outward Europeanization is still far from being a major driver of international policy change; at least in areas such as RES-E and biofuels policy where the EU itself has not yet established a clearly defined policy model and member states are still competing to upload their preferred policy design to the European level.

15.5 EXPLAINING THE DIFFERENTIAL SUCCESS OF RES-E AND BIOFUELS POLICIES

One of the findings of our analysis of RES-E and biofuels policies was that the promotion of RES-E has generally been more successful and more sustainable than the promotion of biofuels. How can this imbalance be explained? First and foremost, our case studies point to the fact that domestic capacities for the production of biofuels were very unevenly distributed among EU member states. While a few countries with a strong agrarian sector and large areas of agricultural land such as France, Germany, Italy and Spain were able to produce first-generation biofuels domestically, most member states were forced to import biofuels, mostly from outside the EU. This had an important impact on the constellation of domestic actors. While in the field of RES-E strong domestic actor coalitions formed in most member states that were in support of effective promotion schemes, the same did not happen with regard to biofuels (see, e.g., Chapter 4 by Hoppe and van Bueren, and Chapter 5 by Dyrhauge). Only a few countries with a strong agrarian sector with surplus capacities, such as France (see Chapter 9 by Bocquillon and Evrard), saw the emergence of an influential pro-biofuels coalition.

Besides impeding the formation of domestic advocacy coalitions, the scarcity of domestic production capacities and the resulting need to import biofuels from non-EU member states was problematic also in a second way. While the EU decided to increase the share of fuels derived from RES, it was not immediately able to set sustainability criteria for their production. Consequently, the growing demand for first-generation biofuels based on energy crops and the resulting competition between the production of food and fuels in non-European countries triggered a fierce public 'food versus fuels' debate that shed a negative light on the ambitious European biofuels targets. This partly moral, partly economic debate weakened the case for ambitious biofuels quotas and constituted another obstacle to the formation of strong biofuels advocacy coalitions in the member states (see, e.g., Chapter 5 by Dyrhauge, and Chapter 6 by Solorio and Fairbrass).

But even in countries with the agrarian potential to produce biofuels domestically, early RES support policies were adopted in the RES-E field rather than with regard to biofuels. This was the case, for example, in Spain and Italy which, in the wake of the oil crises of the 1970s, took first steps towards RES promotion (see Chapter 7 by Di Nucci and Russolillo, and Chapter 8 by Solorio and Fernandez), but even in Poland measures to promote RES-E preceded attempts to foster biofuels (Chapter 10 by Jankowska and Ancygier). A potential explanation could be that the decision-making powers necessary for RES-E support measures were all concentrated in the energy policy domain, while biofuels support would have required the more difficult and time-consuming task of policy coordination between three policy domains: agriculture, transport and energy. The Polish President's veto of the 2002 biofuels law on the grounds that biofuels might be harmful to car engines is a case in point (Chapter 10 by Jankowska and Ancygier).

Arguably the most paradoxical driver of RES-E policies was the promotion of nuclear power by various EU member states, especially in the 1970s and 1980s, and its subsequent decline since the late 1980s. At least three pathways of influence can be distinguished here. Firstly, the pioneering role of countries such as Denmark and Germany in RES-E promotion cannot be explained without a very strong domestic movement that had evolved in opposition to nuclear power and that pushed for RES-E as a clean and less risky alternative to nuclear energy (see Chapter 3 by Vogelpohl et al., and Chapter 5 by Dyrhauge). Conversely, the weakness of the French anti-nuclear movement vis-à-vis a nuclear-friendly policy network centred around the monopolist Électricité de France (EDF) spilled over to the RES-E sector, as Chapter 9 by Bocquillon and Evrard shows. Second, in some countries instruments originally designed to promote nuclear power were opened to RES-E mainly to lend them a 'greener' image. However, as Solorio and Fairbrass (Chapter 6) write with regard to the early UK Non-Fossil Fuel Obligation (NFFO), 'Once the door was opened … it was impossible to impede support for RES-E'. Finally, decisions to phase out nuclear energy in various EU member states in combination with ambitious national climate targets dramatically increased the demand for carbon-free electricity that could only be produced from RES (for Germany, see Chapter 3 by Vogelpohl et al., as well as Mez, 2012 and Glaser, 2012; for Denmark, see Chapter 5 by Dyrhauge; for Italy, see Chapter 7 by Di Nucci and Russolillo).

Another factor that has favoured RES-E promotion over measures to support biofuels is the former's greater compatibility with the aims of international climate policy. Since the late 1990s, the environmental policy domain has increasingly been marked by a predominance of climate mitigation goals and strategies over all other environmental goals. Consequently, the potential to reduce GHG emissions was a decisive criterion for evaluating and comparing different policy options. While there is little doubt about the GHG reduction potential of RES-E compared to electricity from fossil fuels, the same is not true for biofuels.

Land-use change, fertilizer production, agricultural practices and processing are just some of the factors that can impair the GHG reduction potential of biofuels. Consequently, domestic policymakers committed to reducing GHG emissions regularly gave priority to RES-E policies over biofuels promotion (see, e.g., Chapter 6 by Solorio and Fairbrass on the UK).

Policy development may also be constrained by irreconcilable conflicts between opposing actor coalitions. In the case of RES-E promotion, the major divide between EU member states related to the design of support schemes. While the pros and cons of different support schemes were fiercely debated since the 1990s, this did not lead to policy stalemate as the EU could simply refrain from harmonizing national support schemes. Being mainly a question of instrument choice, it was only marginally relevant to the overall aims and legitimacy of the policy. In contrast, the most controversial issue regarding biofuels – the environmental sustainability of biofuels and the question of global food security – was an inherently moral one that questioned both the goals and the legitimacy of the policy as a whole. Here, disagreement between member states pushing for second-generation biofuels (for example, the Netherlands; see Chapter 4 by Hoppe and van Bueren) and those with a strong national interest in the production of first-generation biofuels (for example, Poland; see Chapter 10 by Jankowska and Ancygier) had a greater potential to slow down policy developments at the European and the national levels. Moreover, as in many moral debates, compromise between the opposing views usually does not resolve the underlying conflicts.

15.6 THE ROLE OF DOMESTIC ACTORS: VESTED INTERESTS OF UTILITIES AND THE POWER OF ENGOs

While the Europeanization perspective adopted in this book has been crucial for understanding the complex causal mechanisms of policy change in the interdependent European multi-level polity, one might argue that such an approach underestimates the role of purely domestic factors, in particular of the power, interests and strategic choices of domestic actors. Although we are convinced that our distinction of three mechanisms of Europeanization has been helpful for detecting the role of domestic actors, in particular in our analysis of bottom-up and horizontal Europeanization, this section will take an independent and comparative look at the role of utilities (or incumbent actors) and ENGOs and their support and opposition in the RES-E and biofuels cases.

RES-E policies developed within an energy system dominated by powerful vested interests in fossil fuels and nuclear energy. The analysis of RES policies in the different EU member states has shown that the extent to which governments can put these vested interests under control determines the success or failure of RES-E development. As the cases of France, Poland and the Netherlands demonstrate, RES-E do not get much attention in a political system, if the utilities do not experience any loss of influence or power through, for instance, the liberalization of the energy market. In France and in Poland, vested interests of utilities still have a prominent position in the political system. Both have a state-owned centralized power industry, nuclear and coal-based, which is hostile to the development of RES-E policy and acts accordingly. They have therefore failed to stimulate the large-scale deployment of RES-E (see Chapter 9 by Bocquillon and Evrard on France, and Chapter 10 by Jankowska and Ancygier on Poland).

Utilities do not always adopt a veto position against RES-E from the start, but most of them became active very late, when RES-E started to become competitive on the market and began to replace traditional sources of energy from the electricity mix (see Chapter 8 by Solorio and Fernandez on Spain). Another common characteristic of power utilities is the opposition against FIT schemes and the support of quota models at the domestic and European level. FIT schemes demand a more decentralized energy system with multiple actors, while quotas prevent a more fundamental transformation that might be accompanied by losing their dominant position in the energy landscape. Special cases in this context constitute the power utilities in the new eastern member states, as these states were obligated to adopt the *acquis communautaire* in order to comply with the requirements for EU membership. This might explain why the utilities in these member states did not oppose top-down Europeanization after their EU accession. However, the question is whether conditionality-induced institutional and policy change in the pre-accession phase has been sustainable. As the cases of Bulgaria and Romania show, their utilities did actually start to oppose RES-E development and blamed RES-E support schemes for increases in prices of electricity some years after the accession (see Chapter 12 by Hiteva and Maltby on Bulgaria, and Chapter 11 by Davidescu on Romania). This finding contradicts earlier studies that showed that, even in the post-accession phase, new EU member states maintained their commitment to the policies they had to adopt as a precondition for EU accession (see, e.g., Sedelmeier, 2008). Conversely, the behaviour of incumbent actors for the biofuels case has been less visible than for the RES-E case, given that they are diffused across three policy domains: agriculture, transport and energy (for example, farming associations, car producers and oil distributors).

On the other side, ENGOs were crucial for the rise of RES-E policies in the EU and its member states by, first and foremost, contesting the dismantling of the national FIT schemes via a harmonization along TGCs supported by the European Commission. Strong ENGOs together with interest groups and RES-E producers kept pressing for ambitious RES-E policies and targets on the EU and domestic level. Moreover, ENGOs used European institutions such as the European Court of Justice and the European Commission to express their concerns in order to bring member states back on track towards a rapid energy transition (see, e.g., Chapter 8 by Solorio and Fernandez on Spain, and Chapter 11 by Davidescu on Romania). Several case studies have also demonstrated the importance of ENGOs in the process of disclosing the environmental and social impacts of biofuels. They actively campaigned against biofuels and raised awareness of negative impacts in developing countries.

Overall, RES debates in the EU and its member states show that this is a complex policy domain where a constellation of actors from the different levels of governance (that is, European, national, subnational) converge. This constellation is characterized by a divergence of interests and values that only accentuates the complexity of the policy process, which in this book has been disentangled by means of adopting a Europeanization perspective. In this regard, this book has to be taken as an invitation to further discuss policy change in the EU's energy sector and the structural and practical barriers that an RES-based energy transition presents in Europe and abroad.

REFERENCES

Börzel, T. and T. Risse (2012), 'From Europeanisation to diffusion: introduction'. *West European Politics*, 35 (1), 1–19.

Delreux, T. and K. Van den Brande (2013), 'Taking the lead: informal division of labour in the EU's external environmental policy-making', *Journal of European Public Policy*, 20 (1), 113–131.

Glaser, A. (2012), 'From Brokdorf to Fukushima: the long journey to nuclear phase-out', *Bulletin of the Atomic Scientists*, 68 (6), 10–21.

Kassim, H. (2001), 'Introduction: co-ordinating national action in Brussels', in H. Kassim, A. Menon, B. Guy Peters and V. Wright (eds), *The National Co-ordination of EU Policy: The European Level*, Oxford: Oxford University Press, pp. 1–46.

Knill, C. (2013), 'The study of morality policy: analytical implications from a public policy perspective', *Journal of European Public Policy*, 20 (3), 309–317.

Mez, L. (2012), 'Germany's merger of energy and climate change policy', *Bulletin of the Atomic Scientists*, 68 (6), 22–29.

Sedelmeier, U. (2008), 'After conditionality: post-accession compliance with EU law in East Central Europe', *Journal of European Public Policy*, 15 (6), 806–825.

Index